TO THE STUDENT: *A Study Guide for this textbook is available through your college bookstore under the title* Study Guide for Managerial Accounting *by Sanoa J. Hensley and Geraldine Dominiak. The Study Guide can help you with course material by acting as a tutorial, review, and study aid. If the Study Guide is not in stock, ask the book store manager to order a copy for you.*

USED BOOK

MANAGERIAL ACCOUNTING

FOURTH EDITION

MANAGERIAL ACCOUNTING

GERALDINE F. DOMINIAK

Texas Christian University

JOSEPH G. LOUDERBACK III

Clemson University

Kent Publishing Company
Boston, Massachusetts
A Division of Wadsworth, Inc.

Senior Editor: John B. McHugh
Production Editor: Carolyn Ingalls
Cover Designer: Nancy Lindgren
Production Coordinator: Linda Siegrist

KENT PUBLISHING COMPANY

A Division of Wadsworth, Inc.

Printed in the United States of America

1 2 3 4 5 6 7 8 9 — 89 88 87 86 85

Library of Congress Cataloging in Publication Data

Dominiak, Geraldine F.
  Managerial accounting.

  Includes index.
  I. Managerial accounting.   I. Louderback, Joseph G.   II. Title.
HF5635.D64   1984   658.1′5   84-23395
ISBN 0-534-04185-X

CONTENTS

1 INTRODUCTION   1

Functions of Management   2
Types of Managers   3
Managerial Accounting and Functions of Management   3
    Planning and Budgeting   3
    Decision Making   4
    Controlling   5
    Evaluating   5
    Illustration   6
Managerial Accounting and Financial Accounting   8
Activities of Managerial Accountants   9
Summary   11
Key Terms   11
Assignment Material   11
    Questions for Discussion   11
    Problems   12

PART ONE   VOLUME-COST-PROFIT ANALYSIS AND DECISION MAKING   15

2 PROFIT PLANNING   17

Cost Behavior   18
    Variable Costs   18
    Contribution Margin   19
    Fixed Costs   19
    Emphasis on Expectations   20

Income Statements—Financial Accounting
and the Contribution Margin Approach   21
Average Total Cost per Unit: A Pitfall   21
Relevant Range   22
Volume-Cost-Profit Graph   23
Achieving Target Profits   26
Contribution Margin Percentage   27
Determining Unit Price   28
Changing Plans   29
Summary   30
Key Terms   30
Key Formulas   30
Review Problem   31
Assignment Material   33
Questions for Discussion   33
Exercises   34
Problems   42
Cases   49

3   ANALYZING COST BEHAVIOR   52

Mixed Costs   52
High-Low Method of Estimation   54
Scatter-Diagram Method of Estimation   55
Regression Method of Estimation   56
Estimates and Facts   57
Step-Variable Costs   57
Managerial Action and Fixed Costs   59
Discretionary Costs   59
Committed Costs   60
Selecting a Measure of Volume   62
The Manufacturing Firm   62
Other Examples   64
Income Taxes and Profit Planning   66
Cost Structure and Managerial Attitudes   67
Margin of Safety   69
Summary   69
Key Terms   70
Key Formulas   70
Review Problem   70
Appendix: Regression Analysis   72
Simple Regression   72
Multiple Regression   76
Assignment Material   77
Questions for Discussion   77
Exercises   79

Problems   88
Cases   97

4   ADDITIONAL ASPECTS OF VOLUME-COST-PROFIT ANALYSIS   99

Analysis of Results   99
Multiple Products   102
    Weighted-Average Contribution Margin Percentage   102
    Sales Mix in Units   105
    Overall Planning   106
    Fixed Costs and Multiple-Product Firms   107
Price-Volume Relationships   108
Volume-Cost-Profit Analysis in Not-for-Profit Entities   109
    Benefit-Cost Analysis   111
Summary   112
Key Terms   112
Key Formulas   113
Review Problem   113
Assignment Material   115
    Questions for Discussion   115
    Exercises   116
    Problems   121
    Cases   135

5   SHORT-TERM DECISIONS AND ACCOUNTING INFORMATION   139

The Criterion for Short-Term Decisions   140
    Basic Example   141
    Sunk Costs   142
    Opportunity Costs   143
Developing Relevant Information   144
    Allocated Costs   145
Typical Short-Term Decisions   147
    Dropping a Segment   147
    Make-or-Buy Decisions   152
    Joint Products   153
    Special Orders   157
    Use of Fixed Facilities   159
    A Word of Caution   160
Decision Making Under Environmental Constraints   161
Summary   161
Key Terms   162
Review Problem   162

Assignment Material   164
    Questions for Discussion   164
    Exercises   165
    Problems   172
    Cases   184

PART TWO   BUDGETING   189

6   OPERATIONAL BUDGETING   191

Comprehensive Budgets   191
    Budgets and Planning   192
    Budgets and Control   193
    Organization of Budgets   194
    Developing the Comprehensive Budget   195
Sales Forecasting   196
    Indicator Methods   196
    Historical Analysis   198
    Judgmental Methods   198
    Which Method to Use   198
    Expected Values and Forecasting   199
    Interim Period Forecasts   200
Expense Budgets   200
    Alternative Measures of Activity   201
    Budgeting Discretionary Costs   203
Budgeting and Human Behavior   204
    Conflicts   204
    Imposed Budgets   204
    Budgets as "Check-Up" Devices   206
    Unwise Adherence to Budgets   206
Illustration   206
    Budgeted Income Statement   207
    Purchases Budget   208
Purchases Budget—A Manufacturing Firm   209
Summary   211
Key Terms   212
Key Formulas   212
Review Problem   212
Assignment Material   213
    Questions for Discussion   213
    Exercises   214
    Problems   220
    Cases   228

7 FINANCIAL BUDGETING   230

Illustration of Cash Budget   230
   Cash Receipts   231
   Cash Disbursements   232
   Cash Budget   234
   Revised Financial Statements   235
   Minimum-Cash-Balance Policies   237
   Concluding Comments   238
Annual and Long-Term Budgets   239
   Asset Requirements   240
   Financing Requirements   240
   Illustrations of Annual and Long-Term Budgets   241
   Long-Term Planning   245
   Illustration   246
Budgeting in Not-for-Profit Entities   246
   Zero-Based Budgeting   249
   Program Budgeting   250
Summary   251
Key Terms   251
Review Problem   252
Assignment Material   254
   Questions for Discussion   254
   Exercises   255
   Problems   263
   Cases   273

8 CAPITAL BUDGETING, PART I   276

Capital Budgeting and Resource Allocation   277
   Cost of Capital   277
Types of Capital Budgeting Decisions   278
   Capital Budgeting Techniques   279
   Cash Flows and Book Income   279
Basic Example   280
   Net Present Value Method   281
   Internal Rate of Return Method   281
   Generality of the Analysis   282
Taxes and Depreciation   283
Uneven Cash Flows   284
   Accelerated Depreciation   284
   Salvage Values   287
Decision Rules   288
Other Methods of Capital Budgeting   289
   Payback Period   289
   Book Rate of Return   291

Summary Evaluation of Methods   293
Investing Decisions and Financing Decisions   293
Summary   294
Key Terms   294
Key Formulas   295
Review Problem   295
Assignment Material   297
 Questions for Discussion   297
 Exercises   298
 Problems   302
 Case   311

9   *CAPITAL BUDGETING, PART II*   *313*

Complex Investments   313
 Working Capital Investment   314
 Replacement Decisions   315
Mutually Exclusive Alternatives   319
 Unequal Lives   320
 Ranking Investment Opportunities   322
Sensitivity Analysis   324
Income Taxes—Special Considerations   326
 ACRS   327
 Investment Tax Credit   330
Social Consequences of Decision Making   332
Summary   333
Key Terms   334
Key Formulas   334
Review Problem—Replacement Decision and Investment in Working Capital   334
Review Problem—Determining Required Volume   337
Review Problem—ACRS and Investment Tax Credit   337
Assignment Material   338
 Questions for Discussion   338
 Exercises   338
 Problems   344
 Cases   353

PART THREE   CONTROL
AND PERFORMANCE EVALUATION   *355*

10   *RESPONSIBILITY ACCOUNTING*   *357*

Goal Congruence and Motivation   357
Responsibility Centers   358
 Cost Centers   359

Profit Centers   359
Investment Centers   359
Criteria for Evaluaton   360
Organizational Structure   361
Responsibility Reporting for Cost Centers   362
Responsibility Reporting for Profit Centers   365
Choosing an Organizational Structure   368
Performance Reports and Allocations   369
Behavioral Considerations   370
Examples of Allocations and Transfer Prices   371
Critiques   373
What to Do?   374
Effects on Firm Income   375
Other Uses of Allocations   377
Summary   377
Key Terms   378
Review Problem   378
Appendix: Step-Down Allocations   379
Assignment Material   382
Questions for Discussion   382
Exercises   384
Problems   389
Cases   401

11   DIVISIONAL PERFORMANCE MEASUREMENT   405

Decentralization   405
Measures of Performance   407
Income   407
Return on Investment (ROI)   407
Residual Income   409
Behavioral Problems   411
ROI vs. RI   411
Book Results and Discounted Cash Flows   412
Problems in Measurement   414
Investment in Assets   415
Liabilities   417
Fixed Assets   418
The Subject of Evaluation—Division or Manager   419
Transfer Prices   421
Pricing Policies   421
Illustrations   423
Summary   426
Key Terms   427

Key Formulas   427
Review Problem   427
Assignment Material   430
    Questions for Discussion   430
    Exercises   431
    Problems   436
    Cases   449

12   CONTROL AND EVALUATION OF COST CENTERS   453

Performance Concepts   453
Standards and Standard Costs   454
Standard Costs and Budgets   455
    Illustration of Standard Variable Cost   456
Variances   457
    Labor Variances   457
    Alternative Computation Methods   459
    Variable Overhead Variances   460
    Materials Variances   463
    Interaction Effects   464
Variances and Performance Evaluation   465
Investigation of Variances   466
Setting of Standards—A Behavioral Problem   467
    Engineering Methods   467
    Managerial Estimates   468
    What Standard—Ideal, Attainable, or Historical?   468
    Revising Standards   469
Standard Costs and Performance Reports   470
Variances and Cost Centers   470
Variances and Income Statements   472
Control of Fixed Costs   473
    Budget Variances   473
    Fixed Costs on Performance Reports   474
A Problem Area: Separating Fixed and Variable Costs   474
Standards and Multi-Product Companies   477
Standard Costs for Nonmanufacturing Activities   477
Summary   478
Key Terms   478
Key Formulas   479
Review Problem   479
Assignment Material   481
    Questions for Discussion   481
    Exercises   483
    Problems   488
    Cases   498

PART FOUR   PRODUCT COSTING   501

13   INTRODUCTION TO PRODUCT COSTING: JOB-ORDER COSTING   503

General Approaches   503
Cost Flows   504
The Manufacturing Process   506
Job-Order Costing   507
    Actual Costing   508
    Normal Costing   511
    Misapplied Overhead   512
    Combining Overhead Rates   515
Income Statements, Actual and Normal Costing   517
Absorption Costing in Other Settings   519
Summary   520
Key Terms   520
Key Formulas   520
Review Problem—Actual and Normal Costing   521
Review Problem—Overhead Variances   523
Assignment Material   524
    Questions for Discussion   524
    Exercises   525
    Problems   531
    Cases   541

14   STANDARD COSTING: ABSORPTION AND VARIABLE   545

Standard Absorption Costing   546
    Calculating a Standard Fixed Cost   547
    Income Statements   548
    Review Problem   550
    Multiple Products   551
    Comparison of Standard and Normal Costing   553
Variable Costing   554
Evaluation of Methods   558
    External Reporting   558
    Internal Reporting   559
Summary   560
Key Terms   561
Key Formulas   561
Review Problem   561
Assignment Material   563
    Questions for Discussion   563
    Exercises   563
    Problems   569
    Cases   580

15 PROCESS COSTING AND THE COST ACCOUNTING CYCLE 585

Process Costing 586
  Equivalent Production 587
  Materials and Conversion Costs 590
  Multiple Processes 592
  Summary of Process Costing 594
The Cost Accounting Cycle 594
  Illustration of Actual Process Costing 596
  Illustration of Job-Order Costing 599
  Illustration of Standard Costing 603
  Final Comparative Comments 607
Summary 607
Key Terms 608
Key Formulas 608
Review Problem—Process Costing 608
Review Problem—Standard Costing 609
Appendix: Process Costing—The FIFO Assumption 612
  Illustration of FIFO 612
  Why Choose FIFO? 615
Assignment Material 616
  Questions for Discussion 616
  Exercises 616
  Problems 620

PART FIVE   SPECIAL TOPICS 637

16 QUANTITATIVE METHODS AND MANAGERIAL ACCOUNTING 639

Quantitative Methods—An Overview 640
Statistical Decision Theory 640
  Variance Investigation 642
  Capital Budgeting Application 644
  Payoff Tables 646
  Developing Probabilities 649
Inventory Control Models 650
  The Problem 651
  When to Order—The Reorder Point 652
  Determining Safety Stock 653
  How Much to Order—The Economic Order Quantity 654
Linear Programming 657
  Sensitivity Analysis 662
  Shadow Prices 663
Summary 664
Key Terms 665

Key Formulas   665
Review Problem—Expected Values   665
Review Problem—Inventory Control   666
Assignment Material   667
    Questions for Discussion   667
    Exercises   667
    Problems   671

17   STATEMENT OF CHANGES IN FINANCIAL POSITION   680

The Interest in Resource Flows   680
The Formal Resource Statement   681
    Concepts of Resources   681
    Categories of Resource Flows   683
    Format of the Statement   683
    Data for Illustration   684
Resources as Cash   686
    Reconciliation of Net Income and Cash from Operations   686
    Nonoperating Flows   688
    The Formal Statement   689
Resources as Working Capital   690
    Reconciliation of Net Income and Working Capital from Operations   691
    The Formal Statement   692
Operating Flows—A Special Problem   693
Concluding Comments   694
Summary   696
Key Terms   696
Key Formula   696
Review Problem   696
Appendix: A Worksheet Approach to Preparing Statements
   of Changes in Financial Position   702
    Preparing the Worksheet   702
    Reconstruction of Transactions   704
Assignment Material   706
    Questions for Discussion   706
    Exercises   707
    Problems   712

18   ANALYZING FINANCIAL STATEMENTS   723

The Purpose and Approach of the Analyst   724
General Methods of Analysis   725
    Areas of Analysis   725
    Sample Financial Statements   725

Liquidity   727
   Working Capital and the Current Ratio   727
   Quick Ratio (Acid-Test Ratio)   728
   Working Capital Activity Ratios   729
Profitability   732
   Return on Assets (ROA)   733
   Return on Common Equity (ROE)   734
   The Effects of Leverage   734
   Earnings per Share (EPS)   736
   Price-Earnings Ratio (PE)   738
   Dividend Yield and Payout Ratio   738
Solvency   739
   Debt Ratio   739
   Times Interest Earned   740
   Cash Flow to Total Debt   740
Ratios and Evaluation   741
Summary   743
Key Terms   743
Key Formulas   743
Review Problem   745
Assignment Material   748
   Questions for Discussion   748
   Exercises   750
   Problems   755
   Cases   761

APPENDIX A   TIME VALUE OF MONEY   764

Present Value of a Single Amount   766
Present Value of a Stream of Equal Receipts   767
Streams of Unequal Amounts   768
Computations for Periods Other Than Years   769
Uses and Significance of Present Values   770
Determining Interest Rates   771
Determining Required Receipts   772
Summary   773
Key Terms   773
Key Formulas   774
Review Problems   774
Assignment Material   777
Table A   779
Table B   779

INDEX   781

Preface

The fourth edition, like the first three editions, is designed for an introductory course in managerial accounting. Though the book is written with the undergraduate student in mind, we have had several reports of successful use of earlier editions in both graduate and management development courses. Accordingly, we have made additional efforts to provide a wide variety of assignment material so that instructors can select assignments consistent with the backgrounds of student users.

Because of the book's emphasis on the *uses* of managerial accounting information, we think the book appropriate not only for accounting majors but also for nonaccounting business majors (in marketing, management, finance, etc.), as well as for majors in nonbusiness areas such as engineering, mathematics, and the physical sciences. Our concern for a broader audience is consistent with the information we have received about enrollments in managerial accounting courses across the nation.

We make few assumptions in this book about the background knowledge of the reader. We assume that a reader has had one or two terms of financial accounting or a working exposure to basic financial statements. From this limited, assumed background, we expect only that a reader will have developed some understanding of the most basic principles upon which financial statements are based. The journal-entry/T-account framework appears only in Chapter 15 and is not, with the exception of that chapter, of critical importance to the understanding of the concepts being presented.

Most discussions in the book focus on the important functions of management: planning, decision making, controlling, and performance evaluation. This emphasis is apparent even in the three chapters on product costing (Chapters 13–15), a topic often presented in accounting textbooks but seldom discussed with the nonaccountant in mind. Thus, the product-costing chapters approach that subject from the standpoint of analyzing results under different costing systems, rather than concentrating on cost-accumulation procedures or on the problems that accountants encounter related to those procedures.

Our objectives in this edition remain essentially the same as those for the first three editions:

1. To present clearly and understandably the most important conceptual and practical aspects of managerial accounting;
2. To order the material in a way that allows the reader to build from elementary concepts to more complex topics and thus to integrate and expand early understanding;
3. To help a student to see some of the interrelationships among the several courses that are required parts of a normal business curriculum;
4. To show the reader, through discussion, illustration, and assignment material, what seems to us the almost infinite number of applications of managerial accounting principles to decision making in economic entities of all types (including personal decisions).

In this and earlier editions we had one further objective that was not explicitly stated but was, nevertheless, reflected in the ways we stated, approached, and offered possible solutions in decision situations. We want to encourage the reader to recognize that *people,* not entities, make decisions and are responsible for the results of those decisions, and that unquantifiable factors influence decisions.

We use several means to achieve these objectives. First, we use examples and illustrations liberally. Sometimes we introduce an important concept by means of an example; sometimes we try to give meaning to a rather abstract concept by immediately concentrating on an illustration. Second, we proceed through the text (and its increasingly complex concepts) in a building-block fashion. Thus, we begin with the principles of cost behavior and volume-cost-profit analysis, which underlie virtually all of managerial accounting, and use this basis for approaching the more complex problems encountered in decision making, comprehensive budgeting, responsibility accounting, and product costing. A reader will discern the continued reliance on previously developed concepts by the regularity of text references to earlier chapters. Our frequent text references to the concepts, research, and practices of other business disciplines are intended both to encourage further study and to remind the reader that decision making requires an integration of knowledge from many areas.

The applicability of the concepts of managerial accounting to a wide variety of economic entities is most obvious in the specific sections of the text that refer to nonbusiness situations. But the reader will also see, through examples in other parts of the text and in the decision situations posed in the assignment material, our efforts to demonstrate the many opportunities for using managerial accounting concepts in a nonbusiness context.

Wherever possible, we consider the qualitative and difficult-to-quantify aspects of a topic. As part of the qualitative considerations, we pay a good deal of attention to behavioral problems and point out the implications of such problems. In raising these qualitative issues, our intention is to emphasize that decisions are made by individuals who have personal beliefs and feelings. We expect readers to come away from this book with an appreciation of the role of accounting data: to provide relevant information but not to *dictate* courses of action.

Throughout the book we emphasize that decisions are made on the basis of estimates and that it is difficult to quantify some factors important to a decision. Our intentions are to underscore (1) the presence of the manager's constant companion, uncertainty, and (2) the importance of recognizing all the available alternatives and all the factors relevant to each alternative. Both the text and many of the problems—especially those that come relatively late in the assignment material—emphasize that a major problem in managing any enterprise is determining the right questions to ask and, concomitantly, what kinds of information to seek. In our opinion, students should learn that real-world problems do not present themselves in the form of schedules to be filled in and manipulated. Indeed, sometimes a manager's most difficult task is to discern, from the mass of economic activity taking place all around, exactly what the problem is that requires investigation and resolution.

PLAN OF THE BOOK

We organized this book to emphasize the fundamental importance of cost behavior patterns to all aspects of managerial decision making. Accordingly, after an introductory chapter, Part One, Volume-Cost-Profit Analysis and Decision Making, consists of four chapters that are intended to help the reader develop a clear and firm grasp of the basic implications and applications of this fundamental issue. These chapters introduce different types of cost behavior, the reasons for such behavior, a tool for using information about behavior (volume-cost-profit analysis), and the basic analytical approaches used for making short-term decisions.

Part Two, Budgeting, treats operating, financial, and capital budgeting in four chapters. Chapter 6 concentrates on operating budgets, building on the material in Part One and introducing, on a more formal basis, behavioral considerations. Chapter 7 deals with financial budgeting, including cash budgets and pro forma balance sheets, and considers the special problems of budgeting for not-for-profit entities. Chapter 8 introduces capital budgeting, covering income taxes but dealing only with relatively straightforward types of decisions involving the acquisition of new assets. Chapter 9 considers more complex decisions, such as those involving the replacement or disposing of assets, as well as some of the more technical aspects of the tax laws (especially the Investment Tax Credit and Accelerated Cost Recovery System) as they may relate to capital budgeting decisions. A full understanding of the topics covered in Chapters 8 and 9 requires an understanding of the concepts of present value analysis. Appendix A offers a basic discussion and illustrations of present value analysis, with the emphasis on promoting an understanding of relationships and without the mathematical development of present value factors.

Part Three integrates the topics of control and performance evaluation. Chapter 10 introduces responsibility accounting and alternative organizational structures and emphasizes the behavioral aspects of both topics. Chapter 11 treats divisional performance evaluation—again, with emphasis on behavioral issues. Chapter 12 uses standard variable costs and variance analysis to evaluate cost centers.

Part Four consists of three chapters on product costing. The emphasis in these chapters is on the uses of product-cost information and on analysis of reports that result from applying different product-costing methods. Chapter 13 introduces the general ideas of cost flows, absorption costing, and predetermined overhead rates; both actual and normal costing are illustrated in a job-order context. Chapter 14, building on the standard cost concepts of Chapter 12 and the absorption costing ideas of Chapter 13, contrasts absorption and variable costing as well as developing the idea of a standard fixed cost per unit. Chapter 15 completes the product-costing coverage by introducing the special problems of a process-costing situation and illustrating the flows of costs through accounts. (An Appendix to Chapter 15 illustrates the computational problems of adopting a first-in-first-out cost-flow assumption under process costing.)

Part Five consists of three chapters, the topical coverage in which will fit the plans for some, but not all, courses in managerial accounting. Chapter 16 discusses several quantitative methods of analysis that might be applied to some of the situations presented in earlier chapters of this text. Included in Chapter 16 are basic applications of statistical decision theory and linear programming, as well as an introduction to inventory control models. Chapter 17 deals with the statement of changes in financial position, which is used by decision makers both inside and outside of the entity preparing such a statement. Chapter 18 offers an introduction to the analysis of financial statements, with special attention given to the interpretation (and misinterpretation) of commonly used ratios. Throughout these last two chapters, the topics in which are often considered to be part of financial rather than managerial accounting, the emphasis is on why and how a manager might use the available information.

NEW FEATURES

1. Extensive rewriting and reorganization of Chapters 13 and 15. The changes were designed to simplify the introductory presentations of product-costing concepts and to further the goal of building carefully and deliberately on an understanding of basic concepts. Chapter 13 continues to concentrate on absorption costing, but the presentation is enhanced by an earlier introduction of the general idea of the flows of costs through a manufacturing firm. We also believe that specifying a job-order setting for the initial illustration of absorption costing will help the reader understand the idea and implications of a predetermined overhead rate for manufacturing costs. Chapter 15 now considers the multiple-process manufacturing situation that was covered in an appendix in the third edition. The special problems of adopting the first-in-first-out cost-flow assumption, which were covered in the text of Chapter 15 in the third edition, are now in an appendix to that chapter.

2. Extensive revision of Chapter 9 and considerable rewriting of some sections in Chapter 8. Because we believe that tax considerations are an integral part of capital budgeting decisions, Chapter 8 continues to recognize the most basic tax implications associated with such decisions. Accordingly, *after* covering the other critical concepts of capital budgeting, we offer some specific, though limited, comments on the Accelerated Cost Recovery System (ACRS). The revised Chapter 9 provides further details about ACRS as well as the investment tax credit, but omits several specialized topics considered in the previous edition (e.g., net operating loss carryovers, differential tax rates, and the many issues relating to the special taxation associated with capital gains).

3. Considerable rewriting of sections in Chapters 10 (on responsibility accounting) and 11 (on divisional performance measurement). The goal of the rewriting was

further integration of the coverage of transfer pricing and clarification of the discussions of cost allocations.

4. Change in orientation for Chapter 17. This chapter is now independent of any earlier coverage of cash budgeting. In the second and third editions, the discussion of funds flows incorporated many references to prior study of cash budgeting and called upon the reader's understanding of that topic. Chapter 17 can now be covered at any time.

5. Revisions of Chapters 3 through 7 (and associated assignment material) to incorporate still more examples of the applicability of concepts in a manufacturing setting. These revisions emphasize the broad applicability of the basic concepts of cost behavior and may be helpful to those users who choose a chapter sequencing to provide earlier coverage of product costing.

6. Revisions of, deletions from, and additions to previously used assignment material. There is 15% more assignment material, and, in addition, approximately forty percent of the total assignments are either new or revised. There is more integration of assignments in Chapters 6 and 7, with several new items in Chapter 6 continued in Chapter 7.

ASSIGNMENT MATERIAL

End-of-chapter material includes questions for discussion, exercises, problems, and cases. We believe there are no discussion questions that can be answered simply by referring to a sentence or two, or to a list of points in the chapter. Rather, discussion questions are meant to increase understanding of concepts introduced in the chapter, and for many questions there are no clearly correct answers. Exercises are generally short and cover the most basic applications of one or two key concepts. Problems tend to be longer than exercises, are more challenging, sometimes contain irrelevant information, and often ask the student to state reservations about whatever solutions are proposed. Both exercises and problems are generally arranged in order of increasing difficulty.

Cases normally contain less than all the information needed to develop a single solution, the intention being to emphasize this inconvenient characteristic of real-life situations. For most cases, the student is required to propose an analytical approach appropriate to the available, relevant information. The cases, and the later problems, require the student to determine what principles are relevant and how those principles apply in a given situation. That is, these assignments are designed to encourage the student to think, since a manager must do so.

We believe one of the strongest features of this book is the integration of assignment material and text. We have been told by users of previous editions that judicious choice of assignment material makes it possible to teach this course, and the individual topics therein, at various levels of difficulty. Considering the variety of economic enterprises and the dynamic nature of the economic environment, it is impossible to illustrate every conceivable application of every fundamental principle covered in the text. We do believe, however, that the principles and the variety of situations presented in the text and assignment material provide a student with sufficient background to develop an approach for analyzing almost any economic decision.

ALTERNATIVE CHAPTER SEQUENCING

There is more material in this text than would normally be needed for a one-term course. We recommend covering the chapters in the order presented. Nevertheless, the text offers considerable flexibility in the order of coverage, and several users have found alternative sequencing to be practical.

Chapters in Part Four are the most likely candidates for alternative sequencing. Chapters 17 and 18, on funds flows and financial analysis, are intended primarily for students whose financial accounting backgrounds did not include these topics. The chapters contain only a few, noncritical references to earlier chapters. Accordingly, either one or both of these chapters can be taken up at any time or omitted entirely.

Chapter 16, which discusses several quantitative methods of analysis, can be covered separately at any time after Chapter 12. Or, individual segments of that chapter can be assigned in conjunction with earlier chapters. The section on statistical decision theory (pages 640–650) has illustrations that use materials from Chapters 6, 8, and 12. The illustrations, while concentrating on applying the quantitative methods, draw on topics discussed in these earlier chapters. The concept of expected value could be introduced as early as Chapter 5. The section on inventory control models (pages 650–657) is particularly relevant to Chapter 6, which covers production and purchases budgets. The linear programming section (pages 657–664) extends the material in Chapter 5 on alternative uses of fixed facilities (pages 159–160).

Instructors desiring an earlier and greater emphasis on product costing could move to Chapters 12 through 15 after Chapter 5. A jump to Chapter 12 is also possible after covering Chapter 4 (or even after Chapter 3), but we would recommend additional discussion of joint/common costs if this sequencing is selected. (Note that if early emphasis on product costing is desired, it is necessary to incorporate Chapter 12 in the coverage of product costing rather than as a part of the study of responsibility accounting. This combination is required because some understanding of standard costs is assumed in Chapters 14 and 15.) Some users have increased the time available to cover product costing by omitting Chapters 10 and 11. Alternatively, some users have omitted all product-costing material, or have omitted all or parts of Chapters 14 and 15.

Some instructors have chosen to omit Chapter 4. Following this plan, some coverage of the ideas of joint and separable costs is required for an understanding of the presentations in Chapter 5 (short-term decision-making). It is also possible to omit one or both chapters on capital budgeting (Chapters 8 and 9) without serious loss of continuity, and some users have taken these options.

Appendix A, which deals with present values, was designed to be used with Chapters 8 and 9 on capital budgeting. Previous exposure to the general idea of the time value of money is not assumed, but those who have had such exposure are likely to find this material useful for review.

SUPPLEMENTARY MATERIAL

An Instructor's Manual contains possible time allocations for alternative course lengths and chapter sequencing, a brief statement of the topical coverage of each chapter, suggestions of assignment items for coverage of basic concepts, and, where appropriate, a brief commentary about concepts or approaches that students find difficult to understand. It also suggests some text assignments that may be useful for examination purposes.

A Test Bank, consisting of true-false and multiple-choice questions, and some basic problems, is also available.

The Solutions Manual contains detailed solutions for all assignment material, as well as suggested times for completing assignments. In addition, the Solutions Manual provides notes to the instructor regarding class use of the material. Important features of these notes are (1) presentations of alternative approaches for arriving at solutions; (2) suggestions for eliciting class discussion; and (3) suggestions for expanding individual assignments to cover new issues, pursuing existing issues in more depth, or highlighting relationships between managerial accounting concepts and concepts studied in courses in other business disciplines.

A list of check figures for at least some parts of virtually every exercise, problem, and case is available in quantity from the publisher. In addition, transparencies are available for selected solutions and text illustrations.

A Study Guide, prepared by Sanoa J. Hensley and Geraldine Dominiak, is designed to help students obtain full value from the study of this text. This supplement, which offers key questions or statements to use as guides in reading the chapters, includes not only objective questions but also a variety of short and medium-length problems (solutions included) to test understanding. The final section of the Guide for each chapter identifies those concepts, practices, or approaches that cause the most difficulty or greatest misunderstanding for students.

ACKNOWLEDGMENTS

We wish to thank the many instructors and students whose comments and suggestions have helped us significantly in the preparation of all four editions of this book. In particular, we want to thank the reviewers of the first and second editions, plus the reviewers of the third edition and the revised material for the fourth edition: Don E. Collins, Franklin University; Michael Fetters, Babson University; Maurice L. Hirsch, Jr., Southern Illinois University at Edwardsville; James T. Hood, Northeast Louisiana University; Philip Jagolinzer, University of Southern Maine; Bernard T. Kaylor, Northeast Louisiana University; Robert Koehler, The Pennsylvania State University; W. E. McTeer, Texas A & I University; Thomas A. Morrison, University of Connecticut; Denis T. Raihall, Drexel University; John M. Ruble, Bradley University; and David Weiner, University of San Francisco. Special thanks for their insightful comments and suggestions go to Fara Elikai, Bill Ferrara, Sanoa Hensley, and Bob Koehler.

We also want to express our appreciation to the American Institute of Certified

Public Accountants, and to the National Association of Accountants, for their generous permission to use problems adapted from past CPA and CMA examinations, respectively.

Finally, we offer our thanks to our respective institutions, and to our colleagues at those institutions; for without those colleagues and institutions, the development of this volume, in its current and prior editions, would have been a much less pleasant task.

Geraldine F. Dominiak
Joseph G. Louderback III

CHAPTER 1

INTRODUCTION

Virtually every organization has accountants who develop and communicate much of the economic information needed by the variety of parties interested in the organization's activities. One important aspect of the accountant's function is to provide information to parties external to the organization, such as creditors, stockholders, contributors, and governmental agencies. This aspect of the accounting function is identified as **financial accounting. Managerial accounting,** another important aspect of the accounting function, involves meeting the information needs of internal parties, the organization's managers.

Managers of organizations make decisions about acquiring and using economic resources, and need information to help them make those decisions. The study of managerial accounting deals with much of the information so used, as well as with some of the techniques managers employ in performing the economic aspects of their jobs. There is no reasonably concise definition of managerial accounting that captures all of its aspects. The subject is relatively young and is constantly changing to adapt to a widening spectrum of managers' needs and new approaches to the study of other functional areas of business—marketing, production, finance, personnel, and general management. We can say that managerial accounting is a significant part of the total system that provides information to managers—the people whose decisions and actions determine the success or failure of an organization.

Managerial accounting obviously applies to business firms, for it deals with economic information, and such firms seek profits and other economic goals. Managerial accounting also applies to organizations that do not seek profits—governmental units, universities, hospitals, churches, etc.—because those organizations, like business entities, use economic resources to meet their objectives. Hence, an understanding of the concepts of managerial accounting is important to managers regardless of the type of organization in which they direct the use of economic resources. In this book we do not assume that you plan to major in accounting or to become an accountant. We assume only that you are interested in managing and are familiar with the basic components of financial statements.

FUNCTIONS OF MANAGEMENT

The most important functions of management are planning and control. The **planning function** is the process of setting goals and developing methods for achieving them. It includes the important process of budgeting. **Budgeting** is the relating of goals to the specific means for achieving them. For example, if a goal is set as a particular level of profit, the budgeting process involves determining what machinery, cash, labor force, and other resources will be needed to achieve that goal, and whether the entity has, or can acquire, the required amount of each resource.

Managing requires **decision making,** which is sometimes viewed as a subfunction of planning. A plan for a year, for example, requires decisions about what products or services to sell, and at what prices, as well as about what machinery to acquire, how many people to hire, whether to borrow money or seek additional equity funds, etc.

Often, the planning process involves an important managerial method—**management by objectives.** A management-by-objectives program, in its simplest form, requires that managers and their subordinates define a set of objectives and then try to achieve them. On occasion, the objectives of various units within the firm may conflict, and the managerial accountant may gather relevant information to help resolve the conflict. For example, the sales manager might want increased production of a particular product in order to meet the demand anticipated in his or her sales objective. The production manager might argue that it would be prohibitively expensive—preventing him or her from meeting cost and production objectives—to shift production away from other products to meet this request. The managerial accountant might analyze the effects of the changed production schedule and recommend which manager's view should prevail.

The **control function** is the process of determining whether goals are being met, and if they are not, what can be done. What changes might be made so that existing goals are still achievable? Should the existing goals be modified? Implicit in the control process is **performance evaluation**—managers reviewing the results of work that was done by their subordinates (who might also be managers, though with narrower responsibilities).

The size of most modern corporations precludes close contact among persons who are several levels apart in the organizational hierarchy. Even in relatively small companies, managers are not likely to exercise constant oversight of the activities of their subordinates. The principle of **management by exception** was formulated to help managers perform their control function under these circumstances. Applying this principle, the manager relies on reports to keep informed on operations. The reports reduce the need for minute-by-minute, physical supervision and allow managers time to perform their other functions. If the reports show that results are not in accordance with plans—that is, if there are exceptions—investigation and action might follow. Thus, accounting reports partially substitute for managers' personal supervision of activities for which they have planned and are responsible.

TYPES OF MANAGERS

It is common practice to distinguish between *line* and *staff* functions in an organization. The manager of a **line function** is concerned with the primary operating activities of the firm—usually, acquiring and selling a physical product, or perhaps selling and performing some type of service. A staff manager is one who manages a department that serves other departments. For example, the financial manager is concerned with obtaining sufficient cash to keep operations running smoothly. The manager of the legal department advises other managers regarding the legal ramifications of actions (e.g., whether the firm would be violating a law if it sold some of its products to a particular customer at prices lower than those usually charged).

Accounting is essentially a **staff function,** with the managerial accountant providing information to other managers. The information can relate to financial statements, tax problems, dealings with governmental authorities, and other matters. The managerial accountant, like other staff managers, will often recommend courses of action to those using the information. But neither the managerial accountant, nor any other staff manager, can impose recommendations on line managers. Nevertheless, because of their expertise, staff managers can heavily influence decisions. In fact, there is evidence that "management accountants have votes on some line decisions, and, on certain decisions, their prior approval is sought."[1] Note also that staff managers, like all managers, must make decisions about the activities in their own departments.

MANAGERIAL ACCOUNTING AND FUNCTIONS OF MANAGEMENT

Successful managers require information to plan and control adequately. The managerial accountant is the primary, though certainly not the only, provider of information. The managerial accountant can provide information to which only someone inside the firm would have access. Such information would include the actual prices of materials purchased, wages paid to employees, amounts of rents on leased facilities or equipment, costs of fringe benefits and various taxes. Managers also use information originating outside the firm. For example, statistics on the state of the economy can be helpful in the forecasting of sales; studies of population growth in particular geographical areas are relevant to decisions about the locations for new stores, warehouses, or manufacturing plants; statistics on the state of the industry, or industries, in which a firm operates, are useful in forecasting both sales and related expenses. (Are our profits about as good as those of other firms? Are our selling costs too high?)

Planning and Budgeting

Without proper planning, goals are achieved only by accident. Managerial accounting is closely interwoven in the planning process both because it provides information for decision making and because the entire budgeting process is developed around

[1]Lander, Gerald H., James R. Holmes, Manuel A. Tipgos, and Marc J. Wallace, Jr., *Profile of the Management Accountant,* New York: National Association of Accountants, 1983, p. 10.

accounting-related reports.

If a firm sets a target profit for a year, it must also determine how to reach that target. For example, what products are to be sold at what prices to reach the target? The managerial accountant develops data that will help managers identify the more profitable products. Often, the managerial accountant is asked to determine the effects of alternative prices and selling efforts. (What will profit be if we cut prices 5% and increase volume 15%? Would spending $250,000 on advertising, or offering a 10% sales commission, be wise if such actions led to a 20% increase in sales volume?)

As part of the budgeting process, managerial accountants prepare forecasted financial statements, usually called **pro forma statements.** Among the most important of such forecasted statements is the budget of cash receipts and disbursements. Forecasts of cash requirements are used by the finance department to determine whether some type of borrowing will be necessary in the future. The *management* of cash is one of the most crucial aspects of a firm; more companies fail because they run out of cash due to inadequate planning than because they are unable to make a profit. Making profits and maintaining adequate cash are two very different things, and it is important that every manager understand that success in one does not necessarily mean success in the other.

Decision Making

Much of the information provided by managerial accountants is used in decision making, which is, as we stated earlier, a critical part of the planning process. Some decision making is carried on continually. For example, managers must decide daily or weekly how many units of a product to buy or make, or how much advertising to place in specific newspapers or on specific radio stations. They are also often confronted with a decision about what prices to set for various products or services. Timeliness is critical to the usefulness of reports that contain information needed for such decisions. It is equally important that the information in the reports be relevant to the decisions at hand. A sales manager needs, among other data, information about inventory levels, product costs and margins, and trends of sales. That same manager, given his or her likely responsibilities, does not need extremely detailed information about the cost to make a particular product. On the other hand, the production manager *does* need detailed information about product costs, so it would not be surprising to find reports to production managers that show 20 or more different categories of costs.

Some decisions are made at relatively infrequent intervals, such as whether to build a new factory, buy a new warehouse, introduce a new product line, enter a foreign market, etc. The information needed by managers to help them make decisions like these usually requires that the managerial accountant undertake special analyses of available information. In fact, the data necessary for such analyses may not be readily available in the needed form. The managerial accountant will have to determine what data are needed, present those data in an understandable way, and explain the analysis to the concerned managers.

Although managers use accounting data extensively as they make decisions, it is important to understand that such data do not provide automatic answers to the questions that managers face. *People* make decisions; and people bring to the decision-making process their experience, values, and knowledge that often cannot be incorporated into some type of quantitative analysis. Sometimes, an action that seems best based on an analysis of the accounting data may not be taken because of some factor not captured in those data. For example, because the managers of a firm want the company to have a reputation for innovation, they may launch a new product even though it is expected to be unprofitable. Quantifying the benefits of such things as maintaining a firm's reputation is not easy. It is unlikely that such a quantification would be included in the managerial accountant's analysis of the desirability of bringing out the new product. It is, however, quite likely that a report of that analysis would include a comment about the inability to quantify such benefits. That is, the reports from managerial accountants are very likely to give explicit recognition to those factors whose financial implications have not been incorporated in the reports.

Controlling

For many managers, the most common contact with managerial accounting information comes through their use of **control reports,** that is, reports detailing costs incurred by the managers and their subordinates and usually relating those costs to planned costs. Managers use such reports to determine whether some aspect of their spheres of responsibility requires special attention and perhaps corrective action. The use of control reports follows the principle of management by exception. As a rule, when budgeted and actual results are the same the manager assumes that operations are going according to plan and that no special investigation is needed. When significant differences between planned and actual results arise, a manager will usually investigate to determine what is going wrong and, possibly, what subordinates might need help.

Control reports do not tell managers what to do. The fact that actual results differ greatly from planned results does not tell the manager why the results differed. Control reports simply provide feedback that should help the manager to determine where attention may be required; they do not tell the manager how to correct any problems that might exist.

Control reports should be timely and relevant. A manager might receive one report daily, another weekly, and others monthly, the frequency depending on the position of the manager. The closer the manager is to the actual operations, the more frequently reports will be needed. For example, factory foremen and other such supervisors may receive daily reports on production and costs; but higher level managers may want production reports at less frequent intervals.

Evaluating

Evaluating and controlling are very closely related. Managers will usually be evaluated on the basis of how well they control their operations: whether they achieve planned sales volume, meet planned cost levels, produce planned quantities of product, etc. Because the topmost managers of today's large business firms are far removed from the firm's day-to-day activities, they place great reliance on the information reported by management accountants about the performance of subordinate managers.

Developing a suitable measure of performance for a given manager can be difficult. For example, if sales managers are evaluated on the basis of total sales in their regions, they may concentrate on obtaining the highest dollar sales without regard to the profitability of the items sold. The result may be a very high sales volume but a very low overall profit for the firm. Similarly, if production managers are evaluated based on whether they meet budgeted levels of cost, they may be tempted to ignore the quality of the product, postpone preventive maintenance, or take other actions that could harm the firm in the long run. The problem of selecting an appropriate measure of performance is of constant concern to both managers and managerial accountants.

Illustration

We have diagramed some managerial processes and related accounting activities in Figure 1-1. Usually the top level of management sets overall objectives that can be formalized into profit plans. Objectives, such as 10% growth in sales, 12% growth in profits over the next three or five years, a 20% return on total investment, and a 35% return on stockholders' equity, can be put into profit plans. Other objectives, related to

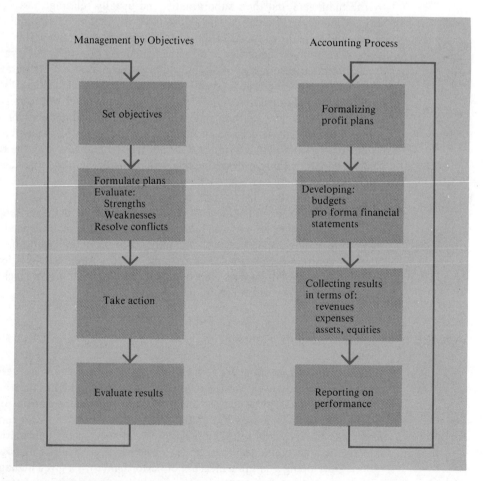

FIGURE 1-1   Management and Accounting

matters such as product quality, pollution abatement, and employee satisfaction cannot formally be described in profit plans but must be taken into account in the development of these plans. For example, top management might believe that a pollution abatement program will add 3% to costs of manufacturing their products. This increase would affect the achievement of profit goals.

Broad objectives are set, followed by detailed plans that will help realize these objectives. What new products can be introduced? What can existing products contribute to future profits and sales? Does our expertise in one area of manufacturing enable us to move into some different markets, and can some of our products be marketed more widely? Should we stress overseas operations or pay more attention to domestic business? Questions like these and others are thrashed out, and planning is then based on the strengths and weaknesses of the firm. Such plans can be expressed in budgets and pro forma financial statements.

Having established plans that are consistent with the broad objectives of the firm, managers implement these designs. They direct research programs on new products, advertising, and other sales efforts toward customers identified in sales plans, add capacity to the plant to meet anticipated demand, and fill requirements for workers, managers, and other personnel. Many results of these actions will show up within the framework of the accounting system. The results of sales efforts show up as revenues, while the efforts of the firm show up as expenses and assets. The financing aspects of the various efforts are reflected in equities—the use of long-term debt, common stock issuances, and increases in retained earnings. Constant evaluation of the varied activities occurs simultaneously with the compilation of results.

In Figure 1-1 we have shown the boxes labeled "Take action" and "Evaluate results" as independent, but there is usually continual feedback. The most recent results are quickly evaluated so that corrective action can be taken if the results do not conform to plans. Moreover, evaluations of results often lead to reconsideration of the original objectives, the plans formulated to meet the objectives, or the actions currently being taken. Thus, it is rare that the cycle shown runs a complete course without any modifications. Plans and budgets are not static; managers change them continually.

Periodically, the collected results of management decisions, in the form of formal financial statements, are distributed outside the firm. But note that such periodic reporting does not change the continuous nature of the process of managing the firm. Indeed, by the time such periodic reports have been prepared and distributed, the firm's managers have already made more plans and decisions.

If the evaluation function is to succeed, the manager being evaluated must know the basis on which he or she is being evaluated, and the information received by both the evaluator and the evaluatee must reflect performance with respect to that basis. For example, if sales managers consistently receive reports emphasizing savings in travel costs, they might conclude that such savings are of critical importance in the evaluation of their work. Such an assumption, if incorrect, could, in much the same way as the earlier examples, lead to actions that are not in the best interests of the company as a whole. An interesting topic, relatively new in managerial accounting, is the question of the extent to which the format and content of accounting reports influence actions taken by managers. A great deal of research has been conducted on the effects of reporting on the performance of managers, and we can expect that the reports developed by managerial accountants will continue to improve as a result of such research. In any case, the likelihood of misdirected managerial efforts is reduced significantly when managers are fully informed about the basis on which their performance will be evaluated.

MANAGERIAL ACCOUNTING
AND FINANCIAL ACCOUNTING

Both managerial and financial accounting deal with economic events. Each requires the quantification of the results of economic activity, and each is concerned with revenues and expenses, assets, liabilities, and cash flows. Both, therefore, involve financial statements in some form, and both suffer from the difficulties of capturing, in quantitative terms, the many aspects of an economic event or decision. The major differences between financial and managerial accounting stem from the fact that they serve different audiences.

Financial accounting serves persons outside the firm, like creditors, customers, governmental units, and equity investors. Hence, financial accounting reports are concerned mostly with the firm as a whole. Managerial accounting reports usually deal with parts of a firm, with particular managers getting information related to their own responsibilities rather than to the entire firm.

Because of the different audiences for financial accounting and managerial accounting information, their uses also differ. Creditors and investors use information to decide whether or not to extend credit to the firm, whether to buy, sell, or hold stock in the firm. (In Chapter 18 we describe some of the steps taken by these individuals as they analyze the information provided by the firm.) Individuals inside the firm use accounting information to make decisions such as which of several products to sell, whether to borrow money or sell stock, which employees to reward for good performance, what prices to charge, etc. The information used by these individuals is the basic subject matter of this text.

The classification schemes used in managerial accounting reports usually differ from those used in financial accounting reports. In financial accounting, costs are usually classified by the *object* of the expense (salaries, taxes, rent, repairs, etc.) or perhaps by the *function* of the expense (cost of goods sold, selling expenses, administrative expenses, financing expenses). In contrast, reports for managerial accounting purposes normally follow a cost classification scheme based on the *behavior* of costs (separating costs that change when activity levels change, from costs that do not change regardless of the level of activity). Or, managerial accounting reports may concentrate on the concepts of *responsibility* and *controllability,* so that costs are classified according to whether or not a particular manager is responsible for the cost and can control it. The three classification schemes of managerial accounting (behavior, responsibility, and controllability) underlie much of the material in this book and are critical to almost all aspects of planning, control, and evaluation.

Information in financial accounting reports may also differ in source and nature from information included in managerial accounting reports. Financial accounting reports are developed from the basic accounting system, which is designed to capture data about completed transactions. Some managerial accounting reports incorporate information not contained in the normal accounting system and related primarily to future transactions, or even to alternatives to past transactions. For example, financial accounting reports (obtainable from the normal accounting system) may include depreciation for a particular building. A managerial accounting report for some purpose could include, instead, the rent that would have to be paid for the building if it were not owned (information not obtainable from the normal accounting system).

To a great extent, managerial accounting reports are specifically designed for a particular user or a particular decision, while financial accounting reports are general purpose reports. For this reason, a particular cost may appear on one internal report and not on another; the cost may be relevant for some kinds of internal decisions and not for others. We can illustrate this point with an example from everyday life. Suppose you own a car and pay $450 insurance per year. That cost is part of the total cost of owning the car, but it is irrelevant if you are trying to determine how much it would cost to take a particular 200-mile trip. Because you pay the insurance whether you take the trip or not, you can ignore its cost in determining the cost of the trip. The phrase "different costs for different purposes" has often been used to describe this characteristic of managerial accounting.

Some have suggested that financial and managerial accounting information differ in that the former is historical while the latter is more concerned with the future. Although many items in financial statements incorporate expectations about the future (e.g., estimated useful life and residual value in the computation of depreciation, estimated warranty work to be done on items sold, and so on), it is true that financial accounting reports concentrate more on the results of past decisions. Internal reports to managers, on the other hand, very often concentrate on what is likely to happen in the future. This particular difference between financial and managerial accounting, however, is becoming less marked, and some firms now present forecasts in their annual reports along with the historical cost financial statements. The increased emphasis on expectations (as opposed to history) stems from the realization that external users of information cannot, any more than can internal managers, plan or control the past or make decisions retroactively.

Managerial accounting has no restrictions such as the generally accepted accounting principles that govern financial accounting. For managerial purposes, relevance is the important concern, and the managerial accountant responds to specific information requirements. For example, market prices or replacement costs or some totally different measure will be used in a managerial accounting report if one of these will help the manager make a better decision. Such alternatives are usually not allowed in financial accounting.

In summary, managerial accounting is different from financial accounting in purpose, orientation, and constraints. In addition, as we noted earlier, there is a difference in the timing and timeliness aspects of internal and external reporting. Financial accounting reports, in the form of financial statements, are developed and distributed externally less often than reports for managers and therefore include information that is less current than that received by managers.

ACTIVITIES OF
MANAGERIAL ACCOUNTANTS

As we stated at the start of the chapter, accountants within an organization perform functions related to both financial and managerial accounting. We concentrate here on those aspects of the internal accountant's activities that involve serving the needs of information users within the organization. Some of the major activities of managerial accountants are as follows: (1) aiding in the design of the total information system of the firm; (2) gathering data; (3) ensuring that the system is performing according to plan; (4) undertaking special analyses for management; (5) interpreting accounting data based on the particular requirements of the manager in a given situation.

The total information system of the firm must be designed to meet the needs of all individuals within the firm who require information for the performance of their jobs. For example, a manager responsible for the sales of a particular product might need to receive sales reports for each territory for each week. His or her supervisor, who also supervises other managers, might need a weekly report for a group of products. The chief sales executive might want monthly reports of sales by product groups and sales territories. The managerial accountant must work to ensure that the total system can meet these varying needs.

The actual recording of transactions in journals and ledgers is commonly done by computer. The accountant is responsible for supervising the gathering of data and for monitoring the system, making sure that the system is functioning as intended. The accountant must also make sure that the output of the information system is understood and used appropriately. Suppose that a particular report was designed for the sales manager to help identify sales trends by geographic area and that the report has subsequently been used as the basis for computing commissions to salespeople. The report might be inappropriate for this second use because the sales data in it fail to reflect customer returns on which no commissions should be paid.

Special analyses are required when management is considering an unusual action. In some cases, such as the possibility of adding a new product to the firm's line, the relevant data may not be available in a form that would enable management to decide on the best course of action. Accountants will use their knowledge of the information system and data-gathering techniques to obtain this special information.

Finally, the accountant frequently explains the results of the accounting process to other managers. Perhaps a manager is unable to understand what has happened. Or the data given to the manager may not be appropriate for the particular purpose he or she had in mind. The latter situation indicates that some change in the system may be appropriate.

Managerial accountants have gained status in recent years as their activities have become concerned more with the analysis of the operations of the firm and less with the problems of recording and computing costs of products. The National Association of Accountants, the principal organization of managerial accountants in the United States, instituted a program designed to provide certification for managerial accountants. The Certified Management Accountant (CMA) examination was first given in 1972. Approximately 4,000 people had successfully completed the examination by the end of 1982. A brief listing of the required subject areas in the CMA examination indicates the breadth of knowledge expected of the professional managerial accountant. The examination consists of the following five parts: Economics and Business Finance; Organization and Behavior, Including Ethical Considerations; Public Reporting Standards, Auditing and Taxes; Periodic Reporting for Internal and External Purposes; and Decision Analysis, Including Modeling and Information Systems.

SUMMARY

Managerial accounting and financial accounting both deal with economic events and reports about them. But the two areas of accounting differ in many ways, primarily because they serve different audiences. Managerial accounting serves managers in functional areas of business. Managers associated with sales, production, finance, and accounting, and top executives all use accounting data for planning and control, including decision making and performance evaluations. Managers of not-for-profit organizations perform many of the same functions and use much of the same accounting data as managers in business entities.

As you study managerial accounting, you will be introduced to some of the activities carried on by managers in several areas of a business firm or other economic organization. Some managerial accounting concept or type of report is related to almost every area of managerial activity, and managerial accounting draws heavily on the concepts from related business disciplines.

KEY TERMS

budgeting
Certified Management Accountant
control function
control reports
decision making
functional area (or classification)
line function

management by exception
management by objectives
performance evaluation
planning function
pro forma statement
staff function

ASSIGNMENT MATERIAL

Questions for Discussion

1-1 Everyday planning and control   In each of the following activities, find an analogy to the planning and control process described in the chapter. Describe the process that would be undertaken in these activities and compare with the process described in the chapter.
(a) Taking a course in college, including preparation and study, taking examinations, and evaluating test results.
(b) Taking a long trip by automobile.
(c) Decorating your own room or apartment.
(d) Being a coach of an athletic team.

1-2 Financial versus managerial accounting information   The chapter illustrates that financial and managerial accounting overlap to some extent, but that managerial accounting uses information not normally used in financial accounting. For financial accounting purposes, the information needed about a particular automobile is its cost, its expected useful life, its residual value at the end of that life, and the method of depreciation to be applied. What other information about a particular business automobile might be important for managerial accounting purposes?

1-3 Who needs financial accounting?   The chapter points out that differences between financial and managerial accounting relate to differences in the decisions made by managers and those made by parties external to the firm. If managerial accounting is intended to serve the information needs of managers, why should managers know and understand financial accounting?

Problems

1-4 Review of financial statement preparation   Below is the balance sheet for Illustrative Company as of December 31, 19X4, followed by selected information relating to activities in 19X5.

Illustrative Company
Balance Sheet
as of December 31, 19X4

Assets

Current assets:		
Cash	$ 10,000	
Accounts receivable	40,000	
Inventory	65,000	
Total current assets		$115,000
Property, plant, and equipment:		
Cost	250,000	
Less: Accumulated depreciation	100,000	
Net		150,000
Total assets		$265,000

Equities

Current liabilities:		
Accounts payable	$ 10,000	
Taxes payable	12,000	
Total current liabilities		$ 22,000
Long-term debt:		
Bonds payable, 7%, due 19X8		100,000
Total liabilities		$122,000
Stockholders' equity:		
Common stock, no par value, 10,000 shares issued and outstanding	90,000	
Retained earnings	53,000	
Total stockholders' equity		143,000
Total equities		$265,000

During 19X5 the following events occurred:
(a) Sales on account were $350,000.
(b) Collections on receivables were $360,000.
(c) Credit purchases of inventory were $180,000.
(d) Cost of goods sold was $150,000.
(e) Payments to suppliers for inventory were $165,000.
(f) Operating expenses paid in cash were $80,000; interest on the bonds was also paid.

(g) Plant and equipment were bought for $70,000 cash.

(h) Taxes payable at December 31, 19X4 were paid.

(i) Depreciation expense was $30,000.

(j) Income taxes are 40% of income before taxes. No payments were made on 19X5 taxes in 19X5.

(k) A dividend of $10,000 was declared and paid.

Required

1. Prepare an income statement for Illustrative Company for 19X5.

2. Prepare a balance sheet for Illustrative Company as of December 31, 19X5.

1-5 **Review of the statement of changes in financial position**   Using the information from 1–4, prepare a statement of changes in financial position for 19X5 for Illustrative Company on (a) a working capital basis; (b) a cash basis.

1-6 **Review of financial statement preparation**   Below is the balance sheet for Example Company as of December 31, 19X4, followed by selected information relating to activities in 19X5.

Example Company
Balance Sheet
as of December 31, 19X4

Assets

Current assets:		
Cash	$ 20,000	
Accounts receivable	50,000	
Inventory	120,000	
Prepaid expenses	8,000	
Total current assets		$198,000
Property, plant, and equipment:		
Cost	350,000	
Less: Accumulated depreciation	130,000	
Net		220,000
Total assets		$418,000

Equities

Current liabilities:		
Accounts payable	$ 40,000	
Taxes payable	25,000	
Accrued expenses	12,000	
Total current liabilities		$ 77,000
Long-term liabilities:		
Bonds payable, 6%, due 19X7		200,000
Total liabilities		$277,000
Stockholders' equity:		
Common stock, $10 par value, 5,000		
shares issued and outstanding	50,000	
Retained earnings	91,000	
Total stockholders' equity		141,000
Total equities		$418,000

Other data relating to activities in 19X5 were as follows:
(a) Sales on account were $480,000.
(b) Collections on accounts receivable were $430,000.
(c) Credit purchases of goods for resale were $220,000.
(d) Cost of goods sold was $240,000.
(e) Payments of accounts payable were $210,000.
(f) Interest expense on bonds payable was paid in cash.
(g) Prepaid expenses at the beginning of the year expired and new prepayments in the amount of $6,000 were made in 19X5.
(h) Accrued taxes payable at the beginning of the year were paid.
(i) Accrued expenses payable are for wages and salaries. Total cash payments for wages and salaries during 19X5 were $95,000. At the end of 19X5, $7,000 was owed to employees.
(j) Other cash payments for expenses during 19X5 were $65,000, not including the $6,000 prepayments in (g).
(k) Common stock was sold for $40,000 (4,000 shares).
(l) Plant and equipment were purchased for $30,000 cash.
(m) Depreciation expense was $40,000.
(n) The income tax rate is 40%. No payments were made in 19X5 on 19X5 income taxes.
(o) A dividend of $5,000 was declared and paid.

Required
1. Prepare an income statement for Example Company for 19X5.
2. Prepare a balance sheet for Example Company as of December 31, 19X5.

1-7 Review of the statement of changes in financial position Using the information from 1–6, prepare a statement of changes in financial position for 19X5 for Example Company on (a) a working capital basis; (b) a cash basis.

VOLUME-COST-PROFIT ANALYSIS AND DECISION MAKING

The first part of this book discusses the most basic principles relating to decision making, the principles of volume-cost-profit analysis. These principles underlie each of the chapters in Part One and nearly all of the material in this book. Much of that material depends on the classification of costs in accordance with their behavior when the volume of activity changes. Though practical considerations can complicate the identification of the behavior of a specific cost, such identification is essential if a manager is to have the best information for making rational decisions.

The principles and techniques developed in this section are primarily discussed and illustrated in a business context. But most of these are applicable to not-for-profit economic entities, such as hospitals, universities, charitable institutions, and governmental units.

CHAPTER 2

PROFIT PLANNING

Managers of business firms are vitally concerned with profits, without which their firms cannot long survive. They want to be able to predict how various managerial actions will affect profits. (For example, what will happen to profits if increasing promotional efforts by $250,000 results in additional sales of 50,000 units?) Managers are also interested in answering questions like these: How many units must we sell to earn $50,000? What selling price should we set? Would it be desirable to hire another salesperson? Would staying open another two hours each day be profitable?

The technique of volume-cost-profit analysis helps us to answer such questions, and many others that managers deal with continually. Essentially, **volume-cost-profit (VCP) analysis** is a method for analyzing the relationships among volume, costs, and profits that managers use as the basis for much of their planning and budgeting.[1] The first step in volume-cost-profit analysis is the classification of costs according to their behavior.

Classifying costs according to their behavioral patterns is a task distinctive to managerial use of accounting information, because reports prepared for external use normally employ a functional classification. That is, in external reports, costs are grouped according to the functional areas of business: production (cost of goods sold); marketing (selling expenses); administration (general and administrative expenses); and financing (interest expense).[2] A functional classification does not provide the type

---

[1]Other terms you may encounter that mean essentially the same thing as VCP analysis are *cost-volume-profit analysis, breakeven analysis,* and *profit-volume analysis.*

[2]In financial accounting the term *cost* denotes the initial expenditure or incurrence of a liability. *Expense* denotes expired costs—costs assigned to the income statement for a period of time. Since *cost* is the more general term, we shall generally use it to refer to both expired and unexpired costs.

of information necessary to predict what is likely to happen to costs and profits if circumstances change, and a manager's tasks include planning for change and taking actions to make changes.

COST BEHAVIOR

A cost is classified as either fixed or variable, according to whether the total amount of the cost changes as volume changes. In this chapter we use sales as the measure of volume and identify costs as either fixed, or variable with sales. Not all costs fall into these categories; other measures of volume are often important, and we shall consider these in Chapter 3.

Variable Costs

Costs that change in direct proportion to changes in volume are called **variable costs.** To illustrate this concept, let us consider Ted's Threads, a retail store.

Ted buys shirts for $3.80 each from a wholesaler and sells them for $10 each. He also incurs a $0.20 cost for wrapping materials for each shirt sold. For now, we shall assume (unrealistically) that he has no other costs. Both the cost of the shirts and the cost of wrapping materials are variable costs: they will be incurred every time a shirt is sold. For our purposes we can treat the two costs as a single variable cost of $4 per shirt, the $3.80 for the shirt and $0.20 for wrapping.

Suppose that in the month of April Ted sells 500 shirts. His income statement would appear as follows:

Ted's Threads
Income Statement for April

Sales (500 units × $10)	$5,000
Variable costs (500 × $4)	2,000
Income	$3,000

Suppose that Ted sells 501 units in May. What will his income be? Instead of preparing a whole new income statement, you may find the additional income that the sale of one more shirt will bring and add it to the income for 500 units. This added income is $10 − $4 = $6. Ted's income will be $3,006. To verify this, let's prepare a new income statement:

Ted's Threads
Income Statement for May

Sales (501 units × $10)	$5,010
Variable costs (501 × $4)	2,004
Income	$3,006

Contribution Margin

The difference between sales price per unit and variable cost per unit is called the **contribution margin.** The term *contribution* is used because the amount left from a sale after variable costs are covered contributes to covering other costs and producing profit. In Ted's case, income increased by $6, his contribution margin per unit, when sales increased by one unit. If Ted sells only 499 shirts in June, his income should drop to $2,994. Sales and income generally increase or decrease in the same direction. In the absence of nonvariable costs, income is computed by multiplying contribution margin per unit by the number of units sold.

Fixed Costs

Some costs will remain the same in *total* over a wide range of volume. These are called **fixed costs** and are generally incurred to provide the capacity needed to operate. Suppose that Ted pays $2,400 per month to rent a store, display counters, a cash register, and other equipment. (It was unrealistic to assume that Ted could sell his product without having a store; the store provides him with capacity—physical assets needed to conduct the business.) These costs will be the same whether he sells 300 or 400 shirts, and may even be the same when he sells no shirts at all. Fixed costs reduce income, but by the same dollar amount regardless of volume. The following income statements for Ted's Threads show the effects of his fixed costs.

Ted's Threads
Income Statements at Various Sales Levels

	499 units	500 units	501 units
Sales	$4,990	$5,000	$5,010
Variable costs	1,996	2,000	2,004
Contribution margin	$2,994	$3,000	$3,006
Fixed costs	2,400	2,400	2,400
Income	$ 594	$ 600	$ 606

Notice especially that the $6 difference in contribution margin at 499, 500, and 501 units is also the difference in incomes for those levels. The presence of fixed costs does not change the significance of the contribution margin per unit. We can predict income by multiplying contribution margin per unit by unit sales, and then subtracting total fixed costs.

Thus, if we want to calculate income if 600 shirts are expected to be sold, we can take the $6 contribution margin per unit and multiply it by 600 shirts. This gives contribution margin of $3,600, and when we subtract fixed costs of $2,400, we find income of $1,200.

An important use of volume-cost-profit analysis is highlighted by the fact that contribution margin per unit is the amount by which income of the firm will change if sales change. If Ted wonders what will happen to his profits if his sales increase by 50 shirts per month, we can tell him that his income will increase by \$300, which is the 50-shirt increase multiplied by \$6 per shirt. This would be true no matter what the current level of sales.

Under our assumption that all costs are either fixed in total or variable with volume, we can predict total costs by adding the two together. The formula is simply

$$\text{Total costs} = \text{fixed costs} + (\text{variable cost per unit} \times \text{unit volume})$$

Emphasis on Expectations

At this early stage we are dealing with a simplified case, looking at the costs in a single time period (a month, a quarter, or whatever), and predicting costs for the following period. Nevertheless, we are dealing with the future, not the past. It is unreasonable to expect, however, that costs—variable or fixed—will remain the same month after month, or year after year. There are many reasons why total fixed costs and/or the per-unit variable costs could change from what they have been in the past.

Inflation is a major cause of changes in both fixed and variable costs. Suppliers might raise their prices. Lessors might raise rents. Salaries might rise, and so on. Profit planning requires that expected changes in costs be taken into account. Volume-cost-profit analysis does not assume that costs remain constant over time; the analysis is based on expectations. Thus, if Ted *expected* the price that he pays for shirts to go up by \$0.10 next month, he would use \$3.90 (instead of \$3.80) in his planning for next month.

The emphasis on expectations is also important because managers can take actions to change some of their costs. Ted could hire a new employee at a monthly salary, increasing his fixed costs. Or, he could advertise (also increasing fixed costs). In a more complex firm, there are many possibilities for cost changes as a result of managerial actions. A large firm could increase (or decrease) its office staff, or change its level of spending on such items as travel and employee training. Thus, the magnitude of fixed costs may change from one period to the next without any change in the nature of those costs (as not varying with the level of activity). For planning purposes, Ted, or any other manager, would predict fixed costs on the basis of what was *expected* for the coming period.

As a general rule, managers can change fixed costs more easily than variable costs, especially over fairly short periods of time (more about this in Chapter 3). Some accountants use the term **nonvariable costs** to describe what we have called fixed costs. Their point is that fixed costs are not fixed in the sense that they cannot be changed, but rather that such costs do not automatically change when volume changes. We call such costs *fixed* because that term is more common; and the term is best thought of as describing those costs that will not change with changes in volume. Regardless of the terminology used, the emphasis in planning is on expectations. If actual conditions (selling prices, prices from suppliers, etc.) do not coincide with expectations, or if managers change their decisions at some later time, there will be differences between actual and predicted costs and profit. Such differences between actuality and expectations are inherent in business but do not reduce the necessity to plan.

Income Statements—Financial Accounting and the Contribution Margin Approach

The approach to developing income statements in this chapter differs from the approaches used in financial accounting. As stated earlier, in financial accounting, costs are usually classified by function or by object. The income statements in Exhibit 2-1 highlight the differences between the two approaches. Notice that the sales and income figures are the same under both approaches, but the costs are different because they are classified using different criteria. The income statements are for a month in which Ted sells 500 shirts.

The major differences between the statements are in terminology and the placement of the cost of wrapping materials. If we had a great many costs, instead of only three, the advantages of the contribution margin format would be more obvious. Even with the few costs used here, you can see that using the financial accounting format requires rearranging costs in order to perform volume-cost-profit analysis.

Exhibit 2-1
Comparison of Income Statements Using the Financial Accounting
and the Contribution Margin Approaches

Financial Accounting Approach		Contribution Margin Approach	
Sales	$5,000	Sales	$5,000
Cost of goods sold (500 × $3.80)	1,900	Variable costs:	
		Purchase cost of shirts (500 × $3.80)	1,900
Gross profit	3,100	Wrapping materials (500 × $.20)	100
			2,000
Operating expenses:			
Wrapping materials (500 × $.20)	100	Contribution margin	3,000
Rent	2,400		
	2,500	Fixed costs:	
		Rent	2,400
Income	$ 600	Income	$ 600

Average Total Cost per Unit: A Pitfall

You should see that because fixed costs in total remain the same at different levels of volume, the average fixed cost per unit will change whenever volume changes. Thus, the average fixed cost per unit when Ted sells 600 units is $4 ($2,400/600), while the average when he sells 800 units is $3 ($2,400/800). The average *total* cost per unit, then, also depends upon the level of volume, with the average total per-unit cost for Ted being $8 ($4 fixed plus $4 variable) when he sells 600 units, and $7 ($3 fixed plus $4 variable) when he sells 800 units.

Failure to recognize the dependence of average total per-unit cost on the level of volume can create problems when a manager attempts—unwisely—to use averages to predict future costs. Use of the average total per-unit cost for one level of volume will not provide a good prediction of total costs at another level of volume.

To illustrate this point, suppose we tried to use the $8 average total cost per unit (associated with a volume of 600 shirts) to predict total costs at a volume of 800 shirts. We would predict costs to total $6,400 ($8 × 800 shirts). But Ted's income statements at volumes of 600 and 800 shirts would be as follows:

	600 Shirts	800 Shirts
Sales	$6,000	$8,000
Variable costs	2,400	3,200
Contribution margin	3,600	4,800
Fixed costs	2,400	2,400
Income	$1,200	$2,400
Average cost per unit	$ 8	$ 7
Profit per unit	$ 2	$ 3

Total costs at a volume of 800 shirts are $5,600 ($3,200 + $2,400). What appears to be an additional profit per unit at the higher level of volume is, in reality, the simple result of spreading the fixed costs over a larger number of units. The nature of the company's costs has not changed at all; variable costs remain at 40% of sales ($4 per unit) and fixed costs remain at $2,400. Using an average total cost per unit to predict total costs is appropriate only if *all* costs are variable. When there are fixed costs, such averages will not give a reasonable prediction at any volume level other than the one on which the average was based.

In the preceding example, notice that income as a percentage of sales varies between the two levels of volume. Perhaps the most common mistake made by managers is to use the prevailing ratio of income to sales in an attempt to predict future income. At a sales level of 600 units, income is 20% of sales, while at a level of 800 units, income is 30% of sales. From the earlier discussion of the nature of fixed costs, you should see that if a company has any fixed costs, income as a percentage of sales (called **return on sales**) will increase as volume increases, and that the percentage increase in income will be greater than the percentage increase in sales. In the income statements shown above, a one-third increase in sales ($2,000/$6,000) produced a 100% increase in income.

RELEVANT RANGE

We have already discussed the fact that per-unit variable costs and total fixed costs may not remain the same over several time periods. Neither can we expect that variable and fixed costs will remain the same at all possible levels of volume. That is, the per-unit variable cost, and even the level of total fixed cost, can be expected to behave as we predict them only over some limited range of volume.

For example, Ted might be able to handle the store himself so long as he sells no more than, say, 900 shirts per month. At some point around that level of sales, he would have to hire additional help. If he paid a new employee a commission on each shirt sold, his variable cost per unit would increase; if he paid a salary (or even an hourly wage that was independent of sales), his fixed costs would increase. There is also a possibility that if Ted began to sell a great many shirts he might be able to get a discount on the purchase price that he pays to the supplier, thus reducing his per-unit variable cost. (Many firms give discounts to customers who order large quantities.)

An important assumption underlying the use of volume-cost-profit analysis is that the firm will operate within a **relevant range,** a range of volumes over which the firm can reasonably expect selling price, per-unit variable cost, and total fixed costs to be constant.[3] Firms will usually have several relevant ranges, and it is risky to use the same value of each factor (price, unit variable cost, total fixed costs) at all levels of volume. For planning purposes, managers attempt to forecast the approximate range of volumes that can be expected and use the costs they believe will hold within that range.

A special case of operating outside the relevant range occurs when a business shuts down altogether. If a firm closes down for a week or a month, it would probably find its total costs to be less than the level of its fixed costs within its relevant range. For instance, a firm might plan for heating costs of $3,000 per month under normal, eight-hour day operations. If the firm were to close for a month, the building would be empty (or nearly empty), and there would be no need to keep the temperature at the normal level of, say, 68 degrees. Heating costs for that month would then be less than $3,000, perhaps considerably less. Similarly, during that month the firm probably would not advertise. Thus, it is not appropriate to interpret *fixed costs* as the costs that the firm would incur at zero volume. Rather, fixed costs are better thought of as the planned costs that will not change in total as volume changes *within the relevant range.* That is, the relevant range is a range of likely operating volumes over which fixed costs in total and variable costs per unit are expected to remain the same.

VOLUME-COST-PROFIT GRAPH

The complete volume-cost-profit picture for Ted's Threads is shown in Figure 2-1. First, we draw a line to show total fixed costs of $2,400. Then, we add variable costs at each level of volume, to give a total cost line. The vertical distance between total costs at any volume and fixed costs at that volume is total variable costs. The revenue line shows total sales at any volume and is simply the price per unit multiplied by the level of unit volume.

Although we have shown the lines on the graph extended to the vertical axis and far to the right, we should point out that it is not usually legitimate to do so because of the known existence of some relevant range. In Ted's case, as suggested earlier, fixed costs could be something smaller than $2,400 if the store were closed for the month (zero volume); and either variable or fixed costs, or both, are likely to change if volume exceeds 900 shirts per month. Thus, extending the lines to zero volume and beyond 900 shirts is unwarranted. But there is no danger in planning on the basis of the estimated relationships as long as the firm does not anticipate operating outside the relevant range. If unusual levels of operations are planned, the cost and pricing structure would have to be reviewed and new relationships developed.

The graphical approach highlights an important point. So long as price exceeds variable cost (contribution margin is positive), selling more units will increase profits

[3]The problem of changing selling prices is considered in Chapter 4.

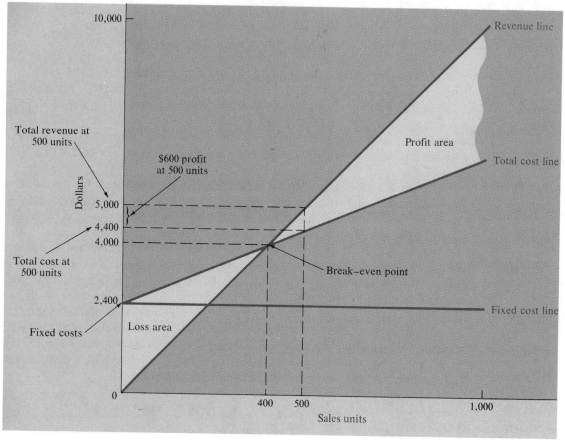

FIGURE 2-1   Volume-Cost-Profit Chart

or *decrease losses.* Thus, the firm might well be better off incurring losses than shutting down. Such is often the case with enterprises whose sales tend to be seasonal. For example, firms operating in summer resort areas might expect to suffer losses during the winter. Similarly, toy companies might expect losses after the Christmas season is over. Many seasonal businesses continue to operate in the off season because they recognize that the contribution margin from the additional, though lower, sales will reduce the losses during the low periods. Chapter 4 considers this point in more detail.

A significant point in the graph is that at which total revenues equal total costs. This is called the **break-even point**—the point at which profits are zero. When the firm operates above the break-even point it makes profits; below that point, the firm will show losses. The vertical distance between the revenue line and the total cost line at any volume is the amount of profit or loss (shaded areas).

Knowledge of the break-even point is important to managers and can be useful for many purposes. For a business firm, breaking even is the first step in the pursuit of profits. Managers of not-for-profit organizations frequently seek to break even, or show only a small profit or loss, on some of their activities. We can derive an equation to give us this point by using relationships we already know. For example, we know that profit is equal to total sales dollars minus total variable costs minus total fixed costs.

That is,

$$
\text{Profit} = \begin{matrix}\text{total}\\ \text{sales}\\ \text{dollars}\end{matrix} - \begin{matrix}\text{total}\\ \text{variable}\\ \text{costs}\end{matrix} - \begin{matrix}\text{total}\\ \text{fixed}\\ \text{costs}\end{matrix}
$$

Identifying the quantity of units sold as Q, we can restate the formula as

$$
\text{Profit} = \left(\begin{matrix}\text{per-unit}\\ \text{selling}\\ \text{price}\end{matrix} \times Q\right) - \left(\begin{matrix}\text{per-unit}\\ \text{variable}\\ \text{cost}\end{matrix} \times Q\right) - \begin{matrix}\text{total}\\ \text{fixed}\\ \text{costs}\end{matrix}
$$

Knowing that selling price per unit less variable cost per unit is contribution margin per unit, we can combine and restate the first two components of the equation, and rearrange the fixed costs to get

$$
\text{Profit} + \begin{matrix}\text{total}\\ \text{fixed}\\ \text{costs}\end{matrix} = \begin{matrix}\text{contribution}\\ \text{margin}\\ \text{per unit}\end{matrix} \times Q
$$

And, since we are looking for the break-even point (where profit is *zero*), the profit term drops out. Now we can solve for Q (the break-even point in units) by dividing both sides by contribution margin per unit, producing

$$
\begin{matrix}Q\ (\text{break-even}\\ \text{sales in units})\end{matrix} = \frac{\text{total fixed costs}}{\text{contribution margin per unit}}
$$

Summarizing the formulation and derivation, identifying the per-unit selling price and variable cost as P and V, respectively, the total fixed costs as F, and contribution margin as CM, we can restate the break-even formula as

$$
Q = \frac{F}{P - V} \quad \text{or} \quad \frac{F}{CM}
$$

Applying this formula to Ted's case, we obtain a break-even point of 400 shirts, computed as follows:

$$
\begin{matrix}\text{Break-even sales}\\ \text{in units}\end{matrix} = \frac{\$2,400}{\$10 - \$4} = \frac{\$2,400}{\$6} = 400 \text{ shirts}
$$

Although the graph in Figure 2-1 and the break-even formula derived above show sales in units, other measures of sales volume could be used just as well. One commonly used measure is sales dollars. The break-even point, if computed in sales dollars, utilizes the **contribution margin percentage** (contribution margin per unit/ selling price per unit) rather than the contribution margin per unit, as follows:

$$
\begin{matrix}\text{Break-even}\\ \text{sales in}\\ \text{dollars}\end{matrix} = \frac{\text{total fixed costs}}{\text{contribution margin percentage}}
$$

Or, in abbreviated terms, the formula could be restated as

$$
\begin{matrix}Q\ (\text{break-even}\\ \text{in dollars})\end{matrix} = \frac{F}{(P - V)/P} \quad \text{or} \quad \frac{F}{CM\%}
$$

In Ted's case, the break-even sales, in dollars, is $4,000, computed as follows:

$$\text{Break-even sales in dollars} = \frac{\$2,400}{(\$10 - \$4)/\$10} = \frac{\$2,400}{60\%} = \$4,000$$

Note that break-even sales in dollars ($4,000) is consistent with the dollars of sales expected at the break-even point in units (400 × $10). We shall see shortly that a firm with several products needs to use the contribution margin percentage, rather than a contribution margin per unit, to make break-even calculations. For a single-product firm, either form of the contribution margin can be used, depending on computational convenience.

For Ted's firm, break-even volume was measured in unit sales and dollar sales. Firms that provide services, rather than goods, often charge their clients for the hours that they work. CPA firms, law firms, and consulting firms are examples. For these firms, chargeable hours (the number of hours worked that are chargeable to client business) could be an appropriate and useful measure of volume, and the horizontal axis of the volume-cost-profit graph would represent varying levels of chargeable hours.

ACHIEVING TARGET PROFITS

The break-even point is of interest, but managers of profit-seeking organizations are also concerned with finding the volume that will yield some desired or **target profit.** The technique for determining the volume needed to achieve a target profit is simply a variation of the break-even situation. The break-even point tells you what sales are required to make no profit and incur no loss; by incorporating into the break-even analysis the amount or rate of profit desired, we can readily determine the sales volume required to achieve that profit.

Suppose, for example, that Ted wishes to earn a profit of $1,200 per month. How many shirts must he sell to achieve that target? We know that total contribution margin must be equal to fixed costs of $2,400 to allow the company to break even. Hence, to achieve a profit of $1,200, total contribution margin must be $1,200 greater than fixed costs, or $3,600. To achieve a total contribution margin of $3,600 when the contribution margin per unit is $6 ($10 sales price − $4 variable cost per unit), he must sell a total of 600 units. Expressed in general terms

$$\text{Target profit} = \left(\begin{array}{ccc}\text{sales, in units,} & & \text{contribution} \\ \text{to achieve} & \times & \text{margin} \\ \text{target profit} & & \text{per unit}\end{array}\right) - \begin{array}{c}\text{fixed} \\ \text{costs}\end{array}$$

Restating this equation to solve for the needed level of sales, we have

$$\text{Sales, in units, to achieve target profit} = \frac{\text{fixed costs + target profit}}{\text{contribution margin per unit}}$$

Using this formula in Ted's case, we have

$$\text{Sales, in units, to achieve target profit} = \frac{\$2,400 + \$1,200}{\$10 - \$4} = \frac{\$3,600}{\$6} = 600 \text{ units}$$

Notice that the numerator of the formula is really the total contribution margin required to earn the target profit, which consists of the contribution margin required for break-even (400 units as computed earlier) plus the contribution margin required for the target profit ($1,200/$6 or an additional 200 units).

Contribution Margin Percentage

In the earlier computation of break-even sales in dollars, contribution margin was expressed as a percentage of sales rather than as a specific amount per unit sold. Some times it is helpful, or even necessary, to use a contribution margin percentage, or ratio, rather than a per-unit contribution margin. This would be true for Ted if he sold shirts at different prices. The analysis is the same as in the per-unit contribution method, provided that variable costs are the same percentage of sales dollars for the differently priced shirts. We will now introduce another kind of shirt that sells for $5. The cost of this shirt is $1.80 and the variable cost for wrapping materials is $0.20 per shirt, making the variable cost per shirt $2.

If the percentage relationship between variable cost and sale price is to be the same for all of Ted's shirts, the relationship of variable cost to sale price for the $5 shirt must be the same as for the $10 shirt. For the $10 shirt, this is 40% ($4/$10), and the variable cost for the $5 shirt is 40% of its sale price ($2/$5 = 40%). Therefore, the contribution margin percentages are both 60% because the contribution margin percentage is simply 1 minus the variable cost percentage.

If Ted's business is to break even in any month, what sales must it achieve? We can no longer use contribution margin per unit, because we have two different per-unit contribution margins. We already computed 400 units as the break-even point if *only* $10 shirts are sold ($2,400/$6). If only $5 shirts are sold, the break-even point is 800 units ($2,400/$3). Many break-even points can be computed, each depending upon the mix of shirts to be sold. But, since the percentage of contribution margin per sales dollar is the same regardless of the type of shirt, the break-even point in terms of sales dollars (computed earlier as $4,000) is still relevant even with this new mix of products. It does not matter how many shirts of each price Ted sells as long as total sales are $4,000. He could achieve that volume by selling 400 $10 shirts or 800 $5 shirts, or any combination that results in $4,000 in sales. The contribution margin percentage merely states contribution margin as an amount per $1 in sales, rather than an amount per unit sold.

We can also find income for any level of dollar sales by using the contribution margin percentage. If Ted has sales of $8,000, what will be his total contribution margin? his income? Contribution margin in total will be $4,800 ($8,000 × 60%) and income $2,400 ($4,800 − $2,400).

Whether a firm sells one or more products, the contribution margin percentage may be useful. Some firms establish target profits stated as a **return on sales**—the ratio of income to sales—rather than as some dollar amount. Just as the contribution margin percentage can be used to determine a break-even point in sales dollars, so it is useful when a firm specifies some target return on sales. Suppose, for example, that Ted has decided that he must earn a profit of 30% on sales. We know that his variable costs are already 40% of sales; what he is saying is that no matter what his sales are, his profit must be 30% of sales. In this context, the profit is much like any variable cost—as sales increase, the total of this item increases proportionately. Therefore, we can treat his desired profit like any other variable cost, and, substituting in the formula, we then find

$$\text{Sales to achieve the target profit} = \frac{\text{fixed costs}}{\text{contribution margin percentage} - \text{profit percentage}}$$

In Ted's situation, the sales required to achieve a target profit of 30% of sales are

$$\text{Sales to achieve the target profit} = \frac{\$2,400}{60\% - 30\%} = \frac{\$2,400}{30\%} = \$8,000$$

At the sales volume of $8,000, Ted's income statement will appear as follows:

Sales	$8,000
Variable costs (40% of sales)	3,200
Contribution margin	4,800
Fixed costs	2,400
Income (equal to 30% of sales)	$2,400

Of course, if we knew that Ted sold only one product, say, the original example in which he sold only the $10 shirt, we could translate Ted's goal of a 30% return on sales to a $3 profit per shirt. Subtracting the variable cost of $4 and the required profit of $3 from the $10 selling price leaves $3 to cover the fixed costs. In a variation of the basic break-even formula (fixed costs/contribution margin), we could determine the sales volume required for the target profit as 800 of $10 shirts ($2,400/$3), or the $8,000 sales determined above. When more than one product is involved, target sales dollars can be determined using the formula that incorporates contribution margin percentage, but we will defer until Chapter 4 a discussion of how to determine the target sales in units of the various products.

Determining Unit Price

If volume of sales in units is given or can be predicted, VCP analysis can also be used to determine what prices must be charged so as to earn the target profits. This analysis can be done in single- or multiple-product situations, but we shall limit the analysis to the single-product firm. Assume that Ted is now selling only the shirts that have a variable cost of $4 and that his fixed costs are $2,400 per month. He wishes to earn profits of $2,000 per month and believes that he can sell 800 shirts per month. What price must he charge to achieve the desired results?

When volume, variable cost per unit, and fixed costs are known, it is easiest to build up an income statement from the bottom:

Sales	?
Variable costs (800 × $4)	$3,200
Necessary contribution margin	4,400
Fixed costs	2,400
Desired profit	$2,000

It can be seen that sales must be $7,600, the amount necessary to provide $4,400 in contribution margin when variable costs are $3,200. The unit selling price will have to be $9.50 ($7,600/800). The analysis cannot stop here; Ted must consider the prices charged by his competitors. His prices cannot be too far out of line with theirs.

Another approach is to determine the necessary contribution margin per unit by dividing the required contribution margin in total by the number of units expected to be sold. This yields $5.50 (i.e., $4,400/800). To have a contribution margin of $5.50 when variable costs are $4, the selling price must be $5.50 greater than variable cost, or $9.50.

This hypothetical analysis may result in an excessive selling price. If Ted wanted to earn $4,000 per month by selling 400 shirts, he would have to price them at $20.00 (required contribution margin is $6,400/400 = $16.00 contribution margin per unit + $4 variable cost = $20.00 selling price). If other stores are selling similar shirts for $10, a monthly profit goal of $4,000 on sales of 400 units is unachievable. This analysis helps show what price is required to reach a profit goal.

In both examples an expected monthly volume in units was used and our objective was to determine a required selling price. In Chapter 4 we will discuss the analysis when the set price and the expected volume are interrelated.

Changing Plans

In addition to helping managers determine selling prices, the concepts of contribution margin, break-even analysis, and target profit are useful when managers are contemplating some change in plans in the hope of increasing profits. A typical example of such a change would be a proposal for increased advertising, with the expectation that the advertising would result in an increase in the number of units sold.

It should be clear that making the expenditure for advertising would not cause profits to increase by the increase in units sold multiplied by the per-unit contribution margin. Why? Though total contribution margin would increase by that amount, the total fixed costs would increase by the cost of the advertising. Thus, the change in profit would be the change in total contribution margin *minus* the change in fixed costs.

Consider, for example, a firm with a per-unit contribution margin of $10 and a proposed advertising campaign that would cost $50,000 and is expected to increase sales by 4,000 units. Total contribution margin will increase by $40,000 (4,000 × $10), but fixed costs will be $50,000 higher, so that profit will actually be lower than it would be without the extra advertising. Using our knowledge of the contribution margin and the break-even formula, we can determine that it will take a volume increase of 5,000 units just to cover the increase in fixed cost ($50,000 fixed costs/$10 per-unit contribution margin). Total profit will increase only if the advertising can increase sales by more than 5,000 units, and will decrease if unit sales increase by less than that.

It is worth noting that the above analysis does not require knowledge of the sales volume that the firm expects without undertaking the advertising campaign. The levels of volume before and after the decision are not necessary pieces of information, only the *change* in volume. That is, it would not matter whether sales without the additional advertising would be 0, 50,000, or 2,000,000 units; so long as the increase in volume is greater than 5,000 units, taking the contemplated action would increase profits over what they would otherwise have been.

SUMMARY

Volume-cost-profit analysis is vital to planning and requires classification of costs by behavior. A cost is either fixed or variable according to whether the total amount of the cost changes as volume changes. After determining variable costs, contribution margin can be computed.

The critical points in the chapter are the recognition of the fixed/variable cost classification scheme, the analytical value of this classification, and the usefulness of contribution margin.

Volume-cost-profit analysis can be used to answer such questions as the following: What profits are earned at different levels of sales? What level of sales is needed to earn a particular profit? How will changes in cost structure affect profit? What are the effects of changes in selling prices? What price should be charged to earn a particular profit?

The validity of volume-cost-profit analysis depends on accurate estimates of assumed revenue and cost behavior within relevant ranges of volume and over short periods of time. It is unwise to view a volume-cost-profit graph as presenting a single set of conditions that is valid over wide ranges of volume. The graph should be viewed as a rough gauge of relationships over the relevant range.

Volume-cost-profit analysis is valuable in planning, selecting alternatives, analyzing results, and incorporating new information into future plans.

KEY TERMS

average total cost per unit
break-even point
contribution margin
contribution margin percentage
cost behavior
fixed costs

nonvariable costs
relevant range
return on sales
target profit
variable costs
volume-cost-profit analysis

KEY FORMULAS

$$\text{Profit} = \frac{\text{total}}{\text{sales}} - \frac{\text{total}}{\text{variable costs}} - \frac{\text{total}}{\text{fixed costs}}$$

$$\frac{\text{Total}}{\text{costs}} = \frac{\text{fixed}}{\text{costs}} + (\text{variable cost per unit} \times \text{no. of units sold})$$

$$\frac{\text{Break-even sales,}}{\text{in units}} = \frac{\text{fixed costs}}{\text{contribution margin per unit}}$$

$$\frac{\text{Break-even sales,}}{\text{in dollars}} = \frac{\text{fixed costs}}{\text{contribution margin percentage}}$$

$$\frac{\text{Sales, in units, to}}{\text{achieve target profit}} = \frac{\text{fixed costs} + \text{target profit}}{\text{contribution margin per unit}}$$

$$\frac{\text{Sales, in dollars,}}{\text{to achieve target}} = \frac{\text{fixed costs}}{\text{contribution margin percentage} - \text{target return on sales}}$$

REVIEW PROBLEM

Volume-cost-profit analysis assumes that important variables (selling price, variable cost per unit, total fixed costs) do not change within the relevant range. Nevertheless, as we saw in the section on unit price determination, a manager may want to know what value for one of these variables is consistent with a particular target profit. Additionally, because prices and costs may change quickly, a manager must be alert to the effects that such changes may bring. The following problem will test your basic understanding of the principles of VCP analysis and the extent to which changes in important variables can affect a firm's planning. You should solve the problem, one part at a time, and check your answers with those provided. Consider each question independently of the others.

Glassman Company sells one product at $20 per unit. Its variable costs are $12 per unit and its fixed costs are $100,000 per month.

1. If the firm can sell 15,000 units in a particular month, what will its income be?
2. What is the firm's break-even point in units?
3. What is the firm's break-even point in sales dollars?
4. What sales, in units, are required for the firm to earn $40,000 for the month?
5. What sales, in dollars, are required for the firm to earn $40,000 for the month?
6. Suppose that the firm must reduce its selling price to $18 because competitors are charging that amount. What is the new break-even point (a) in units? (b) in dollars?
7. Suppose that fixed costs are expected to increase by $10,000 (to $110,000 per month). What is the new break-even point (a) in units? (b) in dollars? Price is $20.
8. Suppose that the firm is currently selling 10,000 units per month. The sales manager believes that if advertising expenditures were increased by $5,000, sales would also increase. How much would sales have to increase, in units, to give the firm the same income or loss that it is currently earning? Although you are told how many units are now being sold, you do not need to know this fact to solve the problem.
9. Suppose that the selling price is reduced to $18, but that variable costs drop to $10 at the same time. What is the new break-even point (a) in units? (b) in dollars?

Answer to Review Problem

1. The firm will earn $20,000. An income statement for sales of 15,000 units would show the following:

Sales (15,000 × $20)	$300,000
Variable costs (15,000 × $12)	180,000
Contribution margin (15,000 × $8)	120,000
Fixed costs	100,000
Income	$ 20,000

A shortcut approach is to multiply contribution margin per unit of $8 by 15,000 units, which gives $120,000 in contribution margin, then subtract fixed costs of $100,000 to get $20,000 income.

2. 12,500 units. The break-even point in units is the result of dividing fixed costs ($100,000) by the $8 contribution margin per unit.

3. $250,000. This amount can be determined either by multiplying the break-even point in units (from part 2) by the sales price per unit (12,500 × $20) or by applying the break-even formula that incorporates the contribution margin percentage ($100,000/40%). The contribution margin percentage is determined by dividing the sales price of $20 into the contribution margin of $8 (sales price of $20 − variable cost per unit of $12).

4. 17,500 units. The profit of $40,000 is added to the fixed costs of $100,000, and the break-even formula is then applied. Thus, the total to be obtained from sales is $40,000 plus $100,000 in fixed costs. If Glassman gets $8 per unit and desires total contribution margin of $140,000, it must sell 17,500 units ($140,000/$8).

5. $350,000. This amount can be determined either by multiplying the 17,500 units in part 4 by the $20 selling price per unit or by applying the break-even formula that incorporates the contribution margin percentage. To return the fixed costs of $100,000 plus a profit of $40,000, when the contribution margin percentage is 40%, requires sales of $350,000 ($140,000/40%).

6. (a) 16,667 units. If fixed costs of $100,000 must be covered when each unit carries a contribution margin of $6 ($18 sales price − variable cost of $12), a total of 16,667 units must be sold ($100,000/$6).

    (b) $300,000. This amount can be determined either by multiplying the number of units (16,667) in part (a) by the selling price of $18 or by utilizing the formula that incorporates the contribution margin percentage. Thus, 16,667 × $18 is $300,000 (rounded) or $100,000/[($18 − $12)/$18] = $300,000.

7. (a) 13,750 units. With fixed costs of $110,000 and a contribution margin per unit of $8, the number of units to produce a contribution margin equal to the fixed costs is 13,750 ($110,000/$8). Still another approach would be to determine what additional sales volume (beyond that required to break even with the current cost structure) would provide sufficient contribution margin to cover the additional fixed costs. It will take the contribution margin from an additional 1,250 units ($10,000/$8 per unit) to cover the added fixed costs, and the break-even point is already 12,500 units, so the total number of units required to cover the new cost structure is 13,750 (12,500 + 1,250).

    (b) $275,000. The most direct approach to this answer is simply to multiply the number of units (13,750) computed in part (a) by the sales price per unit ($20). Or, the answer could be determined by dividing the fixed costs ($110,000) by the contribution margin percentage (40%).

8. 625 units. Current income will not be affected so long as the contribution margin from the additional units is sufficient to offset the expenditure for advertising. Hence, we need only determine what additional sales will produce the contribution margin sufficient to cover the cost of the advertising. Since the contribution margin per unit is $8, the number of units needed to be sold to cover the $5,000 advertising campaign is $5,000/$8 or 625 units. You should note that the current level of sales is irrelevant to the decision of whether or not to

undertake the advertising campaign. As long as the campaign will increase sales by 625 units, the company will be neither better nor worse off than it would have been without the campaign.

9. (a) 12,500 units. The contribution margin per unit remains at $8 ($18 sales price − $10 variable cost) and the fixed costs remain at $100,000. Hence, the break-even point, in units, remains the same as before, or 12,500 units ($100,000/$8).

   (b) $225,000. Although the number of units to break even remains the same as before the changes in selling price and variable cost per unit, the total sales in dollars must change in order to break even. One approach is simply to multiply the break-even sales in units times the sales price per unit (12,500 × $18 = $225,000). Another approach would be to compute the new break-even point in dollars by reference to the new contribution margin percentage. Thus the fixed costs of $100,000 would be divided by the contribution margin percentage of 44.44% ($8/$18).

The emphasis in this review problem has been the possibility of changes in the structure of costs and selling prices. Managers must be alert for such possible changes and their effects on profits. Additionally, managers can analyze proposed changes to see if they will increase profits. Part 8 of this problem gave an important practical example: an increase in a fixed cost was expected to lead to some increase in volume. If the advertising manager believed that the increase in cost would generate additional sales in excess of 625 units, the plan would have been wise.

Volume-cost-profit analysis is used to answer "what if?" questions: What if we increased our prices? What if we sold more units? What if we could make the product at a lower variable cost? These questions are constantly being asked by managers.

ASSIGNMENT MATERIAL

Questions for Discussion

2-1 Significance of average cost   "If selling price is less than the average cost of a unit, the firm should stop operating because it will incur losses." Is this statement true? Explain.

2-2 Economic profit   There is no profit unless all costs are covered. The economist's concept of cost includes a return to the owners of the capital invested in the firm. From the economist's point of view, the return to the owners should be equal to what investors would earn had they invested their capital elsewhere in the economy in an essentially similar venture. In determining a break-even point (in sales dollars) after a return to the owners of capital, how would you incorporate the economist's idea?

2-3 Volume-cost-profit assumptions   You have been trying to convince a friend to use volume-cost-profit analysis in planning her business, a clothing store. She has come up with the following objections to using the analysis and has asked you to explain how to overcome them, if possible.

1. Inflation makes it likely that she will have to pay successively higher prices for the clothing she buys, the salaries she pays employees, utilities, and other operating costs. In addition, she will raise her selling prices as her costs rise. Therefore, she cannot use the current prices and costs to plan future operations.

2. She sometimes advertises heavily, sometimes lightly. Because she can alter the amount of advertising almost at will, she wonders how you can treat the cost as fixed.

3. On occasion, she must sell clothes at greatly reduced prices to make room for new merchandise. Therefore, the percentage of the purchase price to the selling price is not always constant, and she is unsure whether that can be worked into the analysis.

Required: Respond to these objections.

2-4   Misconceptions about VCP analysis   One of your classmates is having some trouble with VCP analysis and has asked for your help. Specifically, he has the following questions:

1. "How can VCP analysis work when you really don't know what's going to happen? You might have to change your selling price. Your suppliers might change their prices. You might not sell the number of units you need to sell in order to earn a target profit. All sorts of things can happen that will invalidate your calculations."
2. "When I took economics, I learned that the higher the price, the less you sell. So how can you draw a straight revenue line?"
3. "I don't see how you can say that some costs are fixed. I'll accept depreciation and a few others, but salaries can be raised or lowered easily, your insurance premiums can go up or down, you can spend more or less on advertising, travel, and all sorts of other elements that you would call fixed."

Required: Answer your classmate's questions.

2-5   Will Sears' stockholders understand?   The following statement appeared in the Sears, Roebuck and Co. report to stockholders for the first quarter of 1983.

> Traditional buying patterns in the merchandise business generally result in the lowest sales of the year in the first quarter, producing a relatively high ratio of fixed costs to sales and lower ratio of income to sales.

Discuss this statement in relation to the concepts introduced in Chapter 2 and the traditional, late-January "white sales" at most department stores.

2-6   Purchases and sales   One of your classmates has just come to you with the following question: "I don't understand how the variable costs are calculated for merchandise that a firm buys and sells. Suppose that a firm buys 2,000 units for $6 each and sells 1,500 of them for $10 each. Why isn't contribution margin calculated like this:

Sales (1,500 × $10)	$15,000
Variable costs (2,000 × $6)	12,000
Contribution margin	$ 3,000

"See what I mean?" Respond to your classmate's question.

Exercises

2-7   Contribution margin statements   Prepare income statements for each of the following situations. Use the contribution margin format shown in the chapter.

		Cases			
	1	2	3	4	5
Selling price per unit	$ 20	$ 16	$ 10	$ 15	$ 5
Variable cost per unit	$ 14	$ 12	$ 4	$ 12	$ 1
Fixed costs	$24,000	$30,000	$100,000	$100,000	$30,000
Unit sales	8,000	10,000	60,000	30,000	6,000

2-8 Contribution margin statements Prepare income statements for each of the following situations. Use the contribution margin format shown in the chapter.

Case	Sales	Variable Cost as Percentage of Sales	Fixed Costs
1.	$170,000	40%	$ 88,000
2.	100,000	75	22,000
3.	50,000	30	41,000
4.	700,000	55	220,000
5.	300,000	60	80,000

2-9 Contribution margin income statements, break-even points, and profit targets Each of the following cases is independent of the others.

Case	Selling Price per Unit	Variable Cost per Unit	Fixed Costs	Sales in Units
1.	$ 4	$3	$ 8,000	12,000
2.	8	5	33,000	18,000
3.	12	8	170,000	40,000
4.	16	8	70,000	15,000

Required
1. For each case, prepare an income statement using the contribution margin format.
2. For each case, calculate the break-even point in units and in dollars.
3. For cases 1 and 2, calculate the unit sales volume to earn a target profit of $30,000.
4. For cases 1 and 2, calculate the unit sales volume needed to earn a 20% return on sales.

2-10 Contribution margin income statements, break-even points, and profit targets Each of the following cases is independent of the others.

Case	Sales	Contribution Margin Percentage	Fixed Costs
1.	$ 40,000	50%	$18,000
2.	120,000	60	60,000
3.	75,000	30	15,000
4.	180,000	25	48,000

Required
1. For each case, prepare an income statement using the contribution margin format.
2. For each case, calculate the break-even point.
3. For cases 1 and 2, calculate the sales dollars needed to earn a target profit of $60,000.
4. For cases 1 and 2, calculate the sales dollars needed to earn a 30% return on sales.

2-11 Relationships among variables Fill in the blanks for each of the following independent situations.

Case	(a) Selling Price per Unit	(b) Variable Cost Percentage	(c) Number of Units Sold	(d) Contribution Margin	(e) Fixed Costs	(f) Income (Loss)
1.	$160	—	2,000	$80,000	—	($10,000)
2.	40	70%	—	—	$60,000	12,000
3.	25	—	15,000	—	25,000	50,000
4.	4	—	26,000	52,000	—	36,000
5.	—	68	4,000	64,000	60,000	—
6.	—	80	15,000	—	22,000	8,000

2-12 Relationships among variables Fill in the blanks for each of the following independent situations.

	1	2	3	4	5	6
Selling price per unit	$ 6	$ 6	—	$ 9	$ 25	—
Variable cost per unit	$ 3	—	$ 6	$ 4	$ 19	$ 6
Number of units sold	—	2,000	3,000	1,000	—	1,000
Total contribution margin	$3,000	$4,000	$12,000	—	—	$2,000
Total fixed costs	$1,500	—	$ 8,000	—	$ 600	—
Income	—	$3,000	—	$3,500	$3,000	$1,200

2-13 Volume-cost-profit graph The graph at the top of page 37 portrays the operations of Richmond Company.

Required: Using the graph as the basis, determine the following.
1. Sales dollars at the break-even point.
2. Fixed costs at 450 units sold.
3. Total variable costs at 400 units sold.
4. Variable cost per unit at 200 units sold.
5. Variable cost per unit at 500 units sold.
6. Selling price per unit.
7. Total contribution margin at 300 units sold.
8. Profit (loss) at sales of 300 units.
9. Profit (loss) at sales of 500 units.
10. Break-even sales, in units, if fixed costs were to increase by $50.

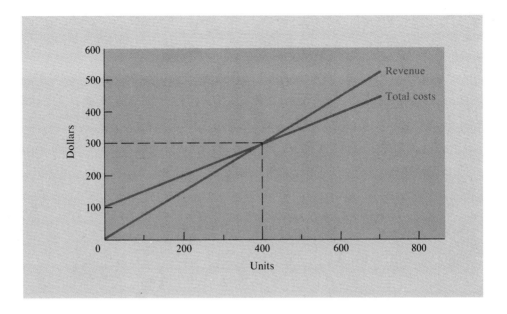

2-14 Graphs of cost behavior   If one were to graph the behavior of costs in relation to volume, the following might result.

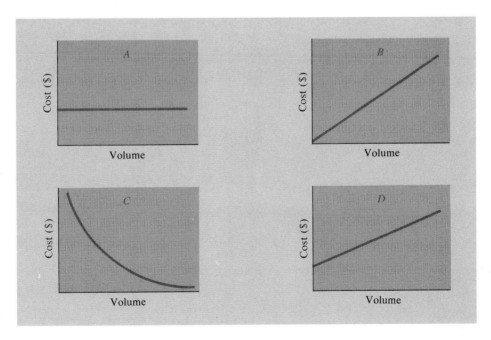

Required: Fill in the blanks using the letters of the graphs above. One letter may be the answer to more than one question.

1.   Which graph shows the behavior of total variable costs? _____
2.   Which graph shows the behavior of total fixed costs? _____

3. Which graph shows the behavior of variable costs per unit? _____
4. Which graph shows the behavior of fixed costs per unit? _____
5. Which graph shows the behavior of total costs? _____

2-15 Volume-cost-profit chart   The chart below portrays the operations of the Weyand Company.

Required: Fill in the blanks with the appropriate letter(s) from the chart. You may have to indicate additions or subtractions.

1. Revenue line   _____
2. Variable costs   _____
3. Fixed costs   _____
4. Profit area   _____
5. Loss area   _____
6. Total cost line   _____
7. Break-even point   _____
8. Contribution margin   _____

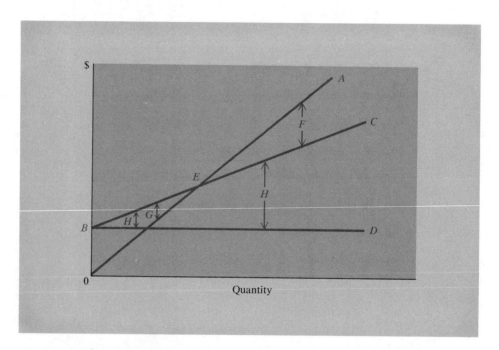

2-16 Volume-cost-profit graph, analysis of changes   You have prepared a VCP graph that reflects the following expectations held by the managers of your company.

Selling price	$50
Unit variable cost	$30
Total fixed costs	$400,000

The managers have been wondering what effects there would be on operations if some changes took place, either by management decision or by some outside force such as a supplier raising its prices to the company. The following specific changes have been raised as the most likely possibilities:

a. a decrease in the selling price resulting from higher-than-expected competition;
b. an increase in unit variable cost arising from a decision to use more expensive materials in the product;
c. an increase in total fixed costs accompanied by a decrease in unit variable cost from introducing labor-saving machinery;
d. an increase in the number of units expected to be sold; and
e. an increase in the selling price combined with an increase in unit variable cost resulting from a decision to increase the quality of the product.

Required: Treat each change independently of the others. For each change, state the effects on (a) the revenue line, (b) the total cost line, and (c) the break-even point. Some changes will have no effect on one or more of the items. In at least one case, the effect on the break-even point cannot be determined without additional information. Note that both the intercept and slope of the total cost line could be affected by a set of changes.

2-17 Pricing and return on sales   Data for the one product of Rogers Company appear below.

Selling price	$5
Variable costs	3
Annual fixed costs	$20,000

Required: Answer each of the following items independently.

1. The firm's managers would like a 20% return on sales. Determine the volume required to earn that return in units and in dollars.
2. The managers believe that the firm can sell 20,000 units and would like a profit of $30,000. What price must they charge?
3. If the firm could sell 30,000 units at $5, how high could variable costs go and the firm earn a $28,000 profit?
4. If variable costs increase to $4 per unit and the firm can sell 40,000 units, what price must it charge to earn a $36,000 profit?

2-18 Volume-cost-profit analysis   At the current time, ABC Company sells its single product for $20 and has variable costs of $12. Fixed costs are $80,000 per year.

Required: Answer the following questions, considering each independently.

1. What are break-even sales in (a) units and (b) dollars?
2. If a $160,000 annual profit is to be earned, what sales are necessary in (a) units and (b) dollars?
3. If sales are 60,000 units, what will profits be?
4. If sales are $250,000, what will profits be?
5. If sales are 30,000 units
    (a) Total variable costs will be how much?
    (b) Total costs will be how much?
6. Write formulas to determine total costs at any level of sales, based on (a) dollars and (b) units.

2-19 Profit planning   Tinney Company, which is a wholesaler of jeans, had the following income statement in 19X5:

Sales (40,000 pairs at $15)		$600,000
Cost of sales		300,000
Gross margin		300,000
Selling expenses	$150,000	
Administrative expenses	90,000	240,000
Income		$ 60,000

Mr. Tinney informs you that the only variable costs are cost of sales and $2 per unit selling costs. All administrative expenses are fixed. In planning for the coming year, 19X6, Mr. Tinney expects his selling price to remain constant, with unit volume increasing by 20%. He also forecasts the following changes in costs:

Variable costs:	
Cost of goods sold	up $0.50 per unit
Selling costs	up $0.10 per unit
Fixed costs:	
Selling costs	up $10,000
Administrative costs	up $15,000

Required
1. Determine the firm's profit for 19X6 if all forecasts are met, and prepare an income statement using the contribution margin format.
2. Determine the number of units that the firm would have to sell in 19X6 to earn the same profit it did in 19X5.

2-20 Volume-cost-profit analysis   Searfoss Company had the following income statement in February:

Sales	$150,000
Costs	170,000
Loss	($ 20,000)

The firm's contribution margin percentage at its current selling price of $20 is 40%.

Required: Consider each question independently.
1. Determine the firm's break-even point in sales dollars.
2. Determine the firm's total costs if it sells 8,000 units.
3. Determine the firm's income if it sells 9,000 units at $18 per unit.
4. Determine whether or not it would be worth the $6,000 cost of a special advertising campaign if, because of the campaign, the firm could increase its sales by 1,000 units per month at $20 per unit.
5. The firm is considering changing its selling price. The president wishes the firm to earn $15,000 per month with a sales volume of 10,000 units. What selling price will achieve this objective?

6. Comment on the president's profit goal in item 5, given the information that is currently available.

2-21 Conversion of income statement to contribution margin basis The following income statement was prepared by the controller of Wassenich Company. Material and labor costs are variable.

Wassenich Company
Income Statement
for 19X4

Sales (10,000 units)		$120,000
Cost of goods sold:		
Materials	$30,000	
Labor	35,000	
Factory overhead:		
Variable	16,000	
Fixed	14,000	95,000
Gross profit		25,000
Selling and administrative expenses:		
Variable	9,000	
Fixed	22,000	31,000
Loss		($ 6,000)

Required

1. Prepare a new income statement showing contribution margin.
2. What is the break-even point in units?
3. The president of the firm believes that sales could be increased by 4,000 units if an additional $7,000 were spent on advertising. His son, the general manager, says that it would be silly to do so because the firm is losing enough already. Would it be wise to undertake the advertising campaign?

2-22 Per-unit data The controller of Walker Company has provided the following per-unit analysis, based on a volume of 50,000 units.

Selling price		$20
Variable costs	$8	
Fixed costs	7	
Total costs		15
Profit		$ 5

Required: Answer each of the following questions independently of the others.

1. What total profit does the firm expect to earn?
2. What is the firm's break-even point in units?
3. If the firm's managers expect to be able to increase volume to 55,000 units by spending an additional $40,000 on salaries for additional salespeople, what total profit will the firm earn?
4. The managers now believe that the firm could sell 60,000 units and desire a profit of $310,000. What price per unit must the firm charge?

2-23 VCP analysis for a CPA firm Bret McConnell, a certified public accountant, has estimated the following fixed costs of operation for the coming year.

Office salaries	$34,000
Rent, utilities	26,000
Other	10,000
Total	$70,000

There are no variable costs as McConnell currently plans operations. He charges clients $50 per hour for his time.

Required

1. How many hours must McConnell work to earn $50,000?
2. McConnell is thinking about hiring one or two senior accounting majors from a local university for $8 per hour to do some routine work for his clients. He expects each to work about 300 hours, but about 30 of those hours (training and temporary idle time) will not be chargeable to clients. McConnell wants each student to provide at least $3,000 profit. What hourly rate must he charge for their time in order to achieve the objective?

Problems

2-24 Pricing decision—nursery school The Board of Directors of First Community Church of Delmar is considering opening a nursery school for four- and five-year-old children. The school would operate in a building that the church owns. The members of the board agree that the school, which would be open to all children, should break even or be within $100 either way of the break-even point.

The treasurer has prepared an analysis of the expected costs of operating the school, based on conversations with members of other churches that run similar programs. The school would be open for nine months each year, with two classes, one in the morning and one in the afternoon.

First Community Church
Expected Costs of
Nursery School Operation

Salaries, teacher and assistant	$10,600 for nine months
Utilities	$400 for nine months
Miscellaneous operating costs	$300 for nine months
Supplies, paper, paint	$2 per child per month
Snacks, cookies, juice	$4 per child per month

The best estimate of probable enrollment is 20 children in each of the two classes, which is all that the teacher and assistant can handle and still achieve the quality that the board feels is essential.

Required

1. Determine the monthly fee per child that would have to be charged in order that the school break even (round to nearest dollar) with its maximum enrollment.

2. Suppose that the monthly fee is set at $45. What is the break-even point in enroll-ment?

2-25 Relationships Considering each situation below independently, answer the questions. You may not be able to answer the questions in the order in which they are asked.

1. A firm had variable costs per unit of $12, a selling price of $20, fixed costs of $100,000, and a net loss of $20,000.
   (a) What was its contribution margin in total?
   (b) What were its sales in units?
   (c) What were its dollar sales?

2. A firm earned $30,000 selling 50,000 units at $5 per unit. Its fixed costs were $180,000.
   (a) What were its variable costs per unit?
   (b) What was its total contribution margin?
   (c) What would its income be if sales increased by 5,000 units?

3. A firm had return on sales of 10%, income of $30,000, selling price of $10, and a contribution margin percentage of 30%.
   (a) What were its fixed costs?
   (b) What were its variable costs per unit?
   (c) What were its sales in units?
   (d) What were its sales in dollars?

4. A firm had return on sales of 15% at sales of $300,000. Its fixed costs were $75,000, and its variable costs were $6 per unit.
   (a) What were sales in units?
   (b) What was its contribution margin per unit?
   (c) What was its income?

5. A firm earned $50,000 selling 100,000 units. Its contribution margin in total was $110,000 and its variable costs were $3 per unit.
   (a) What was its selling price?
   (b) What were its fixed costs?

6. A firm sold 40,000 units with contribution margin of $5 per unit, which is 40% of selling price. Its fixed costs were $220,000.
   (a) What was its income?
   (b) What were its dollar sales?

7. A firm increased its income from $14,000 to $26,000 by increasing its sales $40,000. When it earned $14,000, it had sales of $90,000.
   (a) What were its fixed costs?
   (b) What was its contribution margin percentage?

2-26 Sensitivity of variables The following data relate to the one product of Cranston Company:

Planned sales in units—19X5	30,000
Selling price	$15
Variable costs	$12
Total fixed costs	$60,000

Required: Answer the following questions, considering each independently.

1. Which of the following events would reduce planned profits the most:
   (a) A decrease in selling price of 10%?
   (b) An increase in variable costs of 10% per unit?

(c) An increase in fixed costs of 10%?

(d) A decline in sales volume of 10%?

2. Which of the following events would increase planned profits the most:

(a) An increase in selling price of 5%?

(b) A decrease in variable costs of 10% per unit?

(c) An increase in sales volume of 10%?

(d) A decrease in fixed costs of 15%?

3. If selling prices declined by 10%, how many more units would have to be sold to achieve the planned profit?

4. If selling prices increased by 20%, by how much could variable costs per unit increase and the planned profit be achieved?

2-27 Volume-cost-profit analysis—changes in variables   During two recent months the Thompson Company had the following income statements:

	March	April
Sales	$200,000	$216,000
Variable costs	130,000	120,600
Contribution margin	70,000	95,400
Fixed costs	40,000	40,000
Income	$ 30,000	$ 55,400

You learn that the price of the product sold by the firm is generally changed each month though its purchase cost is stable at $11 per unit. The only other variable cost is a 10% commission paid on all sales.

Required: Determine the selling price, unit volume, and variable cost per unit in each of the two months.

2-28 Volume-cost-profit analysis for a hospital   The administrator of The Caldwell Memorial Hospital is considering methods of providing X-ray treatments to patients. The hospital now refers about 160 patients per month to a nearby private clinic, and each treatment costs the patient $25. If the hospital decides to provide the treatment, it will have to rent a machine for $1,600 per month and hire a technician for $1,200 per month. Variable costs are $5 per treatment.

Required

1. The hospital administrator is considering charging the same fee as the clinic has charged. By how much will the hospital increase its income, or decrease its losses, if it provides the service?

2. How much would the hospital have to charge to break even on the treatments?

2-29 Assumptions of VCP analysis   Last year you were engaged as a consultant to Thompson Products Company and prepared some analyses of its volume-cost-profit relationships. Among your findings was that the contribution margin percentage was 40% at the firm's planned selling price of $20. The firm expected to sell 10,000 at the $20 price, which you estimated would result in an income of $48,000. You told Mr. Thompson, the owner of the firm, that profits would change at the rate of $0.40 per $1 change in sales.

Mr. Thompson has just called to tell you that the results did not come out as you had said they would. The firm earned profits of $63,200 on volume of $226,800. Although variable costs per unit were incurred as expected, the firm had higher fixed costs than expected because of a $2,000 advertising campaign during the year. The campaign was coupled with an increase in selling price, and Mr. Thompson was very pleased at the results. However, Mr. Thompson asks you why profits did not increase by 40% of the added sales volume of $26,800, but rather by somewhat more.

Required
1. Reconstruct the income statement for the year, based on the actual results.
2. Determine (a) the number of units sold and (b) the selling price per unit.
3. Explain to Mr. Thompson why the results were not as you had originally forecasted.

2-30 VCP in a service business   Microprog Company develops programs for microcomputers to customer order, primarily for business applications. The company charges its customers $40 per hour for programming time. The managers of the company have been planning operations for the coming year and have developed the following estimates.

Total estimated chargeable hours	80,000
Total fixed costs, salaries, rent, etc.	$1,750,000

Microprog employs 15 full-time programmers at an average salary of $30,000. These salaries are included in the cost figure given above. Each programmer works about 2,000 chargeable hours per year. The company does not wish to hire additional programmers, but rather to use free-lancers to meet demand. Free-lancers charge an average of $25 per hour.

Required
1. If the company meets its goal of 80,000 chargeable hours, what profit will it earn?
2. How many chargeable hours must it obtain from free-lancers, in addition to the hours its full-time programmers work, to earn a $300,000 profit?

2-31 Income statement construction   The president of Conoy Industrial Products Company has asked for your assistance in preparing a planned income statement for the coming month. He gives you the following data developed by the controller, who has become ill and cannot help the president:

Expected sales	25,000	units
Selling price	$20	per unit
Purchase cost	$8	per unit
Sales commissions	15%	of sales
Shipping costs	$2	per unit
Salaries	$96,000	per month
Rent	$16,000	per month
Depreciation on equipment	$120,000	per year
Advertising	$6,000	per month
Miscellaneous expenses	$4,500	per month

Required
1. Prepare an income statement for the coming month based on the planned data given.
2. Determine the break-even point for the firm, in units per month.
3. Suppose that a doubling of the advertising expense, coupled with a $2 reduction in

price, would increase sales by 5,000 units over the planned volume. Would it be wise to take these actions?

2-32 **Developing volume-cost-profit information** The manager of Sans Flavour Food Store, a franchise operation, is confused by the income statements he has received from his accountant. He asks you to help him with them. He is especially concerned that his return on sales dropped much more than sales from April to May.

Income Statements

	April	May
Sales	$90,000	$75,000
Cost of sales	36,000	30,000
Gross profit	54,000	45,000
Operating expenses:		
Rent	1,200	1,200
Salaries, wages, commissions	31,500	28,500
Insurance	900	900
Supplies	1,800	1,500
Utilities	1,400	1,400
Miscellaneous expenses	4,500	4,500
Total operating expenses	41,300	38,000
Income	$12,700	$ 7,000
Return on sales	14.1%	9.3%

The manager informs you that the salaries, wages, and commissions account includes the salaries of several clerks and himself. All salespersons work on commissions of 20% of sales. Supplies are primarily wrapping paper and tape and vary directly with sales. For various reasons he had expected the $15,000 decline in sales. But he had expected income of $10,575 on those lower sales (that is, 14.1% of his expected sales).

Required: Prepare income statements using the contribution margin format for April and May, and explain to the manager the advantages of this alternative format.

2-33 **New market area** The Whizzer Toy Company has just finished an analysis of its cost and sales picture for 19X6. The analysis indicates the following:

Planned selling price	$40
Variable costs per unit	$32
Total fixed costs	$320,000
Planned sales volume	50,000 units

Required: Answer the following questions, considering each independently.
1. What is the break-even point in units?
2. If sales volume were 10% higher than planned, what would be the break-even point?
3. If the company wanted to increase its profit by $30,000 over that which would be earned at planned sales volume, by how many units would sales have to increase?
4. Suppose the company could undertake a $40,000 advertising campaign in a foreign country where the company has no sales at this time. The campaign is expected to

generate sales of 15,000 units if the price is set at $36. Additional shipping costs of $1 per unit will be incurred. Would the venture be profitable?

5. The preceding question indicates that this would be the first time the company tried to sell in the particular foreign couuntry. What is the importance of the specification that the sales be made in another country?

2-34 Changes in operations   Bart Packard operates the 15th Street Parking Lot, leasing the lot from the owner at $12,000 per month plus 10% of total revenues. Packard is thinking about extending until midnight the hours the lot will be open. It now closes at 7:00 PM. Keeping the lot open would require paying an additional $800 per week to attendants. Increases in utilities and insurance would be another $100 per week. The lot must pay a 5% city tax on its total revenue. The parking charge is $0.80 per hour.

Required

1. Suppose that Packard expects additional business amounting to 2,000 hours per week. Should he extend the hours of operation to midnight?
2. How much additional business, stated in hours, does Packard need to break even on the additional hours of operation?

2-35 Unit costs   Carl Murphy owns a chain of shoe stores. He recently opened a new store in a shopping mall, and he was not pleased with the following results for the first month of operation:

Sales		$80,000
Cost of sales		40,000
Gross margin		40,000
Salaries and wages	$23,000	
Utilities, insurance, rent	3,500	
Commissions at 15% of sales	12,000	38,500
Profit		$ 1,500

Noting that sales were 4,000 pairs at an average price of $20, Murphy calculated the per-pair cost at $19.625 ($78,500/4,000), leaving only a $0.375 profit per pair. He considered this an inadequate profit. He did expect sales to rise to 5,000 pairs at an average price of $20 over the next month or two, but figured that profit would increase only to about $1,875 (5,000 × $0.375), which was still not adequate.

Murphy asked for your advice, and in response to your questions he said that even with the increase in sales there would be no need for additional salaried personnel and that utilities, insurance, and rent would remain about the same. The cost of sales percentage would also remain at 50%.

Required: Prepare an income statement based on sales of 5,000 pairs of shoes. Explain to Mr. Murphy the fallacy in his reasoning.

2-36 VCP analysis and break-even pricing—municipal operation   The City of Gardendale operates a municipal trash collection service. Analyses of costs indicate that the fixed monthly cost is $15,000 and the variable cost is about $0.80 per pickup per customer. The city collects trash in the business district twelve times a month and in the residential district four times a month. The difference in frequency results from the much larger volume of trash in the business district. There are 250 businesses and 1,500 residences served by trash collection.

Required

1. The city manager is aware that other cities charge business customers $20 per month and residential customers $6 per month. What profit or loss would the operation generate at these prices?
2. The city manager would like to break even, or show a small profit on trash collection. She believes it fair to charge businesses three times as much as residences because the businesses get three times as much service. What monthly prices would make the operation break even?

2-37   Volume-cost-profit analysis for a service business   Walker Associates is a market research firm. Companies come to it asking for various types of studies regarding the preferences of consumers, and Walker develops a plan for the study. If the company approves the plan, Walker does the job.

  Most of Walker's business involves interviewing people in or near supermarkets, drugstores, and department stores. Walker hires people part-time to perform the interviews for $8 per hour and pays such expenses as mileage and meals. Expenses average $6 per day per person, and each person generally works about six hours per day. The fixed costs associated with Walker's operation consist largely of salaries to the permanent staff. These, along with rent and utilities for the firm's office, total $300,000 per year.

  Walker would like to develop a pricing policy based on an hourly rate, that is, charging the client company an amount per hour that Walker's part-time employees spend interviewing.

Required

1. Walker's management estimates that it can get enough business to require about 10,000 six-hour days of interviewing. What hourly charge would give the firm a profit of $75,000?
2. Suppose that Walker sets the charge at $16 per hour. How many six-hour days must it achieve to earn a $75,000 profit?
3. Walker is considering using full-time, salaried interviewers rather than part-time people. What are some of the implications of such a change?

2-38   Alternative cost behavior—a movie company (continued in Chapters 3 and 4)   Blockbusters Incorporated, a leading producer of movies, is currently negotiating with Sky Kirkwalker, the biggest box-office attraction in the movie industry at the present time, to star in *War Trek,* a science fiction film. For a starring role, Sky would normally receive a salary of $1,500,000 plus 5% of the receipts-to-the-producer. (The producer normally receives 40% of the total paid admissions wherever the movie is shown.) However, Sky is quite optimistic about the prospects for *Trek* and has expressed some interest in a special contract that would give him only 25% of his normal salary but increase his portion of the receipts-to-the-producer to 20%. Other than Sky's salary, costs of producing the picture are expected to be $2,500,000.

Required: Answer the following questions, assuming that the alternative compensation schemes have been identified by Blockbusters as N (for the normal contract) and S (for the special contract).

1. What are the break-even receipts-to-the-producer under each of the compensation schemes?
2. If total paid admissions in theaters are expected to be $14,000,000, what will be the income to the producer under compensation schemes N and S?
3. At what level of receipts-to-the-producer would Sky earn the same total income under compensation schemes N and S?

2-39 Seasonality, relevant range, and profit opportunities   Royal Ice Cream Company currently has monthly sales varying from $60,000 in the winter to $170,000 in the summer. The capacity of the firm is strained in the summer, because the product must be stored in freezers. The relevant range is wide, varying from about $40,000 to $170,000, and the cost structure is as follows:

Variable costs	40% of sales dollars
Fixed costs	$40,000 per month

An analysis of sales by month shows the following:

November through February	$ 60,000 monthly
March through May	90,000 monthly
June through August	170,000 monthly
September and October	80,000 monthly

Required
1. Prepare income statements for each of the groups of months given (November through February, March through May, etc.).
2. The president has been discussing the possibility of acquiring some new equipment from Whipitup Company, a maker of freezing equipment and storage freezers. The equipment would enable the firm to increase its production in the peak months to $220,000 per month. The president believes that all additional production could easily be sold. The equipment would be rented for $5,000 per month, but must be rented for an entire year. Sales in off-peak months would be unchanged. Variable cost percentages and existing fixed costs would not be affected. Should the new equipment be rented? Explain and support your answer.

Cases

2-40 A concessionaire   Ralph Newkirk is considering entering a bid for the hot dog and soft drink concession at the new athletic stadium. He intends to bid for the concession rights at the 14 football games that will be played during the season. There will be seven college games and seven professional games. Average attendance at college games is 20,000, at professional games 50,000. Ralph estimates that he sells one hot dog and one soft drink for each two persons attending a game.
Revenue and cost data for the products are as follows:

	Hot Dogs	Soft Drinks
Selling price	$0.50	$0.30
Variable costs:		
Hot dog	0.080	
Roll	0.040	
Mustard, onion, etc.	0.005	
Soft drink and ice		0.125

In addition, salespeople are paid a 15% commission on all sales, and all sales are subject to commissions. Fixed costs per game are $4,000 for rentals of heating, cooking, mixing, and cooling equipment.

The stadium management has requested that bids be made in the form of royalties on sales. The highest percentage of sales bid will win the contract.

Required

1. What percentage of sales can Ralph pay as royalty to the stadium and earn $20,000 for the season? (Round to nearest one-tenth of a percentage point.)
2. If Ralph bids 12% of sales as the royalty, what income can he expect if operations go according to plan? (Is this consistent with your answer in item 1?)
3. Assuming a royalty of 12% of sales, what is Ralph's break-even point for the season, based on total attendance?
4. What kinds of information would Ralph want if he were also deciding to bid for the concession at baseball games at the same stadium?
5. Assume that Ralph has made a forecast of attendance for both kinds of games. He then learns that the star quarterback of the local professional team will retire before the coming season. What effect would this information be likely to have on Ralph's planning?

2-41   Soccer camp   Since Jean Longhurst has been head soccer coach at Oldberne College, its team has enjoyed considerable success. Longhurst has coached at summer camps for children and now is considering a summer camp for Oldberne. The college would provide room and board for the campers at a price (see below) and would also take 10% of the revenue. Longhurst has asked you for advice. You have said that some of the important factors are setting a price, estimating enrollment, and estimating costs. After a few weeks, Longhurst returned with the following information, gathered from various sources.

Average enrollment	90 campers
Average price for one-week camp	$ 190
Costs:	
Food, charged by college	$ 50 per camper
Insurance and T-shirts	$ 12 per camper
Room rent charged by college	$ 15 per camper
Coaches' salaries	$ 450 per coach
Brochures, mailing, miscellaneous	$2,800 total

Longhurst also said that other camps had typically employed one coach for each 15 campers, excluding the director (Longhurst in this case). One problem is that you generally need to engage the coaches before you know the enrollment, although it is usually possible to find one or two at the last minute. It is, however, necessary to engage some of the coaches early so that you can use their names in the brochure. Furthermore, while the enrollment and price given above are averages, there is wide variation, with enrollments ranging from 40 to 120 and prices ranging from $160 to $230. As might be expected, the better-known camps have higher enrollments at higher prices, but they also pay coaches better, as high as $800 per week for a well-known coach. Longhurst would keep the profits and suffer the losses, and so wants to be fairly confident before proceeding.

Required

1. If Longhurst hired enough coaches to meet the average enrollment and achieved all of the averages given above, what would her profit be?

2. If Longhurst wished to earn $4,000 and expected 100 campers, what price would she have to set?

3. The college has offered to take over the cost of brochures, mailing, and miscellaneous ($2,800 estimated) in exchange for a higher share of the revenue. If Longhurst achieves the results from item 1 (meets the averages), what percentage of revenue would she be able to pay the college and earn the same profit expected in item 1?

4. What advantages and disadvantages are there to Longhurst and to the college of the proposed arrangement?

CHAPTER 3

ANALYZING COST BEHAVIOR

The situations described in Chapter 2, as we have said, are much simpler than we would expect to find in practice. It is rare that a firm would have perfectly linear revenue and cost lines, even within a given relevant range, and the object classification of a cost (e.g., salaries, rent, supplies) cannot be relied upon to identify its behavior. Some costs have both a fixed and a variable component, as is the case with rental contracts that include a minimum payment plus some amount based on sales volume. Some costs vary with an activity level other than sales volume, such as the cost of materials used in making the product (which varies with production) or the cost of sending sales invoices to customers (which varies with the number of sales orders). A major portion of this chapter focuses on methods used to *determine* how costs behave.

This chapter also looks at the effects of income taxes, a very important cost that does not fit the strict variable/fixed classification scheme. In particular, we show how income taxes can be incorporated in the analyses presented in Chapter 2 relating to target profits and price determinations. Finally, we examine the question of what constitutes a desirable cost structure, exploring the efforts that managers make to balance fixed and variable costs in order to produce a desired level of profit.

MIXED COSTS

Perhaps the most common type of cost encountered in determining how costs behave is the **mixed cost** (or **semivariable cost**), which is a cost that has both a fixed and a variable component. The rental contract described earlier, where the rental payment consists of a fixed amount plus some percentage of sales, is an example of such a cost.

Figure 3-1 shows that a mixed cost behaves in the same way as total costs when there are both fixed and variable costs. To incorporate a mixed cost into our analysis of the operations of Ted's Threads, let us change some of the facts. He still sells shirts for $5 and $10; we shall ignore the wrapping cost and assume, instead, that the shirts cost $2 and $4, respectively. Ted has decided to move his store into a new enclosed shopping mall. Instead of paying $2,400 per month rent for the store and equipment, he will be required to pay a fixed monthly amount of $1,200 *plus* 5% of his dollar sales. This kind of rental agreement exists in many shopping centers.

How does Ted plan his rent expense? He must break down the expense into its fixed and variable components. His variable costs are now 45% of sales (40% cost of shirts plus 5% rent), and his fixed costs are now $1,200 per month. Ted's contribution margin percentage has fallen from 60% to 55%, but his fixed costs have been reduced from $2,400 to $1,200 per month. When the components of a mixed cost are based on contractual arrangements, such as the new rent agreement, there is no problem in separating the fixed and variable components. (Notice that rent will now show in two places in Ted's income statement: as a variable cost and as a fixed cost. In volume-cost-profit analysis, the behavior of the cost is important; its functional classification is secondary.)

Ted's operation, as described so far, is still relatively simple. All of his costs are easy to predict and plan for. Unfortunately, this is not usually the case in business or in any other economic activity.

Suppose that Ted employs a person part-time to help with the store. Each month, the person works about 10 to 15 hours doing routine tasks like tagging merchandise, filling out forms for ordering merchandise, and keeping the records of the business. Ted also arranges to have this person come in when Ted expects sales to be relatively heavy and he needs help to wait on customers. Suppose further that the person earns $5 per hour.

The cost of employing the person (wages expense) is variable with the number of hours worked. But the cost will not be perfectly variable with sales; there will be a fixed component because the person works about 10 to 15 hours per month regardless of the sales level. There will also be some variable component, because the person

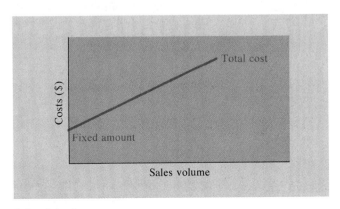

FIGURE 3-1   Mixed Cost Behavior

works more when sales are high than when they are low. It would be useful if Ted could find some relationship between this particular cost and sales, because he will use sales as the basis for planning the amounts of cost he expects to incur. Some methods do exist for developing a cost/sales relationship for costs of this nature.

High-Low Method of Estimation

A relatively unsophisticated but widely used method of estimating the fixed and variable components of a mixed cost is the **high-low method,** or **two-point method.** The high and low points refer to the volume levels at the extremes of the relevant range. Volume and cost at both points are determined, and the difference in volume is divided into the difference in cost to find the variable portion of the cost. The formula for finding the variable cost factor in a mixed cost is

$$\text{Variable cost component in mixed cost} = \frac{\text{cost at high volume} - \text{cost at low volume}}{\text{high volume} - \text{low volume}}$$

Assume that Ted has found the following wages at the extremes of his relevant range of sales of $2,500 and $9,000:

	High	Low	Difference
Sales	$9,000	$2,500	$6,500
Wages for part-time help	$ 408	$ 148	$ 260

With a sales increase of $6,500, wages increased by $260; thus the cost increased at a rate of $0.04 per sales dollar ($260/$6,500). Using the high-low method we say that the variable component of this cost is $0.04 per dollar of sales (or 4% of sales). Using the formula for Ted's situation:

$$\text{Variable cost component} = \frac{\$408 - \$148}{\$9,000 - \$2,500} = \frac{\$260}{\$6,500} = \$0.04 \text{ or } 4\% \text{ of sales dollars}$$

Since the total cost is a combination of the fixed and variable elements, we can compute the fixed component by subtracting the variable component from the total cost of either level of volume. In formula notation this becomes, using the high volume,

$$\text{Fixed cost component of mixed cost} = \text{total cost at high volume} - \left(\begin{array}{l} \text{high} \\ \text{volume} \\ \text{in units} \end{array} \times \begin{array}{l} \text{variable cost per} \\ \text{unit of} \\ \text{volume} \end{array} \right)$$

or

$$= \text{total cost at high volume} - \left(\begin{array}{l} \text{high} \\ \text{volume} \\ \text{in dollars} \end{array} \times \begin{array}{l} \text{variable cost} \\ \times \text{ percentage per} \\ \text{sales dollar} \end{array} \right)$$

At sales of $2,500, the variable component would be $100 ($2,500 × 4%) and the total is $148, so the fixed component must be $48 ($148 − $100). The same answer could be determined by subtracting the $360 variable element at a sales level of $9,000 ($9,000 × 4%) from the total cost of $408 at that volume ($408 − $360 = $48 fixed cost). The formula that Ted might use to predict his total wage cost would be: Total cost = $48 + 4% of sales.

The rationale for the high-low method is this: because variable costs (the dependent variable) change proportionately with changes in volume (the independent variable), the change in total cost between two volumes must be the change in variable cost. Therefore, when you divide a change in cost by a change in volume you are finding the rate of change in cost per unit of volume. In this case, we used sales dollars as the measure of volume, but we could have used units as well.

Although the high-low method is used widely, it does have some disadvantages, which will become more clear as we discuss the next method of cost estimation.

Scatter-Diagram Method of Estimation

The **scatter-diagram method** also involves determining the equation of a line that fits the various points representing costs at various levels of volume. The first step using this method is to develop a scatter diagram that plots the total amount of a particular cost at various levels of volume. Figure 3-2 is such a diagram, showing the wages actually incurred by Ted at various levels of volume. The next step is to draw a line that will

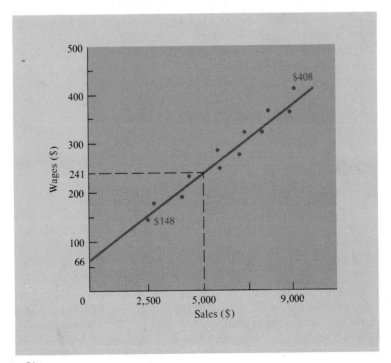

FIGURE 3-2   Scatter Diagram

be as close to all the points as possible. (Note that if the cost of wages were like the cost of Ted's rent, with its fixed and variable components stated by contract, all of the points would be on a single line. Such is not the case with his wage cost; the total cost deviates at some sales level, from any line drawn.) The placement and slope of the line are judgmental. The manager "eyeballs" the data and fits the line visually.

Once a line has been drawn, the fixed and variable components of the cost are found in the following manner. The fixed component is simply that point at which the fitted line hits the vertical axis, $66 in this case. The variable component is found by determining the cost at any point on the line, subtracting the fixed cost, and dividing the remainder by the sales volume. For example, in Figure 3-2, we show the total cost as $241 at a volume of $5,000 of sales. Of that cost, $66 is the fixed component, so the variable component is $175. Dividing the $175 by $5,000 gives $0.035, which is the variable cost per dollar of sales. Thus, the formula that Ted might use to predict his total wage cost would be: Total cost = $66 + 3.5% of sales. (Notice that the $66 fixed cost found by the scatter-diagram method is close to the employee's wages for the 10 to 15 hours worked on nonsales tasks.)

We now have two formulas for predicting Ted's total wage cost. Which of these formulas should Ted use? The high-low method uses only two points to estimate the cost components, while the scatter-diagram method uses many points. If either or both of the time periods used in the high-low method included some unusual event or random oddity, the calculated fixed and variable costs would reflect that event or oddity. The scatter diagram will generally give a better picture of the cost behavior pattern than will the high-low method. Note, however, that even using the formula resulting from the scatter-diagram approach, Ted cannot expect to predict his wage costs exactly. Discrepancies can be caused, for example, by Ted's inability to predict accurately the heavy sales periods when additional help will be needed. Thus, in anticipation of a big selling day, Ted might ask the employee to work some extra hours; but if sales are less than expected, the actual wage cost would be greater than that predicted using the actual level of sales.

In short, in the real world costs do not behave precisely as we predict. A major task of the managerial accountant is to try to develop improved methods and techniques for predicting costs.

Regression Method of Estimation

A more sophisticated method for estimating the fixed and variable components of a mixed cost is **regression analysis.** This statistical method provides an equation like the one used to describe the cost: Total cost = fixed cost + (variable cost per unit × number of units). The equation derived using this method is more precise than an equation gained from a visually fitted line; it minimizes the (squared) deviations from the line representing the equation. Knowledge of some important principles of statistics is required before you can understand and apply regression analysis, but you should be aware that advanced techniques are available for solving these kinds of problems. Those interested in a further discussion of this method are referred to the appendix at the end of this chapter.

Estimates and Facts

We noted earlier that the high-low method is deficient because it considers only two points, the high and low points for the independent variable. The scatter-diagram approach considers more points but relies on the manager's visual analysis of the plotted data. Regression analysis not only uses more than two points but also produces an equation that gives a precise mathematical fit for the observations. What all these methods have in common is that they use past (observable) information about both the dependent variable (the cost to be predicted) and the independent variable (sales or some other measure of activity). It is, therefore, important that this information be gathered and used carefully.

Consider the possibility that the *low* observation reflects the costs when the business is partially shut down. (For example, a firm may shut down for a week in order to avoid the problems of rearranging tasks to cover vacation periods.) Consider the possibility that the *high* observation is associated with an extraordinarily busy period when the firm decides to operate at a two-shift (as opposed to its normal one-shift) level. Both of these observations would seem to be outside the relevant range. If they are considered in developing a cost prediction line, the results are likely to be misleading. In fact, it is possible that lines developed under the high-low method or using regression analysis will show a negative term for fixed costs, which is clearly impossible.

In most cases, the cost prediction lines determined by including unrepresentative observations will not be so obviously wrong. But they will just as certainly lead to serious errors in predicting costs. It is important, then, for managers to review cost and volume data and to understand the operating conditions under which the data were collected. Only then can they apply one of the cost estimation methods that we have discussed. Because plotting the observations, as in the scatter-diagram method, tends to highlight out-of-line points, managers often do such plotting even when they plan to use other methods to determine the prediction formula.

STEP-VARIABLE COSTS

Figure 3-3 on page 58 shows a pattern of cost behavior commonly called **step-variable cost,** which does not fit nicely into the fixed-variable classification scheme. The cost is fixed over a range of volume, then jumps to a new level and remains fixed at that level until the next jump. The width of the range of volume over which the cost remains fixed varies with the particular cost. For instance, a company might hire a mechanic for every 5,000 units expected to be produced, and it might need a supervisor for every 20,000 units. The total cost of salaries for mechanics would jump more often and have narrower ranges than the total cost for supervisors' salaries.

The existence of step-variable costs results from the indivisibility of some resources, ones that must be acquired in fairly large chunks.[1] Such costs can create

---

[1] In reality, nearly all resources are imperfectly divisible. A company must usually acquire labor by the hour, not by the minute; many materials must be purchased by the pound, not by the ounce. But the step-variable behavior associated with indivisibility becomes important only when resources must be acquired in fairly large amounts.

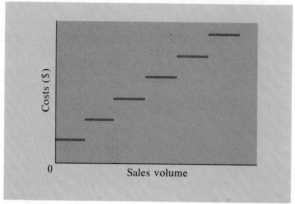

FIGURE 3-3   Step-Variable Cost

serious planning problems because managers cannot adjust their costs as precisely as they would like to as volume changes. For instance, an airline must make a flight or not make it. It cannot provide exactly as many seats as passengers demand. Thus, while volume for an airline is usually measured in passenger-miles (one passenger flown one mile), variable cost must be related to the number of flights. (Crew salaries, fuel, and other costs will depend on the number of flights, not on how many passengers are carried how many miles.) In greater or lesser degree, all companies are confronted with step-variable costs.

How can a firm plan step-variable costs? Should the relevant range consist of only the very small segments over which the cost is fixed? Or should the cost be planned as if it were variable, even though this would result in predictions missing the mark? The usual approach to planning for such costs is to treat them as mixed or entirely variable (as opposed to fixed). Figure 3-4 illustrates the planning of a step-variable cost as if it were variable or mixed.

The three dotted lines show three different philosophies of planning. The top line is conservative. Predicting the cost using this philosophy, you would regularly expect the cost to be less than planned for except at the exact points where the cost

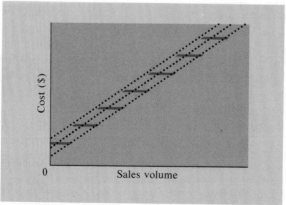

FIGURE 3-4   Planning Step-Variable Costs

jumps. The middle line, which also treats the cost as mixed, connects the midpoints of the small ranges, which means that the predicted cost would equal the actual cost only if the planned and actual volume were both at the middle of one of the small ranges. Use of the lower line, which is the most common, would regularly show unfavorable differences between planned and actual costs except when planned and actual volume were both equal to the high point of one of the ranges.

The method to be used depends on the objectives in a particular situation. If a manager desired never to be confronted with costs higher than planned for (let us call this situation an unfavorable surprise), he or she would plan costs using the top line. Use of the middle line for planning purposes would result in planned costs exceeding actual costs sometimes and being less than actual costs at other times. On the average, you would come the closest to predicting the actual cost. Using the third approach and planning costs based on the bottom line, a manager would expect to have actual costs exceed planned costs most of the time. In this situation, it is important that these differences not be automatically interpreted as overspending or inefficiency, for it is the planning method that ensures the consistent excess of actual over planned costs. This last approach, by producing consistent, unfavorable differences, might serve to remind the manager of the areas where changes in basic operating conditions could increase efficiency. In the examples of salaries, the manager would be reminded that the cost increments result directly from hiring policy.

MANAGERIAL ACTION AND FIXED COSTS

We have considered ways of dealing with costs containing both fixed and variable elements. Fixed costs can be divided into two categories: those that can be altered by managerial action and those that cannot without closing down the business. The first kind are called managed, discretionary, engineered, or programmed costs; the latter are called committed.

A constructive way of looking at fixed costs is to say that they provide the capacity to operate; they must be incurred in order that *any* volume be achieved. Ted, the shirt retailer, needs space to display his merchandise, giving rise to rent. He probably needs some display cases and a cash register, giving rise to depreciation, and he would probably wish to advertise.

Discretionary Costs

You may have noticed a difference between the examples of rent and depreciation and the advertising example. As long as Ted wants to operate, he has to pay rent. He may have a lease for some future period, meaning that even if he liquidates the business he must either pay the rent or find a new tenant for the duration of his lease. These costs are committed. They cannot be changed within relatively short periods of time, such as a year.

Advertising is not necessary to the running of his business, although it may be beneficial. Advertising is an example of a **discretionary fixed cost.** Ted incurs advertising costs as a result of decisions he makes each month about whether to advertise and how much cost to incur. The incurrence and amount of a discretionary cost are subject to managerial action; such costs are **avoidable.**

Discretionary costs are fixed, once incurred. Their amounts are the result of management decisions and actions and they may be changed within fairly short time periods—yearly, monthly, perhaps even weekly. Thus, when VCP analysis is applied, with its need to classify costs over some range, it is assumed that management has decided on the level of discretionary costs.

Because managers can change discretionary costs, they are often the first examined when management is initiating a cost reduction program. This is sometimes unwise. Consider the long-run effects of cutting the following discretionary costs: research and product development; management training programs; programs to upgrade worker skills; advertising; maintenance; and bonuses for highly productive managers.

Research and product development is crucial to companies in such high technology fields as drugs, computers, and aircraft, and in some consumer products. Reducing expenditures associated with personnel development may lead to reduced morale, high turnover, and lessened productivity. Deferral of routine maintenance may result in high repair expenditures when machines finally break down. Many similar examples could be given.

Discretionary costs may fool someone who is attempting to identify fixed and variable costs using past patterns of expenditures. Some discretionary costs are planned on the basis of expected volume, and may therefore *seem* to be variable. A firm may plan to incur advertising expense equal to 5% of sales; or research and product development may be allotted an amount equal to 2% of sales. To one who is studying the pattern of cost incurrence, these expenses may appear to be variable. In one sense they are, but only because management has taken action to make them so. Sales volume does not cause the advertising or research and development in the same sense that sales volume causes salespeople's commissions. It is closer to the truth to say that advertising and research and development are probably causal factors in future sales levels. Without advertising, sales in the future may be lower than expected; without new products, the firm may lose customers to more up-to-date products of other firms.

Committed Costs

A **committed fixed cost** is the minimum that the company must incur to keep operating. In many cases. committed costs arise out of decisions made many years ago. Depreciation is a committed cost. It results from past actions and cannot be changed without disposing of the assets to which it applies. Committed costs are **unavoidable;** their amounts are not subject to managerial review, decision, or action.

The current management may commit future managements to costs by building plants, signing long-term (10-year, for example) leases for machinery or buildings, and negotiating long-term contracts at specified salaries for executives or other employees.

It is not always possible to tell whether a cost is committed or discretionary just by knowing what the cost is (rent, salary, etc.). Some costs have both discretionary and committed elements. If part of the cost of research and product development is depreciation and property taxes on a building occupied by the research and development department, and the remainder is salaries for the staff, the only discretion management may exercise is over the salaries. The depreciation and property taxes are committed as long as the firm owns the building.

Some costs that are committed for some firms may be discretionary for others. A 20-year lease on a building entails a commitment for rent expense whereas a month-to-month lease does not. A firm that leases a machine on a month-to-month basis may cancel the lease at any time. Thus, the time period over which costs are committed may also vary.

Some costs are on the borderline between being committed and discretionary. A firm could not operate without a chief executive, but the number of lower-level managers needed is not always determinable. Some portion of management salaries is committed, some discretionary, but there would be a lot of disagreement among observers as to the precise amounts of each.

There are two major reasons for distinguishing between discretionary and committed fixed costs. One is that they are treated differently for the purpose of analyzing day-to-day operations. Because there is nothing that can be done to change committed costs over short periods of time, they are not watched as closely as are discretionary costs. Secondly, for purposes of decision making, committed costs are treated differently from discretionary costs. More will be said about this subject in Chapter 5. One example will suffice at this point. A firm operates a sales office that shows the following results, which are expected to continue indefinitely:

Sales		$100,000
Variable costs		80,000
Contribution margin		20,000
Fixed costs:		
Salaries	$15,000	
Rent	18,000	
		33,000
Loss		($ 13,000)

Despite the expectation of continued losses, there could be compelling reasons for keeping this particular sales office open: The managers might believe that it is essential to the firm's reputation to have offices in certain geographical areas, and that closing this office could hurt that reputation. That is, policy considerations may override financial concerns.

Policy issues aside, a decision about the future of the loss-producing sales office requires more information than that in the income statement. For example, looking at the names of the costs is not enough; the managers would have to analyze each cost. Perhaps the salaries could be avoided if the firm let the people go, or if it could use them elsewhere and thus avoid having to hire others. However, suppose that the entire $15,000 is the salary of the office manager who has a contract stating that he cannot be transferred and that he must receive the $15,000 whether or not he works. In that case, the $15,000 is committed: the manager cannot be used elsewhere, nor can he be let go.

Thus, even if the rent could be avoided by closing the office, it would be better to keep the office open and lose only $13,000 than to close it and still pay $15,000.

The firm's managers would study the cost of rent in the same way. In all likelihood, there is a lease on the office so that the firm could not move out immediately upon making a decision to close the office. If the lease runs for another year and the firm could not find anyone to move in and take over the lease, the firm would be committed to the $18,000 rent for one more year. In general, then, the question is not whether the office is unprofitable but whether or not the committed fixed costs—the ones that could not be avoided if the office were closed—are greater than the loss incurred by keeping the office open. If they are greater, the firm is better off keeping the office open until the commitments begin to expire.

SELECTING A MEASURE OF VOLUME

In the earliest discussion of cost behavior we described fixed and variable costs as they relate to changes in sales. We saw, through later examples, that a cost does not always vary with sales; it may vary with production, the number of employees, customers, or flights, or with some other measure of operating activity. These costs, like any others, must be planned, but not by considering sales alone. Manufacturing firms provide good examples of these types of costs.

The Manufacturing Firm

A manufacturing firm must make its products before it sells them. Thus, costs to produce the product will be incurred, and hence must be planned for, by reference to production plans. That is, although production plans may depend on expected sales, it is production plans that most directly affect the production costs to be incurred. For this reason, the behavioral classification of costs for planning in a manufacturing firm generally rests on whether the costs are fixed or variable in relation to the volume of production. (Note the importance of this difference for a firm in a seasonal industry, where production must be undertaken several months before the peak selling season. The toy industry is a good example.)

A typical manufacturing firm will have three general types of costs: raw materials, direct labor, and manufacturing overhead. The cost of **raw materials** (sometimes called direct materials, or simply materials), the goods that the firm buys and transforms into its products (steel, wood, etc.), is normally considered to be variable with the volume of production. The cost of **direct labor** (those employees who work directly on the company's product) is also normally considered to be variable with the volume of production. **Manufacturing overhead** (which consists of all production costs not included in materials and direct labor) includes costs that may be fixed, variable, or mixed. Some examples of manufacturing overhead are

Wages of materials handlers (individuals who move materials from one work area to another)
Salaries of foremen and other supervisors

Maintenance and repair costs for work performed on machinery and equipment used to
    make products
Wages of workers assigned responsibility for the storage and control of materials
Heat, light, and other power costs associated with the production areas
Depreciation and property taxes on factory buildings and factory machinery
Salary and office expenses of the manager (and subordinate personnel) responsible for
    production

    From a brief review of the individual manufacturing overhead costs you should
be able to see that *total* manufacturing overhead will be a mixed cost, with some variable component and some fixed component. Total manufacturing overhead can be analyzed into its fixed and variable components using one or more of the methods discussed earlier in this chapter.
    Although many of the costs that comprise manufacturing overhead may vary
with the level of output produced, in a firm that makes a number of different products
it is not usually possible to relate cost behavior to a simple activity measure such as the
number of units produced. A firm that makes, for example, refrigerators, ovens, and
toasters could not expect each type of manufacturing overhead cost to vary with the
total number of units produced because the units are so different. (Presumably, a
toaster would not give rise to as much overhead as a refrigerator.) In such cases, managers usually try to analyze manufacturing overhead as it relates to some *input* factor
in the production process, such as number of hours worked by direct laborers or number of machine hours. The variable component of overhead costs would be expressed,
per unit of product, by relating hours to the products.
    For example, suppose that a manager has found that total manufacturing over-
head is well described by the equation

$$\text{Total cost} = \$40{,}000 + (\$3 \times \text{direct labor hours})$$

Suppose further that a toaster requires 1 labor hour and that a refrigerator requires 20
hours. The variable manufacturing overhead for each product would be as follows:

	Toaster	Refrigerator
Direct labor hours	1	20
Variable overhead per direct labor hour	$3	$ 3
Variable manufacturing overhead per unit	$3	$60

The manager would add the variable overhead to the direct labor and material cost to
get the total variable manufacturing cost for each type of product.
    The managers in a manufacturing firm often face another problem when ana-
lyzing cost behavior so as to apply VCP analysis. For financial accounting purposes,
manufacturing firms must calculate cost of goods sold using fixed manufacturing
costs. From Chapter 2 you know that per-unit fixed costs are of little use in planning
(because they are different at every level of volume). Hence, when analyzing the cost
structure of the manufacturing firm it is necessary to eliminate the effect of fixed costs

from the per-unit manufacturing costs computed for financial accounting purposes. That task can become extremely complicated, and we defer a complete discussion of it to Chapters 13, 14, and 15. For now it is sufficient to show how a manufacturer's income statement would differ from one using the contribution margin format.

Assume the following data for the NMI Manufacturing Company for a period in which the volume is 25,000 units:

Selling price	$20
Variable manufacturing costs	$ 6
Variable selling costs	$ 2
Annual fixed costs:	
Manufacturing	$200,000
Selling and administrative	$ 60,000

The company would produce, at least for persons external to the firm, an income statement much like the one shown at the left of Exhibit 3-1. For comparison, we also show, at the right of the exhibit, an income statement using the contribution margin approach. The incomes shown under the two approaches are the same, but the contribution margin format allows the manager to understand the firm's cost structure and facilitates the use of VCP analysis. For these reasons, the contribution margin format is often used in reports prepared for managers even when such managers also receive copies of the reports prepared for persons outside the firm.

Exhibit 3-1
NMI Manufacturing Company Income Statements for the Year

Financial Accounting Format		Contribution Margin Format		
Sales (25,000 × $20)	$500,000	Sales (25,000 × $20)		$500,000
Cost of sales ($25,000 × $14)[a]	350,000	Variable costs:		
		Manufacturing		
Gross margin	150,000	(25,000 × $6)	$150,000	
		Selling (25,000 × $2)	50,000	
Selling and administrative expenses[b]	110,000			200,000
		Contribution margin		300,000
		Fixed costs:		
		Manufacturing	200,000	
		Selling and administrative	60,000	
				260,000
Income	$ 40,000	Income		$ 40,000

[a]Variable cost of $6 per unit + fixed cost of $8 per unit ($200,000/25,000 units) = $14 manufacturing cost per unit.
[b]Variable cost of $2 per unit + fixed cost of $60,000 = $110,000.

Other Examples

The behavior of many costs other than production costs is related to a volume measure other than sales. Consider, for example, costs of preparing invoices to bill customers for their purchases. Figure 3-5 is a scatter diagram relating the total costs of a firm's billing department to sales volume in dollars and shows a wide spread of values around a line that might be drawn as a result of the diagram. The wide spread of cost values means that predicting the cost of invoice preparation by using dollars of sales is unlikely to be successful. (A moment of thought about the facts should result in some ideas about why this might be so. Would it necessarily take more time or more people to prepare an invoice for $100,000 than it would for an invoice for $10,000?) Some other measure of volume might give better results. The scatter-diagram method of analyzing costs has, as indicated earlier, an important advantage over the high-low method; it allows one to observe that the particular activity measure used in the diagram is probably not a good predictor. The high-low method, because it includes only two points, would not provide this important information until after several unsuccessful attempts to predict costs.

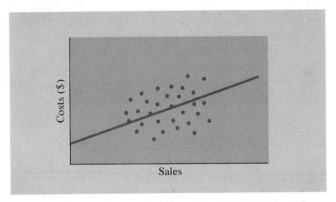

FIGURE 3-5   Scatter Diagram of Invoice Preparation Costs Plotted Against Sales Dollars

Figure 3-6 shows invoice preparation costs plotted against another activity measure, the number of individual sales orders processed. Since it is common to prepare one invoice for each sales order, and since individual sales orders are likely to vary in dollar value, it should not be surprising that the total cost of invoice preparation might vary more directly with the number of sales orders than with the sales-dollar volume represented by the orders.

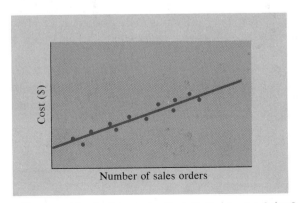

FIGURE 3-6   Scatter Diagram of Invoice Preparation Costs Plotted Against Sales Orders

Sometimes the activities with which costs vary may themselves vary with the volume of sales or production, although perhaps not in direct proportion. For example, consider the costs of carrying inventory. A 10% increase in sales may not lead to a 10% increase in inventory, but some increase in inventory will probably be needed to support the higher level of sales. If increases in inventory are relatively predictable, given increases in sales, it is possible to find the effects of sales increases on costs of carrying inventory, although the relationship is not direct.

Determining the measure of volume with which costs will vary is especially difficult in nonmanufacturing activities. Costs of processing sales orders, mailing invoices, keeping records of accounts receivable and payable, and other administrative activities may show little variation with changes in any single measure of volume. The cost of processing invoices may increase with the number of sales orders; but the number of items ordered by each customer may also affect the cost of invoice preparation, because more typing is required on an invoice with 20 items than on one with three.

In recent years accountants have been more concerned with finding techniques for planning administrative costs, partly because such costs have increased more rapidly than manufacturing costs. One tool that has been employed with some success is multiple regression analysis—the use of two or more independent variables to predict behavior of costs. For interested readers, multiple regression is discussed briefly in the appendix to this chapter.

INCOME TAXES AND PROFIT PLANNING

Income taxes are a cost of doing business and should be considered, as should all business costs, in the planning process. Income taxes are generally based, not on sales, but on the amount of income before taxes. For the purpose of this text, it is reasonable to assume that income taxes are a constant percentage of income before taxes. In most large corporations, that assumption is fairly reasonable, but we hasten to point out that the tax law is exceedingly complex and that generalizations are dangerous.

Assumptions about income taxes take on special importance if a firm's managers plan operations with some idea about an after-tax target profit. Such a plan requires a revision of the basic target-profit formula presented in Chapter 2. The revision requires expressing the *after-tax* target profit as a *pretax* profit, which is computed by dividing the after-tax target profit by a factor equal to 1 minus the income tax rate. For example, suppose that Ted wants to earn an after-tax profit of $1,400 and he anticipates his tax rate as 30%. (We already know that his fixed costs are $2,400 and that his contribution margin percentage is 60%.)

In order to earn $1,400 after raxes, Ted must earn $2,000 before taxes ($1,400/70%). Of the pretax income of $2,000, 30% goes to the government ($2,000 × 30% = $600), leaving $1,400 ($2,000 − $600). Accordingly, we use the basic formula for calculating the volume needed to earn a target profit as follows:

$$\text{Sales to achieve target after-tax profit} = \frac{\text{fixed costs} + \dfrac{\text{after-tax profit}}{1 - \text{tax rate}}}{\text{contribution margin percentage}}$$

or

contribution margin per unit

For a $1,400 profit after taxes, solving for sales dollars gives:

$$\text{Sales} = \frac{\$2,400 + \dfrac{\$1,400}{70\%}}{60\%}$$

$$= \frac{\$2,400 + \$2,000}{60\%} = \frac{\$4,400}{60\%}$$

$$= \$7,333$$

If Ted is selling only $10 shirts with variable costs of $4, then we could calculate the unit sales required by dividing the $6 contribution margin per unit into the $4,400 (fixed costs plus required pretax profit), giving an answer of 733 shirts. The principle involved in planning for income taxes is quite similar to that of contribution margin. Contribution margin is the amount, or percentage, left over after covering variable costs. After-tax income is the amount left over after paying income taxes.

COST STRUCTURE AND MANAGERIAL ATTITUDES

Economic situations can usually be handled in many different ways. A firm may use a great deal of labor and little machinery or vice versa. Salespeople may be on straight salary, straight commission, or a combination of the two. Decisions in business must take into consideration the effects of different methods on the cost structure—that is, on the relative proportions of fixed and variable costs.

The income statements of two firms are presented below. Both have total costs of $80,000 at $100,000 sales, but the makeup of the costs is different between the firms. Hifixed has a higher contribution margin than Lofixed, and so income of Hifixed will increase and decrease faster than that of Lofixed if both firms experience similar changes in sales.

Income Statements

| | Hifixed | | Lofixed | |
	Amount	Percent of Sales	Amount	Percent of Sales
Sales	$100,000	100%	$100,000	100%
Variable costs	20,000	20	60,000	60
Contribution margin	80,000	80	40,000	40
Fixed costs	60,000	60	20,000	20
Income	$ 20,000	20	$ 20,000	20

Figure 3-7 on page 68 shows the cost behavior for the two firms. The break-even points are different for the two firms, and the slopes of the total cost lines are different. Once Hifixed gets beyond the break-even point, its profits increase more rapidly than those of Lofixed, with the firms showing equal profits at $100,000 sales. Beyond $100,000 in sales, Hifixed earns higher profits because of its 80% contribution margin compared to 40% for Lofixed. This difference in profit potential is also reflected in the

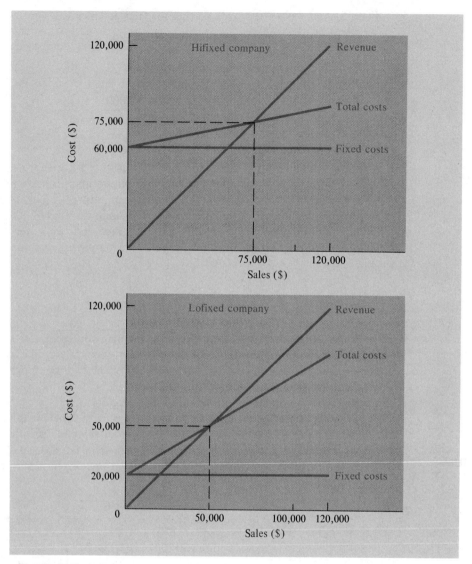

FIGURE 3-7   Volume-Cost-Profit Charts

graphs; the distance between the revenue line and total cost line for Hifixed increases much more toward the right on the horizontal axis than do the distances for Lofixed.

Which cost structure is better? The answer depends on expectations about future sales levels, fluctuations in future sales, and the managers' attitudes toward risk and return. If sales are expected to be higher than $100,000, with little chance of ever being less, then Hifixed is in a better position. If sales are expected to be below $100,000 consistently, Lofixed has the advantage. If sales are expected to fluctuate from $60,000 to $130,000, making a choice becomes more difficult. The profits of Hifixed would fluctuate over a much wider range than would those of Lofixed. Hifixed would suffer losses in bad years while Lofixed would not. Of course, in good years Hifixed would earn much higher profits than would Lofixed.

The cost structure depends on the attitudes of the managers of the firm. Do they prefer stable earnings or are they willing to risk losses for the chance to make high profits? The choice is like that made by investors—to buy bonds or common stocks. The former offer relatively safe, but low returns; the latter may have greater returns, but also higher risks. Much of the investment in stock may be lost in a decline of stock prices.

Margin of Safety

The differing cost structures among firms provide the basis for another measure of risk called the margin of safety. The **margin of safety (MOS)** is the decline in sales that would bring the firm or a product sold by a firm to the break-even point. This margin can be expressed either as a dollar amount or as a percentage of sales. For the Lofixed firm, above, the MOS is $50,000 ($100,000 − $50,000) or 50% ($50,000/$100,000). For the Hifixed firm it is $25,000 ($100,000 − $75,000) or 25% ($25,000/$100,000). As the term suggests, the MOS is a measure of safety, indicating the extent to which sales would have to fall to bring the firm below a profitable level of operation.

The MOS can also be applied to individual products of a firm. For example, suppose that instead of being entire firms, Hifixed and Lofixed are products that a firm is considering bringing out. The fixed costs could be associated with producing the products or could be related to selling efforts such as advertising and promotion. If the volumes of both products were expected to be greater than $100,000, Hifixed would be more profitable, but declines from the expected volumes would hurt Hifixed more than Lofixed because its contribution margin is higher. Again, the selection of which product to introduce would be influenced by the management's attitudes toward risk and reward.

SUMMARY

Costs do not always fit into fixed-variable classifications, and not all variable costs are variable with changes in sales. Some costs, mixed, contain both fixed and variable elements, and some, step-variable, are fixed over small ranges of activity but at different levels for different ranges. Income taxes vary with income, some manufacturing costs will vary with the number of units manufactured, some selling costs may vary with the number of orders placed by customers, and so on. It is not always easy to isolate an appropriate measure of volume to use in the planning of a given cost. But the identification of critical relationships is important to the manager for planning. Scatter diagrams, high-low estimates, and regression analysis are useful tools for analyzing cost behavior, but must be used with care. Actual costs will probably differ from planned costs, and predictions of cost behavior based on a single measure of volume may be inaccurate.

Fixed costs are generally described as either discretionary or committed. Discretionary fixed costs, while not variable with volume, are set by managers at planned levels; these levels may be changed on relatively short notice. Committed fixed costs have been set at particular levels by previous decisions that have long-term effects. In general, only future levels of committed costs may be affected by present management.

The relative proportions of fixed and variable costs in the cost structure of a firm can be greatly influenced by management. Although to some extent the proportions are dictated by the nature of the business, in many cases it is possible to do the same job in different ways. Expected sales, potential for variations from expectations, and the attitudes of managers toward risk-return relationships are some of the factors that will influence management decisions in planning a firm's cost structure.

KEY TERMS

avoidable costs	mixed cost
committed fixed cost	raw materials
cost structure	regression analysis
direct labor	scatter-diagram method
discretionary fixed cost	semivariable cost
high-low method	step-variable cost
manufacturing overhead	two-point method
margin of safety	unavoidable costs
measure of volume	

KEY FORMULAS

Margin of safety = current sales − break-even sales

$$\text{Sales to achieve target after-tax profit} = \frac{\text{fixed costs} + [\text{after-tax profit}/(1 - \text{tax rate})]}{\text{contribution margin percentage (or contribution margin per unit)}}$$

Total costs = fixed costs + (variable cost per unit of sales × number of units sold)

Total costs = fixed costs + (variable cost as % of sales × dollars of sales)

$$\text{Variable cost component in mixed cost} = \frac{\text{cost at high volume} - \text{cost at low volume}}{\text{high volume} - \text{low volume}}$$

$$\text{Fixed cost component in mixed cost} = \frac{\text{total cost at high volume}} - (\text{high volume} \times \text{variable cost factor})$$

REVIEW PROBLEM

The Swanboy Company had the following income statement in 19X2:

Sales (100,000 units at $6)	$600,000
Variable costs (100,000 units at $3.60)	360,000
Contribution margin (100,000 units at $2.40)	240,000
Fixed costs	180,000
Profit before taxes	60,000
Income taxes at 30%	18,000
Net income	$ 42,000

Required

1. The income tax rate is expected to rise to 40% in 19X3. Determine the dollar sales required to earn $42,000 after taxes in 19X3.

2. The firm expects sales of $660,000 (110,000 units) for the next several years. The firm currently rents machinery that can be returned to its owner at any time. If the machinery were returned the firm would save $20,000 in fixed costs per year. However, variable costs would increase to $3.80 per unit. Would it be wise to stop using the machinery?

3. The firm operates several stores in a single city. One of the stores is expected to show the following annual results for the next few years:

Sales (10,000 units)		$60,000
Variable costs		36,000
Contribution margin		24,000
Fixed costs:		
Salaries	$15,500	
Rent	6,000	
Insurance and utilities	2,000	
Miscellaneous	3,000	26,500
Loss before taxes		($ 2,500)

The firm has a 10-year lease on the space occupied by the store and the lease cannot be canceled. Determine the change that would occur in the firm's total profit before taxes if the store were closed.

Answer to Review Problem

1. $625,000. The required profit *before* taxes is $70,000, which is $42,000/60%. The required pretax profit of $70,000 plus fixed costs of $180,000 gives $250,000 required contribution margin, and $250,000 divided by the contribution margin percentage of 40% ($240,000/$600,000) gives $625,000. Alternatively, because the firm needs $10,000 more pretax profit to get the same after-tax profit, it needs $10,000 additional contribution margin, or $25,000 additional sales ($10,000/40% = $25,000).

2. The proposed arrangement would not benefit the firm. Comparative income statements show that profit before taxes would be $2,000 lower under the proposed arrangement:

	Current Arrangement		Proposed Arrangement	
Sales (110,000 units at $6)	$660,000		$660,000	
Variable costs	396,000	($3.60/unit)	418,000	($3.80/unit)
Contribution margin	264,000	($2.40/unit)	242,000	($2.20/unit)
Fixed costs	180,000		160,000	
Profit before taxes	$ 84,000		$ 82,000	

It is not necessary to consider income taxes here. If profit before taxes is higher under one arrangement, it will also be higher after taxes.

Another way to determine the effect would be to determine whether the decrease in contribution margin would be more than the decrease in fixed costs. At 110,000 units the firm would lose $22,000 in contribution margin (110,000 × $0.20) if it stopped using the machinery. This is $2,000 more than the $20,000 saving in fixed costs.

3. Total profit before taxes would drop by $3,500 per year. The $6,000 rent is a committed, unavoidable cost, and the only cost that could not be avoided if the store were closed. The loss for this store would become a loss of $6,000 if the store were closed. An income statement if the store were closed would show no revenues and one cost—the $6,000 rent.

APPENDIX: REGRESSION ANALYSIS

Regression analysis is a technique for fitting a straight line to a set of data. In contrast to the high-low method, regression analysis considers multiple observations, not just two. In contrast to the scatter-diagram method, regression analysis fits a mathematically precise line, not one that depends on the judgment of the manager drawing the line to fit the data.

The procedures for fitting a regression line, or developing a regression equation, may seem laborious to you. There are many computer programs available for doing regression analysis, and even some advanced hand calculators can be used to reduce the number of required computations.

Although regression analysis is used in many different situations, our main interest here is in predicting cost behavior—determining the fixed and variable components of a cost given a measure of volume with which the cost is thought to be associated. The first step, then, in using regression analysis is to decide what measure of volume should be used—sales dollars, production in units, number of sales invoices prepared, hours worked by direct laborers. Once a measure of volume has been selected, the procedures for developing the regression equation are relatively mechanical.

Two basic techniques, simple and multiple regression, will be presented in this appendix. Simple regression involves the development of an equation incorporating the relationship between one dependent and one independent variable. Procedures for developing the equation will be explained at some length. Multiple regression involves the development of an equation incorporating the relationship between one dependent and more than one independent variable. Because of the complexity of this approach, its use will not be required in this text and it will be only briefly discussed.

Simple Regression

Procedures. The developing of a regression equation requires the solving of two equations simultaneously. These equations, which are given below, are called the *normal equations*.

$$(1) \quad \Sigma XY = \Sigma Xa + b \Sigma X^2$$

$$(2) \quad \Sigma Y \ \ = na + b \Sigma X$$

where

X = measure of volume
Y = cost
a = fixed cost
b = variable cost per unit
n = number of observations
Σ = sum of (e.g., ΣX^2 = sum of the squares of the volumes)

In regression analysis, the letter Y is used to designate the *dependent variable,* the one that we are trying to predict. The letter X is used to designate the *independent variable,* the one that we believe affects the value of the dependent variable. In our applications, Y will usually be total cost, and X will be a measure of volume, like production in units, sales in units or dollars, labor hours worked, or sales invoices processed.

We shall use the following data to illustrate the procedures of regression analysis. Each piece of data—the cost in dollars at the particular volume—is called an observation. In this example, the cost is monthly factory operating cost and the volume is expressed as units of product made during the month.

Month	Units of Production	Total Factory Operating Costs
January	80	$350
February	90	390
March	85	365
April	95	405
May	100	410
June	110	425

The following schedule shows the required calculations:

Month	X	Y	X^2	XY
January	80	350	6,400	28,000
February	90	390	8,100	35,100
March	85	365	7,225	31,025
April	95	405	9,025	38,475
May	100	410	10,000	41,000
June	110	425	12,100	46,750
	560	2,345	52,850	220,350

Substituting the appropriate values in the normal equations would give us

$$(1) \quad 220{,}350 = 560a + 52{,}850b$$

$$(2) \quad 2{,}345 = 6a + 560b$$

We have two equations and two unknowns. To determine the values of the unknowns we must use the techniques for solving simultaneous equations. In this case, the most straightforward method is to solve for b first by eliminating a. We can eliminate a by multiplying equation (1) by 6 [the coefficient of a in equation (2)], and equation (2) by 560 [the coefficient of a in equation (1)]. Doing this gives

$$(1) \quad 1{,}322{,}100 = 3{,}360a + 317{,}100b$$

$$(2) \quad 1{,}313{,}200 = 3{,}360a + 313{,}600b$$

Subtracting equation (2) from equation (1) gives

$$8{,}900 = 3{,}500b$$

and $\quad \$2.54 = b$

The value of b, \$2.54, is the slope of the regression equation—the variable component of the cost.

We can now substitute the value of b in either equation and solve for a. We substitute \$2.54 for b in equation (2) and get

$$2,345 = 6a + (560 \times 2.54)$$

$$2,345 = 6a + 1,422.4$$

$$922.6 = 6a$$

$$\$153.77 = a$$

The fixed component of the cost is \$153.77, the value for a. The formula for total cost is then: Total cost = \$153.77 + (\$2.54 × units produced).

Problems and Pitfalls.   A basic assumption in using regression analysis is that the data that have been collected are representative; that is, it is assumed that the conditions under which the observations of costs and volumes were assembled were about the same and can be expected to continue. As we suggested in the chapter, if one or more of the observations used in the analysis are not representative of normal conditions, the regression line would not be as useful a prediction tool as desired.

Consider the scatter diagram in Figure 3-8. The line shown in the figure represents a regression line developed as a result of all of the observations incorporated in the scatter diagram. Notice that the observation at the far left is above most of the other observations and the only low-volume observation to fall above the regression line. The observation is clearly unusual and might best have been ignored in developing the equation. That observation might have been from a month in which the plant was shut down for a considerable period for extensive repair work. The high cost of repairs combined with the low volume of production makes the observation nonrepresentative. Great care must be taken in "throwing out" observations; but if a particular observation occurred for unusual reasons, it is best to ignore it.

It is not sufficient, when developing data for the purpose of regression analysis, that the observations be representative of the normal conditions of the past. If the regression line is to be helpful in predicting *future* costs, it is equally important that the significant conditions affecting the cost in the past be the same as those that are to

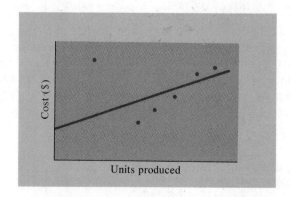

FIGURE 3-8

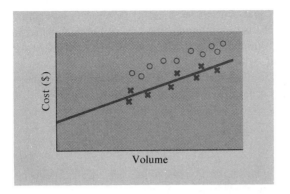

FIGURE 3-9

affect the cost in the future. An example of the failure to meet this requirement is illustrated in the scatter diagram in Figure 3-9. The x's are the observations used to develop the regression equation, which is shown in the figure. The o's are observations subsequently made. All of the subsequent observations fall above the regression line, which means that the firm would have consistently predicted its costs at levels below actual costs. One reason for this could be that some changes have taken place from the time of the x's to that of the o's. If the cost that is being predicted is electricity, it could be that an increase in rates has occurred. Thus, the predictions would generally be too low. Or if the cost being predicted is that of raw materials, perhaps material prices have increased or the product now contains more material per unit. These examples are basically the same; they involve changes in the conditions considered to be normal. If the accountant is aware of such changes in conditions as increased electricity rates, he or she could simply develop the equation by using consumption of electricity in kilowatt-hours, rather than in dollars. The equation would then describe the use of electricity, not the cost. The new rates could then be applied to the predicted use in order to predict the cost. Or more simply, if the cost per kilowatt-hour increased by 10%, the original regression equation could be restated at a 10% higher level for both the fixed and variable components.

One final caution. As is the case with both the high-low and the scatter-diagram methods, the predictions resulting from regression analysis depend for their validity on observations over a particular range of activity, *viz.*, the range over which the observations were gathered. Care must be taken in using any of these methods to predict costs for levels of activity not included within the range over which the observations were gathered. For example, if costs of power to operate machines have been analyzed in a range from 500 to 800 hours of machine time per week, there is no reason to assume that the relationships that held over that range will hold also at, say, 350 hours or 1,100 hours.

Correlation and Association.   Even the sophistication of regression analysis will not ensure completely accurate prediction of costs. As we saw in the chapter, some costs plotted against a particular measure of volume are scattered widely, and there seems to be no association of the cost and the measure of volume. A regression line can be fitted to any set of data no matter how widely dispersed the observations. Hence, the development of the equation does not mean that the equation will give reliable predictions.

There are some statistical procedures that can be used to determine the reliability of the predictions; the results of applying these procedures are measures of the dispersion of the observations around the regression line. One widely used measure is called the correlation coefficient, which measures the extent to which two variables are associated (or how close the actual observations come to the fitted regression line). You will study correlation and other measures of association in your statistics courses.

Multiple Regression

In many cases, there is more than one variable that affects the level of a cost. In such cases, multiple regression analysis might prove helpful in determining the effects of each variable. Essentially, multiple regression analysis is a technique for fitting a least-squares straight line using more than one independent variable.

In a modern business, there are many costs that do not depend strictly on one measure of activity. The cost of heating a factory will depend both on the number of hours that the factory is open and on the outside temperature. Shipping costs will probably depend on both the weight of the goods being shipped and the distance over which the goods must travel. As indicated in the chapter, the costs to prepare invoices to customers are affected not only by the number of sales orders received but also by the number of items covered by each sales order.

A multiple regression equation has the following general form:

$$Y = a + b_1 X_1 + b_2 X_2 + b_3 X_3 \ldots b_n X_n$$

where

$$Y = \text{the dependent variable to be predicted}$$
$$X_1 \ldots X_n = \text{the values of the various independent variables influencing the value of } Y$$
$$b_1 \ldots b_n = \text{the coefficients of the various independent variables}$$
$$a = \text{the fixed component (as in simple regression)}$$

Suppose that the manager of a factory that makes a number of different products has requested an analysis of manufacturing overhead costs. The managerial accountant, working in conjunction with a statistician, might come up with the following information based on historical data:

Fixed component of manufacturing overhead cost	$32,500 per month ($a$)
Variable components (independent variables):	
Direct labor hours (X_1)	$2.40 per hour ($b_1$)
Machine-hours (X_2)	$1.80 per hour ($b_2$)
Weight of materials put into production (X_3)	$0.30 per pound ($b_3$)

Using statistical techniques, the description of which is beyond the scope of this text, the accountant and the statistical consultant have found that variations in three variables (direct labor hours, machine-hours, and weight of material processed) better describe variations in total overhead costs than do variations in any one or combination of two such variables. Such a conclusion is not unexpected when one considers that many overhead costs (fringe benefits, for example) are related to labor time, that some (like power, supplies, and lubricants) are readily associated with machine time, and that still others (like materials handling and storekeeping costs) are heavily dependent on the quantity of materials being used.

Suppose, now, that the factory manager expects the following activity in the coming month:

Direct labor hours	20,000
Machine-hours	15,000
Pounds of material processed	70,000

The manager could predict total manufacturing overhead of $128,500, computed as follows:

$$\text{Total manufacturing overhead} = \$32,500 + (\$2.40 \times 20,000) + (\$1.80 \times 15,000) + (\$0.30 \times 70,000)$$

	= $32,500 +	$48,000 +	$27,000 +	$21,000
	fixed cost	variable with direct labor hours	variable with machine-hours	variable with pounds of material

All of the cautions associated with simple regression also apply here, plus one more. In multiple regression analysis, there is an assumption that the independent variables are not correlated *with each other*. In our example, for instance, it would be important to know whether direct labor hours and machine-hours (or some other combination of the three independent variables) are closely associated. If two (or more) of the independent variables are highly correlated, the results of multiple regression analysis must be used with care and the underlying statistical problems must be understood. You will study such problems in depth in your statistics courses.

In summary, it is very important, when using either simple or multiple regression analysis, that you understand the statistical principles that underlie these approaches. Critical to the production of useful results under either approach is the need for the observations to be representative of conditions expected to prevail during the period for which predictions are being made.

ASSIGNMENT MATERIAL

Questions for Discussion

3-1 Cost classification   For each of the following items of cost, indicate whether it is likely to be discretionary or committed. If in doubt, describe the circumstances under which the cost would fall into one or the other category. If the cost is mixed, consider only the fixed portion.

(a) Straight-line depreciation on building.

(b) Sum-of-years'-digits depreciation on a machine.

(c) Salaries of salespeople.
(d) Salaries of president and vice-presidents for production, sales, and finance.
(e) Research and product development.
(f) Advertising.
(g) Fee for annual audit.
(h) Fees for consultants on long-range planning.
(i) Utilities for factory—heating and lighting.
(j) Repairs and maintenance.
(k) Management development costs—costs of attending seminars, training programs, etc.

3-2 **High-low method**   The controller of your firm recommends the following approach to estimating the fixed and variable components of manufacturing overhead costs like supervision, indirect labor, and supplies.

Estimate the total cost that the firm would incur if it shut down, and treat that amount as fixed cost. Then estimate the total cost if the firm worked at 100% of capacity, stated in direct labor hours. Divide the difference in the two cost figures by the difference in direct labor hours and treat that as the variable component.

Required: Comment on the procedure. Would the formula derived from it work well for the firm if it normally operated between 75% and 90% of capacity?

3-3 **Take or pay contract**   Boulder Chemical Company has a contract that requires it to buy 100,000 tons of a raw material each month. The material is perishable, and if Boulder cannot sell the products that use the material, the unused material must be discarded. In most firms, raw materials costs are variable. Is that so in this case?

3-4 **Cost classification**   Analyze each of the following statements, explaining what is wrong with it:
(a) The controller of a firm tells you that the units-of-production method is used for depreciation of machinery and that depreciation is therefore a variable cost for the firm, not a committed fixed cost.
(b) The same controller tells you that since the firm nearly always operates at full capacity, all fixed costs cannot be reduced and are therefore committed.
(c) A sales manager tells you that without salespeople the firm cannot operate and that therefore salespeople's salaries are committed fixed costs.
(d) Another controller says that if committed costs are those necessarily incurred because the firm is in business, there are no such costs because the firm could reduce its costs to zero by simply closing up.

3-5 **Misconceptions about cost behavior and analysis**   Comment on each of the following statements, pointing out the misconceptions:
(a) "All right, variable costs are the same per unit, while fixed costs change as activity changes. Therefore, variable costs are fixed and fixed costs are variable."
(b) "This 'high-low' method of analyzing cost behavior is no good. I found our total costs last January when we were just starting in business and this past August when we were working three shifts a day to fill some big orders. The formula I got does not help us to predict cost at other levels of activity very well at all."
(c) "Look, buddy, don't tell me about VCP analysis. Last year it worked fine, but I know that our selling prices will be higher this year so it won't do us any good this year."

(d) "Fred, you fire that dumb controller. He just told me that we should cut our prices to sell more units. We are already selling below our total cost per unit and reducing prices will result in even bigger losses."

3-6 Managerial attitudes   It is often said that an enterprise's behavior is to a great extent a function of its cost structure. Why might you say that an enterprise's cost structure is a function of its behavior?

Exercises

3-7 Accuracy of predictions   The scatter diagrams below show costs plotted against production. Which cost would you be able to predict and plan for more easily? Explain.

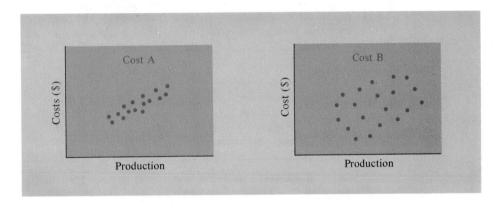

3-8 Mixed costs   The president of Gorman Company has asked you to develop a behavioral classification for indirect labor cost. You have the following data from two recent months:

Direct Labor Hours	Indirect Labor Cost
19,000	$27,800
25,000	33,200

Required: Compute the fixed and variable portions of indirect labor cost based on direct labor hours.

3-9 Basic income taxes   Borden Company is introducing a new product, an electronic game that will sell for $140. Unit variable manufacturing cost is $106 and the firm pays a 10% commission on all sales. The fixed costs associated with the new game are $150,000 per year. The tax rate is 40%.

Required
1. Determine the profit after taxes that the firm would earn selling 11,000 games.
2. Determine the number of games that the firm would have to sell to earn an after-tax profit of $204,000.

3-10 Contribution margin statements, taxes

Case	Unit Selling Price	Unit Variable Cost	Fixed Costs	Unit Sales
1.	$16	$10	$ 4,000	2,000
2.	20	14	36,000	9,000
3.	30	22	220,000	31,000
4.	13	8	115,000	27,000

Required
1. Prepare income statements for each case shown, assuming a 40% income tax rate.
2. Determine the sales, in units, required to double the after-tax income that you computed for each situation.

3-11 Manufacturing company income statements   The chief accountant of Blackman Industries prepared the income statements that appear below:

	June	July
Sales	$350,000	$370,000
Cost of sales	200,000	208,000
Gross margin	150,000	162,000
Selling and administrative expenses	90,000	94,000
Income before taxes	$ 60,000	$ 68,000

Blackman produces and sells a single product. The selling price is $5 per unit.

Required
1. Determine the fixed and variable components of cost of sales and of selling and administrative expenses.
2. Prepare income statements for June and July using the contribution-margin format. Comment on the differences between the statements above and the ones that you prepared.

3-12 Cost behavior   A study of the office supplies used in the regional sales offices of a large manufacturer shows that the cost is semivariable. A record of sales and corresponding supply costs in one of the offices is as follows:

Monthly Sales	Cost of Supplies
$43,000	$1,296
48,000	1,380
35,000	1,050
52,000	1,433
39,000	1,170
39,000	1,161
45,000	1,356
56,000	1,470
50,000	1,392

Required: Determine the variable cost rate and the fixed costs using the high-low point method.

3-13 Relationships and taxes   Considering each situation independently, answer the following questions. You may not be able to solve the questions in the order in which they are asked.

1. A firm earned an after-tax income of $18,000 by selling 10,000 units at $13 per unit. The company is subject to an income tax of 40%. Its total contribution margin was $90,000.
    (a) What was the variable cost per unit?
    (b) What were fixed costs?

2. A firm had an after-tax return on sales of 7½%, net income of $21,000 after a 58% tax, a contribution margin ratio of 45%, and a selling price of $80 per unit.
    (a) How many units did the firm sell?
    (b) What is the variable cost per unit?
    (c) What were fixed costs?
    (d) What was the total contribution margin?

3. A firm experienced a 15% increase in net income when it increased its sales by 10% from 15,000 units to 16,500 units. Income taxes at 45% are deducted to arrive at net income. Net income was $63,250 at sales of 16,500 units. Variable cost per unit is $15.
    (a) What is the selling price per unit?
    (b) What were fixed costs?
    (c) What were the income taxes at sales of 15,000 units?
    (d) What was the total contribution margin at sales of 16,500 units?

3-14 Using per-unit data   Nimmer Company expects the following per-unit results at a volume of 100,000 units.

Sales		$4.00
Variable costs	$1.50	
Fixed costs	2.10	3.60
Profit		$ .40

Required: Answer the following questions independently of one another.
1. How many units must the company sell to earn a profit of $80,000?
2. If Nimmer could sell 60,000 units, what selling price would be needed to yield a profit of $60,000?
3. The company could undertake an advertising campaign for $6,000. Unit volume would increase by 3,000 units at the $4 selling price. By how much and in which direction (increase or decrease) would the company's profit change if it took the action?
4. If the income tax rate is 60%, how many units must the company sell to earn an after-tax profit of $60,000?

3-15 Percentage income statement   The president of Fillmore Industries has developed the following income statement showing expected percentage results at sales of $800,000.

Sales	100%
Cost of sales	40%
Gross margin	60%
Other expenses	50%
Income	10%

The president tells you that cost of sales is all variable and that the only other variable cost is commissions, which are 20% of sales.

Required
1. Determine the profit that the company expects to earn.
2. Determine the break-even point.
3. If sales are $900,000, what would profit be?
4. The president would like to earn a profit of $100,000. The expected unit volume is the same as for the statement above. By what percentage must the company increase its selling price to achieve the goal? Assume that per-unit cost of sales remains constant.

3-16 Cost behavior graphs (AICPA adapted) Graphs and descriptions of cost elements are given below. For each description, select the letter of the graph that best shows the behavior of the cost. Graphs may be used more than once. The zero point for each graph is the intersection of the horizontal and vertical axes. The vertical axis represents *total* cost for the described cost and the horizontal axis represents production in units. Be prepared to discuss any assumptions you might have to make in selecting your answers.

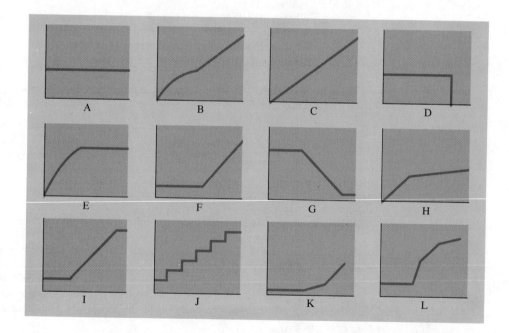

1. Depreciation of equipment, where the amount of depreciation charged is computed by the units-of-production method.
2. Electricity bill, a flat fixed charge plus a variable cost after a certain number of kilowatt-hours are used.
3. City water bill, which is computed as follows:

First 1,000,000 gallons or less	$1,000 flat fee
Next 10,000 gallons	0.003 per gallon used
Next 10,000 gallons	0.006 per gallon used
Next 10,000 gallons	0.009 per gallon used
etc., etc., etc.	

4. Cost of lubricant for machines, where cost per unit decreases with each pound of lubricant used (for example, if one pound is used, the cost is $10.00; if two pounds are used, the cost is $19.98; if three pounds are used, the cost is $29.94; with a minimum cost per pound of $9.25).

5. Depreciation of equipment, where the amount is computed by the straight-line method.

6. Rent for a factory building donated by the city, where the agreement calls for a fixed-fee payment unless 200,000 man-hours are worked, in which case no rent need be paid.

7. Salaries of repairmen, where one repairman is needed for every 1,000 hours of machine-time or less (i.e., 0 to 1,000 hours requires one repairman, 1,001 to 2,000 hours requires two repairmen, etc.).

8. Federal unemployment compensation taxes for the year, where the labor force is constant in number throughout the year and the average annual wage is $6,000 per worker. The tax is levied only on the first $4,500 earned by each employee.

9. Rent for production machinery, where the rental charge is computed as follows:

First 10,000 hours of use	$20,000 flat fee
Next 2,000 hours of use	$1.90 per hour
Next 2,000 hours of use	$1.80 per hour
Next 2,000 hours of use	$1.70 per hour
etc., etc., etc.	

10. Rent for a factory building donated by the county, where the agreement calls for rent of $100,000 less $1 for each hour laborers worked in excess of 200,000 hours, but a minimum rental payment of $20,000 is required.

3-17 **Revenue and cost analysis—high-low method** The controller of your firm is attempting to develop volume-cost-profit relationships to be used for planning and control. He is not sure how this might be done and asks your assistance. He has prepared two income statements from monthly data.

	October	November
Sales	$40,000	$50,000
Cost of goods sold	24,000	30,000
Gross profit	16,000	20,000
Operating expenses:		
Selling expenses	6,600	7,200
Administrative expenses	4,700	5,000
Total expenses	11,300	12,200
Income	$ 4,700	$ 7,800

Required

1. Determine the fixed and variable components of cost of goods sold, selling expenses, and administrative expenses.

2. Prepare an income statement based on sales of $60,000.

3-18 **Target profit—income taxes** Balkan Company sells a product with a contribution margin of $2 per unit. The firm has a target profit of $52,000 before income taxes, and fixed costs are $60,000.

Required

1. How many units must be sold to achieve the target profit?
2. Suppose that the firm pays income taxes of 40% of pretax income. How many units must the firm sell to achieve an after-tax profit of $48,000?
3. If the selling price is $5 per unit, what must dollar sales be to obtain an after-tax profit of $30,000, given a 40% tax rate?

3-19   Interpretation of scatter diagram   The graph below depicts the cost experienced by Magma Enterprises.

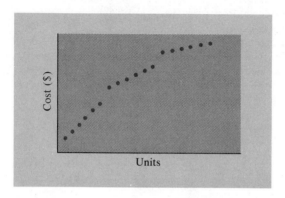

Required

1. Give some possible reasons for the observed behavior of costs.
2. How would you plan for costs that exhibited this type of behavior?

3-20   Profit improvement alternatives   Below is the income statement for Meriwether Company for 19X6.

Sales (100,000 × $10)	$1,000,000
Variable costs (100,000 × $7)	700,000
Contribution margin	300,000
Fixed costs	250,000
Profit	$ 50,000

Leslie Meriwether, president of the company, was not happy with the 19X6 results, and stated that a profit of $100,000 was a reasonable target for 19X7. She instructed the controller to analyze each component of the statement separately and determine what change in that component would be needed for the firm to earn the target profit of $100,000. (For example, what change in per-unit selling price would produce the target profit if sales volume, fixed costs, and per-unit variable costs remained constant; or what change in sales volume would be needed, assuming that prices and costs did not change?)

Required: Comply with Meriwether's request.

3-21   Interpretation of data   The scatter diagram on p. 85 was used by your assistant to separate maintenance expenses into the fixed and variable components. The equation she derived is as follows: Monthly total cost = $350 + ($0.80 × machine-hours), which is represented by the line drawn on the diagram.

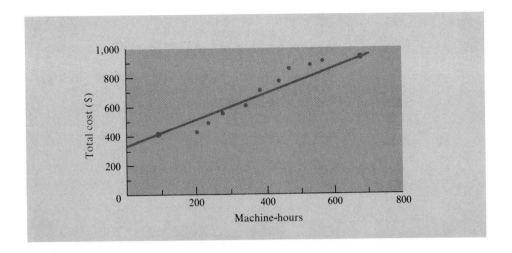

Required: Comment on the way in which your assistant fitted the line to the data and make an alternative recommendation.

3-22 Target profits and unit prices   Tina's Handicrafts sells handmade sweaters at $40 apiece. The firm acquires the sweaters from Ms. Posey at $30 apiece, but the agreement with her also requires an extra fee of 5% (of selling price) for each sweater sold. The firm's monthly fixed costs are $2,000.

Required: Answer each of the following questions.
1. If the firm wants to earn profit of $3,000 a month before taxes, how many sweaters must it sell?
2. If the firm wants to make an after-tax profit of $2,400 and the tax rate is 40%, how many sweaters must the firm sell?
3. If the firm wants to make a before-tax profit of $5,000 and expects to sell 400 of the handmade sweaters, what price must be charged per sweater to obtain the desired level of profit?
4. How many sweaters would the firm have to sell to earn a 9% after-tax return on sales, assuming a 40% tax rate?
5. Suppose that the firm is now selling 450 sweaters per month and making a before-tax profit of $1,600. Ms. Posey offers to renegotiate the buying agreement so that there would be a charge of $24 per sweater plus a 10% (based on selling price) extra fee per sweater sold. How many sweaters would the firm have to sell under the new agreement if it wished to earn the same $1,600 in before-tax profits?

3-23 Cost and contribution margin analysis, with taxes   The data below relate to the operations of Westfall Company for March and April.

	March	April
Sales at $5 per unit	$100,000	$120,000
Costs	80,000	87,000
Profit before taxes	$ 20,000	$ 33,000

Required
1. What is the per-unit contribution margin?
2. What are monthly fixed costs?
3. What is the break-even point?
4. What unit sales would give a $33,000 profit after taxes if the tax rate were 40%?

3-24   Cost analysis, three alternatives   Davis Company makes a single product. One component of the product currently costs the firm $1.80 per unit plus $30,000 per month to rent machinery. At any time, the company can get out of the lease without penalty. An outside supplier has offered to supply Davis's needs for the component at $2.15 each. Additionally, there is a newer machine available that the company could lease month-to-month for $65,000 per month. Using this machine would reduce the unit variable cost to $1.45.

Monthly volume of the product, and component, is now about 50,000, but the managers believe that the volume might rise soon. They are uncertain about how far it will rise. As a matter of policy, the managers do not want to change arrangements (alternatives) more than once a year.

Required (*Hint:* It might be helpful to prepare a graph showing total monthly cost under each alternative.)
1. Determine which alternative is cheapest at a monthly volume of 50,000.
2. At what monthly volume would the company be equally well off buying from the outside supplier or making the component using the existing machine?
3. At what monthly volume would the company be equally well off using the new machine or the existing machine?

3-25   Cost classification   Halton's Flower Shop buys and sells floral arrangements of various types. The average selling price is $25 and average purchase cost is $5. Weekly fixed costs are $4,000. Because the arrangements are perishable, the shop cannot sell any units after they have been in inventory for one week. The shop must order a full week's supply at one time.

Mr. Halton, the owner, would like to earn $1,000 per week from the business. A friend of his has explained VCP analysis to him and made the following calculation.

$$\text{Unit volume required for \$1,000 profit} = \frac{\$4,000 + \$1,000}{\$25 - \$5}$$

$$= 250 \text{ arrangements}$$

Required
1. Is the above equation correct in the sense that if Mr. Halton orders 250 arrangements per week, he will earn $1,000? Why or why not?
2. Is the purchase cost a fixed or variable cost? Explain.
3. Can you tell Mr. Halton how many arrangements he must sell to earn $1,000 if he purchases 300? If he purchases 400?

3-26   Cost behavior—regression analysis (related to Appendix)   The following data have been collected for the purpose of determining the behavior of factory costs:

Month	Units Produced	Factory Costs
January	80	$1,300
February	110	1,640
March	70	1,120

Required
1. Determine the fixed and variable components of factory costs using the high-low method.
2. Repeat, using regression analysis.

3-27 Changes in cost structure   Manfred Company makes a product that has variable product costs of $6 per unit. The production manager has been approached by a salesperson from a machinery maker. The salesperson offers a machine for rent for five years on a noncancellable lease at $24,000 per year. The production manager expects to save $0.40 per unit in variable manufacturing costs using the machine.

Required
1. Determine the annual unit production that would make renting the machine and continuing with currrent operations yield the same profit to the firm.
2. Suppose that the expected volume is 80,000 units per year. Determine the change in the firm's annual profit that would occur if the firm were to rent the machine.
3. Would you be more likely or less likely to rent the machine if the lease were cancellable at your option rather than noncancellable for a five-year-period? Explain your answer.

3-28 Review exercise, Chapters 2 and 3 (continued in Chapter 4)   After reviewing its cost structure (variable costs of $7.50 per unit and monthly fixed costs of $60,000) and its potential market, Forecast Company established what it considered to be a reasonable selling price. The company expected to sell 50,000 units per month, and planned its monthly results as follows:

Sales	$500,000
Variable costs	375,000
Contribution margin	125,000
Fixed costs	60,000
Income before taxes	65,000
Income taxes (at 40%)	26,000
Net income	$ 39,000

Required: On the basis of the information above, answer the following questions independently.
1. What selling price did the company establish?
2. What is the company's contribution margin per unit?
3. What is the company's break-even point in units?
4. If the company determined that a particular advertising campaign had a high probability of increasing sales by 4,000 units, how much could it pay for such a campaign without reducing its planned profits?
5. If the company wanted to make a before-tax profit of $50,000, how many units would it have to sell?
6. If the company wanted to make a before-tax return on sales of 10%, what level of sales, in dollars, would be needed?
7. If the company wanted to make an after-tax profit of $45,000, how many units would it have to sell?
8. If the company wanted to make an after-tax return on sales of 9%, how many units would it have to sell?
9. If the company wanted to make an after-tax profit of $45,000 on its expected sales volume of 50,000 units, what price would it have to charge?

10. If the company wanted to make a before-tax return-on-sales of 16% given its expected sales volume of 50,000 units, what price would it have to charge? (Round answer to nearest cent.)

11. The company is considering offering its salesmen a 5% commission on sales. What would the total sales, in dollars, have to be in order to implement the commission plan and still earn the planned net income of $39,000?

Problems

3-29 Cost formula, high-low method   The owner of Bed and Bath Boutique regularly uses part-time help in addition to the full-time employees. Although some minimum of part-time help is needed for miscellaneous chores, the owner arranges for additional hours based on estimates of sales for the following week. The following is a record of the wages paid to part-time employees at various recent monthly sales volumes.

Sales Volume	Wages Paid to Part-time Help
$ 9,600	$ 870
2,000—	600
6,400	730
17,000	1,260
18,000	1,300
12,800	1,030
15,000	1,350
5,000	650
11,000	960

The owner considers these months to be relatively normal except that in the month with volume of $2,000, the Boutique was closed for about two weeks for repainting and the installation of new carpeting.

Required: Determine the variable cost rate and the fixed costs using the high-low method.

3-30 Fixed costs in decision making   Warren Keith owns a restaurant in a suburb of a large city. The restaurant does not do very much business during the month of August, and Keith is considering closing down and taking a vacation during that month. He has developed the following income statement based on planned operations for that month:

Sales		$25,250
Cost of sales		10,100
Gross margin		15,150
Wages to part-time help	$4,500	
Utilities	1,500	
Rent on building	1,500	
Depreciation on fixtures	750	
Supplies and miscellaneous	6,400	14,650
Income		$ 500

Keith doesn't believe that it is worthwhile to stay open unless he can net at least $2,000 for the month. He works hard when the restaurant is open and believes that he deserves at least that much to compensate him for the work he does.

He also tells you that if he were to close, he would have to pay a minimum utility bill of $350. Supplies and miscellaneous expenses are fixed, but these discretionary fixed costs would fall to zero if he closed.

Required: Advise Mr. Keith about the desirability of staying open for August.

3-31 **Return on investment**   IML Company is considering a new product, a high quality mechanical pencil. The managers of the firm expect volume to be 100,000 units annually. Unit variable cost is $5 and annual fixed costs are $80,000. The firm would have to invest $500,000 in the new venture and wants a 12% after-tax return on that investment. The tax rate is 40%.

Required: Determine the price that the firm must charge to achieve its profit objective.

3-32 **Planning step-variable costs**   Schumpet Company's purchasing department hires clerks as they are needed, and because the firm is growing there has never been a layoff of clerks. It takes one clerk to process 200 purchase orders per week. Clerks are paid $180 per week.

Required
1. Prepare three different formulas for planning clerical costs as volume changes. (You may wish to set up a chart of behavior of the cost from 200 to 2,000 orders per week.)
2. Using each of the methods in item 1 above, compute the variance had 1,840 orders been processed.

3-33 **High-low method, income taxes**   Your assistant has prepared two income statements for your firm, McKenzie Company, at your request:

	February	March
Sales	$260,000	$220,000
Cost of sales	104,000	88,000
Gross profit	156,000	132,000
Operating expenses	76,000	72,000
Income before taxes	80,000	60,000
Income taxes at 40% rate	32,000	24,000
Net income	$ 48,000	$ 36,000

Required
1. Determine the fixed and variable components of each cost element, including income taxes.
2. Explain why income tax expense displays the behavior it does.

3-34 **Average costs**   The sales manager of Cooper Company recently approached the controller with the news that a large chain store wanted to buy 2,000 units of product at a price of $15 per unit. Because that price was below the firm's usual $25 price, he was reluctant to close the deal, but decided to check with the controller.

The controller pulled out the planned income statement for the coming period, which showed the following:

Planned sales, 10,000 units at $25	$250,000
Expected total costs	120,000
Profit	$130,000

The controller saw that the price was above the firm's average cost and would therefore add to profit. But the production manager said that increasing production to 12,000 units would add $15,000 to the firm's fixed costs, for additional supervision and other costs associated with putting operations near to capacity of about 12,800 units. The production manager also said that variable cost per unit was $10, and should remain so at the higher level of ouput.

The controller quickly figured that total costs of $155,000 [$120,000 + $15,000 + ($10 × 2,000)] could be expected, for an average total cost of $12.92 ($155,000/12,000). The controller concluded that the order would definitely increase profits because the price substantially exceeded average cost.

Required: Determine whether or not the controller was correct.

3-35 Alternative cost structures—a movie company (continuation of 2-38)   Lois Lane, the president of Blockbusters Incorporated, has reviewed the preliminary analysis of the two contract alternatives and wishes to give further consideration to the contract arrangements with Kirkwalker. Kirkwalker's agent is also having second thoughts about the alternatives that he has proposed, and is wondering what is best for his client.

Required: Answer the following questions.
1. If total paid admissions are expected to be between $9 and $10 million, which compensation scheme is best for (a) Blockbusters, and (b) Kirkwalker? (*Hint:* Refer to your answers in 2-38 regarding break-even points.)
2. If total paid admissions are expected to be in the neighborhood of $20 million, which compensation scheme would be preferred by: (a) Blockbusters; (b) Kirkwalker?

3-36 Regression analysis (related to Appendix)   Your new assistant has just handed you the following results of a regression analysis.

$$\text{Factory overhead} = \$262,203 + (\$13.19 \times \text{units produced})$$

You are a bit surprised because your company makes several models of lawnmowers and you had not thought it possible to express factory overhead so simply. Your assistant assures you that the results are correct, showing you the following data:

Month	Units Produced	Factory Overhead
January	1,700	$260,000
February	1,100	280,000
March	2,800	300,000
April	2,300	260,000
May	2,000	360,000
June	1,800	320,000
July	2,400	320,000
August	2,000	200,000
September	2,100	300,000

Required: Comment on your assistant's results. You may assume the mathematical accuracy of your assistant's work.

3-37 **Alternative graphical VCP analysis**   The figure below illustrates a widely used technique for graphing volume-cost-profit relationships. Instead of using separate lines for revenue and total costs, it employs a single line to represent profit at various levels of volume. The graph includes both negative and positive dollar values on the vertical axis. The intercept is the fixed cost, the slope is contribution margin per unit, and the break-even point is where the profit line intersects the horizontal axis.

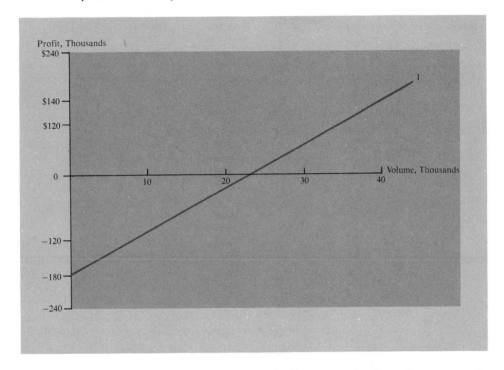

An advantage of this method is that it allows you to plot alternatives more neatly than you could by using separate lines for revenue and total cost. One line suffices to represent any combination of selling price, variable cost, and fixed cost.

The managers of the Sanders Company wish to graph the following alternatives. Each represents a particular strategy and the differences result from alternatives such as salaries versus commissions, different levels of product quality, and different levels of advertising and promotion. Alternative 1 is already plotted.

Alternative	Price	Variable Cost	Fixed Costs
1	$20	$12	$180,000
2	$20	$ 8	$240,000
3	$18	$10	$120,000

Required

1. Plot the profit lines for alternatives 2 and 3.
2. What general conclusions can you draw from the completed graph? Could you select the best alternative based on the graphical results?

3-38   Negative fixed costs   The managers of Kooper Company have observed the following costs and activity:

Month	Direct Labor Hours	Overhead Costs
1	2,200	$3,590
2	2,500	4,210
3	2,800	4,830
4	2,300	3,780
5	3,100	5,400
6	3,200	5,650

Required
1. Find the fixed and variable components of overhead costs using either a scatter diagram or regression analysis.
2. Does the pattern make sense to you? Is it possible to have negative fixed costs? Can you suggest an explanation?
3. How would you handle the negative fixed cost for planning purposes?

3-39   Cost structures and average costs   At a dinner meeting of a local association of company accountants, the following conversation took place.

Ruth Hifixed: "My firm has enormous fixed costs, and volume is our critical problem. My cost per unit is now $6, at 100,000 units, but if I could get 200,000 units, cost per unit would drop to $4. My selling price is also too low, only $6."

Jim Lofixed: "You are lucky. My cost per unit is $5 at 200,000 units, but we can't produce any more than 200,000. At least we're now better off than we used to be when sales were 80,000 units. At that volume we lost $0.50 per unit at our selling price of $6. We were fortunate in being able to keep the same selling price at all volumes."

Required
1. Compute the profit being earned by each firm at its current level of sales.
2. Determine the fixed costs and variable cost per unit and the contribution margin per unit for each firm.
3. Compute the break-even point for each firm.
4. Which firm would earn more at 150,000 units?
5. Which firm would earn more at 100,000 units?
6. Does the way in which each controller describes his or her cost behavior help or hinder analysis of the firm?

3-40   Cost estimation—service business   William Jarvis operates his own firm of Certified Public Accountants. For planning purposes, he is interested in developing information about the cost structure of the firm. At times, he finds it necessary to hire part-time employees, usually accounting majors from the nearby university.

The best measure of activity for the firm is chargeable hours, the number of hours that employees work on client business, and for which the firm charges the clients at hourly rates. Jarvis has the following data regarding wages of part-time employees from recent months:

Total Chargeable Hours	Part-time Wages
3,000	$3,000
3,500	3,100
2,800	2,990
3,200	3,090
4,800	5,400
5,200	6,180
5,600	6,900

Required: Plot the data on a scatter diagram and comment on the results. Can Mr. Jarvis use your results for planning? What reasons might there be for the pattern that you can observe?

3-41 Labor policies—cost behavior   In conversation with the president of Hirsch Industries, you hear the following: "We employ 40 skilled workers and guarantee them 80 hours of work per month even if production doesn't keep them busy. When we crank up production beyond a 40-hour week for all of our employees, we work overtime and pay $6 per hour instead of the usual $4. Each of our workers produces two units of product per hour."

Required
1. Determine the firm's total labor cost at the following monthly volumes of production in units. Assume that a month has four weeks.
    (a) 5,000
    (b) 6,000
    (c) 7,000
    (d) 10,000
    (e) 14,000
    (f) 16,000
2. Draw a line that represents the firm's labor costs, with clearly marked points on the horizontal axis for the volumes where the cost behavior changes.
3. What is the range, if any, over which labor cost per unit behaves like a true variable cost?

3-42 Volume-cost-profit analysis for an airline   Icarus Airlines flies a number of routes in the southwestern United States. The firm owns six airplanes, each of which can hold 150 passengers. All routes are about the same distance, and all fares are $66 one way. The line is obligated to provide 250 flights per month. Each flight costs $4,000 for gasoline, crew salaries, and so on. Variable costs per passenger are $6, to cover a meal and a head tax imposed for each passenger at every airport to which Icarus flies. Other costs, all fixed, are $130,000 per month.

Required
1. How many passengers must Icarus Airlines carry on its 250 flights in order to earn a $70,000 per month profit? What percentage of capacity does this number represent?
2. If the firm could cut its flights to 200 per month, what would be the number of passengers required to earn $70,000 per month? What percentage of capacity would this number represent (using 200 flights as capacity)?
3. Is the $4,000 cost per flight fixed or variable?

4. What is the chief problem faced by an airline or other firm with a similar cost structure?

3-43 Committed versus discretionary cost   Gladack Company makes a number of products and uses a great deal of machinery. A new product this coming year will require the acquisition of a new machine. The machine can only be leased, not purchased. There are two alternative leasing arrangements: (1) a month-to-month lease that can be canceled on 30-days' notice by either Gladack Company or the lessor, at a monthly rental of $6,000; and (2) a five-year noncancellable lease at $5,200 per month. The new product is expected to have a life of five years, during which annual revenues will be $250,000, annual variable costs $100,000. There are no new fixed costs other than the lease payments. The president is concerned that the five-year lease removes a great deal of flexibility: if the product does not pan out as expected, the company is stuck with the machine and there are no other uses for it. He does, however, like the idea of saving $800 per month.

Required
1. Are the rentals, under each of the alternatives, discretionary or committed fixed costs?
2. Why would the president hesitate between the choices? What could happen to make him regret choosing (a) the five-year lease? (b) the month-to-month lease?
3. Suppose Gladack takes the monthly lease option. It is now the end of the fourth year and management expects that sales of the product will be $90,000 in year five, evenly spread over the year. Should the firm use the machine for the fifth year?
4. Answer question 3 again assuming that the firm had signed the five-year lease.

3-44 VCP and cost changes   Barton Products, Inc., has sufficient capacity to produce 1,000,000 square yards of its best-selling floor tile, Mapleshade. The managers of the firm can increase capacity by 200,000 square yards by renting additional machinery for $400,000 per year. Their best estimates are that the company could sell 1,150,000 square yards at $9 each. Unit variable cost is $4 and total fixed costs without considering the $400,000 are $3,600,000.

Required
1. What profit would the company earn without adding the capacity?
2. Would it be wise to increase capacity?
3. Suppose now that the unit variable cost of the tile produced on the rented machinery is expected to be greater than before because the new machinery is not as efficient as the existing machinery. How high could variable cost per square yard go before it would be unprofitable to rent the machinery?
4. Suppose now that Barton could subcontract work on tile in excess of 1,000,000 square yards at $7 each. What would the company's profit be if it did not rent the machinery and, instead, subcontracted production in excess of 1,000,000 square yards? Are there any advantages to the subcontracting, even if unit variable cost would be $4 for tile made with the rented machinery?

3-45 Significance of unit costs   The sales manager of Seagle Company burst into the office of the controller and exclaimed: "This will cheer you up—we just got a big order from Stanley Industries. The price is lower than usual, but the order should still be very profitable." The controller morosely looked up and said that he would have to see it to believe it because the sales manager was so eager to make sales that he would give the firm away if no one kept him under control.

After looking at some data the controller told the sales manager that the order was clearly not profitable. He mentioned the following points: The price per unit offered by Stanley Industries was $12, which was less than the firm's average cost per unit of $16, based on current volume of 100,000 units. Thus, even though the sales to Stanley would not affect sales at regular prices, it was obviously unprofitable.

The sales manager said that because the order was for 20,000 units, the cost per unit should be based on 120,000 units, not 100,000. He argued that fixed costs were included in the unit cost and that unit cost would be reduced if volume increased by 20,000 units. The controller sighed and pulled out his pencil again. He made a few calculations and then said that the cost per unit would indeed drop, but only to $14 which was still above the $12 price being offered. The sales manager shook his head and trudged out of the office. The controller wondered when people would begin to understand that selling below cost was the road to ruin.

Required: Determine the profit or loss that would have occurred had the order been accepted. Comment on the position taken by the controller.

3-46 **Loss per unit**   A firm had a loss of $3 *per unit* when sales were 40,000 units. When sales were 50,000 units the firm had a loss of $1.60 *per unit*.

Required
1. Determine the contribution margin per unit.
2. Determine fixed costs.
3. Determine the break-even point in units.

3-47 **Margin of safety**   Nelson Wallet Company is considering two new wallets for introduction during the coming year. Because of a lack of production capacity, only one will be brought out. Data on the two wallets are given below:

	Model 440	Model 1200
Expected sales	$200,000	$250,000
Expected contribution margin	60,000 (30%)	150,000 (60%)
Expected fixed costs—for production, advertising, promotion, etc.	39,000	120,000
Expected annual profit	$ 21,000	$ 30,000

Required
1. Determine the margins of safety for each wallet, in dollars and as percentages of expected sales.
2. Suppose that the firm is relatively conservative; its top managers do not like to take significant risks unless the potential profits are extremely high. Which wallet would you recommend be introduced? Why?

3-48 **Cost structure**   Wink Company manufactures replacement parts for automobiles and sells them to distributors in the northeastern United States. The president of the firm wishes to begin selling in the Southeast but is uncertain how to expand most profitably. Two alternatives have been selected for final consideration. Under the first, Wink would use the services of independent sales representatives who would sell to distributors for a 15% commission. This plan would increase the clerical costs at the company's central office by $20,000 per year. Under the second alternative, Wink would hire its own salespeople to work on straight salary. It is estimated that salaries for salespeople would be $100,000 per year; additionally, an office would be opened in the region and would cost $25,000 per year to operate.

The variable cost on parts is now 35%. The president is uncertain about demand in the Southeast and wants you to prepare analyses of profitability under both plans at various volumes. He selects $500,000, $700,000, $1,000,000, and $1,200,000 as the sales volumes to be used for comparison.

Required
1. Prepare the requested analyses.
2. Which alternative would you recommend and why? What nonquantified factors are related to the alternatives?
3. Suppose that variable costs on parts were 65%. Which alternative would you recommend and why?

3-49 **Pricing policy, relevant range, lost sales**   The Portland Visigoths, an expansion team in the Constellation Football League, are now playing their home games in Municipal Stadium. The stadium seats 40,000. The Visigoths play ten games including four exhibition games, during the season at home. Tickets are priced at $11 and variable costs are $4 per ticket sold, most of which is the payment to the visiting team.

A major supermarket chain in the area has offered to buy 2,000 tickets for each game at $7. The chain will sell the tickets as part of a promotional campaign to customers who accumulate food purchases of $100. The manager of the Visigoths estimates that about half of these 2,000 tickets will be sold by the chain to people who would attend the game anyway. This fact worries him particularly. He estimates that attendance for the coming season, without special sales, would be as follows:

Number of Games	Paid Attendance at Each
2	40,000
4	36,000
4	32,000

Required
1. What is the total expected contribution margin without the special sale to the supermarket chain?
2. What is the expected total contribution margin if the offer from the chain is accepted?
3. What should the Visigoths do?
4. Would your answer to question 3 be different if all 2,000 tickets for each game were to be sold to people who would not otherwise attend the game?

3-50 **VCP analysis—measures of volume**   Acme Foam Rubber Company buys large pieces of foam rubber (called "loaves") and cuts them into small pieces that are used in seat cushions and other products. A loaf contains 5,000 board feet of foam rubber (a "board foot" is one foot square and one inch thick), of which 10% becomes scrap during the process of cutting up the loaf. A loaf costs $700, including freight, and the firm is currently processing 100 loaves per month.

The firm charges $0.22 per board foot for its good output, $0.07 per board foot for the scrap. Variable costs of cutting the loaf are $100, for labor and power to run the cutting machines. Fixed costs are $18,000 per month.

The president of the firm has asked for your assistance in developing volume-cost-profit relationships.

Required

1. Determine the firm's income when it processes 100 loaves per month.
2. Determine the firm's break-even point expressed as number of loaves processed.
3. The president tells you that your analyses in parts 1 and 2 are not what he had in mind. He says that he is accustomed to thinking in terms of board feet of good output sold. He would like to know how many board feet he would have to sell to earn $6,000 per month. Determine the firm's contribution margin per board foot of good output sold and sales required to earn $6,000 per month.

Cases

3-51 **Regression analysis and managerial judgment (related to Appendix)** Your firm has just hired a recent graduate of the state university. His first assignment was to prepare a regression equation to be used for predicting total factory overhead costs. The equation he developed is: Total cost = $110,328 + $4.40X, where X is the number of units produced. The equation is based on the following observations:

Month	Unit Production	Total Overhead Cost
April	9,000	$146,000
May	10,000	151,000
June	12,000	164,000
July	14,000	178,000
August	3,000	130,000
September	8,000	140,000
October	11,000	156,000
November	13,000	170,000

Other data developed were as follows:

Sum of production ΣX	80,000
Sum of costs ΣY	1,235,000
Sum of squared production ΣX^2	884,000,000
Sum of cost × production ΣXY	12,720,000,000

Required

1. Plot the observations on a scatter diagram.
2. Discuss the equation computed by the new person. Would you make any changes or offer an alternative? If so, what would be your choice for an equation?

3-52 **Measures of volume** The controller of Throckton Company has been to a seminar on VCP analysis and wishes to use some of the techniques she learned. She has given you the following data and requests that you develop analyses of each cost into its fixed and variable components. She plans to use the information you develop in the profit planning of the firm. You prepare the following schedules of costs and measures of volume for the previous six months:

Sales	Labor Hours	Production Costs	Selling Expenses	Administrative Expenses
$12,000	500	$ 9,100	$3,250	$3,200
10,000	700	11,000	2,980	3,300
21,000	1,200	14,300	4,130	4,100
30,000	1,300	15,300	4,950	4,500
33,000	900	11,980	5,370	4,300
35,000	800	11,200	5,560	4,800

Required: Analyze the cost behavior patterns in accordance with the request of the controller. Indicate weaknesses and suggest possible improvement.

CHAPTER 4

ADDITIONAL ASPECTS OF VOLUME-COST-PROFIT ANALYSIS

This chapter completes the study of volume-cost-profit analysis, treating some problems not yet discussed, with special attention to multiple-product firms. VCP analysis has been presented as a powerful planning tool, and it is. But planned and actual results might not coincide for many reasons. This chapter illustrates techniques for analyzing differences between planned and actual results. Finally, we discuss the application of VCP analysis in the special context of not-for-profit entities.

ANALYSIS OF RESULTS

A firm's estimate of income derives from sales projections and assumptions about cost behavior. It is unlikely that planned and actual results will coincide exactly. Managers will be evaluated on the results; thus, methods must be found to assign responsibility for differences between actual and planned results.

The analytical approach in this chapter concentrates on differences between actual and planned contribution margin that arise because of differences between (1) planned and actual sales volume, and (2) planned and actual selling prices. The same general approach can also be used by managers desiring to analyze differences between actual and planned gross margin (sales minus cost of goods sold). In addition, the analysis is often applied to explain differences in the actual results of two periods, such as the current and the prior month. Actual margin can differ from plans because of differences between planned and actual costs. We shall ignore cost differences at this early stage and treat them in detail in Chapter 12.

Suppose that a firm expected to sell 20,000 units at $20 each and incur variable costs of $12 per unit. Actual results were 21,000 units sold at $19 each. These results and the differences appear below:

	Actual	Planned	Difference
Units sold	21,000	20,000	1,000
Sales	$399,000	$400,000	$ 1,000
Variable costs	252,000	240,000	12,000
Contribution margin	$147,000	$160,000	$13,000

We want to explain the $13,000 difference between planned and actual contribution margin. The schedule shows that total revenues were $1,000 less than planned, while total variable costs were $12,000 more than planned. Notice that actual variable cost per unit was $12 ($252,000/21,000). The increase in total variable costs is entirely attributable to the increase in volume. Had the firm sold 21,000 units at $20, it would expect contribution margin to be $8,000 more than planned, which is 1,000 units times the $8 unit contribution margin. (Managers would not expect contribution margin to increase by the selling price times the increase in volume because they know that variable costs should increase as well.)

Two factors caused the difference between planned and actual contribution margin: a difference in selling price and a difference in sales volume. To isolate the monetary effect of each factor, we hold one of the factors (price or volume) constant and look at the effect of the change in the other. One simple way to do this is to prepare a statement that shows what would have happened if the firm had sold the actual volume, but at the planned price. Such a statement appears below:

	Actual Results	Actual Volume at Planned Selling Price	Planned Results
Units sold	21,000	21,000	20,000
Sales	$399,000	$420,000	$400,000
Variable costs	252,000	252,000	240,000
Contribution margin	$147,000	$168,000	$160,000
Differences		$21,000 $8,000	

The difference between the planned contribution margin ($160,000) and the contribution margin if the actual sales volume had been achieved at the planned selling price ($168,000) is $8,000. That difference is called **sales volume variance.** Had the firm been able to sell 21,000 units *and* maintain its selling price at $20 it would have earned $8,000 more than planned, which is the 1,000 additional units sold times the $8 planned contribution margin per unit. Thus the sales volume variance can also be computed as

$$\begin{matrix} \text{Sales} \\ \text{volume} \\ \text{variance} \end{matrix} = \begin{matrix} \text{planned} \\ \text{contribution} \\ \text{margin} \\ \text{per unit} \end{matrix} \times \left(\begin{matrix} \text{actual} \\ \text{sales,} \\ \text{in} \\ \text{units} \end{matrix} - \begin{matrix} \text{planned} \\ \text{sales,} \\ \text{in} \\ \text{units} \end{matrix} \right)$$

$$\$8,000 = \$8 \times (21,000 - 20,000)$$

If a firm sells more units than planned, the variance is positive and is said to be favorable. If fewer units are sold than was planned, the variance is negative (unfavorable). In the example, the variance is favorable. Again, please notice that we are holding unit variable cost constant because we want to determine the effect on total contribution margin of selling more (or fewer) units than planned. We are also holding selling price, and therefore contribution margin per unit, constant.

Now, we look at the difference between planned and actual total contribution margin that is attributable to the difference between the planned and actual selling price. As you know, a change in selling price automatically changes unit contribution margin by the same amount and in the same direction. Thus, changes in selling price affect total contribution margin because they affect contribution margin per unit.

The difference between the $168,000 contribution margin that would have been earned if the $20 price had been maintained and the actual contribution of $147,000 is due to the fact that the firm sold its product at less than $20 per unit. This difference is called the **sales price variance.** The variance in this case is unfavorable, because the actual selling price was less than planned. Contribution margin was $147,000, but it would have been $168,000 if the price had actually been $20.

We can also calculate the sales price variance by determining the actual selling price and multiplying the difference between the actual and planned prices by the actual unit volume. The actual selling price was $19.

$$\begin{matrix} \text{Sales} \\ \text{price} \\ \text{variance} \end{matrix} = \text{units sold} \times (\text{actual price} - \text{planned price})$$

$$\$21,000 = 21,000 \times (\$19 - \$20)$$

Notice that the difference between the planned and actual selling prices is also the difference between planned and actual unit contribution margin. Because changes in selling price translate directly into equal changes in contribution margin, we can use the difference in selling prices. We could also express the sales price variance as the difference between actual total revenue ($399,000) and the total revenue that we would have had at the actual volume and planned selling price ($20 × 21,000 = $420,000). This difference is expressed in the schedule showing planned results, results at actual volume and planned price, and actual results.

A word of caution. An unfavorable variance, either sales price or sales volume, is not necessarily a bad outcome. A firm might deliberately reduce its price in order to sell more units. The total variance in contribution margin is more important than either variance taken separately. This question of pricing policy is discussed in more detail later in the chapter.

MULTIPLE PRODUCTS

In Chapter 2 we discussed a simple situation in which the firm sold two products. Both products had the same contribution margin percentage but different per-unit contribution margins. Most firms, however, sell many products with varying contribution margins, both per unit and as percentages. Such firms can use VCP analysis for each individual product, or even for groups of products where the contribution margins are equal. But firm-wide analysis is also possible, provided that the **sales mix** of the different products is generally the same (that is, provided that the various products are usually sold in about the same proportions).

There are several reasons why firms might experience the same sales mix of products. Some products are sold and used together so that the sales of the products are associated. Examples would be tables and chairs, cups and saucers, wallpaper and paste. In other cases, though the products are not always sold together, they are used together, so that the sales of one product influence the sales of the other. Examples of such products would be cameras and film, razors and razor blades, golf clubs and golf balls. These types of products are called **complementary products.**

Even when there is no apparent relationship among the products of a particular firm, experience may indicate that the sales mix remains fairly constant. For example, a particular department store may consistently derive 40% of its sales from clothing, 25% from furniture and housewares, and 35% from all its other departments. These percentages may be relatively constant over time despite the absence of obvious causes. Where sales mix is, for whatever reason, relatively predictable, VCP analysis uses a weighted-average contribution margin percentage.

Weighted-Average Contribution Margin Percentage

As its name suggests, a **weighted-average contribution margin percentage** is a measure of the overall contribution margin percentage weighted by the sales of the individual products. It is essentially an analytical device for treating a multiple-product company as if it were a single-product firm. For planning purposes, the percentage is computed on the basis of the expected total contribution margin *given* the estimated ratios of sales of the firm's various products. When actual total sales in dollars are multiplied by the expected weighted-average contribution margin percentage, the result should be about equal to the actual contribution as long as the actual sales mix is about the same as the expected mix.

Consider a retail store that sells three products: shirts, shoes, and jeans. Prices and variable costs for these products are as follows:

	Shirts	Shoes	Jeans
Selling price	$10	$20	$15
Variable cost	4	10	9
Contribution margin	$ 6	$10	$ 6
Contribution margin percentage	60%	50%	40%

Suppose that the sales dollars derived from these products are normally 30% from shirts, 20% from shoes, and 50% from jeans, and that the store manager expects total sales for the coming month to be $30,000. His planned income statement would look like the following:

	Shirts	Shoes	Jeans	Total
Sales	$9,000	$6,000	$15,000	$30,000 (100%)
Variable costs	3,600	3,000	9,000	15,600 (52%)
Contribution margin	$5,400	$3,000	$ 6,000	$14,400 (48%)

The individual sales figures are the sales mix percentages multiplied by expected total sales. The variable cost and contribution margin amounts for each product can be derived from the basic price and cost data. The weighted-average contribution margin is 48% (total contribution margin of $14,400/total sales of $30,000).

We could have derived the 48% without first determining total sales and variable costs by product. So long as the expected prices and sales mix hold, the *typical* sales dollar will consist of $0.30 from the sale of shirts, $0.20 from shoes, and $0.50 from jeans.[1] Consequently, the contribution margin on a *typical* sales dollar can be computed by calculating the contribution margin for each segment of that dollar and adding them together. Hence, the weighted-average contribution margin could be computed as follows:

	Shirts	Shoes	Jeans	Total
Typical sales dollar	$0.30	$0.20	$0.50	$1.00
Product contribution margin percentage	60%	50%	40%	
Contribution margin	$0.18	+ $0.10	+ $0.20	= $0.48
Weighted-average contribution margin	($0.48/$1.00)			48%

[1]Because no product sells for as little as $1, it might be more understandable to think of each $100 or each $1,000 (or some other convenient amount) of sales. Using some other typical sales package in the calculation will produce the same results.

A more direct, but equivalent, approach is to deal only with percentages, as follows:

	Shirts		Shoes		Jeans		Total
Contribution margin percentage	60%		50%		40%		
Sales mix	30%		20%		50%		100%
Weighted contribution percentage	18%	+	10%	+	20%	=	48%

Even if a particular firm does not experience a constant sales mix in each period, it can still use the weighted-average contribution margin developed from planned income statements to analyze the actual results. Some firms, for example, may simply forecast sales for each product and build up a planned income statement, by product, for the entire firm. The previous income statement could have been the result of such individual forecasts, in which case the planned weighted-average contribution margin of 48% would be known only after the income statement had been prepared.

The importance of sales mix can be seen if we change the example to reverse the mix percentages of jeans and shirts. Shirts are now 50% of sales and jeans 30%. Recall that jeans have the lowest contribution margin percentage of 40% and shirts the highest at 60%. The new weighted-average contribution margin percentage is calculated below:

	Shirts		Shoes		Jeans		Total
Contribution margin percentage (from previous schedule)	60%		50%		40%		
Sales mix percentage	50%		20%		30%		100%
Contribution margin per sales dollar	30%	+	10%	+	12%	=	52%

The new weighted-average contribution margin percentage is 52%, four percentage points higher than the 48% shown before. Thus, if the firm could sell relatively more shirts and relatively fewer jeans it would earn a higher contribution margin percentage.

Figure 4-1 on page 105 shows the volume-cost-profit chart for the firm, assuming that the fixed costs are $10,000 per month. Note that the horizontal axis shows sales in dollars rather than, as was the case in earlier chapters, in units. We cannot use sales in units because we are dealing with three separate products and the cost and revenue lines would depend on which products made up the number of units sold. Two different total cost lines are shown in this chart, to represent two different sales mixes. The dotted line shows the variable cost percentage of 52% of sales, which holds when the weighted-average contribution margin percentage is 48% (as originally computed when the sales mix was 30% shirts, 20% shoes, and 50% jeans). The solid line for total cost incorporates a variable cost percentage of 48%, which holds when the weighted-average contribution margin is 52% of sales (the second computation, when the sales mix was 50% shirts, 20% shoes, and 30% jeans).

Notice that the break-even point is lower when the contribution margin percentage is 52% than when it is 48%. Note also that at the predicted sales volume of

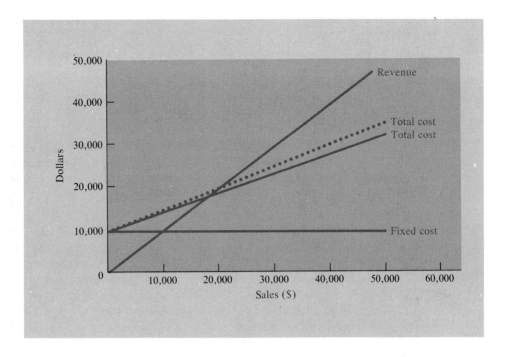

FIGURE 4-1

$30,000, profits are higher when the contribution margin is higher. Both of these results should be expected based on the principles discussed in earlier chapters.

Sales Mix in Units

Sometimes, it is more convenient to state a sales mix in units rather than in dollars. For example, a maker of tables may find that its three kinds of tables, high-priced, medium-priced, and low-priced, sell in unit ratios of 10%, 30%, and 60%, respectively. That is, for every ten tables sold, one will be high-priced, three medium-priced, and six low-priced. Suppose that the data relating to each table are as follows.

	High-priced	Medium-priced	Low-priced
Selling price	$300	$180	$100
Variable cost	120	110	60
Contribution margin	$180	$ 70	$ 40

When the mix is stated in units rather than in dollars the easiest way to find the weighted-average contribution margin percentage is to develop an income statement for a typical (hypothetical) batch of units. (Remember that the calculations using a sales mix in sales dollars rested on analysis of the contribution margin on a typical sales dollar.) In this case, ten units is a convenient figure for a hypothetical batch. If the firm sells ten tables, its income statement will appear as follows.

	High-priced	Medium-priced	Low-priced	Total
Units sold	1	3	6	10
Sales	$300	$540	$600	$1,440
Variable costs	120	330	360	810
Contribution margin	$180	$210	$240	$ 630

The weighted-average contribution margin percentage is 43.75% ($630 total contribution margin divided by $1,440 total sales). Using this percentage, the firm can prepare a planned income statement based on its expected sales volume in units.

Overall Planning

Because of historical trends, managers of a multiple-product firm may have some ideas about the expected sales mix and can use the weighted-average contribution margin for planning purposes. Managers can, however, take some actions that will influence the sales mix. For example, they may approve expenditures for special advertising campaigns or specific sales promotion plans. Managers can also encourage salespeople to concentrate on certain products, either through direct instructions or through special commission plans. When products are complementary, as we discussed on page 102, managers have an additional problem. They must not only plan for volume of one product, but also take into consideration the effects on sales of complementary products.

Before proposing any special programs that could influence sales mix, the manager will want to know the basic sales and cost data for each product. From these data, the manager will have some idea of profitability by product and in what way the sales mix might be better. (In general, a "better" mix would be one that has more sales of the higher contribution margin products.) Often managers will study the sales and cost data for the various products and evaluate alternative strategies by assuming different mixes of sales. A technique that is used in this type of study is called **simulation.** Simulation is a computer-assisted process by which a manager provides the computer with various sets of assumptions about sales mix and other factors, and the computer calculates the level of profit or loss for each combination. Alternative assumptions could relate to, but are not limited to, different selling prices and different sales mixes.

In planning sales mix, managers should be continually evaluating the individual products or product lines. A **product line** is a group of similar products. An example would be a "hair care" line, which could consist of shampoos, conditioners, colorings, creams, tonics, and restorers. In many cases, managers may treat the entire line as a single "product." There are many reasons for taking this simplified approach for analytical purposes.

First, the products might be similar enough in contribution margin percentage that little is gained by looking at them individually. Planning does, after all, involve estimates; moreover, minor differences that may result from grouping products with slightly different contribution margins are not likely to affect decision making. Another reason for grouping products is that the sheer number of them might make analyzing them individually very difficult and time consuming.

A third important reason for grouping products relates to the level of the manager for whom an analysis is being prepared. Different managers make different decisions and therefore need different kinds of information. For example, the president of a full-line department store would seldom, if ever, want to look at the sales and cost details for every single product stocked by the store. A lower-level manager in the store—say the one in charge of sporting goods—would, however, want to look periodically at individual products in that line. That manager would be concerned about each product and would make decisions about adding and dropping individual products. The president, on the other hand, would be more concerned with the product line as a whole, and would make decisions about adding or dropping entire departments.

An important factor in analyzing either an individual product or a product line is an understanding of the nature of the fixed costs associated with that product or line. We explore, in the next section, a few of the concepts necessary for such an understanding. Chapter 5 contains a more extensive discussion of fixed costs and individual products.

Fixed Costs and Multiple-Product Firms

In Chapter 3 we introduced the concepts of discretionary and committed fixed costs and suggested that for some purposes the former might be considered as avoidable and the latter as unavoidable. Further refinement and expansion of the concept of avoidability is required in planning, evaluating, and decision making by managers looking at individual products or lines.

Costs that are discretionary from the standpoint of a firm as a whole may not, in fact, be avoidable from the standpoint of a segment of the firm, such as a product or product line. For example, the salaries of salespeople are to some extent discretionary. Yet if each salesperson handles all of the firm's products, it is unlikely that dropping one or two products would allow the firm to reduce the sales force. The salespeople would still make their rounds of customers and would probably require just about as much time as they had before the firm dropped one or two products. (Of course, if the firm were to drop half of its products, it could probably reduce the sales force because of the loss of customers whose purchases consisted only of products that had been dropped.) The avoidability of fixed costs, then, depends on the specific situation—on *which* products or lines are being considered.

Because the avoidability (or unavoidability) of costs depends upon the segment of the business being looked at, accountants have developed a further distinction between fixed costs—on the basis of whether such costs are separable or joint. A **separable** fixed cost is one that relates directly to the product, product line, or other segment specifically under consideration. A **joint** (or **common**) fixed cost is one that relates to more than one segment.

Some discretionary fixed costs are joint to several products, lines, or other segments. The sales salaries mentioned in the earlier example would be considered joint to most, if not all, products. Because these costs are not avoidable so far as a specific product or product line is concerned, they are not relevant in determining whether or not a specific product or line should be dropped.

Committed fixed costs may also be either separable or joint. If a particular factory makes a single product, the depreciation and property taxes for that factory are committed and are also separable with respect to that product. If, on the other hand, a factory makes several products, depreciation and property taxes on it are common to all of the products it produces.

Exhibit 4-1 presents an income statement suitable for use by a manager in analyzing the relative profitability of the firm's three product lines. Avoidable fixed costs are subtracted from the contribution margin of each line, and the joint and committed costs are shown only in the total column. This format highlights what is often called the **product margin,** the amount by which contribution margin from the product is greater or less than the related avoidable fixed costs. As a general rule, a product (or line) having a positive product margin should be continued unless there are overriding non-quantitative considerations. If the product is dropped, the firm's total profits will fall by the amount of the product margin. If product margin is negative, total profits would rise by that amount if the product were dropped. More specific attention to decision making appears in Chapter 5.

Exhibit 4-1
Davis Department Store
Product-Line Income Statement
19X5
(thousands of dollars)

	Clothing	Housewares	Sundries	Total
Sales	$2,400	$1,800	$1,300	$5,500
Variable costs:				
Cost of goods sold	1,050	900	700	2,650
Commissions	240	180	130	550
Other variable costs	150	120	90	360
Total variable costs	1,440	1,200	920	3,560
Contribution margin	960	600	380	1,940
Separable-discretionary fixed costs:				
Salaries and expenses of				
department managers	80	65	40	185
Other	30	15	10	55
Total separable-discretionary				
fixed costs	110	80	50	240
Product margin	$ 850	$ 520	$ 330	$1,700
Committed and joint fixed costs:				
Depreciation on fixtures				155
Rent on store				300
Salaries of administrative staff				410
Utilities				140
Other				500
Total committed and joint fixed costs				1,505
Income				$ 195

PRICE-VOLUME RELATIONSHIPS

The concept of relevant range, as introduced in Chapter 2, incorporated the assumption that the volume of sales was unrelated to the selling price. (The absence of such a relationship allowed the graphing of total revenue as a straight line.) Selling prices are, in many realistic situations, very unlikely to be constant over wide ranges of sales volume. For example, consider automobile sales. If each car maker doubled the price of every car in its line, its sales and total auto sales would surely fall. Similarly, if the price of each car were halved, total volume might be expected to increase sharply. The described expectations reflect the **law of demand,** which states that as prices increase the quantity sold decreases, and vice versa. In most realistic situations, there is *some* price-volume interdependence, even over the relevant range, and managers must recognize such interdependence in developing their plans.

Consider a company that currently sells 10,000 units of product at $15 per unit. Variable costs are $10 per unit and fixed costs are $20,000. The sales manager believes that if the price were increased to $16, volume would fall to 9,000 units, and the controller has concluded that the stated cost structure is probably applicable to volumes ranging from 8,000 to 16,000 units. (Thus, the relevant range with respect to costs is between 8,000 and 16,000 units; but price/volume interdependence exists, making a single, straight, revenue line inappropriate.) Such a firm could still use the basic concepts of VCP analysis in analyzing, and planning, its operations. It might, for example, use income statements such as those below to show the potential effect of a price increase:

	Sell 10,000 Units at $15	Sell 9,000 Units at $16
Sales	$150,000	$144,000
Variable costs, at $10	100,000	90,000
Contribution margin	50,000	54,000
Fixed costs	20,000	20,000
Income	$ 30,000	$ 34,000

Income would be $4,000 higher at a selling price of $16. The increase in price is large enough to offset the decline in volume brought on by the price change.

The firm might also evaluate its alternatives by considering only contribution margin. The existing price yields $50,000 of contribution margin ($5 × 10,000) whereas the proposed price is expected to yield $54,000 ($6 × 9,000). Suppose the sales manager also believes that volume would increase to 14,000 units if the price were reduced to $14. Would a price reduction be preferable to a price increase? It would appear to be so. Total contribution margin would be $56,000 ($4 × 14,000), which is higher than total contribution margin at either the current price or the proposed higher price.

The possibility of an interdependence between prices and volume must be recognized and allowed for when planning profit and analyzing alternative courses of action.

VOLUME-COST-PROFIT ANALYSIS
IN NOT-FOR-PROFIT ENTITIES

The term "not-for-profit entities" encompasses many different kinds of economic entities, including governmental units, universities, churches, charitable organizations like the Red Cross and American Cancer Society, and various types of clubs and fraternal groups. We use the term "not-for-profit" in preference to "nonprofit" because the former better describes the *intent* of such organizations. (Many business firms turn out to be "nonprofit," but usually not by choice!)

Income is one measure of how well a business has been run. Although maximizing profit is not the only objective of a business firm (survival, growth, product quality, good corporate citizenship being other important objectives), the earning of profits sufficient to attract capital investment is necessary to the continuation of the firm. How then is VCP analysis relevant to entities that do not intend to earn profits?

Remember that the first step in applying the analysis is to classify costs according to behavior. The nature of a cost as fixed or variable (or some combination) does not change because the cost is incurred by a not-for-profit entity. Such entities often have to choose from among alternative ways to accomplish some specific and required task. For instance, a city can choose to do its own trash collection or to contract the task to a private firm. If the outside firm would charge on the basis of the volume of trash collected, the cost would be variable. If the city had its own trucks and personnel, a large portion of the costs would be fixed. Recognizing the implications of the different types of behavior, city officials would want information about the likely volumes of trash, including some estimates about probable growth in that volume.

Many not-for-profit entities do try to earn profits, or at least to break even, on some of their activities. College bookstores and food services often operate profitably and help to defray other costs. Municipalities sometimes run parking lots or utilities like water companies that operate at a profit. When a not-for-profit entity operates a service that benefits only a portion of the members, it might try to break even on that service. For instance, not everyone in a city will take advantage of a municipal golf course. The city's elected officials might believe that the course should "pay its own way" and, therefore, require that the prices charged provide enough revenue to meet the costs.

The situations mentioned so far are relatively straightforward applications of cost analysis or volume-cost-profit analysis. As a rule, however, the major activities of not-for-profit entities are not amenable to such straightforward application because there is often no objective way to determine the value of the services—there is no revenue. Of course, not-for-profit entities do get revenues—taxes, donations, tuition, etc.—but often not from the specific services that they provide. A city or town will have a police force, but the people do not pay for this service on the basis of use; they pay for it in taxes that also support all the other activities of the government.

Despite the difficulties associated with measuring the results of the activities of not-for-profit entities, some evaluations of results are always being made. Proof that some type of evaluation was undertaken is evidenced by the facts that organizations disband, governmental programs are sometimes cut back or even dropped, some charities find their donations decreasing. The creation and dissolution of not-for-profit entities are often instigated by large groups of people (the public ceases to support a particular charity), at other times by small groups (the head of a foundation decides to stop funding a particular program). Essentially, not-for-profit entities are concerned with analyzing the benefits and costs of activities, not so much with the revenues, costs, and profits. Accordingly, they use **benefit-cost analysis.**

Benefit-Cost Analysis

Many actions contemplated by not-for-profit entities are supported by analyses that attempt to make some kind of monetary measurement of both benefits and costs. For instance, governmental studies relating to the construction of a new dam are likely to include not only construction costs but also estimates of benefits resulting from flood control and additional recreational opportunities. Those who oppose the dam might offer an alternative analysis that measures the benefits using different assumptions, attempts to quantify the cost of displacing people who live near the dam site, and states that the proposed dam would do irreparable, unquantifiable harm to some species of wildlife. The proponents and opponents will dispute each other's figures on quantified points and then will argue about how to evaluate the unquantified ones.

In other kinds of situations, especially those relating to ongoing activities such as public education and police and fire protection, it might be even more difficult to measure benefits and costs. Some think a better-educated citizen to be more beneficial to a community than one less well educated, but how much more beneficial? Would a reasonable measure of the difference be the difference between the income taxes that the two would pay, or perhaps the difference between their incomes?

As a practical matter, many public service problems of this type have been approached by the responsible decision makers in one of two basic ways:

1.   Decide on the amount of money to spend on a particular activity and concentrate on getting the most benefit from that level of expenditure.
2.   Decide on the level of service to be provided, and concentrate on providing that level of service at the most reasonable cost.

As an example of the first approach, the city council might decide to spend $500,000 on police protection. The chief of police would then have to decide how best to spend the allotted money. Should the chief increase the number of patrol cars and cut down on police officers walking beats, or would the reverse be better? Should the department send officers to training programs on advanced crime-fighting techniques, and if so, how many officers and which programs? Unfortunately, establishing the level of expenditure does not really avoid the problems of measuring the benefits of public services. The chief must develop criteria for measuring the benefits from alternative plans to provide police protection. The council, meanwhile, must decide whether or not the city is getting its money's worth, which means finding a way to measure variations in the level of accomplishment for the fixed expenditure. Meaningful measures are seldom available. Were the funds well spent if the number of arrests increases? (Probably not, because arrests for minor offenses would count as much as ones for major crimes.) Are the funds being better used this year if there is a drop in the crime rate? (Possibly, but many factors besides the quality and quantity of the police force affect the level of crime.)

The second approach—deciding first on the level of service and then trying to achieve that level at reasonable cost—presents many of the same problems as the first. For example, the citizens of a state might, through their elected representatives, decide that all high school graduates should have the opportunity to attend college whether or not they can afford it. A number of alternatives, with differing costs, are available. Does the mandate require that there be branches of the state university in all large population centers? Should the state establish a large number of community colleges that would prepare students for work at a smaller number of senior colleges? Might it be better to provide money for tuition assistance directly to the students, who could use the funds to attend a college of their choice? How does one evaluate whether the stated level of service has been provided at reasonable cost? (Should the fundable choices include private colleges? Colleges outside the state?) Choosing among the alternatives would involve not only determining the costs but also developing some measures of the benefits of each alternative. Thus, trying to achieve a specified level of service at a reasonable cost does not entirely avoid the problems of measuring the benefits of a public service or evaluating the performance of that service.

In sum, analyzing public service activities is exceedingly difficult because of the lack of objective, unarguable measures of services and performance. Analyzing costs, especially if one is trying to determine whether or not those responsible are spending money wisely, is also difficult, but usually less so. The problems are not limited to not-for-profit entities. Business firms spend a great deal of money on employee training, research, and development, and on other activities where the benefits are not readily measurable in monetary terms. Finding ways to make useful measurements is a constant concern of managers and a goal of much research in universities, business, and government.

SUMMARY

A firm dealing with several products will generally need to compute a weighted-average contribution margin for its volume-cost-profit analysis. This computation requires information about the sales mix, stated either in dollars or units, as well as price and cost data.

The techniques of VCP analysis are helpful in analyzing the results of operations. Differences between planned and achieved contribution margin and income may be attributed to differences in volume, price, and mix. Managers then concentrate on those products or strategies (pricing, promotion, etc.) that can be expected to yield the best results. Managers also use contribution margin information to identify profitable products.

An important assumption in basic VCP analysis is that there is no interdependency between the sales price charged and the volume of sales obtainable at that price. This assumption is often unrealistic, and managers must allow for the potential effect of a price change on volume.

Not-for-profit entities utilize benefit-cost analysis, a counterpart of VCP analysis. It is difficult to define and measure benefits deriving from a particular expenditure in a not-for-profit entity. Despite these difficulties, more and more managers in such entities are finding that adaptations of the concepts of managerial accounting can be helpful in their organizations.

KEY TERMS

benefit-cost analysis
complementary products

joint (common) cost
law of demand

product line

product margin

sales mix

sales price variance

sales volume variance

separable fixed cost

simulation

weighted-average contribution
    margin percentage

KEY FORMULAS

$$\text{Sales volume variance} = \text{planned contribution margin per unit} \times \left(\begin{array}{c} \text{actual} \\ \text{sales, in} \\ \text{units} \end{array} - \begin{array}{c} \text{planned} \\ \text{sales, in} \\ \text{units} \end{array} \right)$$

$$\text{Sales price variance} = \text{units sold} \times \left(\begin{array}{c} \text{actual} \\ \text{price} \end{array} - \begin{array}{c} \text{planned} \\ \text{price} \end{array} \right)$$

REVIEW PROBLEM

Data on the three types of can openers that are sold by McMichael Company are given below:

	Regular	Deluxe	Super
Selling price	$2.00	$3.00	$5.00
Variable costs	1.20	1.50	2.00
Contribution margin	$ .80	$1.50	$3.00
Contribution margin percentage	40%	50%	60%

Monthly fixed costs are $90,000.

Required: Consider each part independently.

1. Suppose that the sales mix in *dollars* is: Regular, 60%; Deluxe, 30%; and Super, 10%. Determine the weighted-average contribution margin percentage and the monthly sales required to break even. Prepare an income statement by product line for sales of $250,000. Assume that, of the $90,000 fixed costs, there are separable-discretionary costs of $10,000 for each product.

2. Suppose now that the sales mix in *units* is: Regular 50%; Deluxe, 30%; and Super, 20%. Determine the weighted-average contribution margin percentage and sales required to earn $20,000 per month before taxes.

3. Suppose that in one month the firm expected to sell 40,000 Regular openers at $2 each. It actually sold 42,000, but the average selling price was $1.85. Compute the sales price variance and sales volume variance.

Answer to Review Problem

1. The weighted-average contribution margin percentage is 45%, computed as follows:

	Regular	Deluxe	Super	Total
Contribution margin percentage multiplied by	40%	50%	60%	
sales mix percentage	60%	30%	10%	
equals				
contribution margin per sales dollar	24% +	15% +	6% =	45%

The sales required to break even are $200,000 per month (fixed costs of $90,000/45%).

	Regular	Deluxe	Super	Total
Sales[a]	$150,000	$75,000	$25,000	$250,000
Variable costs[b]	90,000	37,500	10,000	137,500
Contribution margin	$ 60,000	$37,500	$15,000	$112,500
Separable-discretionary fixed costs	10,000	10,000	10,000	30,000
Product margin	$ 50,000	$27,500	$ 5,000	$ 82,500
Joint fixed costs				60,000
Income				$ 22,500

[a]Based on the stated sales mix of 60%, 30%, and 10%. $250,000 × 60% = $150,000; $250,000 × 30% = $75,000; $250,000 × 10% = $25,000.
[b]These figures can be determined by using the variable cost percentages, which are 60%, 50%, and 40% (all are 1− contribution margin percentages). Or, the number of units of each product can be determined by dividing sales for the product by selling price per unit as given in the problem. Then, the results are multiplied by variable cost per unit as given in the problem. For example, sales of the Regular model are 75,000 units ($150,000/$2). Variable costs are given as $1.20 per unit, so such costs would be $90,000 for 75,000 units ($1.20 × 75,000).

2. The weighted-average contribution margin percentage is 50%, computed as follows by using a typical sales batch of ten units distributed as stated in the problem:

	Regular	Deluxe	Super	Total
Mix	50%	30%	20%	100%
Units	5	3	2	10
Sales (no. of units × stated sales price per unit)	$10.00	$9.00	$10.00	$29.00
Contribution margin (no. of units × stated contribution margin per unit)	$ 4.00	$4.50	$ 6.00	$14.50
Weighted-average contribution margin percentage ($14.50/$29.00)				50%

Sales required for $20,000 profit per month would be computed using the target profit formula from Chapter 2 and amount to $220,000 [(fixed costs of $90,000 + target profit of $20,000)/50% contribution margin percentage].

3. Because of the way in which the information is given, the easiest way to solve the problem is to deal with only the price and volume differences, as follows:

Sales price variance
$$= \frac{\text{quantity}}{\text{sold}} \times \left(\begin{array}{cc} \text{actual} & \text{planned} \\ \text{price} & \text{price} \end{array} \right)$$
$$= 42,000 \times (\$1.85 - \$2.00)$$
$$= 42,000 \times (-\$0.15)$$
$$= \$6,300 \text{ unfavorable}$$

Sales volume variance
$$= \frac{\text{planned}}{\text{contribution}} \times \left(\begin{array}{cc} \text{actual} & \text{planned} \\ \text{volume} & \text{volume} \end{array} \right)$$
$$\text{margin}$$
$$= \$0.80 \times (42,000 - 40,000)$$
$$= \$0.80 \times 2,000$$
$$= \$1,600 \text{ favorable (favorable because actual}$$
volume was greater than planned)

Alternatively, we could prepare the following schedule, similar to the one on page 100:

	Actual Results	Actual Volume at Planned Selling Price	Planned Results
Sales	$77,700 (42,000 × $1.85)	$84,000 (42,000 × $2)	$80,000
Variable costs	50,400 (42,000 × $1.20)	50,400 (42,000 × $1.20)	48,000
Contribution margin	$27,300 (42,000 × $0.65)	$33,600 (42,000 × $0.80)	$32,000

$6,300
unfavorable sales
price variance

$1,600
favorable sales
volume variance

ASSIGNMENT MATERIAL

Questions for Discussion

4-1 Price determination—postal service   What do you think would be the major problem in developing an analysis to determine prices to be charged for the various classes of mail handled by the postal service?

4-2 Volume-cost-profit chart   Explain how preparation of a volume-cost-profit graph would differ between (a) a firm that sells only one product, and (b) a firm that sells several products.

4-3 Volume-cost-profit analysis   "VCP analysis is fine for firms that have very simple operations, but for most firms in the real world it won't work." Identify several problems involved in the use of VCP analysis by firms with complicated operations. How can these problems be overcome?

4-4 Unit costs and governmental performance   The city manager of a medium-sized city was quoted as saying that trash collection service in her city was better than that in many neighboring cities because the unit cost was lower. The unit cost was the total cost of collections divided by the number of tons collected. Does having a low unit cost mean that the city is doing a good job?

Exercises

4-5 Price-volume relationships   Watson Company makes two products, Hicost and Locost. Both products are being sold at $25 per unit and monthly volume is 6,000 units for each. Hicost has variable costs of $15 per unit and Locost has variable costs of $5 per unit. The sales manager believes that volume of either product could be increased by 25% if the price were reduced by 10%.

Required
1. Compute the effects on monthly contribution margin if the proposed price cut were implemented for each product.
2. Should either price be cut?

4-6 Product profitability and selection   The following data relate to the three products sold by Quert Company:

	Flibetts	Wibbets	Hobbits
Selling price	$20	$14	$8
Variable costs	8	7	2
Contribution margin	$12	$ 7	$6

Required
1. Determine which product is the most profitable (a) per unit, (b) per sales dollar.
2. Sales are currently 5,000 Flibetts, 12,000 Wibbets, and 16,000 Hobbits per year. The products are interchangeable to some extent and the sales manager believes that customers can be induced to switch from Wibbets and Hobbits to Flibetts. He believes that an advertising campaign costing $70,000 would result in 3,000 buyers of Wibbets switching to Flibetts, and 8,000 buyers of Hobbits changing to Flibetts. Should the firm undertake the campaign? Support your answer with calculations.

4-7 Variance relationships   Ayres Company had the following planned results for March 19X9:

Sales (12,000 units)	$180,000
Variable costs	108,000
Contribution margin	$ 72,000

Actual contribution margin was $63,000 on sales of 14,000 units. Variable costs per unit were incurred as planned.

Required

1. Compute actual sales in dollars.
2. Compute the actual selling price.
3. Compute the price and volume variances.

4-8 Relationships   Bruton Company sold 11,000 units of its one product. It experienced a sales volume variance that was $3,000 unfavorable and a sales price variance that was $3,300 favorable. It had originally budgeted a selling price of $10 and variable cost of $7.

Required

1. Determine the number of units that Bruton had budgeted to sell.
2. Determine the actual unit price that Bruton received.
3. Determine Bruton's budgeted and actual contribution margins.

4-9 Comparison of monthly performance   Randle Company's results for July and August appear below.

	July	August
Sales	$120,000	$121,540
Variable costs	84,000	82,600
Contribution margin	$ 36,000	$ 38,940

The controller tells you that unit variable cost was the same in both months and that the company sold 12,000 units in July.

Required: Analyze the difference between the contribution margins, showing the difference resulting from sales volume and that resulting from sales price.

4-10 Price and volume variances   Klaxton Company produces a single product, a large plastic wastebasket. Planned results for March were as follows:

Sales (30,000 units)	$210,000
Variable costs	75,000
Contribution margin	135,000
Fixed costs	70,000
Income	$ 65,000

Actual results were as follows:

Sales	$210,000
Variable costs	60,000
Contribution margin	150,000
Fixed costs	70,000
Income	$ 80,000

Variable costs were incurred as expected, per unit.

Required
1. How many wastebaskets did the firm sell?
2. What was the actual selling price?
3. What were the volume variance and price variance?

4-11 **Sales volume and sales price variances** Walker Company budgeted sales of 10,000 units of its product at $20. It actually sold 9,500 units at $20.50. Variable cost is $10 per unit.

Required: Determine the sales price and sales volume variances.

4-12 **Basic sales mix** Allen Company makes two types of facial cream, Allergy-free and Cleansaway. Data are as follows:

	Allergy-free	Cleansaway
Price per jar	$12	$4
Variable cost per jar	$ 3	$3

Monthly fixed costs are $55,000.

Required
1. If the sales mix in dollars is 50% for each product, what is the weighted-average contribution margin percentage? What dollar sales are needed to earn a profit of $30,000 per month?
2. If the sales mix is 50% for each product in units, what is the weighted-average contribution margin percentage? What dollar sales are needed to earn $30,000 per month?
3. Suppose that the firm is operating at the level of sales that you calculated in part 1, earning a $30,000 monthly profit. The sales manager believes that it is possible to persuade customers to switch from Cleansaway to Allergy-free by increasing advertising expenses. How much can the firm spend on additional monthly advertising to change the mix to 60% for Allergy-free and 40% for Cleansaway, while maintaining a $30,000 monthly profit? Total dollar sales will not change, only the mix.

4-13 **Weighted-average contribution margin** Blue-Room Products sells three types of simulated brass soap dishes, the Necessary, the Frill, and the Luxury. Detailed selling price and cost data for the products are as follows:

	Necessary	Frill	Luxury
Selling price	$10	$20	$25
Variable cost	$ 4	$12	50% of selling price

Fixed costs for these products are $280,500.

Required
1. If the company has a choice of selling one more unit of any one of its products, which product should it choose to sell one more unit of?
2. If the company has a choice of selling $1,000 more of one of its products, which product should it choose to sell $1,000 more of?

3. Assume that the sales dollar volume of the company is normally distributed 30% from Necessary, 20% from Frill, and 50% from Luxury.
   a. What is Blue-Room Product's normal weighted-average contribution margin percentage?
   b. What would the break-even point for the company be in sales dollars?
   c. At the break-even point, how many units of Luxury would be sold?
4. Assume, instead, that the company's sales in units are normally distributed 40% for Necessary, 20% for Frill, and 40% for Luxury.
   a. What is the company's normal weighted-average contribution margin percentage?
   b. What would the break-even point for the company be in sales dollars?
   c. At the break-even point, how many units of Luxury would be sold?

4-14 **Pricing policy—public service**   Speebus, the city-owned bus service of Middleville, charges $0.75 for all rides on its buses. The city has a large number of retired citizens, whose incomes are generally lower than those of working citizens. One of the members of the city council has proposed that Speebus reduce its fares for persons over 65 to $0.40.

At the present time, about 1,200,000 rides per month are made on Speebus buses, about 30% of which are by citizens over 65. Buses are rarely crowded. The councilman estimates that the decrease in fares to older persons would increase their use of the bus service by 50%. Other users would remain the same. Even with the increase in riders expected, buses would rarely be crowded.

Required
1. How much will it cost per month for Speebus to reduce fares to riders over 65?
2. Suppose that the bus service is operating at break-even. By how much would regular fares have to be increased to get back to break-even if the reduction is granted?

4-15 **Pricing to break even**   The Student Senate at Western University sponsors a number of programs for students and faculty. Among them is a monthly movie in the school auditorium, which holds 3,200 people. The movies selected would not ordinarily be shown in the one theater in the small town in which the university is located, and attendance at the University showings is high. A one-evening showing of a movie is invariably sold out. When it is shown on two evenings, attendance at each showing averages 2,375.

Movies are rented at a cost of $2,000 for one showing, $3,000 for two showings. Other fixed costs per showing are $400 and variable costs are $0.40 per person for chair rentals, tickets, and miscellaneous items. The Senate wants to break even for the year on the movie program.

Required
1. Determine the prices that must be charged in order that the Senate break even on the movie showings for the year assuming (a) one showing of each movie, and (b) two showings of each movie.
2. Make a recommendation to the Senate regarding the number of times a movie should be shown, explaining the factors that influenced your decision.

4-16 **Market share**   MBT Company produces and sells a number of consumer products. It recently hired a new vice president for sales who is a great believer in increasing the market share of a product. One of his first proposals was to reduce the price of Kleenbrite, a toothpaste that currently had a 15% share of the total market of 2,000,000 tubes monthly in the area where it was sold.

The current price is $1.60 per tube, variable costs are $0.50. The new vice president reduced the price by $0.15 and Kleenbrite increased its share of the market to 16.5% of the 2,000,000 tube market.

Required
1. Was reducing the price to gain market share a wise move? Show separately the effects of the change in price and the change in volume.
2. What share of the market did Kleenbrite need to achieve in order to justify the $0.15 price reduction?
3. Suppose that the firm could increase the market share of Kleenbrite at the $1.60 price by increasing advertising and promotion expenses. What additional expenditures would MBT be able to make to increase market share by one percentage point without reducing its overall profit?

4-17   Variances from plans (extension of 3-28)   Competitive pressures late in February prompted the managers of Forecast Company to reduce its selling price for March to $9.80. Per-unit variable costs, total fixed costs, and income tax rates continued to behave as planned, and the total variable costs for March were $420,000.

Required
1. How many units were sold in March?
2. What was the total contribution margin for March?
3. Was the March sales volume variance favorable or unfavorable?
4. How much of the difference between planned and actual contribution margin was due to the sales volume variance?
5. Was the March sales price variance favorable or unfavorable?
6. How much of the difference between planned and actual contribution margin for March was due to the sales price variance?
7. What net income did the company earn in March?

4-18   Product profitability   Wrynn Company sells three kinds of tobacco jars. The controller has prepared the following analysis of profitability of each of the jars:

	Flavorsaver	Shagholder	Burleykeeper
Selling price	$5.00	$8.00	$11.00
Variable costs	2.00	4.00	6.40
Fixed costs	3.00	3.00	3.00
Total costs	5.00	7.00	9.40
Profit	—	$1.00	$ 1.60
Profit percentage to selling price	0%	12.5%	14.5%
Annual volume	22,000	15,000	13,000

The firm has total fixed costs of $150,000 per year. The controller obtained the fixed cost per unit figure of $3 by dividing $150,000 by 50,000 units (22,000 + 15,000 + 13,000). On the basis of her analysis, the controller suggested that the Flavorsaver model be discontinued if a substitute could be found that would be more profitable. This conclusion upset the sales manager, who understood VCP analysis and had planned to undertake a $10,000 promotional campaign for Flavorsavers. He had calculated that a $10,000 expenditure would increase the volume of the product selected by 25%. Sales of the other products would be unaffected, as would existing fixed costs.

Required: Determine which product should be selected for the special promotion.

4-19 **Variances in a service business**   Earl Torgeson, the managing partner of Torgeson, Watts, and Gold, Certified Public Accountants, was comparing the planned and actual results for the firm for 19X1. Because all employees are on a straight salary, there are no variable costs associated with chargeable hours (hours worked on client business).

Employee Category	*Planned*			*Actual*		
	Hourly Rate	Total Hours	Revenue	Hourly Rate	Total Hours	Revenue
Junior staff	$18	40,000	$720,000	$19	38,000	$722,000
Senior staff	30	12,000	360,000	28	13,000	364,000

Required: For each category, determine the price (rate) and volume variances.

4-20 **Explaining results, accounting methods**   The controller of Walston Company has given you the following income statements for the firm's major product for the two most recent months. She has asked you to develop an explanation of the differences in gross margin between the two months and to present your analysis to the president. You learn that the purchase price of the product, a typewriter, was $111 in June and $117 in July. Additionally, at the end of June there were 3,500 typewriters in inventory bought at $111. The firm uses the first-in-first-out (FIFO) method of accounting for inventory. All units sold in June had cost $111.

	June	July
Sales	$2,269,200	$2,306,350
Cost of sales	1,354,200	1,377,150
Gross margin	$ 915,000	$ 929,200

Required
1. Prepare an explanation for the president, as the controller has requested.
2. The president wonders what monthly gross margin the firm would earn if it maintained its volume and price at the levels for July. Give him the answer.

Problems

4-21 **Costs and profits per unit**   Managers of the Hylman Company, which manufactures a packaged beverage-sweetener, have been trying to decide what price to charge for the product for the coming year. One manager has come up with the following analysis.

		Likely Results	
Price per Case	Case Volume	Average Total Per-case Cost	Per-case Gross Margin
$260	60,000	$225.00	$35.00
$250	70,000	$218.00	$32.00
$240	80,000	$212.75	$27.25

"It seems to me," the manager said, "that we should go with the $260 price, since the per-case gross margin is highest at that price."

Required: Determine the price that would yield the highest total profit to the firm.

4-22   VCP analysis—product mix   Happy Times Brewery produces and sells two grades of beer: regular and premium. Premium beer sells for $4 per case, regular for $3. Variable brewing costs per case are $2.50 (premium) and $2 (regular). Sales of regular beer, in cases, are double those for premium. Fixed brewing costs are $60,000 monthly, and fixed selling and administrative costs are $75,000 monthly. The only variable cost in addition to variable brewing costs is the 10% commission (based on dollar sales) paid to salespeople.

Required
1. Compute the break-even point in sales dollars per month.
2. How many cases of each kind of beer are sold at break-even?
3. The brewery is now running about $660,000 in monthly sales. The advertising manager believes that sales of premium beer could be increased by 20% if an extensive advertising campaign were undertaken. The campaign would cost $4,000 per month. However, sales of regular beer would probably fall by about 5% because some customers now buying the regular grade would merely switch to premium. Should the campaign be undertaken?
4. If the campaign were undertaken, what is the weighted-average contribution margin? Round to three decimal places.
5. What is the new break-even point in dollar sales?

4-23   Pricing a product   Watson Razor Company makes razors, blades, and other shaving accessories. The firm is introducing a new razor this year, the Super-90, which has 30 comfort settings and other features that lead the management to believe that it will be a big seller. The razor has variable costs of $2 per unit. Associated fixed costs are $2,000,000 per year for production, advertising, and administration. The sales manager of Watson believes that if the razor is priced at $3, about 2,500,000 units per year will be sold. If the price is $4, about 1,500,000 units per year would be sold.

Required
1. Determine which price would yield the higher profit to Watson.
2. Suppose that for each razor sold the firm also sells four packages of blades per year. Blades sell for $1.50 per package and the variable cost is $0.60 per package. Would this information affect your analysis in part 1?

4-24   Pricing decision and average costs   The sales manager for Markham Pen Company has been trying to decide what price to charge for a new pen the firm is introducing this year. His staff has prepared a research report that indicates the following price-volume relationships:

Price	Volume
$2.25	800,000 units
2.10	1,000,000
1.95	1,200,000
1.80	1,400,000
1.65	1,600,000

The variable cost per pen is $1.00 and total annual fixed costs are estimated at $500,000. The sales manager believes that any product should be priced at 150% of total cost. He decides to use 1,000,000 units as the volume to determine the average unit cost and computes the cost at $1.50 per pen. He intends to set the price at $2.25.

Required

1. Assuming that the predictions of the staff are correct, determine what profit would be earned if the pen is priced at $2.25.
2. Again assuming the correctness of the staff's predictions, determine which price would yield the highest profit.
3. Suggest what might be wrong with the sales manager's method of setting prices?

4-25 Product profitability   Craven Clothing Company has hired a new assistant controller who recently graduated from the state university. Her first assignment was to prepare a break-even analysis of the firm. She gathered the following data related to operations for the latest year:

	T-Shirts	Sweat-shirts	Jeans
Sales price	$4	$8	$15
Variable costs	3	4	6
Contribution margin	$1	$4	$ 9

Total fixed costs are $840,000. Sales are usually distributed in the following percentages of dollar sales: T-shirts, 40%; sweatshirts, 40%; jeans, 20%.

Required

1. If $1 in advertising expenditures would increase sales of the one product being advertised by one unit, which product should be advertised if advertising funds are limited?
2. What are break-even sales dollars for the firm?
3. By how much will the firm increase its income for each sales increase of $1?
4. What sales are necessary to achieve income of $210,000?
5. The controller has just come from a meeting with the operating managers and says that the sales mix is likely to change to 20%, 30%, and 50%, for T-shirts, sweatshirts, and jeans, respectively.
   (a) Compute the new break-even point.
   (b) Compute the sales volume needed to earn $210,000.

4-26 Sales interdependencies (AICPA adapted)   Breezway Company operates a resort complex on an offshore island. The complex consists of a 100-room hotel, shops, a restaurant, and recreational facilities. Mr. W. E. Blenem, manager of the complex, has asked for your assistance in planning the coming year's operations. He is particularly concerned about the level of profits the firm is likely to earn.

Your conversation with Mr. Blenem reveals that he expects the hotel to be 80% occupied during the 300-day season that it is open. All rooms rent for $40 per day for any number of persons. In virtually all cases, two persons occupy a room. Mr. Blenem also tells you that past experience, which he believes is an accurate guide to the future, indicates that each person staying at the hotel spends $10 per day in the shops, $20 in the restaurant. There are no charges for use of the recreational facilities. All sales in the shops and restaurant are made to guests of the hotel, which is isolated from the only large town on the island.

After talking with Mr. Blenem, you obtain the following data from the firm's controller:

	Shops	Restaurant
Variable costs, as a percentage of sales dollars:		
Cost of goods sold	40%	30%
Supplies	10	15
Other	5	5

For the hotel, the variable costs are $6 per day per occupied room, for cleaning, laundry, and utilities. Total fixed costs for the complex are $1,200,000 per year.

Required
1. Prepare an income statement for the coming year based on the information given.
2. Mr. Blenem tells you he believes if the room rate were reduced to $35 per day, the occupancy rate would increase to 90%. Determine the effect on planned income if the rate were reduced.

4–27   Product line reporting   Kelly Company is a retail store specializing in men's clothing. The firm has three major product lines: suits, sport clothes, and accessories. The firm's most recent monthly income statement is given below:

Kelly Company
Income Statement for April 19X7

Sales		$800,000
Cost of sales		572,000
Gross profit		228,000
Operating expenses:		
Commissions	$48,000	
Salaries	80,000	
Rent	20,000	
Shipping and delivery	15,000	
Insurance	4,500	
Miscellaneous	7,500	175,000
Income before taxes		$ 53,000

The president of the firm would like a product-line income statement. She gives you the following additional data:
1. The sales mix in April was 30% suits, 50% sport clothes, and 20% accessories, expressed in dollars of total sales.
2. The cost of sales percentages are 80% for suits, 75% for sport clothes, and 50% for accessories.
3. Sales commissions are 6% for all product lines.
4. Each product line is the responsibility of a separate manager and each manager has a small staff. The salaries that are directly related to each product line are $12,000 for suits, $8,000 for sport clothes, and $5,200 for accessories. All other salaries are joint to the three lines.
5. Rent is for both office and warehouse space, all of which is in a single building.

6. Shipping and delivery costs are for operating expenses and depreciation on the firm's three trucks. Each truck serves a particular geographical area and delivers all three product lines.
7. Insurance includes a $500 fixed amount for basic liability coverage. The rest of the insurance is for coverage of merchandise at the rate of one-half of one percent of the selling price of the average inventory on hand during the month. In April the average inventories at selling prices were equal to sales for each product line.
8. Miscellaneous expenses are all joint to the three product lines.

Required: Prepare an income statement by product, using the format of Exhibit 4-1 on page 108 and comment on the results.

4-28   Product profitability   Messorman Company produces three models of pen and pencil sets, A, B, and C. Price and cost data are as follows:

	A	B	C
Selling price	$10	$20	$30
Variable costs	6	8	15

Monthly fixed costs are $20,000.

Required
1. Which model contributes the most per unit sold?
2. Which model contributes the most per dollar of sales?
3. Suppose the sales mix in dollars is 40% A, 20% B, and 40% C.
   (a) What is the weighted-average contribution margin?
   (b) What is the monthly break-even point?
   (c) What is the sales volume necessary to earn a profit of $30,000 per month?
4. Suppose the sales mix in dollars is 30% A, 30% B, and 40% C.
   (a) What is the break-even point?
   (b) What is the sales volume necessary to earn $30,000 per month?
5. Suppose that the sales mix in units is 40% A, 20% B, and 40% C.
   (a) What is the weighted-average contribution margin?
   (b) What is the break-even point in sales dollars?
   (c) How many units of each model would be sold at the break-even point computed in (b)?
   (d) What is the sales volume in units of each model necessary to earn a profit of $30,000 per month?

4-29   What is profitability?   Kimbell Company sells three products. Data are given below:

	Product		
	A	B	C
Selling price	$30	$50	$100
Variable cost	20	25	60
Contribution margin	$10	$25	$ 40
Annual unit volume	50,000	10,000	5,000

Required

1. Rank the three products in order of profitability as measured by:
   (a) total annual profit (b) profitability per unit sold (c) profitability per dollar of sales.
2. Explain what the rankings mean and how Kimbell's managers might use the information.

4-30 Product line income statements   The president of Mifflan Tool Company has just received the firm's income statement for January 19X8. He is puzzled because you had told him last year, when working as a consultant to the firm, that sales of $500,000 should produce a profit of about $57,000 before income taxes.

Mifflan Tool Company
Income Statement
January 19X8

Sales		$500,000
Cost of sales		307,500
Gross profit		192,500
Operating expenses:		
Rent	$40,000	
Salaries	70,000	
Shipping and delivery	14,000	
Other expenses	30,000	154,000
Income before taxes		$ 38,500

The firm sells three products and your analysis assumed the following sales mix in dollars: hammers, 30%; screwdrivers, 20%; and chisels, 50%. The actual mix in dollars in January was 40%, 30%, 30%. The firm does not manufacture its products. Cost of sales and shipping and delivery are variable costs. All others are fixed. Data per unit for each product are given below:

	Hammers	Screwdrivers	Chisels
Selling price	$5.00	$2.00	$4.00
Cost of sales	3.00	1.50	2.00
Shipping and delivery	0.20	0.04	0.08
Total variable costs	3.20	1.54	2.08
Contribution margin	$1.80	$ .46	$1.92

None of the fixed costs is directly associated with any particular product line. All costs were incurred as expected, per unit for variable costs, in total for fixed costs. Selling prices were as expected.

Required

1. Prepare a new income statement by product, based on actual results in January. Show both gross profit and contribution margin for each product.
2. Prepare an income statement by product for January, assuming that the expected sales mix had been achieved.
3. Explain the reasons for the differences between the two statements.

4-31 Bus service   Bluebird Bus Company provides service among a number of Northeastern cities. The firm's buses make 300 trips per week with an average distance of 100 miles. Fares are $0.06 per mile per passenger and each bus can carry 40 passengers. The firm has the following cost structure:

Drivers' pay ($300 per week per driver)	$6,000	per week
Other salaries and wages	$8,000	per week
Other fixed costs, including depreciation and maintenance of buses	$13,000	per week
Gas, oil, and other variable costs	$0.50	per bus per mile

Required
1. Determine the break-even point in passenger-miles.
2. Determine the weekly income if the firm operates with its buses 60% full.
3. Suppose that Bluebird is now operating at 50% of capacity. The president believes that if fares were reduced to $0.055 per mile, the buses would run 60% full. Additional advertising and promotional costs to publicize the lower fares would be $1,500 per week. Should Bluebird reduce its fares?

4-32 Decision making for student programs   The Speaker Committee at a large university is in charge of inviting distinguished persons to address students, faculty, and members of the public. Students and faculty are admitted free; members of the public pay $2. Students and faculty must pick up tickets in advance; any tickets left on the day of the speech are sold to the public beginning the morning of the speech. The speaker program is expected to break even for the year.

The committee is trying to decide whether to invite Marvin Gardens, a noted environmentalist, or Cayuga Waters, a famous industrialist. One student member of the committee argues that Marvin Gardens is an ideal speaker. His required fee is $800. The student states that the auditorium, which holds 2,000 people, will be almost completely filled with students and faculty if Gardens speaks. He believes that only about 500 tickets would be available to members of the public and that all available tickets could be sold. One of the other members, an administrative officer of the university, says that Waters would be a better speaker. She estimates that only 500 students and faculty would show up, leaving 1,500 tickets to be bought by the public. These tickets could easily be sold to the public, she believes. Waters charges a fee of $2,000.

Required
1. Assuming that both committee members are correct in their assessments of demand for tickets, which speaker would be more profitable?
2. What other factors should be considered in reaching a decision?
3. What would you recommend?

4-33 Cost analysis in a university   The School of Management at State University currently has 500 students enrolled and 25 faculty members. The school has only juniors and seniors who take all their courses in the school, an average of five courses per semester. The school offers 75 sections per semester with each faculty member teaching three of the sections.

Following are the data for the number of sections, average number of students per section, and "student-sections," which is the total number of enrollments in all sections. Since there are 500 students taking five courses each semester, there must be 2,500 student-sections.

Number of Sections	×	Average Enrollment	=	Student-Sections
20		20		400
30		35		1,050
25		42		1,050
75				2,500

The university's administration is considering allowing the enrollment in the School of Management to increase to 1,000 students. One university officer objects that the cost would be prohibitive. He states that faculty salaries are now $950,000 per year and would double if enrollment were to double because twice the number of faculty now teaching would be required.

Another officer points out that it would not be necessary to double the size of the faculty because the sizes of sections could be increased, although the university policy is that no more than 45 students be enrolled in a single section.

You are assigned the task of determining the additional cost of faculty salaries required to support enrollment of 1,000 students. You determine that demand for the classes now averaging 20 students per section is such that each section would go up to 25 students if enrollment went to 1,000. All other sections would be increased to the 45-student maximum. A faculty member would be hired for each three sections per semester added, at a salary of $30,000 per year.

Required
1. How many sections would be needed if enrollment were increased to 1,000 students? (*Hint:* Because 1,000 students will take five courses per semester, you must account for 5,000 individual enrollments.)
2. How much additional cost would be incurred for faculty salaries, given your answer to question 1?
3. After you performed the analysis in questions 1 and 2, the chancellor of the university became concerned about the large class sizes. She asks you to redo the analysis of required additional faculty salaries assuming that only 40 sections would hold 45 students, 20 would still hold 25 students, and the rest would have a maximum of 36 students.

4-34   Multiple products—movie company (continuation of 2-38 and 3-35)   Both the producing company and prospective star have given further thought to the possible contract terms and concluded that some provision probably should be made for revenues to be earned from contracts authorizing showings of the movie on television. After lengthy negotiations, Kirkwalker's agent proposed the following terms: (a) a payment of $1,000,000, plus (b) 15% of the receipts-to-the-producer from theater admissions, plus (c) 10% of the revenues from sales of television rights. Blockbusters' negotiating team leaves the negotiations in order to study the potential impact of the new offer.

A study of past productions indicates that the producer can expect revenues from sales of television rights to be approximately one eighth (12.5%) of producer's revenues from theater admissions. Ms. Lane is pleased with the opportunity to lower the fixed-payment part of the contract but is concerned about the magnitudes of the two off-the-top percentages.

Required
1. At what level of receipts-to-the-producer will Blockbusters break even under the new contract proposal?

2. Considering the additional information about the sale of television rights, at what level of receipts-to-the-producer will Blockbusters break even under Kirkwalker's normal contract terms ($1,500,000 plus 5% of the producer's receipts)?

3. Assume that, because of Blockbusters' delay in accepting the contract offer, Kirkwalker's agent decides that his client should also receive a percentage of the revenues Blockbusters will derive from the sale of screening rights in foreign countries, which revenues typically amount to 10% of domestic receipts. If the agent proposes a 5% "cut" of those revenues for Kirkwalker, what is the break-even point for Blockbusters Incorporated?

4-35 **Interrelationships between products**   Rapidcal Company manufactures hand-held calculators. The industry is highly competitive and pricing is critical to sales volume. Warren James, sales manager of Rapidcal, has been trying to decide on a price for a new model that the firm will introduce shortly. The new model, the RC-89, is somewhat more sophisticated than the RC-63, which has been successful in recent years. The RC-63 now sells at retail for $20, of which 30% goes to the dealer, 70% to Rapidcal. The other variable costs for the RC-63 are $8 per unit. The variable costs for the RC-89, exclusive of dealer share, are $18 per unit.

James is especially concerned about the effects on sales of RC-63 following the introduction of the RC-89. He believes that if the RC-89 is priced at $44 retail, there would be no loss in sales of the RC-63. However, if the RC-89 were sold at $42, he thinks that some people will buy the RC-89 instead of buying the RC-63. At the $44 price, James expects sales of 150,000 RC-89s per year. For each $2 cut of the price of RC-89s, sales would increase by about 30,000 units, but about 40% of the increased sales of RC-89 would be at the expense of sales of the RC-63. At any price for the RC-89, Rapidcal would receive 70%, the retailer 30%.

Also, James believes that a $38 retail price is rock-bottom for the RC-89. He therefore instructs you to determine the effects on the income of the firm of pricing the RC-89 at $44, $42, $40, and $38.

Required: Comply with the sales manager's request, and determine the price that should be set for the RC-89.

4-36 **Multiple products (extension of 3-28)**   The planned data for Forecast Company, as shown in 3-28, represent the combined plans for the firm's three products: a platter, a cup, and a saucer. The expected sales mix of the three products, in sales dollars, is 40%, 30%, and 30%, for the platter, cup, and saucer, respectively.

Required

1. What are the expected sales, in dollars, for each product?

2. If the contribution margin percentage for cups is 10% and that for saucers is 30%, what is the expected contribution margin percentage for platters?

3. The firm's normal sales mix, in units, is one platter sold for every two cup-and-saucer sets sold, and the planned results reflect that sales mix. If the expected sales of 50,000 units counts each platter, cup, and saucer as a separate unit, what are the planned selling prices and per-unit variable costs for each of the three products?

4. Assume that the actual sales for April were $450,000 and that the sales mix, in dollars, was 60% platters and 20% each for cups and saucers.
    (a) What was the actual total contribution margin earned for April?
    (b) What was the actual weighted-average contribution margin percentage for April?

5. B. J. Douglas, sales manager for Forecast Company, considers the April results to be unusual and not likely to be repeated. That is, she believes that sales and cost data

reflected in the original plans are appropriate as long as there are no changes in costs or selling prices. But she is convinced that the price being charged for plates (in relation to those charged for the other two products) is too high and not in the firm's best interest. Accordingly, she has developed several plans for improving sales, all of which plans involve price reductions for plates. These plans, together with Douglas's best estimates of their effects on sales, are summarized below.

Plan A: Reduce the price of a plate to $19. (Douglas estimates that unit sales of plates will increase by 10% but that the price reduction will have no effect on the sales of the other two products.)

Plan B: Reduce the price of a plate to $16. (Douglas estimates that the unit sales of plates will increase 20% and that the price reduction will result in more customers buying cups and saucers so that three of each of the other products will be sold for every plate sold.)

Plan C: Reduce the price of a plate to $18. (Douglas estimates that the unit sales of plates will increase 20% and that the present sales mix of two cups and two saucers sold for every plate sold would not be changed.)

Which, if any, of the proposed plans should be adopted?

4-37   **Personnel policies and decisions**   Patterson Company operates a chain of hardware stores in a metropolitan area. Each store has a manager, several salespersons, and a clerk or two. The vice president of the firm has reviewed the performance of individual stores and is considering closing the Middleton store. The income statement for that store shows the following for 19X7 and future results are expected to be about the same:

Middleton Store
Income Statement for 19X8

Sales		$500,000
Cost of sales	$350,000	
Salaries	85,000	
Commissions, 10% of sales	50,000	
Rent on building	20,000	
Rent on store equipment	4,000	
Miscellaneous expenses	7,000	516,000
Net loss		($ 16,000)

If Patterson closes the Middleton store, it would transfer all personnel to other stores. The firm is opening several new stores and would have to hire additional people even if the ones from the Middleton store are transferred. The miscellaneous expenses are fixed, but are avoidable if the store is closed. If the store closes, none of its former business would go to any of the existing stores.

Required

1.   Assume that the rentals on building and equipment are for leases that have 12 years to run. Patterson has no other use for the building and equipment and could not sublease to another firm. Determine whether the firm should close the store.

2.   Assume that the rentals are on month-to-month leases so that they can be cancelled at any time. Determine whether the store should be closed.

3.   Assume that the rentals are unavoidable, as in part 1. However, suppose now that the Middleton store has been losing business because the firm has two newer stores relatively close by. The vice president believes that if the Middleton store were closed,

total sales in its other stores would increase by $80,000 per year. The cost of sales and commissions, as percentages of sales dollars, are the same in all of the firm's stores. Fixed costs in the other stores would not be affected by the increases in sales. Determine whether the Middleton store should be closed.

4-38   Line of business reporting (CMA adapted)   Riparian Company produces and sells three products. Each product is sold domestically and in foreign countries. The foreign market has been disappointing to the management because of poor operating results, as evidenced by the income statement for the first quarter of 19X8:

	Total	Domestic	Foreign
Sales	$1,300,000	$1,000,000	$300,000
Cost of goods sold	1,010,000	775,000	235,000
Gross profit	290,000	225,000	65,000
Selling expenses	105,000	60,000	45,000
Administrative expenses	52,000	40,000	12,000
	157,000	100,000	57,000
Income	$ 133,000	$ 125,000	$ 8,000

Management decided a year ago to enter the foreign markets because of excess capacity, but is now unsure whether to continue devoting time and effort to developing the foreign market. The following information has been gathered for consideration of the alternatives that management has identified:

	Products		
	A	B	C
Sales: Domestic	$400,000	$300,000	$300,000
Foreign	100,000	100,000	100,000
Variable manufacturing costs (percentage of sales)	60%	70%	60%
Variable selling expenses (percentage of sales)	3%	2%	2%

All fixed manufacturing costs are joint to the three products. All administrative expenses are fixed and joint to the three products and to the two markets. Fixed selling expenses are separable and avoidable by market, but not by product.

Management believes that if the foreign market were dropped, sales in the domestic market could be increased by $200,000. The increase would be divided 40%, 40%, 20% among products A, B, and C, respectively.

Management also believes that a new product, D, could be introduced by the end of the current year. The product would replace product C and would result in increased fixed costs of $10,000 per quarter.

Required
1. Prepare an income statement for the quarter by product, showing contribution margin for each product.
2. Prepare an income statement for the quarter by market, showing contribution margin and product margin for each market.

3. Determine whether the foreign market should be dropped, assuming that management's estimates of increased domestic sales are valid.
4. Assume that the foreign market would not be dropped. Determine the minimum quarterly contribution margin that product D would have to produce in order to make its introduction desirable.

4-39 Price and volume variances (AICPA adapted)   Bay City Gas Company supplies liquefied natural gas to residential customers. Below are the results, both planned and actual, for the month of November 19X7. Although he knows that the price of gas per thousand cubic feet drops with increases in purchases by a customer, the operations manager is having difficulty in interpreting the report.

	Planned	Actual	Difference
Number of customers	26,000	28,000	2,000
Sales in thousands of cubic feet	520,000	532,000	12,000
Revenue	$1,300,000	$1,356,600	$56,600
Variable costs	$ 416,000	$ 425,600	($ 9,600)

Required: Compute the sales price variance and sales volume variance.

4-40 Sales strategies   Nova Company sells cosmetics through door-to-door salespeople who receive commissions of 25% of selling price. Nova's national sales manager has been evaluating alternative selling strategies for the coming season. She is trying to decide whether any products should be discounted in price by 30%, receive increased promotional efforts, or be left alone. She is now considering four products, data for which are given below:

	Mascara	Eyeliner	Lipstick	Cologne
Normal selling price	$2.50	$2.20	$2.00	$12.00
Variable cost	0.90	1.00	0.80	5.00
Contribution margin	$1.60	$1.20	$1.20	$ 7.00
Expected volumes:				
Without discount or special				
promotion (units)	800,000	750,000	2,000,000	200,000
With 30% discount	1,650,000	1,350,000	3,200,000	380,000
With special promotion	950,000	920,000	2,150,000	240,000

If the special promotion is chosen for a particular product, its selling price and variable cost will remain the same. Additional fixed costs would be $200,000 for each product selected, primarily for advertising and incentive payments to salespeople.

If a product is selected for a price cut of 30%, variable costs will remain the same, per unit, because Nova pays sales commissions on the basis of the normal selling price even during such special sales.

Required
1. For each product, determine which of the following should be done: reduce price, engage in special promotion, or don't do anything.
2. Discuss some additional factors that might influence the sales manager's decisions about each product.

4-41 **VCP for a hospital—patient-days**   The administrator of Brookwood Memorial Hospital has developed the following estimate of costs:

$$\text{Total annual cost} = \$39,000,000 + (\$28 \times P1) + (\$40 \times P2)$$
$$P1 = \text{patient-days on medical wards;}$$
$$P2 = \text{patient-days on surgical wards.}$$

A "patient-day" is one patient occupying a bed for one day. The administrator expects contribution margins, other than from room charges, to be about $25 per day from each medical patient and $60 per day from each surgical patient. These come from pharmacy, blood bank, operating room charges, and other such sources.

Required
1. Suppose that patient-days on medical wards generally run twice the number of those on surgical wards. The room charges are tentatively set at $75 per day for medical patients, $100 for surgical patients. How many total patient-days must the hospital achieve to break even?
2. Suppose now that the administrator forecasts 250,000 medical patient-days and 150,000 surgical patient-days. He would like to set the room rates so that the hospital breaks even and also wants each type of patient-day to provide the same dollar contribution margin. What room rates will achieve these objectives? (The $25 and $60 miscellaneous contributions should be included in determining the contribution margins from room charges.)
3. Repeat part 2 assuming that the administrator wants both types of patient-day to provide the same contribution margin percentage.

4-42 **Comprehensive review of Chapters 2, 3, and 4**   Tacky Company makes three products and sells them in about the same mix each month. Below are income statements for two recent months.

Tacky Company Income Statements
(in thousands of dollars)

	April	May
Sales	$80	$60
Costs	60	52
Income	$20	$ 8

Selling price and cost data by product are as follows.

	A	B	C
Selling price	$20	$10	$5
Variable costs	8	3	3
Contribution margin	$12	$ 7	$2
Contribution margin percentage	60%	70%	40%
Percentage of total sales dollars (mix)	40%	40%	20%

Required
1. Using the income statements for April and May, find total fixed cost, and variable cost as a percentage of sales dollars.
2. Determine the break-even point in sales dollars.

3. Which product is most profitable per unit sold?
4. Which product is most profitable per dollar of sales?
5. What sales dollars are needed to earn $35,000 per month and how many units of each product will be sold at that sales level if the usual mix is maintained?
6. The sales manager believes that he could increase the sales of C by 10,000 units per month if more attention were devoted to it and less to B. Sales of B would fall by 2,000 units per month. What would the change in income be if this action were taken?
7. In June, the sales were $100,000 with a mix of 40% A, 30% B, and 30% C. What is the income?
8. In July the firm had sales of $90,000 and an income of $22,000.
    (a) What was the contribution margin percentage?
    (b) Which product would you think was sold in a higher proportion than the usual mix?
9. Suppose the firm is currently selling 6,000 units of C. It is felt that because this is the least profitable product it should be dropped from the mix. If C is dropped, it is expected that sales of B would remain the same and those of A would rise. By how much would sales of A have to rise to maintain the same total income?

4-43 **Comprehensive problem on volume-cost-profit** You are presented with the following information about Gammon Sales Company, based on plans for the year 19X1:

Sales ($1 per unit)		$100,000
Variable costs:		
Cost of goods sold	$67,000	
Other operating costs	15,000	
Total		82,000
Contribution margin		18,000
Fixed costs		13,140
Planned income before taxes		$ 4,860

Required: Answer the following questions on the basis of the data for the 19X1 plans:
1. What is Gammon's break-even sales volume?
2. The company's officers have analyzed the anticipated cash situation for the year and have determined that it could afford to spend $3,600 on a special advertising campaign. They are not sure, however, that the expenditure would be worthwhile. What would be the break-even point if the campaign were undertaken?
3. If, as a result of the advertising campaign, the number of units sold could be expected to increase in an amount equal to the change in the break-even point in units, would the campaign be financially advisable (that is, to the company's advantage)? Explain.
4. Assume that Gammon has decided not to undertake the advertising campaign and is looking for other ways to improve the financial outlook for 19X1. The purchasing agent determines that there is a supply house (other than the one with which the company now deals) that will allow the company to buy at a price 10% below the anticipated purchase price. The sales manager believes that the new supplier would not be providing a product of equal quality, and he estimates that sales volume would decrease by about 15% if the new supplier were used. The controller has determined that the switch in suppliers will necessitate minor changes in the administrative procedures, which changes will increase fixed costs by approximately $1,000. Would the change of suppliers be wise? Explain your answer with supporting computations.

5. Are there some qualitative considerations that might influence the decision on the change in suppliers?

6. After further investigation, you determine that Gammon has not one but three separate products in its line, each of which has the same selling price. The planned activity for 19X1 in more detail is as follows:

	Product			
	#1	#2	#3	Total
Sales ($1 per unit)	$50,000	$30,000	$20,000	$100,000
Variable costs:				
Cost of goods sold	30,000	21,000	16,000	67,000
Other operating costs	7,500	4,500	3,000	15,000
Total	37,500	25,500	19,000	82,000
Contribution margin	$12,500	$ 4,500	$ 1,000	18,000
Fixed costs				13,140
Planned income before taxes				$ 4,860

Gammon has decided not to dilute the impact of a special advertising campaign by trying to promote more than one product. Which product would the company probably choose to promote in the $3,600 advertising campaign? Explain.

7. The company has found an alternative supplier for each of its products. Each supplier would be willing to sell to the company at a price 10% lower than is currently being paid. In each case, however, the product from the new supplier would probably reduce the total sales of that product by 15%. However, the company can change suppliers for only one of the products at a time. Ignoring any qualitative considerations, decide for which product, if any, Gammon should change suppliers. Support your answer.

8. Assume that Gammon's directors decide to postpone the advertising campaign and continue doing business with current supply sources. At the end of 19X1, despite sales of $110,000, income before taxes was only $360. Analysis of sales by product showed the following:

Sales of Product #1	$ 30,000
Sales of Product #2	20,000
Sales of Product #3	60,000
Total	$110,000

These results surprised the board of directors because operating managers assured the directors that the variable and fixed costs had behaved during the year exactly as expected; sales were in excess of the forecast. Explain the reason or reasons for the disappointing results.

Cases

4-44 Product mix, profit planning, taxes Michael Monte, the new assistant controller of Remley Company, has prepared a volume-cost-profit analysis for the firm based on sales of the firm's three products from 19X7. He will present the analysis to a group of managers later in the week. Data per unit are given below.

	Products		
	101	102	103
Selling price	$3.50	$4.00	$5.00
Variable costs	1.50	3.00	2.00
Contribution margin	$2.00	$1.00	$3.00

On the basis of the sales mix in 19X7, Michael believed that out of every ten units sold, four would be 101s, four 102s, and two 103s. Total fixed costs were predicted to be $90,000. Total sales were expected to be 100,000 units, based on a projection of trends in recent years, and Michael had prepared the following planned income statement for the year 19X8.

	101	102	103	Total
Sales	$140,000	$160,000	$100,000	$400,000
Variable costs	60,000	120,000	40,000	220,000
Contribution margin	$ 80,000	$ 40,000	$ 60,000	180,000
Fixed costs				90,000
Income before tax				90,000
Income taxes (40%)				36,000
Net Income				$ 54,000

At the meeting, Michael demonstrated that his analysis could be used to predict changes in profits that would be expected to follow changes in sales. As an example he said that the break-even point for the firm would be $200,000 in sales, because the contribution margin percentage is 45% and fixed costs are $90,000. He showed the other managers that target profits can also be computed, although the presence of income taxes makes it a bit more complicated than computing the break-even point. He said that if an after-tax profit figure were desired, it would be necessary to divide it by 60%, the percentage of net income to income before taxes. The resulting before-tax profit could be added to fixed costs and the sum divided by 45%. Thus, the sales required for profits of $90,000 would be about $533,300. [Before-tax profits would have to be $150,000, and ($90,000 + $150,000)/45% is $533,333.]

Some of the managers were becoming restless as Michael explained his analysis. Finally, the production manager said that it was all very interesting, but irrelevant. She told the group that labor costs, which are 50% of variable costs, would increase by 20% under a new union contract that she expected would be signed shortly.

The controller said that he was somewhat disappointed with Michael's analysis because it had failed to provide for a $40,000 dividend to stockholders that the president of the firm had said should be a target. The firm has a policy of not allowing dividends to be more than one-third of after-tax profits. The controller had thought that Michael would incorporate the desired dividend into his analysis to show the other managers what had to be done to meet the president's goal.

As the managers began to mumble among themselves about the irrelevance of the analysis, the sales manager announced that the assumed sales mix was no good. He said,

"I don't know how this will affect the analysis, but we expect that each product will be sold in equal amounts during this coming year. The demand for 103s is increasing substantially."

Slapping her forehead, the production manager commented that she had forgotten that the firm would have to rent some additional equipment to increase production of 103s. The rental would be $10,000 per year. She wondered what effect that news would have on Michael's figures.

As he left the meeting, Michael chastised himself for not having obtained more information before going in and looking like a fool.

Required: Prepare a new analysis for Remley, incorporating the goals and changed assumptions learned at the meeting. Show the sales necessary to (a) break even, and (b) meet the profit required to pay the $40,000 dividend without violating the firm's dividend policy.

4-45   Changing product mix (CMA adapted)   Hewtex Electronics manufactures two products—tape recorders and electronic calculators—and sells them nationally to wholesalers and retailers. The Hewtex management is very pleased with the company's performance to date in 19X7. The projected income statement for 19X7 appears below.

Hewtex Electronics
Projected Earnings Statement
for the Year Ended December 31, 19X7

	Tape Recorders		Electronic Calculators		
	Total Amount (000 omitted)	Per Unit	Total Amount (000 omitted)	Per Unit	Total (000 omitted)
Sales	$1,050	$15.00	$3,150	$22.50	$4,200.0
Production costs:					
Materials	280	4.00	630	4.50	910.0
Direct labor	140	2.00	420	3.00	560.0
Variable overhead	140	2.00	280	2.00	420.0
Fixed overhead	70	1.00	210	1.50	280.0
Total production costs	630	9.00	1,540	11.00	2,170.0
Gross margin	$ 420	$ 6.00	$1,610	$11.50	2,030.0
Fixed selling and administrative costs					1,040.0
Income before income taxes					990.0
Income taxes (55%)					544.5
Net income					$ 445.5

Because the tape recorder business has been stable over the past few years, the managers of Hewtex plan to keep the price the same in 19X8 as it was in 19X7. However, it will be necessary to reduce the price of calculators to $20 per unit at the beginning of 19X8. The firm expects to spend an additional $57,000 on advertising and promotion in 19X8 and expects that it will gain 80% of its total revenue from calculators in 19X8.

The managers expect material costs to fall by 20% for calculators and 10% for tape recorders in 19X8, while direct labor costs for both products should increase by 10%. Variable overhead per unit should remain the same as it was in 19X7 for both products, and total fixed manufacturing overhead should be the same as it was in 19X7.

Required

1. How many calculators and tape recorders did Hewtex have to sell in 19X7 to break even, assuming the 19X7 sales mix?
2. What sales volume does Hewtex need in 19X8 to earn an after-tax profit of 9% of sales?
3. What is Hewtex's break-even point for 19X8, in dollar sales?

CHAPTER 5

SHORT-TERM DECISIONS AND ACCOUNTING INFORMATION

Making decisions always means choosing from among alternatives. Even continuing to do what you have been doing implies a decision, if there is some other alternative available. (When there are no alternatives, there is no decision because you have no choice.) Should we raise the price of our product? Should we continue to carry a particular product or drop it? Should we add a new product? Would it be better to compensate salespeople by paying a salary (a fixed cost) or a commission (a variable cost)? Should we make this part in our factory or buy it from an outside supplier? Managers are continually concerned about these and other sets of alternatives.

Another critical characteristic of decisions is that they relate to future actions. That is, they cannot be made retroactively. (You cannot decide in August after the price of a particular stock has consistently increased for six months, to buy that stock the previous February.) There are two important implications of this characteristic. First, managers must make decisions on the basis of estimates of what is likely to occur, recognizing that what happens might not coincide with the estimates. Thus, a decision was not necessarily bad just because some unpredictable change in circumstances caused results to differ markedly from expectations. By the same token, a manager can also never be *sure* that a particular decision was wise, because it is impossible to know what would have happened if he or she had selected a different course of action. But the manager can have a reasonable degree of confidence if the decision was based on the best available information, *and* if the manager understood the significance of the information at hand. Managerial accounting provides some, but not all, of the information needed by managers in making decisions.

The focus of this chapter is short-term decisions, while Chapters 8 and 9 treat long-term decisions. The distinction between these two types of decisions is sometimes hazy. Most managers and accountants consider a decision to be short-term if it involves a period of one year or less. The cutoff is arbitrary, but is in general use. The basic principles that apply to short-term decisions also apply to long-term ones, but long-term decisions require some additional considerations. Perhaps a better distinction between short- and long-term decisions is that the former do not normally require large capital investments. For this reason, short-term decisions are more easily reversible than long-term ones. (You can almost always change prices or the method of compensating salespeople, but you cannot so simply sell a new factory or even a large piece of equipment.) In general, the long-term decisions discussed in later chapters require the commitment of money for a fairly long period of time, with a good deal of uncertainty as to whether the firm can get its money back if the investment turns out poorly.

One final matter before we proceed with the analysis of short-term decisions. Almost every decision involves both quantitative and qualitative considerations. In this chapter we often point out qualitative issues associated with specific decisions, but the analytical approaches that are presented concentrate on the quantitative (economic) aspects of decisions. Qualitative considerations are very important and might even contradict a decision based on only quantitative issues. In many cases, managers will select an alternative that is not as economically sound as others because of "company policy" or a "feeling" that an action just isn't right for the firm. To take one example, it is not uncommon for manufacturers of name-brand products to take their own labels off and sell unlabeled products to discount stores at lower prices. This kind of business can be profitable, but some firms would not accept it because their managers believe that the firm's reputation for quality could suffer if people learned that discount stores were carrying the merchandise under another name (or no name at all). Such managers cannot be called wrong. But it is critical that the managers who make such decisions be aware of the costs, in the form of lost profits. The techniques described in this chapter will help them to determine what such a policy might be costing.

THE CRITERION FOR SHORT-TERM DECISIONS

The economic criterion for making short-term decisions is simple: *Take the action that you expect will give the highest income (or least loss) to the firm as a whole.* The analysis required to facilitate applying this rule is not always simple, and two subrules may be helpful:

1.   The only revenues and costs that matter in decision making are the expected future revenues and costs that will *differ* among the choices that are available. These are called **differential revenues and costs,** or **incremental revenues and costs.**

2. Revenues and costs that have already been earned or incurred are irrelevant in making decisions. Their only use is that they might aid in predicting future revenues and costs.

The term *differential* is more inclusive than *incremental*. The latter term suggests increases, and some decisions result in decreases in both revenues and costs. But the terms used are not as important as what they denote. Essentially, differential costs are avoidable costs, which we introduced briefly in Chapter 4. If the firm can change a cost by taking one action as opposed to another, the cost is avoidable and therefore differential. For example, if the firm stops selling a product in a particular geographical region and can save $50,000 in salaries and fixed costs by doing so, the $50,000 is avoidable. It is also differential because it will be incurred if the firm continues to sell in the region and avoided if it stops selling in that region.

The next section offers a basic example of a business decision so that you can see how the general criterion, as well as its subrules, apply. The example also provides a basis for discussing two important concepts related to decision making—the concepts of sunk costs and of opportunity costs—and these are considered after the example is introduced.

Basic Example

The Arnold Company manufactures large printing presses. In May of 19X5 the company began to make a press for a large publishing company. The price was to be $180,000. In August 19X5, the customer went bankrupt and Arnold had already spent $120,000 building the press. After looking around for a new customer, the marketing manager came to the president and said that he had two offers. Another publisher would buy the press for $160,000 provided that Arnold did a good deal of additional work on it. The added work would cost Arnold about $60,000. The second offer was from a newspaper chain that would buy the press in its current condition for $70,000 and have its own employees make any necessary alterations. What should Arnold Company do?

The analysis for this decision can be approached two ways. First, one could consider only the incremental revenues and costs of the two alternatives, as below:

	Sell Machine As Is	Modify Machine and Sell
Incremental revenues	$70,000	$160,000
Incremental costs		60,000
Incremental profit	$70,000	$100,000

The analysis indicates that Arnold should make the modifications and sell the modified machine to the publisher. The incremental profit from that course of action is $30,000 greater ($100,000 − $70,000) than that to be gained from selling the machine as it is. Notice that the $120,000 already spent on the machine does not appear in the analysis. The $120,000 is irrelevant because it will be the same no matter what the firm does.

Historical costs are irrelevant because they are already incurred and cannot be changed by a subsequent decision.

A second approach to an analysis for this decision, which clarifies the role of historical cost, is to prepare income statements for the sale of the press under both alternatives. The income statements, shown below, tell us nothing that we do not know from the incremental analysis; the difference in losses is still $30,000 in favor of making the modifications.

	Sell Machine As Is	Modify Machine and Sell	
Revenues	$ 70,000		$160,000
Less: Costs—already incurred	120,000	$120,000	
—incremental		60,000	180,000
Loss	$ 50,000		$ 20,000

Including past costs does not change the *difference* between the two alternatives. The overall gains (or losses) are different when we include historical costs, but the advantages of modifying the press remains at $30,000 ($50,000 − $20,000).

We hasten to add that there is a third alternative open to Arnold Company: it could junk the press in its present condition. We ignored that possibility because it was obviously inferior to either of the other alternatives available; it generates no incremental revenue or incremental profit, while both of the other choices do. Outright rejection of an obviously inferior alternative saves analytical time and effort. But managers must be cautious in concluding that a particular alternative is not worthy of further consideration, because serious study of the alternative may reveal revenue (or cost-saving) opportunities not obvious at first glance.

Sunk Costs

We stated above that any cost that will not change as a result of an action is irrelevant in making a decision about that action. Such a cost is called a **sunk cost.** In the example, the $120,000 that had already been spent building the press was a sunk cost. In fact, all historical costs are sunk. The original costs, and net book values of depreciable assets, are sunk, as are salaries, advertising, and any other operating expenses that have already been incurred.

Moreover, any *expected cost* that will be the same under all of the available courses of action that managers are considering is also sunk: the amount cannot be changed by managerial action. That is why we stated the criterion for short-term decisions as expected revenues and costs that will *differ* under the alternatives. For example, suppose that Arnold Company would require 20 labor hours to pack the press for shipment, and that the workers who would do the packing are on salary and would be paid whether they actually work or sit idle, so that they would be paid if they were not going to pack the press. Their salaries are sunk because they would be the same no matter which alternative the firm chooses. (Even if Arnold junks the press, it would have to pay the workers.)

It is not always easy to determine whether or not a particular cost is sunk or incremental. We shall have more to say about this problem shortly.

Opportunity Costs

An **opportunity cost** is the benefit lost by taking one action as opposed to another. For the Arnold Company, the opportunity cost of modifying and selling the press is the $70,000 selling price that it could get without making the modifications. To take an example from everyday life, part of the cost of attending college is the salary that one could be earning if not enrolled. That is, by going to college one forgoes the benefits of earning a salary during the college years.

To tie together the important concepts of differential, sunk, and opportunity costs, let us consider another example. The Griggs Company has on hand 1,000 pounds of a material that it originally purchased for $2 per pound including transportation. The current price per pound is $3, not including a $1 per pound cost to transport the material to the Griggs factory.

In the simplest of circumstances, where Griggs no longer uses the material in making its products, two alternatives are available: (1) continue to hold the material, and (2) sell it to someone else. Whether Griggs holds or sells this material, its purchase price ($2) will not change; the cost is sunk and irrelevant to either alternative. Holding the material (option 1) would change neither the firm's future revenues nor its future costs. Selling the material (option 2) would increase revenues by $3,000 (1,000 × $3) with no change in total costs. The differential revenues and costs under the two options are:

	Option 1 Hold the Material	Option 2 Sell the Material
Differential revenues	0	$3,000
Differential costs	0	0
Differential profit	0	$3,000

To incorporate the above analysis of individual alternatives into a single analysis of the effects of accepting option 1 rather than the only alternative, we would *measure* the cost of accepting option 1 by the revenue lost (opportunity cost) from forgoing option 2. The combined analysis would show the following:

Revenues gained from holding materials	$ 0
Cost of holding materials, measured by current selling price (opportunity cost)	3,000
Disadvantage of holding materials	$3,000

Either way of presenting the case shows that the materials should be sold rather than held.

What if we change the assumptions by stating that Griggs uses this material regularly in the making of products it wishes to continue to sell? The option of selling the material at $3 now carries with it the necessity of replacing that material, at $4 per pound, in order to continue manufacturing the firm's regular products. That is, there would now be a differential cost for the sale option—the cost to buy similar material for regular production. A combined analysis of the two options would show the following:

Revenues gained from selling the material	$3,000
Cost of selling materials, measured by current replacement cost (opportunity cost)	4,000
Disadvantage of selling materials	$1,000

In this case, the cost of selling the materials is measured by the cost of having to replace them.

In summary, the opportunity cost of a resource depends on its next best use. Selling price is one possibility; replacement cost is another; but there still might be others.

Most assets that a firm owns have opportunity costs. They could be sold outright, rented to another firm, or perhaps used in the production of another product. Time is also an asset, though not recorded in the accounts as such, and one task of managers is to determine how best to use their time, as well as the time of workers and available machinery. As we shall be seeing, in the examples in this chapter, opportunity costs play an important role in the analysis of decision alternatives.

DEVELOPING RELEVANT INFORMATION

Managers are usually involved in making many decisions that concern only a relatively small segment, or narrow activity, of the firm: a product, a product line, a single factory, even a single component of one of many finished products. In many cases, the segment (individual activity) that managers are reviewing for possible change may not be one that is separately reflected in accounting reports.

For example, consider a company that makes office equipment. It might make several models each of typewriters, bookkeeping machines, calculators, and copiers, sell them in several countries and to different types of customers (businesses, hospitals, governmental agencies, etc.), and operate several factories, some of which make only one product or line and others of which produce a combination of products. Regularly prepared accounting reports may not reflect information by model of product, by region, by type of customer, and by factory producing the model in question.

Existing accounting reports, as, for example, the product-line income statement illustrated in Chapter 4 (page 108), may give the accountant a good base to begin to analyze a product line (because it highlights avoidable costs). But information in past accounting reports is of interest only to the extent that it helps you to decide whether or not the future is likely to reflect the past. Thus, the development of information for making a decision about the operations of some particular segment of the business may involve the use of information from accounting records and from other sources. Engineers may provide information about materials needs and labor requirements for a new product. People from the marketing department may provide estimates of future sales of a current, or a new, product. Thus, even the availability of a regular accounting report on the segment of the firm for which some change is being contemplated does not mean that the report contains the information needed for making a decision about that change.

It is important also to understand that costs do not come to the accountant, from reports or elsewhere, with labels like *differential* or *avoidable*. The widespread availability and use of computers make it easier to develop some types of information, like the number of units of a particular product sold in each region to each type of customer. But the computer cannot determine what effect the changing or dropping of a particular model would have on various types of costs. Chapter 4 pointed out some of the problems of determining whether costs are joint (and therefore unavoidable) or separable-discretionary (and therefore probably avoidable). Making these determinations requires a great deal of work and close cooperation between the managerial accountant and other managers.

For example, consider the office equipment company described above. If salespeople are paid salaries, concentrate on specific types of customers, *and* sell all of the firm's products, neither sales salaries nor travel costs are avoidable costs in analyzing a particular model of copier. (The salespeople would still call on the same customers.) On the other hand, in analyzing sales to a particular type of customer, sales salaries and related expenses might well be avoidable. It is also quite possible that if salespeople cover specific geographical regions, their salaries and other expenses would be avoidable if one is analyzing for the purpose of evaluating sales by geographical region, through the details of sales territory assignments would have to be known before drawing a conclusion on this point.

The most important point about analyzing segments is that each decision about each segment is likely to be different. There are no magic formulas; each situation will present different problems and the manager—and the manager's information source, the managerial accountant—must treat the problems accordingly. Costs that are avoidable when one segment is under review might be unavoidable when looking at a different segment. *In general, the smaller the segment the fewer the avoidable costs.* Avoidable costs associated with a model of typewriter sold in a particular region would probably be limited to the variable costs of producing that model. Those associated with the entire line of typewriters in the same region would include variable production costs and perhaps some selling expenses. Some fixed manufacturing costs might be saved, especially if typewriters sold in that region are made in a factory that does not make other product lines, but even that conclusion depends on the specific circumstances of that plant. As the segment under study expands to, say, an entire product line, it is likely that more and more costs would be avoidable.

Allocated Costs

The task of identifying joint and separable costs for decison-making purposes is sometimes made difficult by the accounting practice of allocating costs to segments of the firms. For example, because financial reporting requirements (and income tax regulations) call for showing fixed manufacturing costs as part of the cost of units produced, firms regularly allocate these fixed costs to product lines and, ultimately, to individual units of product. Since such allocations must be made anyway, goes the argument, they may as well be included in internal reports and incorporated in reports relating to decision making.

By definition, as stated in Chapter 4, common costs are unavoidable because they relate to more than one segment or activity. And we showed, in Chapter 2, the irrelevance of per-unit fixed costs in predicting future costs. Hence, internal allocations made only to comply with financial accounting (or tax reporting) requirements must be recognized for what they are, and the managerial accountant must remove these allocated costs when trying to determine incremental costs.

There are other reasons why firms might allocate costs. Many managers believe that unless joint costs are allocated to products they will not get a "true picture" of profitability. They argue that without such allocations they will not be able to determine whether a product or product line is bearing a "fair share" of the joint costs. For instance, a company might make several products in a single factory. The costs associated with the factory building, the administrative staff, and other activities relating to the factory as a whole are not separable with respect to any product, much less with respect to specific units of product. Nevertheless, the costs exist and are necessary to the operation of the factory as a whole; the company could not make any one product without incurring these costs. Insisting that each product manufactured in the plant bear its "fair share" of the joint costs is appealing. The problem is that the allocations, however made, not only must be arbitrary but can also interfere with making rational decisions about an individual segment. Again, joint costs, whether or not allocated, are, by definition, unavoidable with respect to a single segment.

Still another aspect of the argument for using allocated costs for decision making is that some managers favor a policy often called *full cost pricing*. Under this policy, joint costs are allocated to specific products, then to units of product, and a selling price is set by adding a profit margin to the computed full cost of a unit. We illustrated this pricing technique for a single-product firm in Chapter 2. Some managers suggest that it is also applicable in multiple-product situations. We saw in Chapter 4 that price and volume are often related. A price that is set based on an analysis that includes an allocation of common costs might be so high that the firm could not sell the product at the volume level used in making the original calculations. Common costs would not change. But actual sales mix will differ from planned, with unfavorable results if the sales decline occurs for products with relatively higher contribution margins. In short, the policy of "full cost pricing" might work well if the firm can sell the required volume of a given product at the price calculated to take into consideration the "full cost"; but for a great many firms the price set on the basis of full-cost pricing may be unacceptable to the majority of purchasers.

Perhaps the most obvious, and least useful, argument for allocating all joint costs is an unfortunate carryover from our earlier training in mathematics, where we were taught that the whole must equal the sum of its parts. Some managers argue that the income for a set of products (or product lines, or parts of the firm), must add up to the income for the entire company. The fact that the individual segments add to the total for the company says nothing about the logic of the allocations or about their legitimacy for decision-making purposes. It is always possible to *make* the segments add to the total simply by allocating the joint costs. That is, the additivity of the parts is contrived, not natural.

The appearance of allocated costs on segment income statements does raise an important point about providing information within a firm. An information system must serve several purposes. It must provide data for preparing financial statements, completing tax and other governmental forms, and analyzing managerial decision alternatives. The system is usually designed around the needs of financial accounting and taxation, because the specific information required for these purposes is known with some certainty and is needed regularly. Adjustments will then be made to meet the needs of internal decision makers. Because the information system and resulting segment reports serve several purposes, a manager should study such reports carefully to ensure that only relevant costs are included in his or her analysis for a particular decision.

The remainder of this chapter is devoted to the most typical examples of short-term decisions. To some extent, all of the general concepts presented thus far are used in the analyses that facilitate the making of these common decisions.

TYPICAL SHORT-TERM DECISIONS

Dropping a Segment

Chapter 4 introduced the idea of evaluating segments such as product lines. As noted before in this chapter, there are many ways to segment a firm. Determining the best mix of segments is a continual problem for managers, who frequently have to decide whether to drop a segment or replace it with another. Consider the following income statement for a recent month for the Moorehead Department Store. Its managers expect these results to continue for the foreseeable future.

	Clothing	Appliances	Housewares	Total
Sales	$40,000	$30,000	$15,000	$85,000
Variable costs	22,000	14,000	11,000	47,000
Contribution margin	18,000	16,000	4,000	38,000
Fixed costs:				
Separable and avoidable	(4,000)	(3,000)	(1,500)	(8,500)
Common, allocated on sales				
dollars	(8,000)	(6,000)	(3,000)	(17,000)
Profit (loss)	$ 6,000	$ 7,000	($ 500)	$12,500

Suppose a manager looked at this report and decided that the housewares line should be dropped because it showed a loss. Is that the right decision? You are correct if you object to the decision because you see the positive *product margin* (contribution margin less separable fixed costs) for housewares. Dropping housewares would mean giving up product margin of $2,500 ($4,000–$1,500) without any savings in the common costs. Does that mean the decision is wrong and the housewares line should be continued? The answer is: *It depends*. How will sales of the other two lines be affected if housewares are dropped? How would Moorehead's managers use the resources now devoted to selling housewares? Let us consider these questions in turn.

In the unlikely event that dropping housewares would have no effect on the sales of the other two lines, total profit would be reduced by $2,500, as computed above. But if some of the current clothing and appliance sales are made to customers who come into the store with the intention of purchasing houseware items, the reduction in profit would be even greater. For example, suppose that a study of customers' purchases suggests that sales of appliances are likely to decline by 5% if the housewares line is dropped. We can approach the analysis required by a decision about dropping housewares in two ways. We can analyze the incremental effects of the decision, or look at the new totals based on selling only clothing and appliances.

First, we examine only the incremental effects of a decision to drop the housewares line. As long as appliances continue to be sold, savings in separable costs for that segment are unlikely. We also know that there will be no decline in common costs. An incremental analysis follows:

	If Housewares Are Dropped
Gain from dropping housewares—	
savings of separable fixed costs	$ 1,500
Costs of dropping housewares:	
Lost contribution margin on	
houseware sales	(4,000)
Lost contribution margin on	
appliance sales (5% × $16,000)	(800)
Decrease in income	$ 3,300

Dropping housewares would cause total income to decline by $3,300. Put in another way, we could say that dropping the housewares line yields an **incremental loss** of $3,300, or that the **incremental profit** from carrying housewares is $3,300.

A longer and less direct approach to the analysis involves preparing a new income statement for the company as a whole, assuming that the segment in question is dropped. Such a statement appears below:

	Clothing	Appliances	Total
Sales	$40,000	$28,500	$ 68,500
Variable costs	22,000	13,300	35,300
Contribution margin	18,000	15,200	33,200
Fixed costs:			
Separable	(4,000)	(3,000)	(7,000)
Common, allocated on sales dollars	(9,927)	(7,073)	(17,000)
Income	$ 4,073	$ 5,127	$ 9,200

The total income is $3,300 less than before ($12,500–$9,200), as was indicated from the earlier analysis. The joint fixed costs have also been reallocated, further reducing the incomes of the remaining product lines. On the basis of the information available, Moorehead's managers should choose to continue carrying housewares. Note, however, that the available information ignores the very reasonable and practical question of what will be done with the resources currently devoted to housewares if that line of products is dropped. Let us direct our attention to this critical question.

The company would almost certainly use the space now occupied by displays of housewares in some other way. Suppose this space could be rented to another company. How much rent would have to be received to make it profitable for the firm to stop selling housewares and rent the space? Because dropping the housewares line would result in a profit decline (incremental loss) of $3,300, it would take at least $3,300 in rental income to offset the loss resulting from the discontinuance. To use a term introduced in this chapter, the opportunity cost of selling housewares is the rental income foregone if the firm continues to sell housewares. A decision can be reached by comparing the incremental profit of the current course of action (selling housewares) with the opportunity cost. *If opportunity cost exceeds incremental profit, the company should take the opportunity; if not, it should continue on its present course of action.*

Let us use this analysis for a more complicated case alternative to the sale of housewares. Suppose that the company could substitute a shoe department, using the same space. Suppose further that, while there would be the expected decline in appliance sales, the shoe department would be expected to generate revenues of $20,000, with variable costs of $8,000 and separable avoidable costs of $3,000. A budgeted income statement incorporating the estimates for the shoe department appears below.

	Clothing	Appliances	Shoes	Total
Sales	$40,000	$28,500	$20,000	$88,500
Variable costs	22,000	13,300	8,000	43,300
Contribution margin	18,000	15,200	12,000	45,200
Separable fixed costs	4,000	3,000	3,000	10,000
Product margin	$14,000	$12,200	$ 9,000	35,200
Joint costs, unallocated				17,000
Income				$18,200

Note that we have identified the product margin for each segment and that we have not allocated the common costs.

The statement shows that dropping housewares and adding shoes would increase total profit by $5,700 ($18,200–$12,500). Following the principle stated earlier, the opportunity cost of selling housewares (the $9,000 product margin from selling shoes) is greater than the incremental profit from selling housewares ($3,300), so it would appear that the firm should switch to selling shoes. The same conclusion would be suggested by the following incremental analysis:

	Sell Shoes Instead of Housewares	
Gains from substituting shoes for housewares:		
Savings of separable fixed costs for housewares	$ 1,500	
Contribution margin on sales of shoes		
($20,000 − $8,000)	12,000	
Total		$13,500
Costs of substituting shoes for housewares:		
Lost contribution margin on housewares	4,000	
Lost contribution margin on appliances	800	
New separable fixed costs for shoes	3,000	
Total		7,800
Advantage of selling shoes		$ 5,700

We must emphasize that the above analysis is based only on the information available about alternatives. That is, the analysis depended on the assumption that the space now devoted to housewares could be used only for shoes. If the store had enough space to accommodate *both* product lines and if it had no other alternatives, it might well be wise to add shoes to the lines that are already being sold (including housewares).

Finally, we remind you that reports prepared for one purpose may not be directly usable for another, and that costs carrying a label in one kind of report may well warrant some other label in a report prepared for some other purpose. For example, in the case of the Moorehead Store, the report by product line could show some costs that would normally be considered as joint but which might decrease if the firm actually dropped one of the product lines (such as housewares). The clerical workers in the firm's payroll department might keep records on employees' hours, payroll deductions, and other matters relating to all departments, and the wages of those employees would be common to all departments. It is quite possible that dropping one entire line of products could result in having one clerk fewer than previously, even if payroll clerks do not work exclusively on individual departments. Thus, the identification of costs as avoidable and joint, and of cost savings likely to accrue because of a particular decision, is not a simple task. The managerial accountant, working with other managers, must look at all costs with a full understanding of the specific decision that is being considered.

Complementary Effects and Loss Leaders.   In the above analyses relating to the decision to continue or drop a product line, we expected a change in the sales of another line (appliances) if one line (housewares) were dropped. When there is such an interrelationship, which is not uncommon, we say that a decision about the one product will have **complementary effects;** that is, that the sales of some products will be affected by the sales of one or more other products being carried.

The magnitude of complementary effects can be considerable, and the analytical approach that emphasizes the effects of a decision on *total* profits is particularly important when such effects exist. Emphasizing total profits may lead managers to sell one or more products at a loss (negative product margin) if such sales will sufficiently increase the sales of other products.

Consider the manager of a local pizza parlor who has been disturbed by a lack of business at lunchtime. He attributes this to the "specials" of competing restaurants at lunchtime and is eager to change the situation. He has prepared the following income statement, based on a normal week, for the 11:00 A.M. to 2:00 P.M. period. The costs shown are all incremental.

	Pizza	Beverages	Total
Sales (200 pizzas @ $1.80)	$360	$100	$460
Variable costs	120	40	160
Contribution margin	$240	$ 60	300
Waitress salaries			80
Income			$220

He is interested in developing his own luncheon special, and is considering offering with each pizza all the free beverages a customer can drink. He believes that such an offer could double his pizza sales at lunchtime. On the basis of his past experience and judgment, he anticipates that beverage consumption would increase to two and one-half times the present level. To take care of the additional business, he believes he will have to hire additional part-time waitresses for $40 per week for the three-hour period during which the special will run. There will be no revenue from beverages, but there will be costs, so he will obviously lose money on beverages. Can he gain enough on the sales of pizza to offset the loss? Using his estimates of the effects of the special (which are the best information available), he can prepare a budgeted income statement.

	Pizza	Beverages	Total
Sales	$720	$ 0	$720
Variable costs	240[a]	100[b]	340
Contribution margin	$480	($100)	380
Waitress salaries			120
Income			$260

[a]Variable costs computed at the same rate as before, one-third or $33\frac{1}{3}$% of selling price.
[b]Variable costs computed two and one-half times the costs experienced previously.

Though one of his products shows a *negative* contribution margin, the manager can increase his total profits by $40 per week ($260–$220) if his expectations about increased sales are realized. A loss leader of this sort can be helpful because the products are complementary.

The potential for complementary effects is more obvious in some cases than in others. For example, one can readily see the relationship between sales of golf clubs and golf balls, razors and blades, or gasoline and motor oil. But the loss-leader rationale is responsible also for many "specials" that involve products only vaguely complementary. What prompts supermarket offers of incredibly inexpensive name-brand items in return for a newspaper coupon? The sale of well-known products for a few pennies to any customer purchasing a specific dollar amount of other merchandise also has an obvious objective.

Emphasizing the total profit picture is also constructive for product evaluation. A product that is selling at a loss (that is, negative product margin) may be so essential to the sales of other products being carried that it should not be dropped. Whenever a firm is contemplating the elimination of a specific product, the potential for complementary effects must be considered.

Make-or-Buy Decisions

Many manufactured products are the result of assembling several component parts into a unit of final product. Most components can be either bought from an outside supplier or made by the assembling firm using its own facilities. Several qualitative factors must be considered when deciding whether to purchase or make a component. Will the quality of the component acquired from the supplier be consistently equal to what can be achieved in the firm's plant? Will the supplier be reliable in meeting delivery commitments? Is it possible that the supplier who quotes a low price now will raise it once he feels you are a captive customer?

The quantitative factors to be considered are the incremental costs to make or to buy and any opportunity costs. Suppose that the XYX Company now makes a major component for its final product. A manager has prepared the following estimates of costs at the expected volume of 20,000 units.

Materials at $2 per unit	$ 40,000
Direct labor at $5 per unit	100,000
Variable overhead at $3 per unit	60,000
Allocated fixed overhead (building depreciation, heat and light, etc.)	120,000
Total costs	$320,000

An outside supplier has offered to provide any number of units that the firm needs at $14 each, which would be $280,000 for 20,000 units. We first need to determine whether or not there are any alternative uses of the space now used to make the component. If there is no alternative use, then the analysis is quite straightforward, focusing on the incremental costs of the two actions:

	Decisions	
	Make	Buy
Materials	$ 40,000	0
Direct labor	100,000	0
Variable overhead	60,000	0
Purchase price	0	$280,000
Totals	$200,000	$280,000

The firm saves $80,000 by making the component. The allocated fixed costs would not change if the firm bought the component, but would simply be reallocated to other activities. We could include the fixed overhead of $120,000 under *both* alternatives, in which case the $80,000 advantage of making would still hold. A handy shortcut analysis in problems like this is to add the unavoidable, allocated costs to the cost of buying the component, and then compare that total with the total cost to make the component. Thus, the unavoidable fixed manufacturing costs of $120,000, plus the $280,000 cost to buy the component externally, equals a total cost of $400,000, which is $80,000 more than the total cost ($320,000) to make the component internally.

The firm is better off making the component unless it can obtain more than $80,000 by using the space in some alternative way. The $80,000 is the minimum profit that the firm would need to earn from an alternative use in order to induce it to buy outside. Such profit could come from renting the space, or using it to produce some product that would bring more than $80,000 in incremental profit, assuming that space is short so that the firm could not make both the component and the product.

The same type of consideration, as well as others, arises when the firm has special-purpose machinery that it uses to make the component. If the equipment cannot be used for any other purpose and cannot be sold, the previous analysis is still appropriate. Both the cost and the present book value of the equipment are sunk costs and hence irrelevant. If the equipment could be rented, or converted to some other use, the rent or the incremental profit from the alternative use becomes the opportunity cost. However, the problem of analyzing the decision becomes more complex: essentially, it becomes a long-term decision of the type that we cover in Chapters 8 and 9.

Joint Products

When a single manufacturing process invariably produces two or more separate products, the outputs are called **joint products.** The process that results in the joint products is called a **joint process.** The refining of crude petroleum results in a number of distinct products, such as gasoline, various grades of oil, and kerosene. The processing of cattle results in hides, hoofs, various cuts of meat, and other items (fat, organs, lips). Some of these joint products are quite valuable; some have little or no value. Some may be sold just as they emerge from the joint process or processed further. A meat packer may sell hides to a tanner. If it has the expertise and the facilities, it may tan the hides and make shoes, gloves, and other products from the hides.

Manufacturers who produce joint products regularly face the decision of whether to sell them at the **split-off point**—the point at which they emerge from the joint process—or to process them further. This decision cannot be based on the total costs of the individual final products, or even on the total variable costs. To produce *any* of the joint products, the firm must undertake the joint process, incurring all the costs to perform that process. Hence, the costs incurred prior to split-off are irrelevant in determining whether the joint products, once produced, should be sold then or processed further. The costs of the joint process (or processes) are relevant only in determining whether that process should be carried on at all. A refiner may incur variable costs for material, labor, and overhead of $32 per barrel of crude oil refined. But this cost does not relate to any one of the outputs, such as gasoline, fuel oil, and motor oil. If it decides to refine at all, it will incur these costs in proportion to the total quantity of crude oil refined, and independently of whether any of the individual products are desired. Thus, in an analysis to determine whether to sell a product at the split-off point or process it further, all costs—fixed and variable—prior to the split-off are sunk. If the joint process operates, both variable and fixed costs must be incurred.

Consider the following example. A chemical company makes two products, Alpha and Omega, in a single joint process. Each 1,000 pounds of raw material put into the joint process yields 600 pounds of Alpha and 400 pounds of Omega. Both Alpha and Omega can be sold at the split-off point or can be processed further. Selling price and cost data per batch (1,000 pounds of raw material) are given below:

	Alpha	Omega
Selling price at split-off	$1,200 ($2 per pound)	$1,600 ($4 per pound)
Selling price after additional processing	$3,600 ($6 per pound)	$2,000 ($5 per pound)
Costs of additional processing, all variable	$900 ($1.50 per pound)	$500 ($1.25 per pound)

Assuming that a batch of each product has already been produced in the joint process, what should be done with each product? We can analyze the results of both alternatives for each product. Alpha is analyzed as follows:

Decision on Alpha

	Sell at Split-off	Process Further
Sales	$1,200	$3,600
Incremental cost	0	900
Incremental profit	$1,200	$2,700

Alpha should be processed further because the firm's profit will be $1,500 higher ($2,700–$1,200) if this course is followed. We can reach the same conclusion by examining just the *changes* in revenues and costs involved in processing Alpha further:

Change in revenue ($3,600 − $1,200)	$2,400
Change in costs	900
Change in profit	$1,500

Similar analysis reveals that Omega should be sold at split-off rather than being produced further.

Decision on Omega

	Sell at Split-off	Process Further
Sales	$1,600	$2,000
Incremental costs	0	500
Incremental profit	$1,600	$1,500

The firm would be $100 worse off ($1,600 − $1,500) if it processed Omega further. Processing further would increase revenues by $400 ($2,000 − $1,600) but would also increase costs by $500, which is greater than the increase in revenues.

The above analytical approaches are appropriate when all incremental processing costs are variable. However, when the additional processing involves some fixed costs, a slightly different approach is necessary. The unit for analysis (in the previous example, one batch of raw material) must be chosen carefully to correlate with the nature of the fixed costs. To see why this is necessary and how it works, let us assume that the further processing of Alpha involves incremental, avoidable fixed costs of $10,000 per month. Note that such costs are *joint* to all units produced during the month and hence cannot be identified with a single batch unless the firm is able to process only one batch per month. Let us assume that ten batches per month are normally processed; the output of Alpha would be 6,000 pounds (10 × 600 pounds per batch). The analysis shown below indicates that the firm should still process Alpha beyond the split-off point.

Decision on Alpha

	Sell at Split-off	Process Further
Sales: 10 × $1,200 per batch	$12,000	
10 × $3,600 per batch		$ 36,000
Incremental costs:		
Variable 10 × $900 per batch		(9,000)
Fixed and avoidable		(10,000)
Incremental profit	$12,000	$ 17,000

The additional revenue from processing further ($36,000 − $12,000) is still greater than the additional costs incurred by undertaking the extra processing ($19,000). We could say that the $17,000 incremental profit from processing further is the opportunity cost of a decision to sell at the split-off point, so this decision yields a $5,000 loss. Similarly, the opportunity cost of processing further is the $12,000 given up by not selling immediately. Including the opportunity cost among the other costs of the decision to process further, this decision yields a profit of $5,000 (revenues of $36,000 and total costs of $9,000 + $10,000 + $12,000).

The general rules for determining whether products should be sold at the split-off point or processed further are as follows: *if the additional revenue gained by processing further is greater than the additional cost of further processing, the product should be processed further; if the additional revenue from further processing is less than the additional cost of further processing, the product should be sold at split-off.*

The decisions resulting from applying the above rules are important, for they are needed for the analysis in support of an even more basic decision: whether to operate the joint process itself, from which the joint products emerge. In deciding whether to operate a joint process, the question is whether the *best* incremental profit that can be earned from the individual products is greater than the incremental cost to operate the joint process.

From the earlier analyses we know that Alpha should be processed further and that Omega should be sold at split-off. These courses of action are wise only if it is profitable to make the products at all. To make that decision, we now need to consider the costs of the joint process itself. Let us assume that these costs are $1,000 per batch of raw material; $8,000 in incremental, avoidable fixed costs per month; and $20,000 in monthly unavoidable fixed costs. With this additional information *and* the results of the earlier decisions about the best use of the individual products, we can construct an analysis showing the incremental profit from operating the joint process:

	Alpha	*Omega*	*Total*
Sales (10 batches):			
Alpha, after extra processing	$36,000		$36,000
Omega, sold at split-off		$16,000	16,000
Total			52,000
Incremental costs of additional processing of Alpha	19,000	0	19,000
Incremental profit on products	$17,000	$16,000	33,000
Incremental costs of joint process:			
Variable ($1,000 per batch)			10,000
Fixed and avoidable			8,000
Total			18,000
Incremental profit from operating joint process			$15,000

The key figure in the above analysis is the last line "incremental profit from operating the joint process." If it is negative, the joint process should not be operated even though the individual joint products might have positive incremental profits considering only their individual revenues and incremental costs (the line "incremental profit on products"). The unavoidable fixed costs of the joint process are irrelevant. Even if the unavoidable fixed costs of the joint process ($20,000) exceed the incremental profit ($15,000), the joint process should be operated. Why? Because without operating the joint process, the firm would still incur the unavoidable fixed costs. Any incremental profit reduces the net cost to the firm.

One final word of caution. Remember that many segment reports include allocated costs. This is particularly common when reports are prepared for joint products; the costs of the joint process are often allocated among the various joint products. A common allocation scheme is to assign the joint costs in proportion to the relative sales values of the products. Such allocated costs are, as stated earlier, irrelevant to decision making on the individual segments and should accordingly be ignored in analyses relating to the joint products.

The joint products case gives us an opportunity to reinforce another critical point made earlier, namely, the idea that the relevance or irrevelance of a cost depends on the specific decision at hand. The variable costs of operating the joint process are relevant in deciding whether or not to operate that process at all. But they are irrelevant in deciding whether to sell a given joint product at the split-off point or to process it further. Thus, a cost can be relevant for one decision, irrelevant for others. It is critical, therefore, that the managerial accountant understand just what decisions managers are trying to make when they call for information. The accountant cannot respond to the question "What does it cost?" without knowing why the manager wants the answer to that question.

Special Orders

Retail chain stores that sell merchandise under their own names influence the decisions of firms that manufacture the products. Many manufacturing companies make both products to be sold under their own brand names and nearly identical products that are sold at lower prices under the brand name of a chain store (called *house brands*). The manufacturer would normally sell to chains at lower prices than to dealers who sell the products under the manufacturer's brand name. Manufacturers also sometimes accept special, one-time orders for their products at lower prices than usual.

The following budgeted income statement is for a manufacturer who has just received an opportunity to sell 20,000 units of a product at $10 per unit to a discount store. Sales of 60,000 units at the regular price are planned. The plant has the capacity to produce 100,000 units. As the controller of the firm, you are asked to evaluate the offer.

Griffith Company, Budgeted Income Statement

	Per unit		Total
Sales (60,000 units)	$15		$900,000
Manufacturing costs:			
Materials	4	$240,000	
Direct labor	3	180,000	
Overhead (one-third variable)	6	360,000	
Total	13		780,000
Gross margin			120,000
Selling, general, and administrative expenses			80,000
Operating income			$ 40,000

The variable portion of selling, general, and administrative expenses is $12,000 for sales commissions. Commissions would not have to be paid for the 20,000 unit special order. The president has some misgiving about accepting the order, even though sufficient capacity is available. He sees that average manufacturing costs are $13 per unit ($780,000/60,000) and that a $10 per-unit price will be below this average cost.

Only the incremental elements should be considered in making a decision.

	Per Unit	Incremental Analysis of Special Order	
Revenues (20,000 units)	$10		$200,000
Manufacturing costs:			
Materials	4	$80,000	
Direct labor	3	60,000	
Variable overhead	2	40,000	180,000
Incremental profit			$ 20,000

Accepting the special order would increase income by $20,000, and, therefore, Griffith should accept it.

In this example, the only incremental costs were variable manufacturing costs.

In another situation there might be some variable selling, general, and administrative expenses connected with any kind of sales, and those variable costs would be included in the analysis. Where the special order requires a large increase in production, it is likely that some additional fixed costs will have to be incurred. Those costs, too, will have to be incorporated in the incremental analysis.

Special orders, either one-shot or continuing (like the house brand arrangement mentioned above), require careful study. Of major importance is the potential effect of the special-order sales on the firm's sales at regular prices. For instance, if an appliance manufacturer agrees to supply a discount chain with 100,000 washing machines, it might find that its sales to regular dealers fall because the ultimate customers for the machines buy from the discount chain instead of the regular dealers. Or, a firm accepting a special order might find that its sales at regular prices could have been higher than originally thought, but that it cannot fill these more profitable orders because the special order has brought the company to full use of its manufacturing capacity. In either case, the issue is one of incorporating into the analysis of the special order the potential for lost sales. We can illustrate the problem of lost sales, and a basic approach for dealing with it, by continuing the example of the Griffith Company.

Suppose that Griffith has capacity for 75,000 units, rather than for 100,000 units as stated earlier, and that the expected sales through regular sources represents the most optimistic estimate of the sales through those sources for the coming period. If it accepts the special order, it would not be able to fill orders for 5,000 units at the regular price (capacity of 75,000 − 20,000 units on the special order leaves capacity for 55,000 units at the regular price, a 5,000 unit shortfall). We could prepare a new budgeted income statement reflecting these facts, or we could simply calculate the lost contribution margin from the 5,000 units and compare it with the profit of $20,000 expected on the special order. The more direct, incremental analysis is shown below:

Profit from special order		$20,000
Lost contribution margin on regular sales:		
Selling price	$ 15.00	
Variable manufacturing cost		
($4 + $3 + $2)	(9.00)	
Commissions ($12,000/60,000)	(0.20)	
Unit contribution margin on		
regular sales	$ 5.80	
Lost sales volume, in units	5,000	
Lost contribution margin		29,000
Net loss from accepting special order		($ 9,000)

When the analysis recognizes the potential for lost sales, the special order no longer appears to be profitable.

If there were no capacity constraint, but the managers of Griffith believed that the firm would lose *some* sales at the regular price through customers buying from the chain, they could at least determine the amount of sales that the firm could lose before the special order became unprofitable. The special order generates $20,000 incremental profit considered in isolation. At a $5.80 unit contribution margin for normal sales, the firm could afford to lose sales of up to 3,448 units ($20,000/$5.80) at the regular price before accepting the order would hurt overall profits. The question then becomes whether the managers believe that actual lost sales are likely to approach this critical number. Such an estimate is very difficult because it involves predicting the responses of customers.

Use of Fixed Facilities

So far we have recognized limitations of capacity in units that can be produced. We have not considered capacity limitations when two or more products could be produced and sold in various combinations. Sometimes a firm has available a fixed quantity of some input factor—machine-hours, space, specialized labor—and could produce different quantities of different products within the limits of the available factor. Suppose a firm can make and sell two products and has a machine that is used in the production of these products. Revenue and cost data for products A and B are as follows.

	A	B
Sales price	$10	$6
Variable costs	6	4
Contribution margin	$ 4	$2

Regardless of which product or combination of products is produced, fixed costs will be the same—costs for use of the machine and productive space.

If the machine time required to produce a unit of A is the same as that required for a unit of B, all available time would be used to produce A. It is more profitable to make A, because its contribution margin is twice that of B. But suppose that a unit of A requires five hours machine time, a unit of B needs two hours, and only 500 machine-hours are available. There are two ways to solve the problem. One is to determine what total contribution margin would be obtained by making only As or only Bs. This would yield the following:

	A	B
Maximum production in units	100 (500 hours/5)	250 (500 hours/2)
Contribution margin per unit	$ 4	$ 2
Total contribution margin	$400	$500

This method determines the total contribution margin that can be obtained by giving all the scarce factor (machine time) to the making of each product in turn. The one with the highest total contribution margin should be made.

The second method determines which product has the highest contribution margin *per unit of the fixed factor*. In the example, the contribution margin per machine-hour that can be earned by making only one or the other product is computed. One must determine how many units, or fractions of units, can be made per hour and multiply this by contribution margin per unit of product.

	A	B
Hours required to make	5	2
Number made in one hour	1/5	1/2
Contribution margin per unit	$4	$2
Contribution margin per hour	$0.80	$1

Product B has a higher contribution margin per machine-hour and should thus be made over product A. Both methods indicate the same choice. Specific results of the two methods can be confirmed by multiplying the contribution margins per hour by the number of available hours. Thus 500 hours × $0.80 = $400, total contribution margin if only product A is made. And 500 × $1 = $500, total contribution margin if only product B is made.

An assumption critical to the example was that the firm could sell as many of either product as could be produced. Suppose that only 200 units of B can be sold, even though 250 can be made. (This is more realistic because a firm is seldom able to sell all of a product that it can produce.) Product B is still more profitable than product A, but only 200 units of B should be produced. Using 400 hours to produce Bs leaves 100 hours to make units of A. In that time, 20 units of A can be produced (100 hours/5 hours per unit). From the sale of all produced units of both products, the contribution margin will be as follows.

	A	B	Total
Sales	$200	$1,200	$1,400
Variable costs	120	800	920
Contribution margin	$ 80	$ 400	$ 480

Contribution margin is $20 less than it would be if 250 units of B could be sold. In some cases there may be several constraints imposed on the firm. A detailed discussion of this problem is reserved for Chapter 16.

A Word of Caution

The approaches that we have presented have many things in common, including the need for the manager to understand volume-cost-profit relationships and the concepts of common/joint and separable costs. But perhaps the most important of the commonalities is that each approach requires the manager, and hence the managerial accountant, to use estimates. There are estimates of future sales volumes, future costs, future cost savings, lost sales, etc.

Estimates (or assumptions) about the future cannot, for obvious reasons, be considered as certainties. Managers are fond of saying that the only thing they can be certain about is the uncertainty associated with the future and with the information used in decision making. Some formal methods of dealing with uncertainty are discussed in Chapter 16, and the typical collegiate program of study presents those and other methods in courses in statistics and management science. At this point in your study of decision making and the use of accounting information, it is important that you recognize the extent to which estimates, and the associated uncertainties, may influence the analyses developed to aid in the decision-making process.

DECISION MAKING UNDER ENVIRONMENTAL CONSTRAINTS

The cost structure of a firm is always a major factor in decisions. There are many other constraints imposed upon the firm that must be considered in decision making, such as total sales potential for its products, product interdependencies, and types of customers. Still other constraints are part of the legal environment of the firm.

The United States has a number of laws that managers must be aware of when deciding among various courses of action. Antitrust laws forbid actions that might reduce competition substantially. Various aspects of environmental protection laws restrict actions that could have detrimental effects on wildlife, increase pollution, etc. At various times economic controls, such as wage and price controls, have forbidden price increases except as costs justified them. The Robinson-Patman Act forbids the charging of different prices to customers unless there are intrinsic cost differences in serving the different customers. We shall limit our discussion to the major law dealing with pricing practices.

Robinson-Patman Act.   This act forbids discriminatory pricing. The Federal Trade Commission is the regulatory agency responsible for enforcing the act. The act does not, of course, forbid charging different prices for different goods. Thus, to ensure compliance with the law, manufacturers who sell private brands usually modify the items offered for private branding. The passing of the act was partially stimulated by the practice of selling to large customers (say, grocery chains) at lower prices than to corner grocery stores, enabling the large chains to charge their customers lower prices and endangering the existence of smaller firms.

Manufacturing costs are not of particular significance when differences in prices of the same products are justified by cost differences. The Federal Trade Commission will not permit a firm to justify lower prices to some customers on the grounds that the incremental cost of production is less than the average cost, including fixed costs. Because fixed costs relate to all products of a firm, the manufacturing cost of all units of the same product comes out the same. Differences in distribution costs can be a valid defense against charges of unlawful discrimination. In the special-order example on page 157, sales commissions did not have to be paid on the special order. This fact could be used as a partial defense against a suit for discrimination.

If a suit alleging price discrimination is filed, the managerial accountant will sometimes help prepare the evidence for the defense. It could be shown, for example, that *distribution* costs are lower for some customers than for others. Or perhaps the accountant can show that larger orders require fewer deliveries and hence result in lower costs.

SUMMARY

Managerial accountants are frequently asked for information to be used in short-term decision making. The essential quantitative factors influencing such decisions are differential revenues and costs, including opportunity costs. Costs and revenues that would be the same whatever action is taken can be ignored. Historical costs, which constitute the majority of sunk costs, are irrelevant for current decisions because they cannot be changed by some current action. Separable discretionary costs will be relevant while joint costs and separable committed costs will not be. Whether or not a cost is relevant to a particular decision does not always depend on whether the cost is variable or fixed.

Typical examples of short-term decisions are: whether to drop a product or product line; whether to produce a component internally or purchase it from an outside supplier; whether to further process one or more joint products; whether to accept a special order; and how to utilize the services available from critical fixed facilities.

As a general rule, the action that is expected to result in the highest income for the firm as a whole should be pursued. This decision rule considers only the quantifiable factors in a given situation. In most decisions, there will be some factors that can have monetary effects but for which no reliable estimates can be made. Still other factors, such as a company policy against certain types of products, may not lend themselves to quantification at all. These unquantified factors should not be ignored.

KEY TERMS

allocated cost	joint products
complementary effects	make-or-buy decision
differential revenue and cost	opportunity cost
incremental revenue and cost	segment analysis
incremental profit (loss)	split-off point
joint (common) cost	sunk cost
joint process	

REVIEW PROBLEM

Andrews Company makes three products. Revenue and cost data for a typical month are as follows.

| | Product | | | |
	X	Y	Z	Total
Sales	$300	$500	$800	$1,600
Variable costs	100	200	400	700
Contribution margin	200	300	400	900
Fixed costs:				
Separable and avoidable	80	100	120	300
Joint, allocated on sales dollar basis	60	100	160	320
Total fixed costs	140	200	280	620
Profit	$ 60	$100	$120	$ 280

Required: Answer each of the following questions independently.
1. If product X were dropped, what would the company's profit be?
2. The firm is considering the introduction of a new product P, to take the place of X. Product P would sell for $7 per unit, have variable costs of $5 per unit, and separable-avoidable fixed costs of $120. How many units of P would have to be sold to maintain the existing income of $280?

3. The firm charges $10 per unit for product Z. One customer has offered to buy 40 units of Z per month at $8 per unit. Fixed costs in total and variable costs per unit would not be affected by the sale. Andrews has the capacity to produce 110 units of Z per month. If the offer is accepted, what will the firm's monthly income be?

4. Closer analysis reveals that X, Y, and Z are joint products of a single raw material that goes through a single process. The cost of the joint process, including raw material, is the $320 joint allocated fixed cost. All other costs are incurred to process the three products beyond the split-off point. If the sales values of X, Y, and Z are $110, $220, and $230, respectively, at split-off, could the firm increase its profits by selling one or more products at split-off? If so, which product or products should be sold at split-off and what would the increase in total profit for the firm be?

5. At the current dollar levels of sales of X and Z, unit sales are 100 and 200, respectively. Both products are made on a single machine that has a limited capacity. The machine can make five units of X per hour, or eight units of Z.

    (a) Assuming that all units made of either product can be sold at existing prices, should the company continue to make both products? If not, which product should it make?

    (b) Assuming that the machine is being operated at its capacity of 45 hours per month, what would happen to the firm's monthly profits if it concentrated on the more profitable product as determined in part (a)? Give the dollar increase in profits that would occur. (*Hint:* Remember that if only one product is made, the firm will save the avoidable fixed costs on the product that is dropped.)

Answer to Review Problem

1. $160. The company would lose the contribution margin from the sale of X but would save $80 by not having to pay separable-avoidable fixed costs. Net reduction in profit is $120 ($200 − $80), which should be subtracted from current profit of $280 to arrive at $160. The $120 is the incremental profit on X.

2. 120 units. To achieve the same profit, the new product must provide the same incremental profit as would be lost by discontinuing the sale of X. Incremental profit from X is $120 (see part 1). The sale of P must provide contribution margin sufficient to cover both the new separable-avoidable fixed costs and the $120 profit. Since the new fixed costs would be $120, the contribution margin needed is $240 ($120 fixed costs plus the desired profit). P carries a contribution margin of $2 per unit ($7 − $5), so a total of 120 units ($240/$2) would have to be sold.

3. $350. It is important to see that if this special order is accepted, the company will have to curtail its regular sales at the regular price. [The firm's capacity is 110 units and planned sales are 80 units ($800/$10 selling price). If 40 units are sold to the new customer, regular sales will be cut by 10 units.] The analysis might proceed as follows.

Gain from contribution margin on special order ($8 − $5[a]) × 40 units	$120
Lost contribution margin because of loss of sales of 10 units at regular price	
($10 − $5[a]) × 10 units	50
Gain on special order	70
Planned profit	280
New monthly income	$350

[a]Variable cost per unit ($400/80 units $5 per unit)

4. The firm could increase its profits by $20 per month by selling product Y at split-off, as shown by the following analysis.

	X	Y	Z
Sales with further processing	$300	$500	$800
Additional processing costs:			
Variable costs	100	200	400
Avoidable fixed costs	80	100	120
Total additional processing costs	180	300	520
Profit if further processed	120	200	280
Split-off values	110	220	230
Advantage (disadvantage) of further processing	$ 10	($ 20)	$ 50

5. (a) The company should concentrate on product Z rather than product X. This can be shown even without knowing the number of hours available; the contribution margin per hour of machine time spent on product Z is the largest.

	X	Z
Contribution margin per unit	$2 ($200/100)	$2 ($400/200)
Units that can be made in 1 hour	5	8
Contribution margin per hour	$10	$16

As long as the company can sell all the units it makes of either product, total contribution margin will be greater by concentrating solely on product Z.

(b) Profit would increase by $200. The analysis involves both contribution margin and incremental profit. If the firm used its capacity of 45 hours to produce only Z, it could make 360 units of Z (45 × 8), which would bring total contribution margin of $720 (360 × $2 per unit). This is an increase of $320 ($720 − $400 contribution margin already anticipated). However, the firm would lose the current *incremental profit* from product X, which is $120 (see part 1). Thus, if the firm concentrated on product Z it would gain $200 ($320 additional contribution margin from Z − $120 incremental profit lost from not producing X).

ASSIGNMENT MATERIAL

Questions for Discussion

5-1 **"Where do you start?"** One of your classmates, who believes that he thoroughly understands the principle of incremental costs, places an advertisement in the school paper that reads as follows:

Wanted—Ride to Linville

I will pay all of the extra costs involved in taking me to Linville. Call Bob at 555-6202.

Linville is 1,200 miles from the university. Did your classmate make a mistake in wording the advertisement the way he did?

5-2 **Cost analysis** While standing in line waiting to use a telephone, you hear the following part of a conversation. "No dear, I'm going to play golf today." (Pause) "Look, sweetie, I know it costs $6 for a caddy and $3 for drinks after the round, but it really does get cheaper the more I play. Look, the club dues are $1,000 per year, so if I play 50 times it costs, ah, let's see, $29 per round. But if I play 100 times it only costs, um, just a second, yeah, about $19 per round." (Pause) "I knew you'd understand, see you at dinner, bye." How did the golfer figure the cost per round? Comment on her analysis.

5-3 **The generous management**   Several years ago, a leading newspaper ran an advertisement for itself. The advertisement stated that the paper, which cost the customer $0.40, cost the publisher $0.53 for paper, $0.09 for printers' labor, $0.05 for ink, $0.15 for salaries of editorial employees (reporters, editors, etc.), and $0.18 for other operating expenses such as executives' salaries, rent, depreciation, and taxes. Thus, the opportunity to buy a paper for $0.40 that had a cost of $1.00 was presented as a great bargain. Is the firm actually charging the buyer less than cost? What assumptions did you make to arrive at your answer? How can the management be so generous to its readers?

Exercises

5-4 **Product selection—capacity constraint**   Winston Company makes three products, all of which require the use of a special machine. Only 200 hours of machine time are available per month. Data for the three products are as follows:

	Gadgets	Supergadgets	Colossalgadgets
Selling price	$12	$16	$21
Variable cost	7	8	10
Contribution margin	$5	$8	$11
Machine time required in minutes	6	10	15
	10	6	4

Winston can sell as much of any product as it can produce.

Required
1. If all products required the same amount of machining time, which product should be made?
2. Given the capacity constraint, determine which product should be made and the total monthly contribution margin that would be earned if that product were made.
3. How much would the selling price of the next most profitable (per machine-hour) product have to rise to be as profitable, per machine-hour, as the product that you selected in part 2?

5-5 **Special order**   Devio Company produces high-quality golf balls. A chain of sporting goods stores would like to buy 25,000 dozen balls at $15 per dozen. The chain would sell the balls for $20, which is $5 less than is usually charged by dealers who normally stock the company's product. The chain would obliterate the Devio name so that customers would not be able to tell who had made the balls.

Devio can produce 200,000 dozen balls per year. Planned results for the coming year, without considering the order from the chain, are given below:

Sales (150,000 dozen at $18 per dozen)	$2,700,000
Cost of goods sold	1,110,000
Gross profit	1,590,000
Selling and administrative expenses, all fixed	600,000
Income	$ 990,000

Cost of goods sold contains variable costs of $7 per dozen balls. The rest of the cost is fixed.

Required
1. Based only on quantitative concerns, determine whether Devio should accept the order.
2. Might your answer to part 1 change if the Devio name were to appear on the balls sold in the chain stores?

5-6 Special order—alternative volumes   Woolen Products Company makes a heavy outdoor shirt in one factory. Revenue and cost data relating to the coming year's operations are budgeted as below.

Sales (230,000 shirts)	$2,300,000
Cost of sales	1,380,000
Gross profit	920,000
Selling and administrative expenses	575,000
Income	$ 345,000

The factory has capacity to make 250,000 shirts per year. The fixed costs included in cost of goods sold are $460,000. The only variable selling, general, and administrative expenses are a 10% sales commission and a $0.50 per shirt licensing fee paid to the designer.

A chain store manager has approached the sales manager of Woolen Products offering to buy 15,000 shirts at $6 per shirt. The sales manager believes that accepting the offer would result in a loss because the average cost of a shirt is $8.50. He feels that even though sales commissions would not be paid on the order, a loss would still result.

Required
1. Determine the income that would result if the company accepts the offer.
2. Suppose that the order was for 40,000 shirts instead of 15,000. What would the firm's income be if it accepted the order?
3. Assuming the same facts as in part 1 above, what is the lowest price that the firm could accept and still earn $345,000?

5-7 Dropping a segment   Colbert Company expects the following results for the coming year.

	Hats	Belts	Jeans	Total MARICA
Sales	$80,000	$120,000	$250,000	$450,000
Variable costs	$30,000	$ 40,000	$100,000	$170,000
Fixed costs	60,000	40,000	120,000	220,000
Total costs	90,000	80,000	220,000	390,000
Profit (loss)	($10,000)	$ 40,000	$ 30,000	$ 60,000

Required: Answer each of the following questions independently.
1. Suppose that the fixed costs are all allocated based on the floor space that each segment occupies and are all unavoidable. What would the firm's total profit be if it dropped the hat segment?
2. Suppose that $25,000 of the fixed costs shown for the hat segment are avoidable. What would the firm's total profit be if it dropped the hat segment?

3. Suppose that the firm could avoid $25,000 in fixed costs by dropping the hat segment (as in part 2). However, the managers believe that if they did drop hats, sales of each of the other lines would fall by 10%. What would the firm's profit be if it dropped hats and lost 10% of the sales of each of the other segments?

5-8 Make or buy   GFA Company is introducing a new product. The managers are trying to decide whether to make one of its components, part #A-3, or to buy it from an outside supplier. Making the part internally would require using some available machinery that has no other use and no resale value. The space that would be used to make the part also has no alternative use.

The outside supplier would sell the part for $5 per unit. An estimate of costs to make the part appears below.

	Cost to Make Part #A-3
Materials	$1.50
Direct labor	2.00
Variable manufacturing overhead	.50
Fixed manufacturing overhead	2.50
Total cost	$6.50

The above estimate reflects anticipated volume of 10,000 units of the part. The fixed manufacturing overhead consists of depreciation on the machinery, and a share of the costs of the factory (heat, light, building depreciation, etc.) based on the floor space that manufacturing the part would occupy.

Required: Determine whether GFA should make or buy part #A-3.

5-9 Short-term decisions   Nickolai Company expects the following results in 19X5.
(VOLKOFF)

	Product A	Product B	Total
Sales	$300	$500	$800
Variable costs	150	150	300
Contribution margin	150	350	500
Fixed costs	90	150	240
Profit	$ 60	$200	$260

Fixed costs are allocated based on relative sales dollars.

Required: Answer each question independently, unless otherwise told.
1. The managers are considering increasing advertising for product A by $30. They expect to achieve a 40% increase in volume for product A with no change in selling price, but some of that increase will be at the expense of product B. Sales of B are expected to decline by 5%. What will the firm's total profit be if it takes the action?
2. What is the maximum percentage decline in volume of product B that would leave the action in part 1 just barely desirable?
3. The firm is considering dropping product A and replacing it with product C. Introducing product C would increase total fixed costs by $30. Its contribution margin percentage is 60%. What dollar sales of product C are needed to maintain the original profit of $260?

5-10 Analyzing data for decisions The expected results for the coming year for Porter Company, which manufactures two lines of products, appear below.

	Kitchenwares	Officewares	Total
	(in thousands of dollars)		
Sales	$3,300	$2,700	$6,000
Variable costs	1,650	810	2,460
Contribution margin	1,650	1,890	3,540
Avoidable fixed costs	650	1,300	1,950
Incremental profit	$1,000	$ 590	1,590
Joint fixed costs			900
Profit before taxes			$ 690

Required

1. Suppose that Porter uses the same productive facilities for both products. Demand is such that the firm could sell $500,000 more of either product line but it would have to reduce output and sales of the other line by the same amount. Which line should the firm make more of and what would be the effect on total profits before taxes?
2. Porter could introduce a new line that would be much more profitable than either of the existing ones. To introduce the new line, however, the firm would have to drop one of the existing lines entirely. The other line—the one not dropped—would continue as originally budgeted, and the fixed costs would not be affected by the change of product lines. Which line should Porter drop?

5-11 Joint products TAB Company produces four joint products at a joint cost of $80,000. The products are currently processed beyond the split-off point, and the final products are sold as follows:

Products	Sales	Additional Processing Costs
M	$150,000	$110,000
N	180,000	60,000
O	45,000	40,000
P	20,000	15,000

The firm could sell the products at the split-off point for the following amounts: M, $80,000; N, $50,000; O, $15,000; and P, zero.

Required

1. Determine which products the firm should sell at the split-off point.
2. Determine what TAB's profit would be if it took the most profitable action with respect to each of its products.

5-12 Dropping a product—complementary effects Kaiser Face Care Company makes three products in the same factory. Revenue and cost data for a typical month are given on page 169, in thousands.

| | Product | | | |
	Razors	Blades	Shaving Cream	Total
Sales	$300	$600	$300	$1,200
Variable costs	200	240	90	530
Contribution margin	100	360	210	670
Fixed costs				
Separable and discretionary	120	150	70	340
Joint, allocated on basis of				
relative sales dollars	50	100	50	200
Total fixed costs	170	250	120	540
Income (loss)	($ 70)	$110	$ 90	$ 130

Required
1. Determine income for the firm if razors were dropped from the product line assuming there would be no effect on sales of other products.
2. Suppose that if razors were dropped, the sales of blades would decline by 20% and those of shaving cream by 10%. Determine the income for the firm if razors were dropped.

5-13 **Inventory values**   James Company has 300 pounds of a chemical compound called bysol, bought at $3.20 per pound several months ago. Bysol now costs $3.80 per pound. The firm could sell the bysol for $3.50 per pound (shipping costs account for the $0.30 difference between the cost to buy and the selling price).

Required
1. Suppose that the firm has stopped making the product that it used bysol for and will sell it unless it uses all of it to make up a special order. The special order has a price of $2,000. Incremental costs, excluding the bysol, are $900. What is the relevant cost of using the bysol in the special order? Should the firm accept the order?
2. Suppose now that the firm does have alternative uses for bysol so that if it accepts the special order it will have to buy additional quantities for its regular production. What is the relevant cost of using the bysol in the special order? Should the firm accept it?

5-14 **Car pool**   You and your neighbor have been carpooling for several years, driving on alternate days. A colleague at work has injured his hand and will not be able to drive for the next three months. He inquires about the possibility of going with you and your neighbor. He could ride a bus for $2 per day, and offers to pay you a "fair price."

From your house it is a 10-mile round trip to work. If you pick up your injured colleague, the round trip is 14 miles. Last year, your car cost you the following for 15,000 miles. (Your neighbor's car cost the same for the same number of miles.)

Gasoline and oil	$1,350
Maintenance	450
New tires (life of 30,000 miles)	300
Insurance and registration	600
Decline in market value	3,000
Total	$5,700

Required

1. Quote a daily price to your colleague that seems fair to you.
2. If you were your colleague, what would you say is a fair price?

5-15 Make or buy (AICPA adapted)   MTZ Company manufactures 10,000 units of part Z-101 annually, using the part in one of its products. The controller has collected the following data related to the part.

Materials	$ 20,000
Direct labor	55,000
Variable overhead	45,000
Fixed overhead	70,000
Total costs	$190,000

Vortan Company has offered to supply the part for $18 per unit. If MTZ accepts the offer, it will be able to rent some of the facilities it devotes to making the part to another firm for $15,000 annually and will also be able to reduce its fixed overhead costs by $40,000.

Required

1. Should MTZ accept the offer based on the available information?
2. What is the maximum price that MTZ would be willing to pay for the part—the price that would give it the same income it would have if it continued making it?
3. Assuming the $18 price from Vortan, at what annual unit volume would MTZ earn the same income making the part as it would buying it?

5-16 Joint products   Grevel Company slaughters cattle, processing the meat, hides, and bones. The hides are tanned and sold to leather manufacturers. The bones are made into buttons and other sundries. In a typical month, about 3,000 cattle are processed. A segmented income statement for such a month follows.

Income Statement
(In thousands of dollars)

	Totals	Meat	Hides	Bones
Sales	$500	$300	$120	$80
Cost of cattle[a]	300	180	72	48
Gross profit	200	120	48	32
Additional processing costs, avoidable	80[b]	40[b]	20[b]	20[b]
Allocated costs[c]	60[b]	30[b]	15[b]	15[b]
Income (loss)	$ 60	$ 50	$ 13	($ 3)

[a]Allocated on the basis of relative sales value (60% of sales).
[b]Deduction.
[c]Allocated on the basis of additional processing costs, all unavoidable.

Required

1. Is the firm losing money by processing the bones into buttons and sundry items? Explain.
2. A tanner has offered to buy the hides as they come off the cattle for $7 each. He has seen the income statement and contends that income from the hides segment would

be $21,000 if hides were sold directly to him (3,000 hides × $7). Should his offer be accepted?

3. If the bones could be sold without further processing, how much would have to be received per month to keep total profits the same as they are now?

5-17 Opportunity cost pricing   Boyett Company makes three products. Data for the products are as follows:

	Product		
	Wallet	Belt	Hat
Current selling price	$10	$15	$25
Variable cost	3	6	10
Contribution margin	$ 7	$ 9	$15
Machine time required, in minutes	10	15	30

The company has only 40,000 minutes of machine time available per week. It can sell all of any of the three products that it can make.

Required

1. Determine which product the firm should make.
2. Determine the selling prices that the firm would have to charge for each of the other two products to make them equally profitable per minute of machine time as the one you selected in part 1.

5-18 Comprehensive review of short-term decisions   The data below relate to the planned operations of Kimble Company before consideration of the changes described later.

	Product		
	Chair	Table	Sofa
Selling price	$ 120	$ 400	$ 600
Variable cost	40	160	360
Unit fixed costs	30	120	180
Total costs	70	280	540
Profit per unit	$ 50	$ 120	$ 60
Annual volume	8,000	3,000	4,000

All fixed costs are separable, but unavoidable.

Required: Answer each of the following items independently of the others unless otherwise instructed.

1. What is total annual profit expected to be?
2. What would happen to profit if the company dropped sofas?
3. What would happen to profit if the company dropped chairs, but was able to shift the facilities to making more sofas so that volume of sofas would increase to 7,000 units? (Total fixed costs would remain constant.)
4. The variable cost per sofa includes $60 for parts that the company now buys outside. The company could make the parts at a variable cost of $45. It would also have to

increase fixed costs by $35,000 annually. What would happen to profit if the company took the proposed action?

5. The company has received a special order for 1,000 tables at $250. There is sufficient capacity to make the additional units, and sales at the regular price would not be affected. What would happen to profit if the firm accepted the order?

6. Repeat part 5 assuming now that the order is for 1,500 tables and that capacity is limited to 4,000 tables.

5-19 Using per-unit data   The managers of Ferrara Company expect the following per-unit results at a volume of 200,000 units.

Sales		$10
Variable costs	$6	
Fixed costs	3	9
Profit		$ 1

Required: Answer each of the following parts independently of the others.

1. The company has the opportunity to sell 20,000 units to a chain store for $8 each. The managers expect that sales at the regular price will drop by about 8,000 units as some customers will buy from the chain store instead of from the regular outlets. What will happen to the company's profit if it accepts the order?

2. Of the total unit variable cost of $6, $2.80 is for a part that the company now buys from an outside supplier. The company could make the part for $2.25 variable cost plus $100,000 per year fixed costs for renting additional machinery. What would happen to annual profit if it made the part?

3. The company is considering a new model to replace the existing product. The new model would have a $6 unit variable cost and the same total fixed costs as the existing product has. The new model has expected sales of 100,000 units per year. At what selling price per unit would the new model give the same total profit as the existing one now gives?

Problems

5-20 Salesperson's time as scarce resource   Lombard Company sells to both wholesalers and retailers. The firm has 30 salespeople and cannot easily increase the size of the sales force. An analysis has shown that a salesperson's call on a wholesale customer yields an average order of $100, on a retailer $60. However, prices to wholesalers are 20% less than to retailers. Cost of goods sold (all variable) is 60% of prices charged to retailers. A salesperson can call on 7 wholesalers or 12 retailers per day. (The greater number of retailers reduces travel time between calls.)

Required

1. Should salespeople concentrate on wholesalers or retailers? Provide an analysis based on one salesperson for one week showing the difference.

2. What other factors require consideration?

5-21 Product pricing—off-peak hours   Marie Angelo, the owner of Gino's Pizzeria, is considering the possibility of introducing a "luncheon special" to increase business during the slow time from 11:00 A.M. to 1:00 P.M. on weekdays. For $1.50 on any weekday, she will give a customer all the pizza he or she can eat. Marie has prepared the following data for current business during those hours for a one-week period:

	Pizza	Beverages	Total
Sales (average pizza price, $2)	$300	$84	$384
Variable costs	100	21	121
Contribution margin	$200	$63	263
Avoidable fixed costs—salaries of students hired			180
Current incremental profit, lunch period			$ 83

She estimates that if she offers the special price, she will be serving about 300 pizzas per week to about 250 customers. (Some customers are expected to eat more than one pizza, given the lower price.) She also anticipates that variable costs per unit will be about 20% higher than they are now because people will want more toppings than they now order (pepperoni, sausage, hamburger, etc.). Beverage sales will bear the same relationship to the number of customers that they do now when each customer eats one pizza. The increase in the number of customers would entail an increase in personnel during the hours of the special, increasing salaries costs by 50%.

Required

1. Evaluate the monetary effects of the proposed "luncheon special."
2. Are there any other critical factors that should be taken into account? If so, what are they?

5-22 Pricing policy   At the Washington National Airport, you enter the departure area of an airline just before a flight to Los Angeles is to take off. The airplane is about 80% full. You offer to pay $50 to take the flight, which is $250 less than the regular fare.

Required

1. If the airline accepted your offer, what would happen to its total profit? Assume that there are no variable costs associated with the number of passengers.
2. Do you think that the airline would accept your offer? Why or why not?

5-23 Special order—capacity limitation   Weston Tire Company has been approached by a large chain store that offers to buy 60,000 tires at $17. Delivery must be made within 30 days. The productive capacity of Weston is 320,000 tires per month and there is an inventory of 10,000 tires on hand. Expected sales at regular prices for the coming month are 300,000 tires. The sales manager believes that about 40% of sales lost during the month would be made up in later months.

Price and cost data are as follows:

Selling price		$24
Variable costs:		
Production	$12	
Selling	3	15
Contribution margin		$ 9

The variable selling costs on the special order would be $2 per unit.

Required
1. Determine whether the firm should accept the special order.
2. Determine the lowest price that Weston could charge on the special order and not reduce its income.
3. Suppose now that the chain offers to buy 50,000 tires per month at $17. The offer would be for an entire year. Expected sales are 300,000 tires per month without considering the special order. Assume also that there is no beginning inventory and that any sales lost during the year would *not* be made up in the following year. Determine whether the offer should be accepted and determine the lowest price that Weston could accept.

5-24   Special orders and qualitative factors   Robinson Company has had a reputation for high-quality phonograph products for many years. The firm is owned by descendants of its founder, Allan Robinson, and continues the policy of producing and selling only high-quality, high-priced stereo components.

Recently James Giselle, president of a chain of discount stores, proposed that the Robinson Company make and sell him a cheaper line of components than it currently produces. Giselle knows that Robinson has excess capacity and that many other firms produce lower-quality lines for sale in discount stores. Giselle believes that, even though the Robinson name will not appear on the components, buyers will become aware that Robinson does in fact make the components. Giselle tries to convince the management that its only potential for growth lies in the private-brand field, because Robinson now sells only to devoted aficionados who would not settle for less than Robinson components.

Giselle proposes that Robinson sell to the chain at 60% of its current selling price to other outlets. Variable costs are now about 60% of normal selling price, but would be reduced by 20% per unit if the cheaper components were made. The first-year order is to be $1,260,000, for which Robinson has enough excess capacity.

Required
1. Evaluate the monetary effects of the proposed deal.
2. How would you evaluate qualitative factors such as the attitudes of the management and the family owners and the reputation of the firm? Do they outweigh the quantifiable factors, in your judgment?

5-25   Processing decisions, constraints on capacity   Moorehouse Solvent Company produces a number of industrial solvents. Most of its products arise from joint processes and may usually be sold as-is or refined through additional processing. Department III has the capacity to refine a total of 110 tons of product per month. There are two joint products that could be refined in Department III. Data on these two products are given below.

	Morgil	*X-zon*
Monthly output in tons	60	80
Price per ton at split-off	$ 80	$120
Price per ton after refining in Department III	$110	$230

The cost of refining either product in Department III is $70 per ton, all variable.

Required
1. What should the firm do with Morgil and with X-zon?
2. Assume that all factors remain constant except for the selling price of Morgil after refining. There are two critical prices for refined Morgil, ones at which the firm would change its processing decisions. What are these two prices and what changes should the firm make?

5-26 **Relevant costs for special order**   Tollman Company makes various types of calculators and other office products. Late in 19X5 the firm had 20,000 units of model Z-345 in stock. The unit cost was $18, of which $6 was allocated fixed overhead. The firm expects to sell 80,000 or so of this model in 19X6, at $30 each, but make only about 60,000 because the model is being discontinued and 20,000 units are currently on hand.

The purchasing agent of a large chain store has approached the sales manager of Tollman with an offer to buy the 20,000 units at $14 each. The sales manager talked to the production manager, who pointed out that costs were increasing and showed the following estimates of production costs for model Z-345 in 19X6.

Materials	$ 8
Direct labor	4
Variable overhead	4
Fixed overhead	7
Total	$23

The sales manager believed that even if he accepted the special order he would be able to sell the 80,000 or so expected for 19X6 because the chain store would sell in areas where Tollman does little business.

Required: Identify the relevant costs and decide whether or not you would accept the order.

5-27 **Cost of being your own boss**   Martha Crain and her husband Jim own a leather goods store in a large city. Their most recent year's income statement showed the following results.

Sales		$108,000
Cost of sales		50,000
Gross profit		58,000
Other expenses		
Rent (monthly lease)	$3,000	
Utilities	1,300	
Advertising	900	
Supplies	700	
Insurance	400	
Licenses and fees	280	
Miscellaneous	620	
		7,200
Income		$ 50,800

Martha and Jim were discussing the results and both were pleased. Martha said that it was nice to own your own business and not have to work for someone else and Jim agreed. He commented that he had been earning $25,000 per year before the store had been opened and that she had been earning $32,000. She replied that it was true, but that their hours were much longer working in the store than when they were employed. "Of course," she went on, "we have $50,000 invested in the business, which is a lot, but we also don't have to fight the traffic to get there."

Required: Assume that the Crains could sell the business for $50,000, invest the proceeds at 12% interest, and go back to their former jobs. Should they do so?

5-28   Pricing policy and excess capacity   Electric utilities face several problems in achieving optimal use of their facilities. First, because electricity cannot economically be stored, the firms must be able to generate enough electricity to meet demand at all times. Second, the use of electricity is seasonal, especially in warmer climates where the use of air conditioning produces high-peak requirements in the summer months.

Executives of Southern Electric Company are evaluating a proposal by the sales manager to offer discounts on electrical service to those customers who will use electrical heating equipment. The controller has amassed some data at the request of the sales manager. These data appear below.

Current generating capacity—monthly	20 million kilowatt-hours (kWh)
kWh sold—typical winter month	7 million
kWh sold—typical summer month	18 million
Price per 1,000 kWh	$35
Variable cost per 1,000 kWh	$19

The proposal is to reduce the price of electricity to $29 per 1,000 kWh if the customer uses electrical heating equipment. It is anticipated that about 5 million additional kWh per month could be sold in the winter, a total of about 22 million additional hours per year. The total annual sales in kWh are now 120 million. Users expected to convert to electrical heating now consume a total of about 30 million kWh per year. Sales to customers currently using electrical heating equipment, who would also qualify for the discount, are about 10 million kWh per year.

Required: Evaluate the monetary effects of the proposed decision.

5-29   Use of facilities   Chapman Company needs a new machine that it can either acquire from another firm for $85,000 or build itself. If the machine is built by the firm, it will require materials costing $20,000 and 2,000 hours of labor time at $5 per hour. The firm incurs other variable costs at the rate of $6 per labor hour. The following analysis shows the relative costs of the methods of acquisition.

	Make	Buy
Purchase price		$85,000
Materials	$20,000	
Labor ($5 × 2,000 hours)	10,000	
Variable overhead ($6 × 2,000 hours)	12,000	
Fixed overhead	40,000	
Totals	$82,000	$85,000

Your assistant explains that he included fixed costs in the analysis because Chapman would lose sales of 4,000 units by making the machine. The number of workers, and of hours worked, cannot be increased; and, since each worker makes two units per hour, using workers for 2,000 hours on the machine reduces units available for sale. Because 4,000 units is 2% of expected sales for the year, he allocated 2% of fixed manufacturing costs to the making of the machine.

Each unit of product sells for $22 and has total variable costs of $8.

Required: Determine whether the machine should be bought or made.

5-30   Sales premiums   Mrs. Nelson's Coffee Company has been experiencing difficulties in achieving sales goals because of increased competition. The sales manager has proposed the following to stimulate sales: The firm will place a coupon in each one-pound can of coffee. A customer who returns ten coupons will receive merchandise that costs the firm $1. In addition, mailing and handling costs will be $0.20 for each $1 of merchandise. The sales manager expects an increase in sales of about 50,000 one-pound cans per month and further predicts that only about 40% of the coupons will be redeemed. The firm currently sells 350,000 one-pound cans per month at $1.50, with variable costs being $0.90.

Required: Should the firm adopt the plan based on the sales manager's estimates?

5-31   Joint products—changes in mix   Brewer Company produces three products from a single raw material. The production process is set up to yield the following quantities of each product from ten pounds of raw material: Nyron, three pounds; Xylon, three pounds; and Krylon, four pounds. Each product can be further processed; price and cost data are given below.

	Nyron	Xylon	Krylon
Selling price at split-off (per pound)	$2	$4	$ 6
Additional processing costs (per pound)	1	3	8
Selling price after additional processing (per pound)	8	6	12

Required
1. Determine which products the firm should sell at split-off.
2. Assume that Brewer is now operating in accordance with your answer to part 1. Suppose that by changing the production process the firm could get eight pounds of Nyron and one pound each of Xylon and Krylon from ten pounds of raw material. There would be additional costs of $60,000 per month to process the raw material. The firm generally processes 100,000 pounds of raw material each month. Should Brewer change the process? Show calculations.
3. At what level of output per month, expressed in pounds of raw material processed, would Brewer have the same income under the existing process and under the changed process as described in part 2?

5-32   Hours of operation   Bronson Book Store is normally open 12 hours per day, six days per week. As an experiment, the owner kept the store open for six hours one Sunday and had sales of $750. The payroll was $110.

In an effort to determine whether it was worthwhile to stay open on Sundays, the owner collected the following additional information on annual results.

Sales		$361,400
Cost of sales		162,700
Gross margin		198,700
Operating expenses:		
Salaries	$88,300	
Rent	36,000	
Utilities	11,500	
Insurance	6,500	
Other	17,200	159,500
Profit		$ 39,200

Doing a few calculations, the owner came up with $511 as the estimated daily cost of operations, exclusive of cost of sales. He therefore concluded that about $930 in sales was necessary to justify staying open.

Required

1. Try to determine just what calculations the owner made to get his figures of $511 and $930.
2. With the information available, does it appear profitable to stay open Sundays?
3. What other information would you wish to get before making a final decision?

5-33 Make or buy Christensen Appliance Company is bringing out a new washing machine. The machine requires a type of electric motor not used for the current line of products. The purchasing manager has gotten a bid of $30 per motor from Wright Motor Company for any number the firm would need. Delivery is guaranteed within two weeks after order.

Christensen's production manager believes that the firm could make the motor by extensively converting an existing model. Additional space and machinery would be required if the firm were to make the motors. The firm currently leases, for $28,000 per year, space that could be used to make the motors. However, the space is now used to store vital materials, so the firm would have to lease additional space in an adjacent building to store the materials. That space could be rented for $42,000 per year. It is suitable for storage, but not for converting the motors. The equipment needed to convert the motors could be rented for $35,000 per year.

The treasurer of the firm has developed the following unit costs based on the expected demand of 14,000 units per year.

√ Materials	$12.20
√ Direct labor	10.00
Rent for space	2.00
Machinery rental	2.50
Other overhead	7.00
Total cost	$33.70

The "other overhead" figure includes $4 in fixed overhead that would be allocated to conversion of the motors.

Required
1. Determine whether the motors should be bought or made.
2. Determine the volume of motors at which Christensen would show the same total income whether it bought or made the motors.
3. Suppose that the firm had decided to make the motors, however wisely or unwisely according to your analysis in part 1. One-year contracts have been signed for the additional space and for the equipment. These contracts cannot be canceled. Determine the price that Wright Motor would have to offer Christensen to induce it to buy the motors.

5-34 **Dropping a product—opportunity costs**   Grothe Company has three product lines. Data for the coming year's operations that reflect the managers' best estimates appear below.

	Cabinets	Shelves	Bureaus
Sales	$450,000	$320,000	$200,000
Variable costs	200,000	180,000	125,000
Contribution margin	250,000	140,000	75,000
Avoidable fixed costs	110,000	60,000	40,000
Product margin	$140,000	$ 80,000	$ 35,000
Investment in receivables and inventories	$350,000	$300,000	$320,000

Unallocated joint costs total $130,000 and plant and equipment is $560,000.
    The managers are not happy with the expected results of the bureau line and are considering dropping it. If they did so, the firm could recover the investment in receivables and inventory related to the line and pay off debt of $320,000 that bears 14% interest.

Required: Determine whether the firm should drop the bureau line, supporting your answer with appropriate calculations.

5-35 **Relevant range**   The president of Ipswick Company has received an offer to purchase 10,000 of the tables made by his firm. The offer is to be filled any time during the coming year and the offer price per table is $55. The planned income statement for the year without this order is as follows.

Sales (45,000 tables @ $100)		$4,500,000
Cost of goods sold:		
Materials	$ 675,000	
Direct labor	900,000	
Overhead	1,575,000	
Total cost of goods		3,150,000
Gross profit		1,350,000
Selling, general, and administrative expenses		1,040,000
Income		$ 310,000

    The president believes that the order should be rejected because the price is below average total cost of $93.11 per table. He asks you to check the matter further because he knows that some costs are fixed and would not be affected by the special order.

In your analysis you find that $900,000 in overhead is fixed, and that a 10% commission on sales is the only variable selling, general, and administrative expense.

Required: Answer the following questions, considering each situation separately.

1. Assuming that the relevant range for the firm is between 30,000 and 60,000 tables, that existing sales would not be affected, and that the 10% sales commission would not have to be paid on the special order, what effect would there be on income if the order were accepted? Should it be accepted?

2. The relevant range is the same as in question 1 and existing sales would be unaffected, but the 10% sales commission would have to be paid. What is your decision? Support with calculations.

3. The relevant range is now 30,000 to 50,000 tables. If the special order is accepted, sales at regular prices would fall to 40,000 units. The 10% sales commission would not be paid on the special order. Should the order be accepted?

4. The relevant range is the same as in question 3, but production could be increased to meet the special order as well as regular budgeted sales. For all units produced above 50,000, labor cost per unit and per-unit variable overhead would be 10% higher than budgeted. Fixed production overhead would increase by $7,000. No sales commission would be paid on the order, and other selling, general, and administrative expenses would remain the same as budgeted. Should the order be accepted?

5-36 Value of new products—effects on sales of other products   Jackman's Grocery is a medium-sized operation in a suburb of a large city. Joe Jackman, the owner, is contemplating the addition of a department to sell either hardware or beer and wine. He has talked to the owners of several similar stores and has reached the following conclusions.

1. A hardware department would generate sales of $40,000 per year with a gross profit of 60%. No other variable costs would be added. Fixed costs added would be $12,000. There would be an increase of 5% in sales of groceries because of increased traffic through the store.

2. A beer and wine department would generate sales of $60,000 per year with gross profit of 40%. No other variable costs would be added, and additional fixed costs would be $18,000. Sales of groceries would increase by 8%.

    The income statement for a typical year for grocery sales alone is as follows.

Sales	$600,000
Cost of goods sold (variable)	240,000
Gross profit	360,000
Other variable costs	120,000
Contribution margin	240,000
Fixed costs	140,000
Income	$100,000

Required

1. Ignore the effects on sales of groceries for the moment. Compute the change in income that would result from adding (a) the hardware department, and (b) the beer and wine department.

2. Recompute the effects on income of adding each department, considering the effects on sales of groceries. Which department should be added and why?

3. What can be learned from this problem?

5-37 **Special orders—effects on existing sales**   Hunt Company makes high-quality calculators that are sold only by department stores and office equipment dealers. A large discount chain has offered to buy 30,000 calculators this year at an average price of $30. The income statement expected for the coming year shows the following without considering the special order.

Sales (90,000 units at average price of $50)	$4,500,000
Variable production costs (average of $20)	1,800,000
Contribution margin	2,700,000
Fixed costs (production and selling, general, and administrative)	2,200,000
Income	$ 500,000

The 30,000 units to be bought by the chain would be in the same mix as Hunt currently sells. The firm has the capacity to produce 140,000 units per year.

Required
1. Should the order be accepted if there would be no effect on sales at regular prices? Support your answer with calculations.
2. Suppose that accepting the order from the chain would result in a 10% decline in sales at regular prices because some current customers would recognize the chain store's product and make their purchases at the lower price. The sales mix would remain unchanged. Should the special order be accepted?
3. By how much could sales at regular prices decline before it became unprofitable to accept the order?
4. Assuming the same facts as in question 2, what other factors should be considered before the order is accepted?

5-38 **Alternative uses of product (CMA adapted)**   So-Clean Corporation manufactures a variety of cleaning compounds and solutions for both industrial and household use. Some of its products share ingredients and some can be refined into others.

Grit 337 is a coarse cleaning powder with industrial uses that sells for $2.00 per pound and has variable costs of $1.60 per pound, all for manufacturing costs. The firm currently uses a portion of Grit 337 in making a silver polish that sells for $4.00 per jar. Each jar requires one-quarter pound of Grit 337. Other variable production costs for the silver polish are $2.50 per jar and variable selling expenses are $0.30 per jar. Monthly avoidable fixed costs associated with making the silver polish are $5,600.

Required
1. Assuming that the firm cannot sell all of the Grit 337 that it can produce, how many jars of silver polish must it sell monthly to justify continuing to sell the polish?
2. Suppose now that the firm can sell all of the Grit 337 that it can make. How many jars of silver polish must the firm sell per month to justify further processing Grit 337 into silver polish?

5-39 **Services of an athlete—jumping leagues**   The Fort Bluff Titans of the Cross Continental Football League have been approached by Flinger Johnson, the star quarterback of the Snidely Whips, a team in the other major football league—the Nationwide Football League. Johnson is unhappy with his current salary and would like to jump leagues if a satisfactory arrangement can be made. His contract has run out, so he is free to negotiate with the opposing league.

The owner of the Titans believes that acquiring Johnson would be a boon to attendance, estimating that he would be worth 10,000 additional admissions in every game he played. No team in the Cross Continental League comes close to filling its stadium, and even with Johnson there would be no sellouts. There are six teams in the league, each playing each of the others twice, for a total of ten games. Each team plays every opponent once at home and once away. Tickets sell for $8 per game and variable costs are about $2 per ticket. The home team collects $6 per admission, the visiting team $2. The home team pays the variable costs.

Required
1. What is the additional annual income to the Titans that would be attributable to acquiring Johnson?
2. What is the additional annual income to all of the teams in the Cross Continental League?
3. Why is it necessary to state that there would be no sellouts even if Johnson were playing? If there were, how would it affect your analysis?
4. Suppose that Johnson demands $400,000. Should the Titans meet his demand?
5. Suppose that the other teams in the league agree to pay part of Johnson's salary. How much could each team pay without reducing its profits below the current level? (Include the Titans and each of the other five teams.)
6. Johnson is now being paid $200,000 per year. Suppose that the teams in the Nationwide League decide to try to keep Johnson. The member teams estimate that if Johnson jumps, 8,000 admissions will be lost for each game in which he would have played. Ticket prices are $11, with $2 variable costs, and each team plays 12 games.
   (a) How much would the total profits of the teams in the league fall if Johnson did jump leagues?
   (b) How much of a raise could be given to Johnson to yield the same total profit that would be earned if he jumped leagues?
   (c) Assume the same facts except that each team has 50% of its games sold out. There are usually 3,000 more requests for tickets than seats available for the sellouts. If Johnson were to jump, the total number of requests for tickets per game in which his old team plays would drop by 8,000. How would this additional information affect your analysis?

5-40 **Product processing**   Taylor Plywood Company makes high-quality wall paneling used in homes and offices. The firm buys walnut logs and processes them into thin sheets of veneer that are glued to sheets of plywood to make the paneling. The firm also makes the plywood from various kinds of wood. Taylor has enough capacity to make 1,000,000 square feet of veneer per month and 1,200,000 square feet of plywood. Capacity in the gluing operation is 1,300,000 square feet per month.

At the present time the firm can sell its paneling for $178 per 1,000 square feet. Veneer and plywood can be sold separately for $74 and $81, respectively, per 1,000 square feet. Cost data developed by the controller are given below, per 1,000 square feet.

	Plywood	Veneer	Paneling
Materials	$18	$16	$ 34
Direct labor	25	20	55
Overhead	32	29	93
Totals	$75	$65	$182

The figures shown for paneling are cumulative. They are the sums of the costs of veneer and plywood plus the additional costs associated with the gluing operation. Thus, no new materials are added in the gluing operation because the paneling cost for materials is equal to the sum of the veneer and plywood costs for materials. Direct labor in the gluing operation is $10 per 1,000 square feet, $55 total minus $25 for plywood operation and $20 for veneer operation.

The controller who prepared the above data stated that Taylor should stop making the paneling because it is unprofitable, and instead make and sell the veneer and plywood.

You learn that the overhead figures given above contain both fixed and variable overhead. The variable portion of overhead is 80% of direct labor cost. All fixed overhead is unavoidable.

Required

1. Determine what the firm should do. How much of each product should be produced and sold?
2. Determine what the firm should do if the price of paneling drops to $164 per 1,000 square feet.
3. Assume that paneling can be sold for $178 and veneer for $74, as in part 1. At what price for plywood would Taylor earn the same profit selling all of its plywood and veneer separately as it would combining them into paneling?
4. Assume the same prices as in part 1. Suppose that the firm could increase its capacity in any of the three operations by renting additional equipment on a month-to-month lease. Determine the maximum monthly cost that the firm could incur in order to increase capacity by 100,000 square feet in each of the three operations, considered independently.

5-41 Special order (CMA adapted) Anchor Company manufactures a variety of jewelry cases. The firm is currently operating at 80% of its capacity of 7,500 direct labor hours per month. Its sales manager has been looking for special orders to increase the use of capacity. JCL Company has offered to buy 10,000 cases at $7.50 per case provided that delivery is within two months. Per-case cost data for the order are as follows.

Materials	$2.50
Direct labor (½ hour at $6)	3.00
Manufacturing overhead	2.00
Total unit cost	$7.50

Variable overhead is $1.50 per direct labor hour and the firm allocates fixed manufacturing overhead to units of product based on their direct labor time. Without the order, Anchor would have enough business to operate at 6,000 direct labor hours $(7,500 \times 0.80)$ in each of the next two months. The normal selling price on the jewelry case is $10.50. JCL would put its own label on the case.

The production manager is concerned about the labor time that 10,000 cases would require. She cannot schedule more than 7,500 labor hours per month because the firm has a policy against overtime. Thus, the firm would have to reduce some regular-price sales of the jewelry case if it accepts the order. (JCL will not take fewer than 10,000 cases.)

Required

1. Determine whether or not Anchor should accept the order.
2. Determine the price per case for the order that would make Anchor indifferent between accepting and rejecting the order (the price that would give Anchor the same profit under both alternatives).

5-42 Processing decision   Most beef bought in stores comes from cattle that have been fattened on feedlots. A feedlot is an area consisting mainly of pens and barns in which cattle are closely packed and fed on diets designed to increase their weight rapidly. The cattle are bought from ranchers when they weigh about 500 pounds, at a cost of $260, including freight. After the cattle are fattened, their selling price is $0.50 per pound and the buyer pays the freight.

The average animal gains weight in the following pattern:

First month	140 pounds
Second month	130
Third month	120
Fourth month	100
Total potential gain	490 pounds

For each month that an animal is on the feedlot, it eats $52 worth of feed. The lot can hold 5,000 head of cattle at a time.

Required

1. Assume that there is a shortage of animals available for fattening. The lot is only able to buy 600 head per month. Determine the number of months that each animal should be kept on the lot before being sold.
2. Suppose that the supply of animals is very high so that the lot is operating at full capacity. Determine the number of months each animal should be kept.

Cases

5-43   Peanuts for peanuts*

The Time:	Hopefully never, but then everybody knows the outcome of wishful thinking.
The Scene:	A small neighborhood diner in a small New Jersey town about twenty-five miles from New York City. The operator-owner, Mr. Joseph Madison, is preparing to open for the day. He has just placed a shiny new rack holding brightly colored bags of peanuts on the far end of the counter. As he stands back to admire his new peanut rack, his brother-in-law, Harry, a self-styled efficiency expert, enters from the back door.

Harry. Morning Joe. What're you looking so pleased about?

Joe. I jus' put up my new peanut rack—the one I tole you about the other night.

Harry. Joe, you told me that you were going to put in these peanuts because some people asked for them. But I've been thinking about it and I wonder if you realize what this rack of peanuts is costing you.

Joe. It ain't gonna cost. Gonna be a profit. Sure, I hadda pay $25 for a fancy rack to hol'

*Used with the permission of Rex H. Anderson, Senior Vice-President, INA Reinsurance Company.

the bags, but the peanuts cost 6¢ a bag and I sell 'em for 10¢. I figger I can sell 50 bags a week to start. It'll take twelve and a haf' weeks to cover the cost of the rack and after that I make a clear profit of 4¢ a bag. The more I sell, the more I make.

Harry (shaking his finger at Joe). That is an antiquated and completely unrealistic approach. Fortunately, modern accounting procedures permit a more accurate picture which reveals the complexities involved.

Joe. Huh?

Harry. To be precise, those peanuts must be integrated into your entire operation and be allocated their appropriate share of business overhead. They must share a proportionate part of your expenditures for rent, heat, light, equipment depreciation, decorating, salaries for waitresses, cook . . .

Joe. The cook? What's he gotta do wit' the peanuts? He don' even know I got 'em yet.

Harry. Look, Joe. The cook is in the kitchen; the kitchen prepares the food; the food is what brings people in; and while they're in, they ask to buy peanuts. That's why you must charge a portion of the cook's wages, as well as a part of your own salary to peanut sales. Since you talked to me I've worked it all out. This sheet contains a carefully calculated cost analysis which clearly indicates that the peanut operation should pay exactly $1,278 per year toward these general overhead costs.

Joe (unbelieving). The peanuts? $1,278 a year for overhead? That's Nuts!

Harry. It's really a little more than that. You also spend money each week to have the windows washed, to have the place swept out in the mornings, to keep soap in the washroom and provide free cokes to the police. That raises the actual total to $1,313 per year.

Joe (thoughtfully). But the peanut salesman said I'd make money—put 'em on the end of the counter, he said—and get 4¢ a bag profit.

Harry (with a sniff). He's not an accountant; and remember, he wanted to sell you something. Do you actually know what the portion of the counter occupied by the peanut rack is worth to you?

Joe. Sure. It ain't worth nuttin'. No stool there—just a dead spot at the end.

Harry. The modern cost picture permits no dead spots. Your counter contains 60 square feet and your counter business grosses $15,000 a year. Consequently, the square foot of space occupied by the peanut rack is worth $250 per year. Since you have taken that area away from general counter use, you must charge the value of the space to the occupant. That's called opportunity cost.

Joe. You mean I gotta add $250 a year more to the peanuts?

Harry. Right. That raises their share of the general operating costs to $1,563 per year. Now then, if you sell 50 bags of peanuts per week, these allocated costs will amount to 60¢ per bag.

Joe (incredulously). What?

Harry. Obviously, to that must be added your purchase price of 6¢ a bag, which brings the total to 66¢. So you see, by selling peanuts at 10¢ per bag, you are losing 56¢ on every sale.

Joe. Something's crazy!!

Harry. Not at all. Here are the figures. They prove your peanut operation just can't stand on its own feet.

Joe (brightening). Suppose I sell lotsa peanuts—thousand bags a week, mebbe, 'stead of fifty?

Harry (tolerantly). No, Joe, you just don't understand the problem. If the volume of peanut sales increased, your operating costs will go up—you'll have to handle more bags, with more time, more general overhead, more everything. The basic principle of accounting is firm on that subject: "The bigger the operation the more general overhead costs must be allocated." No, increasing the volume of sales won't help.

Joe. Okay. You so smart, you tell me what I gotta do.

Harry (condescendingly now). Well—you could first reduce operating expenses.

Joe. Yeah? How?

Harry. You might take smaller space in an older building with cheaper rent. Maybe cut salaries. Wash the windows biweekly. Have the floor swept only on Thursdays. Remove the soap from the washrooms. Cut out the cokes for the cops. This will help you decrease the square-foot value of the counter. For example, if you can cut your expenses 50%, that will reduce the amount allocated to peanuts from $1,653 down to $781.50 per year, reducing the cost to 36¢ per bag.

Joe. That's better?

Harry. Much, much better. Of course, even then you'd lost 26¢ per bag if you charged only 10¢. Therefore, you must also raise your selling price. If you want a net profit of 4¢ per bag, you would have to charge 40¢.

(Harry is looking very confident, now, but Joe appears flabbergasted.)

Joe. You mean even after I cut operating costs 50%, I still gotta charge 40¢ for a 10¢ bag of peanuts? Nobody's that nuts about nuts! Who'd buy 'em?

Harry. That's a secondary consideration. The point is, at 40¢, you'd be selling at a price based upon a true and proper evaluation of your then reduced costs.

(Joe does not look convinced; then, he brightens.)

Joe. Look! I gotta better idea. Why don't I jus' throw the nuts out—so I lost $25 on the rack. I'm outa this nutsy business and no more grief.

(Harry is shaking his head vigorously.)

Harry. Joe, it just isn't that simple. You are in the peanut business! The minute you throw those peanuts out, you are adding $1,563 of annual overhead to the rest of your operation. Joe—be realistic—can you afford to do that?

Joe (by now completely crushed). It's unbelievable! Last week I wuz makin' money. Now I'm in trouble—jus' becuz I think peanuts onna counter is gonna bring me some extra profit. Jus' becuz I believe 50 bags of peanuts a week is easy.

Harry (by now smiling and satisfied that his brother-in-law will not be so quick to argue with him in the future). That is the reason for modern cost studies, Joe—to dispel those false illusions.

Curtain falls.

Required
1. Who's nuts?
2. Identify and evaluate the position(s) expounded by Harry.

5-44   **Dropping a segment**   Tom Johnson, the owner of Johnson's Drugstore, is opposed to smoking and would like to drop the tobacco counter from the store. He has determined from industry statistics and opinions of other drugstore managers that the tobacco counter creates a good deal of other business for the store because many people who come in just for cigarettes, cigars, and pipe tobacco buy other articles. Moreover, some people will go elsewhere for drugs and sundries if they know that tobacco is not being sold.

The manager estimates that sales of drugs would drop by 5%, and sundries by 10% if the tobacco counter were removed. The space now occupied by the tobacco counter would be devoted to greeting cards, which are not now sold in the store. Estimated annual sales for greeting cards are $8,000, with an associated cost of goods sold of $3,000.

If the tobacco counter is dropped, one clerk earning $4,000 could be dropped. But a pharmacist would have to handle the greeting card sales which would result in a further drop in drug sales of 2% (from the current level).

Carrying costs of the inventory of greeting cards are expected to be about $300 less per year than those associated with tobacco.

You have been asked by the manager to advise him in this decision. He has provided you with an income statement for the coming year showing his expectations if tobacco products are retained.

Johnson's Drugstore
Expected Income Statement
for Coming Year

	Tobacco	Drugs	Sundries	Total
Sales	$27,000	$120,000	$33,000	$180,000
Cost of goods sold	9,000	50,000	11,000	70,000
Gross profit	18,000	70,000	22,000	110,000
Operating expenses:				
Salaries	6,700	36,000	7,300	50,000
Occupancy costs (rent, utilities,				
maintenance, etc.)	3,000	7,000	4,000	14,000
Miscellaneous	1,500	6,700	1,800	10,000
Total operating expenses	11,200	49,700	13,100	74,000
Income before taxes	$ 6,800	$ 20,300	$ 8,900	$ 36,000

You learn that occupancy costs are allocated to each product group based on percentages of space occupied for display of those products. These costs will not change in total if greeting cards are substituted for tobacco. The salary of the manager, $18,000, is arbitrarily allocated to departments and is included in the salaries amount in the income statement. Miscellaneous expenses are allocated based on relative sales volume and would be unaffected by the change except for the cost of carrying inventory.

Required: Comment on the cost to Mr. Johnson of implementing his convictions about smoking.

5-45 Alternative uses of space Several years ago the Star Department Store began leasing some of its space to Clothes Horse, Inc., a chain of boutiques specializing in high-priced women's clothing and accessories. The boutiques are usually separate stores in shopping centers, but the management of Clothes Horse wished to experiment with an operation in a department store and Star was willing, as the space was then not needed for its own operations.

Clothes Horse pays Star a monthly rental of $3,000 plus 5% of its gross sales, and the arrangement has been profitable for both parties. Star pays all electricity, gas, and other costs of occupancy, which are negligible when considered incrementally because the space would have to be lighted and heated anyway. The lease is about to expire and Clothes Horse is eager to renew it for another year on the same terms. However, some of Star's department heads have indicated a desire to take over the operation of the boutique, and others have requested the use of the space to expand their selling areas.

After reviewing all the requests, Ron Stein and Bill Rausch, Star's executive vice president and general manager, respectively, have narrowed the range of choices to the following: (1) renew the lease with Clothes Horse; (2) keep the boutique, but place it under the women's wear department head, Margot Miller; (3) use the space to expand the shoe department, which is located next to the boutique.

The boutique had total sales of $400,000 in the first ten months of the current year, and the monthly rate is expected to double for the last two months, which come at the height of the Christmas season. Stein and Rausch expect a 10% increase in sales in the coming year if Clothes Horse continues to operate the boutique. Ms. Miller has presented the following expected income statement for the coming year, which she believes she could achieve if she took over the operation of the boutique:

Sales		$380,000
Cost of sales		171,000
Gross profit		209,000
Salaries	$75,000	
Advertising and promotion	14,000	
Supplies	7,000	
Miscellaneous	8,000	
		104,000
Profit		$105,000

Mr. Stein commented that Ms. Miller is generally too optimistic and that her estimate of sales volume was probably about 10% too high. He noted that she had provided for fewer salespeople than were employed by Clothes Horse and that the somewhat reduced level of service would not help business. He felt that expenses other than cost of sales would probably be about as she had estimated, even at the lower volume which he thought would be achieved.

The manager of the shoe department believed that if the space were used to expand his department his sales would increase by about $200,000 with a gross profit ratio of 45%. He would only need to add one salesperson, who would work on a 10% commission, like the other employees in that department. Virtually all other store employees worked on salary, not commission.

Rausch and Stein both brought up the subject of traffic through the store and both agreed that traffic had increased since Clothes Horse opened the boutique. They were uncertain about the effects of the increased traffic on sales in the store's own departments, and so Rausch told Stein that he would investigate the matter.

Rausch instructed several of his assistants to interview people in the store, particularly in the boutique, regarding their shopping habits. Several days later the results were in and he went to Stein's office to discuss them. The following major conclusions were contained in the reports Rausch had received:

1. About 40% of the dollar sales made in the boutique are to people who come especially to shop there. These people have to walk through parts of the store to get to the boutique and spend about 20% as much in the store as they do in the boutique.
2. The remaining 60% of the boutique's dollar sales is made to people who come for other reasons. Many seem to drop in on their way in or out of the store, some plan to shop in the store's other departments as well as in the boutique. These people spend about twice as much in the store's own departments as they do in the boutique.

After a discussion lasting nearly an hour, Stein and Rausch decided that the people who came in especially to shop in the boutique would not patronize the store at all if Clothes Horse did not operate it. The executives believed that only the popularity of the Clothes Horse name induced these people to come in.

Of the other group, they believed that about 10% of the patronage would be lost if Clothes Horse did not operate the boutique. This loss of sales would be spread fairly evenly throughout the store. The average gross profit ratio in the store is 45% and other variable costs are an additional 8% of sales.

Required: Determine the best course of action for the store.

PART TWO

BUDGETING

The activities of a typical enterprise require not only planning but also coordination of plans. A myriad of activities is carried on in an individual enterprise; the relationships among those activities are explored in this part.

The comprehensive budget is a tool to make planning effective, and provides a means for monitoring whether activities are going according to plan. The budget captures and reflects, in a formal and integrated way, the results of managers' planning decisions, from decisions about product mix and cost structure, to those about dividends and major new investments.

Both volume-cost-profit analysis and knowledge of cost behavior are important in budgeting for basic operations for the relatively near future—the coming year—and in analyzing the potential of longer-term projects the expenditures for which might have to be made in the near future. You will also be able to apply some of the principles from financial accounting, because a comprehensive budget includes the normal financial statements associated with reports to outsiders.

The budgeting process is more than a technical or mechanical exercise. It is people who plan and people who act (according to or contrary to plans). Thus the ways in which budgets are developed and used can have an effect on the behavior of people and vice versa. Some behavioral problems entailed in the budgeting process are introduced in this part. A more comprehensive treatment of these problems is given in Part Three.

CHAPTER 6

OPERATIONAL BUDGETING

Because the functional areas of a business (marketing, production, purchasing, finance) are interdependent, all areas must work in harmony to achieve profit goals. The production department must make enough units for marketing to achieve its sales objectives, but not so many that some go unsold or can be sold only at drastically reduced prices. There must be a balance between having too much inventory, which causes excessive costs for storage, insurance, taxes, and interest, and too little inventory, which may result in lost sales.

Similarly, the purchasing manager must ensure that enough of the right kinds of material are available to meet production schedules. The finance department must make cash available for paying for material, labor, and other operating costs. Cash must also be available for dividend payments, acquisitions of major assets, and repayments of borrowed funds. Cash planning is vital because many disbursements must be made in advance of collections from sales, and the plans of the various managers have implications for cash inflows and outflows.

The overall plans of the business, then, must be so specified that the manager of each functional area knows what must be done to ensure smooth performance for other areas and for the firm as a whole. Managers use comprehensive budgets to coordinate all of these activities.

COMPREHENSIVE BUDGETS

A **comprehensive budget** is a set of financial statements and other schedules showing the *expected*, or pro forma, results for a future period. A comprehensive budget normally contains an income statement for the period, a balance sheet as of the end of the period, a cash flow statement, production and purchases schedules, and schedules of fixed asset acquisitions. The budget package may have many other components, depending on the needs of the firm, but the foregoing constitute a minimum for a manufacturing firm.

Comprehensive budgeting depends heavily on the principles of VCP analysis. For example, both require careful studies of costs, including the estimation of cost behavior patterns, and the "planned" income statements of VCP analysis and short-term decision making are very similar to the budgeted income statement that is part of a comprehensive budget. But budgeting involves more than VCP analysis. For instance, the budgeting of cash collections requires both predicting sales *and* estimating the pattern of cash collections (how much do we collect within 30 days? within 60 days?). Predicted cash collections combine with cash receipts from planned borrowing to become a cash receipts budget. If the sales forecast proves accurate, and if customers pay their bills at the expected times, and if negotiations with lenders result in loans as planned, then cash receipts will be as budgeted. If customers pay less quickly than expected, sales do not materialize as forecast, or negotiations with lenders are unsuccessful, cash receipts will be less than budgeted.

Comprehensive budgeting is also more complex than VCP analysis because a change in a single assumption will affect results throughout the whole set of budgets, not just in one or perhaps more items in an income statement. For example, a change in the forecasted sales for a particular month would affect not only the variable costs (cost of sales and other variable costs such as sales commissions) and profit, but also the expected cash receipts, the plans for purchasing the items to be sold, the amount of cash needed to pay for the items that need to be purchased (for subsequent sale), and perhaps even the amount of loans that must be negotiated.

All levels of management are involved in putting together some part of the collection of interrelated statements and schedules that make up the comprehensive budget. However, individual managers deal only with segments of the total package, and the degree of detail in the schedules they use varies with the breadth of the manager's responsibilities. Thus, while top managers will be interested in overall results, the schedules used by the production manager might deal only with production data, in total and by product. In general, most managers will have budgets showing what is expected of *them*—what objectives *they* are to achieve and at what costs.

Budgets and Planning

The comprehensive budget is the most conspicuous evidence of an overall plan for a business firm. It ties together a set of diverse activities that are related to specific goals, and specifies the means for their achievement. Thus the business has a formal plan in contrast to an intuitive approach to operations.

A principal benefit of formal planning is that it requires explicit statements of objectives such as sales volume and profit, and of the means to achieve those objectives. Some of the objectives initially considered feasible may prove not so in light of the budget. Suppose the budget specifies high sales in the early part of the year. When the production manager uses the sales budget as a basis for planning production, he or she may recognize that there will not be sufficient productive capacity to attain the budgeted level of sales. Or perhaps sufficient production and inventory to meet the budgeted level of sales are possible *only* if the firm obtains a great deal of short-term financing. If securing the necessary financing is undesirable (or even impossible), the budgets would have to be modified to be consistent with the amount of cash available for investment in inventory.

Figure 6-1 shows how the budgeting process uses the financial statements and other schedules a firm normally prepares, and coordinates all of these statements and schedules into a comprehensive system. Chapter 5 showed that decision making, which can be considered part of the overall planning process, relies on estimates about future results under different alternative courses of action. Budgeting is an obvious part of the overall planning process, and is related to decision making in that managers consider the status quo as one alternative and compare it with possible alternatives (such as special orders). To make good decisions, managers need reliable information about the future, and the information in carefully prepared budgets is likely to be as reliable as that from any other source.

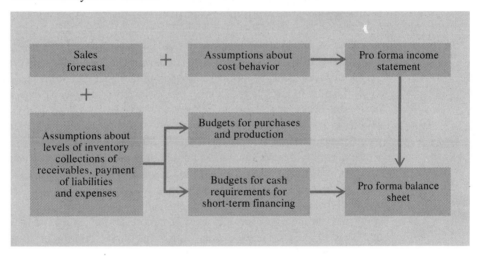

FIGURE 6-1   Relationships Among Financial Statements in Budgeting

Budgets and Control

A budget expresses targets or goals; actual results express achievements. Thus a comparison of the budget and actual results is a basis for evaluating performance and helps control future operations. Corrective action can be taken to eliminate problems that show up in the comparisons.

The preceding statements are oversimplified, but they are nevertheless a fair statement of the role of budgets in control and performance evaluation. Actual performance is best judged by comparison with expected rather than past performance. This is true if expectations are reasonable, carefully formulated, and based on all available information. Using past performance to judge current performance is inappropriate because circumstances change. Moreover, comparisons with past performance cannot reveal whether current performance is as good as it should have been.

Although improvement over past results is desirable, it is more important to know if the improvement has been as great as it could have been. (A student who gets a 38 on one examination and follows it up with a 42 on the next has improved, but is still not performing adequately.)

The budgeting process incorporates all the managerial functions that we have associated with managerial accounting. Planning, control, decision making, and performance evaluation are integrated in the budgeting cycle.

Organization of Budgets

Budgets usually cover specific time periods, such as a month, a year, or a 5-year period. Virtually all companies prepare a budget for the fiscal year, and the annual budget is normally broken down into shorter time periods—quarters, months, or even weeks. Budgets are also prepared for periods of longer than a year, usually for three, four, or five years, broken down into 1-year units. It is, of course, more difficult to forecast several years into the future, so longer-term budgets tend to be less detailed than annual budgets.

It is also likely to be more difficult to forecast in detail for very short periods, such as a month, or a week, than for a quarter, even if the period is in the near future. This is because many random factors may influence results for short time periods. You might be able to budget your expenditures for entertainment fairly well on a monthly basis. But breaking down that budget on a day-by-day basis is difficult. Similarly, a retailer of women's clothing may be able to predict sales for a quarter quite closely, but would have difficulty in pinning down the sales pattern week by week.

Despite these problems, an annual budget is normally broken down into shorter time periods for several reasons. First, managers want to gauge their progress toward meeting the goals set in the annual budget; monitoring progress is easier if benchmarks are available during the year. More important, what actually happens is often different from what is incorporated into even the most sophisticated plans, so that managers may need to make changes in operating plans for the remainder of the period.

Consider the following situation. The sales manager sees that actual sales for the first month of the fiscal year are higher than budgeted. She must try to decide whether the additional sales in this month will be offset by lower sales later, or whether the high sales are an indication that the *total* expectations were too low. Suppose she concludes that sales for the rest of the first quarter, or even for the year, will be in excess of budgeted amounts. The original production budget was based on budgeted sales. If the original production plan is followed, inventory will be less than budgeted at the end of the first month and shortages may develop. The sales manager may then want to have production increased to meet the expected increases in sales. An increase in production may require the hiring of more employees, the acquisition of greater quantities of material, and other actions by various managers. Changes in plans—such as increased production—will go more smoothly and more effectively if they can be accomplished well in advance of the point at which a crisis develops.

Even if the sales manager concluded from these early results that sales for the year will not be materially greater than budgeted, the fact that sales are higher than expected in the first month means that inventory will be lower than budgeted. It might then be necessary to plan a temporary increase in production sufficient to maintain the desired level of inventory. Perhaps some overtime work could be scheduled, but perhaps not. Whether the sales in excess of expectations are a temporary or a longer-lasting phenomenon, there are new plans to be made, with implications for production and cash flows.

When business is seasonal, the firm must acquire large quantities of goods in advance of the selling season, thus creating a need for funds prior to the receipt of cash from customers. But even if there is no seasonality in a firm's operations, cash requirements will vary over the year because some costs fluctuate throughout the year. For example, property taxes for the year can normally be paid in two installments, some insurance premiums are due only annually, interest payments can be made quarterly, semiannually, or annually, and dividends are seldom paid on a monthly schedule. (It makes a big difference whether a $100,000 payment for taxes or dividends must be made in January or July, because the funds must be available when the payment falls due.) Cash budgets are an important part of the total budget package, and budgets prepared for the year as a whole fail to identify these irregular funds requirements and so are not useful for monthly planning.

Continuous budgets.   Most managers like to have plans for at least a year in advance. If budgets are prepared only for fiscal years, as the year goes by the period for which a budget is available will shorten until the budget for the next year is prepared. To alleviate this problem some firms use continuous budgets. Under such a system, a budget for a month (or quarter) will be added as one of these periods goes by. Thus there would be a 12-month budget at all times. Managers are then kept aware of the needs for the next 12 months, regardless of the time of the year.

Project budgets.   Some kinds of budgets are not oriented to time periods but to stages in the completion of projects. For example, a firm building a new plant is concerned with getting the plant on stream according to a time schedule (finish the exterior by March, the interior by August, begin production by December). The time periods selected, which may be of unequal length, are dependent on the project, but of no importance in themselves. The focus is on completing each of the various stages of the project. Of course the project budget does have implications for periodic budgeting. The project will probably require the expenditure of cash at various times, and these expenditures must be considered in preparing the cash budget.

Capital budgets.   Virtually all firms prepare budgets of expenditures for fixed assets, often for many years into the future. Such budgets are called **capital budgets.** Like project budgets, capital budgets are required periodically because there will be expenditures associated with acquiring fixed assets. These expenditures must be incorporated into the cash budgets for the appropriate time periods.

Developing the Comprehensive Budget

The comprehensive budget is generally developed well in advance of the period being budgeted for. This is necessary because budgets often must be extensively revised for reasons already discussed. In every case, the budget begins with a sales forecast, because expected sales will determine production requirements, labor and material needs, cash flows, and financing requirements. The ways in which each of these various elements are related depend on managerial policies (how many months' supply of inventory should be kept, what credit terms are offered to customers) and operating characteristics (costs, production time).

You are already familiar with the preparation of pro forma income statements based on sales forecasts and cost behavior. The preparation of a budgeted income statement is, with minor exceptions, an extension of VCP analysis. Other budgets, especially the pro forma balance sheet and statement of cash flow, present some technical difficulties because of the leads and lags involved. For example, revenue is generally *recorded* at the point of sale, though cash may not be collected for some time after the sale. The cost of goods sold is recognized at the time that revenue is recorded. But the costs to purchase or produce the inventory are incurred prior to the sale. Liabilities are recorded as they are incurred, but cash payments may be delayed for varying periods of time. These leads and lags give rise to the critical technical problems in comprehensive budgeting.

In the remainder of this chapter we shall discuss and illustrate sales forecasts, purchase budgets, and expense budgets. These budgets are usually called **operating budgets.** In Chapter 7 we will complete the process by considering **financial budgets** (pro forma balance sheet and cash budget).

SALES FORECASTING

The sales forecast is critical to budgeting because virtually everything else depends on it. Firms use many methods to forecast sales. Not all firms can use all of these methods, but it is likely that most firms can use one or more.

Indicator Methods

The sales of many industries are closely associated with some factor in the economy. Sales of long-lasting consumer goods (cars, washing machines, furniture, etc.) generally correlate well with indicators of economic activity like the Gross National Product and personal income. Sales of baby food are associated with the number of births, general foods with population increases, and housing units with the formation of new households.

A firm in such an industry might find it fairly easy to predict total sales for the industry and then forecast its own sales by estimating its share of the total market. Both scatter diagrams and regression analysis find wide use in forecasting sales, just as they do in predicting costs.

The sales in many industries depend to a great extent on the sales of some other industries. Textile firms watch closely the sales of clothing and take note of forecasts of sales of various kinds of clothes. Makers of cans and bottles look at forecasts for sales of beer and soft drinks. Steel companies and tire companies keep abreast of developments affecting the auto industry. In these situations, a firm tries to develop a forecast for its industry and then for itself, the key being forecasts from *other* industries.

The use of an indicator as a basis for sales forecasting requires, of course, that the indicator itself be predictable. Suppose you have observed over time that the sales in your industry correlate well with Gross National Product. You can use GNP to predict industry sales (and then your sales) only if you are able to predict GNP. Thus, once the relationships have been determined as well as possible (probably using regression equations) and a forecast of the indicator is available, the relationships can be used to forecast sales for the industry or firm.

Figure 6-2 is a scatter diagram showing the number of automobiles sold plotted against per capita income (PCI). See if you can develop an equation of the form: Auto sales = constant + (PCI × ?). If per capita income is forecast to be $4,800 for the coming year, what do you forecast for automobile sales? If your firm makes parts for automobiles, what could you do with your forecast of auto sales?

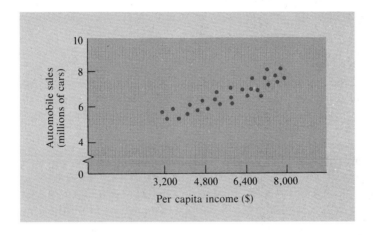

FIGURE 6-2

A line fitted to the points would hit the vertical axis at about 4 million cars. The slope would be about 0.5 million cars per $1,000 in per capita income. The line is at 5.5 million cars at $3,200, 7.9 million at $8,000, a difference in cars of 2.4 million for a $4,800 difference in income. Thus car sales would rise about 500 (2.4 million cars/$4,800 change in income) for each rise of $1 in per capita income. At $4,800 per capita income, sales would be forecast as follows: 4 million + (500 × $4,800) = 4 million + 2.4 million = 6.4 million cars.

Sometimes managers can obtain predictions of industry sales directly. Many trade associations publish studies that provide guidance in sales forecasting. For example, an association of appliance dealers may conduct studies to determine what kinds of appliances are likely to sell, and in what quantities. A study for the purpose of forecasting the sales of washing machines could take into account the overall economic outlook, previous sales of washing machines, the average age of machines currently in use (to see whether replacements will be significant), and the forecasts for new housing units. Although the study would not indicate the effects of these factors on the sales of any single dealer, each dealer should gain a more accurate picture of what is likely to happen to industry sales and thus apply it to his or her own sales forecasts.

Historical Analysis

The past is not always a good guide to the future, but it usually provides a starting point. Some firms analyze their sales from previous years and project the trend to arrive at a forecast. Thus, if sales have been rising at an average of 10% per year, the firm will start with a forecast based on last year's sales plus 10%. This is only a start. Are there any factors that suggest higher or lower sales? Were last year's sales abnormally high or low because of a strike, unusual weather conditions (ice cream, beer, golf balls, and many other products sell better in hot weather)? Are there discernible changes in taste that would affect our sales? The past can be used for guidance on what might happen, but differences in conditions might cause the future to differ from the past.

A number of sophisticated statistical techniques can be used to make predictions from historical data. These techniques are beyond the scope of this book, but you will learn about some of them in later courses in your curriculum.

Judgmental Methods

Some firms forecast sales using judgment based on experience with the company's customers and products. Each regional sales manager may, in consultation with sales staff, estimate the expected sales in that area, by customer or product line. The chief sales executive will review the regional forecasts, discuss them with the regional managers, and develop a forecast for the entire company.

The analysis underlying these judgment-based forecasts may proceed along the lines of the other methods described here, except that the procedures will be less formal. Instead of using regression analysis or some other mathematical tool, the manager will develop a forecast of the prospects for the industry and for the firm by relying on his or her experience and personal perceptions of changing circumstances. The manager may, for example, take note of several newspaper and magazine articles about the decreasing length of the work week and reason that people will have increased leisure time. If the firm makes products associated with leisure-time activities, the manager may correctly conclude that sales for the industry and for the firm will be higher than previously forecast.

Which Method to Use

The applicability of any of the methods discussed depends on the characteristics of the firm. Most firms will use a combination of methods. The use of judgmental methods alone might reflect unwarranted optimism of the sales manager and sales force. The indicator methods might not be applicable to particular firms. Moreover, where indicators are used, there is a danger if such methods are relied on to the exclusion of other factors. (Current conditions may differ from those in force when the relationships among economic indicators and the sales of the firm or industry were first developed.) Successful planning is the result of combining sound and experienced business judgment with the judicious use of the quantitative tools available.

Whatever methods are used to forecast, the sales budget for the firm as a whole is likely to have evolved from several forecasts made on a smaller scale. The original forecasts may be by individual product or product line, by geographical area, by department, or by some combination of these. A large company could have several regional sales offices, each with a manager in charge of a particular product line. The product line managers would submit forecasts to the regional sales manager, who would assemble and add them, then pass on the regional budget to company headquarters where all of the regional forecasts would be added up to obtain a budget for the firm as a whole. Alternatively, the product managers could submit budgets directly to headquarters so that the aggregation would be by product line, rather than by region. The method followed depends on the organization of the firm and should be the most effective to obtain the desired information in the form most adaptable for planning.

Expected Values and Forecasting

As just indicated, several different managers are usually involved in preparing the sales forecast. It is also possible that a firm will develop different forecasts by using different indicators or methods. When different methods are used, or different persons are preparing forecasts, the resulting forecasts are likely to differ. Indeed, even a single manager may come up with several different forecasts based on different assumptions and on his or her judgment about the conditions in the coming period. In such cases, the concept of expected value is sometimes used to reach a single forecast figure for use in budgeting.

Determining an **expected value** involves identifying available alternatives, assigning probabilities to each, and computing a single outcome. To illustrate, suppose that the sales vice president of a firm has been given three forecasts: one has been developed from forecasts by regional sales managers; another has been prepared by the firm's market research department; and the third originated with the firm's chief economist. The vice president will assign to each forecast a probability expressing his confidence in the accuracy of that forecast. Say that he decides to assign the probabilities 20%, 30%, and 50% to the three forecasts respectively. Below is a calculation of the expected sales using the forecast amounts and his opinions.

Source of Forecast	(1) Sales Forecast in Dollars	(2) Assigned Probability	(1) × (2) Expected Value
Regional sales managers	$6,000,000	0.20	$1,200,000
Market research department	$4,500,000	0.30	1,350,000
Chief economist	$5,000,000	0.50	2,500,000
Expected value		1.00	$5,050,000

Notice that the probabilities assigned must add up to 1, or 100%. The concept of expected value has its origins in statistical decision theory and has many more sophisticated uses. In most cases, the assignment of probabilities is based on the manager's judgment and experience, sometimes refined by other statistical techniques. The probabilities are, therefore, termed subjective: different managers might assign different probabilities. As with any other managerial tool, the quality of the final information or decision rests heavily on the quality of the manager's judgment.

Interim Period Forecasts

The forecasting methods discussed apply to sales forecasting of three distinct types: (1) annual forecasts, (2) longer-term forecasts (three to five years), and (3) quarterly or monthly forecasts. Once a forecast for the year has been approved as a basis for planning, it is necessary to break it down into shorter periods.

Often the data used to forecast annual sales (economic indicators, sales for other industries) are already broken down by quarters. Where such data are available, the manager can base his or her quarterly forecast on the same indicator used for the annual forecast. Many firms have developed reliable criteria for breaking down annual forecasts. Their experiences may show that particular percentages of yearly sales occur in particular quarters or months (15% of annual sales are concentrated in March, 40% in the first quarter, and so on).

Managers revise budgets when they obtain more information. For example, if the firm used a forecast of housing starts as the basis for its sales forecast, then saw that housing starts were significantly higher or lower than originally forecasted, it would alter the budget accordingly. A budget is a plan, not a straitjacket; changing it in the face of changing conditions is usually sound practice.

EXPENSE BUDGETS

Specific managers are responsible for specific tasks and expenses, and the budgeting process must recognize this. Each manager should have a **budget allowance** that sets forth the acceptable limits of expenses that the manager may incur in accomplishing his or her assigned tasks.

There are two general ways to develop budget allowances. One approach sets the budget for a particular cost at a single amount without any reference to or consideration of the volume of activity. An allowance set this way is called a **static budget.** This approach would be used with fixed costs. The other approach sets a variable, or **flexible budget allowance,** based on volume of activity. Budgets are set in this fashion for variable costs and mixed costs. Budgets for some discretionary fixed costs could also be flexible. For example, a flexible budget allowance would be appropriate if it is the firm's policy to spend an amount equal to some percentage of sales on advertising, research and development, bonuses, and other discretionary elements of cost.

A static budget is generally set for fixed cost elements, both committed and discretionary. The budget allowance for committed costs can generally be set by reference to existing obligations (because costs to be incurred have largely been set by actions already taken). Discretionary cost allowances would generally be set by managerial policy, and the manager responsible for controlling the cost would participate with higher management in determining the amount to be allowed. (See the discussion below for further problems relating to the budgeting of discretionary costs.)

Managers set flexible budget allowances using procedures similar to those employed in predicting costs. The variable cost component per unit of volume would be found by using one or more procedures outlined in Chapter 3 and the fixed component by managerial policy or reference to commitments arising out of previous decisions.

Alternative Measures of Activity

As indicated in Chapter 3, the amount of a particular cost may vary not with sales volume or units of output but with some other measure of activity. The originally budgeted amounts for such costs, and the subsequent flexible budget allowances, must be based on the activity measure determined to be the best in predicting the behavior of the particular cost in question.

The most obvious example of the need for a measure of volume other than sales is the case of a production manager. The production budget for the period must be related to production volume rather than sales. Whether units are sold or not, the cost to make them is incurred at the time of production. The production manager will incur costs before they become expenses in the income statement. Thus the budget allowance would be some fixed amount plus the variable costs of production times the number of units produced.

Suppose that a department manager and his superior have agreed on the following flexible budget allowance for factory overhead:

Cost	Fixed Amount per Month	Variable Amount per Hour of Direct Labor
Indirect labor	$1,200	$0.50
Supplies	200	0.40
Maintenance	2,400	0.10
Depreciation	1,200	0
Miscellaneous	700	0.05
Totals	$5,700	$1.05

Suppose further that 1,000 direct labor hours are budgeted for the coming month. The original budget allowances for the month will be determined and reported as in the first column of Exhibit 6-1 on page 202. Budgeted amounts for each cost element are computed by using the following formula:

$$\text{Flexible budget allowance} = \text{fixed cost per month} + \left(\text{direct labor hours} \times \text{variable cost per hour} \right)$$

For example, the budget amount for indirect labor is computed as $1,200 + (1,000 \times \$0.50)$ or $1,700. This exhibit is actually the beginning of a performance report which will be completed later when actual labor hours are known.

Exhibit 6-1
Production Performance Report

Month _March_   Department _Mixing_
Manager _E-Jones_

| | Budget Allowances | | | |
	Budgeted Hours	Actual Hours	Actual Costs Incurred	Variance
Direct labor hours	1,000			
Indirect labor	$1,700			
Supplies	600			
Maintenance	2,500			
Depreciation	1,200			
Miscellaneous	750			
Totals	$6,750			

If actual hours during the month turned out to be 1,300, we would need a *revised* budget allowance for each cost element, taking into consideration the higher production. For example, for indirect labor, the flexible budget allowance for the month would now be $1,850 [$1,200 + (1,300 hours × $0.50)]. In Exhibit 6-2, we have completed the performance report by inserting the flexible budget allowances for the achieved level of production, inserted some assumed actual costs, and computed a variance (difference between the *revised* budget and the actual costs).

When actual costs are less than the budget allowance, the variance is said to be favorable; when the reverse is true, the variance is said to be unfavorable. Hence, the variances for supplies, maintenance, and total costs were favorable. In Chapter 12 we shall discuss methods for analyzing variances.

It should be noted that in our example we assumed that the cost prediction formulas for the various cost elements applied to the actual level of hours worked. But we know from Chapter 3 that cost behavior tends to be predictable over a certain range of

Exhibit 6-2
Production Performance Report

Month _March_   Department _Mixing_
Manager _E-Jones_

| | Budget Allowances | | | Variance Favorable (Unfavorable) |
	Budgeted Hours	Actual Hours	Actual Costs Incurred	
Direct labor hours	1,000	1,300		
Indirect labor	$1,700	$1,850	$1,870	($20)
Supplies	600	720	705	15
Maintenance	2,500	2,530	2,470	60
Depreciation	1,200	1,200	1,200	—
Miscellaneous	750	765	780	(15)
Totals	$6,750	$7,065	$7,025	$40

volume and also that a choice must be made among cost formulas when faced with step-variable costs. For this reason, some firms will prepare schedules of flexible budget allowances for several different levels of volume. These allowances will normally take into consideration the changes in cost formulas resulting from large differences in volume. Then, at the end of a period when actual volume is known; the firm will compute its flexible budget allowances based on the cost formulas relevant to that general volume range. Although the computations may be more numerous, the principles underlying the use of alternative production budgets are the same as those presented for a single budgeted production level.

Of course, careful cost analysis may show that the costs for a particular department vary with a measure of activity other than sales, in dollars or units, or labor hours, or production. Budgeting for such costs depends on establishing budget allowances based on whatever independent variable can be determined as having a predictable relationship with actual costs. Suppose, for example, that we want to establish a budget allowance for the manager of the customer billing department, and that the only costs that vary in that department are the costs of billing forms and postage. Sales in units or in dollars are not good measures of the volume of activity in that department, because the form and postage costs will be the same for each order, whether the order is for one or ten units, $30 or $500. If the cost of a billing form and postage is $0.40, the budget allowance might be the monthly fixed costs plus $0.40 per bill processed. Here again, the analytical methods discussed in Chapter 3 can be helpful in identifying an activity measure that would be useful for budgeting purposes.

Budgeting Discretionary Costs

Establishing budget allowances for discretionary costs presents some of the most difficult problems in budgeting. As explained in Chapter 3, no one really knows for sure the optimal amount of funds to spend on most discretionary activities. (How much is an appropriate investment in employee development? in improving current products? in research on potential products?)

Unfortunately, costs incurred for discretionary items seldom produce immediately measurable output. Research and development activities do not normally show results for several years; employee training, especially the training of managers, does not bear fruit quickly. In some cases, budgets for discretionary items will be, as in the case of some variable costs, related to some input factor, such as the number of employees being given training or the number of products being studied by research scientists and engineers. (But, of course, the decision about how many employees to train or how many products are to be studied is open to discussion.) In some cases, it may be possible to specify, at least qualitatively, what benefits the firm could get from a particular level of spending on a discretionary item. For example, the manager of data processing may be able to say that providing a budget sufficient to lease a particular software package would speed customer billing by one or two days. The value of getting bills out quicker would be that payments would probably come in sooner. (But, of course, there remains the question of whether the benefits of speeded up collections—the opportunity cost of money tied up in accounts receivable—would exceed the cost of leasing the software package; and there is no assurance that the more timely billing will produce collections at an earlier date.)

Because of the inability to determine optimal levels of spending on discretionary items, the setting of budget allowances for such items often involves negotiations between the affected managers and the budget director, or perhaps between those managers and upper levels of management. In many instances, budgets for these areas are established as a result of specific policy decisions on the part of top management. "We shall increase spending on research and development by 10% per year for the next five years" is an example of a policy statement that would guide the preparation of budget allowances. Such a statement is likely to be the result of top managers having set a particular goal for the firm, such as the goal to be viewed as an innovator in the industry. Whatever the goal accepted by top management, it is important that the managers of the affected areas understand the reason behind a stated policy, so that those managers authorize actions (and the related expenditures) most likely to be consistent with the goal.

BUDGETING AND HUMAN BEHAVIOR

Budgeting necessarily entails behavioral problems. These problems include the following: conflicting views, imposed budgets, budgets as check-up devices, and unwise adherence to budgets.

Conflicts

We can illustrate the problem of conflicts in budgeting by considering a matter of importance to almost any firm—inventory policy. The sales manager wants inventory to be as high as possible because it is easier to make sales if the goods are available to the customer immediately. The financial manager would like to keep inventories as low as possible because there are costs associated with having inventory: storage, insurance, taxes, interest, and so on. If a manufacturing process is involved, the production manager is not interested in inventory per se, but does have an indirect interest. He or she wants long runs of production, steady production, no rush orders, no overtime, because these conditions will minimize the costs of production. Thus three managers will have different views on the desirable level of inventory. Each will be evaluated by reference to how well the individual does his or her job, so each has a lot at stake in the determination of inventory policy. The conflict is resolved with great difficulty, if at all. The managerial accountant may be called in to determine the best level of inventory for the firm. Such a determination must weigh the costs of having inventory with the cost of lost sales resulting from not having enough inventory. The task is difficult, but the objectives of the individual managers must all be considered, together with the general concern for the welfare of the firm.

Imposed Budgets

We have assumed in this chapter that cost levels, production levels, and so on were determined rather mechanically. But this is seldom the case. Managers and workers determine cost levels by how well they perform their assigned jobs. It is not uncommon for higher levels of management to *set* performance standards for the individuals below them. When such is the case, the standards are said to be imposed, and serious behavioral problems can arise or be avoided depending on the managers' attitudes.

Some managers believe that performance standards should be set very high (costs very low)—so high that almost no one could be expected to meet the budget. This position is sometimes justified on the grounds that it "keeps the managers and workers on their toes," and assumes that people will slacken their performances if they can easily meet a budget. Others say that budgets should be set so that they are achievable given a good, but not exceptional, performance.

Significant problems can result from the imposition of unachievable budgets. Managers tend to become discouraged and do not commit themselves to achieving budgeted goals. They may act in ways that *seem* to help achieve goals (such as scrimping on preventive maintenance to achieve lower costs in the short run). But such actions are likely to be harmful in the longer run (when machinery breaks down and production must be halted altogether). The imposition of unachievable goals may also have serious financial effects. Management actions based on such a budget may be improper; that is, the budget will be useless for planning, when facilitating planning is one of its primary purposes.

Consider, for example, the implications of setting unrealistically high sales goals. Based on those goals, production plans will be made, including perhaps commitments for materials and the hiring and training of factory workers. Based on sales goals, production plans, and inventory policies, storage areas for inventory will be acquired. Based on sales goals, cash receipts will be planned, and the firm will estimate and perhaps negotiate certain amounts of short-term financing.[1] Now what if the sales goals are not realized? Inventory levels will be higher than expected, and additional space may have to be contracted for at unfavorable rates, or production efficiency may be interfered with to accommodate the extra inventory. Cash receipts will not materialize as planned, and additional short-term financing may have to be negotiated on terms unfavorable to the firm. If production schedules are subsequently adjusted to bring them into line with lower sales and to reduce inventory, employee relations may suffer as workers are laid off, and relations with suppliers may be harmed as delays in delivery of materials are requested.

We could say that the firm's planning based on its budget has been ineffective. At their worst, unrealistic budgets can have serious and detrimental financial effects on the firm. At the very least, unrealistic budgets will probably simply be ignored.

It is possible that imposed budgets can reflect achievable, realistic performance goals. There are, however, at least two reasons for adopting another approach, which involves participation in standard-setting by the individuals expected to meet those standards. First, although particular managers may be generally aware of the problems associated with the tasks performed by people responsible to them, they cannot be as well informed as the persons performing the tasks. Second, a considerable body of empirical evidence suggests that allowing individuals a say in their expected levels of performance is conducive to better performance than when those individuals are not consulted. While the managers, including the top-level managers, must take the final responsibility for establishing goals, their methods of arriving at those goals can have a significant effect on the performance of individuals affected by those goals.

---

[1]One of the advantages of the cash portion of the comprehensive budget is that it allows the firm to identify financing needs before they occur, so the managers have time to seek the best financing sources. More of this in Chapter 7.

Budgets as "Check-Up" Devices

Behavioral problems do not arise solely because of the procedure followed for developing budget allowances. Comparisons of budgeted and actual results and subsequent evaluation of performance also introduce difficulties. In ideal circumstances managers would use actual results to evaluate their own performance, to evaluate the performance of others, and to correct elements of the operations that seem to be out of control. The budget serves as a feedback device, letting managers know the results of their actions. Having seen that something is wrong, they can take steps to correct it.

Unfortunately, budgets are often used more for checking up on managers, and the feedback function is ignored. Where this is the case, the manager is constantly looking over his or her shoulder and trying to think of ways to explain unfavorable results. The time spent on thinking of ways to defend the results could be more profitably used to plan and control operations. Some evaluation of performance is necessary, but the budget ought not to be perceived as a club to be held over the heads of managers. More attention will be given to behavioral problems of performance evaluation in Chapters 10, 11, and 12.

Unwise Adherence to Budgets

In our discussion of expense budgets we pointed out that the budget sets limits on cost incurrence, allowances beyond which managers are not expected to go. This can cause managers to spend either too little or too much.

There are times when exceeding the budget may be beneficial for the firm. A sales manager may believe that a visit to several important customers or potential customers will result in greatly increased sales. However, if taking the trip would result in exceeding the travel budget, he or she will be reluctant to do so.

At the other extreme, a manager who has kept costs well under the budget might be tempted to spend frivolously in order to get expenditures up to the budgeted allowance. The manager may fear that the budget for the following year will reflect the lower costs for the current year. Not wishing to be given a lower budget next year, the manager will take an undesirable action in order to protect personal interests.

ILLUSTRATION

We shall illustrate the preparation of a comprehensive budget by working with Cross Company, a retailing firm. The illustration will be done in two parts. In this chapter we shall prepare the sales forecast, purchases budget, and tentative pro forma income statement. In Chapter 7 we shall prepare the cash budget, which requires some of the data in the budgets developed here. We shall then see how the operating and financial budgets are related, especially how the results of the cash budget may induce the managers to look again at the operating budgets and possibly make changes in them. The example uses dollar amounts that are unrealistically small because we want to avoid long and arduous computations.

The managers of Cross Company are developing its comprehensive budget for the first six months of 19X4. As the first step, they have developed the sales forecasts

ILLUSTRATION   207

below, which extend to August 19X4. (As we shall see shortly, a firm must budget sales beyond the six-month period in order to complete the purchases budget for June.)

Month	Sales Forecast	Month	Sales Forecast
Jan.	$ 400	May	$1,200
Feb.	600	June	800
Mar.	800	July	700
Apr.	1,000	Aug.	800

Sales are obviously seasonal; sales increase through May and then drop off, with May sales budgeted at three times those of January.

Budgeted Income Statement

We wish first to develop a budgeted or pro forma income statement. To do so, additional assumptions are necessary, and we shall assume that the managers of Cross have decided that the following assumptions about cost behavior will provide a good basis for planning:

Cost of goods sold will be 60% of sales dollars.

Other variable costs will be 15% of sales.

Total fixed costs will be $240, of which $120 is depreciation expense.

With this information we can develop the budgeted income statements for the six months.

Exhibit 6-3
Cross Company
Budgeted Income Statements
Six Months Ending June 30, 19X4

	Jan.	Feb.	Mar.	Apr.	May	June	Six-Month Period
Sales	$400	$600	$800	$1,000	$1,200	$800	$4,800
Cost of goods sold (60% of sales)	240	360	480	600	720	480	2,880
Gross profit	160	240	320	400	480	320	1,920
Other variable costs (15% of sales)	60	90	120	150	180	120	720
Contribution margin	100	150	200	250	300	200	1,200
Fixed costs (depreciation, rent, etc.)	40	40	40	40	40	40	240
Income	$ 60	$110	$160	$ 210	$ 260	$160	$ 960

It is not necessary to prepare a separate income statement for each month; a statement for the six-month period would suffice. However, the other budgets will be broken down by month, and the monthly income statements will facilitate the preparation of those budgets.

Purchases Budget

Our next step is to determine what inventory level is considered desirable. In an actual situation, this determination can be extremely complex. We shall assume here that the interested managers have already reached agreement that inventory should be kept at a level of two months' budgeted sales. (That is, the managers have decided that at the end of each month the firm should have on hand enough inventory to cover the sales of the following two months.) An inventory policy related to expected sales levels is in keeping with the fact that a firm stocks in anticipation of sales. Hence, if sales are expected to increase in the next period, inventory should also increase.

You should recognize that as you move from budgeting sales to budgeting inventory and purchases you must also move from considering selling prices to considering costs. (Remember that inventory is carried at cost.) We can determine purchasing requirements for the six months by using the general formula for cost of goods sold (from financial accounting):

$$\text{Cost of goods sold} = \text{beginning inventory} + \text{purchases} - \text{ending inventory}$$

Adding ending inventory and subtracting beginning inventory from both sides, we obtain

$$\text{Purchases} = \text{cost of goods sold} + \text{ending inventory} - \text{beginning inventory}$$

Exhibit 6-4 shows the purchases budget by month for the period.

Exhibit 6-4
Purchases Budget

	Jan.	Feb.	Mar.	Apr.	May	June	Six Months
Ending inventory required	$ 840	$1,080	$1,320	$1,200	$ 900ᵃ	$ 900ᵇ	$ 900
Cost of sales for month (Exhibit 6-3)	240	360	+ 480	600	720	+ 480	2,880
Total requirements	1,080	1,440	1,800	1,800	1,620	1,380	3,780
Beginning inventory	600ᶜ	840	1,080	1,320	1,200	900	600
Purchases required	$ 480	$ 600	$ 720	$ 480	$ 420	$ 480	$3,180

ᵃJune and July cost of sales, 60% × ($800 + $700).
ᵇJuly and August cost of sales, 60% × ($700 + $800).
ᶜInventory at January 1 is assumed to be consistent with company policy.

Note that the sum of the cost of sales for two consecutive months is the inventory required at the beginning of that two-month period. For example, the inventory required at the end of January ($840) is the sum of the cost of sales for February

($360) and March ($480). The circled items show the derivations of the ending inventory for January and April.

The total requirement for any one month is the amount needed to cover that month's sales plus the amount that the company has determined must be on hand at the end of that month. The total requirements can be met from two sources: goods already on hand (beginning inventory) and purchases during the month. Thus purchase requirements are total requirements less beginning inventory. You should work through the budget to be sure you understand the calculations.

The rows for cost of sales and purchases add across to the totals, but the inventory rows and total requirements row do not. The beginning inventory in the total column is the beginning inventory for the six-month period. The ending inventory is the required ending inventory for the last month being budgeted. The final column is the result you would obtain if you were budgeting *only* for the six-month period as a whole.

The inventory account may be reconciled just as is done in financial accounting. The beginning balance is $600, purchases are $3,180, and cost of sales is $2,880, leaving an ending balance of $900. The ending balance, derived as part of the purchases budget, will also be used for the June 30 pro forma balance sheet. The purchases budget is also important in preparing the cash budget.

PURCHASES BUDGET—A MANUFACTURING FIRM

Just as a retailer must budget purchases to meet sales goals and adhere to inventory policy, so a manufacturer must budget production in keeping with expected sales and inventory policy. That is, the manufacturer must *produce* sufficient units to meet the sales goals, while the retailer must *purchase* those units. Moreover, the manufacturer must purchase sufficient raw materials to meet production goals. Thus, both types of firms must plan purchases, and the basic idea of such planning is the same. But the development of the final budget is somewhat more complex for the manufacturer because such a firm must first develop a budget for production in units before developing a purchases budget in dollars. Units must be used first because both variable and fixed costs are associated with the production process, and the presence of the latter makes the use of dollars difficult without an intermediate budget in units.

Suppose that Brandon Company, a manufacturer, wishes to keep an inventory of the firm's product equal to the budgeted sales for the following two months (much like the retailer in the earlier example). Brandon's managers have gathered the following budgeted data for 19X8.

Units of product on hand at December 31, 19X7	200 units
Pounds of material on hand, December 31, 19X7	3,000 pounds

Budgeted sales for the next five months:

January	120 units	April	280 units
February	180 units	May	336 units
March	240 units		

Variable costs of production per unit:	
Materials, 8 lbs. at $0.50	$4.00
Labor	3.00
Manufacturing overhead:	
Fringe benefits	0.40
Power	0.30
Supplies	0.30
Total	$8.00
Fixed costs of production per month:	
Rent of machinery	$ 400
Supervisory salaries	600
Insurance	100
Managerial salaries	800
Total	$1,900

The company has identified its costs as variable or fixed, as did the retailer. But, for the manufacturer, the variable production costs will vary with the number of units produced, not with the number of units sold. A production budget shows the number of units that must be produced each period to meet sales and inventory requirements. The budget appears in Exhibit 6-5.

Exhibit 6-5
Production Budget
(In Units)

	Jan.	Feb.	Mar.	Three Months
Ending inventory required	420	520	616	616
Expected sales	120	180	240	540
Total units required	540	700	856	1,156
Beginning inventory	200	420	520	200
Required production	340	280	336	956

Note that even though a sales forecast is available for the first five months of 19X8, we can prepare a production budget for only the first three months. This is true because the firm's inventory policy for finished units is based on the expected sales for the following two months, and we do not know the expected sales beyond May.

A manufacturing firm rarely buys its materials only as they are needed for production; it usually has a policy regarding how much material should be on hand, just as it has a policy about a desired inventory of finished units. Referring to the original data, we see that the $4 material cost per unit of product consists of eight pounds of material at $0.50 per pound. Let us assume further that the managers of Brandon Company desire to keep a materials inventory equal to 150% of the coming month's budgeted production needs. (It is reasonable to set the inventory policy for materials based on production, not on sales, because materials are needed when the product is made, not when it is sold.)

Exhibit 6-6 shows a budget for materials purchases in January and February. Note that the firm's inventory policy for materials makes it impossible to budget pur-

Exhibit 6-6

Purchases Budget—Materials

	January	February	March
Budgeted production, from Exhibit 6-5	340	280	336
Ending inventory, 150% of coming month's production needs (280 × 8 × 1.5 and 336 × 8 × 1.5)	3,360	4,032	?
Needed for current production, budgeted production × 8	2,720	2,240	2,688
Total pounds of material needed	6,080	6,272	
Beginning inventory	3,000	3,360	
Required purchases, in pounds	3,080	2,912	
Required purchases at $0.50	$1,540	$1,456	

chases for March because such purchases depend on an unknown, the budgeted production for April. This example offers further evidence of the problem that lead times can create, and of the need for planning if the firm is to operate efficiently.

In a retailing firm, the purchases budget is important for the development of a cash budget, since the payments for purchased units are not likely to be made at exactly the time of purchase. In a manufacturing firm, both the production and the materials purchases budgets are important for the budgeting of cash, because it is likely that required payments for materials purchases will not occur at the same time as the payments for other costs associated with production. The development of a cash budget, one of the most important of the schedules included in a comprehensive budget, will be discussed in detail in Chapter 7. At this point you need only to recognize the need for developing purchases (and production) budgets to reflect the lead times required to meet sales goals.

SUMMARY

Comprehensive budgeting is vital to effective planning and control. The comprehensive budget is perhaps the major planning document developed by the firm and consists of a set of financial statements and other schedules showing the expected results for a future period. The development of a comprehensive budget formalizes management objectives and helps coordinate the many activities performed within a single firm.

Sales forecasting is critical to the budgeting process; it underlies all other budgets. Several approaches are used for forecasting sales. The approach adopted depends on the reliability of available data, the nature of the product, and the experience and sophistication of the managers. The sales forecast and assumptions about cost behavior and inventory policy are used to prepare the purchases and expense budgets and a pro forma income statement. A flexible budget allowance is recommended in dealing with variable costs; it is advantageous for subsequent performance evaluation and identifying problems requiring action.

The budgeting process entails numerous behavioral problems, which can be particularly severe if managers do not participate in the development of the budget, or if budget goals are perceived as unachievable. However, used wisely, the budgeting process can help resolve conflicts among managers.

KEY TERMS

capital budgets
comprehensive budget
expected value
expense budget
financial budgets
flexible budget allowance

operating budgets
production budget
purchases budget
sales forecast
static budget

KEY FORMULAS

Budgeted purchases[a]	=	desired ending inventory	+	cost of current sales	−	beginning inventory

Budgeted production, in units	=	desired ending inventory	+	units needed for current sales	−	beginning inventory

[a]For budgeting purchases in a manufacturing firm, "cost of current sales" becomes "cost of units of material needed for current production."

REVIEW PROBLEM

Using the following data for Exempli Company, prepare a budgeted income statement and a purchases budget in units and dollars for January 19X4.

Budgeted sales for January	5,000 units at $20	$100,000
Budgeted sales for February	6,000 units at $20	$120,000
Cost data:		
Purchase price of product		$5 per unit
Commission to salespeople		10% of sales
Depreciation		$2,000 per month
Other operating expenses		$40,000 per month plus 5% of sales

Inventory policy is to maintain inventory at 150% of the coming month's sales requirements. Inventory at December 31, 19X3, is $30,000 (6,000 units at $5), which is less than budgeted.

Answer to Review Problem

Purchases Budget for January 19X4

	Units	Dollars
Desired ending inventory (6,000 × 150%)	9,000	$45,000
Cost of sales	5,000	25,000
Total requirements	14,000	70,000
Beginning inventory	6,000	30,000
Purchases required for the month	8,000	$40,000

Exempli Company
Budgeted Income Statement
for January 19X4

Sales		$100,000
Cost of sales (5,000 units at $5)		25,000
Gross profit		75,000
Variable costs:		
Commissions (10% × $100,000)	$10,000	
Variable operating expenses (5% × $100,000)	5,000	15,000
Contribution margin		60,000
Fixed costs:		
Depreciation	2,000	
Other operating expenses	40,000	42,000
Income		$ 18,000

ASSIGNMENT MATERIAL

Questions for Discussion

6-1 "Why bother with budgets?" Evaluate the following statement: "I suppose that budgets are fine for firms that can plan ahead, but I cannot. Things are too uncertain for me to make plans, and besides, I have to spend my time looking after the day-to-day operations and trying to figure out what is wrong."

6-2 Expense budgeting What would be the major factors to be known in setting the budgeted amounts for the following:
(a) commissions to salespeople
(b) electricity
(c) taxes on land and buildings
(d) taxes on personal property (inventory, machinery, assets other than land and buildings)
(e) charitable contributions
(f) office salaries

6-3 Relationships of selling expenses and sales The chapter suggests that there are disadvantages in budgeting such expenditures as advertising, research and development, and product promotion based on some fixed percentage of sales. What disadvantages do you see if the firm is forecasting: (1) a strong demand for its products during the coming year with a substantial increase in sales over the prior year, and (2) a relatively weak demand for its products with a decline in sales from the prior year?

6-4 Sales forecasting—effects of external events For each of the following situations, indicate what effect, if any, there would be on the sales forecast that you have already prepared. Explain your reasoning.
(a) Your firm makes building materials. The federal government has just announced a new program which is designed to assist low-income families to buy their own homes.

    (b)   Your firm makes toys. The government announces that the economic outlook is better than had been thought. Personal income is likely to increase and unemployment decrease.

    (c)   You make parts for the automobile industry. A strike against your major customer is announced by the head of the union.

    (d)   You process baby food. The number of marriages is expected to drop sharply because of poor economic conditions.

    (e)   You make heating and air conditioning equipment. The prices of electricity, heating oil, and natural gas are expected to rise rapidly.

    (f)   You make insulation for houses and other buildings. The prices of electricity, heating oil, and natural gas are expected to rise rapidly.

    (g)   Your firm is a publisher of college textbooks. Recent statistics show that the numbers of high school seniors and juniors have fallen off from previous years.

    (h)   Your firm makes plumbing pipe from copper. The major source of copper is Chile, which has just gone to war with one of its neighbors.

6-5 Budget requests   Some organizations follow the practice of cutting back all budget requests by some set percentage, ignoring the merits of the specific requests. For example, the total budget for each department may be reduced by 5% or each line item in each department might be reduced by 5%. Explain how this practice could be considered beneficial. Is there any way in which this practice could be considered harmful?

6-6 Six months is already too long   The owner of a retail store tells his controller: "Seems pretty silly to me to make budgets for more than a month or two in advance. You make a purchases budget based on a sales forecast and an inventory policy. Ha! Inventory policies are fine; but you know as well as I do that a month's sales are never exactly what we have forecast, so within a month our actual inventory is different from the budget. All the time we spend putting together budgets for more than two months in advance is a waste." How would you respond to the owner's comments?

6-7 Sales forecasting—value of indicators   The following conversation took place between two company presidents:

    Grant: "We hired a consultant to help us with our sales forecasting and he has really done a good job. As you know, we make ballpoint pen refills and he found that our sales are very closely correlated with sales of refillable pens from four months previous. He says that four months seems to be the average life of the cartridge that most firms use in their original pens. Of course, we don't make pens, but our refills will fit the pens that nearly every firm makes."

    Harrison: We've done the same thing. Our major product is baby bottles and our consultant found that the number of bottles we sell is very closely related to the number of births about a month later. People seem to buy bottles about a month before the baby is born."

Required: Determine which firm seems to be in the better position to forecast its sales. Explain your answer.

Exercises

6-8 Purchases budget (continued in Chapter 7)   The following data refer to the operations of Jordan Company, a retail store.

Sales Forecast—19X9

January	$70,000
February	70,000
March	90,000
April	80,000

Other data:
1. Cost of sales is 60% of sales.
2. Inventory is maintained at one and one-half times budgeted sales for the coming month (at cost).
3. The beginning inventory is $45,000.

Required: Prepare a purchases budget for each of the first three months of 19X9, and for the quarter as a whole.

6-9 Budgeted income statement and purchases budget (continued in Chapter 7)   The following data relate to the operations of Thomas Company, a retail store.

Sales Forecast—19X4

January	$100,000
February	120,000
March	150,000
April	160,000

1. Cost of sales is 40% of sales. Other variable costs are 30% of sales.
2. Inventory is maintained at twice budgeted sales requirements for the following month. The beginning inventory reflects this policy.
3. Fixed costs are $25,000 per month.

Required
1. Prepare a budgeted income statement for the first quarter of 19X4. (Do not prepare separate statements for each month.)
2. Prepare a purchases budget, by month, for the first quarter.

6-10 Budgeting manpower and costs   Kramwer Company has established a policy of having a foreman for every nine workers; whenever the number of foremen divided into the number of workers is greater than nine, a foreman is hired. The firm is expanding output and has budgeted production as follows:

January	4,800 units
February	5,400 units
March	6,100 units
April	6,800 units
May	7,300 units
June	7,500 units

A production worker can produce 100 units per month. Both workers and foremen are hired at the beginning of the month in which they are to be added. Workers are paid $1,500 per month, foremen, $2,800.

Required: Prepare a budget of requirements for workers and for foremen, by month, in number and dollar cost.

6-11   **Purchase budget—units and dollars**   Warner Company expects the following sales by month in units for the first six months of 19X6:

	Jan.	Feb.	Mar.	Apr.	May	June
Sales	1,900	2,500	2,500	2,000	1,900	1,500

The firm has a policy of maintaining an inventory equal to budgeted sales for the following two months. The beginning inventory reflects this policy. Each unit costs $4.

Required
1. Prepare purchases budgets for as many months as you can (a) in units, and (b) in dollars.
2. Explain why you had to stop where you did.

6-12   **Interim period sales forecasts**   Rashad Company has prepared its annual sales forecast, expecting to achieve sales of $650,000. The controller is uncertain about the pattern of sales to be expected by month and asks you to prepare a monthly budget of sales. You collect the following data from last year. The pattern of sales is representative of a normal year.

Month—Prior Year	Sales
January	$22,000
February	23,000
March	20,000
April	28,000
May	36,000
June	45,000
July	52,000
August	66,000
September	68,000
October	70,000
November	40,000
December	30,000

Required: Based on the data given, prepare a monthly sales budget for the first six months of the coming year.

6-13   **Budgeted income statements**   Weinstock Building Supply operates a chain of lumberyards in a large metropolitan area. The sales manager has retained a prominent economist to develop sales forecasting methods to enable the firm to plan better. The economist, for a substantial fee, has developed the following equation that he says will forecast sales quite well based on past patterns of behavior:

$$\text{Monthly sales in dollars} = \$136,000 + \left(\$52 \times \frac{\text{number of building permits}}{\text{issued in prior month}} \right)$$

The sales manager is confused and asks your advice. He presents you with the following data regarding actual and forecast issues of building permits. The forecasts were developed by the Association of Builders in the area and have generally been quite accurate.

March	2,300 (actual)
April	3,000 (forecast)
May	4,500 (forecast)
June	7,100 (forecast)
July	6,500 (forecast)

It is now April 3rd and the sales manager would like forecasts of sales and income for as many months as you can prepare. He also states that cost of goods sold, which is all variable, is 45% of sales. Other variable costs are 8% of sales, and fixed costs are $140,000 per month.

Required: Prepare budgeted income statements for as many months as you can, given the data available.

6-14 Flexible budget and variances   Adams Company makes a single product. Materials for a unit of the product cost $4, labor is $3, and manufacturing overhead is $20,000 per month fixed, plus $5 per unit variable (with production). In one month, production was 18,000 units and costs incurred were as follows: materials $71,800, labor $56,100, variable overhead $89,000, and fixed overhead $20,000.

Required
1. Prepare a flexible expense budget formula.
2. What should costs have been to produce 18,000 units? (Consider each element of cost separately.)
3. What were the variances between actual and budgeted costs?

6-15 Production and purchases budgets   Genware Company makes inexpensive dishes. It expects to sell 20,000 sets in April, 22,000 in May, and 25,000 in June. It keeps inventory of finished sets at twice the coming month's budgeted sales. It requires 20 pounds of material to make a set and keeps an inventory of materials equal to 150% of the coming month's budgeted production needs. At the beginning of April the company had inventories of 37,000 sets of dishes and 410,000 pounds of material.

Required
1. Determine budgeted production for April and for May.
2. Determine budgeted purchases of materials for April.

6-16 Production and purchases budgets   Feemsdel Company manufactures a product that sells for $20 per unit. The manufacturing process requires 5 pounds of material and one and one-half hours of labor to produce one unit of product. The material costs $0.60 per pound and laborers are paid $6 per hour. The company's policies are to maintain an inventory of completed units equal to the sales needs for the next two months, and to maintain an inventory of raw materials equal to one-and-one-half times what will be needed for production for the next month.

At December 31, 19X7, there are 2,200 units of finished products on hand and 10,500 pounds of raw materials on hand. Sales for the first four months of 19X8 have been forecasted at $20,000, $24,000, $28,000, and $26,000.

Required
1. Determine the number of units that should be produced (a) in January, and (b) in February.
2. Determine the budgeted raw material purchases for January (a) in units, and (b) in dollars.

6-17 Modifying a production budget   The sales and production budgets for McPherson Company are shown below. It is now the end of January, during which actual sales were 12,000 units. The sales manager expects the sales for each of the remaining months of the year will also be 20% higher than originally budgeted. She wishes to increase production to take advantage of the higher demand. The firm has a policy of keeping inventory equal to budgeted sales for the following two months. Actual production in January was 14,000 units and the beginning inventory was 30,000 units. Below are budgeted data based on previous estimates:

	Jan.	Feb.	Mar.	Apr.	May	June
Budgeted sales	10,000	12,000	14,000	15,000	14,000	13,000
Budgeted production	14,000	15,000	14,000	13,000	12,000	

Required: Prepare a modified sales budget and production budget through April.

6-18 Budgeting production and purchases   The production manager of Crass Company wishes to maintain an inventory of raw materials equal to budgeted production needs for the next two months. Each unit of product takes five pounds of raw material which costs $2 per pound. Inventory of finished goods is usually maintained at 150% of the following month's budgeted sales. The sales budget for the first six months of the coming year, given in units, is as follows:

Month	Budgeted Sales	Month	Budgeted Sales
January	12,000	April	16,000
February	14,000	May	20,000
March	10,000	June	12,000

As of December 31, there were 170,000 pounds of raw material on hand and 17,000 units of finished product.

Required: Prepare budgets for production and purchases of raw materials in units and pounds, respectively, for as many months as possible.

6-19 Relationships   The following data relate to Habib Company operations for April. No change in inventories is planned.

Budgeted Income Statement
Month of April

Sales (900 units at $50)		$45,000
Variable costs:		
Materials ($5 per unit)	$4,500	
Labor ($7 per unit)	6,300	
Overhead—manufacturing ($4 unit)	3,600	
Selling expenses ($2 per unit)	1,800	16,200
Contribution margin		28,800
Fixed costs:		
Manufacturing	8,000	
Selling and administrative	9,600	17,600
Income		$11,200

Required: Fill in the blanks.

1.   Budgeted production for April is _____ units.
2.   Total variable manufacturing costs for April are $_____.
3.   The sale of an additional 10 units would increase income by $_____.
4.   Total costs and expenses if 920 units were sold would be $_____.
5.   Break-even volume in units is _____.
6.   If variable manufacturing costs increased by $2 per unit, income at 900 units sold would be $_____.
7.   If fixed costs increased by $2,400, and the firm wanted income of $11,200, sales in units would have to be _____.
8.   If ending inventory were to be 20 units higher than beginning inventory, manufacturing costs incurred during the period would be $_____.

6-20   Multiple materials—manufacturing firm   Williams Company expects the following sales by month, in units, for the first eight months of 19X9.

	Jan.	Feb.	March	April	May	June	July	Aug.
Budgeted Sales	1,500	1,800	1,900	2,500	1,900	2,000	2,000	1,800

The company's one product, the Tow, requires two raw materials: Tics and Tacs. Each Tow requires three Tics and two Tacs. Williams follows the policy of having finished goods equal to 50% of budgeted sales for the following two months. Raw material inventories are maintained at 150% of budgeted production needs for the coming month. All inventories at December 31, 19X8, reflect these policies.

Required

1.   Prepare a production budget for Tows for as many months as you can.
2.   Prepare purchases budgets for Tics and Tacs for as many months as you can.

6-21   Budgeted production and purchases   Alco Company makes a single product. It keeps an inventory of finished units equal to budgeted sales requirements for the following two months and inventory of materials equal to twice the coming month's budgeted production requirements. Materials cost $4 per gallon and each unit of product requires 4 gallons of material. Budgeted sales in units are: January 2,000; February 3,000; March 2,800; April 2,500; May 2,600; June 3,000.

Required

1.   Determine budgeted production for March.
2.   Determine budgeted purchases of materials for March, in units and in dollars.

6-22   Smoothing production   Maynard Company makes bathing suits, with its sales falling heavily in the April–June period, as shown by the sales budget below (in thousands).

	January	February	March	April	May	June
Sales	100	100	110	160	200	250

The firm's normal inventory policy has been to have a two-month supply of finished product on hand. The production manager has criticized the policy because it requires wide swings in production, which add to costs. He estimates that per-unit variable manufacturing cost is $3 higher than normal for each unit produced in excess of 180,000 units per month. Maynard's treasurer is concerned that increasing production in the early months of the year would lead to high costs of carrying inventory. He estimates that it costs the firm $0.80 per unit per month in ending inventory, consisting of insurance, financing, and handling costs. He emphasizes that these costs are incremental.

All of the managers agree that the firm should have 450,000 units on hand by the end of April. The production manager wants to spread the required production equally over the four months, while the treasurer believes that the firm should stick to its current policy unless it turns out to be costlier.

Required
1. Prepare a budget of production for January through April following the firm's current policy. Inventory at January 1 is 200,000 units.
2. Prepare a production budget using the production manager's preference.
3. Determine which budget gives lower costs.

6-23 Relationships among sales and production budgets Partially completed sales and production budgets for Firmin Company are shown below. The firm maintains an inventory equal to 150% of the budgeted sales for the coming month. Fill in the blanks.

Sales Budget In Units

Jan.	Feb.	Mar.	Apr.	May	June	July
3,000	3,400	___	___	___	5,800	___

Production Budget (In Units)

	Jan.	Feb.	Mar.	Apr.	May	June
Ending inventory	___	6,300	___	___	8,700	___
Sales	3,000	___	___	___	___	5,800
Total requirements	___	___	___	13,900	___	___
Beginning inventory	___	5,100	___	6,900	___	___
Production	3,600	___	___	7,000	___	5,200

Problems

6-24 Budgeted income statements—expected values Burke Company is preparing its comprehensive budget for 19X7. The sales manager has said that he does not wish to pin down a single estimate of sales, but would prefer to give three forecasts, along with his estimates of the probabilities he attaches to them.

Sales Forecasts	Probabilities
$ 500,000	0.6
$ 800,000	0.3
$1,000,000	0.1

Variable costs are 60% of sales and total fixed costs are budgeted at $250,000.

Required
1. Prepare budgeted income statements based on each of the three forecasts.
2. Prepare a budgeted income statement based on the expected value of sales.

6-25 Budgeting in a C.P.A. firm   Donald Ebit is a certified public accountant practicing in a large city. He employs two staff accountants and two clerical workers. He pays the four employees a total of $6,100 per month. His other expenses, all fixed, for such items as rent, utilities, subscriptions, stationery, and postage are $3,400 per month.

Public accounting is, for most firms, highly seasonal, with about four months (January through April) that are extremely busy, eight months of less activity.

The most relevant measure of volume in a C.P.A. firm is charged hours—the hours worked on client business for which the clients are charged. Mr. Ebit expects his two staff accountants to work an average of 120 charged hours each month during the eight slower months, and 200 hours each per month during the January–April busy season. Clerical personnel work about 600 charged hours each per year and Mr. Ebit works about 1,400. For both the clerical personnel and Mr. Ebit, approximately 40% of their charged hours fall in the four-month busy season.

Mr. Ebit charges his clients $50 per hour for his time, $25 for the time of a staff accountant, and $10 for the time of clerical personnel.

Required: Prepare a budget of revenues and expenses for a year for Mr. Ebit's firm. Separate the budgets for the periods January–April and May–December.

6-26 Deficiencies of high-low method   The assistant controller of Cowden Company has just given you the following equation for developing the monthly flexible expense budget for supplies:

$$\text{Supplies expense} = \$1300 + (\$0.10 \times \text{units produced})$$

She also shows you the data from which she developed the equation.

Month	Units of Production	Supplies Expense
1	17,400	$2,260
2	19,100	3,210
3	11,900	2,760
4	15,300	2,170
5	9,800	2,280

Required
1. Comment on the flexible budget formula developed by the assistant controller.
2. What reasons might there be for the cost incurrence pattern for supplies?

6-27 Sales forecasting—scatter diagram and regression   Ridley Carpet Company has engaged you as a consultant to help in its sales forecasting. After a long discussion with Robert Ridley, president of the firm, you develop the following data.

Year	Housing Units Built (In Thousands)	Sales of Ridley Company (In Thousands)
19X1	1,300	$2,440
19X2	1,400	2,610
19X3	1,900	3,380
19X4	1,500	2,760
19X5	2,000	3,520
19X6	1,600	2,875

Required

1. Develop an equation to be used to forecast sales for Ridley Company. Use a scatter diagram and regression analysis.
2. Mr. Ridley has learned that housing units to be built in 19X7 will be about 1.8 million. What is your forecast for Ridley's sales? Are you relatively confident about your forecast? Why or why not?

6-28 Comprehensive budget (continued in Chapter 7)   The managers of Calco Products Company have been developing information for the comprehensive budget for the coming year. They have decided to use the following estimates and policies for planning.

Sales forecast, in units:	
January	20,000
February	24,000
March	30,000
April	25,000
May	22,000
Selling price	$30 per unit
Material cost	$8 per unit of product
Direct labor and variable overhead	$6 per unit
Variable selling expenses	$2 per unit
Fixed manufacturing costs	$120,000 per month
Fixed S, G, & A expenses	$60,000 per month

The company plans to keep inventory of finished goods equal to budgeted sales for the following two months, and inventory of materials equal to twice budgeted production for the coming month. The December 31 inventories are: finished goods 35,000 units, materials 66,000 units (one unit of material per unit of product).

Required

1. Prepare budgeted income statements for January, February, and the two-month period, using the contribution margin format.
2. Prepare production budgets for January, for February, and for March.
3. Prepare purchases budgets for materials for January and for February.

6-29 Budgeting for a hospital (AICPA adapted)   The administrator of Taylor Memorial Hospital, Dr. Gale, has asked for your assistance in preparing the budget for 19X7, which budget he must present at the next meeting of the hospital's board of trustees. The hospital obtains its revenues through two types of charges: charges for use of a hospital room and charges for use of the operating room. The use of the basic rooms depends on whether the patient undergoes surgery during the stay in the hospital. Estimated data as to the types of patients and the related room requirements for 19X7 are as follows:

Type of Patient	Total Expected	Average Stay in Days	Percentages Selecting Kinds of Rooms		
			Private	Semiprivate	Ward
Surgical	2,400	10	15%	75%	10%
Medical only	2,100	8	10%	60%	30%

Basic room charges are $50, $40, and $30 for private, semiprivate, and ward, respectively.

Charges for use of the operating room are a function of the length of the operation and the number of persons required to be involved in the operation. The charge is $0.15 per man-minute. (A "man-minute" is one person for one minute; if an operation requires three persons for 40 minutes, there would be a charge for 120 man-minutes at $0.15 per man-minute, or $18.) Based on past experience the following is a breakdown of the types of operations to be performed:

Type of Operation	Number of Operations	Average Number of Minutes per Operation	Average Number of Persons Required
Minor	1,200	30	4
Major—abdominal	400	90	6
Major—other	800	120	8
	2,400		

Required

1. Prepare a schedule of budgeted revenues from room charges by type of patient and type of room.
2. Prepare a schedule of budgeted revenues from operating room charges by type of operation.

6-30 Selecting an activity measure   Your company has been having difficulty with overhead costs. Control is poor and differences between budgeted and actual costs are large. The plant manager has asked you to look at the present method of budgeting, based on direct labor hours. Your assistant prepares the following data from the past six months' operations:

Month	Direct Labor Hours	Machine-Hours	Total Overhead Costs
1	8,600	12,000	$38,000
2	9,000	13,200	40,700
3	8,700	14,100	42,800
4	9,300	12,800	41,100
5	10,500	14,700	45,500
6	9,800	13,600	42,600

Required: Prepare a recommendation regarding the activity measure likely to be most useful for budgeting purposes. Support with calculations.

6-31 Inventory policy—carrying costs   The managers for production, sales, and finance of the Steele Company are discussing production and inventory policies. The sales manager would like the firm to increase production in order to stock more units in inventory. The production manager is willing to do so. The financial manager argues that the cost of storing, insuring, and financing the additional inventory would be prohibitive; it costs the firm $4 per month per unit to cover these costs and they are variable with the number of units on hand.

The sales manager states that if inventory were increased by 5,000 units, sales would be 2,000 units per month higher. Contribution margin per unit is $7.

Required

1. What is the value (per month) of the additional sales that would be generated by the increased inventory?
2. What are the additional monthly costs associated with carrying the additional 5,000 units in inventory?
3. What decision should be made regarding production and inventory?

6-32 **Flexible and static budget**   Wilkinson Company prepares budgets for each month of its fiscal year. Budgeted amounts, along with actual results, are shown in reports that are circulated to the managers whose operations are being reported on *and* to their superiors. Excerpts from the report of the latest two months for one production department are given below.

	April			**May**		
	Budget	*Actual*	*Variance*	*Budget*	*Actual*	*Variance*
Production in units	8,000	7,000	1,000	10,000	10,500	(500)
Costs:						
Material	$16,000	$14,600	$1,400	$20,000	$20,800	($800)
Direct labor	24,000	21,600	2,400	30,000	31,300	(1,300)
Indirect labor	4,000	3,900	100	5,000	5,300	(300)
Power	7,000	6,700	300	8,000	8,400	(400)
Maintenance	5,200	4,700	500	6,000	6,200	(200)
Supplies and other	4,600	4,580	220	5,000	5,050	(50)
Total costs	$60,800	$56,080	$4,720	$74,000	$77,050	($3,050)

Required

1. Using the budgeted amounts, determine the fixed and variable components of each cost.
2. Prepare new reports showing in the budget columns the amounts of cost that you would expect to be incurred given the actual production achieved. Use the same format as is shown above.
3. Comment on the desirability of Wilkinson's method of providing information to its managers.

6-33 **Manufacturing cost budget**   Horton Company makes a variety of products, usually in about the same mix. On the average, each unit requires $3 in materials and $2 in variable manufacturing overhead. Direct labor averages $4 per unit up to 100,000 units. Above that level, direct labor rises to $6 per unit for units over 100,000, because of overtime premium. The remainder of manufacturing overhead is step-variable, with the following pattern.

Unit Production	*Other Costs*
Up to 100,000	$230,000
100,001–120,000	245,000
120,001–140,000	275,000

The pattern of these costs reflects increased supervision, utilities, and other costs associated with operating beyond the normal eight-hour day.

Budgeted unit production for the next few months is:

March	90,000
April	115,000
May	130,000
June	105,000
Total	440,000

Required
1. Prepare budgets for manufacturing cost for each month, and in total.
2. What would total production costs be for the four-month period if the company could equalize production at 110,000 units per month?
3. If the company needs only to produce 440,000 units for the entire four-month period, how should it produce by month to obtain the lowest possible total production cost?
4. What reasons might there be for the company to stick to the original monthly production budget despite its higher costs?

6-34 Preparation of flexible budget—high-low, scatter diagram, and regression analysis Hensley Company has used flexible budgets for some years and is now reviewing the rate it uses to budget variable overhead. The following data have been collected:

Month	Direct Labor Hours	Total Overhead
1	7,000	$22,000
2	8,200	24,700
3	9,100	26,700
4	8,600	25,800
5	7,800	23,800
6	7,300	23,000

Required
1. Estimate the variable overhead rate per direct labor hour using the following:
   (a) the high-low method
   (b) the scatter-diagram method
   (c) regression analysis
2. Prepare a formula for budgeting overhead costs.

6-35 Indicators for sales forecasting The following economic indicators and other data might be useful in forecasting sales for certain kinds of firms: income per capita, population, car sales, and rate of unemployment.
   For each of the types of firms listed below, state which, if any, of the listed indicators you think would be relevant in forecasting sales. Indicate briefly why you think each indicator is relevant or irrelevant.
   (a) food company
   (b) maker of outboard motors
   (c) home construction firm
   (d) tire maker
   (e) textbook company
   (f) jewelry maker
   (g) maker of proprietary drugs (drugs sold without prescription)

6-36   Budgeting and behavior   Rydell Company sets sales budgets for its salespeople who are evaluated by reference to whether they achieve budgeted sales. The budget is expressed in total dollars of sales and is $200,000 per salesperson for the first quarter of 19X3. The firm makes two products, for which price and cost data are given below.

	Wiffers	Trogs
Selling price	$10	$15
Variable costs	4	10
Contribution margin	$ 6	$ 5

During the first quarter of 19X3, all salespeople met the $200,000 sales budget. Wiffers are a new product that the firm's president thinks should become a big seller, while Trogs are the standard model that has been popular for some years. The products are sold to different kinds of customers; the customers who have been buying Trogs for years are not expected to buy Wiffers. Customers for Wiffers must be sought out by the salespeople and convinced of the high quality of the product. The $200,000 budgeted sales per person is a fairly high goal, but is attainable.

Required
1. Which product should salespeople stress?
2. Under the circumstances described, which product do you think sold most?
3. If your answers to questions 1 and 2 conflict, what would you suggest be done in the firm's budgeting process?

6-37   Production and purchases budgets—units and dollars   Drummond Company manufactures several products, including a frying pan with a wooden handle. The sales forecasts for the frying pan for the next five months are given below.

	April	May	June	July	August
Budgeted sales	2,500	3,100	2,800	3,500	2,400

Each frying pan requires a blank sheet of iron that Drummond buys from a single supplier and molds into the appropriate shape. The handles are purchased in ready-to-use condition from another supplier. The firm's policy is to keep finished goods inventory at twice the coming month's budgeted sales, blank iron sheets at budgeted production requirements for the coming two months, and handles at budgeted production requirements for the coming month.

Each sheet of blank iron is made into one frying pan and costs $2. Handles cost $0.40. Labor costs for shaping the iron and putting on a handle are $1.50 and variable manufacturing overhead costs are $0.80. Fixed manufacturing costs are $4,500 per month.

At the end of March the firm expects to have the following inventories:

Finished pans	5,300
Blank iron sheets	5,600
Handles	4,600

Required
1. Prepare production budgets for as many months as you can, in units and dollar costs.
2. Prepare purchases budgets in units and dollars for blank iron sheets and handles for as many months as you can.

6-38 Budgeting administrative expenses   The controller of Kaufman Company has asked you to prepare a flexible budget for costs in the purchasing department. It has been determined that the typists in the department can type about 100 lines per hour and the average purchase order has 10 lines. Typists are paid $4 per hour and work a 35-hour week. When there is not enough typing to keep them busy, the typists file and perform other work in the office. There are order clerks who prepare purchase orders to be typed. They are paid $6 per hour for a 35-hour week and generally take 20 minutes to prepare an order for typing. They also work at other tasks when purchase orders are slack. The purchasing agent is paid $300 per week. Supplies, stationery, and so on average $0.40 per purchase order.

Required
1. If normal volume in the purchasing department is 800 orders per week, how many order clerks and typists are required?
2. Based on your answer to question 1, how much slack time do clerks and typists have available to perform other duties?
3. If salaries for clerks and typists, and costs for supplies and stationery are to be budgeted as variable costs, what is the flexible budget formula?
4. What variance from the budget would you expect if 800 orders were processed during one week? (Use the data for personnel requirements developed in question 1.)
5. What is the capacity of the purchasing department given the personnel requirement derived in question 1?
6. What is the flexible budget formula if the personnel requirements in question 1 are treated as fixed costs?

6-39 Sales forecasting, budgeted income, and budgeted production (continued in Chapter 7)   Richards Company manufactures ignition systems used in automobile engines. The firm has developed a forecasting tool that has been successful in predicting sales for the firm. Written in equation form, sales = 80,000 + (0.009 × automobile sales). This coming year's automobile sales are expected to be 8,000,000.

Each system contains material costing $5. Direct labor is $10 per unit and variable manufacturing overhead is $12. Besides the variable manufacturing costs, there are commissions to salespeople of 10% of dollar sales. The system sells for $80 per unit. Fixed costs of manufacturing are $1,200,000 per year; fixed selling and administrative expenses are $1,800,000 per year. Both are incurred evenly over the year.

Sales are seasonal; about 60% of sales are in the first six months of the fiscal year, which begins June 1. The sales forecast by month, in percentages of annual sales, is as follows.

June	5%
July	8
August	9
September	12
October	14
November	12
December	9
January	8

Richards has a policy of keeping inventory of finished product equal to budgeted sales for the next two months. Materials are bought and delivered daily, so no inventory is kept. The inventory of finished product at May 31 is expected to be 19,000 units.

Required

1. Prepare a budgeted income statement for the coming year.
2. Prepare a budgeted income statement for the first six months of the year.
3. Prepare a production budget by month for the first six months, in units.
4. Determine the firm's break-even point (in units) for a year. How might the managers of the firm interpret that information in light of their successful sales predictions using the given formula?

6-40 **Comprehensive budget (adapted from a problem prepared by Professor Maurice L. Hirsch, and continued in Chapter 7)**   Banana City is a wholesaler of bananas and nuts. Mr. Bertram A. Nana, the president of the firm, has asked for your assistance in preparing budgets for fiscal year 19X7, which begins on September 1, 19X6. The following information has been gathered for your use:

1. Sales are expected to be $880,000 for the year, of which bananas are expected to be 50%, nuts 50%.
2. Sales are somewhat seasonal. Banana sales are expected to be $77,000 in November, with the rest spread evenly over the remaining eleven months. Sales of nuts are expected to be $40,000 per month except in October and November when they are expected to be $25,000 per month and in April and May when they are expected to be $35,000 per month.
3. Cost of sales, the only variable cost, is 40% for both products.
4. Inventory of bananas is generally kept equal to a one-month supply. Inventory of nuts is usually held at a two-month supply.
5. Income taxes are 40% of income before taxes.
6. Fixed expenses for the year, all incurred evenly throughout the year, are expected to be as follows:

Rent	$ 24,000	Depreciation	$ 36,000
Insurance	12,000	Interest	6,000
Wages and salaries	120,000	Other fixed expenses	156,000

7. Inventories at August 31, 19X6, are expected to be: bananas, $14,300; nuts, $27,500.
8. The firm expects to sell some land that it owns. The sale, which is expected to have a price of $6,000, will take place in October. The cost of the land on the balance sheet is $8,000.

Required

1. Prepare a budgeted income statement for the fiscal year ending August 31, 19X7.
2. Prepare a budgeted income statement for the first quarter of the fiscal year, by month, and in total.
3. Prepare a purchases budget by product for each of the months of the first quarter of the fiscal year and for the quarter as a whole.

Cases

6-41 **Production budgeting with constraints**   Firms do not commonly hire and lay off workers when moderate changes in production are contemplated. Among the reasons for this are an increased feeling of responsibility to provide regular employment; the potential decline in the available work force if skilled workers left the community permanently because they were laid off; and union contracts providing for guaranteed employment. Under these conditions stable production becomes more desirable. For these same reasons, firms that have high degrees of seasonality may try to stabilize production to keep workers busy all year.

Robertson Company has the following sales forecast by month for the first eight months of 19X5 (in units): 3,000, 3,800, 4,200, 5,000, 5,400, 5,900, 4,800, 4,200.

The work force is now 100 men, who can produce 4,000 units per month. Overtime can be used to increase output by 10%. Since a five-man team works together, workers can be hired only in groups of five. The company's policy is to keep inventory equal to a two-month supply, and the beginning inventory is 6,800 units.

Required: Prepare a production budget for the first six months, including budgeted numbers of workers. Prepare to defend your answer.

6-42   Budgeting step-variable costs   Corman Company manufactures several products using a great deal of machinery. Since it is critical to keep the machines running well, Corman pays a good deal of attention to maintenance. The chief engineer has determined that routine maintenance requires a complete shutdown and cleaning every 200 hours a machine has been running. This job costs $250. Excluding these major cleanings, maintenance costs for ten machines have been as follows for the past eight months. Each machine runs about the same amount of time each month as every other machine.

Month	Hours for 10 Machines	Maintenance Costs
1	2,200	$1,400
2	2,100	1,380
3	1,950	1,260
4	2,000	1,290
5	1,700	1,190
6	2,400	1,505
7	2,300	1,455
8	1,800	1,200

Required

1. Using the high-low method, prepare a flexible budget formula for maintenance costs, excluding the major cleaning at 200 hours.
2. Determine the budgeted cost levels for 1,600 hours and 100-hour intervals up to 2,500 hours, including the major cleaning costs. What can you say about the use of flexible budgets when such costs are present?

CHAPTER 7

FINANCIAL BUDGETING

In Chapter 6 we discussed comprehensive budgeting and illustrated the operating budgets of the total budget package. The financial budgets are equally important to the package. In this chapter we complete the illustration by developing the cash budget and pro forma balance sheet.

We shall also show how financial statement data are used in the preparation of annual budgets and long-term budgets. Finally, we look at the special issues associated with budgeting in not-for-profit entities.

ILLUSTRATION OF CASH BUDGET

We have prepared the budgeted income statement and purchases budget for Cross Company and can now proceed to the cash budget and pro forma balance sheet. Following are the balance sheet as of December 31, 19X3 and the budgeted income statement for the six-month period after that date (from Exhibit 6-3):

Cross Company
Balance Sheet as of
December 31, 19X3

Assets	
Cash	$ 60
Accounts receivable	576
Inventory	600
Plant and equipment	600
Total	$1,836

Equities

Accounts payable (merchandise)	360
Accrued expenses	50
Common stock	1,000
Retained earnings	426
Total	$1,836

Cross Company
Budgeted Income Statement
January 1, 19X4 to June 30, 19X4

Sales	$4,800
Cost of goods sold (all variable, at 60% of sales)	2,880
Gross profit	1,920
Other variable costs (15% of sales)	720
Contribution margin	1,200
Fixed costs (including $120 of depreciation)	240
Income	$ 960

We need the balance sheet at the beginning of the budget period because it shows both resources (assets) that have already been acquired and can be used during the period and liabilities that must be paid during the period. For example, we used the inventory figure at December 31 in preparing the purchases budget.

Cash Receipts

To develop the budgeted income statement we relied on the sales forecasts by month, as follows:

	Jan.	Feb.	Mar.	Apr.	May	June
Sales	$400	$600	$800	$1,000	$1,200	$800

To forecast cash receipts we need more information. Does the company sell on credit or for cash only? How soon do credit customers pay their accounts? Assume that experience (adjusted for any *expected* changes in conditions) indicates that 20% of sales are collected in the month of sale, 48% in the month after sale, and the remainder (32%) in the second month after sale. The beginning accounts receivable consists of $400 of December sales and $176 of November sales. Can you determine what the total sales were for December? for November?

Since 20% of December sales were collected in December, the $400 now in accounts receivable must be 80% of December sales. Thus, December sales were $500 ($400/80%). The $176 still uncollected from November is 32% of November sales, so November sales must have been $550 ($176/32%). The $176 will be collected in January but only $240 (48% of December sales of $500) will be collected in January on December sales. The remaining receivables from December sales, $160 ($500 × 32%), will be collected in February. The ability to recognize relationships among accounts helps understanding of the budgeting process.

We shall first determine cash inflows for the six-month period, before proceeding to cash outflows and the pro forma balance sheet. Exhibit 7-1 is a good general format for budgeting cash receipts from sales.

Exhibit 7-1
Cash Receipts

	Jan.	Feb.	Mar.	Apr.	May	June	Total
Sales for the month	$400	$600	$800	$1,000	$1,200	$ 800	$4,800
Collections from Sales							
20% of total sales for the month	$ 80	$120	$160	$200	$240	$ 160	$ 960
48% of prior month's sales	240	192	288	384	480	576	2,160
32% of second prior month's sales	176	160	128[a]	192	256	320	1,232
Total cash collections	$496	$472	$576	$776	$976	$1,056	$4,352

[a]$400 = total January sales, collected in January, February, and March ($80 + $192 + $128).

The circled items show the pattern of collection of January sales; the total is given below the schedule. Notice that cash receipts increase, but that there is a lag. Cash receipts exceed sales only in January and June, when sales have declined and collections are being made from the prior months in which sales were considerably higher. A firm can run out of cash while its sales are rapidly increasing, because it is very likely spending to pay for the goods to be stocked in advance of sales and is collecting cash well after the point of sale. This situation will become clearer when we examine cash disbursements.

As cash receipts are related to sales, but do not coincide with sales except accidentally, so cash disbursements are related to the incurrence of costs, but do not always coincide. For example, if the firm pays sales commissions in the month after salespeople earn them, the expense and the cash payment would not be the same for any month (unless the amount earned is the same in both months).

Cash Disbursements

The major component of cash disbursements for the Cross Company is payments for purchases. To determine cash payments for purchases, we use the purchases budget developed in Chapter 6 (page 208) and the timing of payments for those purchases. If the company paid cash on delivery of goods, cash payments for purchases would equal purchases in each month. Suppose, however, that Cross Company takes full advantage of the 30-day credit terms extended by its suppliers so that purchases are paid for in the month after purchase. (If Cross were granted 60-day credit, payments would be made in the second month after purchase, and so on.) To derive cash payments it is necessary only to lag payments a month behind purchases, as in Exhibit 7-2.

Exhibit 7-2
Cash Disbursements for Purchases

	Jan.	Feb.	Mar.	Apr.	May	June	Total
Budgeted purchases	$480	$600	$720	$480	$420	$480	$3,180
Payments	$360	$480	$600	$720	$480	$420	$3,060

The January payment is for December purchases as reflected in accounts payable for December 31, 19X3. The other amounts come from the purchases budget developed in Chapter 6 (page 208) and summarized here. Purchases are paid for in the month after purchase, so accounts payable at the end of any month will be equal to that month's purchases. And cash disbursements for purchases will be equal to accounts payable at the beginning of the month, which is the same as accounts payable at the end of the prior month.

Two parts of the cash budget are now complete: cash receipts from sales and cash disbursements for purchases. Other cash disbursements may be determined more easily than those for purchases. You will remember that variable expenses other than cost of sales are 15% of sales. Assume that one-third is paid in the month of incurrence, and two-thirds in the following month. (The portion paid in the month after incurrence could be for commissions to salespersons, who are paid in the first week of a month for the commissions they earned in the previous month.) Thus in each month, cash disbursements related to variable costs will be 5% of that month's sales, plus 10% of the sales of the previous month. A schedule of disbursements, by month, for variable costs appears in Exhibit 7-3.

Exhibit 7-3
Cash Disbursements—Variable Costs

	Jan.	Feb.	Mar.	Apr.	May	June	Total
5% current month's sales	$20	$30	$ 40	$ 50	$ 60	$ 40	$240
10% previous month's sales	50[a]	40	60	80	100	120	450
Total	$70	$70	$100	$130	$160	$160	$690

[a]December accrued expenses.

The total cash disbursements for variable costs ($690) do not correspond with variable costs on the income statement ($720) because of the timing of the payments for variable costs. This difference is explained by examining the Accrued Expenses. The disbursement made in January ($50) was accrued in December (10% × $500 sales in December). This payment is not an expense in 19X4. At June 30, 19X4, $80 is owed for commissions on June sales of $800. The cash disbursement for June commissions is made in July. Total disbursements of $690 include $50 for expenses of 19X3, and do not include $80 of June expense that will be paid in July ($690 − $50 + $80 = $720).

Suppose that the cash component of fixed costs is paid evenly over the six-month period. Depreciation, a noncash expense, is $120 out of the $240 fixed costs, so the cash portion is $120 ($240 − $120), or $20 per month. The complete cash disbursements budget is shown in Exhibit 7-4.

Exhibit 7-4
Cash Disbursements—
All Costs

	Jan.	Feb.	Mar.	Apr.	May	June	Total
For purchases (Exhibit 7-2)	$360	$480	$600	$720	$480	$420	$3,060
Variable costs (Exhibit 7-3)	70	70	100	130	160	160	690
Fixed costs	20	20	20	20	20	20	120
Total	$450	$570	$720	$870	$660	$600	$3,870

Cash Budget

We are now ready to prepare a tentative cash budget. The budget is tentative because we would not know, until after preparing this schedule, whether revisions might be necessary because of potential cash shortages. Such a tentative budget is shown below:

Cash Budget

	Jan.	Feb.	Mar.	Apr.	May	June	Six Months
Beginning balance	$ 60[a]	$106	$ 8	($136)	($230)	$ 86	$ 60
Collections (Exhibit 7-1)	496	472	576	776	976	1,056	4,352
Total available	556	578	584	640	746	1,142	4,412
Disbursements (Exhibit 7-4)	450	570	720	870	660	600	3,870
Ending Balance	$106	$ 8	($136)	($230)	$ 86	$ 542	$ 542

[a]From 12/31/X3 balance sheet, page 230.

The total column covers the six-month period so that the beginning balance is the balance at December 31, 19X3. Although the firm will complete the six months with a good deal more cash than it had at the start of the period, it has budgeted cash deficits in March and April, and a balance of only $8 at the end of February. If the firm had prepared a budget only for the entire six-month period, the managers would not have become aware of the deficits, and plans would not have been made for dealing with the problem. Budgets should therefore be broken down into relatively short time periods.

What could Cross do now? It could consider borrowing cash to tide it over the period during which the deficits appear. It could also reconsider its inventory policy, reduce its purchases, and consequently reduce its needs for cash. But this action might adversely affect sales.

Assume that Cross can borrow cash at 12% interest. If the firm decides to borrow to offset the expected cash deficits, the cash budget must be revised. Assume that any borrowings must take place at the beginning of the month in which they are needed, and that repayments are made at the earliest possible time, which is at the end of a month in which a surplus of cash is budgeted. Under these circumstances, a loan must be outstanding for at least two months. Suppose that borrowings must be in multiples of $10, and that interest is paid at the time of repayment. Assume that the firm has a policy of maintaining a minimum cash balance of $50 at all times. (Many companies maintain a minimum cash balance as a matter of policy. A minimum cash balance is usually established to make room for variations from planned cash flows and unexpected cash requirements.) A revised cash budget appears in Exhibit 7-5.

Exhibit 7-5
Revised Cash Budget

	Jan.	Feb.	Mar.	Apr.	May	June	Six Months
Beginning balance	$ 60	$ 106	$ 58	$ 54	$ 50	$ 78	$ 60
Collections	496	472	576	776	976	1,056	4,352
Total available	556	578	634	830	1,026	1,134	4,412
Disbursements	450	570	720	870	660	600	3,870
(1) Indicated balance	106	8	(86)	(40)	366	534	542
(2) Minimum required cash	50	50	50	50	50	50	50
1 − 2 = (3) Excess (deficit)	56	(42)	(136)	(90)	316	484	492
(4) Borrowings		50	140	90			280
(5) Repayments					(280)		(280)
Interest					(8)^a		(8)
4 + 1 − 5 = (6) Ending balance	$106	58	54	50	78	534	$ 534
Cumulative borrowings		$ 50	$190	$280	$—0—	$—0—	

^{a}12% × 4/12 (four months) × $ 50 = $2.00
12% × 3/12 (three months)× $140 = 4.20
12% × 2/12 (two months) × $ 90 = 1.80
                                 $8.00

The revision of the cash budget produces the need to revise the original budgeted income statement because the original budgeted income statement did not include interest expense.

Revised Financial Statements

A revised budgeted income statement for the six-month period is shown in Exhibit 7 - 6 (page 236). The income statement shows the interest expense necessary to finance the budgeted level of operations. A separate pro forma income statement for the first three months of the period is provided in the exhibit so that you may check your understanding, and because a firm would ordinarily prepare pro forma statements more frequently than once every six months.

Exhibit 7-6
Cross Company
Budgeted Income Statements

	Three Months Ending March 31, 19X4	Six Months Ending June 30, 19X4
Sales	$1,800	$4,800
Cost of goods sold (60% of sales)	1,080	2,880
Gross profit	720	1,920
Other variable costs (15% of sales)	270	720
Contribution margin	450	1,200
Fixed operating costs	120	240
Operating income	330	960
Interest expense	2.40^a	8
Income	$ 327.60	$ 952

^{a}At March 31, loans were outstanding for $190. Accrued interest was:

$$\$ 50 \times 2/12 \times 12\% = \$1.00$$
$$\$140 \times 1/12 \times 12\% = \underline{\quad1.40}$$

Total accrued interest and interest expense $\underline{\underline{\$2.40}}$

A pro forma balance sheet for June 30 is shown in Exhibit 7-7. Here again, a pro forma balance sheet at an interim date—March 31—is included to facilitate your understanding and to recognize normal practice. In this instance, one important reason for having pro forma statements (income statement and balance sheet) prior to the end of the six-month period is that this firm has to obtain a short-term loan. A potential lender would want to see monthly cash budgets and pro forma statements at least each quarter, if not each month. The lender will want information to help it decide whether the firm can repay the loan and will also be interested in whether the management makes good use of budgets. The manager can compare the actual balance sheets at March 31 and June 30 with the pro forma ones as a check on whether operations are proceeding as planned. For example, if the sales forecast proves accurate, but accounts receivable are higher than budgeted, cash inflows from collections would be lower than budgeted. This could be a danger signal; if customers pay less quickly than anticipated, the firm could run into a cash shortage. Additionally, increasing receivables might be a sign that the firm is extending credit to less worthy customers in an effort to boost sales. This could be a costly move: bad debts might increase, and the need for financing might become more acute, as well.

Exhibit 7-7

Cross Company Pro Forma Balance Sheets

Assets	As at March 31, 19X4	As at June 30, 19X4
Cash (from cash budget, Exhibit 7-5)	$ 54	$ 534
Accounts receivable (credit sales for month		
plus 32% of prior month's credit sales)	832	1,024
Inventory (from purchases budget, Exhibit 6-4)	1,320	900
Plant and equipment (beginning balance		
less depreciation for 3 and 6 months)	540	480
Total assets	$2,746	$2,938
Equities		
Accounts payable (from purchases budget,		
Exhibit 6-4)	$ 720	$ 480
Accrued expenses (10% of the month's sales)	80	80
Short-term loan (from cash budget, Exhibit 7-5)	190	0
Accrued interest on loan (Exhibit 7-6)	2.40	0
Common stock (beginning balance sheet, page		
231)	1,000	1,000
Retained earnings (beginning balance plus income		
for period)	753.60	1,378
Total equities	$2,746	$2,938

Minimum-Cash-Balance Policies

The minimum cash balance in our illustration ($50) is, of course, an assumed figure. In actual situations, the chief financial officer of the firm would devote considerable attention to determining this amount. As with almost all decisions that managers must make, there is a trade-off involved, and two conflicting factors must be considered. First, the lower the minimum required balance, the greater the probability that the firm will run out of cash. Remember we are budgeting—dealing with the future and with estimates. If customers pay more slowly than expected, or cash outflows are higher than expected (or include unanticipated expenditures), the firm could run out of cash.

Conflicting with a desire to ensure that the firm has sufficient cash to pay its bills is the fact that the firm's cash maintained in a business checking account earns no return. Keeping a high cash balance is costly because the firm *could* be investing the cash elsewhere to earn additional income or, perhaps, saving interest costs by retiring outstanding debt. The lost income (or savings foregone) that accompanies a high cash balance is an opportunity cost, and the manager must weigh carefully the conflicting objectives and decide on a reasonable compromise.

There are some sophisticated techniques, as well as some rules of thumb, for approaching the problem of determining an optimal minimum cash balance. For now it is enough to say that many firms will just set a policy of carrying cash equal to, for example, budgeted cash disbursements for the coming two weeks or month. Under such a policy, the firm would have different minimum required balances at different times, depending on budgeted disbursements. You will study closely the important topic of determining minimum cash balances in your financial management course(s).

Concluding Comments

Now that we have presented all the statements and schedules that make up the comprehensive budget we can point out other advantages that accrue from the budgeting process.

The cash budget and pro forma balance sheets are a basis for asset management. The managers can see that a large amount of cash will be available at the end of June and can begin to look for profitable uses for this cash. At the very least, the firm can buy marketable securities like government bonds and earn safe, though low, returns. (*Idle* cash earns *no* return and should be put to some use in the business, or paid to stockholders as dividends.)

Knowing well in advance that extra cash will be needed, the firm is more likely to be able to find financing to carry it over the months in which deficits are budgeted. It will be able to explain to potential lenders why it needs the money and how a loan will be repaid. If the firm waits until its cash balance is precariously low before seeking a loan, it may have to pay a higher interest rate or it may not get a loan on any terms.

The budgets are interrelated; the cash budget, which is prepared next to last, just before the pro forma balance sheet, shows that the previously prepared pro forma income statement must be modified to include interest expense. The original profit goal of $960 cannot be achieved. The firm must either seek short-term financing, attempt to get along with less inventory, or take some other action to ensure that it does not run out of cash, injure its credit rating, or go bankrupt.

Our example is much simpler than would be the case in practice. If a company's experience indicates that some portion of its credit sales will never be collected (become bad debts), the receipts budget would be prepared to reflect only the expected collections. There could, and probably would, be some special receipts and disbursements. For example, many firms receive interest or dividends on some investments, and, as was mentioned earlier, there are many expenses, such as taxes and insurance, that are not paid monthly. In addition, a firm may be obligated to make periodic repayments of outstanding long-term debt.

Perhaps the single, most commonly found item that is missing from the example budget is planned expenditures for new, long-lived assets. Because such expenditures are usually relatively large, their inclusion is critical if the budget is to fulfill its functions of identifying the timing of financial needs and providing as realistic as possible a picture of planned activities. Once managers have decided that certain major investments are to be made, it is, of course, simple to incorporate the expenditures into the cash budget. Making those decisions is not quite so simple, and the next two chapters consider the analyses that managers use to make them. At this point, you need only recognize that a firm's budget would not be complete without consideration of planned expenditures for new assets, as well as the firm's plans for financing those expenditures.

The firm in the illustration does not do any manufacturing. Chapter 6 shows that development of a budget for a manufacturer is more complex than for a nonmanufacturer, but that the principles are virtually the same. For example, as we showed in Chapter 6, the production budget for Brandon Company, a manufacturer, is very similar to the purchases budget for a retailer. If we know when the costs of production are paid, we can easily compute cash requirements for production. Let us continue the example started on page 209, with Brandon showing a production budget as follows:

Month	No. of Units Produced
January	340
February	280
March	336

The breakdown of production costs was as follows: materials at $4 per unit, other variable costs at $4 per unit, and fixed costs of $1,900.

Let us deal with the simplest of the assumed situations for Brandon Company, where materials are bought as needed (no inventory is maintained) and let us assume also that materials are paid for in the month after purchase. All other production costs requiring cash are paid in the month incurred. Assume that production in December was 300 units. (Why must we make some assumption about December production?) The budget for cash disbursements for manufacturing costs would be as follows:

	Jan.	Feb.	Mar.
Units produced	340	280	336
Cash disbursements:			
Materials ($4 × prior month's production)	$1,200	$1,360	$1,120
Other variable costs ($4 × current production)	1,360	1,120	1,344
Fixed costs	1,900	1,900	1,900
Totals	$4,460	$4,380	$4,364

The totals would be included in the computation of total disbursements for the cash budget. The remainder of the budget package would be completed accordingly.

In principle there is little difference between the budgets for the retailer and the manufacturer. In practice, the manufacturer's budget is likely to be more complicated. For example, some production costs may not require cash outlay (depreciation). Also the materials used for production may be purchased in advance of production needs. In such a situation the cash disbursements for materials will be determined by a separate materials-purchases budget, as was the case in the example on page 211.

ANNUAL AND LONG-TERM BUDGETS

The techniques of financial statement analysis can assist managers in budgeting for longer periods of time and in assessing long-term asset requirements and financing requirements—long-term debt and stockholders' equity. "Long term" usually means a period of more than one year.

Asset Requirements

We have shown how operating and financing budgets relate to each other in the short term. Using budgeted sales and relationships of certain current assets to sales, we developed budgets of purchases and pro forma balance sheets showing budgeted amounts of cash, accounts receivable, and inventory. What was shown on the asset side of these balance sheets was essentially a statement of asset requirements—the amounts of various assets required to enable the firm to meet its goals of sales and income. The firm might have to reconsider its sales and profit goals if it could not obtain the financing needed to carry its planned levels of assets.

Managers make similar analyses when developing **long-term budgets.** If the firm forecasts increasing sales, it must also plan for the assets that will support the planned level of sales. Sales can seldom be increased significantly without having to stock more inventory, provide additional production capacity, and allow receivables to increase. In addition, the desired minimum cash balance will probably increase with higher sales volume.

In the long term, the planned levels of sales usually dictate the necessary levels of assets. Thus, we shall be using ratios of various assets to sales to determine required amounts of those assets. Recognize, however, that the analyses undertaken and numbers used for long-term budgeting are less precise than when budgeting for the shorter term. Moreover, there is more opportunity for circumstances to change. Managers must make allowances for changes in selling prices, purchase costs, and general economic conditions, which changes are extremely hard to predict over relatively long periods of time. The predictions made are more general, with managers trying to see what the firm's needs will be in broad terms. As time passes, managers refine their budgets of asset needs.

Financing Requirements

A firm requires financing, in the form of liabilities or stockholders' equity, because it has assets that are used to generate sales. The need for assets creates the need for financing—the items listed on the equity side of the balance sheet. The elements on the equity side of the balance sheet are often referred to as the *sources* of the elements on the asset side. As the need for assets increases because of increased sales, so does the need for sources to finance the required assets. A few sources of financing are available almost automatically. For example, most firms do not pay cash on delivery of merchandise; they incur a liability for accounts payable. When a vendor does not demand immediate payment for the goods sold to the firm, it is providing a source of financing. The firm does not pay cash on receipt of goods, so it has, in effect, obtained a short-term loan—a source of financing. Similarly, if the firm earns income and does not distribute assets in an amount equal to net income, retained earnings will increase. Increases in retained earnings are also sources of financing.

Most firms cannot meet all financing needs through funds provided by operations and trade creditors. Cross Company used short-term credit. However, firms cannot use short-term loans too liberally. If working capital (current assets − current liabilities) and the current ratio (current assets/current liabilities) get too low, creditors will be reluctant to lend to the firm. Thus, firms will seek more permanent financing.

For more permanent financing, firms issue long-term debt or additional stock. A growing firm generally requires higher and higher levels of assets to support its increased sales and therefore needs more financing than a firm that is not growing. Sometimes the goals and objectives expressed in a budget cannot be met because the means are not available; such means include productive capacity, personnel, and availability of materials, as well as financing. A firm might not be able to obtain the loan needed to support its short-term requirements and would therefore have to scale down its purchases of goods; this could, in turn, reduce sales and profits. The same situation occurs in long-term budgeting. The firm might not be able to obtain the long-term financing to support the asset levels believed to be necessary to reach the levels of sales projected.

In most cases, managers find that advance planning is needed to obtain financing. For example, potential long-term lenders might demand that the borrower maintain some particular minimum ratio of equity capital to long-term debt. Thus, the firm might have to seek new stock financing before it is able to secure additional long-term debt.

Illustrations of Annual and Long-Term Budgets

Two types of procedures are used in budgeting for long periods: those that are used for a one-year period and those that are more appropriate for three- to five-year periods broken down into annual periods. Differences between the two types are primarily matters of detail; the composition of assets and equities for a one-year budget is more detailed than for longer periods.

Following is a set of financial statements for the Style Shop, a retailer of men's and women's clothing. The balance sheet shows percentages that each asset and two of the current liability items bear to sales. These percentages are used to develop the pro forma balance sheet as of the end of the coming year.

Style Shop

Income Statement

for Year Ending December 31, 19X3

Sales	$400,000
Cost of goods sold (60% of sales)	240,000
Gross profit	160,000
Other variable costs (20% of sales)	80,000
Contribution margin (20% of sales)	80,000
Fixed costs	30,000
Income before income taxes	50,000
Income taxes (40% rate)	20,000
Net income	$ 30,000

Style Shop
Balance Sheet
as of December 31, 19X3

			Item as Percentage of Sales in 19X3
	Assets		
Current assets:			
Cash	$ 25,000		6.25%
Accounts receivable	60,000		15.0
Inventory	80,000		20.0
Total current assets		$165,000	41.25%
Fixed assets:			
Building and equipment	120,000		30.0
Less: accumulated depreciation	60,000		15.0
Total fixed assets		60,000	15.0
Total assets		$225,000	56.25%
	Equities		
Current liabilities:			
Accounts payable	$ 40,000		10.0%
Accrued expenses	10,000		2.5
Accrued income taxes	15,000		
Short-term loan	30,000		
Total current liabilities		$ 95,000	
Long-term bank loan (6%)		30,000	
Total liabilities		125,000	
Stockholders' equity:			
Common stock	60,000		
Retained earnings	40,000		
Total stockholders' equity		100,000	
Total equities		$225,000	

We are assuming that the relationships in 19X3 will hold for 19X4. If available information suggested that this would not be the case, managers could easily make appropriate adjustments. For instance, if variable costs as a percentage of sales were expected to increase or decrease, the new percentage would be used in the preparation of the pro forma income statement.

First, we prepare a budgeted income statement for 19X4 (page 243) based on a sales forecast of $440,000, a 10% increase in sales over 19X3.

Assume for the present that the firm will not pay a dividend in 19X4; thus, it is possible to determine the retained earnings on the pro forma balance sheet as $74,800 ($40,000 beginning balance plus $34,800 net income).

All the items in the asset section of the pro forma balance sheet at the end of 19X4 can be computed by taking their percentages of sales for 19X3 and multiplying these percentages by 19X4 sales of $440,000.

Style Shop
Budgeted Income Statement
Year Ending December 31, 19X4

Sales	$440,000
Cost of goods sold (60% of sales)	264,000
Gross profit	176,000
Other variable costs (20% of sales)	88,000
Contribution margin (20% of sales)	88,000
Fixed costs	30,000
Income before income taxes	58,000
Income taxes (40% rate)	23,200
Net income	$ 34,800

We have now established asset requirements based on the 19X3 relationships of assets to sales. How much financing is available for these assets? We assume that current liabilities for accounts payable and accrued expenses will also bear their historical relationships to sales. This assumption is a bit weak for accounts payable, because one might expect payables to vary with purchases and not sales; however, because inventory is increasing in the same percentage as sales, we can reasonably expect that accounts payable will do likewise. If inventory is expected to increase by 10%, purchases will also be 10% higher in 19X4 than they were in 19X3. We have no information about 19X3 purchases and will assume, for simplicity, that 19X4 purchases are 10% more than those of 19X3.

Such a simplifying assumption about accrued income taxes would not be reasonable. This liability will depend on the net income of the firm and the amounts that are paid to the government during the year. (Firms pay estimated taxes throughout the year, much as individuals have taxes withheld from their paychecks.) A reasonable assumption would be that accrued income taxes at December 31, 19X4 will bear the

Style Shop
Partial Pro Forma Balance Sheet
as of December 31, 19X4

Assets			Percentage of 19X4 Sales
Current assets:			
Cash	$ 27,500		6.25%
Accounts receivable	66,000		15.0
Inventory	88,000		20.0
Total current assets		$181,500	41.25%
Fixed assets:			
Building and equipment	132,000		30.0
Accumulated depreciation	66,000		15.0
Net fixed assets		66,000	15.0
Total assets		$247,500	56.25%

same relationship to net income as they did at December 31, 19X3. Accrued income taxes at the end of 19X3 were 50% of 19X3 income ($15,000/$30,000), so they would be $17,400 at the end of 19X4 (50% × $34,800). The short-term loan was paid during 19X4.

Assuming that long-term debt and common stock remain the same, we can now fill in the available sources of financing on the equity side of the pro forma balance sheet as below. At this point, the balance sheet amounts are only tentative because the firm requires additional sources of financing if it is to have the asset amounts already derived. The equity side of the balance sheet would, at this stage, equal the asset side only by chance.

Style Shop
Pro Forma Statement of
Available Equities as of December 31, 19X4

Current liabilities:		
Accounts payable	$44,000	
Accrued expenses	11,000	
Accrued income taxes	17,400	
Total current liabilities		$ 72,400
Long-term bank loan		30,000
Total liabilities		102,400
Stockholders' equity:		
Common stock	60,000	
Retained earnings	74,800	
Total stockholders' equity		134,800
Total available equities		237,200
Total assets required		247,500
Difference—financing required		$ 10,300

Testing the firm's tentative plans has revealed that required assets are greater than available equities, given the cash balance desired and the assumptions regarding other balance-sheet items. What now? There are several options. The deficiency in equities could be offset by reducing the desired cash balance from $27,500 to $17,200. Total assets would be reduced to $237,200, matching total available equities. (This is what would occur if no other action were taken.) Or, management might decide to reduce other assets (inventory, for example) or postpone purchasing fixed assets. The firm might also obtain additional long- or short-term financing.

The first two suggestions could prove unwise. A cash balance of $17,200 could be too low for safety, and reducing other asset requirements could adversely affect sales in 19X4 or later. Seeking additional long-term financing may prove desirable, or it may not, but the manager now knows that if the assumptions are borne out by experience, he or she must take some action to prevent the cash balance from becoming too low. There is no provision for dividends. A dividend payment would reduce cash and retained earnings in equal amounts, thus creating an even greater strain on cash requirements.

This balance sheet is not being prepared completely on expected transactions. The objective was to determine what, if any, additional financing must be secured in order to have $247,500 in total assets at December 31, 19X4. The procedures used are similar to those used in developing the month-by-month cash budget, where a tentative budget is prepared and revision is required because of deficits. Cross Company's initial cash budget (page 234) allowed us to determine how much short-term financing was needed to operate as we wished. The same holds true when budgeting for longer periods using the broader approach of the Style Shop. If available equities exceed required assets, the difference is an increase in cash over the amount budgeted. This excess could be used to reduce debt, pay dividends, or make investments in marketable securities that will earn interest.

In an actual situation, the managers of a firm would probably have developed many relationships for use in budgeting, sometimes much more sophisticated than those shown here. The material presented here is introductory.

Long-Term Planning

In the previous section the firm had options for financing anticipated requirements for assets. If long-term financing were sought, there were two major alternatives—debt and equity. The choice can be critical. A poor decision is difficult to correct because long-term debt or equity cannot be issued frequently.

The choice between debt and equity financing is similar to that between fixed and variable costs. Debt financing requires periodic interest payments and, probably, periodic repayment of principal. These periodic payments can cause bankruptcy if the firm does not generate sufficient cash inflows to service the debt. Equity financing relates to variable costs in that the payments for equity capital (dividends) can be expected to vary to some extent with income; investors generally expect to receive dividends. However, equity financing does not *require* periodic payments. If sufficient cash is not available, no dividend has to be paid. Consequently, equity financing is less risky to the firm than debt financing.

Judicious use of debt can increase the return earned by stockholders. You will remember from the discussion of cost structures that if revenues are rising, a firm with a preponderance of fixed costs will show a faster increase in profits than one with a large proportion of variable costs. The question, then, is usually not *whether* to use debt, but how much to use. Finding the answer to this question is the province of managerial finance. The point to understand here is how the budgeting process can be used in developing and assessing the financial strategy of the firm. The proportion of debt that a firm can carry depends largely on the same factors that govern the desirable proportions of fixed and variable costs—namely, expected levels of revenues, stability of revenues, and managerial attitudes toward risks (see Chapter 3).

One way to develop long-range financing plans is to predict asset requirements, determine available financing from current liabilities and existing stockholders' equity, find an acceptable amount of long-term debt, and finally determine whether sufficient equities are available from these sources. If not, there is a **financing gap,** a difference between asset requirements and available equities. This gap must be filled with additional equity, or debt and equity, in a mix considered desirable.

In the illustration that follows, expenditures for fixed assets are also incorporated in the budget.

Illustration

The process of long-term financial planning is illustrated in this section, based on the following data, assumptions, and policies of the Klep Company.

Sales forecast in 19X4	$ 800,000	Current asset requirements are expected to be 30% of sales budgeted for the following year.
19X5	$1,000,000	
19X6	$1,300,000	
19X7	$1,700,000	Net fixed assets are expected to be 75% of sales budgeted for the following year.
19X8	$2,100,000	
Stockholders' equity		Depreciation is 10% of beginning of year net fixed assets.
12/31/X3	$ 412,000	
Net fixed assets		Desired current ratio of 3 to 1, so that current liabilities cannot exceed one-third of current assets.
12/31/X3	$ 600,000	
Net income is expected to be 10% of sales over the period of the forecast.		
		Desired ratio of long-term debt to equity of 0.5 to 1 (long term cannot exceed 50% of stockholders' equity).
Dividends of 40% of net income will be paid each year.		

These data are the bases of Exhibits 7-8 (page 247) and 7-9 (page 248) which determine year-by-year financing requirements and required expenditures for fixed assets. Exhibit 7-8 shows the analysis for 19X4 and 19X5 and how the numbers were derived. See if you can complete the rest of the table. (Answers appear in Exhibit 7-9.) Such a schedule gives the manager an idea of future financing needs, as well as future asset requirements. A plan can now be devised for seeking additional debt and equity financing to satisfy line (13), "Additional requirements." It is generally expensive and undesirable to obtain equity financing frequently; therefore the firm might obtain funds from a large issue of common stock in 19X4, an issue that would enable it to finance without additional debt until 19X8 or so. Funds received in excess of the amounts currently needed might be invested or used to retire debt. As needs become more pressing, additional debt could be issued up to the limit prescribed by the 0.5 to 1 debt/equity ratio.

BUDGETING IN NOT-FOR-PROFIT ENTITIES

Not-for-profit entities, especially governmental units, make extensive use of budgeting, but the budgeting process is not usually of the type described earlier. First, such entities are likely to budget on the basis of cash flows (expenditures and receipts) as opposed to revenues and expenses. Second, the process is more likely to begin with expenditures as opposed to receipts. That is, in most cases, the problem will be to determine what receipts are required to support the budgeted level of expenditures, as opposed to what costs will be incurred as a result of the budgeted level of revenues.

Budgets for not-for-profit entities are not usually as geared to activity levels as are budgets for businesses. Nevertheless, some kinds of activity analysis might be used in determining budget allowances for a particular category. For example, a university might budget faculty positions by applying some formula based on student enrollment.

Exhibit 7-8

Financing Requirements for Klep Company

(In Thousands of Dollars)

		19X4	19X5	19X6	19X7
	(1) Sales	$800	$1,000	$1,300	$1,700
(1) × 10%	(2) Net income	80	100		
(2) × 40%	(3) Dividends	32	40		
(2) − (3)	(4) Add to stockholders' equity	$ 48	$ 60		
(1) for next year × 30%	(5) Current assets required	$300	$390		
(5) ÷ 3	(6) Permissible current liabilities	100	130		
(5) − (6)	(7) Working capital to be financed from long-term sources	200	260		
(1) for next year × 75%	(8) Net fixed assets required	750	975		
(7) + (8)	(9) Total long-term financing required	950	1,235		
	(10) Stockholders' equity [prior year plus (4)]	460	520		
(10) × 50%	(11) Permissible long-term debt	230	260		
(10) + (11)	(12) Total available long-term financing	690	780		
(9) − (12)	(13) Additional requirements	$260	$ 455		
(8) + year's depreciation − beginning-of-year fixed assets	(14) Expenditures for fixed assets	$210	$ 300[a]		

[a] $975 + ($750 × 10%) − $750 = $300

Thus, an academic department might be given one position for each 300 credit hours expected to be taught. If the department is expected to teach 2,800 credit hours during the coming year, it would be authorized nine and one-third positions (2,800/300). The one-third position would probably be filled by part-time instructors.

On the revenue, or receipt, side, budgeting by governmental and other not-for-profit entities could be relatively simple or quite complex. School districts and some municipalities like towns and cities rely chiefly on property taxes for their revenues. Property taxes are levied based on the assessed valuation of real property (land and buildings) in the area. Once the entity has determined the total assessed valuation, it can set the tax rate by dividing the required revenues by the assessed valuation. If a school district requires $4,580,000 in revenues and the assessed valuation of property in the district is $54,000,000, the rate would be 0.08482 ($4,580,000/$54,000,000), which is $84.82 per $1,000 of assessed value. You should note that the required revenue is determined on the basis of the budgeted expenditures, which partially explains the need for careful planning and monitoring of budgeted expenditures.

For governmental units that depend heavily on income and sales taxes, as do most states, the determination of required tax rates would be more complex. Estimates of total incomes subject to the income tax and of transactions subject to the sales tax would be required. Forecasting methods such as those described in Chapter 6 may

Exhibit 7-9
Financing Requirements for Klep Company
(In Thousands of Dollars)

		19X4	19X5	19X6	19X7
	(1) Sales	$800	$1,000	$1,300	$1,700
(1) × 10%	(2) Net income	80	100	130	170
(2) × 40%	(3) Dividends	32	40	52	68
(2) − (3)	(4) Add to stockholders' equity	$ 48	$ 60	$ 78	$ 102
(1) for next year × 30%	(5) Current assets required	$300	$ 390	$ 510	$ 630
(5) ÷ 3	(6) Permissible current liabilities	100	130	170	210
(5) − (6)	(7) Working capital to be financed from long-term sources	200	260	340	420
(1) for next year × 75%	(8) Net fixed assets required	750	975	1,275	1,575
(7) + (8)	(9) Total long-term financing required	950	1,235	1,615	1,995
	(10) Stockholders' equity [prior year plus (4)]	460	520	598	700
(10) × 50%	(11) Permissible long-term debt	230	260	299	350
(10) + (11)	(12) Total available long-term financing	690	780	897	1,050
(9) − (12)	(13) Additional requirements	$260	$ 455	$ 718	$ 945
(8) + year's depreciation − beginning-of-year fixed assets	(14) Expenditures for fixed assets	$210	$ 300	$397.5[a]	$427.5[b]

[a]$1,275 + ($975 × 10%) − $975 = $397.5
[b]$1,575 + ($1,275 × 10%) − $1,275 = $427.5

be used, and individual states may develop and use very sophisticated forecasting models.

The problems of developing the receipts budget for nongovernmental not-for-profit entities are probably more related to those of business entities. The variety of such entities rivals the variety of business entities, and the need for forecasts of revenue-related factors is no less. For example, tuition charges in a private school must be set by utilizing forecasts of enrollments and contributions. The various service charges of a hospital must be established by forecasting expected utilization. All the forecasting methods discussed in Chapter 6 are used in making such forecasts.

Governmental units like towns, states, school districts, and the federal government usually require voter or legislative approval of their budgets. Once adopted, the budget must be strictly adhered to; overspending is often illegal. In addition, budget authorizations tend to be on a line-by-line basis. That is, specific amounts are authorized for specific categories of expenditures, such as salaries, equipment, supplies, travel, postage, etc. (The detail in such budgets can be overwhelming, with specified amounts for categories such as Grade II Typists and Grade IV Carpenters.) The budgeting process used in most governmental units tends to have two major disadvantages in practice. The first relates to the line-by-line approval procedure, and the second relates to the ways of arriving at the amounts for each line.

Because of the line-by-line approval, individual managers within a governmental unit often cannot exercise discretion in how they use the budgeted funds to achieve the expected objectives. The managers are usually not allowed to increase spending on one item even if they can make equivalent decreases in the spending on other items. This inflexibility can lead to actions inconsistent with the objectives of the entity. For example, suppose that an accounting instructor in a public university is invited to a worthwhile seminar on a contemporary accounting topic; the dean and faculty are in favor of the trip but the travel budget is exhausted. Even if funds remain in the budget allowances for supplies, or telephone, or secretarial help, the trip cannot be authorized. Such a situation could occur even if the receipts budget had been devised to cover the total budgeted expenditures. The problem lies in the concentration on individual items and types of cost rather than on the objectives to be accomplished.

A further problem that can result from line-by-line approval is that it tends to encourage the setting of current budget allowances based on prior year's (or an average of prior years') budget allowances or actual expenditures for each item. This general approach is called **incremental budgeting.** Under this approach, each department might be given a 5% increase (or decrease) in some or most of its line items. In a somewhat broader application of incremental budgeting, each department might be given a 5% increase (or decrease) and allowed to spread the total increase (or decrease) over whatever items are available. Either variation ignores the question of objectives. More important, either variation assumes that the increased or decreased benefits of changes in one segment of the total entity are equal to the increased or decreased benefits of any other segment. Further, when the current budget allowance is based on prior expenditures, there is a tendency to spend right up to the allowance in order to avoid cuts in the next period's budget. (The media have been known to report particularly interesting examples of such actions, as, for example, an end-of-year purchase of a five-year supply of toilet tissue or waste baskets.)

We hasten to point out that the use of line budgeting and incremental budgeting is not limited to not-for-profit entities; many businesses also use these techniques, especially in areas of discretionary spending, like employee training, and some general and administrative areas.

Recent years have seen increasing attention focused on the problems of budgeting in governmental and other not-for-profit entities. Two alternative budgeting approaches, zero-based budgeting and program budgeting, discussed in the next sections, have been suggested as possible means of alleviating some of the problems.

Zero-Based Budgeting

Strictly interpreted, **zero-based budgeting** implies that a manager must justify every dollar that he or she requests in a budget proposal for any given year. Past budget allowances are irrelevant and the manager must start from scratch to convince higher-level managers that the current request is necessary. In a strict but practical application of the zero-base concept, each budget unit develops its budget request as a series of (three, or perhaps more) **decision packages.** The most basic of the unit's services would constitute the first package, and incremental packages would represent higher levels of service and/or additional services. A critical aspect of the decision packages is that each is associated with a *definable* level or quantity of services.

Higher level managers will perform cost/benefit analysis and, of course, exercise their judgment about the organization's needs, to evaluate and rank the packages from all units. The final budget, then, might include the basic packages from all budget units, plus some incremental packages. This approach helps to circumvent any assumption that increased (or decreased) expenditures in all units are equally beneficial (or harmful) to the entire organization. Moreover, forcing managerial review of even the most basic functions of a budget unit may help to show that some budget unit has outlived its usefulness. (That is, managers may conclude, after reviewing all the decision packages and considering the quantity of potentially available resources, that even the most basic service level of a particular budget unit contributes less to achieving desired goals than do higher-than-basic service levels in other units.)

Because a full review of each and every budget request every year is very costly, most organizations require such a review of some, or all, budget units only every few years. But the goals of these periodic reviews are the same as under the more strict application of the zero-base concept: to make sure that there is still a need to spend money for a particular service, and that the money being spent is being spent wisely. **Sunset legislation,** which requires that a program or regulatory agency approved by the legislature receive a full, regular review and be dropped if it has served its purpose, is a variation of this second approach to the implementation of zero-based budgeting.

Program Budgeting

Program budgeting requires that a budget indicate not only what the requested funds are to be spent for, but also *why* the funds are to be spent. A program budget emphasizes the desired results of the unit's efforts and normally provides the unit's manager with considerable discretion in shifting expenditures from one category to another as long as the shift will increase the likelihood of achieving the desired results. For instance, a traditional budget for a school district would probably show the objects of the district's expenditures, such as teachers' salaries, textbooks, supplies, etc. A program budget for the district would also show expenditures by such categories as reading, mathematics, remedial work, student activities, and support services. Similarly, a program budget for a police department might show amounts requested for crime prevention, juvenile work, and detection.

Budgeting by program should permit the people who supervise the spending (the citizens, the contributors, etc.) to make better decisions regarding the use of resources. One feature of program budgeting that should be particularly beneficial is that managers making budget requests are expected to be able to state clearly what would happen if their requests were cut by, say, 10%. Thus, the director of parks and recreation for a city should be in a position to say that such a cut would reduce the hours that a swimming pool would be open, or require that grass be cut every ten days instead of once a week. This feature of program budgeting is, in its result, somewhat similar to what would be accomplished with zero-based budgeting, since different levels of service are associated with each level of requested funding.

The increasing interest in and use of program and zero-based budgeting probably owes much to an increasing public demand for accountability from governmental and other not-for-profit organizations. Taxpayers appear to have become dissatisfied with the performance of some governmental units; donors to charitable causes have expressed concern about the proportion of contributed funds devoted to administrative expenses. Program budgets that specify goals clearly allow people to see where their money is going and, eventually, to see whether or not it was spent effectively. (If a school district requests money "to raise the average reading levels of its pupils," board members can later see whether the levels rose.)

Both program and zero-based budgeting are applicable to business entities as well as not-for-profit organizations. For example, corporate executives have become more concerned with the productivity of research and development, general administration, and other such activities, and some have adopted variations of these alternative approaches to budgeting for all or some portions of their organizations. In the typical business use, however, program budgets are developed in addition to, rather than as a substitute for, the more traditional budgets, and zero-based budgeting would include an expenditure request identified as the current level of service.

SUMMARY

Financial budgets, like operating budgets, use forecasts and assumptions about the behavior of the various factors incorporated in them. Financial budgeting develops detailed budgets of cash receipts and cash disbursements, and a pro forma balance sheet. Effective financial budgeting depends on good operational budgeting. The detailed cash budgets utilize data from the purchases and expense budgets and from the pro forma income statement.

Once the preliminary cash budget is completed, it may become apparent that additional financing is needed; managers can plan in advance to meet this need. Financial budgets are often prepared for relatively long time periods. Such budgets are less precise than those prepared for the short term, but do assist managers in assessing long-term asset and financing requirements.

The presentation of the budgeting process is now complete. Comprehensive budgeting brings together and coordinates the plans of many managers and many levels of management. A comprehensive budget is the most conspicuous process of communication within a firm, and facilitates the coordination of major functional areas—production, sales, and finance.

Budgeting takes place in not-for-profit entities as well as businesses. Although many of the same principles apply, there are some identifiable differences, the most significant difference being that receipts are normally budgeted based on budgeted expenditures. Two additional budgeting approaches, program and zero-based budgeting, have been introduced for governmental units, to help offset the tendency in not-for-profit budgeting to concentrate on detailed expenditures rather than objectives.

KEY TERMS

cash budget
decision package
financial budgets
financing gap
incremental budgeting
long-term budget

minimum cash balance
pro forma financial statements
program budgeting
sunset legislation
zero-based budgeting

REVIEW PROBLEM

This problem continues the review problem from Chapter 6. Using the following additional data, prepare a cash budget for January 19X4 and a pro forma balance sheet for January 31, 19X4. Prepare supporting budgets for cash receipts and cash disbursements.

Exempli Company
Balance Sheet
December 31, 19X3

Assets		Equities	
Cash	$ 20,000	Accounts payable	
Accounts receivable	30,000	(merchandise)	$ 12,000
Inventory (6,000 units)	30,000	Common stock	200,000
Building and equipment (net)	200,000	Retained earnings	68,000
Totals	$280,000		$280,000

1. Sales are collected 40% in month of sale, 60% in the following month.
2. Purchases are paid 40% in month of purchase, 60% in the following month.
3. All other expenses requiring cash are paid in the month incurred.
4. The firm will declare a $3,000 dividend on January 10 and pay it on January 25.
5. The budgeted income statement and purchases budget from the solution in Chapter 6 (pages 212–13) are given below for convenience.

Exempli Company
Budgeted Income Statement
for January 19X4

Sales		$100,000
Cost of sales		25,000
Gross profit		75,000
Variable costs:		
Commissions	$10,000	
Other variable expenses	5,000	15,000
Contribution margin		60,000
Fixed costs:		
Depreciation	2,000	
Other operating expenses	40,000	42,000
Budgeted income		$ 18,000

Purchases Budget for January 19X4

Desired ending inventory	$45,000
Cost of sales	25,000
Total requirements	70,000
Beginning inventory	30,000
Budgeted purchases	$40,000

Answer to Review Problem

Cash Budget

Beginning balance	$20,000
Receipts, see below	70,000
Cash available	90,000
Disbursements, see below	86,000
Ending balance	$ 4,000

Cash Receipts Budget

Collection from December sales	$30,000
Collection from January sales	
($100,000 × 40%)	40,000
Total	$70,000

December sales will all be collected by the end of January. Because sales are collected by the end of the month following sale, all accounts receivable at the end of a month are expected to be collected in the coming month.

Cash Disbursements Budget

Merchandise ($40,000 × 40%) + $12,000	$28,000
Commissions	10,000
Various operating expenses	45,000
Dividend	3,000
Total	$86,000

Exempli Company
Pro Forma Balance Sheet
January 31, 19X4

Assets		Equities	
Cash (cash budget)	$ 4,000	Accounts payable^c	$ 24,000
Accounts receivable^a	60,000	Common stock	200,000
Inventory (purchases budget)	45,000	Retained earnings^d	83,000
Building and equipment^b	198,000		
Totals	$307,000		$307,000

^{a}60% of January sales of $100,000 (40% was collected in January).
^{b}$200,000 beginning balance less $2,000 depreciation expense.
^{c}60% of January purchases of $40,000 (40% was paid in January).
^{d}Beginning balance of $68,000 plus budgeted income of $18,000 minus dividend of $3,000.

Notice that cash declined by $16,000 (from $20,000 to $4,000) even though income was $18,000. The budgeted cash balance of $4,000 might be too low in management's judgment, and the firm might wish to seek a short-term bank loan.

ASSIGNMENT MATERIAL

Questions for Discussion

7-1   **Cash budgeting—effects of external events**   You are controller of a large manufacturing company and have recently completed your cash budget for the coming year. You now learn of each of the following events, which you are to consider independently. For each event, indicate (1) whether you would expect it to influence your cash receipts or disbursements, and (2) in which direction. Explain your answer and state any assumption you make.
1.   The sales manager informs you that customers are not paying their bills as quickly as usual because of high interest rates.
2.   The sales manager informs you that, due to a strike at the plant of a competitor, your firm's sales should be higher than budgeted.
3.   Your suppliers, whom you have been paying 45 days after purchases were made, are now requiring payment in 30 days.
4.   Inventory policy is being changed from the carrying of the next two months' requirements to 150% of the next month's requirements.

7-2   **Publication of budgets**   In financial accounting you studied the composition of the various financial statements usually distributed to persons, or groups of persons, outside the economic enterprise. Included among these statements were the balance sheet and the income statement. In this chapter it is suggested that a comprehensive budgeting program involves the preparation of the same statements using budgeted data. Budgeted financial statements are not normally made available to persons outside the organizations. Do you see any advantages to publishing these budgeted statements as part of the annual reports? Do you see any disadvantages?

7-3   **"Something is enough."**   The owner of a small chain of shoe stores has expressed his dissatisfaction with the request from his budget director that he establish a policy regarding a minimum acceptable cash balance to be incorporated in the firm's planning for the coming year. "I see no reason for such a policy," he has said. "As long as the monthly budgets show that we can expect to have some cash on hand at the end of the month, why put still another assumption into the budget. There are far too many assumptions in the budget already." Comment on the owner's position about specifying an acceptable cash balance for budgeting purposes.

7-4   **Philanthropy or business sense?**   In the last several years, public utilities have begun to offer "level-payment plans" for their customers. For example, individuals purchasing natural gas for heating purposes from Consumers Power in Michigan, and individuals purchasing electricity from Texas Electric Service Companies, have been offered the opportunity to spread the payments for their purchases over the entire year. The normal plan is for a given month's payment to be $1/12$ of the total cost of service provided in the twelve months ending with the current month.

Required: Discuss the reasons for a company to offer a level-payment plan.

7-5   **Behavior of cash balances and profit**   Randolph Growing and Harry Declining were talking about the performances of their respective companies in recent months.

Growing: We have seen rapid increases in monthly sales and are making profits hand over fist. We had expected this growth and have been keeping our inventories up to meet the increasing demand. I was careful to say that we are making profits because our cash balances have been a problem. We have borrowed a lot of money lately.

Declining: Things have not been going as well for us. We have entered our slow season and sales have been falling. Of course, we knew it would happen and planned accordingly. We are not making much profit, but do we have cash. Our balance has risen every month.

Required: Explain why cash is going in the opposite direction from profit for each of these companies.

Exercises

7-6 Cash receipts budget Jasica Company expects the following sales for the first six months of 19X7. Figures are given in thousands of dollars.

	Jan.	Feb.	Mar.	Apr.	May	June
Budgeted Sales	$1,600	$2,200	$1,100	$900	$1,600	$2,500

Cash collections expectations are as follows: 2% of sales become bad debts, 30% of sales are collected in the month of sale, 40% in the first month after sale, and 28% in the second month after sale. Sales in November 19X6 were $800, in December $1,200.

Required: Prepare a schedule of budgeted cash receipts for the six-month period ending June 30, 19X7, by month.

7-7 Production and cash disbursements budgets The following data relate to Corr Company and its single product, a desk lamp.
(a) Sales forecast, January through June, 19X9 (in units): 1,200; 1,400; 1,700; 2,000; 2,400; and 1,800.
(b) Inventory policy: inventory is maintained at 150% of budgeted sales needs for the coming month.
(c) Cost data: materials $8 per unit; direct labor $7 per unit; and variable overhead $5 per unit.
(d) Materials are purchased daily and are paid for in the following month; all other costs requiring cash disbursements are paid as incurred.
(e) The beginning inventory for January is 1,500 units.

Required
1. Prepare a budget of production for each month of the period for which you have data (in units).
2. Prepare a budget of cash disbursements for each month for which you have data. Production in December 19X8 was 1,200 units.

7-8 Cash receipts and cash budget—continuation of 7-7 Refer to the data in the preceding exercise. The lamp sells for $25 per unit. All sales are on account with 40% collected in the month of sale, 60% in the month after sale. Sales in December 19X8 were 1,000 units.

Required
1. Prepare a schedule of budgeted cash receipts for each of the months for which you have data.
2. Prepare a cash budget for each month for which you have data. Cash at January 1 is $8,000.

7-9 Cash budget—continuation of 6-8   The Jordan Company (see 6-8) has no variable costs except for cost of sales. Its fixed costs are $10,000 per month, all paid as incurred. It pays for its purchases 40% in the month of purchase, 60% in the following month. December 31, 19X8, accounts payable were $18,000. It collects its sales 60% in the month of sale, 40% in the following month. December 31, 19X8 receivables were $30,000.

Required
1. Prepare a cash receipts budget for each of the first three months of 19X9 and for the quarter as a whole.
2. Prepare a cash disbursements budget for each of the first three months of 19X9 and for the quarter as a whole.
3. Prepare a cash budget for each of the first three months of 19X9 and for the quarter as a whole. Beginning cash was $20,000. If the budgeted cash balance goes below zero, assume that you borrow the exact amount needed to bring the balance to zero. Repay also in exact amounts. Ignore interest.

7-10 Pro forma balance sheet—continuation of 7-9   The Jordan Company balance sheet as of December 31, 19X8 appears below.

Jordan Company
Balance Sheet as of
December 31, 19X8

Assets		Equities	
Cash	$20,000	Accounts payable	$18,000
Receivables	30,000		
Inventory	45,000	Stockholders' equity	77,000
Totals	$95,000		$95,000

Jordan Company rents all of its fixed assets.

Required: Prepare a pro forma balance sheet as of the end of March, 19X4, using your results from 7-9.

7-11 Cash budget—continuation of 6-9   Thomas Company has the following information available, in addition to that given in 6-9.

Sales are collected 30% in the month of sale, 70% in the following month. Receivables at December 31, 19X3 are $63,000. The company pays for its purchases in the month after purchase. Accounts payable at December 31, 19X3 are $35,000. All other expenses require cash disbursements (no depreciation) and are paid as incurred. The cash balance at December 31, 19X3 is $25,000.

Required
1. Prepare a cash receipts budget for January and for February.
2. Prepare a cash disbursements budget for January and for February.

3. Prepare a cash budget for January and for February. Should budgeted cash go below $15,000, assume borrowing and repayment in multiples of $5,000 to maintain at least $15,000. Ignore interest.

7-12 Pro forma balance sheet—continuation of 7-11   The Thomas Company balance sheet as of December 31, 19X3 appears below.

Thomas Company
Balance Sheet as of
December 31, 19X3

Assets		Equities	
Cash	$ 25,000	Accounts payable	$ 35,000
Receivables	63,000		
Inventory	80,000	Stockholders' equity	133,000
Totals	$168,000		$168,000

Thomas Company rents all of its fixed assets.

Required: Prepare a pro forma balance sheet as of the end of February, 19X4, using your results from 7-11.

7-13 Cash budget—quarters   Walton Company expects the following results by quarters in 19X4 in thousands of dollars:

	1	2	3	4
Sales	$2,400	$3,000	$3,600	$2,100
Cash disbursements:				
Production costs	1,800	2,800	2,200	1,700
Selling and general	400	600	200	320
Purchases of fixed assets	0	400	600	400
Dividends	20	20	20	20

Accounts receivable at the end of a quarter are one-third of sales for the quarter. The beginning balance in accounts receivable is $700,000. Cash on hand at the beginning of the year is $120,000, and the desired minimum balance is $100,000. Any borrowings are made at the beginnings of quarters in which the need will occur, in $10,000 multiples, and are repaid at the ends of quarters. Ignore interest.

Required
1. Prepare a cash budget by quarters for the year.
2. What is the loan outstanding at the end of the year?
3. Can the firm be operating profitably in view of the heavy borrowing required?

7-14 Pro forma balance sheet   The controller of Lamb Industries has been developing an analysis to see whether the firm will be able to pay off some long-term debt by the end of the current year. So far the controller has come up with the data that are shown below.

Budgeted Income Statement for Year
(In Thousands of Dollars)

Sales	$1,000
Cost of sales	700
Gross profit	300
Operating expenses	180
Income	$ 120

Outline of Pro Forma Balance Sheet
as of Year End (In Thousands of Dollars)

Assets			Equities		
Cash	$	30	Current liabilities	$	?
Accounts receivable		?	Long-term debt		?
Inventory		?	Stockholders' equity		1,400
Plant, net		1,300			
Total	$	?	Total	$	?

The firm's experience has been that accounts receivable are typically about 25 percent of sales, inventory about 30 percent of cost of sales. The firm expects to have about the same income-statement results for the next few years.

The controller would like to hold current liabilities to about one-half of current assets. Long-term debt is now $350,000. The stockholders' equity figure given in the pro forma statement reflects expected profit and dividends for the year.

Required: Complete the pro forma balance sheet, using long-term debt as the balance figure, and determine how much long-term debt the firm will be able to retire by the end of the year.

7-15 Basic cash budget Before being called out of town on urgent company business, Sandy Banks, the controller of Vidgame, Inc., had developed the following information for the company's cash budget for the next few months.

	Unit Sales	Unit Production	Material Purchases
January	10,000	14,000	$130,000
February	12,000	16,000	150,000
March	14,000	13,000	110,000

The company's one product, a home video game unit, sells for $75. Customers pay 40% in the month of sale, 60% in the following month. Material purchases are paid for in the month after purchase. Variable production costs, excluding materials, are $15 per unit; materials are $10 per unit of product. Fixed production costs are $150,000 per month, including $30,000 depreciation. Selling and administrative expenses are $40,000 per month, all cash, paid as incurred. Production costs other than those for materials are paid as incurred.

At January 1, the company had $360,000 in accounts receivable from December sales and owed suppliers of materials $100,000. Cash at January 1 was $35,000.

Required: Prepare a cash budget for January and for February. If you show a negative cash balance, assume borrowing to bring it to zero. Ignore any interest.

7-16 Comprehensive budget   The following data apply to the Borden Hardware Store, which is preparing its budgets for 19X7.

Forecasted Sales		Balance Sheet Data December 31, 19X6	
January	$60,000	Cash	$ 8,000
February	60,000	Accounts receivable:	
March	80,000	November sales	16,000
April	80,000	December sales	50,000
		Inventory	54,000
		Accounts payable (merchandise)	27,000

Other data are as follows:
(a)   Sales are on credit with 60% of sales collected in the month after sale, 40% in the second month after sale.
(b)   Cost of sales is 60% of sales.
(c)   Other variable costs are 10% of sales, paid in the month incurred.
(d)   Inventories are to be 150% of next month's budgeted sales requirements.
(e)   Purchases are paid for in the month after purchase.
(f)   Fixed expenses are $3,000 per month; all require cash.

Required
1.   Prepare budgets of purchases for each of the first three months of 19X7.
2.   Prepare separate budgets of cash receipts and disbursements and a cash budget for each of the first four months of 19X7.
3.   Prepare a budgeted income statement for the four-month period ending April 30, 19X7.

7-17 Cash budgeting—account analysis   Using the following information, prepare cash budgets and supporting schedules for all months that you can. The beginning cash balance is $12,000.

	January	February	March	April
Sales	$90,000	$110,000	$100,000	$115,000
Accounts receivable, end of month	$36,000	$ 44,000	$ 45,000	$ 46,000
Purchases	$70,000	$ 60,000	$ 70,000	$ 50,000
Accounts payable, end of month	$21,000	$ 21,000	$ 28,000	$ 15,000

At the beginning of January, receivables were $28,000 and accounts payable were $20,000.

7-18 Understanding budgets   On page 260 are the Blaisdel Company balance sheet at December 31, 19X0, and information regarding the company's policies and past experiences.

Balance Sheet Data, 12/31/X0

Cash	$35,000	Accounts payable	$ 12,000
Inventory	63,000	Income taxes payable	5,000
Receivables	16,000	Common stock	160,000
Fixed assets, net	96,000	Retained earnings	33,000
Total	$210,000	Total	$210,000

Additional information:
1. All sales are on credit and are collected 70% in the month of sale and 30% in the month after sale.
2. Expected sales for January, February, March, April, and May are $50,000, $60,000, $70,000, $66,000, and $65,000, respectively.
3. Inventory is maintained at a level equivalent to the sales requirements for the following two months.
4. Purchases are all on credit and are paid 80% in the month of purchase and 20% in the month after purchase.
5. Other variable costs are 15% of sales and are paid in the month incurred.
6. Fixed costs are $7,000 per month, including $1,000 of depreciation. Cash fixed costs are paid in the month incurred.
7. The firm's income tax rate is 40%, with taxes being paid in the month after they are accrued.
8. Cost of goods sold is expected to be 60% of sales.

Required
1. What are budgeted cash receipts for January 19X1?
2. What is the budgeted inventory at January 31, 19X1?
3. What are budgeted purchases for January 19X1?
4. What is budgeted net income for January 19X1?
5. What is the budgeted cash balance at the end of January 19X1?
6. What are budgeted accounts receivable at February 28, 19X1?
7. What is the budgeted book value of fixed assets at March 31, 19X1?
8. What are budgeted accounts payable at March 31, 19X1?
9. If the company declared a cash dividend of $1,200 during January, payable in February, what would be the balance reported for retained earnings in a pro forma balance sheet as at January 31, 19X1?
10. What amount would show as the liability for income taxes as of March 31, 19X1?

 7-19 **Comprehensive budget**   The following data pertain to Dipsy Company, a retail store.

Sales Forecasts—19X8

January	$ 80,000	48,000
February	90,000	54,000
March	110,000	66,000
April	120,000	72,000
May	100,000	60,000

Balance Sheet
December 31, 19X7

Cash	$ 15,000	Accounts payable	$ 28,000
Accounts receivable	60,000	Accrued sales commissions	7,000
Inventory	102,000	Common stock	160,000
Net fixed assets	200,000	Retained earnings	182,000
Totals	$377,000		$377,000

Other data are as follows:
(a) All sales are on credit with 40% collected in the month of sale, 60% in the month after sale.
(b) Cost of sales is 60% of sales.
(c) The only other variable cost is a 7% commission to salespeople that is paid in the month after it is earned. All sales are subject to the commission.
(d) Inventory is kept equal to sales requirements for the next two months' budgeted sales.
(e) Purchases are paid for in the month after purchase.
(f) Fixed costs are $10,000 per month, including $4,000 depreciation.

Required
1. Prepare a budgeted income statement for the three-month period ending March 31, 19X8.
2. Prepare a cash budget for each of the first three months of 19X8 and all necessary supporting budgets.
3. Prepare a pro forma balance sheet as of March 31, 19X8.

7-20 Investing idle cash—extension of 7-19 (adapted from a problem prepared by Professor Robert W. Koehler)   The president of Dipsy Company was pleased with the cash budget you prepared, but felt that the firm might be able to invest some of its available cash and thereby earn an additional return. He knows that if the funds are invested in a money-market fund the firm will be able to earn 1% per month interest and to withdraw the money at any time. He believes that a $10,000 cash balance is sufficient and asks you to redo the cash budget to reflect the investing of excess cash at 1% per month. (Thus, you can invest $5,000 on January 1, because the $15,000 balance is $5,000 over the required minimum.) Assume that you invest at the ends of months (except for January 1).

Required: Respond to the president's request.

7-21 Cash budget for a student   Bo Phelps is a junior majoring in mathematics at a large university. At the beginning of the school year Bo wants to develop a cash budget for the fall term, which runs from September 1 through November 30. He has collected the following information.

Cash at September 1	$ 900
Tuition, due September 15	1,900
Room rent, due September 15 (for entire term)	600
Cost of meals, per month	250
Clothing expenditures, per month	50
Textbook purchases, due September 15	190

Bo has been awarded a scholarship of $2,000, the check for which should arrive by the end of the first week of September. He estimates that expenditures for dates and miscellaneous other items should total about $300 for the term, spread about evenly over each month. He also expects that he can get a part-time job that pays $8 per hour and that he will be able, for the most part, to set the hours he will work each month. The employer, a local business, must withhold 10% of Bo's earnings for income and social security taxes.

Required: Determine how many hours Bo must work each month to be able to maintain a $100 cash balance for emergencies.

7-22 **Spreadsheet analysis**   The controller of Winnie Industries has been using a computer-based spreadsheet to prepare the company's budgets. She has been called away to take care of a problem in one of the company's plants, and the president of the company does not understand the program listed below. The president wants you to explain what the program seems to do and how you might change it to test the effects of different estimates and policies.
The program is:

```
70 PRICE = 20
80 VARIABLE COST = 12
90 FIXED COST = 300000
100 SALES = 100000,110000,120000,130000,90000
110 ENDING INVENTORY = FUTURE SALES * 2.5
120 BEGINNING INVENTORY = PREVIOUS ENDING INVENTORY
130 PRODUCTION = LINE 100 + LINE 110 − LINE 120
140 RECEIPTS = SALES * .3 * PRICE + PREVIOUS SALES * .7 * PRICE
150 DISBURSEMENTS = PRODUCTION * VARIABLE COST * .9 + PREVIOUS PRODUCTION *
    VARIABLE COST * .1 + FIXED COST
160 CASH = PREVIOUS CASH + RECEIPTS − DISBURSEMENTS
```

Required
1. Tell the president generally what the program appears to do.
2. Tell the president the policies and estimates reflected in the program, e.g., the patterns of cash receipts and disbursements.
3. The president is considering a change in credit policy that he expects would increase sales by 5% in each month, but would change the collection pattern to 20% in the month of sale and 78% in the following month, with 2% bad debts. Modify whichever lines of the program you need to in order to test the effects of the proposed change.

7-23 **Production and purchases budgets**   Spellman Company makes a single product. Materials for the product cost $3 per unit of product. The company keeps its finished goods inventory at twice the coming month's budgeted sales and its materials inventory at budgeted production requirements for the following two months. The sales budget for the coming six months shows, in units: January 10,000; February 12,000; March 13,000; April 16,000; May 11,000; and June 14,000.

Required
1. Determine budgeted production for February.
2. Determine budgeted purchases of materials for February.

Problems

7-24 Municipal budgeting—revenues   The City of Wentworth is preparing its budget for 19X9. Total required revenues are $36,000,000. The city has two major sources of revenue, sales taxes and property taxes. The sales tax is 2% of taxable retail sales, which includes virtually all sales except for food and medicine. The assessed valuation of taxable property is $560,000,000.

   An economist hired by the city has forecast total taxable retail sales $860,000,000 for 19X9.

Required
1. Determine the property tax rate needed to meet the city's revenue objective, assuming that the estimate of retail sales is correct.
2. The city council is considering a proposal to reduce property taxes on homes owned by people over 65 years of age. It is proposed that the rate on such homes be set at $30 per $1,000 assessed valuation. The total assessed valuation of homes owned by people over 65 is $45,000,000. Determine the rate that would have to be set on the remaining taxable property in order to meet the revenue objective if the proposal is adopted.

7-25 Manufacturer's cash budget—three months   Tompkins Company produces a single product that sells for $15 per unit. Cost data are:
(a)   Variable manufacturing costs, all requiring cash, $7 per unit.
(b)   Variable selling and administrative expenses are $1 per unit.
(c)   Fixed manufacturing costs requiring cash are $50,000 per month. Depreciation is $12,000 per month. Fixed selling and administrative expenses are $40,000 per month, all requiring cash.
Other data are:
(d)   The firm maintains a two-month supply of finished goods. The beginning inventory (January 1) is 42,000 units.
(e)   The firm buys raw materials as needed, maintaining no inventory. The cost of raw materials is included in the variable manufacturing cost of $7.
(f)   The firm makes all sales on credit, collecting 30% in the month of sale, 70% in the month after sale. The beginning balance in accounts receivable is $140,000.
(g)   All manufacturing costs are paid for in the month of production.
(h)   The firm pays 80% of selling and administrative expenses in the month of sale, 20% in the following month. At January 1 the firm owed $14,000 from December expenses.
(i)   The minimum desired cash balance is $40,000, which is also the amount on hand at the beginning of January. If the firm needs to borrow, it does so in multiples of $10,000. It must borrow at the beginning of the month and repay at the end, if sufficient cash is available. The interest rate is 18% and Tompkins pays interest when it repays loans, or portions of them.
(j)   The sales budget for the first six months is, in units: January, 20,000; February, 26,000; March, 30,000; April, 32,000; May, 30,000; June, 28,000.

Required
1. Prepare a cash budget and any necessary supporting schedules for the first three months of the year, by month and in total.
2. Given your results in part 1, does it appear that the firm is profitable? Explain.
3. Suppose that sales stabilized at 25,000 units per month. What would the monthly cash collections from sales be? What would be monthly cash disbursements for manufacturing costs and for selling and administrative expenses?

7-26 Manufacturer's cash budget—changes in assumptions   Using the data from the previous problem, prepare new budgets assuming that sales budgeted for March are 28,000 units; for April, 30,000 units; and for May, 28,000 units. All other information remains the same.

7-27 Manufacturer's cash budget—modification of 7-25   Solve part 1 of 7-25, assuming the following information.
(a)   Of the $7 variable manufacturing cost, $3 is for raw materials, the remainder for direct labor and variable overhead. Each unit of product requires one pound of material, which costs $3 per pound.
(b)   The firm usually maintains raw material inventory at budgeted production requirements for the next two months.
(c)   At January 1, the firm has $201,000 (67,000 pounds) of raw material inventory.
(d)   The firm pays for its purchases of raw material in the month after purchase. The accounts payable at January 1 is $85,000.
(e)   Budgeted sales for July are 26,000 units.

7-28 One month cash budget—discounts   Stony Acres Department Store makes about 20% of its sales for cash. Credit sales are collected 20%, 30%, 45% in the month of sale, month after, and second month after sale, respectively. The remaining 5% become bad debts. The store tries to purchase enough goods each month to maintain its inventory at two and one-half times the following month's budgeted sales. All purchases are subject to a 2% discount if paid within ten days and the store takes all discounts. Accounts payable are then equal to one-third of that month's net purchases. Cost of goods sold, without considering the 2% discount, is 60% of selling prices. The firm records inventory net of the discount.

The general manager of the store has asked you to prepare a cash budget for August and you have gathered the following data:

Sales:	
May (actual)	$230,000
June (actual)	240,000
July (actual)	310,000
August (budgeted)	330,000
September (budgeted)	290,000
Inventory at July 31	455,700
Cash at July 31	65,000
Purchases in July (gross)	210,000
Selling, general, and administrative expenses	
budgeted for August	91,000 (includes $18,000 depreciation)

The firm pays all of its other expenses in the month incurred.

Required: Prepare a cash budget for August.

7-29 Long-range financial budget   Millard Company has retained you to develop a financing plan for the next few years. You collect the following information about the firm's expectations, goals, and policies.

Sales Forecasts

19X4	$1,200
19X5	1,650
19X6	1,800
19X7	1,950

Millard expects a return on sales of 12%. The directors of the firm would like to maintain the policy of distributing dividends in an amount equal to 50% of net income each year. The directors would also like to have a current ratio of at least 2 to 1 and do not want long-term debt to exceed 60% of stockholders' equity.

Current asset requirements are 40% of expected sales in the coming year, net fixed assets are 75% of budgeted sales for the coming year. At the end of 19X3, net fixed assets are $960, stockholders' equity is $750, and working capital is $190.

Required: Prepare a schedule showing financing requirements for 19X4, 19X5, and 19X6 and propose a plan for meeting the requirements.

7-30 Budgeting equations (CMA adapted) Your firm has just acquired a new computer, and one of the first things that the president wants it to be used for is the preparation of the firm's comprehensive budget. He assigns you the task of formulating a set of equations that can be used to write a program to perform the computations required for the budgets. You consult with the chief programmer, and the two of you decide that the following notation should be used, which will make it easy for the programmer to prepare the necessary programs.

S_0 = sales in current month (units)
S_1 = sales in coming month (units)
S_{-1} = sales in prior month (units)
S_{-2} = sales in second prior month (units)
P = selling price per unit
CGS = cost of goods sold per unit (purchase price)
OVC = other variable costs per unit
FC = total fixed costs per month
FCC = fixed costs per month requiring cash disbursements
PUR = purchases in current month (units)
PUR_{-1} = purchases in prior month (units)

You examine the records of the firm and decide that the firm's policies or experienced relationships are as follows:

1. Collections on sales are 30% in the month of sale, 50% in the month after sale, and 20% in the second month after sale.
2. Inventory is maintained at twice the coming month's budgeted sales volume.
3. Purchases are paid for 60% in the month after purchase and 40% in the month of purchase.
4. All other costs are paid as incurred.

Required: Prepare equations that can be used to budget for the following:

1. Income for the current month.
2. Cash receipts in current month.
3. Purchases in current month in units.
4. Purchases in current month in dollars.
5. Cash disbursements in current month.

7-31 Comprehensive budget—continuation of 6-40 (adapted from a problem prepared by Professor Maurice L. Hirsch)   The following information about Banana City is available, in addition to that given in 6-40.

1. Sales of bananas are for cash only. Sales of nuts are on credit and are collected two months after sale.
2. Banana City's suppliers give terms of 30 days for payment of accounts payable. Banana City takes full advantage of the 30-day payments. (Assume that all months have 30 days.)
3. The firm must make quarterly payments on its income taxes. The payment for the first quarter of fiscal year 19X7 is due on January 15, 19X7. The liability for taxes payable shown on the balance sheet below is to be paid on October 15.
4. The fixed expenses of the firm that require cash disbursement are paid as incurred with the following exceptions: (a) insurance premiums are all paid on November 1 in advance for the next 12 months; and (b) interest payments are all made on January 1. The $156,000 "other fixed expenses" shown in part 6 of Problem 6-40 all require cash disbursements evenly over the year.
5. The balance sheet for August 31, 19X6 is given below.

Assets		Equities	
Cash	$ 15,000	Accounts payable (merchandise)	$ 26,000
Accounts receivable	75,000	Taxes payable	31,000
Inventories	41,800	Accrued interest	4,000
Prepaid insurance	2,000	Long-term debt, 6%	100,000
Land	8,000	Common stock	150,000
Equipment (net)	210,000	Retained earnings	40,800
Totals	$351,800		$351,800

6. Sales in the last part of fiscal year 19X6 are given below.

	June	July	August
Bananas	$31,000	$34,000	$32,500
Nuts	37,000	41,000	34,000

7. The firm expects to pay a dividend of $12,000 in October.

Required
1. Prepare budgets of cash receipts and disbursements for each of the first three months of fiscal year 19X7 and for the quarter as a whole.
2. Prepare a cash budget for the quarter, by month and in total.
3. Prepare a pro forma balance sheet for November 30, 19X6.

7-32 Pro forma balance sheet and financing requirements   Using the following data for Caldwell Company, prepare a statement of asset requirements and available equities as of December 31, 19X6. Balance the two either by adding to cash or to long-term debt, depending on whether assets are less than equities or vice versa.

Caldwell Company
Budgeted Income Statement
for 19X6

Sales	$300,000
Cost of goods sold	210,000
Gross profit	90,000
Selling, general, and administrative expenses[a]	36,000
Income before taxes	54,000
Income taxes (40% rate)	21,600
Net income	$ 32,400

[a]Includes $10,000 depreciation expense

Balance Sheet Data, December 31, 19X5

Plant and equipment	$150,000
Accumulated depreciation	50,000
Common stock	200,000
Retained earnings	83,000
Asset requirements:	
Cash—minimum desired balance	$ 25,000
Accounts receivable	30% of sales
Inventory	40% of cost of sales
Plant and equipment—net	70% of sales
Equities available:	
Accounts payable	50% of inventory
Income taxes payable	50% of income tax expense

A dividend of $22,000 will be paid during 19X6.

7-33 **Comprehensive budget**   On page 268 the balance sheet of your firm, Flybynite Industries, at December 31, 19X5 is shown. Also shown is a projected income statement for the first three months of 19X6, prepared by your chief accountant, Robert Cratchit. You are happy with the projection and gloat about it to your banker, Gettin Hirates. Mr. Hirates, always eager to lend money, has asked if you will need any cash to get through the first quarter. "Of course not" is your reply. Later, back at your office, Cratchit informs you of the following.

1. Sales are all on credit and are collected 50% in the month of sale, 50% in the month after sale.
2. It is company policy to build up inventory so that inventory is always equal to the next two months' sales in units. However, at December 31, 19X5 your inventory is depleted because of the dock strike.
3. You pay for purchases 50% in the month of purchases, 50% in the following month.
4. You are committed to paying the recorded cash dividend of $2,000 in March.
5. All cash expenses are paid in the month incurred, except for purchases.
6. The accounts receivable at December 31, 19X5 will be collected in January; the accounts payable at December 31, 19X5 will be paid in January.
7. The monthly breakdown of projected sales is as follows: January, $20,000; February, $30,000; and March, $50,000. In addition, April sales are expected to be $20,000, and May sales $20,000.
8. Cash should not go below $5,000.

Flybynite Industries
Balance Sheet
December 31, 19X5

Cash	$ 5,000		Accounts payable	$16,000	
Accounts receivable	10,000		Dividend payable	2,000	$18,000
Inventory	24,000	$39,000	Owner's equity		61,000
Plant and equipment net of					
accumulated depreciation	40,000				
Total assets	$79,000				$79,000

Projected Income Statement
Three Months Ending March 31, 19X6

Sales (10,000 units @ $10)		$100,000
Cost of sales (10,000 units @ $6)		60,000
Gross profit		40,000
Operating expenses:		
Wages and salaries	$9,000	
Rent	3,000	
Depreciation	3,000	
Other expenses	1,500	16,500
Income		$ 23,500

Required: Do you regret your reply to Mr. Hirates? Explain by preparing the appropriate schedules. (If borrowings are necessary, assume that they are in $1,000 multiples at the beginning of the month and that repayments are at the ends of months with 12% annual interest on the amount repaid.)

7-34 **Comprehensive budget—continuation of 6-28**   The managers of Calco Products Company in 6-28 have the following additional information.

Sales should be collected 30% in the month of sale, 70% in the following month. Purchases are paid 40% in the month of purchase, 60% in the following month. Fixed manufacturing costs include $20,000 per month depreciation. All manufacturing costs requiring cash disbursements are paid as incurred. All selling and administrative expenses require cash disbursements, with 80% paid as incurred, and the remaining 20% paid in the following month. The balance sheet at December 31 appears opposite.

Required
1. Prepare the following budgets for January and for February:
    (a) cash receipts
    (b) cash disbursements
    (c) cash
    The company desires a minimum cash balance of $60,000 at the end of each month. If operating projections show that borrowing is necessary to meet the minimum balance and cover a month's cash activity, such borrowings occur at the beginning of the month, in multiples of $10,000. Repayments, in multiples of $10,000, are made at the end of the month, as soon as cash balances permit them, and the bank charges interest at 1% per month. Interest payments are made only at the time a repayment occurs, and then only for the interest due on the amount being repaid.

Calco Products Company
Balance Sheet as of December 31, 19X5

Assets

Cash	$ 75,000
Accounts receivable	280,000
Finished goods (35,000 × $14)	490,000
Materials (66,000 × $8)	528,000
Net plant	1,200,000
Total assets	$2,573,000

Equities

Accounts payable	$ 96,000
Accrued S, G, and A expenses	18,000*
Stockholders' equity	2,459,000
Total equities	$2,573,000

*$12,000 of the total relates to fixed costs.

2. Prepare a pro forma balance sheet as of the end of February. (Remember that interest accrues on loans outstanding, and that the income statement prepared for 6-28 does not yet reflect interest expense on any borrowed funds.)

7-35 Cash budget—continuation of 6-39   Richards Company (see 6-39) collects its sales 30% in the month of sale, 30% in the next month, and 40% in the second month after sale.

Fixed production costs not requiring cash are $40,000 per month. All selling, general, and administrative expenses require cash and are paid in the month incurred, except for sales commissions, which are paid in the month after incurrence.

All production costs requiring cash are paid 80% in the month of production, 20% in the month after production. This includes payments for materials, of which no inventory is kept since they are delivered daily.

Selected balance sheet data at May 30 are as follows.

Cash	$120,000 (equals the desired minimum balance)
Accounts receivable:	
from May sales	336,000
from April sales	120,000
Liabilities:	
Sales commissions	48,000
Production costs	66,000

Required: Prepare a cash budget for Richards Company for the first six months of the fiscal year, by month. If the need arises, show borrowings required to maintain the desired minimum balance of cash, in multiples of $10,000. Repayments are made at the ends of months and interest at 1% per month is paid when a repayment is made.

7-36 Analysis of budgets   On pages 270 and 271 are shown various budgets for Simpson Company for the first three months of 19X6. Answer the following questions about the assumptions and policies used in formulating them.

1. What are variable manufacturing costs per unit?

2. What are monthly fixed manufacturing costs requiring cash disbursements?
3. What are the firm's expectations about cash collections from receivables? (All sales are on account.)
4. What were sales in December 19X5?
5. What are accounts receivable at March 31, 19X6?
6. What proportion of variable selling and administrative expenses is paid in the month incurred and what proportion is paid the following month? (*Hint:* Variable selling costs are 25% of sales.)
7. What are accrued expenses payable for selling and administrative expenses at March 31, 19X6?
8. How much cash does the firm expect to have at March 31, 19X6? (The balance at January 1 is $1,800.)
9. If the firm could sell 2,000 additional units in the three-month period, what would income be? (Ignore interest expense.)
10. Look at the production budget. From comparisons of inventories, sales, and so on, determine the firm's inventory policy.
11. Does the beginning inventory for January reflect the firm's policy? Show why or why not.
12. What are budgeted sales for April?

Simpson Company Budgeted Income Statement
for Three Months Ending March 31, 19X6

Sales (10,000 units)		$30,000
Variable costs:		
Production	$8,000	
Selling and administrative	7,500	15,500
Contribution margin		14,500
Fixed costs:		
Production	1,800	
Selling and administrative	2,400	4,200
Income		$10,300

Production Budget (in units)

	January	February	March
Desired ending inventory	4,500	7,500	6,000
Units sold	2,000	3,000	5,000
Total requirements	6,500	10,500	11,000
Beginning inventory	2,500	4,500	7,500
Production	4,000	6,000	3,500

Cash Receipts Budget

	January	February	March
Collections:			
December sales	$ 750		
January sales	1,500	$4,500	
February sales		2,250	$ 6,750
March sales			3,750
Total collections	$2,250	$6,750	$10,500

Cash Disbursements Budget

	January	February	March
Production costs:			
Variable	$3,200	$4,800	$2,800
Fixed	600	600	600
Selling and administrative:			
Variable—current month	600	900	1,500
—prior month	150	900	1,350
Fixed	800	800	800
Totals	$5,350	$8,000	$7,050

7-37 Variable minimum cash balance The chief financial officer of Bland Company has asked for your help in preparing a cash budget. He plans to maintain a minimum balance based on the budgeted disbursements for the coming month and is unsure how to proceed. He tells you the following about his policy. "If the coming month's budgeted receipts are greater than budgeted disbursements, I want to hold a balance equal to 10% of budgeted disbursements and invest any excess cash in short-term government notes. If budgeted disbursements are greater than budgeted receipts, I want to have enough cash to make up the budgeted deficit and have 20% of budgeted disbursements on hand to begin the month. We will borrow if the indicated balance is less than required."

The budgets for sales and purchases in the coming months are as follows:

	Sales	Purchases
April	$500,000	$470,000
May	$780,000	$550,000
June	$900,000	$560,000
July	$600,000	$480,000
August	$650,000	$600,000

Sales are collected 30% in the month of sale, 70% in the following month. Purchases are paid for 50% in the month of purchase, 50% in the following month. Sales in March were $450,000, and accounts payable for merchandise at March 31 were $185,000. Cash at March 31 was $140,000. Fixed expenses requiring cash disbursements are $110,000 per month.

Required

1. Prepare a schedule by month for the April–July period indicating the amounts that would have to be borrowed, or would be available for investment, in each month. Borrowings would be repaid as soon as possible and are not included in the determination of disbursements for the purpose of setting the desired balance. Borrowings would be repaid before investments were made and investments would be sold before borrowings are made. Ignore interest.
2. Discuss the policy. What advantages or disadvantages does it have in comparison to a policy of having a set number of dollars as the desired minimum balance?

7-38 Qualifying for a loan The president of Stern's Department Store has requested your assistance. He will be seeking a large bank loan in a couple of months for the purpose of opening a new store and has been told by his banker that the March 31, 19X8 balance sheet should look good if the loan is to be granted. The banker said specifically that working capital (current assets minus current liabilities) should be at least $500,000 and that the current ratio (current assets divided by current liabilities) should be at least 2.5 to 1.

The end of January is now approaching and the president is becoming anxious. He asks you to prepare a cash budget for February and March and a pro forma balance sheet as of March 31. The balance sheet at the end of January is expected to be about as follows, in thousands of dollars:

Assets		Equities	
Cash	$ 110	Accounts payable (merchandise)	$ 410
Accounts receivable	240	Notes payable	40
Inventory	680	Common stock	2,000
Building and equipment (net)	1,830	Retained earnings	410
Totals	$2,860		$2,860

The sales forecasts for the months of February, March, April, and May are, respectively, $780,000; $650,000; $600,000; and $820,000. Cost of sales averages 60% of sales. Receivables are collected 60% in the month of sale, 40% in the following month. Inventory is normally maintained at budgeted sales requirements for the following two months. Purchases are paid for in 30 days.

The notes payable shown in the balance sheet are due on March 15. Although the firm normally keeps a minimum cash balance of $80,000, the president asks you to disregard this for purposes of the budgets. He also informs you that monthly fixed costs of operation are $265,000, of which $30,000 is depreciation. All fixed costs requiring cash are paid as incurred.

Required

1. Prepare the cash budget and pro forma balance sheet that the president wants.
2. Determine whether the firm will be likely to meet the criteria set by the bank.

7-39 Comprehensive budget—annual period   Larsen Company makes fertilizer in a midwestern state. The firm has nearly completed a new plant that will produce twice as much as the old plant, which is being scrapped. Swen Larsen, the owner, has consulted you about his financing requirements for the coming year. He knows that he will require additional financing because of the doubling of production and he intends to obtain a loan as soon as possible. He is on good terms with local bankers and anticipates no difficulty in obtaining the loan, but is anxious that it not be too large or too small.

The production process in the new plant is highly automated and can be carried out with a work force of the same size as that used last year in the old plant. The income statement for last year and the year-end balance sheet are as follows:

Larsen Company
Income Statement
for 19X4

Sales	$600,000
Cost of goods sold	420,000
Gross profit	180,000
Selling, general, and administrative expenses	120,000
Income	$ 60,000

Larsen Company
Balance Sheet
December 31, 19X4

Assets		Liabilities and Owner Equity	
Cash	$ 22,000	Accounts payable	$ 10,000
Accounts receivable	40,000	Common stock	400,000
Inventory of materials	140,000	Retained earnings	122,000
Plant and equipment—old plant	0		
—new plant	330,000		
Totals	$532,000		$532,000

You learn that depreciation expense on the old plant was $10,000 per year, all of which was included in cost of goods sold. The new plant will be depreciated at $30,000 per year. Wages paid last year to production workers were $100,000. Material purchases were $200,000, which is also the amount of material cost included in cost of goods sold (the beginning and ending inventories of materials were the same). Factory overhead, other than depreciation, was $110,000 last year. It is expected that factory overhead, other than depreciation, will be $140,000 in the coming year.

Selling, general, and administrative expenses are expected to be $130,000 during the coming year. Sales will be only 120% of last year's sales because it will take some time to reach the full output of the new plant. Mr. Larsen expects to spend $90,000 buying new equipment to complete the plant. This expenditure will be made as soon as he obtains the new loan. The factory will be operating at full capacity the last few months of the year, so ending requirements for current assets should be double the beginning amounts. Accounts payable are closely related to the amount of inventory carried. The firm ships its products on completion so that all inventory is raw materials.

Required: Prepare a budgeted income statement for 19X5, and a pro forma balance sheet (as far as possible) for December 31, 19X5. State any assumptions you have to make and indicate how much Mr. Larsen must borrow from the bank.

Cases

7-40 Cash budgeting—a lender's viewpoint   You are the chief assistant to Mr. Barnes, the loan officer of Metropolitan National Bank. In December 19X4 Mr. Barnes discussed a loan with Mr. Johnson, manager-owner of a local dry goods store. Mr. Johnson has requested a loan of $250,000 to be repaid at June 30, 19X5. The store is being expanded and additional inventory is needed. From the proceeds of the loan, $200,000 will be spent on remodeling and new fixtures. The rest will be spent for additional inventory. At Mr. Barnes's request, Mr. Johnson submitted a budgeted income statement for the six months ending June 30, 19X5.

Sales	$900,000
Cost of goods sold	360,000
Gross profit	540,000
Selling, general, and administrative expenses, including $15,000 interest	310,000
Income	$230,000

Mr. Johnson said that since $50,000 in depreciation was included in selling, general, and administrative expenses, the firm would generate more than enough cash to repay the loan with $15,000 in interest (12% annual rate). Mr. Barnes asks you to check out the forecast; you obtain the following information:

1. Sales are expected to be $100,000 in January, $140,000 in February, and $165,000 in each of the rest of the months of the entire year.
2. Merchandise is held equal to two months' budgeted sales.
3. Accounts payable are paid in 30 days.
4. About half of sales are for cash. The rest are collected in the second month after sale (60 days).
5. Cost of goods sold is variable, and 15% of sales is the variable portion of selling, general, and administrative expenses. All selling, general and administrative expenses, except depreciation, are paid in the month incurred.
6. At December 31, 19X4, the following balance sheet is expected.

Johnson Store, Inc.
Pro Forma Balance Sheet
December 31, 19X4

Cash (desired minimum)	$ 20,000	Accounts payable	$ 30,000
Accounts receivable	40,000	Common stock	200,000
Inventory	60,000	Retained earnings	115,000
Building and equipment	375,000		
Accumulated depreciation	(150,000)		
Totals	$ 345,000		$345,000

Required: Determine whether the firm can repay the loan with interest at the end of the first six months of 19X5. If not, explain why in terms that will make Mr. Johnson understand where he made his mistakes.

7-41 Budgeting and industry data   Ralph Robertson is considering opening a menswear store in a new shopping center. He has had a great deal of experience in men's stores and is convinced that he can make a success of his own store. He has asked you to develop a financing plan that he can take to a bank to obtain a loan. He knows that a bank manager will be more receptive to an applicant who has made careful plans of his needs. He gives you the following data obtained from a trade association's study of stores of the kind and size he plans to open (1,200 square feet of selling space).

Average sales per square foot	$70 per year
Average rent	$500 per month plus 5% of sales
Average gross profit	45% of sales
Average annual operating expenses (excluding rent and depreciation):	
at $60,000 sales annually	$19,200
at $90,000 sales annually	$26,700
Inventory requirements	four-month supply
Investment in fixtures and equipment (useful life of five years)	$22,000

Ralph plans to sell for cash only. He will have to pay cash for his first purchase of inventory, then he can get 30 days' credit from suppliers. His other operating expenses, including rent, will be paid in the month incurred.

Ralph expects to have a steady growth in sales for the first four months of operation (January through April 19X8) and to reach the monthly average for the industry in May. His projections for the first four months are as follows: $4,000; $4,500; $5,200; and $6,100.

Required

1. Prepare a budgeted income statement for the year 19X8.
2. Prepare a schedule showing his total financing requirements through April. Ralph will invest $10,000 of his own money.

CHAPTER 8

CAPITAL BUDGETING, PART I

The comprehensive budget, the unifying topic of Chapters 6 and 7, reflects the results expected from a wide variety of planning decisions, such as those about product mix, cost structure, pricing, and the like. Many of those decisions have as their goal achieving the best possible results using the firm's existing resources. That is, such decisions did not require large commitments of cash to investments in land, plant, machinery, or other long-lived assets. But a comprehensive budget must also incorporate the results of those planning decisions that do involve such long-term commitments, called **capital budgeting decisions.** Planned expenditures for new, long-lived assets may well be among the largest items in the cash disbursements budget.

Capital budgeting decisions are the subject of this and the next chapter. Such decisions entail sizable commitments of cash, and relate to returns—normally, income or cost savings—that will last for more than one year. (Recall from Chapter 5 that a one-year cutoff is customary in distinguishing short-term and long-term decisions. The rule is arbitrary, but useful nonetheless.)

For two reasons, capital budgeting decisions are generally more risky than short-term decisions. First, the firm will recoup its investment, if at all, over a longer period of time. That is, there is a longer waiting period between the time a decision and its related expenditure are made and the time funds are received as a result of that decision and expenditure. Second, it is much more difficult to reverse a capital budgeting decision than a short-term decision. For example, suppose that a firm raises its prices expecting to improve its profits, and sales fall so much that profits fall. Usually the firm can simply lower its prices. Thus, the firm may suffer a decline in profits for a short period of time, but it can recover fairly quickly once the managers see their error. But suppose a company buys land and constructs and equips a building especially to make a particular product. The plant may have little value in any other use (a low opportunity cost). If the product is unsuccessful, the firm will have made a large, nearly worthless investment.

Managers use the analytical techniques discussed in this and the following chapter to decide whether or not to undertake specific long-term projects. The expenditures on those projects selected by management would then be incorporated into short-term and long-term budgets such as those presented in the preceding chapter. We cover only briefly the issues surrounding decisions about how to finance long-term investments. You will study in more detail the problems of selecting from among financing alternatives in managerial finance.

CAPITAL BUDGETING AND RESOURCE ALLOCATION

In short-term decision making, considering only quantifiable factors, an action is desirable if incremental revenues exceed incremental costs. In the long term, the firm must find the best uses for its capital. In capital budgeting decisions, an action is desirable if the expected rate of return is greater than the rate that must be paid to the suppliers of capital; the latter rate is called cost of capital. The study of cost of capital is the province of managerial finance. We give here only a brief introduction to the concept in order to provide you with a more complete understanding of the capital budgeting process.

Cost of Capital

Cost of capital is the cost, expressed as a percentage, of obtaining the capital resources to operate the firm. Capital is obtained from two sources, creditors and owners, corresponding to the divisions of liabilities and owners' equity on the balance sheet. The cost of capital supplied by creditors is the effective interest rate on borrowings. For example, if the firm would have to make annual interest payments of $80,000 in order to obtain $1,000,000 from a sale of bonds with that face value, the effective interest rate is 8% ($80,000/$1,000,000).[1]

The cost of equity capital is more difficult to determine, for it is based on how much investors expect the firm to earn. In a simple situation this cost may be approximated by finding the expected earnings and dividing this by the market value of the stock. Thus, if a firm is expected to earn $3 per share and the market price of the stock is $30 per share, the cost of equity capital is 10% ($3/$30).

---

[1]You may recall the determination of bond prices and effective interest rates from financial accounting. There are complications if bonds are issued at prices other than face value, but these problems are not important for our purposes.

We are interested in cost of capital primarily because it is the *minimum rate of return on investment that should be acceptable for a new project*. This rate serves as a **cutoff rate of return.** Any project not expected to yield this rate should be rejected; projects expected to yield higher rates should be accepted.

Determining the cost of capital for a firm is usually a complex task. Because of the practical difficulties of the task, a manager might simply set a minimum acceptable rate. A rate so set is often called a **target rate of return,** and the firm will use this rate in deciding which projects to accept. In this chapter we will assume that cost of capital has been estimated and is to be used in the decision to accept or reject a project.

Before you go any further, be sure that you understand the material in Appendix A at the back of the book. The concepts of compound interest and discounting are critical to the evaluation of long-term investments. For the answers to specific questions you can refer to available tables (such as those at the end of Appendix A), but you must understand what discounting accomplishes.

TYPES OF CAPITAL
BUDGETING DECISIONS

This chapter considers two general types of capital budgeting decisions. One type involves making investments to increase volume, either by increasing the output of an existing product or by making a new product. The second type of decision relates primarily to costs: the goal is to find the least-cost way to accomplish some specific objective. Both types of decisions require the same basic analysis, but circumstances surrounding them are somewhat different. Firms need not take advantage of opportunities to increase capacity; they can continue to operate with what they have. Investments made to reduce costs are different; here, the decision implies that the management has already decided to operate in a particular fashion and seeks the least costly way of doing so.

Cost minimization situations can be further subdivided into two basic types. First, in some situations where there is an opportunity for reducing costs there is no choice whether the operations will be performed—the operation must be performed if the firm is to remain in business. An automobile maker must assemble its cars; it cannot simply produce the parts and sell them to consumers. The necessity of assembly follows from a *decision* that the firm will be an automobile maker. Given this decision, the firm must find the least expensive method of performing an essential function: whether to use large amounts of labor or large amounts of machinery; whether to use existing machinery or replace it with more efficient equipment.

The second type of cost minimization situation covers projects not related to essential operations. There may be a top-level management decision to provide a cafeteria or a parking lot for employees. The firm will be seeking the least-cost method of providing the service. Although the firm may gain benefits from a cafeteria (through improved employee morale), future costs will increase rather than decrease. Nonessential investments do not increase cash available to the firm, but they are, nonetheless, important, and should be scrutinized at least as carefully as other potential investments.

Capital Budgeting Techniques

In a typical investment situation, a manager authorizes an investment with the intention of receiving returns sufficient to both recoup the original investment and adequately reward the company for the risk taken. But the returns are to come in the future, often over a period of many years. That is, he must wait for both the return *of* the investment and the return *on* it. Hence, when making an investment decision, the manager tries to determine, considering the **time value of money,** whether the rate of return associated with a particular investment is greater or less than the minimum acceptable rate—cost of capital. There are two ways to do this: (1) find the rate of return associated with the project and compare that rate with the cost of capital, or (2) using the cost of capital, find the present value of the future returns and compare it with the cost of the investment.

The second method is usually easier to apply. Using this method, we compare the present value of future returns from an investment with the cost of obtaining those returns—the required investment. This method is called the **net present value** method, or **excess present value** method. The alternative approach, finding the rate of return on a project and comparing it with a specified minimum acceptable rate, is usually called the **internal rate of return** method. It utilizes the same basic concepts as the net present value approach. Later in this chapter, we shall consider two other commonly used techniques for analyzing long-term investments. These additional techniques are conceptually inferior to either the net present value or the internal rate of return method because neither of the additional techniques considers the time value of money.

In three of the four analytical approaches to capital budgeting decisions discussed in this chapter, returns are defined as **cash flows.** In light of the emphasis given to income in prior chapters, and probably in your first course in accounting, we should take some time to explain why, in capital budgeting, cash flows are so important.

Cash Flows and Book Income

In Chapter 5, related to short-term decisions, the emphasis in each decision problem was on the change in total income for the period as a result of the decision to be made. Changes in revenues, in variable costs, and in avoidable fixed costs were considered. These changes share one important trait: *they affect the current cash flows of the enterprise.* With minor exceptions resulting from the leads and lags associated with the accrual versus the cash bases of accounting, the incremental profits determined for a particular decision were also the incremental cash inflows. That is, changes in income because of the particular decision *were* changes in cash flows because of that decision. None of the decisions involved changes that would affect income but not cash flows, or vice versa.

Long-term decisions differ in one important respect from the decisions covered in Chapter 5. If the investments required by the long-term decisions involve the acquisition of depreciable assets, the changes in incomes resulting from those decisions invariably are *not* also changes in cash flows. This is because of the accounting treatment of depreciation. Future incomes *will* be affected by the acquisition of depreciable assets, but the change in future incomes will *not* be equivalent to the changes in future cash flows. For, as you know from financial accounting, depreciation expense reduces income but does not require a cash outlay in the year in which it affects income.

When a depreciable asset is acquired, a cash outlay occurs in the year of acquisition. Though the cost of that asset may be allocated over the years in which the asset is used, there is no associated outlay of cash in those years even though the incomes of those years are reduced by the depreciation expense. Hence, the change in incomes of year 19X5 or 19X6 as a result of a particular long-term investment decision in 19X1, will not be the same as the change in cash flows of years 19X5 and 19X6 as a result of that same decision. The change in income will be smaller than the change in cash flow because income will be reduced by depreciation expense which requires no cash flow. For this reason, when decisions involve depreciable assets and future incomes, we must be more specific in our analyses. We cannot use income as a substitute for cash flows (as we did in Chapter 5), because income will not be a good measure of cash flows.

Depreciation is, of course, a legitimate deduction in arriving at reportable net income. Were it not for tax laws, we could derive the cash flows associated with a particular investment decision by simply adding the reported depreciation expense back to the net income and arrive at the operating cash flow for the year. Or, we could simply determine the cash flows, and ignore the net income amount because it would be influenced by depreciation. However, depreciation is also a legitimate deduction for income tax purposes. Hence, the income taxes to be paid in a given year, which *are* a cash outflow in that year, are affected by the depreciation expense assigned to that year. So to determine the cash flows for a year, we must know what the depreciation expense will be for that year for tax purposes. Later in this chapter we shall explain how to deal with the special problems resulting from the relationship between depreciation and income taxes.

There is one final and important point that you should bear in mind as we proceed. As with all management decisions that deal with the future, the numbers that will be used (for cash flows, useful lives, etc.) are *estimates*. They are almost never known with certainty. In Chapter 9, we illustrate several techniques that are used because of this uncertainty in dealing with the future.

BASIC EXAMPLE

The principle introduced in Chapter 5, that the only relevant data for decisions are differential revenues and costs, also governs capital budgeting decisions. The relevant data for capital budgeting decisions are the incremental (or differential) cash flows expected from a decision. The following example illustrates the main points:

A firm with cost of capital of 12% has the opportunity to introduce a new product. The best available estimates are that the firm will be able to sell 3,000 units per year for the next five years at $14 each. Variable costs should be $5 per unit. The firm will have to buy some machinery to make the product. The machinery will cost $60,000, have a 5-year life with no salvage value, and require annual fixed cash operating costs of $5,000 for maintenance, insurance, and property taxes. Notice that we have not included depreciation as a cost because it does not require a cash payment. We ignore income taxes for now.

The annual cash flows appear below:[2]

		Annual Cash Flows Years 1–5
Revenues ($14 × 3,000)		$42,000
Variable costs ($5 × 3,000 units)	$15,000	
Cash fixed costs	5,000	20,000
Expected net cash inflows		$22,000

Using this information, we analyze the proposed investment in two basic ways.

Net Present Value Method

When using the *net present value (NPV) method* the question to be answered is whether it is wise to invest $60,000 today in order to receive $22,000 per year for five years. The investment will be worthwhile if the present value of the $22,000 to be received per year for five years is greater than the $60,000 outlay required today (which, obviously, has a present value of $60,000). The present value of the future cash flows of $22,000 minus the $60,000 required investment is called the *net present value* or the *excess present value*. If it is positive (present value of the future cash flows is greater than the required investment), the investment is desirable. If it is negative, the investment is undesirable.

To determine the net present value we must first find the present value of $22,000 per year for five years at 12%. Looking at an appropriate present value table (Table B), we see that the factor for a series of payments of $1 for five years at 12% is 3.605. Multiplying this factor by $22,000 we obtain $79,310 as the present value of the future cash flows. This means that if you put $79,310 in a bank that paid 12% interest, it would grow sufficiently to allow five annual withdrawals of $22,000. Put still another way, if a 12% return is desired and payments of $22,000 annually for five years are expected, you would be willing to pay up to $79,310 for this investment. Therefore, you would be more than happy to pay only $60,000, and the investment is desirable. The net present value is $19,310 ($79,310 − $60,000). In general terms, an investment is worthwhile if the net present value is positive. Below is a summary of the analysis:

Present value of future cash flows ($22,000 × 3.605)	$79,310
Investment required	60,000
Net, or excess present value	$19,310

Internal Rate of Return Method

Another approach to analyzing investment opportunities is to find the expected *internal rate of return (IRR)*. This method poses the question "What return are we earning

[2]Notice that net income, using straight-line depreciation of $12,000 per year ($60,000/5), would be $10,000 per year.

if we invest $60,000 now and receive $22,000 annually for five years?" The investment is desirable if the rate of return is higher than the cost of capital. The internal rate of return is also called the **time-adjusted rate of return** or the **discount rate.**

Where net cash flows are equal in each year, the internal rate of return is not difficult to find. The rate equates the present value of the future cash flows with the amount to be invested now. Consider that the computation of the present value of the future flows is as follows:

$$\begin{array}{l} \text{Present value of} \\ \text{future flows} \end{array} = \begin{array}{l} \text{annual cash} \\ \text{returns (flows)} \end{array} \times \begin{array}{l} \text{the factor related to the discount rate} \\ \text{and the number of periods of returns} \end{array}$$

In computing the internal rate of return, we assume that the present value, above, *is* the cost of the investment and try to determine what discount rate is associated with the factor that, when multiplied by the known annual returns, equals the cost of the investment.

The first step is to find the factor related to both the discount rate and number of periods of returns. From the equation above, we know that

$$\frac{\text{Present value of future flows}}{\text{annual cash returns}} = \begin{array}{l} \text{factor related to the discount} \\ \text{rate and number of periods} \end{array}$$

In our example

$$\frac{\$60,000}{\$22,000} = 2.727$$

We know that this factor, 2.727, relates to some discount rate; we also know that the number of periods involved is five. Hence, we can find the discount rate by looking at the factors listed in the 5-period row in Table B. In the 5-period row under the 24% column, the factor is 2.745; in that row, under the 25% column, the factor is 2.689. Hence, the rate of return on this project is between 24% and 25%. (You should have been able to tell that the rate of return on this project was greater than 12% because the net present value, as computed in the previous section, is positive.)

Although we could interpolate to find a more exact rate, it is obvious that it falls between 24% and 25%, and is higher than the cost of capital, thus showing that the investment is desirable. Because we are dealing with estimates of future cash flows, we should avoid unwarranted precision.

Generality of the Analysis

Our example uses a new product, but it could just as well relate to expanding the productive capacity for an existing product. In fact, it could also be a case of reducing costs. Suppose that instead of the investment being for a new product, it was for labor-saving machinery that would reduce variable production costs of a product now being sold by $9 per unit. (This change in variable costs would increase the contribution margin on the old product by $9, which is equal to the contribution margin expected to result from the new product in the original example.) Assume further that the sales volume on the existing product is 3,000 units per year, and that the additional cash fixed costs for the new machinery would be $5,000 (the same as in the original example). The cash flows would then be

Savings in variable costs ($9 × 3,000)	$27,000
Less incremental cash fixed costs	5,000
Net change in cash flow per year (savings)	$22,000

Thus, the pattern of analysis is the same for both cases: find the incremental cash flows and then apply one of the methods described. Whether the cash flows result from selling new products, expanding output of existing products, or saving on operating expenses, we treat them the same way. *How* the cash flows come about is irrelevant; the important thing is to estimate what the cash flows will be.

Not-for-profit entities are often confronted with long-term decisions involving the acquisition of long-lived assets. For example, a city might want to decide whether or not to purchase additional buses or build a new municipal building. For such entities, which are not concerned with income taxes, the analytical approaches we have illustrated are adequate. However, managers in for-profit entities must also consider, as noted earlier, the fact that income taxes, a relevant cash outflow, can be affected by depreciation on an asset whose acquisition is an important aspect of a long-term decision. The next section presents a refinement of the analytical process by taking into account the effects of taxes.

TAXES AND DEPRECIATION

In order to take income taxes into account, we must perform further calculations to obtain cash flows. Continuing with the example of the new product, assume a 60% income tax rate and straight-line depreciation for income tax calculations. The initial outlay of $60,000 remains the same, but now the annual cash flows are different because the added income from the project is subject to income taxes. The net cash flow for each of the five years is computed below:

Net Cash Flow for Each Year

	Tax Computation	Cash Flow
Revenues	$42,000	$42,000
Cash expenses	20,000	20,000
Cash flow before taxes	22,000	22,000
Depreciation	12,000	
Taxable income	$10,000	
Tax at 60%	$ 6,000	6,000
Net cash flow per year		$16,000

Depreciation on the asset reduces taxes. The $12,000 in depreciation expense saves $7,200 in taxes (60% × $12,000). This saving is called the **tax shield** or **tax effect of depreciation.**

The schedule above does not show net income because we are concerned with cash flows, not net income. However, you might find it easier, and more understandable, to develop an income statement and then add depreciation back to get net cash flow. (This is a calculation frequently used by both accountants and financial managers.) The income statement converted to a cash basis appears below, along with the determination of the net present value of the investment:

Revenues	$42,000
Cash expenses	20,000
Cash flow before taxes	22,000
Depreciation	12,000
Income before taxes	10,000
Tax at 60%	6,000
Net income	4,000
Add back depreciation	12,000
Net cash flow per year	$16,000
Present value factor for 5 years at 12%	3,605
Present value of future cash flows	$57,680
Investment required	60,000
Net present value	($ 2,320)

Using either approach, the cash flows are now $16,000 per year (rather than $22,000), which, when discounted at 12%, have a present value of $57,680. The net present value is a negative $2,320; the investment is not desirable. To compute the internal rate of return, we find the present value factor which, when multiplied by $16,000, equals $60,000. The factor is 3.75 ($60,000/$16,000). The factor closest to this in the 5-year row in Table B is 3.791, the factor for 10%. The rate of return is therefore a little over 10%. (You should have expected a rate of return less than 12%, since the net present value at a 12% cost of capital is negative.)

UNEVEN CASH FLOWS

The basic example assumed that all net cash inflows were received equally each year. But it would not be unusual for revenues, or cash expenses, or both, to vary from year to year. For example, revenues from a new product might grow in the early years and decline in later years, or it might take several years for the revenues to reach a particular, expected level. Too, if depreciation is not taken on a straight-line method for tax purposes, the tax paid each year (and, hence, the cash outflow for taxes) will vary. Or perhaps the investment has a salvage value that would increase the cash flow in the last year. Although the unevenness of cash flows complicates the mathematics of the analysis for a project, the basic principles of the analysis are not affected.

Accelerated Depreciation

One of the most common reasons for uneven cash flows is the tax law. For many years the tax law permitted the depreciation of business property using accelerated methods such as sum-of-the-years'-digits or double-declining balance. In general, speeding up the recognition of expenses for tax purposes is desirable even though the total tax paid over the life of the investment is the same. The reason, as you have probably figured out, is that reduced taxes in the near term—even if they are offset by higher taxes in the longer term—increase the present value of the cash flows. (This is an application of the basic principle that the earlier you get cash, the better.) For obvious reasons, then, business entities were likely to use accelerated methods for tax purposes, while using straight-line for financial reporting purposes.

Although the law no longer allows a choice of a specific accelerated method of depreciation, it does permit acceleration of depreciation deductions by allowing tax-payers to write off (depreciate) assets over a relatively low number of years. (That is, a tax write-off is allowed over a period shorter than the economic life of the asset.) The new method is known as **ACRS** (for **Accelerated Cost Recovery System**). The specific requirements of the law are treated in Chapter 9. For now, let us assume that the machinery in our example must be depreciated, for tax purposes, over three years rather than five.[3]

The tax law permits the three-year write-off, but not in equal amounts. The percentages of cost that are accepted for tax purposes are: 25% the first year, 38% the second year, and 37% the third year (a total of 100%). Exhibit 8-1 shows the yearly cash flows and present values for our illustrative investment given the new information.

Exhibit 8-1
Cash Flows and Present Values—ACRS Depreciation

| | Year | | | | | |
	1	2	3	4	5	Total
(1) Pretax cash flow	$22,000	$22,000	$22,000	$22,000	$22,000	$110,000
(2) Tax depreciation*	15,000	22,800	22,200	0	0	60,000
(3) Increase (decrease) in taxable income (1) − (2)	7,000	(800)	(200)	22,000	22,000	50,000
(4) Increase (decrease) in income taxes (3) × 60%	4,200	(480)	(120)	13,200	13,200	30,000
(5) Net cash flow (1) − (4)	$17,800	$22,480	$22,120	$ 8,800	$ 8,800	$ 80,000
(6) Present value factors, Table A	.893	.797	.712	.636	.567	
(7) Present values (5) × (6)	$15,895	$17,917	$15,749	$ 5,597	$ 4,990	$ 60,148

*$60,000 × .25; $60,000 × .38; $60,000 × .37

The present value of cash inflows from the example project is now, considering the accelerated depreciation allowed by the tax law, $60,148, compared with only $57,680 using the straight-line method. You should not be surprised that the present value of the inflows is higher; the higher present value is consistent with the idea that cash flows in the near future are more valuable than flows in later years.

Let us examine further the $17,800 net cash flow in the first year of the project.

[3]Generally speaking, machinery does not qualify for a three-year ACRS life. We are using this life to illustrate accelerated depreciation.

The $17,800 cash flow in year 1 could be viewed as consisting of two parts:

Pretax cash savings	$22,000	
Less, tax on cash savings, 60%	13,200	
Net cash flow from operations		$ 8,800
Depreciation	$15,000	
Tax savings resulting from de- preciation, 60%		9,000
Net cash flow for year		$17,800

Analysis of the cash flows reveals that they consist of two things: (1) the $8,800 after-tax cash flow from changes in revenues and expenses, and (2) the tax shield from depreciation. The first of these items constitutes an annuity of $8,800 per year for the five years of the investment. Hence, we could compute the present value of the future flows on this investment as follows:

5-year annuity of $8,800 × 3.605		$31,724
Depreciation tax shield:		
Year 1 $15,000 × .60 × .893	$ 8,037	
Year 2 $22,800 × .60 × .797	10,903	
Year 3 $22,200 × .60 × .712	9,484	
Present value of tax shield		28,424
Total present value		$60,148

The advantage of this two-part approach is a reduction in the number of calculations required to obtain the answer. The annuity covers all five of the years in the life of the investment and takes into consideration the tax effect of the change in cash flows. The calculations for the tax shield of depreciation involve only the first three years, because the tax shield is available in only those years. Thus, instead of calculating separate cash flows for each year and multiplying by an appropriate present value factor for each of those years (five separate calculations), we need only compute the present value for the annuity and the present values for the three years in which a tax shield was available (four separate calculations).

The reduction in the number of calculations from five to four may not seem important in this situation. But the two-part approach could significantly reduce the number of calculations in two circumstances. First, the difference between the economic life of the asset and the number of years over which an ACRS write-off is available may be far greater than in the example. (It is possible, for example, that the ACRS write-off period may be three years while the economic life of the asset may be ten or fifteen years.) Second, as we shall show in Chapter 9, it is possible to develop a separate, easily usable table that reflects a single present-value factor that can be used in computing the present value of the tax shield of depreciation for an asset with a given ACRS life.

Finding the internal rate of return on an investment is a relatively difficult task when there are uneven cash flows. Trial-and-error and interpolation will give a close approximation of the rate, and many computers (and some hand-held calculators) have programs that will make the calculations. Because the net present value is positive

($60,148 present value of future cash flows, versus a cost of $60,000), the internal rate of return *must* be greater than the 12% discount rate used in the calculation of present values. Because the net present value is relatively low ($148) compared to the investment ($60,000), the internal rate of return is very close to 12%. (It is, in fact, about 12.09%.)

The illustrations and most of the problems at the end of this and the next chapter use straight-line depreciation for tax purposes simply because it is easier to work with. (You will be able to use the annuity table instead of having to discount each cash flow separately.) However, you should recognize that the depreciation-acceleration provisions of the tax law will increase the present value of future cash flows from any given project. Thus, a project with a positive net present value assuming straight-line depreciation for tax purposes will be even more desirable considering the acceleration provisions of current tax law. By the same token, a project that may not appear desirable assuming straight-line depreciation, must be further evaluated considering the depreciation-acceleration allowable under present tax laws.

Salvage Values

The cash flows for most projects involving the acquisition of depreciable assets could be uneven because of the salvage values of the assets at the ends of their useful lives. To incorporate this factor into the analysis, it is necessary only to find the after-tax cash flow from the salvage value and discount it separately.

Assume, for example, that the new asset purchased in the earlier example has an expected salvage value of $5,000 at the end of its useful life. How would this expectation affect the analysis of the investment? Although you may be inclined, because of your knowledge of financial accounting, to suggest that the depreciation of this asset will be changed because of the known salvage value, there are two important reasons why such is not likely to be the case. First, because salvage values are estimates of what will happen in the not-very-near future, it is quite common for an entity to ignore such values in the calculations of depreciation. Second, the law that established ACRS as an acceptable system for determining the amounts of depreciation for tax purposes also specified that salvage values should be ignored. For these reasons, it is highly probable that the proceeds received from the sale of a fixed asset at the end of its useful life will be subject to taxation at the normal income tax rate.

Using straight-line depreciation and incorporating the expected salvage value into the analysis, we get the following.

Cash Flows Years 1–5

	Tax Computation	Cash Flow
Revenues	$42,000	$42,000
Cash expenses	20,000	20,000
Cash flow before taxes	22,000	22,000
Depreciation ($60,000/5)	12,000	
Taxable income	$10,000	
Tax, at 60%	$ 6,000	6,000
Net cash flow per year		$16,000

Summary of Present Value of Investment

Operating cash flows ($16,000 × 3.605)		$57,680
Salvage value:		
Total salvage value	$ 5,000	
Tax on salvage value 60%	3,000	
After-tax cash flow from salvage value	$ 2,000	
Times present value factor for 5 years hence at 12%	.567	
Present value of salvage value		1,134
Total present value		58,814
Investment required		60,000
Net present value		($ 1,186)

The original net present value was ($2,320), and the new net present value is ($1,186). Incorporating the salvage value into the analysis that used the ACRS rules, we would have the following.

Present value of future flows, based on ACRS	$60,148
Present value of salvage value	1,134
Total present value of future cash flows	61,282
Investment required	60,000
Net present value of project	$ 1,282

Those who supported the adoption of ACRS, and prior systems that allowed accelerated depreciation for tax purposes, claimed that their proposal would increase capital expenditures. As you can see from the above analysis, their claim is justified in the sense that the availability of accelerated tax write-offs can increase the attractiveness (desirability) of opportunities for capital investment.

DECISION RULES

The decision rules associated with the two methods of analysis we have described are simple. Using the net present value method, any project having a positive net present value should be accepted; others should be rejected. Using the time-adjusted rate of return method, a project having a rate of return greater than the firm's cost of capital should be accepted. The relationship of the two criteria is as follows.

1. If the internal rate of return is less than the cost of capital (or cutoff rate), the net present value will be negative.
2. If the net present value is greater than zero, the internal rate of return is greater than the cost of capital (or cutoff rate).

When analyzing any single project for acceptance or rejection, both methods will lead to the same decision. The problem of multiple investment opportunities will be discussed in Chapter 9.

As in other decision areas, qualitative factors may override a capital budgeting decision that seems desirable given only quantifiable data. A project may show a positive net present value and still be rejected by the firm. For example, a firm committed to producing high-quality, high-priced products may reject a project if the proposed product is relatively cheap. Or a firm that manufactures toys might not make toy guns because of the personal convictions of its top managers. On the other hand, a firm might undertake an investment that showed a negative net present value if the project would bring the firm considerable prestige or perhaps enhance its image as an innovator. Where qualitative reasons support the undertaking of a project, analysis of the quantitative factors should not be ignored, because it will give managers a better idea of the *cost* to the firm of accepting a particular qualitative goal as paramount.

OTHER METHODS OF CAPITAL BUDGETING

Though the net present value and internal rate of return methods are theoretically sound, it is sometimes argued that their use is not practical because of the many estimates involved (cost of capital, cash flows, useful lives, etc.). Critics of these methods advocate other methods, which we shall now cover. Interestingly, each of these methods requires most of the same estimates as do the net present value and internal rate of return methods.

Payback Period

One of the most commonly used methods of capital budgeting is the **payback period** technique under which the manager estimates future net cash inflows from an investment and determines how long it will take for the investment to be recovered. If a project requires an outlay of $10,000 and will generate annual net cash inflows of $4,000, it has a payback period of 2.5 years ($10,000/$4,000). Thus, if the annual flows are equal,

$$\frac{\text{Payback}}{\text{period}} = \frac{\text{investment required}}{\text{annual cash returns}}$$

The payback computation ignores the possibility of a payback period longer than the life of the project. Payback thus evaluates only the rapidity with which an investment will be recovered. Obviously, a project would not be acceptable if the computed payback period exceeded the life of the project.

Decision rules when using the payback technique may be stated in several ways. A firm may set a limit on the payback period beyond which an investment will not be made. A firm might also use payback to decide among available investments so that the investment with the shortest payback period would be selected.

The payback method has a very serious fault. It does not indicate the profitability of the investment. *It emphasizes the return* of *the investment but ignores the return* on *the investment*. The life of the project after the payback period is ignored altogether.

Consider the two investment possibilities that are described below:

	A	B
Cost	$10,000	$10,000
Useful life in years	5	10
Annual cash flows over the useful lives	$ 2,500	$ 2,000

Investment A has a payback period of four years ($10,000/$2,500), and B one of five years ($10,000/$2,000). Under the payback criterion, then, investment A would be better than investment B because its payback period is shorter. Yet it should be obvious that investment B is superior; the returns from A will cease one year after the payback period, while B will continue to return cash for five more years.

The payback method has another serious fault in that it ignores the *timing* of the expected future cash flows. This fault, like the method's failure to consider years after the payback period, can also be an impediment to good decision making. Consider two investments, X and Y, as described below:

	X	Y
Cost	$10,000	$10,000
Cash flows by year:		
1	$ 2,000	$ 6,000
2	6,000	3,000
3	2,000	1,000
4–8	3,000	3,000

Both X and Y have payback periods of three years, with equal returns over years four through eight. But the investment in Y will be recovered much more quickly than that in X, which is desirable. If two investments promise equal total returns, the one that generates the returns more quickly is the more desirable. The rate of return on investment X is approximately 29%, whereas that on investment Y is about 31%.

Despite its faults, payback does have some uses. Knowing the payback period can be particularly important if the firm is especially concerned about liquidity. Also, payback can be a rough screening device for investment proposals because a relatively long payback period will usually mean a low rate of return. As a practical matter, the payback period is automatically computed in the process of calculating the time-adjusted rate of return on an investment with equal annual cash flows. For example, suppose an investment opportunity has a cost of $100,000, a life of 15 years, and a promised annual cash flow of $25,000. To compute the internal rate of return on this project, you would begin by dividing the cost by the annual returns and you would get the factor 4.0 ($100,000/$25,000). This factor is the payback period, four years. You would then proceed to look up, in Table B, the interest rate associated with 15 periods such that the factor in the table was approximately 4.0. The factor for 24% and 15 periods is 4.001. Thus, this project promises a 24% rate of return and a payback period of four years.

Payback is also useful as a measure of risk, because, in general, the longer it takes to get your money back, the greater the risk that the money will not be returned.

As the time horizon lengthens, more uncertainties arise. Inflation might ease, or it might get worse; interest rates could rise, or they could fall; new techniques might be developed that would make the investment obsolete. Essentially, all this really means is that a manager might prefer a project that will pay back the investment in two years to one that would take ten years, even though the one with the 10-year payback period might have a higher expected NPV and IRR.[4]

Let us illustrate the point with an admittedly extreme example. Suppose that you have $1,000,000 to invest and are considering two possibilities, both of which involve buying a cargo of merchandise and shipping it to a distant country. One voyage will take a year to complete, the other five years. The expected after-tax returns at the ends of the periods are $1,160,000 for the 1-year voyage and $3,713,000 for the 5-year voyage. The expected rates of return on the voyages are 16% and 30%, respectively; and, using a cost of capital of 10%, the NPVs are $54,545 and $1,305,481.

A lot can happen to a ship on a 1-year voyage; storms, piracy, collisions with icebergs or with rocks, etc. Considering the hazards, it is hard to conceive of an individual who wouldn't feel that it was a lot safer tying up his or her money for one year rather than five despite the advantage of the 5-year voyage as determined under the normal techniques of analysis. Whether you would choose to invest in the 1-year or the 5-year opportunity would depend on your attitude about risk and return. The payback method of evaluation would, because of its emphasis on the rapidity of return of investment, give higher priority to the 1-year voyage. There are other, more formal ways of dealing with the risk associated with investment opportunities, but payback is one of the most common.

Book Rate of Return

Another commonly used capital budgeting method that does not take account of the time value of money is the **book-rate-of-return** technique. Under this method, the average annual book income is divided by the average book investment in the project. That is,

$$\text{Average book rate of return} = \frac{\text{average annual future book income}}{\text{average book investment}}$$

To illustrate, assume a $20,000 investment offering an opportunity for pretax cash flows of $5,000 per year for eight years, and a tax rate of 40%. The book income for each of the eight years, assuming straight-line depreciation is used, would be as follows:

Pretax cash flows	$5,000
Depreciation ($20,000/8 years)	2,500
Pretax income	2,500
Income taxes	1,000
Net income	$1,500

---

[4]A former student of one of the authors informed us that her firm, a very large one, requires a 2-year payback period as the sole criterion for investment.

The average book investment in this project will be $10,000 ($20,000/2). (Note that the book investment in the project declines each year because of the annual depreciation charge.) With an annual net income of $1,500, and an average book investment of $10,000, the average book rate of return is 15% ($1,500/$10,000).[5] This return is an *average* rate of return because we have used the average book investment. In each year, the computed rate of return using book amounts will be different because the book investment in the project will change with each year's depreciation. By using book investment at the beginning of the year, in year one the rate of return will be 7.5% ($1,500/$20,000); in the last year, the rate of return will be 60% ($1,500/$2,500).

Let us compare these results with those obtained using the internal rate of return method. The net cash flows for the project would be $4,000 (net income of $1,500 plus depreciation of $2,500). Dividing the cost by the annual cash flows yields a factor of 5 ($20,000/$4,000). The factor closest to 5 in the 8-period row of Table B is 4.968, which is associated with 12%. Hence, the internal rate of return on this project is approximately 12%.

The following example illustrates the deficiencies of the book-rate-of-return method. Investments A and B require identical investments ($10,000), produce identical total net incomes, and therefore identical average net incomes, and identical average rates of return of 26.7%. However, investment A is clearly superior to investment B; the flows come in faster for A.

	A	B
Pretax cash flows by year:		
1	$10,000	$ 2,000
2	5,000	5,000
3	1,666	9,666
Totals	16,666	16,666
Depreciation	10,000	10,000
Income before taxes	6,666	6,666
Income taxes (40%)	2,666	2,666
Total net income	$ 4,000	$ 4,000
Average net income	$ 1,333	$ 1,333
Average book rate of return ($1,333/$5,000)	26.7%	26.7%

Assuming straight-line depreciation, the internal rate of return on investment A is about 23%, whereas that on investment B is only about 15%. When firms use one method to compute depreciation for their income statements and a faster method to compute depreciation for their tax returns, the book rate of return will differ even more markedly from the IRR.

The book-rate-of-return method almost always misstates the true rate of return because it ignores the timing of the cash flows. This flaw renders it an unsatisfactory method of capital budgeting.

[5]Others may prefer to use the original investment in the denominator.

SUMMARY EVALUATION OF METHODS

The critical difference between the net present value and internal rate of return methods and the payback and book-rate-of-return methods is the attention given to the timing of the expected cash flows. The first two methods, called **discounted cash flow (DCF) techniques,** consider the timing of the cash flows; the last two methods do not. Because they recognize the time value of money, the DCF techniques are conceptually superior. Nevertheless, both payback and book rate of return are in wide use.[6]

It is sometimes argued that the DCF techniques are too complex, or that they require too many estimates to make them useful in practice. There is, we believe, little merit in these charges. All four methods require about the same estimates. DCF methods require estimates of future cash flows and the timing of those flows. The book-rate-of-return method requires estimates of future net incomes, which necessitates making essentially the same estimates as those required to estimate cash flows. The payback method requires the estimation of cash flows but not of useful life. One point in favor of the payback method is that it emphasizes near-term cash flows. Near-term cash flows are usually easier to predict than flows in later years. However, as we pointed out, unless consideration is given to useful life, the payback method could lead to very poor decisions.

The net present value method does require an estimate of the cost of capital or at least a decision as to a minimum acceptable rate of return; this is true also of the internal rate of return method. But the book-rate-of-return method requires such a decision also. And the payback method requires a decision regarding the minimum acceptable payback period. In short, DCF techniques do not seem to be any more unrealistic or impractical than the other two approaches, and the conceptual superiority of the former argues strongly for their use.

INVESTING DECISIONS AND FINANCING DECISIONS

None of the examples offered thus far has considered the specific way that the firm would finance the project in question. That is, we did not say that the firm would issue debt, common stock, some combination of the two, or finance the investment using cash flows from ongoing operations. The omission was deliberate. The investing decision is separate from the financing decision.

It might be tempting to argue that if the firm plans to finance an investment with debt at 9%, this rate should be used to discount the expected cash flows. It might also be tempting in such a case to subtract the interest payments as part of the cash flow computation. Resist these temptations!

A firm should not accept projects that will return less than the cost of capital,

[6]Klammer found that 57% of firms responding to a survey used DCF techniques in 1970, which was up from 19% in 1959. Thomas Klammer, "Empirical Evidence of the Adoption of Sophisticated Capital Budgeting Techniques," *Journal of Business,* October 1972, pp. 387–397.

because it must earn a satisfactory return for *all* investors in the firm—both creditors and stockholders. Both types of capital suppliers are concerned about the safety of their investments and therefore monitor firm solvency by such factors as the ratio of debt to equity. If a firm makes too liberal use of debt because it has investment opportunities the returns on which exceed the interest rate but not cost of capital, it will find itself unable to raise *any* capital except at exorbitant rates. (Stockholders raise the rate by selling their stock, which reduces the price and thus raises the cost of equity capital. Lenders will insist on higher interest rates, thus raising the cost of debt capital.)

The temptation to include interest payments as part of the cash flow computation reflects a misunderstanding of the concept of discounting. The use of cost of capital as the discount rate automatically provides for not only the recovery *of* the investment, but also a return *on* the investment at least equal to the cost of capital. If interest payments are subtracted to arrive at the net cash flow, the cost of debt is provided for twice—once by subtracting the interest payments, and again by using a discount rate that includes the cost of obtaining both debt and equity capital.

SUMMARY

Decisions to commit resources for time periods longer than a year are called capital budgeting decisions. To evaluate such decisions, the investment required must be identified together with its resulting cash flows. Future cash flows may occur because of additional revenues, additional costs, or cost savings. Critical to capital budgeting is the fact that most, if not all, of the numbers used in the analyses are estimates. Also critical is recognition of the effects of depreciation.

Effective evaluation of capital budgeting decisions uses present value analysis. The two approaches recommended are the net present value and the internal rate-of-return methods. Other methods often used are conceptually inferior because they fail to consider the time value of money. But such methods may be useful as rough screening devices for investment opportunities.

Discounted cash flow methods are used to decide on undertaking an investment. The solution is based on the firm's cost of capital. The interest rate that must be paid on borrowings for making the particular investment is not relevant to the analysis.

KEY TERMS

accelerated cost recovery system (ACRS)
book rate of return
capital budgeting decisions
cash flows
cost of capital
cutoff rate of return
discounted cash flow techniques
discount rate
excess present value

internal rate of return
net present value
payback period
present value
target rate of return
tax shield (effect) of depreciation
time-adjusted rate of return
time value of money

KEY FORMULAS

Present value of future flows = annual cash returns × present value factor

Net present value = present value of future flows − required current investment

$$\text{Payback period} = \frac{\text{investment required}}{\text{annual cash returns}}$$

$$\text{Average book rate of return} = \frac{\text{average annual future book income}}{\text{average book investment}}$$

REVIEW PROBLEM

Dwyer Company has the opportunity to market a new product. The sales manager believes that the firm could sell 5,000 units per year at $14 per unit for five years. The production manager has determined that machinery costing $60,000 and having a 5-year life and no salvage value would be required. The machinery would have fixed operating costs requiring cash disbursements of $4,000 annually. Variable costs per unit would be $8. Straight-line depreciation would be used for both book and tax purposes. The tax rate is 40% and the firm's cost of capital is 14%.

Required

1. Determine the increase in annual net income and in annual cash flows expected from the investment.
2. Determine the payback period.
3. Determine the book rate of return on the average investment.
4. Determine the net present value of the investment.
5. Determine the internal rate of return of the investment.
6. Suppose that the machinery has salvage value of $5,000 at the end of its useful life. The firm does not consider the salvage value in determining depreciation expense. (Annual depreciation is the same as before.) The tax rate on the gain at the end of the asset's life is 40%. What would your answer to be part 4?
7. Assume that the investment has *no* salvage value and falls in the three-year ACRS class. Determine the net present value of the investment opportunity.

Answer to Review Problem

1.

	Tax Computation	Cash Flow
Sales (5,000 × $14)	$70,000	$70,000
Variable cost (5,000 × $8)	40,000	40,000
Contribution margin (5,000 × $6)	30,000	30,000
Fixed cash operating costs	4,000	4,000
Cash flow before taxes	26,000	26,000
Depreciation ($60,000/5)	12,000	
Increase in taxable income	14,000	
Income tax at 40% rate	5,600	5,600
Increase in net income	8,400	
Add depreciation	12,000	
Net cash flow per year	$20,400	$20,400

2. Payback period, about 2.941 years, which is $60,000 divided by $20,400.
3. The book rate of return on the average investment is 28%, which is annual net income of $8,400 divided by the average investment of $30,000 ($60,000/2).
4. $10,033, calculated as follows:

Net cash flow per year	$20,400
Present value factor, 5-year annuity at 14% (Table B)	3.433
Present value of future net cash flows	$70,033
Less investment	60,000
Net present value	$10,033

5. The internal rate of return is a little over 20%. The factor to seek is 2.941, which is the payback period calculated in part 2. The closest factor in the 5-year row of Table B is 2.991, which is the 20% factor. Because 2.941 is less than 2.991, the rate is more than 20%. (Notice that the higher the rate, the lower the factor.)
6. The only change required is the determination of the present value of the salvage value less tax on the gain.

Salvage value	$ 5,000
Tax at 40%	2,000
Net cash flow, end of year 5	$ 3,000
Present value factor for single payment,	
5 years at 14% (Table A)	.519
Present value of salvage value	$ 1,557
Net present value from part 4	10,033
Net present value	$11,590

Notice that we did not have to recompute annual net cash flows. The firm still used $12,000 for depreciation expense. Therefore, at the end of five years the machinery would have a book value of zero and the gain on disposal would equal the salvage value.

7. Approximately $11,800. One approach is to compute the cash flows for each year and discount them separately.

	1	2	3	4	5
Cash flow before taxes	$26,000	$26,000	$26,000	$26,000	$26,000
ACRS writeoff (25%, 38%, 37%)	15,000	22,800	22,200	—	—
Increase in taxable income	11,000	3,200	3,800	26,000	26,000
Increase in income taxes (40%)	4,400	1,280	1,520	10,400	10,400
Net cash flow	$21,600	$24,720	$24,480	$15,600	$15,600
Present value factors	.877	.769	.675	.592	.519
Present values	$18,943	$19,010	$16,524	$ 9,235	$ 8,096
Total present value of future cash flows			$71,808		
Cost of investment			60,000		
NPV			$11,808		

A second approach would be to compute the after-tax cash flow without regard to the tax shield from depreciation, and compute the present value of that shield separately.

Five-year annuity of cash savings without		
regard to depreciation:		
Cash savings		$26,000
Tax on cash savings, at 40%		10,400
Cash flows ignoring depreciation		$15,600
PV factor for a five-year annuity at 14%		3.433
Total present value of savings		
without regard to depreciation		$53,555
Depreciation tax shield:		
Year 1 $15,000 × .40 × .877	$5,262	
Year 2 $22,800 × .40 × .769	7,013	
Year 3 $22,200 × .40 × .675	5,994	
		18,269
Total present value of future flows		71,824
Cost of investment		60,000
NPV		$11,824

The difference in NPV between this approach ($11,824) and the first ($11,808) is due to rounding.

ASSIGNMENT MATERIAL

Questions for Discussion

8-1 Rental payments and installment purchase   Is there any difference between the cost of (a) renting a car for $60 per month and (b) buying a car for $3,600 which you expect will have no value at the end of five years and for which you make payments of $60 per month for five years?

8-2 Interest rates and economic activity   The federal government is concerned with regulating the level of economic activity—especially with encouraging production and investment to maintain high employment while not allowing excessive inflation. The government attempts to do this by changing interest rates through the Federal Reserve Board. How can this ability to influence interest rates be used to stimulate or discourage investment?

8-3 Capital budgeting—effects of events   A particular capital expenditure proposal for a new machine has been analyzed, based on currently available information. In what way(s) would each of the following events (not anticipated at the time the original analysis was done) affect the analysis? Consider each event independently.
1. The interest rate on long-term debt increases.
2. The company signs a new contract with its union. The contract includes a negotiated wage rate for all categories of workers that is higher than the prevailing rate.
3. The company raises the selling prices of its products.

4. Congress approves the use of a depreciation rate that provides much faster recognition of depreciation expense than was previously available.

Exercises

8-4 **Discounting**

1. Find the approximate internal rates of return for each of the following investments.
   (a) Investment of $30,000 with annual cash flows of $5,000 for fourteen years.
   (b) $36,000 investment with annual cash flows of $9,000 for 15 years.
   (c) An investment of $90,000 with a single return of $120,000 at the end of three years.

2. Find the net present values of the following investments using discount rates of 8%, 12%, and 16%.
   (a) Annual flows of $30,000 for ten years are produced by an investment of $150,000.
   (b) An investment of $120,000 with annual cash flows of $20,000 for 12 years.
   (c) An investment of $28,000 with annual flows of $8,000 for four years and a single return of $6,000 at the end of the fifth year.

3. Repeat part 2 above using a discount rate of 10% and a 40% income tax rate. Assume straight-line depreciation on the amount of the investment over the entire life of the cash flows.

8-5 **Comparison of net present value and rate-of-return methods**   Jones Company is thinking of buying some new equipment that promises to save $5,000 in cash operating costs per year. The equipment will cost $25,000. Its estimated useful life is 10 years, and it will have zero disposal value. Ignore taxes.

Required
1. Compute the net present value if the minimum desired rate of return is 10%.
2. Compute the time-adjusted rate of return.

8-6 **Discounting**   Solve each of the following independent problems.

1. Harry Smith will be starting college in one year. His father wishes to set up an investment for Harry to use for the $4,200 he will need each year for four years. Harry will make withdrawals at the beginnings of the school years. If Mr. Smith can invest at 9%, how much must he invest today to provide for Harry's college expenses?

2. Brute McGurk is a senior in high school who weighs 450 pounds and runs the 100-yard dash in 8.7 seconds. He has been offered $250,000 per year to play professional football, but would like to go to college. He believes that if he does go to college he will be able to earn $400,000 per year playing football after he graduates. In either case, his playing career will be over at 30, which gives him 12 years if he turns professional immediately. Assuming that going to college would cost him nothing and that his football salary would be paid at the ends of years, what should he do if the interest rate is 10%?

3. Henry Jackson is about to retire from his job. His pension benefits have accumulated to the point where he could receive a lump-sum payment of $120,000 or $20,000 per year for ten years, paid at the ends of years. Jackson has no dependents and fully expects to live ten years after he retires. If he can invest at 10%, which option should he take?

8-7 Time value of money   Answer the following questions.

1. A person received a single payment of $6,440 as a result of having invested some money five years ago at an interest rate of 10%. How much did the person invest?

2. An investment opportunity requiring $5,000 is available. It will return a single payment at the end of ten years. The interest rate is 14%. How much will be received at the end of ten years?

3. An investment of $2,000 returned a single payment of $5,400. The interest rate earned was 18%. How many years elapsed between the investment and the return?

4. A person received seven annual payments of $1,000 from an investment made seven years ago. The interest rate was 12%. What was the amount of the investment?

5. An investment of $1,000 returned $343 annually for some years. The rate of interest earned was 14%. How many payments were received?

6. A $12,000 investment made today will provide a 12% return. The returns will be paid in equal amounts over twelve years. What is the amount of the annual payment?

8-8 Comparison of methods   Using after-tax data, the Jason Company has three investment opportunities, summarized below.

	A	B	C
Cost	$50,000	$50,000	$50,000
Cash inflows by year (after tax):			
Year 1	25,000	35,000	4,000
Year 2	25,000	10,000	8,000
Year 3	0	45,000	10,000
Year 4	5,000	20,000	98,000
Totals	$55,000	$110,000	$120,000

Required

1. Rank the investment opportunities in order of desirability using (a) payback period, (b) average book rate of return (use average net book value of the investment as the denominator), and (c) net present value using a 10% discount rate.

2. Comment on the results.

8-9 Tax shields and present values   Your boss is considering a new parking lot for employees that will cost $200,000. The company is in the 40% tax bracket and your boss says "It will only cost us $120,000 after taxes to put in the lot." The firm has a 14% cost of capital and would depreciate the lot over 10 years using the straight-line method.

Required: Tell your boss the net cost, in present value terms, to put in the parking lot.

8-10 Basic alternatives   Widmer Company is considering an investment opportunity involving a cash outlay of $96,000 for a new machine that would last about ten years and have a residual value of $1,000. The machine would reduce annual cash operating costs by $25,000. The firm's tax rate is 40% and its cost of capital is 14%. The company considers scrap value when computing depreciation (straight line).

Required: For this project compute (1) the payback period; (2) the approximate internal rate of return (ignore the residual value); (3) the net present value.

8-11 NPV and IRR   Morison Company makes high-quality wallpaper. Its managers believe that the company can increase productivity by acquiring some new machinery, but are unsure whether it would be profitable.

The machinery would cost $800,000, have a four-year life with no salvage value, and save about $420,000 in cash operating costs annually. The company would use straight-line depreciation. Morison has a 40% income tax rate and a 14% cost of capital.

Required
1. Calculate the net present value of the investment.
2. Calculate the approximate internal rate of return.

8-12 Comparison of methods   Below are data relating to three possible investments.

	X	Y	Z
Cost	$40,000	$10,000	$20,000
Useful life—years	10	4	20
Annual cash savings	$ 7,668	$ 3,717	$ 3,278

Required: Rank the investments according to their desirability using the following: (1) payback period, (2) internal rate of return, and (3) net present value using a discount rate of 12%. (Ignore taxes and depreciation.)

8-13 Comparison of book return and NPV   Welton Company is introducing a product that will sell for $10 per unit. Annual volume for the next four years should be about 200,000 units. The company can use either of two machines to make the product. Data are as follows:

	Machine X	Machine Y
Per unit variable cost	$ 4	$ 2
Annual cash fixed costs	$725,000	$ 850,000
Cost of machine	$800,000	$1,400,000

Both machines have four-year lives and no anticipated salvage value. The firm uses straight-line depreciation, has a 40% income tax rate, and a 14% cost of capital.

Required
1. Determine which machine would give the higher book rate of return on the average investment.
2. Determine which machine has the higher net present value.
3. Which machine should the firm acquire? Why?

8-14 Effects of ACRS   You have been telling a friend about the benefits of ACRS, in contrast to straight-line depreciation over a longer asset life. He is unimpressed, saying that so long as the total tax savings are the same, it makes no difference when those savings arrive.

Required: Respond to your friend, using as an example a $100,000 asset with no salvage value and a life of five years. Assume that the tax rate is 40%, the cost of capital 20%, and the appropriate ACRS period 3 years. (The deduction for the three years is 25%, 38%, and 37% of cost, in years one, two, and three, respectively.)

8-15 Yesterday's decisions   Mark Quinton, president of Ajax Industries, is talking with Dan Weber, a salesman for a machinery company, about a new model of a machine currently used by Ajax. Quinton is staring, unbelieving, at Weber and saying, "But it was just yesterday that I spent $60,000 for what you now call your 'old model.' I sure am not interested in buying another machine to do the same job. The machine I just bought will last for one year and cost me $45,000 to operate for that year. Agreed, it has no resale value. But after putting out $60,000 I am not about to buy your $25,000 model even though it will do the same job as mine will for $12,000 for the year. Next year, when I have to replace the one I just bought, I'll be glad to talk to you; but I would lose $60,000 if I bought what you're trying to sell me now."

Required: As Dan Weber, respond to Mr. Quinton's remarks and support your reply with calculations.

8-16 Relationships   Fill in the blanks for each of the following independent cases. In all cases the investment has a useful life of ten years and no salvage value. Ignore income taxes.

	(a) Annual Cash Inflow	(b) Investment	(c) Cost of Capital	(d) Internal Rate of Return	(e) Net Present Value
1.	$ 45,000	$188,640	14%	——	$_____
2.	$ 80,000	$_____	12%	18%	$_____
3.	$_____	$300,000	——	16%	$ 81,440
4.	$_____	$450,000	12%	——	$115,000
5.	$100,000	$_____	——	14%	($ 38,300)

8-17 Paying off a mortgage   This problem is based on an experience of one of the authors, although the numerical values have been changed for convenience in calculations.

Joe L. Back was moving from one city to another. His house had a $30,000 mortgage bearing 6 percent interest, with 10 years to run. Payments were made annually in the amount of $4,076.09 ($30,000/7.36, the present value factor for a 10-year annuity at 6 percent). The mortgage was assumable: that is, when Joe sold his house, the buyer could assume the liability for the mortgage as part of the purchase price. Put differently, the bank could not force Joe to pay off the mortgage when he sold the house.

Interest rates for mortgages were then about 16 percent. Joe approached the bank suggesting that it might be worthwhile for him to pay off the mortgage at a discount (pay less than $30,000 to liquidate the liability).

Required

1. Given that the bank could reinvest the proceeds of Joe's paying off his mortgage at 16 percent, how much should it be willing to accept in full satisfaction of the liability?
2. In the actual case the bank refused Joe's offer. He sold the house, and the buyer assumed the mortgage. Did the bank make a bad decision? Why might the bank have rejected Joe's offer?

8-18 New product decision   Cavala Company has the opportunity to introduce a new product with the following expected results:

Annual unit volume	10,000
Selling price	$ 100
Unit variable cost	$ 60
Annual cash fixed costs	$235,000

The product requires equipment that would cost $270,000 and have a three-year life with no salvage value. The company has a 20% cost of capital. The income tax rate is 40%, and straight-line depreciation will be used.

Required
1. Determine the net present value of the investment.
2. Determine the approximate internal rate of return of the investment.
3. For the investment to yield just 20%, what annual unit volume is required?

Problems

8-19 Installing a sprinkler system   Walton Company operates several factories, one of which was built some 30 years ago and is not in good condition. That factory has a fire insurance policy covering machinery, inventory, and the building itself. Premiums on the policy are $15,000 per year.

Recently, a fire inspector from the insurance company has recommended that the premium be increased to $35,000 per year because the factory's fire protection has been diminished. The reason is that its existing sprinkler system has stopped functioning and cannot be repaired at a reasonable cost. The plant manager was told by the inspector that a new system, costing $120,000 and with a 12-year life and no salvage value, would be needed to continue the existing premium of $15,000 per year.

The system would be depreciated on a straight-line basis. The tax rate is 40% and Walton's cost of capital is 12%.

Required: Determine whether the sprinkler system should be bought. ·

8-20 Employment options   Bob Wiblek is a college senior and an All-American football player. Drafted by the Bay City Beasts of the Tri-Continental League, he has been pondering two alternatives that the team has offered. The first is that Bob receives $500,000 per year for 10 years, the second is that he receives $300,000 per year for 30 years. Either way, Bob and the team both expect his playing career to be over in 10 years. Under either alternative, he would get the prescribed amounts whether or not he plays.

Bob would have an income tax rate of 50%. The team has a 40% income tax rate. Bob believes that a 10% discount rate is appropriate. The team has a 14% cost of capital.

Required
1. Which offer should Bob take?
2. Which offer is better for the team?
3. If your answers to parts 1 and 2 differ, explain why. You need not make any calculations.

8-21 **Retirement options**   Mr. Ralph Mathews will retire in a few months, on reaching his 65th birthday. His firm provides a pension plan that offers two options: (1) a lump-sum payment of $150,000 on the day of retirement; and (2) annual payments of $20,000 per year beginning on the date of retirement and ending at death. Mr. Mathews is not sure which option he should select and asks for your assistance. He tells you that he has no savings now, that he could earn a 14% return if he invested part of the lump-sum payment, and that he would like to spend $25,000 per year during his retirement. He has no relatives or other heirs and is not concerned about leaving an estate. He tells you that he could live on $20,000 per year, but would much prefer to spend $25,000 and be more comfortable.

  If he chose the lump-sum payment, he would take out $25,000 to live on during the first year of retirement and invest the remainder. He would then draw $25,000 at the beginning of every year until the money ran out.

Required: Advise Mr. Mathews on how long he could afford to keep up a $25,000 per year standard of living.

8-22 **Expanding a product line**   Kiernan Company makes office equipment of various sorts, such as tables, desks, chairs, and lamps. The sales manager is trying to decide whether to introduce a new model of desk. The desk will sell for $500 and have variable costs of $320. Volume is expected to be 4,500 units per year for five years. To make the desks the firm will have to buy additional machinery that will cost $1,500,000, have a 5-year life, and no salvage value. Straight-line depreciation will be used. Fixed cash operating costs will be $300,000 per year.

  The firm is in the 40% tax bracket and its cost of capital is 10%.

Required

1. Determine, using the net present value method, whether the new desk should be brought out.
2. Compute the payback period.
3. Determine the approximate internal rate of return that the firm expects to earn on the investment.

8-23 **New product—a textbook**   After reviewing selected chapters and detailed outlines, Raven Publishing Company is considering bringing out a new textbook on managerial accounting. Raven expects volume over the 3-year life of the first edition to be 25,000, 18,000, and 13,000 books, respectively. The book will sell for $12 at retail, of which Raven gets 75%. (College bookstores will keep 25% of the retail price.) Variable costs associated with each book are as follows:

Paper and cover	$1.50
Royalties to author	1.40
Other (printing, etc.)	1.10
Total	$4.00

  Fixed costs directly associated with the book will be $20,000 per year. In addition, it costs about $75,000 to set up and print a new book. Moreover, special advertising and promotion costs of $25,000 will be incurred almost immediately upon signing a contract for the book, and approximately $12,000 will be spent at the end of the first and the second years to advertise and promote the book ($12,000 for each campaign).

The company's tax rate is 40%, and setup and promotion costs are deductible in the year such costs are incurred. The company's cost of capital is 16%.

The author desires a $9,000 initial payment, which amount is deductible for tax purposes equally over the three years.

Required

1. Determine whether the book should be published.
2. A survey suggests that sales would be 10% higher if the book were more expensively produced (more artwork and use of color). Variable costs would increase to $4.50 per book, fixed costs would remain the same, and setup costs would be $85,000. Should the more expensive version of the book be published?

8-24 Capital budgeting and reported earnings The president of Wallco Industries has been disturbed by reports that the firm's stock is not considered a good buy. Wallco has been a rapidly growing company in a field that stresses swift technological advances. Wallco has an extensive research program and an ambitious building schedule, with $10 million plant and equipment expenditures planned for next year. The firm's stock is currently selling at $125, about 25 times earnings per share of $5 last year. Increased growth in earnings per share is viewed as necessary to sustain the price of the stock.

Wallco has a cutoff rate of return of 20% after taxes, using discounted cash flow techniques. The president wonders whether to institute another capital spending constraint: by the second year of operations a project must be expected to increase earnings per share by at least $0.40 for each $1,000,000 invested. He feels that such a requirement would help to keep the price of the stock from falling because of disenchantment of stockholders and financial analysts whose recommendations are often acted on.

He shows you the following proposal:

Investment	$2,000,000
Cash inflows by year (before taxes):	
1	$ 600,000
2	800,000
3	1,050,000
4	1,110,000
5	1,500,000

The tax rate is 40%. There are 500,000 shares of common stock outstanding. Straight-line depreciation is used for both tax and book purposes:

Required

1. Determine whether the investment meets the 20% rate of return criterion.
2. Determine the effects of the investment on earnings per share.
3. What suggestions can you make to resolve the conflict?

8-25 Charitable donation Mrs. Jan Williamson is a wealthy entrepreneur who wishes to make a substantial donation to her alma mater, Arkwright University. She is considering two alternatives, a $5,000,000 gift now, or an equal annual amount in each of the next 10 years.

In discussions with the president of Arkwright University, she has learned that the university earns a 10% return on its endowment fund and of course pays no income taxes. The president would be equally happy with either the $5,000,000 now, or equal annual amounts having a present value of $5,000,000. Mrs. Williamson is able to earn a

9% after-tax return investing in tax-free securities. She faces a combined state and federal tax rate of 55%.

Required
1. Determine the annuity that would yield a $5,000,000 present value to the university.
2. Should Mrs. Williamson make the lump-sum donation or pay the annuity that you determined in part 1?

8-26 When-to-sell decisions   Smooth Scotch Company has a large quantity of Scotch whiskey that is approaching its sixth anniversary. When it reaches age six it can be sold for $700 per barrel. If it is held until it is ten years old it can be sold for $1,100 per barrel.

Required
1. Determine the internal rate of return that would be earned if the Scotch were held until it was ten years old.
2. Suppose that the firm has cost of capital of 16%, that the price of six-year-old Scotch is $700 per barrel, but that the price of ten-year-old Scotch in four years is in doubt. What is the minimum price per barrel that the firm would have to receive four years from now to justify keeping the Scotch until it is ten years old?
3. Suppose now that the following schedule of prices is expected. Determine the point at which the Scotch should be sold using the criterion of highest internal rate of return. (Assume that the cutoff rate of return is low enough that all of the rates you compute would be acceptable. That is, the best decision is not to sell now.)

Years of Age	Expected Price
6	$ 700
7	800
8	950
9	1,200
10	1,400

4. Redo part 3 assuming that cost of capital is 9% and the net present value criterion is to be used to make the decision.

8-27 Funding a pension plan   Knowles Company has reached an agreement with the labor union that represents its workers. The agreement calls for the firm to pay $100,000 per year for the next ten years into a pension fund for the benefit of employees. Payments would begin one year from now.

Knowles has excess cash on hand from the sale of some of its assets, so the treasurer approaches the head of the union and asks if it would be all right to make a single, lump-sum payment to discharge the 10-year obligation. Before the head of the union gives a reply, the treasurer decides to determine the maximum amount that Knowles could pay right now. The company is in the 60% tax bracket and has cost of capital of 16%. The annual payments would be deductible for tax purposes in the years in which they were made and the single payment would be deductible in the current year.

Required: Determine the maximum amount that Knowles could pay in a lump-sum settlement of the obligation.

8-28   **New product decision**   Avetta Company, a maker of sporting goods, has the opportunity to introduce a new soccer goal with the following expected results.

Annual unit volume	10,000
Selling price	$ 100
Unit variable cost	$ 60
Annual cash fixed costs	$100,000

Making the goal requires equipment that costs $585,000 and has a three-year life with no salvage value. The company has a 20% cost of capital, but would borrow the money for this investment from its local bank at 10% interest. Ignore income taxes.

Required
1. Determine the net present value of the investment.
2. Determine the internal rate of return on the investment.
3. Determine the number of units that the company must sell to make the investment just barely profitable, considering the time value of money.

8-29   **Bond refunding**   Expost Company has outstanding a $1,000,000 (par value) issue of bonds bearing a 14% interest rate. The bonds mature in ten years. Current interest rates are lower than they were when this issue was sold and the firm can now raise cash on a 10-year bond at 10%. The directors of the firm are considering retiring the outstanding issue and replacing the old bonds with 10%, 10-year bonds. The firm would have to pay a premium of 12% over par value to buy back the currently outstanding issue. It would also have to spend $60,000 in legal fees and other costs to market the new issue. The premium is tax deductible in the year of refunding, but the costs of issuing the new bonds must be amortized evenly over ten years. The tax rate is 40%, and the company's cost of capital is 18%.

Required: Should the old issue be replaced?

8-30   **Capital budgeting by a municipality**   The City Council of Alton is considering the construction of a convention center in the downtown area. The city has been losing employment to surrounding suburbs, and tax revenues have been falling. The proposed center would cost $22,000,000 to build, and the city would incur annual cash operating costs of $500,000. The city controller has prepared the following estimate of receipts from the center over its estimated useful life of 30 years.

Rentals of space for trade shows, convention, etc.	$1,800,000

The controller states that the estimated revenues were based on total annual convention attendance of 200,000 persons.

He reports that at 8% interest, the rate the city would have to pay on bonds to build the center, it would be a losing proposition. The present value of $1,300,000 ($1,800,000 – $500,000) annually for 30 years at 8% is $14,635,400, well below the cost of the center. (Assume this computation is correct.)

One member of the council comments that the rentals are not the only source of revenues to the city. To support this position she offers studies showing that the average person attending a trade show or convention spends $500 in the city in which the event is being held. Because of the various taxes in effect, the city receives, on the average, about 1% of all of the money spent in it.

Required
1. Prepare a new analysis, incorporating the additional tax receipts expected if the center is built.
2. Why is 8% used as the discount rate when it is the interest rate, not cost of capital? (Is the interest rate the same as the cost of capital to a city?)

8-31 Choosing a depreciation method—rising tax rates   Burke Company has the opportunity to invest $60,000 in machinery that will save $30,000 per year in cash operating costs. The useful life of the machinery is four years and no salvage value is expected. The controller has suggested that a three-year ACRS life be used, but the financial vice president thinks that straight-line depreciation would be better because the tax rate is expected to increase substantially over the next few years. In the first year of the life of the investment the tax rate is expected to be 30%, in the second year 40%, in the third year 50%, and 60% in the fourth year. The firm's cost of capital is 10%.

Required
1. Compute the net present value of the investment using straight-line depreciation.
2. Repeat part 1 using ACRS, with 25%, 38%, and 37% of cost deducted in the first three years.

8-32 Comparison of NPV and profit   Graham Company is bringing out a new product and has two choices with respect to the manufacturing process. No matter which choice it makes, it expects to sell 10,000 units per year for four years at $50 per unit. Data on the two processes are:

	Process A	Process B
Per unit variable cost	$ 10	$ 20
Annual fixed cash operating costs	$ 60,000	$ 40,000
Investment in equipment	$600,000	$400,000

Neither set of equipment is expected to have salvage value at the end of four years. The firm uses straight-line depreciation. Cost of capital is 20% and the tax rate is 40%.

Required
1. Which process will give the higher annual profit?
2. Which process will give the higher net present value?
3. Which process would you select and why?

8-33 Buying company cars   Salvo Company is a large distributor of household products. The firm employs salespeople who drive their own automobiles on company business and receive $0.25 per mile from the firm. Each salesperson drives about 25,000 miles per year on company business.

The company's controller has been looking into the possibility of buying cars for the salespeople. After checking on prices and operating costs, he developed the following information:

	Year			
	1	2	3	4
Operating costs per car:				
(based on 25,000 miles per year)				
Gas and oil	$1,650	$1,650	$1,650	$1,650
Insurance and taxes	250	250	250	250
Replacement parts and maintenance	50	250	550	330
Depreciation	2,500	2,500	2,500	2,500
Totals	$4,450	$4,650	$4,950	$4,730

The depreciation expense is based on a $12,000 original cost per car, with provision for $2,000 expected resale value at the end of four years. The controller added the total operating costs for each year, getting $18,780, and divided by the 100,000 total expected miles to get a per-mile cost of about $0.1878. He concluded that the cars should be bought because the average cost per mile was less than what was currently being paid to salespeople for using their own cars.

The firm is in the 40% tax bracket and its cost of capital is 14%.

Required: Determine whether the firm should purchase cars or continue paying salespeople for using their own cars.

8-34 Capital budgeting for a computer service firm   Many firms are in the business of selling computer time to others. Customers include other business firms, universities, hospitals, and so on. One such computer service firm, Compuservice, Inc., currently has a Whizbang 85, a high-speed machine that it rents from the manufacturer for $25,000 per month. The firm is considering the purchase of a Zoom 125, which is the fastest machine of its type available. The Whizbang 85 would be kept even if the Zoom were bought. Cal Kulate, president of Compuservice, believes that a number of new customers would be attracted if the firm acquired the Zoom 125. He estimates additional revenues of $38,000 per month. Additional costs requiring cash would be $3,000 per month for maintenance and salaries for added operators. The Zoom sells for $1,200,000 and has a useful physical life of about 15 years. However, computer experts have estimated that the Zoom will probably be technologically obsolete in six years.

The firm would use straight-line depreciation of $150,000 per year in order to depreciate the computer to its estimated salvage value of $300,000 at the end of six years. The firm's tax rate is 40% and its cost of capital is 16%.

Required: Evaluate the proposed purchase.

8-35 Reevaluating an investment   Ten years ago the Kramer Company, of which you are the controller, bought some machinery at a cost of $200,000. The purchase was made at the insistence of the production manager. The machinery is now worthless and the production manager believes that it should be replaced. He gives you the following analysis, which he says verifies the correctness of the decision to buy the machinery ten years ago.

He bases his statement on the 24.6% return he calculated, which is higher than the firm's cutoff rate of return of 20%:

Annual cost savings:	
Labor	$ 32,000
Overhead	29,000
Total	61,000
Less straight-line depreciation ($200,000/10)	20,000
Increase in pretax income	41,000
Income taxes at 40%	16,400
Increase in net income	$ 24,600
Average investment ($200,000/2)	$100,000
Return on investment	24.6%

Required: Do you agree that the investment was wise? Why or why not?

8-36 Purchase commitment   Ralston Company buys copper from a number of suppliers, including the Boa Copper Company. The president of Boa has offered to sell Ralston up to 1,000,000 pounds of copper per year for five years at $0.80 per pound if Ralston will lend Boa $2,000,000 at 8% interest. The loan would be repaid at the end of five years with the interest being paid annually.

Ralston uses at least 1,800,000 pounds of copper per year and expects the price to be $1.00 per pound over the next five years. The tax rate is 40% and Ralston's management considers the relevant discount rate to be 12%.

Required
1. Determine whether the offer should be accepted by Ralston Company.
2. Determine the price at which copper would have to sell, per pound, over the next five years to make accepting the offer worthwhile.

8-37 New product—complementary effects   Elmendorf Company makes a variety of cleaning products. The firm's research and development department has recently come up with a new glass cleaner that is superior to all of the products on the market, including the one that Elmendorf currently makes. The new cleaner would be priced at $6 per case and would have variable costs of $2 per case. Elmendorf would have to buy additional machinery costing $10,000,000 to make the new cleaner. The machinery would have a 10-year life. Expected volume of the new cleaner is 800,000 cases per year for ten years. In addition to the variable costs, there would be increased fixed costs of $200,000 per year requiring cash disbursements.

The machinery would be depreciated using the straight-line method with no provision for salvage value. There is about $100,000 expected salvage value at the end of ten years. The tax rate is 40% and cost of capital is 14%.

One problem with making the investment is that sales of the firm's existing cleaner would be affected. Volume of the existing cleaner is expected to fall by 300,000 cases per year. A case of the existing cleaner sells for $5 and has variable costs of $3.

Required: Determine the net present value of the proposed investment.

8-38 Cost savings, increases in volume, and ACRS (continued in Chapter 9)   Cardiff Tool Company produces a number of items, including a die that it sells to industrial customers. Sales of the die now run about 40,000 per year, but the company could sell 50,000 per year if it had the capacity to produce that many.

A necessary part of the manufacturing process is the grinding operation, which is now performed manually. The company could acquire a machine that would reduce somewhat the time required for grinding, so that about 60,000 units could be produced per year. The machine costs $500,000, has a five-year life with no salvage value, and could be depreciated using a three-year ACRS period at 25%, 38%, and 37% in each year respectively.

The die sells for $50, and the current per-unit variable cost is $18. Use of the new machine would reduce variable cost to $16 per unit, but would increase fixed cash operating costs by $230,000. The tax rate is 40%, and the cost of capital is 14%.

Required: Determine whether the company should invest in the grinding machine.

8-39   **Uses of space (AICPA adapted)**   Lansdown Company manages large office buildings in the downtown area of a major city. One of the buildings it manages has a large unused lobby area. A manager of the firm believes that a newsstand should be placed in the lobby. He has talked to managers of several other office buildings and has projected the following annual operating results if the company establishes a newsstand.

Sales	$49,000
Cost of sales	40,000
Salaries of clerks	7,000
Licenses and payroll taxes	200
Share of heat and light bills on the building	500
Share of building depreciation	1,000
Advertising for the newsstand	100
Share of Lansdown's administrative expense	400

The investment required would be $2,000, all for equipment that would be worthless in ten years. Before presenting the plan to his superiors, the manager learned that the space could be leased to an outside firm that would operate the same kind of newsstand. The other firm would pay $750 rent per year for each of the ten years. Because the lobby is heated and lighted anyway, Lansdown would supply heat and light at no additional cost. Lansdown's cost of capital is 12%. (Ignore taxes.)

Required
1. Determine the best course of action for Lansdown.
2. Determine how much annual rent Lansdown would have to receive to equalize the attractiveness of the alternatives.

8-40   **New product (CMA adapted)**   Crampton Company makes toys and other products that have relatively short lives.

The firm's management is considering the introduction of a promotional gift for office equipment dealers. Sales personnel have reported a great deal of interest in such an item and the firm has received commitments for the product for a 3-year period, at the end of which there will no longer be a demand for the product.

To produce the required quantities Crampton will have to buy some machinery and rent some additional space. Space requirements will be about 25,000 square feet; the firm has 12,500 square feet of unused space now that it is leasing for $3 per square foot. The lease has ten years to run. Another 12,500 square feet adjoining the Crampton plant could be rented at $4 per square foot per year for three years.

The cost of equipment required would be $900,000. Additional costs would be $30,000 for modification, $60,000 for installation, and $90,000 for testing. These activities would be carried out by an independent engineering firm. All of the above costs would be capitalized and depreciated over three years using ACRS with no provision for the estimated $180,000 in salvage value.

The following estimates, in thousands of dollars of revenues and expenses for the three-year period, have been developed:

	19X6	19X7	19X8
Sales	$1,000	$1,600	$800
Materials, labor, and other variable costs	400	750	350
Allocated general overhead	40	75	35
Rent	88	88	88
Depreciation (ACRS)	270	410	400
Total costs	798	1,323	873
Profit before taxes	202	277	(73)
Income taxes at 40% rate	81	111	(29)
Net income	$ 121	$ 166	($ 44)

The firm has a cutoff rate of return of 20%.

Required: Determine whether the project should be accepted.

8-41 **Long-term special order**   Nova Company makes indoor television antennae that sell for $8 and have variable costs of $3. The firm has been selling 200,000 units per year and expects to continue at that rate unless it accepts a special order from the Acme Television Company. Acme has offered to buy 40,000 units per year at $5, provided that Nova agrees to make the sales for a 5-year period. Acme will not take fewer than 40,000 units.

Nova's current capacity is 230,000 units per year. Capacity could be increased to 260,000 units per year if new equipment costing $80,000 were purchased. The equipment would have a useful life of five years, no salvage value, and would add $24,000 in annual fixed cash operating costs. Variable costs per unit would be unchanged.

Nova would use straight-line depreciation for tax purposes. The tax rate is 40% and cost of capital is 16%.

Required: Determine the best course of action for Nova Company. (Be sure to consider all of the available alternatives.)

Case

8-42 **Introduction of new product**   Jerry Dollink, the controller of Radsiville Industries, Inc., tells you about a meeting of several top managers of the firm. The topic discussed was the introduction of a new product that had been undergoing extensive research and development. Jerry had thought that the product would be brought out in the coming year, but the managers decided to give it further study.

The product is expected to have a market life of ten years. Sales are expected to be 40,000 units annually at $90. The following annual costs were presented by James

Barker, the manager of the division that would produce and sell the product.

Materials	$18 per unit
Direct labor	12
Overhead (manufacturing)	22
Selling and administrative expenses	12
Total costs	$64 per unit

Barker went on to point out that equipment costing $2,000,000 and having an expected salvage value of $100,000 at the end of ten years would have to be purchased. In addition, receivables would be expected to increase by 25% of annual sales revenues ($900,000) because the firm generally collects its receivables in 90 days. Inventory could be expected to increase by $1,000,000. Adding the $900,000 that had already been spent on research and development brought the total outlay related to the new product to $4,800,000.

Depreciation of $190,000 per year would reduce taxes by $76,000 (40% rate). The $26 per-unit profit margin would produce $1,040,000 before taxes, $624,000 after taxes. The net return would then be $700,000 annually, which is a rate of return of less than 8%, far below the firm's cost of capital at 14%. Barker concluded that the product should not be brought out.

Jerry tells you that Barker is a strong believer in "having every product pay its way." The calculation of the manufacturing overhead cost per unit includes existing fixed costs of $300,000 allocated to the new product. Selling and administrative expenses were also allocated to the product on the basis of relative sales revenue. Commissions of $4 per unit will be the only incremental selling, general, and administrative expenses.

Required

1. Prepare a new analysis. The increases in receivables and inventory should be treated as part of the initial investment. They will be recovered in full at the end of the life of the product.
2. Explain the fallacies in Barker's analysis. Comment on why you might treat items differently from the way he did.

CHAPTER 9

CAPITAL BUDGETING, PART II

The capital budgeting decisions discussed in Chapter 8 all involved the purchase of new productive assets. In this chapter we consider some other kinds of decisions, but the basic principles remain the same. In all cases the new features to be discussed require somewhat different methods of computing the net cash flows from the investment or of computing the amount of investment required; but the analyses still concentrate on cash flows and consider the time value of money.

Because of the importance of the many estimates in any capital budgeting decision, we introduce an analytical technique to help identify the most critical estimates. We also give special attention to certain aspects of income tax law that affect capital budgeting decisions. Finally, because budgets reflect planning decisions and many of those decisions have social consequences, we conclude the chapter (and Part Two) with a discussion of the social consequences of decision making and a brief look at the special problem of decision making in the public sector.

COMPLEX INVESTMENTS

For many investment opportunities, the required investment is not simply a single cash outflow for the acquisition of some new depreciable asset. The determination of the required investment may be complicated if the opportunity requires an additional investment in working capital or involves the replacement of already existing assets. These cases will be considered here.

Working Capital Investment

An investment opportunity that requires an increase in noncurrent assets, such as equipment and plant, often also requires an increase in current assets such as accounts receivable and inventory. You witnessed exactly that situation, though only with short-term increases in sales, in the preparation of the comprehensive budget for the Cross Company in Chapter 6. Sales were expected to increase consistently during the first five months of the year (page 207) and higher levels of inventory were needed to accommodate the expected increases (see Exhibit 6-4, page 208). Unless all sales are for cash, increases in sales will be accompanied by increases in the total amount of accounts receivable. Also, unless all inventory purchases are for cash, an increase in inventory will produce an increase in the total amount of accounts payable, a current liability. However, the increase in accounts payable will not be as large as the combined increases in inventory and accounts receivable.

When an investment opportunity offers an increase in sales, the accompanying *net* increase in current assets is normally called an investment in **working capital.** (Remember that working capital = current assets − current liabilities.) Investments in working capital are just as important as investments in plant and equipment, and a capital budgeting opportunity must provide an acceptable return on *all* of the investment that it may require, whether in current or noncurrent assets.

There is one difference between investments in working capital and in noncurrent assets. At the end of the useful life of a physical asset there is often salvage value to be recovered through the sale of the used asset. Working capital investments are typically recovered *in full,* or nearly so, because the larger receivables and inventory will be turned into cash during the final operating cycle in the life of the project. Remember the lags, discussed in Chapters 6 and 7, between the times purchases are made and payments required, and the times sales are made and receivables collected. In the final year of a particular project, the expectation of reduced sales reduces the required inventory, thereby reducing the required purchases, which in turn reduces the amount of cash needed to pay for purchases and frees such cash for other uses. Similarly, cash collections in that final year should exceed sales related to the project, because of the delay in collecting for sales made in the previous year.[1]

It is not particularly difficult to deal with projects that require investment in working capital. It is, however, important to recognize that *there are no tax effects* associated either with the initial increase in working capital, or with its recovery at the end of the useful life of the project. (Remember that taxes are levied on reported income, which is normally computed on the accrual basis.)

Consider an investment for a new product that is expected to have a useful life of five years. Additional revenues from the product are estimated to be $20,000

---

[1] As a practical matter, the return of the net investment in current asset items may extend one or two months after the end of a project because of the lags in (1) collections for sales (through accounts receivable), and (2) payments for purchases (through accounts payable). When dealing with the discounting of cash flows several years hence, a difference of a month or two is not usually significant and can be ignored.

annually, with additional cash costs of $6,000. The investment required is $30,000 in equipment and $35,000 in working capital. Straight-line depreciation is to be used, the equipment has no salvage value, the firm's cost of capital is 12%, and the tax rate is 40%. The cash flows and present value of the project are computed below.

Cash Flows Years 1–5

	Tax Computation	Cash Flow
Revenues	$20,000	$20,000
Cash expenses	6,000	6,000
Pretax cash flow	14,000	14,000
Depreciation ($30,000/5)	6,000	
Taxable income	$ 8,000	
Tax at 40%	$ 3,200	3,200
Net cash flow per year		$10,800

End of Year 5

Recovery of working capital investment	$35,000

Summary of Present Value of Investment

Operating cash flows	
$10,800 × 3.605	$38,934
Recovery of working capital investment	
$35,000 × 0.567	19,845
Total present value	58,779
Investment required ($30,000 + $35,000)	65,000
Net present value	($ 6,221)

The investment is undesirable. If only the noncurrent asset investment were considered, the investment would appear to be desirable because it would show a positive NPV of $8,934 ($38,934 – $30,000). Failure to consider the working capital requirements would lead to a bad decision.

When an investment opportunity requires an increase in working capital, the major change in the analysis involves the computation of the investment and of the cash flow in the final year of the project. The second case to be considered, the replacement decision, is special because it involves additional calculations to determine cash flows.

Replacement Decisions

Businesses frequently face the problem of whether to replace existing assets. This is called a **replacement decision.** Such decisions are made when economic or technological factors make it possible to perform tasks at lower cost. Faster and more efficient machines and labor-saving devices enable the firm to earn higher returns by replacing existing assets. Replacement decisions typically involve essential operations. The focus is on how to perform those operations.

Cash-flow analysis is more complex in replacement decisions than in decisions on whether to purchase new assets because (1) there are tax differences if depreciation on the replacement is different from that on the existing assets; and (2) the determination of the net cost to purchase the replacement can be complicated if the existing asset can be sold. We shall illustrate two methods for evaluating replacement decisions: the incremental approach and the "total project" approach.

The **incremental approach** focuses on the differences between the cash flows, given the alternatives of keeping the existing assets or replacing them. The **total-project approach** looks at the total cash flows and total present values under each alternative and compares the present values. Choosing one approach or the other does not change the decision. The two approaches give the same results, as we shall see, and selecting one or the other is a matter of computational convenience.

Your firm now owns a machine for which it paid $100,000 five years ago. Other data relating to this machine are as follows:

Remaining useful life	5 yrs
Current book value	$50,000
Annual depreciation	$10,000
Expected sales value–now	$20,000
–in 5 yrs.	$10,000
Annual cash operating costs	$30,000

If you continue to use the machine for the next five years, there will be a tax (at an expected rate of 40%) on the expected salvage value, because that value was not included in the depreciation calculation. If the machine is sold now, the loss for tax purposes will be $30,000 ($50,000 book value − $20,000 sales price).

Suppose that a new machine has come on the market that sells for $60,000, has an estimated useful life of five years with no salvage value, and costs only $15,000 per year to operate. The new machine would be depreciated over five years using the straight-line method. Suppose further that your firm's cost of capital is 16%. Would it be wise to replace the old machine now?

As with any capital project, there are two considerations: initial investment and future cash flows. In a replacement decision, the computation of each of these is different from the computations we have made thus far. First we determine the initial investment as shown below.

	Tax Computation	Cash Outlay
Purchase price of new asset		$60,000
Book value of old machine	$50,000	
Sale price, which is a cash inflow	20,000	(20,000)
Loss for taxes, which can be offset against regular income	$30,000	
Tax saved (40%)	$12,000	(12,000)
Total cash benefit from sale		(32,000)
Net outlay for new asset		$28,000

The book value or cost of an existing asset is sunk and irrelevant to decisions. However, book value *does* affect taxes if the asset is sold and so must be considered in determining those taxes.[2] A net outlay of $28,000 is required to buy the new asset. The sale of the old asset reduces the outlay for the new one by $32,000 because the firm will receive $20,000 from the sale of the old asset and save $12,000 in income taxes. Lest it appear that sales at a loss are always desirable because they reduce taxes, consider that if the old asset could be sold for $60,000, creating a taxable gain of $10,000 and additional taxes of $4,000, the sale would bring in $56,000, substantially more than the $32,000 shown above.

Incremental Approach   Below is the computation of future cash flows, using the incremental approach.

Annual Cash Savings Years 1–5

		Tax Computations	Cash Flows
Pretax cash savings:			
Cash cost of using old asset		$30,000	
Cash cost of using new asset		15,000	
Difference in favor of replacement	(1)	15,000	$15,000
Additional depreciation:			
Depreciation on new asset ($60,000/5)		12,000	
Depreciation on old asset		10,000	
Additional tax deduction for depreciation	(2)	2,000	
Total increase in taxable income (1) − (2) =	(3)	$13,000	
Additional tax ($13,000 × 40%)	(4)	$ 5,200	5,200
Additional cash flow (1) − (4)			$ 9,800

Salvage Values—End of Year 5

	Tax Computation	Cash Flows
Old asset	$10,000	
New asset	0	
Difference in favor of not replacing	$10,000	$10,000
Less: Tax on difference	$ 4,000	4,000
Difference in favor of not replacing		$ 6,000

The $9,800 per year for five years is then discounted at 16%, yielding a present value of $32,085 ($9,800 × 3.274). The $6,000 difference in cash flows from salvage values is

---

[2]In practice, the book value of an asset might not be the same as its carrying value for tax purposes (called its *tax basis*). For simplicity, in this section and in most of the assignment material, the book value and tax basis of the asset in question are equal. If there were a difference between the two, the tax effect of the gain or loss on disposition of an asset would be computed using the tax basis for that asset. But the principles of the calculation would remain unchanged: the carrying value of the asset is relevant only to the extent that it affects the cash flow for taxes.

discounted at 16%, yielding $2,856 ($6,000 × 0.476), which is subtracted from the present value of the $9,800 annual flows.

Summary of Present Values of Investment—Incremental Approach

Present value of savings from using new machine	$32,085
Less: Present value of difference in salvage values	2,856
Present value of future net savings	$29,229
Required investment	28,000
Net present value of replacing	$ 1,229

The present value of future net savings from making a replacement now ($29,229) is greater than the net outlay required ($28,000), and so the replacement is desirable. (If the new asset had had some salvage value, the present value of future cash flows would have been greater and the investment even more desirable; and if that salvage value were greater than the salvage value of the old asset, the difference in favor of the new asset would have been added to the $32,085.) The decision rule, then, using the incremental approach, is to replace when the net present value of the replacement alternative is positive.

Total-Project Approach   A replacement decision can also be analyzed using a total-project approach (instead of making comparisons of the incremental cash flows). In the total-project approach we calculate, individually, the present values of the future outflows using the existing asset and using the replacement asset. The decision rule, using the total-project approach, is to accept the alternative with the *lower present value of future outflows*. This is because, in the analysis of both alternatives, we are dealing with costs (cash outflows), not revenues (cash inflows); the alternative with the lower present value is the one that minimizes costs.

For the example just given, the present value of the future outflows if the existing machine is used is calculated as follows.

Decision—Operate Existing Machine

	Tax Computation	Cash Flow
Annual operating costs	$30,000	$30,000
Depreciation	10,000	
Total tax-deductible expenses	40,000	
Tax savings expected (40%)	16,000	16,000
Net cash outflow expected per year		$14,000
Present value factor for 5 years at 16%		3.274
Present value of future operating flows		$45,836
Less: Present value of salvage value ($6,000 × 0.476)		2,856
Present value of future cash outflows on existing machine		$42,980

Consider, now, the present value of the future cash flows if the new machine is purchased.

Decision—Sell Existing Machine, Buy New Machine

	Tax Computation	Cash Flow
Annual operating costs	$15,000	$15,000
Depreciation	12,000	
Total tax-deductible expenses	27,000	
Tax savings expected (40%)	10,800	10,800
Net cash outflow expected per year		$ 4,200
Present value factor for 5 years at 16%		3.274
Present value of future operating flows		$13,751
Net outlay required for the new machine (page 316)		28,000
Present value of buying new machine		$41,751

Comparing the two alternatives, we find

Present value of using existing machine	$42,980
Present value of buying new machine	41,751
Difference	$ 1,229

The present value of the outlays associated with using the existing machine is greater than that of the outlays associated with acquiring and using the new machine. Note that the $1,229 difference is equal to the NPV we computed using the incremental approach (page 318). The two approaches should give the same results, and the choice between them is a matter of convenience.

In the replacement decision considered here, it was possible to continue using the currently owned asset. The same two analytical approaches could be used if one of the firm's essential assets has reached the end of its useful life and alternatives exist as possible replacements. For example, suppose that a firm needs a new fork-lift truck because one of its existing trucks is about to be scrapped. Perhaps two different models are available as replacements, each with a different acquisition cost and associated annual operating costs. Because the firm has committed itself to replacing the old truck, the decision becomes one of how to minimize the future costs. Either the incremental or the total-project approach could be used in the analysis.

MUTUALLY EXCLUSIVE ALTERNATIVES

The analytical techniques (and associated decision rules) presented in Chapter 8 and thus far in this chapter identify investments that are wise without regard to the funds available for investment. Recognize, however, that the total resources available (internally and externally) to a given firm are not limitless. Investments that are wise under the decision rules already presented remain so even when resources are limited. But a limitation on resources means, in a sense, that all of the firm's investment opportunities are competing with each other for the available resources. In some cases, the competition among alternative opportunities is even more specific, as when the firm has two or more ways of accomplishing a given goal so that selection of any one precludes the selection of the others. When this situation exists, we call the competing proposals **mutually exclusive alternatives.**

Some of the decisions already considered would fit this definition—the replacement decision, for example. If the firm keeps its present equipment it does not buy the newer model or models, or vice versa. Mutual exclusivity can also arise as a matter of policy. For example, a firm may have a policy of introducing no more than one new product in a particular year.

Whether exclusivity is inherent in the proposals or is the result of management policy, it is not unusual that the competing alternatives have unequal lives. It has also been suggested that still another evaluation technique, the profitability index, can be particularly useful in ranking and deciding among alternatives. These two special topics are discussed in the next sections.

Unequal Lives

When alternative investment opportunities have different useful lives, the standard analytical techniques can be used, but the analysis must go further. We shall illustrate one of the several ways to deal with this special problem. Assume the following facts about two mutually exclusive investment opportunities, different versions of a machine that is required for a particular job essential to the firm's operation.

	Model G-40	Model G-70
Purchase price	$40,000	$70,000
Annual cash operating costs	8,000	6,000
Expected useful life	4 years	8 years

Neither machine has any expected salvage value at the end of its useful life. The firm's cost of capital is 14% and its tax rate is 40%. It plans to use straight-line depreciation for tax purposes on either machine.

Since the alternatives represent investments for different periods of time, we must seek a way to make the two alternatives comparable. The method we shall illustrate, in effect, equalizes the useful lives of the two opportunities by assuming that we replace the one with a shorter life at the end of its useful life. In this case the equating of useful lives is accomplished by assuming the purchase of one G-40 now and another one at the end of the four years. (In more complex cases it might be necessary to select some point in time that does not coincide with the ends of the useful lives of the investments in question.)

Let us assume that a G-40 will cost $44,000 at the end of the first four years, but that the operating costs and useful life of that asset would be the same as those associated with a similar asset bought today. Calculation of the present value of the future flows associated with acquiring the longer-lived model is shown as follows.

G-70

	Tax Computation	Cash Flow	Present Value
Annual operating costs	$ 6,000	$6,000	
Depreciation ($70,000/8 years)	8,750		
Total tax-deductible expenses	14,750		
Tax savings at 40%	5,900	5,900	
Net cash operating outflows		$ 100	
Present value factor for 8-year annuity at 14%		4.639	
Present value of future operating flows			$ 463
Purchase price			70,000
Total present value of future outflows			$70,463

Calculating the present value of the future flows associated with the shorter-lived model (see below) is somewhat more complicated because the cash flows in the first four years of the time period are not the same as those in the last four years of the

G-40

	Tax Computation	Cash Flow	Present Value
Annual operating costs, years 1–4	$ 8,000	$8,000	
Depreciation, years 1–4 ($40,000/4)	10,000		
Total tax-deductible expenses	18,000		
Tax savings at 40%	7,200	7,200	
Net cash operating outflows per year, years 1–4		$ 800	
Present value factor, 4-year annuity at 14%		2.914	
Present value of operating outflows, years 1–4			$ 2,331
Present value of replacement at end of year 4 ($44,000 × .592, single payment factor, 4 years)			26,048
Annual operating costs, years 5–8	$ 8,000	$8,000	
Depreciation ($44,000/4 years)	11,000		
Total tax-deductible expenses	19,000		
Tax savings at 40%	7,600	7,600	
Net operating cash outflows per year, years 5–8		$ 400	
Present values of operating flows, years 5–8:			
Year 5 $400 × .519			208
Year 6 $400 × .456			182
Year 7 $400 × .400			160
Year 8 $400 × .351			140
Purchase price of G-40 at present time			40,000
Total present value of future outflows			$69,069

time period. This situation is true because of the higher cost of the replacement model and the resulting difference in the tax shield from depreciation. The situation is not unrealistic, however.

The flows associated with years five through eight are, as you can see, discounted separately; that is, the flow for each year is discounted to its present value by using the present value factor from Table A. There are some shortcut methods available that your instructor may wish to illustrate.

Notice in the analysis that the present value of the replacement G-40 ($26,048) is substantially less than its actual cost ($44,000). This is to be expected because replacement will not be needed for four years.

Comparing the present values of the future outflows for each alternative, it appears that the least expensive alternative is to buy two G-40s, one now and one at the end of the four years. However, the two present values are not significantly different ($69,069 versus $70,463), and the firm will wish to consider other factors. For example, how confident is the firm in its forecast of the replacement cost of the G-40 in four years? What is the likelihood of a significant change in technology? These and other factors will influence the final decision.

Ranking Investment Opportunities

In Chapter 8 we stated that the two discounted cash flow techniques (NPV and IRR) were conceptually superior to other methods (payback period and book rate of return). It is possible, however, that if two or more proposals are *ranked* using each of the two conceptually superior methods, the *rankings* might not be the same. That is, the proposals ranking first and second using NPV might rank second and first using IRR. If the proposals are mutually exclusive there is now a conflict; the decision rule for NPV requires acceptance of one proposal while the decision rule for IRR requires acceptance of the other.

To deal with such a situation, some accountants and financial specialists have expressed a preference for still a third analytical approach, the profitability index, which, it is argued, would be as useful as NPV and IRR in most situations but which would be more useful than either of the other approaches in the evaluation of mutually exclusive alternatives. The **profitability index (PI)** is the *ratio* of the present value of the future cash flows to the investment that is required to obtain those cash flows. In general terms,

$$\frac{\text{Profitability}}{\text{index}} = \frac{\begin{array}{c}\text{present value of}\\ \text{future cash flows}\end{array}}{\text{required investment}}$$

Thus, an investment with present value of future cash flows of $118,000 and a required investment of $100,000 would have a profitability index of 1.18. The decision rule associated with this third approach to evaluating investments is: accept projects with a PI greater than 1.0.

Note that the decision rule for using PI will, in the case of simple acceptance/rejection decisions, produce the same results as the rules covering NPV and IRR. An investment with a positive NPV and an IRR greater than the cost of capital will also carry an index value of greater than 1.0. Also, unlike the payback-period and book-rate-of-return approaches, PI considers the problem of the timing of the cash flows (time value of money) and is therefore conceptually superior to those methods.

However, except under very special circumstances, NPV is preferable to either IRR or PI when it comes to the ranking of competing alternatives. Let us see how the three criteria would perform in an example, and explain those special circumstances.

Below are data for two mutually exclusive investment opportunities confronting a firm that has a cost of capital of 10%:

| | Investment Opportunities | |
	X	Y
Investment required	$50,000	$10,000
Life of investment	1 year	1 year
Cash flows, end of year 1	$55,991	$11,403
Present value of cash flows at 10% cost of capital		
(.909 × cash flow)	$50,896	$10,365
Net present value of project	$ 896	$ 365
Internal rate of return:		
Discount rate associated with factor .893 ($50,000/$55,991)	12%	
Discount rate associated with factor .877 ($10,000/$11,403)		14%
Profitability index:		
$50,896/$50,000	1.018	
$10,365/$10,000		1.037

Project Y has both a higher internal rate of return and a higher profitability index number than does project X, which is higher using only the NPV criterion. *Provided that the 10% cost of capital is the rate at which alternative investments could be made,* project X should be selected. The simplest way to show this is as follows.

For both opportunities X and Y to be considered, at least $50,000 (the investment required for X) must be available for investment. If project Y is accepted (outlay of $10,000), $40,000 will be available for other projects. Now assume that another, hypothetical project, Z, is available and that Z requires an investment of $40,000 and shows an expected return of 10%, the cost of capital. What cash would the firm have at the end of the year if it selected Y and invested the additional funds in Z? The firm's cash position is summarized below.

Cash provided by investment in project Y		$11,403
Cash provided by investment in Z:		
Investment returned	$40,000	
Earnings on the investment (10%)	4,000	44,000
Total cash available to firm at end of year		$55,403

From the two projects, the firm would have available, at the end of the year, $55,403. But, had the firm invested the entire $50,000 in project X, it would have had $55,991 at the end of the year. Accepting project Y and using the excess funds for another project would have produced a smaller return than would have resulted from accepting only project X.

The only time that the project with the higher PI or higher IRR should be chosen in preference to the one with the higher NPV is when investing in the former will enable the firm to invest additional cash at a rate *greater* than the cost of capital *and* that opportunity is not available if the firm chooses the higher net present value project. Thus, in our example situation, we would choose project Y only if there were additional available investments with returns that were in excess of 10%, which investments would have to be foregone if the extra $40,000 were invested in project X. In selecting its evaluation criterion, each firm will have to consider its particular circumstances.

SENSITIVITY ANALYSIS

In Chapter 5 we issued a word of caution about all decision making. We emphasized that decision analysis involves the use of many estimates, errors in one or more of which could lead to an unwise decision. Because of the importance of estimates in decision making, many managers analyze the sensitivity of decisions to changes in one or more variables. This testing of the estimates, called **sensitivity analysis,** involves trying to find out how much a variable would have to rise or fall before a different decision would be indicated.

Although sensitivity analysis applies to all types of decisions, for several reasons it is especially beneficial when applied to capital budgeting decisions. First, a relatively small change in a variable in a capital budgeting opportunity can have significant effect on the final outcome. Remember that the annual cash flow is multiplied by the present value factor. Hence, for a project with a 10-year life in a firm where the cost of capital is 20%, a $1 drop in annual cash flow produces a drop of $4.192 in the present value of those flows (the present value factor is 4.192).

A capital budgeting decision also involves a time period longer than a year, which fact is, by definition, not involved in short-term decision making. Suppose that an investment of $12,000 is expected to generate cash flows of $3,000 per year for ten years and that the appropriate discount rate is 12%. The project has a positive NPV, but considering the uncertainties surrounding estimates for years far into the future, a manager may wonder just how long the investment must continue producing an annual flow of $3,000 in order to earn at least the required 12% return. Dividing the investment by the annual cash flow gives a present value factor (also the payback period) of 4 ($12,000/$3,000). Knowing the discount rate (12%) and the present value factor (4.0) we can consult Table B, look down the 12% column, and see that 3.605 is the factor for five years, 4.111 for six years. Hence, the project must yield its annual flows of $3,000 for nearly six years in order to earn the required 12% return. In this case then, the estimated useful life of the project would have to be in error by 40% (from ten to six years), a rather large error in the original estimate, before the decision about the project would change, so the decision is not very sensitive to the estimate of useful life.

The outcome of analysis of a capital budgeting decision can also be affected significantly by a difference in a basic estimate of the sales volume to be achieved under the proposed project. (A magnification effect occurs because each unit of volume is multiplied by contribution margin per unit.) Hence, managers may wish to determine how sensitive a particular decision is to the volume estimates that they have. For example, suppose that a firm with a cost of capital of 14% and in the 40% tax bracket can bring out a new product to sell at $22. Variable costs on the product are expected to be $4 per unit; fixed costs requiring cash outlays are estimated at $100,000 annually, and the estimated annual sales volume is 10,000 units. Bringing out the new product requires an investment of $200,000, all for depreciable assets with a 5-year life and no salvage value, and the firm uses straight-line depreciation. The initial analysis for this decision is shown below.

		Tax	Cash
Expected contribution margin			
(10,000 × $18)		$180,000	$ 180,000
Fixed costs:			
Cash	$100,000		(100,000)
Depreciation	40,000		
		140,000	
Taxable income		$ 40,000	
Tax at 40%		16,000	(16,000)
Income after taxes		24,000	
Add back depreciation		40,000	
Net cash flow per year		$ 64,000	$ 64,000
Present value factor, 5-year			
annuity at 14%			3.433
Present value of cash flows			$ 219,712
Investment required			200,000
Net present value			$ 19,712

Based on the available estimates, the project has a positive NPV and should be accepted. But how far can volume fall before the investment becomes only marginally desirable?

First, for the project to achieve a present value *equal* to the investment, the required after-tax cash flow would have to be $58,258 ($200,000/3.433). Because depreciation can be added back to net income to get cash flow, we can, instead, subtract depreciation from the *required* cash flow in order to obtain required after-tax income. We then divide the after-tax income by (1 − tax rate) to get the required pretax income, just as we did in Chapter 3. From then on, ordinary volume-cost-profit analysis is used to determine the required volume. The full computation is shown in the table below:

Required after-tax cash flow	$ 58,258
Less: Depreciation	40,000
Equals: Required after-tax income	$ 18,258
Divided by 60%, which is (1 − 40% tax rate)	
gives required profit before taxes	$ 30,430
Add fixed costs including depreciation	140,000
Equals: Required contribution margin	$170,430
Divided by $18 contribution margin per unit	
gives required sales volume of	9,468 units

In this calculation we have essentially prepared a cash flow schedule and tax computation schedule from the bottom up, a technique used in very early chapters. Please notice that 9,468 units is only 532 units less than the estimated volume, or 5.32% below the estimate. The margin for error here is not very large and a relatively small decline in volume would render the investment undesirable even though it had a fairly high NPV when the 10,000 unit estimate was used.

Sensitivity analysis gives management an idea of the extent to which unfavorable occurrences like lower volumes, shorter useful lives, or higher costs are likely to affect the profitability of a project. It is used because of the uncertainty that prevails in almost any real-life situation. There are other ways to deal with uncertainty, some of which will be introduced in Chapter 16.

INCOME TAXES—SPECIAL CONSIDERATIONS

Throughout this book, we have treated income taxes rather generally. We have assumed that a flat tax rate applies to all of the firm's revenues and expenses, and that only revenues and expenses affect the firm's taxes.

In reality, the tax law is far more complex than can be presented in an introductory text in managerial accounting. The special considerations of ACRS introduced in Chapter 8 are only a small part of the requirements associated with using an alternative depreciation basis for tax purposes (versus financial accounting purposes). Moreover, neither of the simplifying assumptions made about taxes is always true.

There are at least two important reasons why the assumption of a flat (single) tax rate is not always valid. First, the tax rates relevant to a business entity are graduated (progressively higher) according to the level of the entity's or the owners' income. At this writing, taxes on income of incorporated entities begin at 15% (for the first $25,000 of income) and rise to a rate of 46% on income over $100,000. For unincorporated entities, the relevant tax rates are those applicable to the incomes of the individual owners of such entities, which could range from 12% to 50% depending not only on the owners' income levels but also on marital status and other personal matters.

Another reason why the use of a flat tax rate is sometimes invalid is that certain types of income, including what are called capital gains, may be subject to different tax rates from those on other types of income. Moreover, the tax treatment of such gains is different for incorporated and unincorporated entities. For example, 60% of a capital gain experienced by an unincorporated entity whose owners must, therefore, report such business gains as part of their individual incomes, is not subject to tax at all. Although a lower-than-normal tax rate applies to equivalent gains for a corporation, there are entirely different tax rules about combining gains and losses and other matters affecting how such gains can be treated on the entity's tax return in the year of gain or any other year.

For many purposes, however, the assumption of a flat tax rate is perfectly valid. Most large companies earn enough profit to pay income taxes at the highest rate. Therefore, that rate is appropriate for capital budgeting decisions because we are concerned with incremental income taxes. The rate on a large company's incremental income is likely to be flat.

Income taxes do not depend solely on revenues and expenses for a given tax year. One feature of tax law, called the operating loss carryback/carryforward, allows businesses to offset profits in one year against losses in another. For example, if a qualifying company lost $200,000 in 19X4, then earned $50,000 in 19X5, it would not have to pay any taxes on the $50,000 because of the loss in 19X4. In fact, with some restrictions, the company would not have to pay income taxes until it had earned over $200,000 cumulatively after 19X4. For our purposes, the most important of the provisions we are discussing is the investment tax credit (ITC). The ITC is a special feature of tax law that has been in existence (though not continuously) since the early 1960's. The ITC allows businesses (corporations, partnerships, and proprietorships alike) to deduct from their income taxes a percentage of their expenditures on "qualifying assets." We cover this feature in more detail shortly.

To give even superficial coverage to all of the segments of the tax law that affect decision making would require several chapters; in fact, there are books which are devoted entirely to the tax aspects of decision making. What we do in this section is to present the basics of just two of these aspects. What that coverage, and the above comments, should produce for the reader is the knowledge that an expert in tax matters, whether from within or outside the entity, should be consulted about the tax implications and complications of almost any business decision.

We have selected two tax topics, ACRS and the investment tax credit, for brief consideration in this chapter. The coverage is brief because the discussions ignore many of the complications that surround their use in a particular entity. The topics were selected because they are relevant to the capital budgeting decisions of the vast majority of business enterprises.

ACRS

For more than a decade prior to 1981, the tax law allowed business entities to use a different, and faster, depreciation method for tax purposes than was used for financial accounting purposes. An entity could choose one of the accelerated methods of depreciation, and then switch from the chosen method to the straight-line method when it was advantageous for tax purposes. Thus, an entity could use, say, the sum-of-the-years'-digits method until a switch to straight-line would produce higher depreciation charges.

The Economic Recovery Tax Act (ERTA), enacted in 1981, continued to provide tax benefits from accelerated depreciation. But it also narrowed the options available. Specifically, the Act introduced **ACRS,** a system that stipulates cost recovery (depreciation) percentages for specific years of an asset's life.

Under ACRS, the taxpayer classifies assets into various categories according to rules given in ERTA. There can be some very complex issues in classification, but the following general principles hold for most industrial and service companies.[3]

3-Year Property: This class consists of automobiles, light trucks, equipment used for research and development, and other short-lived personal property. (Personal property consists of assets other than real property; real property is land and buildings.)
5-Year Property: This class includes all tangible personal property not specifically assigned to some other class. Most machinery and equipment and furniture and fixtures fall into this class.
15-Year Property: This class includes buildings and other depreciable real property.

Exhibit 9-1 shows the stipulated cost recovery percentages for three- and five-year property. The percentages approximate the depreciation when using a 150% declining-balance method with a half-year taken in the first year, and with a switch to the straight-line method when the switch would be advantageous (that is, produce more depreciation than the declining-balance method). The schedule of percentages for 15-year property is relatively complex because it includes percentages that depend on the exact month of the year in which the asset is acquired.

Exhibit 9-1
ACRS Cost Recovery Percentages

Year	3-Year Class	5-Year Class
1	25%	15%
2	38%	22%
3	37%	21%
4		21%
5		21%

ACRS simplifies the tax law because a firm no longer has to (1) estimate a useful life for the asset, (2) choose a depreciation method, or (3) estimate the asset's salvage value. The depreciable life is specified for each class. The acceptable depreciation method is incorporated in the tables of recovery percentages for each year. And salvage values are ignored until received, at which time they are fully taxable. The primary alternative available to the taxpayer is to choose straight-line depreciation

---

[3]Public utilities such as electric, natural gas, and telephone companies fall under special rules for some of their assets.

over the ACRS life or a limited number of other, specified lives.[4] (For example, a 3-year class asset could be depreciated over 5 or 12 years instead of 3.

On the whole, the depreciation deductions mandated under ACRS (or even the optional straight-line method) are more advantageous than those previously available, because of the relatively short lives now acceptable for tax purposes. Note, however, that the shorter lives are unlikely to be used to compute depreciation for financial reporting purposes because they are unlikely to coincide with the useful life of the property. An important result of ACRS is that the tax basis of an asset seldom equals its book value. This fact must be considered in calculating the taxable gain (or deductible loss) when the asset is sold. For capital budgeting decisions involving replacements of existing assets, the analysis of both current cash outlay and cash inflow from salvage value requires a calculation of the tax basis of the asset at the time of disposition.

In Chapter 8 we showed that using accelerated depreciation for tax purposes is one of the most common reasons for uneven cash flows over the life of an asset. We gave an example of an investment in a three-year class asset. For convenience, the basic facts of the example are repeated here so that we may introduce you to a time-saving device for dealing with the uneven flows that result from using ACRS.

Your firm has the opportunity to acquire, for $60,000, some special-handling devices that would be used in producing a new food product. The expected life of these devices, and of the product, is five years; operating cash flows without regard to taxes are expected to be $22,000 per year. The firm's tax rate is 60%, and its cost of capital is 12%.

In Exhibit 8-1 (page 285) we showed a year-by-year calculation of the present value of the cash flows for the five years. Later (page 286), we summarized the flows as follows:

Pretax cash savings	$22,000	
Less, tax on cash savings, 60%	13,200	
Annual cash flow from operations without regard to depreciation		$ 8,800
Present value of cash flow, a 5-year annuity of $8,800 × 3.605		$31,724
Depreciation tax shield:		
Year 1 $15,000 × .60 × .893	$ 8,037	
Year 2 $22,800 × .60 × .797	10,903	
Year 3 $22,200 × .60 × .712	9,484	
Present value of tax shield		28,424
Total present value of future flows		$60,148

By separating the cash flows into an annuity component and a tax-shield component, we were able to reduce, from five to three, the number of years for which separate present-value factors had to be used. Because the ACRS percentages are fixed, we can construct a table that will give a single present-value factor for an asset of a given class at a given discount rate. Such a table is Exhibit 9-2.

---

[4]The only other option that might be relevant to businesses is to choose a depreciation method not based on years, for example, the units-of-production or machine-hours methods.

Exhibit 9-2
Present Values of ACRS Tax Shields*

Discount Rate	Recovery Periods	
	Three Years	Five Years
8%	.851	.792
10%	.819	.750
12%	.790	.711
14%	.761	.676
16%	.735	.643
18%	.710	.613
20%	.686	.585
22%	.664	.559
24%	.642	.535

*Factors in this table are simply the sums of the percentages in each period multiplied by the present-value factors for single payments.

To see how this table can be used, let us continue with our example. The asset is in the three-year class, and cost of capital is 12%. The present-value factor that corresponds to an interest rate of 12% in the three-year column is .790. We multiply the cost of the new asset ($60,000) by the present-value factor (.790) and then by the tax rate (60%) to arrive at a present value for the tax shield of $28,440. (The difference between this amount and the $28,424 computed above is due to rounding.) The cash flows from the investment can be resummarized as follows:

Present value of annuity for flows regardless of depreciation ($8,800 × 3.605)	$31,724
Present value of tax shield from depreciation ($60,000 × .790 × .60)	28,440
Total present value of future cash flows	$60,164

Using a separate table to determine the present value of the tax shield has reduced the number of separate discountings to two.[5]

Investment Tax Credit

At various times since 1962, the tax law has allowed businesses to reduce their taxes by making investments in certain types of assets. This tax benefit is called the **investment tax credit (ITC)**. The types of qualifying investments and the size of the credit have varied, but the mechanics of the credit have remained essentially unchanged. If a firm acquires an asset that qualifies for the credit, it can deduct, directly from its tax pay-

---

[5]Those who might ask why the table doesn't reduce the calculations further by incorporating the tax rate are referred to the prior discussion of the variety of tax rates to which an entity might be subject.

ment, an amount equal to some specified percentage of the acquisition cost of that asset.

ERTA, which, as previously stated, introduced ACRS, provided for a credit of 6% for assets in the three-year class and a credit of 10% for qualified property in other classes. (Qualified property includes virtually all depreciable assets except for certain types of real property.) A critical revision of the rules for the ITC occurred with the passage of the Tax Equity and Fiscal Responsibility Act (TEFRA) in 1982. Under that Act, a taxpayer who takes advantage of the full ITC must reduce the depreciable basis of the asset by half of the ITC taken. That is, the ITC is available and the taxpayer can use ACRS percentages, but the basis to which the ACRS percentages can be applied is not the full cost of the asset.

For example, suppose a firm invests $100,000 in an asset with an ACRS life of five years. The relevant ITC is 10% or $10,000 ($100,000 × 10%). The firm can still depreciate the asset over five years and use the ACRS percentages; but the basis for such depreciation, and, hence, the total amount of such depreciation, would be $95,000 ($100,000 cost, less half of the $10,000 ITC).

What TEFRA did, then, was to reduce future depreciation by half of the ITC and, hence, reduce the tax shield. TEFRA allowed a taxpayer an option: keep the full cost of the asset as the basis for depreciation and reduce the ITC (from 6% to 4%, or from 10% to 8%). In almost all circumstances, a taxpayer is better off taking the full credit and losing some of the future tax shield. A short example demonstrates this point.

Consider a $100,000 investment in the three-year ACRS class. The available ITC is (A) 6% if the firm accepts a reduction in the depreciable base, and (B) 4% if no reduction in depreciable base is accepted. Comparing the present values of the available tax benefits, assuming a tax rate of 40% and a cost of capital of 16%, we have the following.

| | Alternative | |
	A	B
Present value of ITC (100% of ITC):		
$100,000 × 6%	$ 6,000	
$100,000 × 4%		$ 4,000
Present value of tax shield from depreciation:		
[$100,000 − (50% × $6,000)] × 40% × .735	28,518	
$100,000 × 40% × .735		29,400
Total present value of tax savings	$34,518	$33,400

The present value of Option A (taking a larger ITC now and reducing the basis for subsequent depreciation) is higher and indicates the wiser choice. The ACRS class of the asset, the firm's cost of capital, and the tax rate are all major factors in selecting an alternative. But there are very few situations where Option B (taking a smaller ITC now and not reducing the depreciable basis) will be the better choice.

Most of the assignment material for this chapter ignores the ITC, basis reduction alternatives, and ACRS. Our goal in presenting these special tax considerations is not to emphasize the application of some particular section of the tax law but rather to underscore the importance of understanding the effects that the tax law can have on the analysis of a capital budgeting decision. The peculiarities of the tax law affect the calculations of the cash flows relating to particular investment opportunities. They do not change the principles involved in the analysis.

SOCIAL CONSEQUENCES OF DECISION MAKING

Throughout this book, and particularly in this and Chapters 5 and 8, we have, for the most part, assumed that the consequences of an action were limited to the entity taking that action. Such an assumption is not always warranted. The action of a single entity may have many effects, desirable or detrimental, for other entities or persons not associated with the deciding entity.

For example, a firm might find that the use of a particular machine that saves labor time is justified on economic grounds. But the decision to use the machinery may put people out of work. The workers who lose their jobs will suffer if they cannot find other jobs within fairly short periods of time. If they do not find work, they will receive unemployment compensation or some other type of payment that is borne by the taxpayers of the state. If they move away from the area to find work, they must incur moving costs; and there may be problems in uprooting their families. The reduced payroll of the plant may adversely affect the community because of declines in economic activity such as retail sales. Other jobs may be lost as a result of the layoffs. Although some of these implications have been referred to in previous discussions of "qualitative considerations" of decision making, they were not specifically incorporated into the analyses.

Costs that are not borne directly by the entity making a decision and taking an action are called **social costs** or externalities. **Social benefits** (also called externalities) are benefits not accruing directly to the entity making a decision. A firm that decides to hire additional workers who are currently unemployed (as opposed to hiring them away from other firms) will provide benefits to the workers in the form of income and increased self-esteem, to the community in the form of increased economic activity and higher taxes to the government, and to the taxpayers in the form of reduced expenditures for unemployment compensation. The firm will not benefit directly from these other benefits, even though its action caused them. Although it may not be possible for business managers to give direct and monetary recognition to externalities, it should be possible to at least try to recognize their existence as individual decisions are studied.

The question of social benefits and costs is critical in decisions made by governmental units like municipalities, states, and the federal government. Decision making for these and for other not-for-profit entities should be based on estimates of discounted benefits and costs, just like those of business firms. The major differences between the techniques used by business firms and governmental units are of several types. One difference is that governmental units do not pay income taxes, which makes their decision making somewhat simpler than that of business firms. But other factors in the governmental decision-making process make decisions much more difficult.

These special factors fall into three general categories: (1) measurement problems; (2) problems in determining whether a particular effect is a benefit or a cost; and (3) problems in the distribution of benefits and costs.

Measurement problems arise in the decisions of governmental units because, as we mentioned in Chapter 4, the benefits and costs are not just monetary. If an unemployed person obtains a job, the government will benefit from additional taxes paid by the employed worker. But other benefits like increased self-esteem of the worker are not readily measurable. Cleaner air is economically beneficial to the people because of fewer deaths from respiratory ailments, less sickness, and reduced cleaning bills for clothing and buildings. But the monetary value of the increased pleasantness that would accompany cleaner air is not readily measurable.

The second factor, determining whether an effect is beneficial or costly, may well depend on one's point of view. The government has sanctioned actions that have reduced the populations of wolves and coyotes in sheep and cattle-raising states. These programs have been favorably received by ranchers, but deplored by conservationists. Programs that result in growth in population of a particular area may also receive mixed reviews. Some states and towns have actively sought industrial development, while others have discouraged it.

The problem of the distribution of benefits and costs has been a difficult social question since the beginning of government. A city or town might be considering the construction of a municipal golf course. Analyses may show that the fees received will be insufficient to earn the minimum desired rate of return, which means that the taxpayers would be subsidizing those who use the golf course. The town government might still decide to build the golf course because it feels that the people who would use it deserve some recreation even if the general taxpayers must pay some of the costs. Similar reasoning could apply to municipally owned bus services, zoos, libraries, and parks.

The criterion that is most generally advocated for decision making by governmental units is the maximizing of "social welfare." Because of the many problems in identifying and quantifying social benefits and costs, the application of this decision rule has generally meant the maximizing of economic benefits—those subject to monetary estimates. To the extent that this can be done, the same general analytical approaches proposed for business decision making can be used in the public sector. And, like the business manager, the decision maker in the public sector must make an effort to at least identify and consider the unquantified but relevant factors before reaching a final decision.

SUMMARY

A proper analysis of investment requirements and future cash flows is critical if the manager is to make good decisions about investing available funds. Required investment should include consideration of any required increases in the firm's working capital. Where the decision involves a replacement, the analysis may be particularly complex.

Mutually exclusive investment alternatives may bring certain analytical problems. A third DCF technique, the profitability index, has been suggested to assist in decision making. This technique can be useful, but the firm's special circumstances in terms of available funds and investment opportunities should be considered before selecting a single capital budgeting technique for general use.

Whatever technique is used, many firms have found it helpful to perform sensitivity analysis in connection with investment opportunities. The use of sensitivity analysis is prompted partially by the number of estimates involved in a typical capital budgeting situation.

Computations of the cash flows for any investment opportunity require knowledge of the many special features of the current income tax laws. Features that are relevant to all businesses are the investment tax credit (ITC) and the Accelerated Cost Recovery System (ACRS). But many other factors, such as the special treatment given to capital gains and the existence of differing tax rates for different levels of income in different types of businesses, can influence both the amounts and the timing of cash flows from a particular investment opportunity.

Qualitative issues are associated with almost every investment opportunity. This is true in both the private and the public sectors. Decision makers in both sectors should make every effort to identify and quantify as many factors as possible, and give full consideration to those factors that remain unquantified.

KEY TERMS

accelerated cost recovery
   system (ACRS)
incremental approach
investment tax credit (ITC)
mutually exclusive alternatives
profitability index (PI)

replacement decision
sensitivity analysis
social benefit
social cost
total-project approach
working capital investment

KEY FORMULAS

$$\text{Profitability index} = \frac{\text{present value of future flows}}{\text{required investment}}$$

Working capital = current assets − current liabilities

REVIEW PROBLEM—Replacement Decision and Investment in Working Capital

Eamon Company owns a machine with the following characteristics.

Book value	$55,000
Current market value	40,000
Expected salvage value at end of 5-year remaining useful life	0
Annual depreciation expense, straight-line method	11,000
Annual cash operating costs	18,000

The firm's cost of capital is 14% and the tax rate is 40%. The firm is considering replacing the machine with one that has the following characteristics.

Purchase price	$80,000
Useful life	5 years
Expected salvage value	$ 5,000
Annual cash operating costs	$ 3,000

Straight-line depreciation at $15,000 per year would be taken on the new machine. Additionally, because the new machine is more efficient, the firm could reduce its investment in working capital by $15,000.

Required: Determine whether the new machine should be bought. Ignore ACRS and the investment tax credit.

Answer to Review Problem

The new machine should be bought and the existing one sold. The incremental investment of $19,000 is less than the present value of the future cash flows of $31,200.

Investment Required

	Tax	Cash Flow
Purchase price of new machine		$80,000
Selling price of existing machine	$40,000	(40,000)
Book value of existing machine	55,000	
Loss for tax purposes	15,000	
Tax saving at 40%		(6,000)
Reduction of working capital requirements		(15,000)
Net required investment		$19,000

Notice that the reduction in working capital requirements is treated as a reduction of the required investment. At the *end* of the five years we would have an increase in working capital. The example in the text showed additional working capital requirements at the beginning and recovery at the end. This reverses the example.

We shall calculate the annual cash flows and present values using both the total project and incremental approaches.

Incremental Approach—Annual Cash Flows

	Tax	Cash Flow
Savings in cash operating costs ($18,000—$3,000)	$15,000	$15,000
Additional depreciation ($15,000—$11,000)	4,000	
Increase in taxable income	11,000	
Increased tax at 40%	4,400	4,400
Net annual cash flow		$10,600
Present value factor for 5-year annuity at 14%		3.433
Present value of annual cash flows		$36,390
Add, present value of recovery of salvage value [$5,000 × .519 (factor from Table A)]		2,595
Subtotal		$38,985
Less increase in working capital at end of 5 years ($15,000 × .519)		(7,785)
Present value of future cash flows		$31,200
Required investment		19,000
Net present value		$12,200

Because depreciation expense taken over the five years is $75,000 (5 years × $15,000), the new asset would have a book value of $5,000 at the end of its life, which is equal to its expected salvage value. There is no tax effect because there is no expected gain or loss.

Total-Project Approach
Keep Existing Machine

	Tax	Cash Flow
Cash operating costs	$18,000	$18,000
Depreciation	11,000	
Total expenses	29,000	
Tax savings at 40%	11,600	11,600
Net cash outflow		6,400
Present value factor for 5-year annuity at 14%		3.433
Present value of annual operating flows		$21,971

Buy New Machine

Cash operating costs	$ 3,000	$ 3,000
Depreciation	15,000	
Total expense	18,000	
Tax saving at 40%	7,200	7,200
Net cash *inflow*		4,200
Present value factor for 5-year annuity at 14%		3.433
Present value of annual inflows		14,419
Add, present value of salvage value (p. 335)		2,595
Subtotal		$17,014
Less, present value of increase in working capital at end of 5 years (p. 335)		7,785
Net present value of future inflows		$ 9,229

The existing machine has a present value of *outflows* of $21,971, while the new machine has a present value of *inflows* of $9,229. The net present value is again $12,200.

Present value of inflows—replace	$ 9,229
Present value of outflows—keep existing machine	21,971
Total present value	31,200
Required investment	19,000
Net present value of replacing	$12,200

Using the new machine would result in net annual cash inflows rather than outflows. This happens because depreciation is so high that the tax saving is greater than the annual cash operating costs. You should *not* conclude that if a replacement asset would yield a positive cash flow it is automatically a wise investment. In the example used here, if we changed the working capital investment from a negative $15,000 to a positive $15,000 the replacement would not be wise.

REVIEW PROBLEM—Determining Required Volume

Chapman Products Company is considering a new product that would sell for $10 and have variable costs of $6. New equipment costing $150,000 and having a 5-year useful life and no salvage value would be needed, and would be depreciated using the straight-line method. The machine would have cash operating costs of $20,000 per year. The firm is in the 40% tax bracket and has cost of capital of 12%. (Ignore the investment credit.)

Required: Determine how many units per year the firm would have to sell in order that the investment earn 12%. Round calculations of required after-tax cash flow and required pretax profits to the nearest $100.

Answer to Review Problem

Annual sales would have to be about 17,325 units. The first step is to calculate the after-tax cash flow per year that would be required to meet the firm's minimum rate of return of 12%. The required flow is $41,600 ($150,000 investment/3.605, the factor for an annuity of five years at 12%). From this amount we proceed to total required contribution margin and the required volume, as follows:

Required after-tax cash flow per year	$41,600 (rounded)
Less, yearly depreciation ($150,000/5) which would reduce income but would not affect cash flow	30,000
After-tax profit required	11,600
Divided by 1 − 40% tax rate	.60
Pretax profit required	$19,300 (rounded)
Fixed costs ($20,000 + $30,000)	50,000
Contribution margin required	$69,300
Contribution margin per unit ($10 − $6)	$4
Number of units of sales necessary to obtain required contribution margin ($69,300/$4)	17,325

REVIEW PROBLEM—ACRS and Investment Tax Credit

The Strock Company is considering investing in a new machine that costs $100,000, has a five-year expected life, and no salvage value. The machine is expected to save about $50,000 per year in cash operating costs and falls in the three-year ACRS class. The available investment tax credit is 6%. Cost of capital is 14% and the tax rate is 40%.

Required: Determine the net present value of the investment, discounting the operating flows and the tax shield of depreciation separately. Use Exhibit 9-2 (page 330) to find the present value of the tax shield.

Answer to Review Problem

Operating flows $50,000 × (1 − .40) × 3.433	$102,990
Tax shield of depreciation	
[$100,000 − ($6,000 × .50)] × .40 × .761	29,527
Total present value	132,517
Less, investment [$100,000 − (6% × $100,000)]	94,000
NPV	$ 38,517

ASSIGNMENT MATERIAL

Questions for Discussion

9-1 Returns and income   If all the forecasts for a specific capital project turn out as estimated, will the reported annual net income for the project be equal to the returns used in the analysis of the project?

9-2 Factors in capital budgeting   The government frequently takes action that alters the economic climate. For each of the events listed below, indicate whether firms would be more inclined, less inclined, or the same, regarding their capital spending plans. Comment on what particular kinds of firms would be affected and how. Consider each independently.
1. Gasoline engines are outlawed for automobiles; electric cars only are approved for production.
2. For some years the price of cotton has been kept artificially high by government price supports. These supports are to be removed.
3. A high tariff is levied on foreign automobiles.
4. Corporate income taxes are raised from 46% to 50%.
5. All nations of the world sign a treaty to outlaw war, and they mean it.
6. Persons with low incomes are given cash grants for attending college.

9-3 Capital budgeting—effects of events   A particular capital expenditure proposal for a new machine has been analyzed, based on currently available information. In what way(s) would each of the following events (not anticipated at the time the analysis was done) affect the analysis? Consider each event independently.
1. A proposal to increase taxes on real property (land and buildings) is approved by the voters of the city in which the firm has its manufacturing plant.
2. Congress passes a law that provides for a credit against corporate income taxes; the credit is to be computed as a specified percentage of the cash invested in new long-lived assets.
3. The *Wall Street Journal* carries a report of a new product that is likely to be a good substitute for the product made by the machine being considered.

Exercises

9-4 Comparison of alternatives   Stanley Company must make a choice between two machines that will perform an essential function. Machine A costs $40,000, has a 10-year life, no salvage value, and costs $12,000 per year to operate (cash costs). Machine B costs

$80,000, has a 10-year life with $10,000 salvage value, and costs $3,000 per year to operate. The tax rate is 40% and cost of capital is 10%. Straight-line depreciation will be used for either machine.

Required: Determine which machine should be bought and explain your answer.

9-5   Comparison of methods—extension of 8-8 and 8-12   In both 8-8 and 8-12 three investment opportunities are presented. Determine the profitability index for each opportunity in each exercise and rank the investments based on the computed index numbers.

9-6   Basic sensitivity analysis   Cunningham Company has an opportunity to purchase a new machine that would reduce annual cash operating costs by $42,000. The cost of the new machine is $170,000, and after its useful life of ten years it is expected to have no residual value. The firm's tax rate is 40% and its cost of capital is 14%. The company uses straight-line depreciation.

Required
1. What is the net present value for the project?
2. What amount of cash savings in annual operating costs would make this project return exactly 14%?
3. Assuming that operating savings are $42,000, as stated, what useful life must the machine have to make the investment worthwhile?
4. Assume that the project is not really a new investment but rather is a replacement for one of the company's current machines that has a remaining life of ten years and a current book value of $66,000. The old machine could be sold now for $12,000 and would have no residual value if retained to the end of its useful life. Annual depreciation is $6,600. Should the company replace the old machine with the new one?

9-7   Basic replacement decision   Bevis Company, which manufactures truck axles, has the opportunity to replace one of its existing lathes with a new model. The existing lathe has a book value and tax basis of $20,000 and a market value of $12,000. It has an estimated remaining useful life of four years, at which time it will have no salvage value. The firm uses straight-line depreciation of $5,000 per year on the lathe and its annual cash operating costs are $42,000.

   The new model costs $65,000 and has a 4-year estimated life with no salvage value. Its annual cash operating costs are estimated at $19,000. The firm would use straight-line depreciation on the new lathe. The tax rate is 40% and cost of capital is 16%. (Ignore the investment tax credit.)

Required
1. Determine the investment required to obtain the new lathe.
2. Determine the present value of the net cash flows expected from the investment and the net present value of the investment.
3. Suppose that the new lathe should have a salvage value of $5,000. The firm would ignore the salvage value in determining annual depreciation and so would have a gain at the end of the life, which would be taxed at 40%. What would the net present value of the investment be?

9-8   Basic working capital investment   The managers of DeCosmo Enterprises are considering a new product. They expect to be able to sell 50,000 units annually for the next five years at $7 each. Variable costs are expected to be $3 per unit, annual fixed costs requiring cash disbursements $80,000. The product requires machinery and equipment costing $150,000 with a 5-year life and no salvage value. The firm would use straight-line depreciation. Additionally, accounts receivable would increase about $60,000, inventory about $20,000. These amounts would be returned in full at the end of the five years. The tax rate is 40% and cost of capital is 16%.

Required: Determine the net present value of the investment. (Ignore the investment tax credit.)

9-9   Relationships   Miller Company invested $180,000 in depreciable assets and earned a 14% internal rate of return. The life of the investment, which had no salvage value, was five years.

Required
1. Determine the net cash flow that Miller earned in each year, assuming that each year's was equal.
2. Assume now that the tax rate is 40% and that Miller used straight-line depreciation for the investment. Determine the annual pretax cash flow that would have been earned to provide a 14% after-tax return.
3. The investment related to a new product that had a selling price of $10, variable costs of $4, and cash fixed costs of $25,000 per year. Assuming a 40% tax rate and straight-line depreciation, determine how many units would have to be sold to earn an 18% internal rate of return.

9-10   Replacement decision—working capital   Thomas Company has the opportunity to replace a machine. Data on the existing and proposed machines are as follows.

	Existing Machine
Current book value and tax basis	$50,000
Annual cash operating costs	$80,000
Current market value	$30,000
Annual depreciation	$25,000
Remaining useful life	2 years
	Proposed Machine
Price	$90,000
Annual cash operating costs	$20,000
Useful life	2 years

The company uses straight-line depreciation. Neither machine is expected to have salvage value at the end of its useful life. Using the proposed machine would require increased inventories of $40,000. The company has a 20% cost of capital and a 40% income tax rate.

Required: Determine the net present value of the proposed investment.

9-11   Basic ACRS and investment tax credit   ORM Company has the opportunity to buy a machine for $1,500,000. The machine is expected to save $400,000 annually in cash operating costs over its estimated 10-year life. For tax purposes, the company would depreciate the machine using a five-year ACRS period. The machine qualifies for a 10% investment tax credit. The company would take the full credit, so that the amount to be depreciated would be reduced by half of the tax credit.

The company has a 14% cost of capital and a 40% tax rate.

Required: Determine the net present value of the proposed investment in the machine.

9-12 **Sensitivity analysis, ACRS, and investment tax credit—extension of 9-11** The managers of ORM Company are not sure of the annual savings in cash operating costs that the machine would generate. One manager has asked how low the savings could be and the company still earn the 14% target rate of return.

Required: Determine the annual savings in cash operating costs that would yield a 14% return, with all other factors remaining constant.

9-13 **Working capital** The sales manager of Watlin Company has received an offer from a company overseas. The overseas company wants to buy 10,000 units of Watlin's major product for $20 per unit, well below the usual $35 price. The sales manager is convinced that Watlin would not lose any domestic sales if it accepted the offer. Unit variable cost of the product is $18. The only drawback the sales manager sees is that, while Watlin would make the units now, incurring $180,000 in cash costs, the customer would not pay for the goods until one year from now because of restrictions on taking money out of the foreign country. Watlin's cost of capital is 16%. Ignore taxes.

Required: Determine whether Watlin should accept the order.

9-14 **Mutually exclusive investments** Miro Manufacturing Company needs additional productive capacity to meet greater demand for its products. Two alternatives are available. The firm can choose either one, but not both.

	A	B
Required investment in depreciable assets	$1,000,000	$2,000,000
Annual cash operating costs	$ 450,000	$ 230,000
Useful life	10 years	10 years

Under either alternative the company expects additional revenues of $750,000. Additional variable costs are included in the cash costs given above. Straight-line depreciation will be used for either investment and neither is expected to have any salvage value.

The tax rate is 40% and cost of capital is 10%.

Required
1. For each alternative, compute:
   (a) net present value
   (b) approximate internal rate of return
   (c) profitability index
2. Make a recommendation on which alternative should be chosen.

9-15 **Timing of depreciation deductions** The controller of NMC Company has given the treasurer the analysis on page 342 regarding the proposed purchase of a new fleet of light trucks. The trucks are expected to last three years with no salvage value.

The trucks cost $300,000 and qualify for a 6% investment tax credit, making the net cost to purchase them $282,000 [$300,000 − ($300,000 × .06)]. The depreciable basis for tax purposes must be reduced by one-half of the ITC, giving $291,000 to depreciate ($300,000 − $9,000). Cost of capital is 16% and the tax rate is 40%.

Annual cash savings, years 1–3	$145,000	
Less 40% income tax	58,000	
After-tax cash savings	87,000	
Present value factor, 3 years, 16%	2.246	
Present value of savings		$195,402
ACRS Tax shield:		
Year 1 $291,000 × .25 × .40 × .862	$ 25,084	
Year 2 $291,000 × .38 × .40 × .743	32,864	
Year 3 $291,000 × .37 × .40 × .641	27,607	
Total present value of tax shield		85,555
Total present value		$280,957
Cost to purchase		282,000
Net present value (negative)		($ 1,043)

On seeing the analysis, the treasurer had the following comments. "Look, I don't agree with the calculation of the present value of the tax shield. It is now late November, and if we buy the trucks, they will arrive before year-end. That means that we get the first year ACRS deduction *now*, not in one year. We will incorporate the deduction in our January payment of estimated taxes, just as we will do with the ITC. So what we really have is a deduction right now, one a year hence, and the last one two years hence. In other words, given the facts of this situation, the delay in recognizing the tax shield is too long. Don't you agree?"

Required: Prepare a new analysis incorporating the treasurer's comments. That is, move the tax shield deductions up one year each and recalculate the net present value of the proposed investment.

9-16   Relationships   Fill in the blanks for each of the following independent cases. In all cases there are no salvage values for the investments and income taxes are to be ignored.

	(a) Years of Project	(b) Annual Cash	(c) Initial Invest-	(d) Cost of	(e) Internal Rate of	(f) Net Present	(g) Profit- ability
Case	Life	Flows	ment	Capital	Return	Value	Index
1	15	$40,000	$ ____	____ %	14%	$ ____	1.109
2	8	$ ____	$238,920	18%	16%	$ ____	
3	12	$ ____	$215,292	16%	____ %	$36,762	____
4	____	$80,000	$361,600	12%	____ %	$ ____	1.25

9-17   Working capital investment   The managers of Rawson-Harmon Company, a whole-saler of paper products, have been approached by managers of Clark Paper Products Company. Clark has offered Rawson-Harmon exclusive rights to distribute its products in the Denver area. The contract would run for three years, after which time either company could terminate the arrangement.

Rawson-Harmon's managers expect revenue from Clark's products to be about $200,000 per month, with variable costs (all cost of goods sold) about 85% of revenue. Incremental monthly fixed costs should be about $8,000. Additionally, Rawson-Harmon would have to carry inventory approximating a three-month supply and would have accounts receivable of about three months' sales. Rawson-Harmon would pay cash on delivery of Clark's products. Cost of capital is 20%. Ignore taxes.

Required: Determine whether Rawson-Harmon should accept Clark's offer.

9-18 Replacement decision   Charles Company, which makes a variety of gardening products, is considering replacing a machine. The firm uses straight-line depreciation, has a 20% cost of capital, and is in the 40% income tax bracket. Neither piece of equipment is expected to have salvage value at the end of its useful life. If the firm makes the replacement it would finance the investment with debt bearing 10% interest. The existing machine could now be sold for $25,000.

Existing Machine	
Book value and tax basis	$ 60,000
Remaining useful life	3 years
Annual cash operating costs	$ 80,000
Annual depreciation	$ 20,000 each of next 3 years
Proposed Machine	
Price	$150,000
Useful life	3 years
Annual cash operating costs	$ 20,000

Required: Determine the net present value of the proposed investment.

9-19 Asset acquisition, ACRS, investment tax credit   Peyton Company is considering a new asset that costs $500,000 and that its managers expect to reduce cash operating costs by $200,000 per year over its five-year estimated life. The asset qualifies for three-year recovery under ACRS and a 6% investment tax credit. The company would take the full credit, and therefore would be able to depreciate 97% of the cost. Cost of capital is 16% and the tax rate is 40%.

Required: Determine the net present value of the investment.

9-20 Unit costs   Ramor Company manufactures running shoes. Its managers are considering entering the market for low-priced shoes and have been looking at several alternatives. The model they wish to introduce will, they believe, sell 200,000 pairs annually at $22. Estimates of unit costs for two alternative production methods are as follows.

	Use Existing Facilities	Buy New Machinery
Materials	$ 3.50	$ 3.40
Direct labor	7.50	6.45
Variable overhead	2.50	2.15
Fixed overhead	3.75	4.225
Total unit costs	$17.25	$16.225

Company policy is to charge each product with both fixed and variable overhead. The basic charge for fixed overhead is $0.50 per direct labor dollar. The amount of fixed overhead shown for the new machinery includes $1.00 per unit for depreciation of $200,000 per year ($600,000 cost) on the new machinery, which has a three-year life. Thus, the $4.225 is $1.00 plus the normal overhead charge of $0.50 times $6.45 direct labor cost. One of the managers points out that the $1.025 difference in unit cost works out to $205,000 per year, which is a significant saving. He also points out that the after-tax saving is $123,000 (the tax rate is 40%), which gives a rate of return of 41% on the average investment of $300,000. Cost of capital is 18%.

Required:
1. Determine the net present value of the investment.
2. Determine the approximate internal rate of return on the investment.

Problems

9-21   **Pollution control and capital budgeting**   Craft Paper Company operates a plant that produces a great deal of air pollution. The local government has ordered that the polluting be stopped or the plant will be closed. The firm does not wish to close the plant and so has sought to find satisfactory ways to remove the pollutants. Two alternatives have been found, both of which reduce the outflow of pollutants to levels satisfactory to the government. One, called the Entrol, costs $1,000,000, has a 10-year life with no salvage value, and has cash operating costs of $180,000 annually. The other, the Polltrol, costs $2,000,000, has a 10-year life with no salvage value, and has cash operating costs of $210,000 annually. However, the Polltrol compresses the particles it removes into solid blocks of material that can be sold to chemical companies. Annual receipts from selling the material are estimated at $250,000.

Either device would be depreciated on a straight-line basis. Cost of capital is 16% and the tax rate is 40%.

Required: Determine which device the firm should buy.

9-22   **Replacement decision and sensitivity analysis**   Hutson Company owns a machine that cost $80,000 five years ago, has a book value of $40,000, and a current market value of $12,000. The machine costs $35,000 per year to operate and will have no market value at the end of five more years.

Hutson has an opportunity to buy a new machine that costs $65,000, will last five years with no salvage value, and costs $18,000 per year to operate. It will perform the same functions as the machine currently owned.

The firm has a cost of capital of 14%. Ignore income taxes.

Required
1. Determine whether the new machine should be purchased.
2. Determine the approximate internal rate of return on the investment.
3. Suppose that the production manager knows that the new machine is more efficient than the old, but not how much more. What annual cash savings would be necessary for the firm to earn 14%?
4. Suppose that the estimate of annual cash flows is considered reliable, but that the useful life of the new machine is in question. About how long must the new machine last in order that the firm earn 14%?

9-23   **Sensitivity analysis**   The managers of Boston Products Company have been trying to decide whether or not to introduce a new product, a deluxe birdfeeder. They expect it to sell for $30 per unit, and have unit variable costs of $14. Fixed costs requiring cash disbursements should be about $500,000 per year. The feeder also requires machinery costing $400,000 with a four-year life and no salvage value. The company uses straight-line depreciation. Its cost of capital is 16%.

The one point that the managers are not sure of is the annual unit volume. Estimates made by individual managers range from 40,000 to 65,000 units.

Required

1. Ignoring income taxes, determine the number of feeders per year the company would have to sell to make the investment yield just 16%.
2. Redo part 1 assuming a 40% income tax rate.

9-24 Determining required cost savings   Grunch Company has an opportunity to buy a machine that will reduce variable production costs of a product that sells 10,000 units annually. The machine costs $80,000, has no salvage value, and should last for five years. Annual operating costs requiring cash are $20,000. Cost of capital is 16%.

Required

1. Ignoring taxes, what reduction in unit variable production costs would be necessary to make the investment desirable?
2. Answer part 1 above assuming a tax rate of 40% and straight-line depreciation.
3. Suppose now that the machine would reduce unit variable production costs by $4, but that annual volume is in doubt. What annual volume would be needed to make the investment desirable? Consider income taxes.

9-25 Benefit/cost analysis   The Department of Health has made studies regarding treatments for two diseases, a type of kidney disease and a type of heart disease. The following data have been assembled.

	Kidney Disease	Heart Disease
Cost to save one life	$100,000	$150,000
Average age of victim at death	40 years	50 years
Average annual income of victims	$ 15,000	$ 25,000

The heart disease appears to be caused partly by stresses that affect higher-income people, which accounts in part for the difference in incomes between the two types of victims.

The department believes that a discount rate of 10% is appropriate. It also assumes that a person will work until age 70 (30 additional years for persons cured of kidney disease, 20 for those cured of heart disease).

Required

1. Compute the net present value of saving a single life from each disease. The cost to save the life is incurred immediately and the annual incomes are assumed to be received at the ends of years.
2. Suppose that a lack of trained personnel makes it impossible to pursue treatment for both diseases. Whichever disease is selected for treatment, the same amount will be spent. Which disease would you prefer to see treated and why?

9-26 Increased sales and working capital   Baker Company now makes several products in a labor-intensive fashion. The products, which are made in about equal quantities, average $4.50 in variable costs of which labor is $2.25. Fixed costs are $100,000 annually. The firm has had difficulty in expanding production to meet increased demand and is considering purchasing a large machine that will enable a production increase to 105,000 with the same size work force. Sales are currently 80,000 units at $8 average selling price. The firm expects to sell all its production at $7 per unit if the machine is bought.

Variable costs per unit other than labor will remain the same and fixed costs will increase by the amount of depreciation on the new machine. The machine costs $80,000 and has a useful life of ten years. There will be increased working capital requirements of $80,000. Straight-line depreciation will be used for tax purposes, the tax rate is 40%, and cost of capital is 14%.

Required: Determine whether the machine should be bought.

9-27 **Backing a play**   Kent Clark, a famous playwright, proposes that your company back his forthcoming play, *I'll Fly Tomorrow*. He has prepared the following analysis.

Investment:	
Sets and other depreciable assets (straight-line basis)	$200,000
Working capital	100,000
Total investment	$300,000
Annual gross receipts, expected to continue for 4 years	$600,000
Annual salaries of actors and other personnel	$200,000
Rent, $20,000 + 5% of gross receipts	
Royalty to Clark, 10% of gross receipts	
Other cash expenses	$140,000

Your company has a cost of capital of 14% and a tax rate of 40%.

Required
1. Should your firm back the play on the basis of the information given?
2. By how much could annual gross receipts increase or decline before you would change your decision?

9-28 **Book values and tax bases**   Your company owns two machines that are identical in all respects except that they have different book values and tax bases because of the use of different useful lives and methods of depreciation for book and tax purposes. Data summarizing the two machines are as follows:

	Machine A	Machine B
Net book value	$20,000	$40,000
Tax basis	$ 0	$30,000

The firm can depreciate $15,000 in each of the next two years for machine B for income tax purposes. It has no future depreciation available for machine A for tax purposes.

Your company needs only one machine now and its managers are deciding which one to sell. Either machine would bring $15,000 in selling price. One manager has argued that the firm should sell machine A because it would then show a loss of only $5,000 ($15,000 − $20,000) while selling machine B would give a $25,000 loss ($15,000 − $40,000). The company has cost of capital of 20% and is in the 40% tax bracket.

Required: Using a net present value approach, determine which machine the firm should sell.

9-29   Replacement decision   The management of Bettel Metals Inc. is considering acquiring a new production machine. The new machine would be more efficient than the one currently in use and would save the firm $6,000 annually because of its greater operating speed. To keep the old machine operating at the present level of efficiency, some repairs costing $5,000 would have to be made now. The repair cost is tax deductible this year. The annual depreciation charge on the old machine, which is expected to last ten years, is $1,800. No scrap value is expected at that time.

The cost of the new machine is $37,300, including freight and installation charges. The old machine now has a book value of $18,000 and a market value of $12,000. The new machine has an expected useful life of 10 years and no expected scrap value. Straight-line depreciation would be used on the new machine.

The firm is in the 40% tax bracket.

Required
1. Compute the net cash outlay if the new machine is purchased.
2. Evaluate the proposal, assuming a minimum required rate of return of 10%.

9-30   Buying an athletic team   Generally speaking, a large portion of the purchase price of an athletic team is allocated to the value of the contracts of the individual players. This amount can be amortized for income tax purposes. Some have argued that the principal value is the monopoly right to operate and earn revenues from television, ticket sales, etc. If this view prevailed, the amount allocated to the monopoly right would not be amortizable for tax purposes, much as the cost of land is not depreciable.

Suppose that you were in the 55% tax bracket and were considering buying the Midlands Maulers of the Transam Football League. You expect the operations of the team to generate pretax cash inflows of $4,000,000 annually. You also expect the league to fold up in 10 years, at which time your investment will be worthless. Your discount rate is 14%.

Required
1. Determine the maximum that you would be willing to pay for the team assuming that the entire investment could be amortized evenly over 10 years for tax purposes.
2. Determine the maximum that you would be willing to pay for the team if you could not amortize the cost. (You would then have a lump-sum tax deduction at the end of year 10 equal to your original investment.)

9-31   Lease/purchase and obsolescence   In some industries companies lease, rather than purchase, certain kinds of equipment. One reason has been that leasing makes it easier for the user to acquire newer equipment if technological progress is rapid. The user may not be committed for as long a period of time in some leases as it would be if the equipment were purchased. One type of equipment that has been leased a great deal is computer hardware—a central processing unit and various peripheral devices.

The controller of Stockton Company has been analyzing the firm's policy regarding computers, which are now being leased on a one-year basis. She is convinced that the firm is acting unwisely and should buy the equipment. Selected data related to currently leased equipment are as follows.

Cost of equipment	$1,500,000
Annual lease payment	$ 400,000
Physical life of computer	10 years
Tax rate	40%

Based upon these data, the controller calculates a net present value of purchasing the equipment at $64,800, using straight-line depreciation for tax purposes and a 14% discount rate. (The lease payments are fully deductible for tax purposes.)

The director of the computer center argues that the controller has not considered that Stockton has had to upgrade its equipment every three or four years, leasing newer, faster computers because of the growth in the use of the computer. Anticipating that the growth in use will continue, the director suggests that a 4-year economic life be used, rather than the 10-year physical life. He believes that if the equipment were purchased, it could be sold at the end of four years for 20% of its purchase price.

Required

1. Verify the controller's computation of the net present value of purchasing the computer.
2. Prepare a new analysis based on the director's comments. Equipment should be depreciated down to salvage value over four years (no gain or loss on disposal).

9-32 **Attracting industry** Minerla is a small town with little industry and high unemployment. The mayor and members of the town council have been trying to interest businesses in locating factories in Minerla. Newman Industries has agreed to the following proposal of the town government. The town will build a $4,000,000 plant to Newman's specifications and rent it to Newman for its estimated useful life of 20 years at $100,000 per year provided that Newman employs at least 600 currently unemployed citizens of Minerla.

An economist from the state university has projected the following annual results if the plant is built.

Increases in retail sales in Minerla	$6,000,000
Increase in property tax base	4,400,000

The mayor expects some increases in the cost of town government to result from the additional employees that Newman would transfer to the new factory.

Additional fire and police protection	$30,000
Additional school costs	40,000
Additional general governmental costs	15,000
Total annual additional	$95,000

The town levies a 1% tax on all retail sales and taxes property at a rate of $80 per $1,000. The relevant discount rate is 9%.

The mayor has been told that the state spends about $2,000 per year for each unemployed person in the form of direct support. He also has been told by the economist from the university that total unemployment is likely to fall by about 1,500 persons because the presence of the factory would help to create other jobs in the town.

The council feels that the factory should be built provided that the benefits to the town government do not exceed the costs.

Required

1. Determine whether the additional receipts to the town, less the additional costs, justify the building of the factory.
2. Assuming that your answer to part 1 is no, list and discuss other factors that might be considered and other actions that might be taken.

9-33 Modification of equipment Pride Company has a number of machines that have been used to make a product that the firm has phased out of its operations. The equipment has a total book value of $600,000 and remaining useful life of four years. Depreciation is being taken using the straight-line method at $150,000 per year. No salvage value is expected at the end of the useful life.

Pride can sell the equipment for $320,000 now. The equipment can also be modified to produce another product at a cost of $400,000. The modifications would not affect the useful lives or salvage value and would be depreciated using the straight-line method. If the firm does not modify the existing equipment it will have to buy new equipment at a cost of $800,000. The new equipment would also have a useful life of four years, no salvage value, and would be depreciated using the straight-line method. The product that would be made with the new equipment or modified existing equipment is essential to Pride's product line.

The cash operating costs of new equipment would be $50,000 per year less than with the existing equipment. Cost of capital is 16% and the tax rate is 40%.

Required: Determine whether the new equipment should be bought or the old equipment modified.

9-34 Replacement, volume increases, and ACRS—extension of 8-38 Assume that the Cardiff Tool Company (see 8-38) is already using a machine as part of its grinding process, so that the new machine is actually a replacement. The old machine has a book value of $200,000, a remaining life of five years, and would have no salvage value at the end of that time. The company uses straight-line depreciation on the old machine, for both book and tax purposes, and the machine could be sold at the present time for $150,000.

Required
1. Determine whether the old machine should be replaced, ignoring the effects of the investment credit.
2. Determine whether the old machine should be replaced, assuming that the firm would be entitled to a 6% investment credit on the purchase of the new machine.

9-35 Dropping a product Stracke Company makes a number of products in several factories throughout the country. The sales manager is unhappy with the results shown by Quickclean, a spray cleaner for household use. Quickclean is made in only one factory. A typical income statement for Quickclean shows the following annual results.

Sales	$4,400,000
Variable costs	3,800,000
Contribution margin	600,000
Fixed costs	775,000
Loss	($ 175,000)

The production manager tells the sales manager that about $520,000 of the fixed costs shown above require cash disbursements. These are all avoidable. The remaining $255,000 in fixed costs consists of $100,000 in depreciation on equipment used only to make Quickclean, and $155,000 in allocated costs. The equipment used to make Quickclean has a useful life of five more years and no salvage value is expected at the end of five years. The book value is $500,000 and straight-line depreciation is being used.

Stracke has a cost of capital of 16% and the tax rate is 40%.

Required

1. Assume that the machinery used to make Quickclean has no resale value. If the product is dropped the machinery will be scrapped. The loss is immediately tax deductible. Determine whether Quickclean should be dropped.
2. Assume that the machinery could be sold for $180,000. Determine whether Quickclean should be dropped.

9-36   New product—complementary effects   Ralph Berger, general manager of the McKeown Division of Standard Enterprises, Inc., is considering the introduction of a new product. It will sell for $20 per unit and have variable costs of $9. Volume at that selling price is estimated at 120,000 units per year. Fixed costs requiring cash disbursements would increase by $300,000 annually as a result of adding the product, mainly in connection with operating some machinery that would be purchased for $2,000,000. The machinery would have a useful life of ten years, no salvage value, and would be depreciated using the straight-line method.

The new product would be made in a section of the factory that is physically separate from the rest of the factory and is now being leased to another firm for $120,000 per year. The other firm has expressed an interest in renewing the lease, which expires this month, for an additional ten years.

Berger expects inventories to increase by $500,000 if the new product is brought out. He also expects customers to pay for their purchases two months after purchase, but is uncertain how or whether to consider these factors.

The cost of capital is 20% and the tax rate is 40%.

Required

1. Determine whether the new product should be introduced.
2. Suppose that if the new product were brought out the sales of an existing product would increase by 30,000 units per year. The existing product sells for $10 and has variable costs of $6. The increase in sales of this product would lead to increases in inventories and receivables of $60,000. Determine whether the new product should be brought out.

9-37   Sensitivity analysis   Carter Pen Company makes several models of ballpoint and soft-tip pens. A model of soft-tip pen currently being made is the Scribbler, which has been moderately successful. The machinery used to make the Scribbler now requires replacement and the firm is trying to decide whether to continue its manufacture.

The alternative to continuing to produce the Scribbler is to bring out a more expensive soft-tip pen, the Brush. Carter's managers believe that if both pens were produced, they would take sales from each other and so only one should be produced. Data on the two investments are as follows.

	Scribbler	Brush
Selling price	$0.80	$2.20
Variable costs	0.40	0.90
Additional annual cash fixed costs	$300,000	$ 800,000
Required investment, all depreciable assets	$800,000	$1,500,000
Expected annual volume of sales, in units	2,000,000	1,250,000

Neither investment would have salvage value at the end of the useful life, which is four years for both investments. Straight-line depreciation would be used for tax purposes. The tax rate is 40% and cost of capital is 16%.

Required

1. Using the net present value criterion, determine which product should be made.
2. The president is concerned about the effects on profitability of declines in volume from the expected figures. Determine the unit volume for each product that would give the firm a 16% return on each. (Round the required after-tax cash flows and pretax incomes to the nearest thousand dollars.) Determine the percentage decline from the original estimates that each volume represents. Would the new information have any effect on your decision in part 1?

9-38   Closing a plant—externalities   Fisher Manufacturing Company operates a plant in Vesalia, a small city on the Platte River. The firm has been notified that it must install pollution control equipment at the plant, at a cost of $4,000,000, or else close the plant. The plant employs 400 people, virtually all of whom would lose their jobs if the plant were to close. Fisher would make a lump-sum payment totaling $80,000 to the people put out of jobs if the plant were closed.

A buyer would be willing to purchase the plant for $400,000, which equals its book value. Fisher could shift production to the Montclair plant if it closed the Vesalia plant, with no increase in total cash production costs. (That is, the increase in Montclair's cash production costs would equal the cash operating costs of the Vesalia plant.) However, shipping costs would increase by $900,000 annually because the Montclair plant is much farther away from customers than the Vesalia plant.

The equipment, if purchased, would have a 10-year useful life with no salvage value. Straight-line depreciation would be use for tax purposes.

The tax rate is 40% and cost of capital is 14%.

Required

1. Considering only monetary factors, determine whether Fisher should install the pollution control equipment or close the plant.
2. What other factors might be considered by those interested in the decision?

9-39   Product modification (CMA adapted)   Williams Company manufactures office equipment and sells it through wholesalers. All sales are for cash.

The general manager of the firm recently learned that a patent on a semiautomatic paper collator could be bought for $60,000. The collator is much faster than a manually operated model that Williams now sells. If the patent were bought, Williams would have to spend $40,000 modifying existing production equipment to make the semiautomatic model and would no longer be able to make the manual model. The modifications would not change the remaining useful life of the equipment (four years), nor would they change the salvage value, which is expected to be negligible.

Variable costs to produce the semiautomatic model would be $1 more than for the manual model, but fixed costs other than depreciation on the modifications and amortization of the patent would be unchanged.

The company currently sells 100,000 units of the manual model at $4 each, with variable costs of $1.80 and total fixed costs of $120,000 per year. The fixed costs include $20,000 in depreciation expense on the existing equipment. The firm has a tax rate of 40% and cost of capital of 20%.

The firm's market research analysts have come up with three important findings relating to the decision: (1) the patent will be worthless in four years because of expected technological advances; (2) if Williams does not buy the patent, a competitor will, with the result that sales of the manual model would decline to 70,000 units per year; and (3) at a $4 price, sales of the semiautomatic model would be 190,000 units per year for four years.

Williams's engineering department has concluded that inventory requirements would be $12,000 more if the semiautomatic model were produced than if the firm were to keep making the manual model.

The firm will use a 3-year ACRS life on the modifications to production equipment, straight-line amortization for the patent. Ignore the ITC.

Required: Determine the course the firm should take.

9-40   **Evaluating an investment proposal**   Your new assistant has just brought you the following analysis of an investment opportunity the firm is considering. The investment relates to a new manufacturing process that would be used to make one of the firm's major products.

Required Investment

New machinery (10-year life, no salvage value)	$350,000
Research and development	60,000
Administrative time	10,000
Total investment	$420,000

Annual Cash Flows (10 Years)

Savings in cost over old process:	
Labor	$ 75,000
Materials	80,000
Variable overhead	40,000
Depreciation	(35,000)
Total operating savings	160,000
Less: Interest on debt to finance investment	35,000
Net savings before taxes	125,000
Less: Income taxes at 40% rate	50,000
Net cash flow after taxes	$ 75,000

Your assistant tells you that the new machinery would replace old machinery that has a 10-year remaining useful life with no salvage value. The existing machinery would be scrapped if the new machinery is bought, and the salvage value would be equal to the cost of having it removed. The existing machinery has a book value of $110,000. Straight-line depreciation is used for the existing machinery and would also be used for the new machinery.

Your assistant also tells you that the listed costs for research and development and for administrative time relate solely to this project and contain no allocations. The costs have been incurred already, so their amounts are certain. The item in the analysis for interest on debt is for $350,000 at 10%, which would be borrowed if the new machinery is acquired.

Based on his analysis and the firm's cost of capital of 16%, he recommends that the project be rejected.

Required: Determine whether the investment should be made, supporting your answer with appropriate calculations.

Cases

9-41 Alternative uses of assets (AICPA adapted)   Miller Manufacturing Company has been producing both toasters and blenders in its Syracuse plant for several years. The rent for the Syracuse factory building is $80,000 per year. When the lease expires at the end of four years, the company intends to cease all operations at that location and scrap the equipment.

Blender production is approximately 50,000 per year and the company expects to continue production at that level. However, because of intense competition and price erosion, the company has decided to stop making toasters.

Two areas of the Syracuse plant, making up about 30% of the total plant floor space, are devoted to the production of toasters. The equipment used to make toasters has a current book value of $140,000 and is being depreciated at $35,000 per year. The company has received a firm offer of $20,000 for all the equipment now used in toaster production, and the buyer is not interested in anything less than all the equipment. If the equipment were sold, the space now used for toaster production could be subleased for $12,000 per year.

Because the production of blenders is to be continued, the production manager was asked if he had need of the space and/or equipment now devoted to toaster production. He said that though he had no need for additional productive capacity for tasks currently being undertaken at the plant, he would be interested in using the space and equipment for the manufacture of a blender part now being purchased from an outside firm. The part is a blade assembly that the firm purchases for $5 per unit. The contract with the outside vendor runs for four more years and requires that Miller buy at least 5,000 assemblies per year.

Either of the two areas now used for toaster production could be converted to facilitate the production of the blade assemblies. The production manager estimates that the variable cost to produce an assembly would be $3.60 and no additional fixed costs requiring cash would be incurred. However, the equipment now used would have to be converted. He estimates that it would cost about $40,000 to convert enough of the equipment to make 35,000 assemblies per year and $80,000 to convert enough equipment to make 60,000 assemblies. Because the prospective buyer of the equipment wants all or none of it, conversion of any of it means the company must forego the sale.

The company's tax rate is 40% and its cost of capital is 14%. Straight-line depreciation would be used on costs of converting equipment.

Required: Determine the best course of action for the company.

9-42 Mutually exclusive investments   Seagle Company requires some machinery for an essential task that will be carried out for the next ten years. Two machines that meet the firm's needs are available. Data on them are as follows.

	Rapidgo 350	Rapidgo 600
Purchase cost	$50,000	$90,000
Annual operating expenses, exclusive of depreciation	12,000	15,000
Salvage value at end of useful life	5,000	10,000
Useful life	5 years	10 years

Either machine would be depreciated using the straight-line method and provision would be made for salvage value. The firm expects to have to pay $60,000 to replace the Rapidgo 350 at the end of five years, if that machine is selected. The other data applicable to the Rapidgo 350 given above would be applicable to the replacement model as well.

Cost of capital is 16% and the tax rate is 40%.

Required: Determine the course of action the firm should take.

9-43   **Expanding a factory**   Fisher Company needs more space and machinery to increase production. The production manager and president have been trying to decide which of two alternative plans to accept. Data on the two plans are as follows.

	Plan A	Plan B
Investment required	$4,000,000	$5,500,000
Additional fixed cash operating costs per year	600,000	800,000
Additional capacity in machine-hours per year	200,000	280,000

Both investments would be depreciated using the straight-line method. No salvage value is expected for either investment at the end of their 10-year useful lives.

The production manager believes that Plan B should be accepted because the cost-per-machine-hour and investment-per-machine-hour figures are lower than for Plan A. The president is unsure about this and asks the sales manager whether the capacity would be fully utilized. The sales manager provides the following data.

	Product		
	101-X	201-X	305-X
Potential increased sales, in units	30,000	40,000	30,000
Contribution margin per unit	$18	$24	$40
Machine-hours required per unit	2	4	5

Fisher pays income taxes at a 40% rate and has cost of capital of 12%.

Required: Determine which, if either, expansion plan should be accepted and how the increased capacity should be used (that is, how much of each product should be made).

PART THREE

CONTROL AND PERFORMANCE EVALUATION

Part Three concentrates on the management functions of control and performance evaluation. Both functions are more effectively carried out through the principles and techniques incorporated into a responsibility accounting system. An essential step in the development of such a system is fixing responsibility for each cost. Fixing responsibility for cost elements is also important if the fullest advantage is to be derived from comprehensive budgeting. In this part, the emphasis shifts from planning to control, and to evaluating actual results in relation to planned or budgeted results.

Human behavior and the ways in which accounting methods prompt particular kinds of behavior are treated extensively in the three chapters in this part. The major thrust of responsibility accounting is behavioral; the critical factor in its success is the extent to which the system encourages or discourages behavior consistent with the best interests of the firm.

CHAPTER 10

RESPONSIBILITY ACCOUNTING

Planning and decision making were the focus of attention in earlier chapters; the basic concepts of managerial accounting were developed and illustrated with applications for these management activities. We are now ready to look more closely at the managerial control process, particularly at the area of performance evaluation. Control is exercised through a management control system, which is a set of policies, procedures, and processes that managers use to determine whether or not operations are going as planned; and if not, to suggest possible courses of action designed to correct the situation. **Responsibility accounting** is the name given to that aspect of the overall management control system that deals with the reporting of information to facilitate control of operations and evaluation of performance. The responsibility accounting system is usually the most formal communication system within the overall management control system.

Nonquantifiable factors are at least as important to effective control and evaluation as they are to planning and decision making. Of particular concern is the potential for the organization and content of accounting reports to influence the actions of managers.

GOAL CONGRUENCE AND MOTIVATION

A major objective of management control is to encourage **goal congruence,** in which managers and workers strive toward the goals of the firm, not just toward their own goals. Employees must have some *incentive* to work toward the goals of the firm. The task of management is to motivate employees to work toward the firm's goals, and the responsibility accounting system should assist managers in accomplishing this task. Because managers at any level will evaluate their subordinates at least partly on the basis of reports that the responsibility accounting system generates, such reports must be carefully designed and thoroughly understood.

A good responsibility accounting system will report only on factors that managers can control. Thus, uncontrollable costs either should not appear at all in performance reports, or should be carefully segregated and labeled so as not to be considered in the evaluation of the employee/manager. Moreover, the system should give sufficient feedback for the manager to be aware of what has been happening, what trends might be expected, and, to the extent possible, why things have happened the way they did.

Most of the major problems in developing an effective responsibility accounting system are behavioral. Managers must trust the reporting system; they must believe that it provides an accurate picture of their performances. Managers must also believe that the system is fair. Accordingly, the evaluation system should use performance evaluation criteria that are under the control of the managers. But if the system is to perform its function for the company as a whole, the feedback provided to, and the criteria used for, evaluating the managers should also motivate them to act in such a way as to advance the overall goals of the firm.

A basic step in implementing responsibility accounting is the establishment of responsibility centers within the firm.

RESPONSIBILITY CENTERS

If managers are to be held accountable for their performances, they must have clearly defined areas of responsibility—activities over which they exercise control. A **responsibility center** is, as the words imply, a center (position) at which some responsibility is exercised, the location of the responsibility for some activity. It might appear to be relatively easy to identify activities with specific managers. A plant manager is in charge of a plant and is responsible for producing required quantities of specific products within budgeted cost limits. A sales manager is responsible for getting orders from customers, and so on. In many cases, however, it is no simple task to isolate the responsibilities of managers.

The performance of one manager can be affected by the performance of others. The best salespeople in the world cannot sell poorly made products; by the same token, no production manager can minimize costs if production schedules change daily because of poor forecasting of sales of individual products. Because such interdependencies cannot be eliminated entirely, it is critical that their effects be minimized by careful selection of responsibility centers, by appropriate use of rewards and penalties, and by proper use of performance reports by managers who understand the information that they receive.

For example, to reduce the potential for conflict between sales and production because of the quality of the output produced, a firm might make the production manager responsible for the quality of output as well as for production costs. Requiring the sales manager to give reasonable notice to the production manager when a change in product mix is needed would help the production manager to meet budgeted costs and thus minimize the potential for conflict. Each specific situation where conflicts might arise must be considered by itself and appropriate procedures and responsibilities assigned to the managers potentially in conflict; there are few general rules to which one can turn for good guidance.

There are three basic types of responsibility centers: cost centers, profit centers, and investment centers. The type of responsibility center should coincide with the breadth of control on the part of the manager. Each of these types of center is described below and considered in more detail in this and the following chapter.

Cost Centers

Cost centers are segments where the managers are responsible for costs incurred but have no revenue responsibilities. A cost center can be relatively small, like a single department with a few people who perform one or several operations on a product. A cost center can also be quite large, such as the administrative area for a very large firm. An entire factory could be a cost center if its manager is responsible for controlling costs but has no responsibility for sales. Some cost centers are composed of a number of smaller cost centers; for example, a factory may be segmented into many departments, each of which is a cost center.

Profit Centers

Profit centers are segments in which the managers are responsible for controlling both costs and revenues. In such a center it is possible to compute a residual figure, like net income, contribution margin, or incremental profit, for evaluating performance.

A profit center can be either natural or artificial. A **natural profit center** sells its output outside the firm. It operates in external markets and therefore earns revenues much the same as does an entire firm. A single firm may have one or more subunits that operate independently in most respects. An **artificial profit center** sells its output primarily within the firm. The selling price in such cases is called a **transfer price.** A firm that mines iron ore, makes it into steel, fabricates the steel, makes products out of the fabricated steel, and sells the products to outsiders could establish profit centers at various stages. The mining operation could "sell" the ore to the steel-making division, which could in turn "sell" the steel to the fabrication division, and so on. The output of a profit center need not be a physical product; a computer center could charge operating units for computing services, and the maintenance department could charge operating departments for repair work. Because there are advantages to operating an area as a profit center, artificial profit centers are becoming more common.

Investment Centers

An **investment center** is a segment in which the manager can control not only revenues and costs but also investment. Thus, for an investment center it is possible to compute a residual figure, such as income, *and* a return on investment.

The concept of an investment center is popular because the manager of such a center is treated much as if he or she were the chief executive of an autonomous company. The manager of an investment center has much wider responsibility than does the manager of a particular functional area within a firm, and it is often possible to evaluate performance with a higher degree of reliability. The choice of a type of responsibility center for a particular activity (or group of activities) is unique to each firm. Such factors as size, industry, operating characteristics, and managerial philosophy influence organizational structure.

Criteria for Evaluation

The selection of criteria for measuring and evaluating the exercise of responsibility is important because the criteria by which managers are evaluated will influence their actions. The most commonly found deficiencies in performance measurement are (1) using a *single* measure that emphasizes only one objective of the organization, and (2) selecting measures that either misrepresent the firm's objectives or don't reflect them at all.

Managers would like to be able to use a single, comprehensive measure of performance, but the search for such a measure is seldom successful. Consider an example reported from the Soviet Union. It is said that the government was once unhappy with the output of nails and decided to evaluate managers of nail factories by the weight of the nails produced. The managers could produce much greater weight by making only large spikes, and they did. Once the government saw that its performance measure was not producing the desired results, it changed the basis of evaluation to the number of nails produced—and the factories began to pour out carpet tacks and small brads.

Although profit is a common measure of performance, and a more comprehensive measure than most others, not only is its use limited to responsibility centers that have both revenue and cost responsibilities, but it too can suffer from overemphasis. For example, managers should know that emphasizing profits in the current period might be detrimental to profits in future periods. But a responsibility accounting system that emphasizes short-run profits will tempt managers to increase short-run profits at the expense of the long run. (Some ways that they might do so are by postponing maintenance and repairs; failing to modernize plant and equipment; reducing spending on research and development and employee training; and paying limited attention to the quality of products while emphasizing cost reductions.) In recent years, many commentators have argued that managers of U.S. companies concentrate too much on the short term and pay insufficient attention to long-term issues. These commentators have suggested that the failure to take a longer-term view was the principal factor in making U.S. businesses less competitive in world markets than, say, the Japanese.

Perhaps the best way to encourage managers to act in the firm's best interests is to measure their performance in relation to budgeted results. Managers of cost centers that are production departments would be evaluated on whether they produced the required quantities of product at budgeted costs. Managers of nonmanufacturing departments, such as a computer center or market research group, could be evaluated on whether budgeted costs were met. Managers of profit centers would normally be evaluated on a comparison of actual and budgeted profit. And investment centers might be evaluated on the basis of return on investment. (The special problems of evaluating investment centers are taken up in the next chapter, but most of the comments on profit centers are applicable to investment centers also.)

Of course, whether or not it is legitimate and useful to evaluate a manager's performance by comparing budgeted and actual results depends on (1) how the budgeted amounts were determined, and (2) to what extent the comparisons consider the controllability of differences. As discussed in Chapters 6 and 7, budgeted amounts must reflect *attainable* performance if managers are to take them seriously and strive to meet them. We also noted earlier that managers tend to react more favorably to an evaluation based on a budget *they* helped to set. But even with budget amounts that are agreed upon in advance as attainable, an uncontrollable change in conditions can influence results, and managers will not react favorably to a reporting and evaluation system that fails to allow for variations due to circumstances beyond their control.

There are other bases for evaluating performance. Some companies evaluate managers on the basis of improvement over some prior period, or by comparison with other segments of the same firm. (Did this factory manager produce at a lower cost than did the manager of the same factory last year? Did this salesperson sell more this year than did other salespeople?) Whatever bases are used for evaluation, it is critical that both the evaluator and the evaluatee know what those bases are and understand the implications of using those criteria.

ORGANIZATIONAL STRUCTURE

The way that the firm is organized influences its reporting system. Different organizational structures result in different groupings of responsibilities. That is, the way in which the company is structured will affect the areas controlled by individual managers. For instance, in one firm a manager of a factory might also have responsibility over the sales force that sells the products from that factory (would control both revenues and expenses) and so would be in charge of a profit center. Another firm, similar to the first in product lines, factories, and other physical aspects, might assign the responsibility for the sales force to a corporate vice president of sales. The factory managers in such a firm would then be managing cost centers. The reporting requirements for the two firms would be quite different.

In general terms, a firm's organization is characterized as *centralized* or *decentralized* on the basis of the extent of the responsibilities granted to individual managers within the entity. If managers have a good deal of authority and can make many types of decisions without the approval of higher levels of management, the organization is said to be **decentralized.** Where managers are more constrained (can act less freely on their own), the structure is said to be **centralized.** We take up the question of decentralization more fully in Chapter 11. For now it is sufficient to note that, in general, profit and investment centers are more commonly associated with decentralization than are cost centers. (This is because managers of profit and investment centers have broader authority than do managers of cost centers.) That is, as we explore the basics of responsibility accounting, the issue is not whether an organization is centralized or decentralized but how the structure affects the reports developed for whatever responsibility centers there may be.

The organizational structure depicted in Figure 10-1 shows a great many cost centers, with the structure of the company following functional lines (production, marketing, administration, finance). Figure 10-2 shows an alternative organizational structure, with many profit or investment centers in which managers of each region are responsible for both production and sales. Note that the finance function is not delegated to the individual managers even in the alternative structure. It is extremely rare that the responsibility for financing the entity rests at other than the corporate (all-entity) level. One of the reasons for not delegating financing decisions to lower levels is a legal consideration: the issuance of bonds and/or stock commits the entire corporation and must be approved by managers with commensurate responsibilities. Legal issues aside, a firm's capital requirements can normally be met at less cost if the needs of its segments are consolidated and filled as a unit. As a practical matter, even if the financing needs of a particular segment can be met through a local source, the arrangement usually requires the approval of a management group with entity-wide responsibilities.

Responsibility Reporting for Cost Centers

Exhibit 10-1 (page 364) shows the interrelationships among reports developed for cost centers. For the company whose reports are being exhibited, there is a factory that has

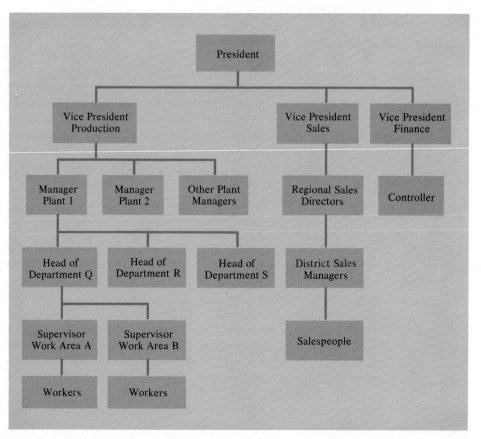

FIGURE 10-1   Sample of Organizational Structure

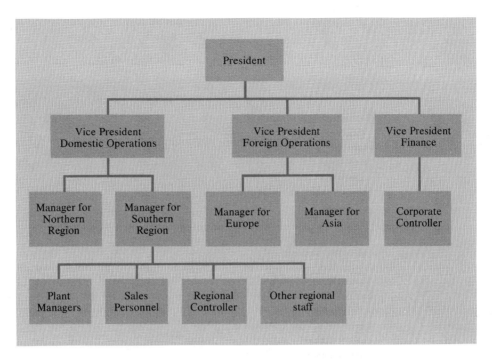

FIGURE 10-2   Sample of Organizational Structure

three levels of supervision: (1) work stations, which are relatively small units under the control of foremen; (2) departments, which are collections of work stations and under the control of a departmental supervisor; and (3) the factory as a whole, which is under the control of the factory manager. In addition, though not reflected in the reports, the factory managers are all subordinates of the vice president of manufacturing.

As stated earlier, an important characteristic of good responsibility reporting is that its reports include only controllable costs. Whether or not a particular cost is controllable—and hence includable in the report to a particular manager—depends on the level of that manager in the hierarchy. For example, in Exhibit 10-1 you can see that the total cost reported to the department supervisor is greater than the sum of the costs reported to the foremen who are subordinates of that supervisor. The supervisor is responsible for all costs that are identifiable with the work stations under his or her supervision. But he or she is also responsible for those costs that are joint (in the sense of not controllable by an individual work-station foreman) with respect to the work stations within the group. In the exhibit, such joint costs are general supervision (which probably includes the salary of the department supervisor), cleaning, and "other."

Similarly, the plant manager is responsible for some costs that the departmental supervisors are not: engineering, heat and light, building depreciation, and general administration. The reports would show more detail in a realistic situation, with more itemizations of individual costs. We have restricted the number of items for simplicity.

An important feature exhibited by the sample reports is that the amount of detail decreases as the reports reach higher and higher levels of management. Departmental managers would probably not receive regular reports detailing all of the costs of

Exhibit 10-1

Responsibility Reports for Cost Centers

	Current Month		Year to Date	
	Budget	Over (Under)	Budget	Over (Under)
Report to Foreman of				
Work Station 106—Drill Press				
Materials	$ 3,200	$ (80)	$ 12,760	$ 110
Direct labor	14,200	170	87,300	880
Supervision	1,100	(50)	4,140	(78)
Power, supplies, miscellaneous	910	24	3,420	92
Totals	$ 19,410	$ 64	$107,620	$1,004
Report to Supervisor of				
Fabrication Department				
Station 106—Drill Press	$ 19,410	$ 64	$107,620	$1,004
Station 107—Grinding	17,832	122	98,430	(213)
Station 108—Cutting	23,456	876	112,456	1,227
Total work stations	60,698	1,062	318,506	2,018
Departmental costs (common to work stations):				
General supervision	12,634	0	71,234	0
Cleaning	6,125	324	32,415	762
Other	1,890	(67)	10,029	(108)
Totals	$ 81,347	$1,319	$432,184	$2,672
Report to Manager of Factory				
Fabrication department	$ 81,347	$1,319	$432,184	$2,672
Milling department	91,234	(2,034)	405,190	(4,231)
Assembly department	107,478	854	441,240	1,346
Casting department	78,245	(433)	367,110	689
Total departments	358,304	(564)	1,645,724	476
General factory costs (common to departments):				
Engineering	14,235	261	81,340	842
Heat and light	8,435	178	46,221	890
Building depreciation	3,400	0	20,400	0
General administration (includes accounting, travel, plant manager's office, etc.)	23,110	340	126,289	776
Total factory costs	$407,484	$ 215	$1,919,974	$2,984

the work stations. If the managers wanted such detailed information, they could get it, and they might well seek it if they were concerned about some particular elements of cost. In general, the regular—say, monthly—reports to departmental managers would show only totals for the work stations, just as the regular reports to the factory manager would show only totals for the departments. There are several reasons for the reduction in detail as reports go to higher levels of management:

1. Excessive detail can interfere with understanding. To give the president a report showing individually the costs incurred by hundreds of work areas in scores of departments would interfere with his or her efforts to understand the operations as a whole.
2. Managers are usually concerned with the performance of those who report directly to them. Thus, there is no need to draw attention to the specific performances of the subordinates of the managers' subordinates.
3. The principle of management by exception implies that a manager should be concerned with problem areas—segments in which operations are not going according to plan. A manager is normally in a position to judge operations only one level below.

One other aspect of the sample reports in Exhibit 10-1 deserves further discussion. Two of the three reports show certain costs as joint (or common) to work stations, or to departments. There are always *some* costs that are common to two or more segments within an organization, but the managerial level at which a particular cost is controllable varies from firm to firm. For example, we show the costs of heating and lighting as joint to departments, which suggests that individual departmental supervisors cannot control these costs. In another firm, each department might have a meter to monitor the consumption of these utilities, in which case their cost might well be controllable at the departmental level. Similarly, one company might require that requests for operating supplies identify the specific work station at which they are to be used, while another might require only that the overall operating department be noted on the request. Thus, a cost is not always joint by its nature, but may be so because the organization follows procedures that do not produce information by segments below a certain level.

Large amounts of costs that cannot be assigned (and, of course, controlled) at lower levels can be frustrating to managers whose task is to evaluate performance of subordinates. Remember that the reports to subordinates are likely to include only those costs assignable to them, though their *actions* could influence joint costs that appear only on the reports to higher levels of management. (Using the earlier example, the use of operating supplies may be controllable by the manager of a work station, even though the existing procedures do not identify costs at that level.) Whether it is worthwhile to adopt procedures to assign responsibility for a particular cost to lower levels of management depends not only on the nature of the cost but also on the benefits to be gained by doing so. Benefits might include the savings derived because lower level managers will be more careful in the use of a particular item (supplies, repair services, whatever). But the benefits must be weighed against the cost of obtaining the additional information (new meters; time required to fill out more detailed requisition forms and to produce more, or more detailed, reports, etc.). In any case, the facts in a particular firm determine whether a cost is controllable at a given level of management, and the responsibility reporting system should follow, as closely as possible, the principle of including only controllable items.

Responsibility Reporting for Profit Centers

The principle of controllability also applies to responsibility reporting for profit centers (and for investment centers, which we consider in more detail in Chapter 11). Exhibit 10-2 provides sample reports for a firm that organizes profit centers around product lines and geographical areas. The managers at the lowest level of profit center are those who manage product lines. They are subordinate to the managers of the broad geographical areas that the firm services. In turn, those area managers are responsible to the executive vice president.

The unallocated costs—regional expenses joint to product lines, or corporate expenses common to regions—could consist of many different kinds of items. For instance, the regional expenses could include the salaries of people at regional headquarters, including those in accounting, personnel, finance, and other functions administered from regional headquarters. These costs are not separable by product lines and product managers cannot control them. In addition, advertising of the "image-building" variety, not aimed at particular product lines, could also be under the control of a regional manager. At the total-firm level, the same kinds of joint costs might be encountered.

Exhibit 10-2

Responsibility Reports for Profit Centers (thousands of dollars)

	Current Month		Year to Date	
	Budget	Over (Under)	Budget	Over (Under)
Report to Product Manager—Appliances, European Region				
Sales	$122.0	$1.5	$387.0	$3.2
Variable costs:				
Production	47.5	3.8	150.7	5.9
Selling and administrative	12.2	1.8	38.7	1.9
Total variable costs	59.7	4.6	189.4	7.8
Contribution margin	62.3	(3.1)	197.6	(4.6)
Separable fixed costs	36.0	(1.2)	98.5	(3.1)
Product margin	$ 26.3	($1.9)	$ 99.1	($1.5)
Report to Manager—European Region				
Product margins:				
Appliances	$ 26.3	($1.9)	$99.1	($1.5)
Industrial equipment	37.4	3.2	134.5	7.3
Tools	18.3	1.1	59.1	(2.0)
Total product margins	82.0	2.4	292.7	3.8
Regional expenses (common to all product lines)	18.5	0.8	61.2	(1.3)
Regional margin	$ 63.5	$1.6	$231.5	$ 5.1
Report to Executive Vice President				
Regional margins:				
European	$ 63.5	$1.6	$231.5	$ 5.1
Asian	78.1	(4.3)	289.4	(8.2)
North American	211.8	(3.2)	612.4	(9.6)
Total regional margins	353.4	(5.9)	1,133.3	(12.7)
Corporate expenses common to all regions	87.1	1.4	268.5	3.1
Corporate profit	$266.3	($7.3)	$864.8	($15.8)

For simplicity, the report we have shown concerning the regional manager includes only product margins for each of the product groups sold in the region. In some companies, such managers would be provided more detail, such as sales, and some firms would also report the amounts of expenses that may be of special concern, such as advertising and promotion. Similarly, reports could also show critical percentages, like contribution margin or profit to sales.

Exhibit 10-3 shows an approach that provides more detail on individual components of the appliance segment in the European region. This approach draws attention to the presence of costs common to the different categories of appliances. To focus attention on the format, we have shown only the actual year-to-date figures. The critical point in performance reporting is conveying the best information; the selections of the elements to include and the format are secondary. Notice that the amount of detail is greater in the alternative format and that some of the costs that were shown as separable by product line in Exhibit 10-2 are shown as common to the components of the line in Exhibit 10-3.

Exhibit 10-3
Alternative Responsibility Reporting Format
Report to Product Manager—Appliances, European Region

	Total	Small Home Appliances	Large Home Appliances	Commercial Appliances
Sales	$390.2	$126.3	$109.5	$154.4
Variable costs:				
Production	156.6	41.1	31.2	84.3
Selling and administrative	40.6	14.2	18.1	8.3
Total variable costs	197.2	55.3	49.3	92.6
Contribution margin	193.0	71.0	60.2	61.8
Separable fixed costs	27.4	9.5	11.2	6.7
Margin	165.6	$ 61.5	$ 49.0	$ 55.1
Costs common to products in the appliance line	68.0			
Product margin	$ 97.6			

In both Exhibit 10-2 and Exhibit 10-3, the sample reports to the manager of appliance sales for the European Region include production costs. The implication of such reporting is that the manager for the region can control, and is responsible for, such costs. Control of production is not necessary to justify this type of reporting scheme. For example, suppose that a company has sales offices in several regions, and that the manager of a region can control salespeople's salaries, administrative costs of the regional sales office, and the relative emphasis given to particular products or product lines. From earlier chapters you know that decisions about individual products or product lines are based on profitability, and that profitability is affected by factors other than sales volume and direct selling costs. For decision-making purposes, then, it is important that regional sales managers be aware of the costs of the products being sold. Accordingly, reports to managers who are responsible only for sales and regional selling costs very often include some charge for the products sold, even though such reporting does not follow strictly the principle of controllability. As long as the product cost included in the report to the sales manager is not affected by the efficiencies (or inefficiencies) of the managers who *can* control production costs, there is no harm in reporting product costs to the sales manager, and better decision making might well result. One method commonly used for measuring such product cost is its budgeted cost.

Another relatively common practice that is not consistent with developing reports on the basis of the principle of controllability is the inclusion of some committed costs in performance reports. Such costs are not relevant for making decisions about whether to drop a segment in the short run, and are not controllable in the short run either. However, they are relevant for long-run decisions, because they will not be committed forever; they are renewed periodically as machinery and buildings are replaced and top managers retired. Moreover, it may be impractical to separate the committed and discretionary portions of some cost items, which difficulty might prompt the inclusion of both types of fixed costs on a performance report. If the situation in a particular firm necessitates the violation of the controllability principle in responsibility reporting, the managers in that firm must exercise care in using the reports for performance evaluation.

Choosing an Organizational Structure

Should a firm organize into profit and investment centers, or into cost centers? Should it centralize or decentralize decision making? The answers to these questions depend on many factors, not the least of which are the attitudes and philosophies of top managers. A company president who is uncomfortable with having subordinates make many critical decisions would tend to centralize decision making; another, who prefers to give subordinates a great deal of responsibility and emphasize accountability, would tend to decentralize.

Another principal consideration in selecting an organizational structure is the extent of common costs; this factor is influenced heavily by the types of operations that the firm carries on. A firm that makes many products in a single factory would find it difficult to decentralize along product lines. The performance reports in Exhibit 10-2 show costs that are joint to product lines within regions. Such reporting indicates that some plants make products in more than one line, and that the firm does not allocate all production costs to the individual product lines. Similarly, we see common selling and administrative expenses both by region and at the corporate level. The costs that are joint to the regions probably emanate from corporate headquarters (offices of the executive vice president, treasurer, etc.) and other general sources having nothing directly to do with activities within regions.

Even after a firm has decided to use profit centers there remains the question of how to make the separations. The segmentation could be along product lines, geographical areas, types of customers (industrial, governmental), or broad markets (leisure, household products, mining) that would encompass a number of product lines. The choice should be influenced by how readily useful performance reports can be developed to facilitate evaluation; and that, too, depends to some extent on the amount of common costs that would occur with each alternative structure. If each factory serves a particular geographical region and makes many products, it would be more reasonable to segment by region than by product line. If factories each produce a single product or product line, serving all regions where the firm operates, it would be more reasonable to segment by product or line. (Of course there could be sales managers in each region, but the profit centers would be the product lines, not the regions.)

Choosing an organizational structure is difficult in all but the most obvious situations where only one structure makes sense. Nor is there any reason to believe that a particular structuring found useful at one time, by one set of managers, will remain useful or appropriate as the managers act with and react to the dynamics of the business environment. Managers, including top managers, change; products and product lines are dropped, added, or regrouped; manufacturing activities are transferred among plants or otherwise changed, perhaps because of technological innovations. Hence, the structure of the organization, for responsibility reporting as for operating purposes, is an evolutionary matter that requires regular review, monitoring, and decision making. But there are no simple rules for discerning the optimal and for-all-time organizational structure, a point that will be emphasized and further explained in your later courses in business policy and strategy.

PERFORMANCE REPORTS AND ALLOCATIONS

The principle that performance reports should show only controllable costs is not always easy to apply. As we mentioned earlier, practical difficulties may prompt the inclusion of committed fixed costs in regular reports, even though such costs may not be controllable for the period covered by the report. But many firms deliberately violate the principle of controllability in order to make calculations of, and draw attention to, the *full cost* of an activity such as a production department. The term *full cost* is used by managers to mean a combination of the costs that are separable, or *direct* to the activity, and what the managers consider to be a "fair share" of the joint, often called *indirect,* costs. The terms *direct* and *indirect* are commonly used in describing costs that we have called, in earlier chapters, separable and joint costs. The term *traceable* is often used as a synonym for *direct*.

The attempt to develop a "full cost" is, as we have mentioned in earlier chapters and will consider in later ones, related primarily to the issue of product costing—determining the unit cost of products for the purposes of determining inventory and cost of goods sold for financial reporting and income tax reports. Determining such a unit cost requires that the firm make a number of allocations. Because such allocations, however arbitrary, must be made for product-costing purposes, there has been a tendency to use these already-made allocations in internal reports that have as their purpose the evaluation of performance. This tendency is most common in **service departments**—those departments that provide services to operating departments but that do not themselves work directly on products.

Operating departments use the services of many other departments. For example, a firm might have a separate maintenance department that performs work on the equipment used by the operating departments, or a personnel department that handles the screening and hiring of factory (and office) employees, etc. The difficulty in applying the concept of controllability to reports for managers of operating departments is that while those managers receive the benefits of the services from the service departments, those managers do not necessarily control either the costs of the services provided or the amount of the services received. For example, the manager of a production department, say the department that does the final assembly of the product, benefits from services provided by the personnel department, building security, maintenance, and a host of other groups. If the firm did not have these other, service departments, the manager of the assembly department would have to provide the service and incur the cost. (The manager would need to keep additional payroll records, hire people to repair and maintain the machinery, etc.)

Because the absence of service departments would increase the costs of the service-using departments, many accounting and other managers argue that it is appropriate to charge the operating manager for some share of the cost of these services. The "full-costers" have a valid point if the quantity (though not necessarily the quality) of services used by an operating manager is controllable. Departmental supervisors might be responsible for the use and misuse of machinery and have the choice of using, or not using, maintenance services. But even where managers control the use of a service, they are not likely to control the cost of the service. For instance, the supervisor of the maintenance department probably assigns people to different jobs, so that one operating manager might have a job done by a very efficient maintenance worker, while another operating manager might have a similar job done by a less efficient worker.

There are two approaches used to *assign* costs of service departments to the departments using the service. A very common approach is to *allocate* the costs of service departments according to some prearranged allocation scheme based on the number of units of the service used in the serviced department. The second approach involves developing a transfer price, a term introduced earlier in connection with the discussion of artificial profit centers. A **transfer price** is a charge made to one segment of an entity for a unit of product or service of another segment. For example, there might be a $30 per hour price for using the firm's computer. The distinction between an allocation and a transfer price becomes less clear when a transfer price is used even though a using manager cannot control the use of the service. What the two approaches have in common is that they are simply different methods of *assigning* costs of service departments to departments being serviced. Under either approach, the result is the assigning of joint costs.

The idea of holding managers responsible for the services they use is appealing, and there have been many suggestions on how to develop appropriate and fair schemes for implementing this idea. (See the Appendix to this chapter for one method of allocating.) Yet any scheme for assigning *all* common costs must, at some point, introduce arbitrariness. And the more that managers view costs assigned to them as arbitrary and unfair because they cannot control such costs, the less those managers will trust the system of performance evaluation. Thus, the primary problem associated with responsibility reports that involve charges for service departments is behavioral.

Behavioral Considerations

It should not surprise you to hear that the behavioral consequences of a cost assignment method are the most important consideration. If a method encourages managers to operate in the best interests of the firm, it is beneficial; if it does not, it is harmful. A particular method might be good for one firm at one time, but bad for that firm at a different time. The usefulness (and hence legitimacy) of the method used depends on the objectives of the firm at the time.

Let us consider a simple example. The costs of a data-processing department are largely fixed. (Most firms rent computers at a fixed monthly or annual rate; professional personnel are normally salaried; and it is normal to keep the computer running for about the same number of hours each day.) If the top managers of the firm wished to encourage lower-level managers to experiment with different ways to use the available computer facilities to help in running the operations, those top managers might set a very low per-hour rate for the use of computer time. Such a rate might be based on only the variable costs of operating the computer.

Later on, when actual computer use begins to approach capacity, those top managers might raise the charges so as to discourage all but essential use. Lower-level managers would then be encouraged to give more careful consideration to their requests for computer services and deterred from seeking computer services for tasks that could be accomplished more efficiently by other means. If actual use, even with the higher charges, came very close to computer capacity, the firm might have to consider more expensive equipment.

Examples of Allocations and Transfer Prices

In this section we offer some examples of common methods of charging for the services of a service department. Examine the proposed methods and try to decide if any or some methods would have the behavioral consequence of inviting abuse of the provided service. After all of the methods have been described, we will provide an evaluation of the alternatives.

Assume that a firm has a maintenance department and two operating departments: fabrication and assembly. The maintenance cost that would be assigned to each of the operating departments under the various methods will be calculated. The following data relate to the activities of the operating and maintenance departments for a given year.

Operating Departments	Hours of Maintenance Service Used
Fabrication	20,000
Assembly	10,000
Total hours	30,000

Costs of the Maintenance Department for the Year

	Budgeted	Actual
Fixed	$ 75,000	$ 90,000
Variable:		
$5 per hour	150,000	
$5.50 per hour		165,000
Total costs	$225,000	$255,000

Assume further that the cost of obtaining similar service from an outside maintenance firm is $8 per hour.

Method 1.   Allocate all maintenance costs to operating departments pro rata based on the number of hours of maintenance work performed in each department. Using this method, the per-hour cost to be allocated for the year would be $8.50 ($255,000 actual cost divided by 30,000 hours of maintenance service), and the total cost would be assigned as follows.

Fabrication	(20,000 × $8.50)	$170,000
Assembly	(10,000 × $8.50)	85,000
Total maintenance cost allocated		$255,000

Method 2.   Allocate to each operating department a fixed amount, regardless of use of maintenance. The total cost incurred by the maintenance department could, under this method, be allocated to the two departments in any amounts so that the combination added up to $255,000.

Method 3.   Charge each operating department a per-hour rate (a transfer price) for maintenance based on what it would cost the department to obtain the services from outside the firm. This would make the maintenance department an artificial profit center. Using this approach, the charge to each department for maintenance service would be as follows.

Fabrication	(20,000 × $8)	$160,000
Assembly	(10,000 × $8)	80,000
Total maintenance cost allocated		$240,000

Using this method, the maintenance department would show revenues of $240,000, costs of $255,000 and therefore a loss of $15,000. This transfer price does not change the actual cost incurred but simply spreads that cost around differently. The total cost of $255,000 has been incurred; $240,000 would be charged to the operating departments and the maintenance department would show the remainder as a $15,000 loss.

Method 4.   Charge each department a per-hour rate based on budgeted variable costs[1] predetermined for maintenance costs. Charge the fixed cost budgeted for maintenance to other departments in amounts based on some criterion like the expected long-run use of maintenance service. Because fixed costs usually reflect the building up of capacity or ability to serve, this method seems to have found a good deal of favor. If we estimate that the expected long-run use of maintenance is 40% for assembly and about 60% for fabrication, we would have the cost allocations shown below. Note that only the $225,000 budgeted costs are allocated. Variable costs are being charged at the rate of $5 per hour, the budgeted variable cost per maintenance hour.

[1]The term *standard* is often employed to describe budgeted variable costs.

		Fixed	Variable	Total
Fabrication	(60% × $75,000)	$45,000	$100,000	$145,000
Assembly	(40% × $75,000)	30,000	50,000	80,000
Total		$75,000	$150,000	$225,000

Critiques

The first method has serious drawbacks. When actual rather than budgeted costs are allocated, the inefficiencies of the maintenance department will be passed on to the operating departments. The maintenance department spent $30,000 more than budgeted, and the entire cost was allocated to the operating departments. When actual costs are allocated, the maintenance department manager knows that the costs, however high, will be spread over the operating departments, and may not be evaluated separately. The manager is not motivated to fulfill his or her responsibility efficiently.

The system also may induce undesirable behavior from the managers of operating departments. Under method 1 the allocation of maintenance costs to the two departments was as shown on page 372. Suppose that in the next year the fabrication department uses 20,000 hours again, but that assembly uses only 5,000 hours. The costs incurred by the maintenance department in the second year are $90,000 fixed (the same as the prior year) and $5.50 per hour variable (also the same as in the prior year). Total variable costs incurred are $137,500 (25,000 × $5.50) and total costs are $227,500 ($90,000 + $137,500). For the second year, the charge for maintenance service would be $9.10 per hour ($227,500 total maintenance cost divided by 25,000 hours) and the costs would be allocated as follows.

Fabrication	(20,000 × $9.10)	$182,000
Assembly	(5,000 × $9.10)	45,500
Total maintenance cost allocated		$227,500

The fabrication department has had more costs allocated to it even though it used the same number of hours of maintenance service as in the prior year. *Fixed costs per hour* were higher in the second year because the total hours of maintenance service used were lower. The manager of the fabrication department is allocated more cost even though he or she used the same amount of service, because the manager of the assembly department used fewer hours. Such an allocation method could prompt a manager to postpone desirable maintenance. Each operating manager knows that the less the service is used, the less the charge, and that the use fellow managers make of the service also affects the amount he or she is charged. Under this allocation method, there is a tendency to underuse the service.

Method 2 produces a tendency to overuse the service. Since each manager knows that his or her charge will not vary with use, he or she will try to get as much work performed as is possible. While having the work done may be good for the firm, the situation can also lead to conflicts and to strains on the maintenance department. This method does encourage the use of services, which might be an objective of the firm.

For example, a firm may have installed a new computer system that is believed to be beneficial for planning and control purposes. Managers might not wish to use the computer until they can be sure the benefits outweigh the costs. One way to encourage their using it is to charge little or nothing. Another is to charge a flat amount unrelated to use. Either way, managers will be more inclined to use the computer than if there were some charge based on the amount of use they order.

Method 3 treats the maintenance department as a profit center. It also treats the operating managers as if their departments were separate firms in the sense that their charges are based on what they would have to pay to obtain the services if there were no internal maintenance department. A problem with this method is that the outside cost might not be easy to determine. The outside cost, used as a transfer price, might also be so high that it would discourage the use of the service.

If reliable outside market prices are available, there is a significant potential advantage to treating a service department as a profit center. If the department consistently shows losses, the manager is alerted to the possibility that the firm could benefit from shutting down the department and buying outside. Such a decision would have to take into consideration the structure of fixed costs (avoidable and unavoidable) and would be made along the lines described in Chapter 5 in connection with make-or-buy decisions.

Method 4 is perhaps the best under most circumstances. The operating managers are being charged at budgeted rates, with an additional lump sum based on budgeted fixed costs; current inefficiencies of the maintenance department are not passed on to the operating managers. The budgeted variable cost might be low enough to encourage necessary use of the service; but because there is a charge based on use, overuse may be discouraged.

There is no answer to the question of which transfer price/allocation approach is best. No single method will serve all decision-making and performance evaluation needs.

What to Do?

Ideally, a manager should be charged with the incremental cost associated with carrying out his or her function. Thus, if some amount of cost of a service department, or portion of cost of a joint activity, is attributable to the manager of a particular department, it should thus be charged.

If allocations are to be made, amounts allocated should reflect budgeted costs, not actual costs. This prevents managers from being charged for inefficiencies in the departments that provide the services. There should be charges for the quantity of the service received based on standard variable costs of providing the services. Budgeted fixed costs could be allocated in lump sum amounts, not based on use of services, but on some idea of the long-run percentages of the service capacity required by each operating department. Thus, the budgeted fixed costs of the personnel department could be allocated based on expected numbers of employees in the operating departments, the costs of the accounting department by the expected volume of transactions originating in the operating departments, and the costs of maintenance by the expected number of machine-hours in each department.

It is important that the allocation to a particular department not be affected by what other departments do. If the amount allocated to a particular department increases or decreases, while the total cost being allocated remains about the same, the change should be because the manager used more or less of the service than previously.

Compromises are possible. The performance report could show controllable and uncontrollable (allocated) costs separately. If the higher-level managers, the ones evaluating the performance reports, recognize the distinction, there is less likelihood of misunderstanding and complaining from the lower-level managers.

There are similarities between the principles described here and those given in Chapters 5, 8, and 9. You will recall that joint costs were ignored in decisions involving a segment to which they were allocated. These costs are ignored because they would not change as a result of future action. The rationale for focusing on controllable costs is the same; the manager cannot do anything about costs that are arbitrarily allocated; to include them in performance reports as if they were under the manager's control obscures analysis and does not facilitate controlling of operations.

The use of allocations or transfer prices gives opportunities to apply the responsibility principle. Consider a situation where the sales manager has control over the credit terms offered to customers and the level of inventory. Normally, the sales manager would like to have a high inventory and liberal credit terms. It would be reasonable to assign to him or her a charge (at the cost of capital) on the investment in receivables and inventory. The sales manager would be less likely to allow receivables and inventory to increase excessively if he or she were charged with the cost of carrying these assets. However, the major objective of a new, growing company might be to establish a strong demand for its products by getting as much market penetration as early as possible. Under these circumstances, it might be wise to allow receivables and inventory to increase more than would be tolerable in an older, more established firm.

One further alternative should be considered when trying to develop a reasonable and acceptable transfer price or allocation scheme that might be useful in performance reporting. The firm can try to increase the extent to which a manager can control the costs for which he or she will be held responsible. We mentioned this point earlier, using the examples of separate utility meters and more detailed requisition forms and reporting of supplies use. The higher the total amount of a cost that might be brought under better control by additional efforts, the more likely it is that the firm would benefit from undertaking the efforts.

We should emphasize that, with all the reservations and suggestions considered, the performance reports used and their content are specific to the particular circumstances that a company faces and to the preferences of its managers. No set of simple rules governs all conceivable situations or leads to reports that would satisfy all managers.

Effects on Firm Income

One final point bears remembering. Allocations and transfer prices are managerial accounting devices, and changes in them cannot, by themselves, change the total income of the firm. Changes in the firm's income *may* occur because a change in an allocation or transfer price induces managers to change their operations in some way. But so long as the managers of the individual segments continue to operate as they have been, the firm's total income will not be affected. We can illustrate this with an example.

Suppose a firm is organized into two segments, manufacturing and selling, and each segment is a profit center. The manufacturing segment "sells" to the marketing segment which, in turn, sells to outsiders. Data for the two segments are as follows.

	Manufacturing	Marketing
Selling price	$20	$30
Variable costs:		
Manufacturing costs	$12	
Selling costs		$3
Fixed costs	$100,000	$50,000

The variable costs for the marketing division are the $3 selling costs plus the $20 the segment is charged by the manufacturing division. If the firm produces and sells 20,000 units, an income statement by segment would show the following.

	Manufacturing	Marketing
Sales 20,000 × $20	$400,000	
20,000 × $30		$600,000
Variable costs at $12 per unit	240,000	
at $23 per unit		460,000
Contribution margin	160,000	140,000
Fixed costs	100,000	50,000
Income	$ 60,000	$ 90,000

Toal income is $150,000 ($60,000 + $90,000). Suppose now that the transfer price is lowered to $15 per unit. This will reduce the revenues of the manufacturing segment and the costs of the marketing segment, but will not affect income. An income statement for 20,000 units with the $15 transfer price is given below.

	Manufacturing	Marketing
Sales 20,000 × $15	$300,000	
20,000 × $30		$600,000
Variable costs at $12 per unit	240,000	
at $18 per unit		
($15 + $3)		360,000
Contribution margin	60,000	240,000
Fixed costs	100,000	50,000
Income (loss)	($ 40,000)	$190,000

The income for the firm is still $150,000 ($190,000 − $40,000), even though the incomes for the segments have changed. The reduction in revenues to the manufacturing division of $100,000 ($400,000 − $300,000) is exactly offset by the reduction in variable costs of the marketing division ($460,000 − $360,000 = $100,000). Because a transfer price is revenue to one segment and a cost to the other segment, the price does not affect total income for the firm *unless* a change in the transfer price induces the manager of some segment to make some change in the operations of the segment.

OTHER USES OF ALLOCATIONS

In our discussion of why allocations might appear on performance reports, we pointed out that the need for such allocations for external purposes is influential. Although we commented on product costing (for financial reporting and income tax purposes), there are a number of other areas where allocations are necessary. For instance, public utilities like electric and telephone companies are required to justify price increases to state commissions. Part of the justification for an increase is increases in costs, and these costs must be allocated among different classes of customers (residential, commercial, industrial) to determine the increases that each will bear. Reimbursements to hospitals under Medicaid are based on costs that include allocations, as are payments to cities, counties, and states under some grants that the federal government makes.

Perhaps the most potent force for making allocations in recent years has been the Cost Accounting Standards Board (CASB), which specified rules for allocating costs by firms that do certain kinds of business with the federal government. The CASB issued a number of regulations regarding many aspects of allocation, including the bases to use for allocations and the costs to include in or exclude from the pool of costs to be allocated. (CASB pronouncements use the terms *allowable* and *not allowable* to indicate which types of costs—direct or allocated—may be included in reports for reimbursement.)

When organizations allocate costs for one or more of the purposes that demand such allocations, they are, as we stated previously, trying to develop a "full cost," with each activity or segment bearing its "fair share" of the indirect costs. The allocations may have to be made for the purpose of reporting on a particular contract, for preparing external financial statements, or in order to abide by some law. For example, society's interests may be served by reimbursing a hospital for an operation on the basis of the full cost of the operation (including the costs incurred to provide and maintain an operating room). But the fact that a contract, generally accepted accounting principles, some regulatory agency, or a legislative mandate, demands the allocation of joint costs does not make that allocation any the less arbitrary.

SUMMARY

Managers need accounting information to control their operations; and their efforts must be evaluated on bases that are consistent with the goals of the firm. Responsibility accounting should assist in achieving goal congruence and in motivating managers. No single responsibility accounting system is appropriate for all firms, or for the same firm over its lifetime. The responsibility accounting system must parallel the structure of the organization. The structure of the organization depends on the nature of the firm's operations and on the attitudes and management styles of top managers.

The reporting segments of a responsibility accounting system may be cost centers, profit centers (either natural or artificial), or investment centers. Most firms use all three types of responsibility centers. Whatever the plan for segmenting the firm for reporting purposes, the individual managers can be made responsible for only that which they can control.

Cost allocations may be a troublesome aspect in responsibility accounting as they have been shown to be in previous discussions of decision making. Conflicting objectives of cost allocation are charging managers for benefits they receive, and reporting on the controllable aspects of the manager's operations in order to increase their motivation. Transfer prices, the selling prices established for artificial profit centers, can produce problems similar to those associated with cost allocations. The pervasive behavioral considerations in responsibility accounting make it difficult to draw general conclusions about the best or most useful approaches to follow.

KEY TERMS

artificial profit center
centralized organization structure
cost center
decentralized organization structure
goal congruence
investment center
natural profit center

performance report
profit center
responsibility accounting
responsibility center
service department
traceable cost
transfer price

REVIEW PROBLEM

Wolfert Company makes and sells air conditioners and operates in three regions: the Northeast, Southeast, and Southwest. Data for 19X5 are given below, in thousands of dollars.

	Northeast	Southeast	Southwest
Sales	$2,400	$5,600	$3,800
Variable cost of sales	1,220	2,200	1,700
Variable selling costs	170	330	240
Traceable fixed costs:			
Selling	240	400	280
Administrative	320	440	380

Joint fixed costs for administration were $450,000 and for selling were $110,000. The firm operates four plants. Data regarding those plants are given below, again in thousands of dollars.

	New Orleans	Houston	Atlanta	Philadelphia
Fixed production costs for 19X5	$780	$340	$310	$210
Region(s) in which product sold	Southwest and Southeast	Southwest	Southeast	Northeast

Required: Prepare a performance report by region, showing contribution margin and regional profit. Show allocated costs as lump-sum deductions in the total column.

Answer to Review Problem

| | *(In Thousands of Dollars)* | | | |
	Northeast	*Southeast*	*Southwest*	*Total*
Sales	$2,400	$5,600	$3,800	$11,800
Variable costs:				
Production	1,220	2,200	1,700	5,120
Selling	170	330	240	740
Total variable costs	1,390	2,530	1,940	5,860
Contribution margin	1,010	3,070	1,860	5,940
Traceable fixed costs:				
Production	210	310	340	860
Selling	240	400	280	920
Administrative	320	440	380	1,140
Total traceable fixed costs	770	1,150	1,000	2,920
Regional profit	$ 240	$1,920	$ 860	$ 3,020
Joint fixed costs:				
Production*				780
Selling				110
Administration				450
Total joint costs				1,340
Income				$ 1,680

*Joint to Southeast and Southwest regions

Notice that the fixed production costs of the New Orleans factory are shown as joint to the regions. They are actually joint to the Southeast and Southwest, which makes them joint if one is looking at either region, rather than the two regions together. The footnote in the report tells the reader that production cost data for the Northeast area are totally traceable.

APPENDIX: STEP-DOWN ALLOCATIONS

As indicated in the chapter, allocations of joint costs *must* be made for some purposes. Allocation schemes have become a topic of considerable interest. A distinguishing feature of many allocation schemes, particularly those specified under cost-reimbursement contracts, is the use of a multistep allocation. The process is called **step-down allocation,** or simply, **step-down.** This process is seen in the legislated or regulated methods for determining how much to reimburse hospitals for services performed for citizens.

Basically, the step-down method allocates the costs of service departments *one department at a time.* Consider the General Manufacturing Company, which has, for simplicity, two operating departments and three service departments. The operating departments, forging and machining, receive services from personnel, housekeeping, and general administration. The personnel department keeps all employee records and handles payrolls; the housekeeping department provides cleaning, maintenance, and other basic services; while general administration handles all other duties. Each service department provides services to each of the other service departments as well as to the two operating departments. Data for the most recent month appear below.

Department	Total Direct Costs	Square Feet Occupied	Number of Employees
Personnel	$ 200,000	2,000	10
Administration	500,000	3,000	30
Housekeeping	300,000	1,000	20
Forging	1,800,000	10,000	100
Machining	3,000,000	15,000	300
Total costs	$5,800,000		

Because the step-down approach to allocations involves allocating one department at a time, we have to decide which department's costs should be allocated first, second, and so on. The rule used most often is to begin with the department that provides services to the most other *service* departments. Another common approach is to begin with the department that provides the greatest percentage of its services to other service departments. The idea behind both of these rules is to get an equitable allocation of the costs of the service departments to one another before finally allocating the costs of all service departments to the operating departments.

In our example, all service departments provide services to one another so that we must select the order of allocation on another basis. Let us suppose that the managers of this firm have elected to make the allocations in the following order: housekeeping; administration; personnel. The bases for allocation are: housekeeping, square feet occupied; administration, total direct costs before allocation; and personnel, number of employees. We begin with the allocation of housekeeping costs.

	Administration	Personnel	Forging	Machining	Total
Square feet occupied	3,000	2,000	10,000	15,000	30,000
Percentage of total	10%	6.67%	33.3%	50%	100%
Housekeeping costs allocated	$ 30,000	$ 20,000	$ 100,000	$ 150,000	$ 300,000
Previous total departmental cost	500,000	200,000	1,800,000	3,000,000	5,500,000
New total departmental costs	$530,000	$220,000	$1,900,000	$3,150,000	$5,800,000

We now allocate the new departmental cost of the administration department, $530,000. We shall not allocate any costs to housekeeping even though the administration department serves the housekeeping department. Once the costs of a service department are allocated to other departments, we ignore it in the remaining steps. We allocate the administration costs based on the direct costs of the departments (that is, we use the costs before the allocation of the housekeeping costs).

	Personnel	Forging	Machining	Total
Total direct costs	$200,000	$1,800,000	$3,000,000	$5,000,000
Percentage of total	4%	36%	60%	100%
Allocation of administration department costs	$ 21,200	$ 190,800	$ 318,000	$ 530,000
Previous totals	220,000	1,900,000	3,150,000	5,270,000
New total departmental costs	$241,200	$2,090,800	$3,468,000	$5,800,000

The final step is to allocate the accumulated costs of the personnel department ($241,200) to the forging and machining departments on the basis of the number of employees in these departments. Again, the total to be allocated consists of the total accumulated costs, including the amounts allocated from the housekeeping and administration departments.

	Forging	Machining	Total
Number of employees	100	300	400
Percentage of total	25%	75%	100%
Allocation of personnel costs	$ 60,300	$ 180,900	$ 241,200
Previous totals	2,090,800	3,468,000	5,558,800
Final totals	$2,151,100	$3,648,900	$5,800,000

The costs of all the service departments have now been allocated to the two operating departments. We can check this by referring to the final total for the two operating departments. The total cumulative costs for those departments is $5,800,000, which equals the total direct costs of all of the departments before any allocations were made.

Presented with the final total costs for the two operating departments, some managers might be tempted to compute some type of unit cost for each department, based perhaps on the number of direct labor hours worked in each. Such temptations should be avoided. By their nature, allocations introduce some degree of arbitrariness to the results. These results are always influenced by the allocation basis chosen. Had we selected different bases for allocating the costs of any of the three service departments, the final results would be different. In the present case, the results are also influenced by the *order* in which allocations were made. That is, had we chosen to allocate administration or personnel costs first, the final total costs for each operating department would have been different. In summary, the allocation process succeeds in assigning the costs of all departments to the two operating departments, but does not change the fact that the costs of service departments are joint to the departments serviced.

The schedule below summarizes the procedures and shows the "step-down" explicitly, as each department's costs are allocated.

	House-keeping	Adminis-tration	Personnel	Forging	Machining	Total
Direct costs	$300,000	$500,000	$200,000	$1,800,000	$3,000,000	$5,800,000
Housekeeping	(300,000)	30,000	20,000	100,000	150,000	
Administration		(530,000)	21,200	190,800	318,000	
Personnel			(241,200)	60,300	180,900	
Totals				$2,151,100	$3,648,900	$5,800,000

ASSIGNMENT MATERIAL

Questions for Discussion

10-1   Relationships with previous material   What similarities do you see between (a) the material in this chapter, and (b) the emphasis on cost behavior in Chapters 2, 3, and 4 and the material in Chapters 5 and 8 on the data used in short-term and long-term decision making?

10-2   Responsibility versus control   In a conversation between the manager of one store in a large chain of supermarkets and the controller of that chain the store manager said the following:

> My son, who is taking a managerial accounting course at CU, has been telling me about something called responsibility accounting and how it can help to motivate employees. How come we don't have some kind of responsibility accounting in our stores? I've got a meat manager who pretty much keeps that department in my store going. My son says the meat department might even be a good candidate for what he calls a profit center. What do you think?

What do you think?

10-3   Responsibility centers—universities   What problems would there be in establishing and evaluating responsibility centers in the following: (a) universities, (b) colleges or schools within universities, and (c) departments within colleges?

10-4   Responsibility reporting   The annual report of a major manufacturer carried the following paragraph (paraphrased):

> Specialization also continues within each marketing force as we increase the number of personnel. We are experiencing a steady rise in the number of customers as well as in the variety and complexity of products and equipment. As a result, an increasing proportion of our salespeople are now concentrating on just one or a few industries—or on certain product categories.

Suppose that in the past the salespeople sold all products made by the firm to all kinds of customers in different industries. What effects would the new method of directing the efforts of the individual salespeople have on the responsibility reporting system?

10-5 Organizational structure The letter from the chief executive officer in an annual report of Genesco Inc. included the following paragraphs and chart.

NEW ORGANIZATION STRUCTURE

In many ways the most significant internal change has been Genesco's new management organization structure. At the Board meeting at the end of February, the Directors designated me the chief executive officer of the corporation. I then designed and implemented a new management structure. As shown in the chart below, the chief operating officers and the chief administrative officer report directly to me. Each officer is responsible for a major area of Genesco's operations.

Reporting to the chief operating officers are the group presidents, each of whom is responsible for a number of related operating companies. Reporting to the group presidents are the presidents of the operating companies.

In this chain of command, each executive knows his responsibilities, has the authority to take the action necessary to produce results, and knows that he is accountable for those results. This organization permits the rapid, decentralized decision making necessary in the apparel industry.

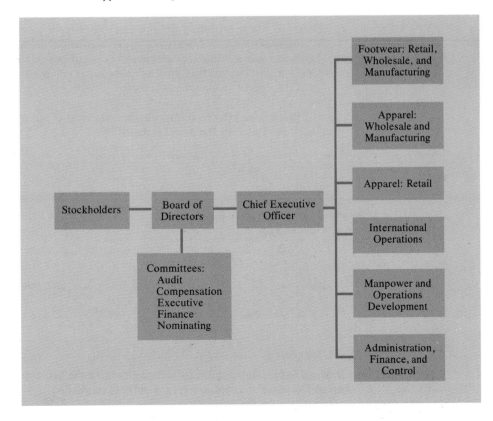

Which of the group presidents is likely to be designated as responsible for an investment center? a profit center? a cost center?

10-6   Pricing, timing, allocations, and public relations   For many years telephone companies did not charge for directory assistance (calling an operator to get a number). When they began to charge for this service (usually 10 cents per request after three free requests per month), a commentator said: "This is ridiculous. They have to have operators on duty anyway, so there is no additional cost for their giving out a number. Ma Bell has just found another way to get into our pockets."

Required: Comment on the quotation.

10-7   Artificial profit centers   A national trade association held a seminar for chief executives and one of the topics discussed was responsibility accounting and the profit-center concept as a means of "correctly evaluating departments." Two executives who attended the conference returned to their respective offices and made the following statements to their respective chief accounting officers.

1.   "I want you to set up as many profit centers as possible, beginning with the legal department. From now on, departments using the services of the legal department will be charged at $40 per hour. That's about twice the average lawyer's salary and ought to cover the nonsalary costs of the legal department. We haven't even allocated the costs of the legal department up to now, and we might as well do something to let our managers know that when they ask for legal advice they can expect to pay for it."
2.   "Well, you accountants have done it again. Like all the other high-priced professionals you insist on coming up with special names for something that everyone already understands. For years now we've been allocating the costs of the legal department, like all other corporate departments, to the operating units in our company, and now I'm told that what we need to do is set up a 'transfer price.' That's just a fancy name for allocating the costs."

Do you foresee any problems with the first executive's intentions? Do you agree with the position taken by the second executive?

Exercises

10-8   Alternative allocation bases   The following data refer to the three departments of ABC Company.

	A	B	C
Sales	$400,000	$200,000	$400,000
Square feet of space occupied	8,000	7,000	5,000
Number of employees	90	60	150

Total joint costs for the year are $100,000.

Required: Allocate the joint costs to departments on the bases of (a) sales dollars, (b) square feet of space occupied, and (c) number of employees.

10-9 Cost allocations Bremen Company allocates costs among its three products on the basis of relative sales dollars. Data from 19X6 are as follows.

	W	X	Y	Total
Sales	$120,000	$180,000	$300,000	$600,000
Joint costs	24,000	36,000	60,000	120,000

In 19X7, joint costs were again $120,000. However, sales of product Y increased to $370,000 while those of W and X declined to $70,000 and $160,000, respectively. The changes were in unit volume only; prices were the same in both years.

Required: Allocate the joint costs for 19X7 using relative sales dollars, and comment on the usefulness of this basis for allocation.

10-10 Cost allocations Cooper Company allocates maintenance costs based on relative use of the service. Last month its three operating departments had the following activity cost allocations.

	Finishing	Fabricating	Assembly	Total
Maintenance hours	2,000	3,000	3,000	8,000
Cost allocated	$20,000	$30,000	$30,000	$80,000

Data for the current month are as follows:

	Finishing	Fabricating	Assembly	Total
Maintenance hours	2,000	2,000	2,000	6,000
Costs	?	?	?	$72,000

You learn that maintenance expense is a mixed cost, with a fixed component of $48,000 per month and a variable component of $4 per hour.

Required
1. Allocate the maintenance cost for the current month using the method followed by the firm.
2. Evaluate the method used, citing the results in part 1 above and those for the prior month as examples.

10-11 Effects of allocations Grange Company has two service departments: building services and administration. The firm has three operating departments. Some data associated with the operating departments are presented below.

	Operating Departments		
	A	B	C
Square feet of space occupied	5,000	7,500	12,500
Machine-hours worked	42,000	70,000	88,000
Sales value of production	$1,200,000	$1,000,000	$1,800,000

Costs for the service departments are as follows: building services $160,000; administration $300,000.

Required
1. Allocate service department costs on three different bases.
2. Comment on the results in part 1 above.

10-12   Allocations and decisions   Cramer Company has a number of product lines, each under the control of a different manager. Each manager is evaluated partly on profit. The expenses charged to each line are the direct costs of the line plus 15% of sales. (The 15% is intended to cover costs not directly associated with the lines, such as salaries of the corporate staff, interest on corporate debt, and service functions like personnel, building security, and cafeteria. These costs are virtually all fixed.) The president of the company estimated that the 15% amount would cover these expenses at budgeted sales of $6,000,000 for the coming year. Each year the percentage is adjusted based on the budgeted costs and budgeted sales for the entire company.

The manager of the small appliances line has the opportunity to sell 20,000 units to a chain store at $30 each. Per-unit variable costs are $27, ignoring the 15% charge. There would be no incremental fixed costs associated with the order and there is sufficient capacity to make the additional units.

Required
1. Given the existing plan for evaluating performance, would the manager of small appliances accept the order? Why or why not?
2. Would it be in the company's best interests for the manager to accept the order? Why or why not?

10-13   Comparison of allocation methods (related to Appendix)   Mott Company has two service departments, Personnel and Administration, and two operating departments, Foundry and Assembly. The schedule below shows the percentages of activity that each service department provides each of the other departments, both service and operating.

Department Providing Service	Department Receiving Service			
	Personnel	Administration	Foundry	Assembly
Personnel	0%	50%	10%	40%
Administration	20%	0%	70%	10%

The costs of Personnel and Administration were $200,000 and $300,000 respectively. One of the staff made the following allocations.

	Foundry	Assembly
Personnel:		
$200,000 × (.10/.50)	$40,000	
$200,000 × (.40/.50)		$160,000
Administration:		
$300,000 × (.70/.80)	262,500	
$300,000 × (.10/.80)		37,500
Totals	$302,500	$197,500

The controller is wondering whether it would make any difference to use the step-down method, instead of the simple direct method shown above.

Required: Allocate the service department costs using the step-down method, beginning with Personnel costs.

10-14   Allocations—actual versus budgeted costs   Merion Turf Products produces lawn fertilizers and grass seed. The company's research department, which works to improve both types of products, had budgeted costs, virtually all fixed, of $450,000. These costs were to be allocated to the two product lines based on the relative amounts of time spent on each. All of the scientists keep time sheets showing which projects they work on each month.

At year end the research department had actually spent $496,000 as a result of unanticipated cost increases and some inefficiencies in the department. The manager of the fertilizer department had budgeted $225,000 for allocated research costs, but found that he was actually charged with $276,760. The final allocation was based on actual costs and actual relative time spent on work for his department. He was not happy with the situation, especially when he learned that the manager of the grass seed department had canceled a major project, resulting in lower-than-budgeted research on grass seed.

Required

1. Determine the actual percentage of use of research for the fertilizer department.
2. Suggest a way to allocate research costs that will not unduly penalize the managers of the fertilizer and grass seed departments.

10-15   Hospital allocations and decisions   Blake Memorial Hospital is a full-service hospital with several departments. Departments that perform services directly for patients are called *revenue centers,* and include the medical, surgical, and emergency departments. Other departments, such as admissions, patient records, laundry, and housekeeping, are called *service centers.* Costs of service centers are allocated to revenue centers. Below is a schedule showing the percentages of costs allocated from two service centers to two revenue centers, together with the direct costs of each of the service centers.

Service Center		Revenue Center	
	Costs	Medical	Surgical
Admissions	$300,000	70%	30%
Records	$400,000	20%	80%

The hospital receives reimbursements from Blue Cross, Medicaid, and other "third parties" for services performed for some patients. The reimbursement contracts typically allow recovery of both direct and indirect costs. Such reimbursements amount to about 30% of total medical department costs, but about 90% for surgical costs. Thus, at the present time, the hospital is being reimbursed for $144,000 of its Admissions costs, calculated as follows:

Through Medical Reimbursements	
$300,000 × 70% × 30%	$ 63,000
Through Surgical Reimbursements	
$300,000 × 30% × 90%	81,000
Total	$144,000

The hospital administrator is considering some different procedures that would increase the cost of Records by $10,000, while reducing Admissions costs by $6,000.

Although the change is obviously not beneficial on cost grounds, the administrator is well aware of the differing reimbursement rates.

Required

1. Calculate the total reimbursement that the hospital is now receiving for the indirect costs of Admissions and Records.
2. Calculate the total reimbursement that the hospital would receive if the new procedures were adopted.

10-16   Transfer prices and goal congruence   The controller of Calvert Company has set a number of transfer prices for service departments within the firm, all of which used to be cost centers. One is for stenographic services. The charge is $13 per hour, which is based on total budgeted hours of available service and total budgeted costs for the stenographic pool. The manager of one operating department, a profit center, has obtained a price of $10 per hour for stenographers' time from an outside agency. The task will take about 50 hours. The manager informs the controller and the manager of the stenographic pool of the outside price and is told to take it if he so wishes; the price set internally will not be lowered.

Required: Comment on the position taken by the controller and the manager of the stenographic pool. (Budgeted costs for the pool are about 90% fixed.) Make a recommendation.

10-17   Cost centers, profit centers, and behavior   State University has a motor pool that operates a fleet of automobiles. Faculty and staff use the cars on official university business and their departments are charged $0.22 per mile. The motor pool is considered a cost center and its manager is evaluated partly on whether he meets his cost budget, which is a fixed amount plus $0.13 per mile the cars are driven. The $0.13 is a good approximation of the variable cost of operating a car.

A local car rental agency has recently announced that it will rent cars at $0.19 per mile. Professor Richardson of the Accounting Department needs to make a 500-mile round trip and has told his department head about the $0.19 deal. The department head tells him to rent the car from the agency unless the motor pool reduces its charge to $0.19 per mile. "At 19 cents per mile, it doesn't matter where we rent the car," the head says, "but since the cost comes out of our travel budget, I want the best deal we can get."

The manager of the motor pool does have some discretion in setting mileage rates.

Required

1. Would it be in the best interests of the university for the motor pool to reduce its charge to $0.19 per mile for Professor Richardson's trip?
2. Would the manager of the motor pool be inclined to reduce the charge?
3. Suppose now that the motor pool were a profit center, with its manager evaluated partly on the profit generated by the pool. His revenue is charges to departments and he has discretion over mileage rates. Assume further that the motor pool has some excess capacity (i.e., some cars are always sitting in the parking lot). Would it be wise from the university's point of view for the motor pool to reduce its charge? Would the manager of the motor pool be inclined to do so?

10-18   Development of performance report   Stratton Company is organized by functional areas: sales, production, finance, and administration. The sales department has product managers who are responsible for a particular product and who are evaluated based on the following typical performance report.

Product Zee Activity Report
May 19X4—Manager, J. Harrison

Sales (30,000 units)		$300,000
Cost of goods sold		172,000
Gross profit		128,000
Other expenses:		
Advertising	$28,000	
Travel	17,000	
Depreciation	6,000	
Office expenses	19,000	
Administrative expense	23,000	93,000
Product profit		$ 35,000

The following additional information about the above report is available.

(a) Because of problems in the production process, cost of goods sold is $11,000 higher than budgeted.

(b) The product manager spent $16,000 on advertising for the product. The remainder is an allocated share of general advertising costs incurred by the firm.

(c) Depreciation charges consist of the following: 20% on furniture and fixtures in the product manager's office, and 80% for the building in which all the firm's activities take place.

(d) Office expenses include $3,000 allocated from the expenses of the vice president for sales (salaries, data processing, etc.)

(e) Administrative expenses are allocated to each product based on relative sales.

Required: Revise the performance report for product Zee to reflect the principle of controllability.

Problems

10-19 Where did the income come from?   The income statement in the 1982 annual report for Pitney Bowes, Inc., shows total revenues of $1,455 million and net income of $83 million. The report also shows the following information.

	Operating Profit (In Millions)
Industry segments:	
Business equipment	$122.3
Retail systems	18.6
Business supplies	8.1
Total	$149.0
Geographic areas:	
United States	$125.2
Europe	7.3
Other (principally Canada)	14.6
Total	$147.1

Another table in the report shows revenues, using the same categories (segments and areas), but the breakdowns in both parts of that table add up to $1,455 million.

Required: Explain why the details in the breakdown of revenues add up to the amount shown in the income statement, while the totals of neither of the two categories in the above table agree with the total net income in the income statement.

10-20 Step-down allocation (related to Appendix)   Walker Company has two operating departments, machining and assembly. It also has the following service departments: personnel, data processing, and general administration. The controller wishes to allocate the service department costs using the step-down method, beginning with data processing, then personnel, and lastly, general administration. She wants to use the following bases: data processing, number of transactions; personnel, number of employees; general administration, total direct costs (before any allocation of service department costs).

The controller has assembled the following data:

Department	Total Direct Costs	Number of Employees	Number of Data Processing Transactions
Data processing	$ 200,000	20	0
Personnel	150,000	30	20,000
General administration	300,000	100	30,000
Machining	2,000,000	300	40,000
Assembly	3,000,000	600	10,000

Required: Prepare a step-down allocation.

10-21 Effects of cost allocations   Below are performance reports for two months for the supervisor of the assembly department of Berkey Manufacturing Company. Maintenance costs are allocated to operating departments by taking the total maintenance costs incurred each month, dividing them by the number of hours worked by maintenance personnel, and multiplying the resulting cost per hour by the number of hours worked in each operating department.

	March			April		
	Budget	Actual	Variance	Budget	Actual	Variance
Materials used	$1,200	$1,210	$ 10U	$1,500	$1,480	$ 20F
Direct labor	3,400	3,420	20U	4,250	4,220	30F
Maintenance	1,200	900	300F	1,200	1,000	200F
Other overhead	2,000	2,050	50U	2,300	2,350	50U
Totals	$7,800	$7,580	$220F	$9,250	$9,050	$200F

Required
1. How is maintenance expense budgeted? What kinds of occurrences could account for the actual charges, given the allocation method used?
2. How might the performance report be improved?

10-22 Responsibility for rush orders   Howard Company's sales manager often requests rush orders from the production department. Howard's production process requires a great deal of setup time whenever changes in the production mix are made. The production manager has complained about these rush orders, arguing that costs are much lower when the process runs smoothly. The sales manager argues that the paramount consideration is to keep the goodwill of the customer and that therefore all sales orders should be made up as quickly as possible.

Required
1. Identify the responsibilities of each manager.
2. What steps might be taken to effect a satisfactory solution?

10-23 Performance measurement   The sales manager of Warner Company is evaluated on the basis of total sales. Exceeding the sales budget is considered good performance. The sales budget and cost data for 19X3 are shown below.

| | Product | | | |
	Alpha	Beta	Gamma	Total
Sales budget	$150,000	$300,000	$550,000	$1,000,000
Variable costs	75,000	135,000	165,000	375,000
Contribution margin	$ 75,000	$165,000	$385,000	$ 625,000

Actual sales for the year were as follows:

Alpha	Beta	Gamma	Total
$500,000	$400,000	$200,000	$1,100,000

Actual prices were equal to budgeted prices, and variable costs were incurred as budgeted (per unit).

Required
1. Did the sales manager perform well? Support your answer with calculations.
2. What suggestions do you have regarding the performance measurement criterion used by the firm?

10-24 Responsibility for factory costs   It is usually not possible to tell whether a cost is the responsibility of a specific manager simply by knowing the object classification of the cost (rent, wages, salaries, shipping, etc.). For each of the following costs, indicate some circumstances under which it would, or would not, be the responsibility of the following: (a) foreman, (b) department manager, and (c) plant manager.
1. Wages of factory workers
2. Rent on equipment
3. Electricity for machinery
4. Cost of materials
5. Cost of forms used for reporting hours worked by laborers, production results in each area, and performance reports for those areas.

10-25 Allocations and performance reporting   Koehler Company allocates common costs to product lines. Before the beginning of each fiscal year, it develops budgeted rates for both manufacturing and selling costs based on budgeted common costs and budgeted company-wide revenues. At year-end, it reallocates common costs based on the actual results for the year. For 19X6, the budgeted rates were: manufacturing, 30% of revenue; selling, 10% of revenue. The actual rates turned out to be 35% for manufacturing, 12% for selling.

Budgeted and actual results reflecting these rates as well as the controllable costs for the Jensin line of apparel appear below, in thousands of dollars.

	Budget	Actual
Sales	$100.0	$110.0
Cost of sales	65.0	76.0
Gross margin	35.0	34.0
Selling expenses	20.0	23.7
Product line margin	$ 15.0	$ 10.3

The manager of the Jensin line was puzzled by the results. He was fairly sure that most controllable costs, fixed or variable, were reasonably on target, given the higher sales volume. He would have to explain the results to his superior in a few days and was concerned about what to say.

Required: Prepare a new report that separates controllable costs from allocated costs. Give the manager of the Jensin line some comments to make to his superior.

10-26 **Compensation plan (CMA adapted)**   Parsons Company compensates its salespersons with commissions and a year-end bonus. The commission is 20% of a "net profit," which is computed as the normal selling price less manufacturing costs. (Such costs contain some allocated fixed overhead.) The profit is also reduced by any bad debts on sales written by individual salespersons. The granting of credit is the responsibility of the firm's credit department, and credit approval is required before sales are made.

Salespeople can give price reductions which must be approved by the sales vice president. Commissions are not affected by such price concessions.

The year-end bonus is 15% of commissions earned during the year provided that the individual salesperson has achieved the target sales volume. If the target is not reached, there is no bonus. The annual target volume is generally set at 105% of the previous year's sales.

Required
1. Identify which features of the compensation plan are likely to be effective in motivating the salespeople to work in the best interests of the firm. Explain your answers.
2. Identify which features of the plan would seem to be least likely to be effective or may even be counterproductive in motivating salespeople to work in the interests of the firm. Explain your answers.

10-27 **Assignment of responsibility**   Johns Company is organized by function: sales, production, finance, and administration. The production manager is upset about his latest performance report (see page 393). He contends that costs of about $8,000 were incurred solely because the sales manager ordered changes in production for rush orders from customers.

Performance Report
Production Department

	Budgeted	Actual	Variance
Controllable costs:			
Materials	$ 80,000	$ 79,000	$ (1,000)
Direct labor	160,000	162,000	2,000
Other labor	46,000	53,000	7,000
Idle time*	1,000	4,000	3,000
Other production costs	21,000	20,000	(1,000)
Totals	$308,000	$318,000	$10,000

*Wages paid to workers while they are idle, as when machines are being reset because of a change from one product to another.

The report, argues the production manager, shows $3,000 in idle time caused by changing the production process to meet the special orders. In addition, about $5,000 in other labor was for costs incurred to make the necessary changes and for the overtime premium paid to workers to get the work finished.

Required: What is wrong and what do you recommend?

10-28 Performance measures   Below are six job titles and the measure by which performance in that job is judged. Comment on each.

Job or Job Title	Performance Measure
(a) Director of the county's mental health program.	The number of patients released from treatment.
(b) Director of a program to reduce unemployment.	The number of jobs found for persons on the unemployment rolls, as a percentage of the total unemployed persons.
(c) Director of a regional program to rehabilitate substandard housing.	The number of homes now meeting local building codes that had previously been classified substandard.
(d) The operator of a particular machine.	The number of hours the machine is running.
(e) A salesperson.	The dollars of sales orders written divided by the number of customers visited.
(f) A college professor.	The enrollment in the professor's classes.

10-29 Evaluation of compensation plans (AICPA adapted)   Gibson Company was established some years ago to bring several new products to the market. Its founders believed that if customers would try the products, they would become well accepted. For the first several years, Gibson grew at a rate the founders considered to be satisfactory. In recent years some problems have developed both in the area of the firm's profitability and in the morale of and harmonious relationships among the firm's salespeople. Since the company began, salespeople have been paid a base salary plus an 8% commission. The following data are available for two of the firm's salespeople for the most recent year.

	Ronald McTavish	James Christy
Gross sales orders written	$250,000	$180,000
Commissions	20,000	14,400
Sales returns	17,500	9,000
Cost of goods sold—all variable	139,500	68,400
Discretionary expenses of salesmen (travel, entertainment, etc.)	19,200	21,500

Required

1. Using the available information, explain what may be causing the difficulties that the firm has identified. Support your answer with appropriate calculations.
2. What changes, if any, would you recommend be made in the company's compensation method?

10-30 Motor pool versus employees' cars   Pascal Company owns 25 automobiles that employees use when they travel on company business. Costs of the pool are assigned to company departments by charging using departments $0.25 per mile. The budgeted costs of operating a pool car for the year are as follows.

Annual depreciation	$3,500
Gas, oil, tires	1,600
Regular maintenance, at prescribed mileage intervals	800
Licenses and insurance	1,000
Administrative costs of pool	600
Total annual cost	$7,500

Pool cars are expected to have average annual mileage of 30,000 miles, hence the $0.25 charge ($7,500/30,000 miles).

  The head of one department has asked for permission to let employees use their own cars for business travel, and he proposes that the employees be paid $0.21 per mile for using their personal cars.

Required

1. Would the company as a whole be better off paying employees $0.21 per mile than making them use company cars?
2. Assume that all employees have the same model cars as the motor pool's and the same cost structure (except for the administrative costs of the motor pool, of course). Would employees using their own cars be penalized at $0.21 per mile?
3. Under what circumstance(s), if any, might the company accede to the department head's request?
4. What two previous company decisions laid the foundation for the current situation?

10-31 Cost allocations and performance measurement   Edwards Company allocates joint costs to its three products, each of which is the responsibility of a different manager. The three managers are evaluated based on the pretax incomes generated by their respective products. Income statements for a typical month are as follows, in thousands of dollars.

	Product			
	Toasters	Ovens	Dishwashers	Total
Sales	$1,200	$800	$400	$2,400
Variable costs	720	420	150	1,290
Contribution margin	480	380	250	1,110
Joint costs—allocated	450	300	150	900
Income	$ 30	$ 80	$100	$ 210

The manager for toasters believes that if he increases his price from $20 per unit to $25 per unit, sales will drop from 60,000 to 32,000 units. Variable costs per unit would remain the same as they are now. Sales of the other products would not be affected.

Required
1. Determine whether the price increase would benefit the firm, showing calculations.
2. Prepare a new set of income statements based on the manager's estimates. Be sure to reallocate the joint costs based on the new dollar sales figures. Is it in the manager's best interest to raise the price? Comment on the advisability of allocating joint costs the way the firm does it.

10-32 Assignment of responsibility   The controller of Baldwin Company is authorized to charge the sales departments with any overtime premium paid to production workers when one of the sales managers requests an order that requires overtime. (Overtime premium is the difference between the wage rate paid when workers are on overtime and the regular rate they are paid.) There are four sales managers, each responsible for a different product.

During March budgeted production is, in total, 20,000 units; capacity production, without overtime, is 22,000 units. An increase in demand for all the company's products is experienced early in the month, and, on March 10, each of the four sales managers requests additional production of 1,000 units. The production manager reports that the extra 1,000 of two products, A and B, were made during regular working hours while the extra production of C and D was carried out after normal hours when overtime rates were paid. Each unit of any product takes one hour to produce, and overtime premium is $2 per hour.

Required: Which sales manager(s) should be charged with the overtime premium and how much?

10-33 Performance reporting—alternative organizational structure (CMA adapted)
Cranwell Company sells three products in a foreign market and a domestic market. An income statement for the first month of 19X2 shows the following results.

Sales		$1,300,000
Cost of goods sold		1,010,000
Gross profit		290,000
Selling expenses	$105,000	
Administrative expenses	72,000	177,000
Income		$ 113,000

Data regarding the two markets and three products are given below.

	Products		
Sales:	A	B	C
Domestic	$400,000	$300,000	$300,000
Foreign	100,000	100,000	100,000
Total sales	$500,000	$400,000	$400,000
Variable production costs (percentage of sales)	60%	70%	60%
Variable selling costs (percentage of sales)	3%	2%	2%

Product A is made in a single factory that incurs fixed costs (included in cost of good sold) of $48,000 per month. Products B and C are made in a single factory and require the same machinery. Monthly fixed production costs at that factory are $142,000.

Fixed selling expenses are joint to the three products, but $36,000 is separable with respect to the domestic market and $38,000 for the foreign market. All administrative expenses are fixed. About $25,000 is traceable to the foreign market, $35,000 to the domestic market.

Required

1. Assume that Cranwell has separate managers responsible for each market. Prepare performance reports for the domestic and foreign markets.
2. Assume that Cranwell has separate managers responsible for each product. Prepare performance reports for the three products.

10-34 Cost allocations, transfer prices, and behavior   Several top executives of Millard Company are discussing problems they perceive in the company's methods of cost allocation. For each of the costs discussed below, indicate what changes would help accomplish the objectives stated by the executives.

(a)   Computer cost, which is 95% fixed, is allocated using a transfer price of $100 per hour of use. The executives are concerned that lower-level managers do not use the computer enough. The firm is growing rapidly and the executives are worried that other managers will not have the computer expertise essential for a manager.

(b)   Maintenance costs, which are budgeted at $10 per hour variable and $200,000 per year fixed, are allocated by dividing total incurred cost by total maintenance hours worked and distributing the resulting per-hour cost to operating departments according to the number of hours of maintenance work done in that department. The executives believe that operating managers request maintenance work only when emergencies arise (i.e., when machinery is about to break down). Production has been halted in the past because repairs were being made on critical machines. Operating managers have been complaining that the per-hour cost is too high.

(c)   Millard has a consulting department that advises operating managers on various aspects of production and marketing. The costs of the consulting department are fixed but discretionary, and have been rising in recent years because of heavy demand for the services. The costs are not allocated because it was felt that managers should be encouraged to use the service. One executive commented that the operating managers call the department to find out where to go to lunch.

10-35 Reporting of variances   John Flowers, assistant controller at Steiner Company, is impressed with the idea of management by exception and is looking for ways to use this principle. The company uses the following format for reporting budgeted and actual data and variances.

Performance Report
Operations of the Assembly Department
(Clyde Williams, Foreman)

	Budget	Actual	Variance
Material:			
Stock #926-4873	$ 8,000	$ 8,800	$ 800
Stock #926-5436	27,000	31,000	4,000
Direct labor:			
Assemblers	64,000	63,000	(1,000)
Indirect labor:			
Material handling	2,000	2,100	100
Inspection	500	600	100
Maintenance	260	300	40
Setup	90	110	20
Supplies	200	160	(40)
Lubricants	40	30	(10)
Small parts	400	420	20
Totals	$102,490	$106,520	$4,030

Budgeted amounts shown in the report are for production achieved. The "actual" amounts are really actual quantities at budgeted prices because the department managers do not control prices.

John feels that there is too much detail on this report and that a manager's real concern should be the variance. He proposes to substitute a report of the following format, showing only the actual results as a percentage of budgeted results.

Performance Report
Operations of the Assembly Department
(Clyde Williams, Foreman)

	Budgeted Results as a Percentage of Actual Results
Material:	
Stock #926-4873	90.9%
Stock #926-5436	87.1
Direct labor:	
Assemblers	101.5
Indirect labor:	
Material handling	95.2
Inspection	83.3
Maintenance	86.6
Setup	81.8
Supplies	125.0
Lubricants	133.3
Small parts	95.2
Total	96.2%

Required: Comment on the reporting method that John is recommending.

10-36 Performance report   The controller of Caldwell Department Store is developing performance analyses for the managers of the store's three major lines—housewares, clothing, and sporting goods. He has prepared the following:

Segmented Income Statement
(In Thousands of Dollars)

	Housewares	Clothing	Sporting Goods	Total
Sales	$900	$1,200	$400	$2,500
Cost of goods sold	500	680	180	1,360
Gross profit	400	520	220	1,140
Other expenses:				
Salaries	60	90	40	190
Advertising	45	60	20	125
Rent	40	40	20	100
Depreciation	20	16	12	48
General and administrative	90	120	40	250
Miscellaneous	60	85	32	177
Total expenses	315	411	164	890
Profit	$ 85	$ 109	$ 56	$ 250

You learn the following about the data in the above statements:
(a)   Cost of goods sold is separable.
(b)   Salaries expense includes allocated salaries of $75,000 for employees whose work takes them into different departments. The controller believes that relative sales is the best measure of volume to use for allocation.
(c)   Advertising is partly allocated. Each department is charged at standard market rates for newspaper space, radio time, and television time that its manager requests. The cost of general advertising ordered by the sales vice president was $50,000 and was allocated based on sales dollars.
(d)   The rent allocation is based on floor space occupied. The three departments occupy 100,000 square feet. The sporting goods department is in the basement, the others on the first floor. Similar property in the city rents for $1.05 per square foot for first floor space, $0.80 for basement space. Rent on space occupied by the administrative offices is included in general and administrative expenses.
(e)   Depreciation is all for furniture and fixtures within the departments.
(f)   General and administrative expenses are allocated based on sales dollars.
(g)   Miscellaneous expenses are partly separable, partly allocated. The allocated amounts by department are as follows: housewares, $28,000; clothing, $36,000; and sporting goods, $16,000.

Required: Prepare a new performance report using the principle of controllability. Include a column for unallocated costs, as well as one for each department.

10-37 Transfer prices and behavior   All operating departments of Jacson Company are profit or investment centers, and a number of service departments are artificial profit centers. The maintenance department is an artificial profit center that charges $10 per man-hour for maintenance work that it does for operating departments. The variable cost per man-hour is $4 and fixed costs are $40,000 per month.

The manager of department A, an operating department, has just determined that some changes in the production process can be made. If the changes are made, maintenance requirements will drop from 2,100 man-hours per month to 1,600. However, the variable cost to produce a unit of product will increase from $6 to $7. Department A produces 4,000 units of product per month.

Required

1. Determine the change in monthly profit for department A if the production process is changed.
2. Determine the change in profit of the maintenance department if department A changes its production process.
3. Determine the effect on the firm's monthly profit of the change in department A's production process.
4. Suppose that the manager of department A was prompted to study possible changes in the production process because he had heard that the transfer price for maintenance work was to be raised to $12 per hour. The higher price was proposed by the manager of the maintenance department because he expected a $1 increase in variable cost per man-hour and had approved other expenditures that would raise his department's fixed costs by $8,000 per month. For the last several months, the maintenance department has shown a profit of $8,000, and the proposed new transfer price was designed to maintain that profit level.
   (a) How many hours of maintenance work per month is currently being done by the maintenance department?
   (b) If the manager of department A decides to implement the change in the production process, what profit will the maintenance department show for a month?

10-38 Performance report Budgeted and actual results for the carpet line of Glenn Products appear below, along with selected other data. The firm makes a wide variety of products, with each line under a single manager.

Carpet Line
January 19X6 (In Thousands of Dollars)

	Budget	Actual	Over (Under)
Sales	$434.0	$446.4	$12.4
Cost of sales	262.0	279.1	17.1
Gross margin	172.0	167.3	(4.7)
Operating expenses	97.0	100.0	3.0
Profit	$ 75.0	$ 67.3	($ 7.7)

Other data:

1. The carpet line is manufactured in several plants, all of which make other products using fabric and other materials that go into carpets. The fixed costs of all of these factories, totaling about $8 million per month, are allocated to product lines based on relative variable manufacturing costs. Budgeted variable manufacturing costs for the carpet line were about 38% of sales, while actual costs were about 39% of sales because of some price reductions.
2. The carpet line had budgeted and actual fixed operating expenses traceable to its operations of $32,600. Variable operating expenses, both budgeted and actual, were

6% of sales. The remaining costs shown on page 399 were allocated expenses common to the entire business of the firm. These costs are allocated based on relative sales.

Required: Prepare a report on the carpet line that identifies the responsibility of the manager in charge. Use the format of Exhibit 10-2 but include a column for actual results as well as for budget results and amounts over or under.

10-39 **Assignment of responsibility** Peckman Company has one manager in charge of purchasing and another in charge of production. The purchasing manager is responsible for acquiring raw materials at the lowest possible cost consistent with quality standards. The production manager is responsible for meeting production quotas at the least possible cost. The raw materials used by the firm fluctuate in price, and the purchasing manager attempts to take advantage of these fluctuations by buying large quantities when he believes that prices will rise in the near future, and holding off on purchases when he believes that prices will fall. The production manager complains that these buying habits adversely affect his performance. He cites the following reasons:

(a) Bottlenecks frequently develop because raw materials are unavailable when the purchasing manager is waiting for better prices.

(b) Efficiency is reduced when large purchases are made: it is difficult to get to needed materials because there is so much stored in a limited space. Workers frequently have to help the storekeepers find the required materials.

 The production manager suggests that limits be placed on the quantities of materials that can be bought at any one time and that certain minimum levels be set for each type of material so that sufficient quantities will always be available. The purchasing manager feels that these limitations will adversely affect profits because purchases will have to be made at unfavorable times.

Required
1. Discuss the issues involved.
2. How can their responsibilities be separated?
3. What recommendations do you have?

10-40 **Cost allocations in a university** Ed Cranston, the new dean of the School of Business at Midstate University, is concerned. It is only early February, and he has just received a report from the university's printing and duplicating service showing that the school has exceeded its budget for duplicating for the academic year. The report appears as follows:

Printing and Duplicating Department Statement of Budget and Charges
for the School of Business September through January

Annual Budget	Actual Charges	Over (Under)
$4,200	$4,350	$150

 An enclosed note states that Ed must either stop using the service or obtain approval of a supplemental budget request from the chief fiscal officer of the university. Ed pulls out his latest statement, from December, and finds that actual charges at that time were $1,830. Since the school was on vacation during a good part of January, he wonders how $2,520 could have been incurred in January.

 He finds out that costs for the printing and duplicating department in January were $6,300, of which $700 was for paper, $2,000 for salaries, $2,000 for machine rentals, and $1,600 general overhead (allocated share of all university utilities, depreciation, etc.). A total of 35,000 copies was made in January, a relatively low number because of the vacation period. However, several faculty members in the School of Business had a substantial amount of printing done for scholarly papers that they were circulating to other professors throughout the country. The School of Business was responsible for 14,000 of the 35,000 copies and so was charged $2,520. The charge was computed by dividing total department costs for the month by the number of copies produced ($6,300/35,000) to arrive at a charge of $0.18 per copy. Ed also learns that during a typical month about $8,600 in cost is incurred and 150,000 copies are processed. Paper is the only item of variable cost.

Required: Evaluate the cost allocation system used and recommend changes if you think any are necessary.

10-41 Allocation of costs—distribution channels Weisner Company sells its products through wholesalers and retailers. Eric Stern is in charge of wholesale sales and Ralph Pike manages retail sales. Frederick Weisner, president of the firm, has ordered an analysis of the relative profitability of the two channels of distribution to determine where emphasis should be placed. The following data show the operations for the last six months.

	Wholesalers	Retailers
Sales	$2,000,000	$3,000,000
Cost of sales—all variable	1,600,000	2,000,000
Sales commissions (3% of sales)	60,000	90,000
Managers' salaries	18,000	18,000
Advertising (allocated as a percentage of sales dollars)	12,000	18,000
Selling expenses—salespeople's expenses, delivery, order processing, credit checking (allocated on the basis of number of orders from each group)	80,000	160,000
General expenses (allocated as a percentage of sales dollars)	40,000	60,000
Total expenses	1,810,000	2,346,000
Income	$ 190,000	$ 654,000

The same products are sold to both wholesalers and retailers, but prices to wholesalers are about 20% less than those to retailers.

Required
1. Comment on the reasonableness of the allocation methods used.
2. Recast the statement based on the principle of controllability.
3. What further information would help in assigning costs to the responsible managers?

Cases

10-42 Allocation of earnings—interaction effects[2] Two students have been hired to grade examination papers in elementary accounting. Jim is a very fast and usually accurate worker who can grade 20 examinations per hour. Jill is always accurate, but some-

---

[2]Adapted from Arthur L. Thomas, *Financial Accounting: The Main Ideas,* Belmont, Calif.: Wadsworth Publishing Company, Inc., 1972. Used with permission.

what slow; she can grade only 15 papers per hour. By concentrating on the parts that they can each grade best, Jim and Jill together are able to grade 50 papers per hour.

The pay for grading is $0.20 per paper.

Required
1. Determine how much Jim and Jill can earn per hour if they grade papers together.
2. If you were Jim, how would you want to divide the pay? Justify your answer.
3. If you were Jill, how would you argue the pay should be shared? Justify your answer.
4. What other possibilities are there for allocating pay?

10-43 Performance measurement   Tenspeed Company has been in the business of repairing bicycles for many years. Average profits have been $60,000 annually with revenues of $150,000. The firm recently began to sell bicycles and provide free repairs and adjustments, for one year after sale. As a result, total profits have increased as shown in the income statement below:

Tenspeed Company, Income Statement
for a Typical Year

	Bicycle Sales	Repairs and Adjustments	Total
Revenues	$400,000	$100,000	$500,000
Variable costs	160,000	75,000	235,000
Contribution margin	240,000	25,000	265,000
Separable fixed costs	80,000	15,000	95,000
Income	$160,000	$ 10,000	$170,000

The manager of the repair and adjustment department has complained that his performance looks bad solely because he is charged with the costs of repairing bicycles sold by the firm, while not being credited with any revenue for this work. He contends that he should be credited with revenue of 200% of variable costs of the repair work on sold bicycles, which is consistent with the revenue earned on regular repair and adjustment work.

The bicycle sales manager says that such a markup is too much, but that he is willing to accept a transfer price equal to variable cost of work done on bicycles sold. The mix of work in the repair department is two-thirds regular repairs, one-third repairs on bicycles sold by the firm.

Required
1. Recast the income statement to reflect the repair department manager's position. (Add the revenues credited to the repair department to variable costs of the bicycle sales department.)
2. Recast the income statement to show results if the repair department were credited with revenue equal to the variable cost of repair work done on bicycles sold.
3. What recommendations would you make? Give reasons.

10-44 Performance measurement in an automobile dealership   In automobile dealerships the sales managers of new and used cars are commonly evaluated according to the profits on sales of new and used cars, respectively. A new-car sales agreement may include some allowance for a traded-in used car. Assume that the trade-in allowance is based upon what the used-car manager is willing to pay the new-car manager for the car. For example, suppose that the customer wants to buy a new car that has a list price of $5,000, and trade in a used car. If there were no trade-in, perhaps the price of the car would be $4,400. If the used-car manager would give $1,800 for the used car to be traded in, the new-car salesperson would allow up to $2,400 to the customer, because the net price would still be satisfactory. The $2,600 cash paid ($5,000 list price − $2,400 allowed on the old car) is the same as the difference between the $4,400 desired price and the $1,800 that the used-car manager will pay for the car.

Sometimes the used-car manager will offer lower prices than at other times, say if his lot is full and sales are slow. If the used-car manager would pay only $1,500 for the car, the salesperson could give only a $2,100 trade-in allowance to obtain $4,400.

Required

1. Assuming that each manager is evaluated on profits in his respective area, what is the disadvantage to the new-car manager? Is there a disadvantage to the used-car manager?
2. Suppose that the dealership's policy provides that if the new-car manager is unhappy with the price offered by the used-car manager, the former can try to sell the car to another used-car dealer. In the second example, suppose the new-car manager believed that the trade-in automobile could be sold to another used-car dealer for $1,800. The $4,400 deemed acceptable for the new car would be obtained ($2,600 from the customer plus $1,800 from selling the trade-in), so this deal for the new car would be accepted despite the lower bid from the used-car manager. What conflicts could arise under this system? Does the system encourage the managers to act in the best interests of the total firm?

10-45 Home office allocations and decisions   Worcester Manufacturing Company has 14 sales offices throughout the United States and Canada. Each sales office is a profit center, with the local manager able to set prices and offer special discounts to obtain new customers. Many functions like checking creditworthiness of customers, billing, and others are centralized in the home office in Toledo. A few years ago, the president of the firm decided to charge the sales offices for these functions. After some thought, he set the charge at 8% of revenue. In general, the home office costs are almost all fixed.

The firm's factories "bill" the sales offices for goods at prices established annually. The charge includes both variable manufacturing costs and a margin added on to cover fixed costs. Variable manufacturing costs average about 40% of revenue at the current prices.

Lee Mott, manager of the Miami office, has come to you for advice. He is considering a price reduction that he expects would add considerably to unit volume, but is unsure of the effects on profit. He begins by showing you an income statement that reflects his expectations for the coming year without the price reduction.

Miami Office Budgeted Income Statement for 19X2

Sales		$2,400,000
Cost of sales		1,200,000
Gross margin		1,200,000
Salaries and commissions	$490,000	
Rent, utilities, insurance	86,000	
Home office charge	192,000	768,000
Profit		$ 432,000

Mott believes that it is possible to obtain the following increases in unit volume given the associated decreases in selling prices.

Decrease in Price (Percentage)	Increase in Unit Volume
5%	20%
10%	35%

Mott tells you that the only variable costs of running the office are the 15% commissions that salespeople earn. Of course, his "cost of sales" is variable also because it depends on unit volume, as is the home office charge because it depends on total revenue. Mott is evaluated on the profit that his office generates.

Required

1. Determine whether or not Mott should reduce prices, and if so, by how much.
2. Determine which action (hold prices, reduce by 5%, reduce by 10%) is in the best interests of the firm.

CHAPTER 11

DIVISIONAL PERFORMANCE MEASUREMENT

The responsibility accounting system provides information that helps a manager control operations and also serves as the basis for higher-level managers to evaluate the manager's performance. This chapter studies the control and evaluation functions in the context of investment centers, which are usually large enough to be divisions[1] of a large firm. Much of what is discussed is also applicable to profit centers, and some to cost centers. The chapter deals with the more autonomous units of a firm—units that may act almost as independent firms. The investment center concept has been developed largely on the premise that higher-level managers should be evaluated as nearly as possible as if they were chief executive officers of firms. Several criteria can be used to evaluate performance. We shall discuss three of these.

DECENTRALIZATION

It is customary to use the term **decentralized** to refer to companies that make extensive use of investment centers. Individual managers of such centers are responsible for and control revenues, expenses, and investment. Under any kind of organizational struc-

---

[1]The term *division* can refer to any large operating unit of a firm, but in this chapter it refers to an investment center.

ture, subordinate managers will have responsibilities and exercise control. Thus, in a broad sense, almost any firm could be said to be decentralized. However, the term normally is used only when managers have responsibility for profit and return on investment, rather than for either costs or revenues.

In highly decentralized firms, operating units (usually called divisions) are almost autonomous; division managers are responsible for both production and marketing, as well as such other functions as personnel and accounting. Normally division managers also prepare capital budgets and submit them to central headquarters for approval. However, division managers usually have no control over long-term financing, which is administered by central headquarters.

The principal advantage of decentralizing is generally argued to be better decision making. It is believed that managers who are closest to an operation can make better decisions because they are better able to gather and evaluate information than are centrally located corporate managers. Managers at the scene can also act more quickly because they do not need to report to headquarters and wait for approval of their proposed actions.

In a modern business firm of any complexity, it is impossible to operate without delegating some authority to lower-level managers. Given the interdependence of functional areas, conflicts between functional managers are inevitable. Hence it is deemed wise, wherever possible, to make some managers almost entirely responsible for both revenues and costs. Then, when conflicts occur, one of those managers becomes responsible for resolving the problems. When the firm's chief executive is the only manager whose span of responsibility includes both conflicting functions, arbitration and settlement of disputes must necessarily take place at the top. Decentralization allows for conflicts among managers of functional areas to be resolved at a lower level in the firm. Top management can also make better evaluations of managerial performance if the interdependencies and conflicts are resolved by managers responsible for the component elements of profit and return on investment.

A benefit that flows from the increased ability to evaluate performance and fix responsibility is that top management does not need to be heavily involved in day-to-day decision making. With decentralization, top management can use the principle of management by exception, monitoring the activities of almost autonomous managers.

Decentralization is also advantageous when firms have divisions that operate in different industries. A president or other chief operating officers of a corporation cannot be expected to be knowledgeable about textiles, furniture, appliances, automobile supplies, movies, and sporting goods. Over the past few decades, firms have greatly widened their range of products, and this diversification makes it necessary to have divisional managers with broad responsibility.

There is evidence that decentralization also increases motivation. Experiments in the behavioral sciences suggest that an individual who is involved in the entire production process takes more interest in the work and performs better than one who does the same operation repeatedly. Good performance in a single repetitive task may appear as wasted effort to the worker because the individual cannot control other tasks that affect the quality of the final product. Similarly, a manager who is responsible for virtually all aspects of the operation of a division may feel more in control of his or her performance than if he or she were responsible only for production or sales.

Managing a nearly autonomous division is also good preparation for higher positions with a firm. Such a manager has an appreciation for all aspects of a company's operations, instead of only one. The chief executive of Container Corporation of America, in an annual report, commented on the advantages of decentralization:

> The corporate organization consists of over 21,000 men and women, working in plants and offices, laboratories, forests and paperboard mills in the U.S. and six other countries. Its 140 plants and mills operate as relatively independent businesses, under a management system that delegates authority and responsibility to local managers. This decentralized organization, which provides for successful development of local markets, also constitutes an environment which encourages individual self-development. One measure of its success, over the years, is that virtually all of the company's present senior management team is a product of this system.

Decentralization has its problems. The major one is that managers operating in nearly autonomous fashion might make decisions that harm the firm. Indeed, perhaps the most formidable problem of decentralization is achieving goal congruence while at the same time promoting and maintaining divisional autonomy. Two managerial accounting issues are related to this important problem of decentralization. First, there is the need to develop methods of evaluating performance that work to the benefit of the firm as a whole. Second, there is a need to develop transfer prices that, as far as possible, produce decisions that are in the best interests of the firm. We turn first to the problem of selecting performance measures for divisions, beginning with descriptions and proceeding to the related behavioral problems.

MEASURES OF PERFORMANCE

Income

Although income, the "bottom line," is the most widely examined (and least understood) financial datum, it is unsatisfactory for measuring the performance of divisions. First, net income includes some expenses such as interest and taxes that are not normally under the control of divisional managers. Second, any income figure, be it pretax or before interest and taxes, tells only part of the story. A division that earns $10 million might be far less successful than one earning $3 million. The other part of the story is the investment that the manager used to generate the income.

Although a single number such as income is not a useful performance measure, income is hardly irrelevant. Indeed, the performance measures that have been proposed and will be discussed in this chapter all consider **divisional income** or **divisional profit,** so we cannot say that an income number is unimportant. But its importance is as a part of other measures rather than as a measure in itself.

Return on Investment (ROI)

Return on investment (ROI) is the general term used to describe a ratio of some measure of income to some measure of investment. In financial accounting you may have seen this ratio: net income divided by stockholders' equity. This ratio is usually called *return on equity* (ROE). ROE is one type of ROI. Another is *return on assets* (ROA), usually measured as income before interest and taxes divided by total assets.

The choice of an ROI ratio depends on the user's focus of interest. Both long-term debt and interest arise because of financing decisions, not operating decisions; and income taxes depend on a host of decisions not made by operating managers. ROA, therefore, is viewed as a measure of operating performance, because it excludes interest, taxes, and long-term debt. On the other hand, stockholders are concerned with both operating and financing decisions, so they look at ROE, which includes the effects of both types of decisions. No single measure of return on investment can satisfy all parties interested in a firm, and both managers and investors use many different measures of income and of investment.

Generally speaking, corporate managers will use an ROI measure of the following form:

$$\text{ROI} = \frac{\text{divisional income}}{\text{divisional investment}}$$

There are many variations in practice, with firms defining and measuring divisional income and divisional investment in different ways. Some firms use the term *return on capital employed* to distinguish internal measurements from measurements for the firm as a whole. We shall use the term ROI to mean whatever ratio the firm calculates that incorporates, however defined and measured, income and investment numbers for segments of the firm.

ROI is the most frequently used criterion for divisional performance measurement. It has a distinct advantage over divisional profit for this purpose, because it is likely that a company has divisions of different sizes. A division earning $100,000 on an investment of $1,000,000 is more efficient than one earning the same profit on an investment of $5,000,000. ROI makes it possible to compare the *efficiency* of different-size divisions by relating output (*income*) to input (*investment*).

Some managers find it helpful to restate the ROI formula when they are analyzing operating performance and trying to identify actions to improve performance. The restatement expands the basic formula, income ÷ investment:

$$\text{ROI} = \frac{\text{income}}{\text{sales}} \times \frac{\text{sales}}{\text{investment}}$$

As you can see, the expanded version produces the same final answer because "sales" appears in the numerator of one factor and the denominator of the other and thus cancels out.

The expanded form can help to focus the manager's attention on the two components of ROI. The first, income ÷ sales, is the familiar **return-on-sales** ratio. The second, sales ÷ investment, is called **investment turnover.** From this expanded version it is clear that an increase in sales, by itself, will not increase ROI because sales cancels out. But a decrease in investment, with other factors remaining the same, will increase ROI (as will an increase in income with other factors held constant). The manager can also determine the effect on ROI of a decision expected to change two factors. Suppose that return on sales is now 15% and investment turnover is 2 times; ROI is now 30% (15% × 2). If the manager is considering changing the product mix to items with lower margins and faster turnover, which would increase turnover to $2\frac{1}{2}$ times, while reducing return on sales to 10%, he or she could see that ROI would fall to 25% ($10\% \times 2\frac{1}{2}$).

The values of the two components of ROI often give clues to the kinds of strategies used by firms or divisions. For example, a single firm might operate both conventional department stores and discount stores. Both kinds of stores may earn the same ROI, but do so using very different strategies.

Assume the following data:

	Conventional Department Store Division	Discount Division
Sales	$2,000,000	$2,400,000
Divisional profit	240,000	192,000
Divisional investment	1,000,000	800,000

The ROI computations are as follows:

$$\text{Conventional store division} \qquad \frac{\$240,000}{\$2,000,000} \times \frac{\$2,000,000}{\$1,000,000} = 12\% \times 2 = 24\%$$

$$\text{Discount division} \qquad \frac{\$192,000}{\$2,400,000} \times \frac{\$2,400,000}{\$800,000} = 8\% \times 3 = 24\%$$

The discount operations produce a lower return on sales but obtain a higher sales volume for each dollar invested.

While the advantages of ROI in taking into consideration relative sizes and alternative strategies are obvious, absolute size is still of concern to the total firm. Recall from Chapter 8 that the firm was wise if it accepted all proposed investments where expected returns were in excess of cost of capital. The same general principle prevails in evaluating divisions.

Questions about what should or should not be included in the numerator and denominator for making an ROI calculation occupy a substantial portion of this chapter and are very important. Also important to the calculation is the way in which each component is measured. (As one example at this early stage, firms could use historical cost, replacement cost, or some other alternative for measuring the amount of investment in plant and equipment.)

Residual Income

Residual income is a measure of the amount of income that a division produces in excess of the **minimum desired** (sometimes called **target**) **rate of return** for the firm. Top management establishes the minimum desired rate of return. This is because the responsibility for long-term financing rests with the top management of the entire entity, and the cost of capital is determined on an entity-wide basis. The minimum desired rate of return should always be equal to or greater than the cost of capital. In general form, residual income (RI) is computed as follows:

$$RI = \text{income} - (\text{investment} \times \text{target ROI})$$

The argument for using RI to evaluate divisional performance is that it measures the amount of profit that the division provides to the firm over and above the profit to be expected (the minimum required) for the amount invested. The parenthetical term in the formula is essentially the profit that must be earned to satisfy the minimum requirements. Anything over that amount benefits the firm. (Of course, *any* income benefits the firm, but the minimum required ROI is needed simply to keep the firm going. If the firm earns less than investors demand, they will invest their capital elsewhere and the firm will cease to operate.)

RI offers an important advantage as a measure of divisional performance. Applying it shows that a division with the highest ROI may be less valuable *to the firm as a whole* than one with a lower ROI. Suppose that in a given firm, Division A produces a $200,000 income on an investment of $1,000,000, an ROI of 20%; Division B of that firm earns a profit of $1,500,000 on an investment of $10,000,000, ROI of 15%. The contributions of the divisions to the firm as a whole will appear quite different depending on the desired ROI for the firm. Let us consider two possible situations: (1) when desired ROI is 10%, and (2) when desired ROI is 18%. The RIs for each division are determined as follows:

	1 Desired ROI Is 10%		2 Desired ROI Is 18%	
	Division A	Division B	Division A	Division B
Investment	$1,000,000	$10,000,000	$1,000,000	$10,000,000
Divisional income	$ 200,000	$ 1,500,000	$ 200,000	$ 1,500,000
Desired minimum return (investment × minimum return)	100,000	1,000,000	180,000	1,800,000
Residual income	$ 100,000	$ 500,000	$ 20,000	($ 300,000)

If the minimum desired ROI is 10%, Division B makes a greater contribution to the firm than does Division A despite the fact that Division B's ROI is lower. In this situation we could say that Division B was more valuable to the firm. On the other hand, if the firm has established a minimum ROI of 18%, Division A contributes more and is more valuable under the RI criterion.

Generally speaking, using RI as the criterion for evaluating divisional performance, the division rated highest is the one with the greatest positive difference between profit and the minimum desired return. In some ways it is similar to the use of net present values as the criterion for evaluating capital expenditures. Under that criterion, the most desirable (valuable) capital project is the one with the highest net present value after discounting future returns at the cost of capital (or the minimum desired rate of return).

Because calculating RI involves the same factors as does ROI (namely, divisional income and divisional investment), the same questions arise about what should or should not be included in those numbers and how to measure the components. These questions are discussed later in the chapter.

BEHAVIORAL PROBLEMS

ROI vs. RI

Unlike the approach recommended in Chapter 8, in this chapter we have accepted the use of book values for investment and book income for return in the computation of ROI. Although the use of book value for investment can create problems, it is the measure of investment most commonly used in evaluations of divisional performance. Moreover, over relatively long periods of time, book ROI may well approximate the ROI that would be computed using only cash flows. Recognizing the difficulties of using book ROI, we can still say that the firm should expand if it can earn an ROI in excess of its cost of capital.

Using ROI as the criterion for divisional performance evaluation can encourage managers to pass up projects that promise returns in excess of cost of capital (or the minimum desired return) if the promised return is lower than the ROI currently being earned by the division. Consider a division manager who currently expects an income of $300,000 on present investment of $1,000,000 (ROI of 30%) and who is presented with an opportunity offering a $75,000 incremental profit on an incremental investment of $300,000 (ROI of 25% on the investment). Suppose further that the firm's minimum desired rate of return is 20%, and that the proposed new investment would be in receivables and inventory and would be recoverable at the end of the life of the investment. (Under these circumstances, the internal rate of return on the new investment would equal the book rate of return.)

If the performance of the division (and its manager) is to be evaluated on the basis of ROI, the manager would be inclined to reject the new investment opportunity because ROI for his division would fall, as can be seen in the following computations.

Investment before new project		$1,000,000
Additional investment for the project		300,000
Total investment		$1,300,000
Divisional profit:		
Current	$300,000	
From new project	75,000	
Total divisional profit		$ 375,000
Divisional ROI after new investment		28.8%

From the point of view of the entire firm, the proposed investment should be undertaken because it promises an ROI in excess of the minimum desired. To encourage the division manager to make the decision that would be advantageous to the firm as well as to the division, the evaluation criterion for the manager's performance must take into account the firm's policy with respect to minimum returns. The residual income approach to evaluation incorporates this important factor.

Applying the RI approach to the situation just described would show the following:

	Without New Project	With New Project
Divisional investment	$1,000,000	$1,300,000
Minimum required ROI	20%	20%
Divisional profit	$ 300,000	$ 375,000
Less, minimum required	200,000	260,000
Residual income	$ 100,000	$ 115,000

A division manager evaluated on the basis of RI would undertake this project because performance would improve. The ROI criterion encourages the maximizing of the *ratio* of profit to investment. The RI criterion encourages the maximizing of total *dollars* of profit in excess of the minimum required dollar return.

Using ROI as the divisional performance measure might also encourage a manager to make an investment that would be poor from the standpoint of the firm, but desirable from the view of the division because it would raise a currently low ROI. Suppose that a firm has a minimum required ROI of 20% and that a divisional manager currently expects income of $200,000 on an investment of $2,000,000, for a 10% ROI. What would the manager's response be to an opportunity to increase income $15,000 by investing $100,000 in receivables and inventory? The divisional ROI would increase to 10.2%.

$$\text{New ROI} = \frac{\$200,000 + \$15,000}{\$2,000,000 + \$100,000} = \frac{\$215,000}{\$2,100,000} = 10.2\%$$

Yet the proposed action would actually generate negative residual income of $5,000 because a $100,000 investment requires income of $20,000 to meet the 20% minimum required rate of return. If the manager is being evaluated on the basis of ROI, he or she would be encouraged to accept the investment, but that would not be the case if RI were the evaluation criterion. The current negative RI of $200,000 [$200,000 − ($2,000,000 × 20%)] would be even worse if the investment proposal were accepted.

Book Results and Discounted Cash Flows

In examples used in the previous section, book ROI equaled the internal rate of return on the proposed investment. That is seldom the case, especially with investments in plant and equipment. First, we should point out that very few divisional managers have the authority to make large capital investments without getting approval from officers at the corporate level. Therefore, it is unlikely that a divisional manager who is earning a low ROI could make a capital investment that would raise divisional ROI even though its internal rate of return was below the firm's cost of capital. But both ROI and

RI can, because they involve measures of *book* income, occasionally produce results that lead managers to avoid investments that would benefit the firm.

Consider the following example. A manager is considering a project that requires a $100,000 investment and will provide pretax cash flows of $40,000 per year for five years. The company requires a pretax return of 25% on investment. The present value of the $40,000 stream of payments discounted at 25% is $107,560 ($40,000 × 2.689). Under the decision rules developed in Chapter 8, the investment is desirable because it promises a return of $107,560 for an investment of $100,000 (a positive net present value of $7,560). But, book values are used in practice. The book rates of return and RIs for the first two years of the investment are as follows, assuming that the firm uses the straight-line method of depreciation for the new investment.

Year	Additional Cash Flow	Additional Depreciation	Increase in Book Income	Average Additional Investment[a]	ROI on Additional Investment	RI[b]
1	$40,000	$20,000	$20,000	$90,000	22.2%	($2,500)
2	$40,000	$20,000	$20,000	$70,000	28.6%	$2,500

[a]Book value of investment at beginning of year plus book value at end of year, divided by two.
[b]Income of $20,000 minus 25% required return on average additional investment.

Book ROI is below the minimum required in the first year, and RI for that year is negative. The division manager, seeing that undertaking the project would penalize his or her showing in the first year, would not be encouraged to accept the project. When book values are used for the computations, the conditions of lower ROI and negative RI could, for some investments, persist for several years.

Both book ROI and book RI will rise over time unless the cash flows from the investment decline sharply. The falling book investment (resulting from depreciation) is the cause of this pattern of returns, and the pattern is more extreme if the firm uses one of the accelerated methods of depreciation. Even if cash flows, and therefore book income, decline, the pattern of increasing ROI is likely to occur.

The rise in ROI based on book values is even more pronounced in more realistic situations because many investments do not begin to produce returns immediately or do not reach their peak cash flows in the early years. Ordinarily some lead time is required—to build a plant, install machinery, test the operation, remove "bugs," and generally get the operation going. If a new product is involved, its sales in the first year or two may well be substantially lower than those in later years. It is also not uncommon to incur heavy start-up costs in the opening of a new plant or even the remodeling of an existing one. The returns are likely to increase over the first few years as the plant gains efficiency.

Thus, there are actually two factors working against the manager who wishes to make substantial investments—lower income in early years, and the natural tendency of ROI to rise as the book value of the investment falls because of depreciation charges. What can be done to encourage the manager to pursue worthwhile investments?

One way to avoid the first-year drop in ROI and thereby encourage managers to accept desirable investments is to leave the new investment out of the base for calculating ROI until the new project is on stream and running well. A version of this approach is used by Burlington Industries, Inc., which bases ROI calculations on the amount of investment at the end of the previous six months; this mitigates the effects of large amounts of construction in progress.[2] Of course, many major projects will take a relatively long time before they could be said to be running well.

Another approach is to amortize start-up costs over several years instead of reporting them all in the income statement in the first year of an investment's life. A third possibility, seldom observed in practice, is to base depreciation charges on budgeted income to be earned over several years; this would result in lower depreciation in the early years and higher charges in the later years. Although top-level corporate managers may not object to leaving assets out of the base or to amortizing start-up costs, there is not much support for the use of increasing-charge depreciation methods. Perhaps the main reason for lack of interest in such depreciation methods is that they are almost never used in financial accounting, and using them for internal purposes would require maintaining additional, alternative records.

Still another approach to encourage managers to accept desirable investments despite the potential negative effects on ROI is to use gross (that is, original) cost of assets, rather than net book values, for evaluating performance. Some companies do use gross cost, but that approach has some serious deficiencies, as we shall see in a later section.

Essentially, the problem just described is one of the conflicts between the long and the short term. As has been stated many times in this book, there are many actions that can help meet some short-term goal but work to the detriment of the entity in the long run. Such actions (like deferring maintenance, employee training, or other discretionary items) could reduce profits, ROI, and RI in the long term, but by then the manager might have been promoted to another job. Conversely, a manager who takes actions that will benefit the division and firm in the long run, while hurting short-term performance, could be fired. The manager who takes over could well reap the benefits of the predecessor's good decisions. Obviously, then, it is unwise to evaluate divisions and their managers simply by reference to ROI, RI, or any other quantitative measures taken by themselves. Qualitative factors must enter into the evaluation process.

PROBLEMS IN MEASUREMENT

Whether ROI or RI is used as the evaluation criterion, we still must determine what revenues, costs, and investments are to be included and excluded in the calculations. Essentially, the determinations should be made along the lines of responsibility, with controllability as the criterion for inclusion of cost and investment. If a division manager is to be held responsible for earning returns (income) on investment, he or she should have control over the elements of both income and investment.

To compute the income for which the division's manager is responsible, it is necessary to identify variable costs and those fixed costs that we have previously described as separable. Fixed costs that are joint to several divisions should not be used in the computation because the division has no control over them. Opinions differ as to

---

[2]As reported by Donald R. Hughes, then assistant controller of Burlington Industries, Inc., in Thomas J. Burns, ed., *The Behavioral Aspects of Accounting Data for Performance Evaluation* (Columbus, Ohio: College of Administration Science, Ohio State University, 1970), p. 56.

what to include in and how to measure divisional investment. As a start, investment will at least include those assets that are used only by a particular division.

Investment in Assets

Under normal circumstances, most assets can readily be identified with specific divisions. Virtually all plant and equipment, for example, will be under the control of divisions (although divisions sometimes share productive assets). Inventory and receivables, which also constitute investment, are generally under divisional control because the divisional manager controls production and credit terms. Cash may or may not be under divisional control. Division managers usually have some cash under their control, but in many cases the central headquarters receives payments directly from customers and pays bills submitted by the divisions.

Some of the firm's assets are controlled only at the highest level of management. The central headquarters controls the headquarters building and equipment, investments in the securities of other firms, and such intangible assets as goodwill and organization costs.

Suppose we have analyzed the revenues, costs, and assets of Multiproducts, Inc., and have identified these by divisions as shown in Exhibit 11-1. The firm has three operating divisions, A, B, and C, and a central corporate office. The president has decided that the minimum desired ROI for the firm is 10%.

From the data in Exhibit 11-1 we can compute both ROI and RI for each division and for the firm as a whole. The latter computation should be based on an investment defined as the total assets of the firm. Note that no performance measurement is given for unallocated assets.

Although the firm earns an ROI a bit over 10%, only one division earns so low a

Exhibit 11-1

(In Thousands)

| | Divisions | | | | |
	A	B	C	Unallocated	Total
Investment in Assets					
Cash	$ 20	$ 30	$ 60	$ 30	$ 140
Accounts receivable	60	80	90		230
Inventory	100	180	240		520
Prepaid expenses	10	15	20	20	65
Plant and equipment—net of depreciation	200	320	440	60	1,020
Investments	10	—	—	100	110
Total assets	$400	$625	$850	$210	$2,085
Elements of Income					
Sales	$100	$400	$700		$1,200
Variable costs	30	220	400		650
Contribution margin	70	180	300		550
Fixed costs—separable	30	90	140		260
Divisional profit	$ 40	$ 90	$160		290
Fixed costs—joint					80
Income					$ 210

| | Divisions | | | Firm as |
	A	B	C	a Whole
Computation of ROI				
Profit of the segment	$ 40,000	$ 90,000	$160,000	$ 210,000
Investment for the segment	400,000	625,000	850,000	2,085,000
ROI (profit/investment)	10%	14.4%	18.8%	10.1%
Computation of RI				
Profit of the segment	$ 40,000	$ 90,000	$160,000	$ 210,000
Required return—investment × minimum				
return of 10%	40,000	62,500	85,000	208,500
RI (profit − required return)	$ —	$ 27,500	$ 75,000	$ 1,500

rate. *Because of unallocated costs and assets, the divisions must earn considerably more than the minimum desired ROI in order for the firm as a whole to do so.* The combined RI of the divisions is partly consumed by the unallocated costs and assets, so that although the divisions earn residual income of $102,500 ($0 + $27,500 + $75,000), the firm earns only $1,500 in excess of a 10% return on total assets.

When top management establishes an overall target ROI for the firm, there are two strategies available to encourage division managers to help achieve that target. One approach is to set divisional target ROI higher than the overall desired rate. Another is to allocate as much cost and investment as possible to divisions. Managers favoring this strategy argue that divisional managers should be made aware of the substantial costs of running the firm as a whole, which costs each of the divisions must work to offset.

There is another justification suggested for following the strategy of allocating joint costs and joint assets to divisions. Corporate managers are often interested in whether a particular division is earning returns comparable to those of independent firms operating in the same industry. If the division is to be treated more or less as an independent, autonomous entity, so the corporate managers argue, it should bear the costs and assets that an independent entity would require. An independent firm would have to incur many costs, and maintain many assets, that a division often does not. For example, an independent firm would perform research and development, while a division may be able to rely for such work on a centrally administered R&D organization. Similarly, an independent firm would have to maintain some cash, while a division may be able to rely for its needs on a centralized cash management function. To make reasonable comparisons between the division and an outside firm, then, corporate management might allocate central costs and assets to divisions (thus reminding the divisional managers of the needs met by the central administration).

Firms that allocate corporate costs among their divisions do so in many different ways. In some firms, the central headquarters charges each division a management fee for the services provided to the divisions. For instance, the divisions would need financing if they were separate firms, and the charge would reflect that service. The fee might be a percentage of revenue, or of total investment in the division, or of some other base. One large firm charges each division at 2% of gross sales.

The effort to make division managers realize that they must consider the performance of the entire firm may be worthwhile, but the assignment of central costs and assets to divisions must be understood for what it is—an allocation. Whatever the allocation methods used, managers at both the divisional and corporate levels must constantly remain aware that the allocations in no way change the nature of the costs or assets as joint and not controllable at the divisional level.

Liabilities

We noted in the general discussion of ROI that stockholders consider return on equity (ROE) to be more important than return on assets (ROA) because ROE incorporates the effects of financing decisions as well as of investing decisions. Someone viewing the top managers in an organization as investors in its divisions might assume a similar preference. However, important practical issues make it unlikely that an internal equivalent of ROE will be used for divisional performance measurement.

There usually is no satisfactory way to assign all liabilities to divisions. Some *current* liabilities (payables, accrued expenses) are readily identifiable with a particular division. However, the responsibility for deciding on methods of long-term financing normally rests with the highest level of management, and the choices are based on the overall needs and problems of the organization. Even if it were possible to identify a specific financing alternative as having been undertaken at the same time as a given investment was accepted, we know from Chapter 8 that the investment was determined to be acceptable without regard to the financing alternative to be selected. Recognizing the "joint" nature of most long-term financing decisions, for performance measurement purposes many firms will seek out liabilities that are definitely (not arbitrarily) related to divisions, and will define divisional investment as controlled assets minus divisional liabilities.

Using *any* liabilities in the determination of divisional investment will naturally cause the ROI of the divisions to increase. This is true because the denominator in our computation (the investment base) will decline, while the profit (the numerator) remains the same. If we were to apply this new definition of investment in the example used on page 416, the computations of ROI and RI would be as follows, given the assumptions about identifiable liabilities.

	Divisions			Firm as
	A	B	C	a Whole
Computation of ROI				
Profit of the segment	$ 40,000	$ 90,000	$160,000	$ 210,000
Total assets	400,000	625,000	850,000	2,085,000
Divisional liabilities (assumed)	60,000	170,000	310,000	540,000
Divisional investment	340,000	455,000	540,000	1,545,000
Unallocated liabilities (assumed)				730,000
Total investment	$340,000	$455,000	$540,000	$ 815,000
ROI	11.8%	19.8%	29.6%	25.8%
Computation of RI				
Profit of the segment	$ 40,000	$ 90,000	$160,000	$ 210,000
Required return—investment above × minimum return of 10%	34,000	45,500	54,000	81,500
RI	$ 6,000	44,500	$106,000	$ 128,500

Both RI and ROI are higher for all divisions and for the firm as a whole when liabilities are included in the computations.

From a behavioral standpoint, the question whether or not to include liabilities is undecided. In favor of their inclusion is that most current liabilities (like trade payables and accruals) are related to the operating level of the division and provide financing to it and to the firm. On the negative side, divisional managers could be encouraged to allow liabilities to rise too high in order to reduce investment and increase ROI. If divisional managers are able to delay payments to suppliers, the credit rating of the firm as a whole might suffer. A reasonable compromise might be a corporate policy that allows managers to carry, say, trade payables up to the length of time specified by the suppliers. Then, if a division had 40 days' purchases in accounts payable and suppliers offered 30-day credit, the division would not be able to deduct the extra 10 days' worth of liabilities to determine divisional investment. Then the manager would have no incentive to allow payables to extend beyond the suppliers' credit terms.

Fixed Assets

In all computations to this point you have been given the amount of the investment in assets. In Exhibit 11-1, for example, the investments in cash, inventory, and fixed assets were given, but there was no mention of how these amounts were determined. There are many views on what constitutes an appropriate valuation method to be used for assigning fixed assets to divisions. Some of the valuation bases used include: original (gross) cost; original cost less accumulated depreciation (often called net cost, or *net book value*); and current replacement cost. The method used can have a significant effect on the calculation of ROI or RI.

Each basis for valuation has advantages and disadvantages. The most popular by far is net book value. Its principal advantages are that it conforms to financial accounting practice and that it recognizes the decline in productivity that usually accompanies increasing age. It is also felt to be the most reasonable basis given that the income number computed for the division usually includes a depreciation charge. And, if depreciation is recognized for determining income, it should also be recognized in computing investment. The major disadvantage of net book value is that it gives, as shown earlier, rising ROI and RI over time.

Using gross (original) cost for valuing fixed assets overcomes the objection about rising ROI and RI. DuPont, one of the firms that uses gross book value, has stated its views as follows:

> Since plant facilities are maintained in virtually top condition during their working life, we believe it would be inappropriate to consider that operating management was responsible for earning a return on only the net operating investment. Furthermore, if depreciable assets were stated at net depreciated values, earnings in each succeeding period would be related to an ever-decreasing investment:. . . [3]

[3]Frank R. Rayburn and Michael M. Brown, "Measuring and Using Return on Investment Information," *The Managerial and Cost Accountant's Handbook,* James Don Edwards and Homer A. Black, eds. (Homewood, Illinois: Dow Jones-Irwin, 1979), p. 331. The authors were quoting from Solomons, *Divisional Performance: Measurement and Control* (Homewood, Illinois: Richard D. Irwin, 1965), pp. 134–135, as modified by letter from E.I. DuPont dated August 8, 1978.

Yet it is true that virtually all assets will lose productivity as they age, and the use of gross cost does not consider that decline.

Both gross and net book values suffer from the defect that they reflect costs that the firm has already incurred, perhaps many years ago. Managers who have older assets generally have lower investment bases (either gross or net) than managers whose assets are newer, and, in all likelihood, costlier. For this reason, many accountants and managers advocate the use of replacement costs to improve the evaluation of divisional performance.

Replacement cost has been defined in many ways. Some consider replacement cost to be the current cost of assets now being used. Under this interpretation, current cost might be measured as the acquisition cost of new assets just like those currently in use, or as the cost of acquiring assets of the same age and condition as those being used. Others consider replacement cost to be the cost of obtaining similar productive capacity or service. Under this interpretation, the emphasis is on how the firm would, at the present time, choose to accomplish a particular task. For example, suppose that a company has a fleet of fork-lift trucks to move material within its factory. Under the second interpretation, the replacement cost of that fleet would be the cost of an automated conveyor system if the division were to replace the fleet with such a system. Because managers should always be evaluating the alternatives available for accomplishing tasks, we believe the second interpretation (equivalent productive capacity) to be more appropriate for purposes of evaluating divisional performance. There is, however, disagreement among managerial accountants on this point.

Whatever definition of replacement cost is adopted, the use of replacement cost for measuring assets included in divisional investment eliminates the problems of different depreciation methods and also allows for changes in prices. Thus, managers are not penalized or rewarded simply because of the depreciation methods used or the respective ages of their divisions. The normal accounting system does not automatically provide information about current replacement costs, and for many years it was thought that the practical difficulties and associated costs of determining replacement costs were too great to warrant developing them. In recent years, however, the Securities and Exchange Commission and the Financial Accounting Standards Board have required the reporting of some replacement cost information. If these requirements continue, more firms may begin to use replacement costs for internal purposes, because the information will be available at no additional cost. Despite the disadvantages, the most popular approach for determining the value of fixed asssets to be assigned to divisions is original cost less accumulated depreciation.

THE SUBJECT OF EVALUATION—
DIVISION OR MANAGER

There is a very important distinction between the use of ROI and RI as diagnostic tools and as performance measures. As diagnostic tools, they serve to evaluate divisions but not necessarily their managers. They give clues to where the firm might be wise to increase, maintain, or reduce investment. Other things being equal, higher ROI and RI are desirable. However, for evaluating managers of divisions, both ROI and RI have drawbacks, or at least present potential problems, depending on how the results for a division are interpreted. The critical issue is the standard used for comparison: with what should we compare a division's results?

There are several bases on which comparisons can be made; each has its strengths and weaknesses. These bases include comparisons among divisions within the same firm, with historical results in the same division, with industry averages, and with budgets.

Divisions within the same firm can be ranked in terms of relative profitability. The ranking also may provide some insight into the relative contributions of the divisions. But such a ranking should *not* be used to rank the managers of the respective divisions, because different kinds of divisions should be *expected* to have different ROIs. ROI is generally higher for divisions (and entire firms) operating in consumer markets than for those selling mostly to other industrial firms. Both ROI and RI should be higher for divisions taking on high risks. (For example, a division making microcomputers, a very risky field, should do better than one making children's clothing.) The performance of the manager of a particular division must not be obscured by intrafirm comparisons that do not consider the nature of the division. A mediocre manager might be able to earn a respectable ROI in a division operating in a traditionally high-return industry. On the other hand, an excellent manager might be saddled with a division operating in a declining industry, and be doing a great job if he can maintain an ROI of 5%.

Comparing current results with historical results in the same division would overcome one difficulty associated with intrafirm comparisons. Differences due to diversities in industries are allowed to some extent. And, if there is a change in managers, the relative performance of two managers may be compared. On the other hand, historical comparisons suffer from the same objections as do intrafirm comparisons and should be interpreted carefully. That is, there is no way to tell whether historical experience is good or bad. Nevertheless, historical comparisons can indicate relative improvement or decay.

Comparisons of divisional results with industry averages can solve some of the problems associated with other measures of performance. Obviously, differences among divisions due to differences in industry no longer influence the performance measure. A division (and its manager) can be seen as better or worse than the firms with which it competes. Such comparisons present their own problems, however, because, as noted earlier, a division should probably earn a higher ROI than an entire firm operating in the same industry. A division will obtain some benefits from being part of a larger organization. Even when an entire firm operates in a single industry, a corporate staff will be required and some costs will be incurred that might not be reflected in the operating results for a single division. As the trend to diversification continues, it becomes increasingly difficult to find companies to which the performance of a single division can be compared.[4]

Budgets that are developed with considerable participation by divisional managers are valuable tools for assessing the performance of division managers. In such a situation, managers commit themselves to meeting the goals reflected in the budgets,

---

[4]Even if there are independent firms in essentially the same industry, it is no simple matter to compare them with a division. In fact, as Chapter 18 shows, comparisons among independent firms are not easy because of such factors as different accounting methods (first-in-first-out versus last-in-first-out is one example), different degrees of diversification, and different ages of plant assets.

and comparisons of actual and budgeted results are usually thought to be the best possible comparisons for evaluation purposes. Exhibit 11-2 shows budgeted and actual statements of income and financial position for a division.

Exhibit 11-2
Divisional Performance Report
(Millions of Dollars)

	Budget	Actual	Variance
Sales	$573.0	$591.0	$18.0
Variable costs			
(perhaps detailed)	246.0	251.2	5.2
Contribution margin	327.0	339.8	12.8
Separable fixed costs	140.0	141.4	1.4
Divisional profit	187.0	198.4	11.4
Allocated costs	12.0	15.0	3.0
Profit	$175.0	$183.4	$ 8.4
Assets employed:			
Cash	$ 15.5	$ 17.0	$ 1.5
Receivables	110.0	141.0	31.0
Inventory	90.0	122.5	32.5
Fixed assets, net	450.0	453.4	3.4
Total assets employed	$665.5	$733.9	$68.4
ROI	26.3%	25.0%	1.3%

Controllable costs are shown separately from allocated costs. There are no allocations of assets; all assets shown are controlled by the division's manager. The exhibit also shows why budgeted and actual ROI were not the same. The division earned more profit than budgeted, but its receivables and inventories climbed much higher than budgeted, resulting in a reduced ROI. This report gives more information than simple comparisons of ROI or of profit.

TRANSFER PRICES

In decentralized firms there may be a great deal of intrafirm buying and selling, which necessitates the setting of transfer prices. Firms in the food industry can have farming operations that supply their own processing plants as well as those of others. A textile mill might sell some of its cloth to divisions within the same firm for further processing and some to outsiders. An automobile manufacturer might establish divisions to produce transmissions or windows, which it sells to divisions that assemble cars.

Pricing Policies

Transfer prices are of critical importance in evaluating performance because prices influence both revenues of the selling division and costs of the buying division. We know from Chapter 10 that changes in transfer prices do not, in themselves, affect the total profits of the firm. It is only if individual managers, acting differently because of a change in transfer prices, make some change in their operations, that the total profits of the whole firm are affected. Because of their *potential* for promoting actions that might (or might not) be consistent with the interests of the total firm, transfer prices are important factors in divisional performance measurement. The following examples explore the implications of several transfer-pricing policies.

1. *Transfers could be made at cost plus a markup for the selling division.* This pricing scheme provides no incentive for the selling manager to keep costs down. Under such a pricing policy, the selling manager would make more profit by allowing costs to rise. The manager of the buying division would naturally object that costs (and hence apparent performance) could be adversely affected.
2. *Transfers could be made at budgeted cost, with or without a markup.* This method would encourage the selling manager to keep his or her costs down and, if there is a markup, provide a profit. The buying manager would appreciate not having cost inefficiencies passed on from the selling division but would prefer no markup at all. Thus discussions would center on whether budgeted cost and markup percentages, if any, were too high.
3. *Transfers could be made at market prices.* This method puts both the buying and selling managers on an independent basis, providing they are free to buy or sell on the outside instead of within the firm. Given this freedom, the managers are in the same position they would be in if they were the chief executives of autonomous firms. This method is generally considered the best. One major difficulty in implementing this policy is that there may not be outside market prices available for the division's products; or the prices that are available may not be representative. For instance, prices available may reflect relatively small transactions, whereas the divisions deal in very large quantities. Under such circumstances, the buying manager might contend that the outside prices are artificially high and that he or she should pay less than those prices because of the quantities bought. In many cases, the transfer price would be somewhat less than the market price to reflect cost savings from dealing internally. For instance, a division might pay a 15% commission on outside sales, none on inside sales. The transfer price would then be 85% of the market price so as to reflect that saving in cost. Market prices might not be a good choice as a transfer price if the selling division is operating below capacity.
4. *Transfers could be made at incremental cost.* Such a price would be the best, theoretically, when the selling division is operating below capacity. The manager of the selling division will object to this approach because it allows no profit at all to that division.
5. *Transfers could be made at prices negotiated by the managers.* This method would alleviate the problems that arise with the use of market prices. If there were outside markets, the manager who is dissatisfied with the price being offered could buy or sell in the outside market.

Despite our suggestion that a market-based transfer price is generally best, we hasten to point out that the autonomous division manager who is setting a transfer price must use judgment and understand the information available. Like the managers involved in making decisions discussed in earlier chapters, division managers must understand the concepts of contribution margin and incremental costs, and the implications of those concepts in light of the alternatives available to them.

For example, in Chapter 5 you read of the analysis underlying a decision about whether to accept a special order at less than the normal price. Critical to that analysis was whether or not the firm had an alternative use for the facilities. When excess capacity existed, the analysis suggested that the order should be accepted if it would bring in contribution margin in an amount greater than any incremental fixed costs. In that same chapter, you studied the analysis underlying a decision among various alternative uses of limited facilities, a situation that is consistent with what could be described as operating at full capacity (having no excess capacity). When there were alternative uses for the facilities, the relevant analysis suggested that the facilities be used in a manner producing the largest total contribution margin in excess of any incremental fixed costs.

The same principles apply when an autonomous division manager has to propose a transfer price on an order from another division. When the division has excess capacity, its results (and hence the manager's reported performance) will be improved by obtaining additional business at a price large enough to cover variable costs and incremental fixed costs; and the manager should offer a transfer price accordingly. When the division's capacity can be fully utilized without taking on the order from the other division, the manager should offer a transfer price at least as high as the alternative offering the greatest contribution margin in excess of associated fixed costs. That is, the transfer price should reflect the opportunity cost, which, in the case of the division manager, is the market price.

Summarizing, then, division managers, if treated as the heads of autonomous units, should be free to develop offers of transfer prices, which offers should reflect the cost structures of their divisions and the available alternatives. When the division is operating at full capacity, with some sales being made to customers outside the firm, a market-based transfer price is nearly always best. When the division is operating at less than full capacity, a transfer price that falls between incremental cost and the market price may be more appropriate. Hence, the division managers must understand the cost structures of their divisions, and use that knowledge in setting transfer prices. If they have the freedom to negotiate prices, the resulting actions are likely to be also in the best interests of the firm. To see why this is true, let us consider an example.

Illustrations

Division A sells a product for $50 that has variable costs of $30. The division buys a component for the product from an outside supplier for $10 per unit, and the supplier has just informed the manager of Division A that the price will soon be increased to $13 per unit. The manager has contacted several other outside suppliers and received similar price quotes. The component is one that could be produced with the equipment present at Division B, another division of the same firm, and the manager of A has asked B for a price for a possible intracompany sale. The manager of A expressed to the manager of B the hope that Division B could supply the component at the old price of $10. Division B now sells its output to outside customers. The budgeted income statements for the coming year for the two divisions and the firm are shown on page 424.

Budgeted Income Statements

	Division		Total for Firm
	A	B	
Sales to outsiders:			
A: 6,000 × $50	$300,000		$300,000
B: 10,000 × $15		$150,000	150,000
			450,000
Variable costs:			
A: 6,000 × ($20 + $13)ᵃ	198,000		(198,000)
B: 10,000 × $7		70,000	(70,000)
Contribution margin	102,000	80,000	182,000
Fixed costs	60,000	30,000	90,000
Income	$ 42,000	$ 50,000	$ 92,000

ᵃThe budget reflects the expected price of the component.

Let us assume, for simplicity, that Division B could make the component needed by A with no change in fixed costs and with the same variable cost per unit as the product it makes now. How should the manager of B respond to the request for a price quotation? What price would serve the best interests of the divisions and of the firm? The answer depends on the alternatives available to the manager of Division B, and on his understanding of those alternatives and costs.

If Division B's capacity is the 10,000 units it is now selling to outsiders at $15 per unit, meeting the needs of A at any price lower than that, even at the market price of $13 (the price that the outside supplier will charge Division A), would not be in the best interests of either the divisions or the firm. Below is a budgeted income statement for the firm (and its divisions) if a transfer takes place at $13.

Budgeted Income Statements
(Component Purchased Internally for $13)

	Division		Total for Firm
	A	B	
Sales to outsiders:			
A: 6,000 × $50	$300,000		$300,000
B: 4,000 × $15		$ 60,000	60,000
Sales to A: 6,000 × $13		78,000	
	300,000	138,0000	360,000
Variable costs:			
A: 6,000 × $20	120,000		120,000
6,000 × $13	78,000		
B: 10,000 × $7		70,000	70,000
	198,000	70,000	190,000
Contribution margin	102,000	68,000	170,000
Fixed costs	60,000	30,000	90,000
Income	$ 42,000	$ 38,000	$ 80,000

Division B would have to give up 6,000 units at the $15 price. Notice that we do not show the revenues and expenses of $78,000 that are associated with the intrafirm business in the total column because they do not represent transactions with outside firms. (Including them in the total column would not change the firm's budgeted income of $80,000 because the revenue to Division B is also an expense to Division A.) The profit that Division A expects does not change; so its manager is indifferent to the source from which it obtains the component. The profit of Division B declines (from $50,000 to $38,000), so its manager would not be willing to participate in an intercompany transaction at the market price. And the income of the firm is affected unfavorably, so the top-level managers would not want to see the transfer take place.

Suppose, however, that Division B can produce 20,000 units, but can sell only 10,000 to outsiders. If fixed costs will not be affected by the production of additional units for sale to Division A, Division B's results would be improved by sales of units at any price greater than the $7 variable cost to produce them. For example, a budgeted income statement for the firm (and its divisions) if a transfer takes place at as little as $8 per unit follows.

Budgeted Income Statement
(Component Purchased Internally for $8)

	Division A	Division B	Total for Firm
Sales to outsiders:			
A: 6,000 × $50	$300,000		$300,000
B: 10,000 × $15		$150,000	150,000
Sales to A: 6,000 × $8		48,000	
	300,000	198,000	450,000
Variable costs:			
A: 6,000 × $20	120,000		120,000
6,000 × $8	48,000		
B: 16,000 × $7		112,000	112,000
	168,000	112,000	232,000
Contribution margin	132,000	86,000	218,000
Fixed costs	60,000	30,000	90,000
Income	$ 72,000	$ 56,000	$128,000

The manager of Division A will be happy to accept an $8 price, for his division's results will be improved considerably (an increase of $30,000 in contribution margin and income). The manager of Division B should be willing to quote such a price, for its results will be improved by the amount of contribution margin [($8 − $7) × 6,000 additional units]. And the firm's top managers would want to see the transfer take place because the firm's total income will increase by $36,000 ($128,000 versus the original budgeted income of $92,000).

It would be unfortunate if the manager of Division B did not understand the division's cost structure and considered a price of $8 to be unacceptable. For example, suppose the manager had reviewed the original budgeted income statement and concluded that the cost was $10 per unit (variable costs of $70,000 plus fixed costs of $30,000, divided by the 10,000 units of planned production). The decision not to sell at $8 would, as indicated by the income statements, have been detrimental to Division A and to the firm, and would not have been in Division B's own interests either.

As a matter of fact, as long as excess capacity exists in Division B, any price less than the market price of $13 and greater than B's variable costs of $7 would be advantageous to the divisions and to the firm as a whole. Division A would be acquiring the component at a lower price than it would have to pay to an outside supplier. Division B would be gaining some contribution margin. And the firm would benefit from having the total cost of the product *to the firm* (the $7 variable cost from Division B, plus the $20 variable cost added by Division A) lower than would be the case if the component were purchased from some outside supplier. Indeed, even a transfer price of $7 should be acceptable. Division B would not lose anything and may gain some advantage by being able to retain the services of good workers who might otherwise have left the area for other jobs, or by keeping good relations with suppliers who might currently be concerned about the low levels of B's orders for materials.

In summary, then, the major issue from the standpoint of the company as a whole is not the choice of a transfer price but whether the transfer should take place at all. In many respects, the decision is much like that described in Chapter 5 regarding whether or not to subject some joint product to further processing. The manager deciding whether or not to buy an item from a sister division, spend money to process it further, and, finally, sell it to an outsider, should analyze the decision from the viewpoint of the company as a whole. Is the revenue to be gained by delaying the sale to an outsider (revenue after processing versus revenue at "split-off point") greater than the cost of the additional processing? When the selling division has excess capacity, the revenue available at the "split-off point" is zero. When the selling division is operating at capacity, the revenue available at the "split-off point" is the price to be gained from a sale to an outsider at that point. If it is profitable for the transfer to take place from the standpoint of the company as a whole, the transfer pricing system, including the information made available to managers who must make the decisions, should prompt the managers to make a decision in the best interests of the firm as a whole. Thus, the establishment of transfer prices requires judgment and a full understanding of the circumstances and of the managerial accounting information available.

SUMMARY

The evaluation of investment centers, like that of cost centers, requires determining what the manager can control. Commonly used performance measures are return on investment (ROI) and residual income (RI). ROI is the most popular measure, but RI is advantageous from a behavioral point of view. With either criterion there are difficult questions to be answered about what items should be included in divisional income and investment, and different opinions about how some items should be measured.

Intrafirm sales and purchases introduce the problem of transfer prices, which is more acute in investment centers than in cost centers. Such prices may encourage managers to take actions not in the best interests of the firm.

KEY TERMS

allocated assets
allocated costs
decentralization
divisional profit (income)
investment center
investment turnover

minimum desired (target) rate of return
residual income (RI)
return on investment (ROI)
return on sales
transfer price

KEY FORMULAS

$$\text{Return on investment (ROI)} = \frac{\text{divisional income}}{\text{divisional investment}}$$

$$\text{Return on investment (ROI)} = \frac{\text{income}}{\text{sales}} \times \frac{\text{sales}}{\text{investment}}$$

$$\text{Return on sales} = \frac{\text{income}}{\text{sales}}$$

$$\text{Investment turnover} = \frac{\text{sales}}{\text{investment}}$$

$$\text{Residual income (RI)} = \text{income} - (\text{investment} \times \text{desired return on investment})$$

REVIEW PROBLEM

The manager of the Bartram Division of United Products Company has given you the following information related to budgeted operations for the coming year, 19X5.

Sales (100,000 units at $5)	$500,000
Variable costs at $2 per unit	200,000
Contribution margin at $3 per unit	300,000
Fixed costs	120,000
Divisional profit	$180,000
Divisional investment	$800,000

The minimum desired ROI is 20%.

Required: Consider each part independently.
1. Determine the division's expected ROI using the second formula on page 408.
2. Determine the division's expected RI.
3. The manager has the opportunity to sell an additional 10,000 units at $4.50. Variable cost per unit would be the same as budgeted, but fixed costs would increase by $10,000. Additional investment of $50,000 would also be required. If the manager accepted the special order, by how much and in what direction would his RI change?

4. Of its total budgeted volume of 100,000 units, Bartram expects to sell 20,000 units to the Jeffers Division of United Products. However, the manager of Jeffers Division has received an offer from an outside firm. The outside firm would supply the 20,000 units at $4.20. If Bartram Division does not meet the $4.20 price, Jeffers will buy from the outside firm. Bartram could save $25,000 in fixed costs if it dropped its volume from 100,000 to 80,000 units.
   (a) Determine Bartram's profit assuming that it meets the $4.20 price.
   (b) Determine Bartram's profit if it fails to meet the price and loses the sales.
   (c) Determine the effect on the total profit of the firm if Bartram meets the $4.20 price.
   (d) Determine the effect on the total profit of the firm if Bartram does not meet the price.

Answer to Review Problem

1. 22.5%

$$\frac{\text{income}}{\text{sales}} \times \frac{\text{sales}}{\text{investment}} = \frac{\$180,000}{\$500,000} \times \frac{\$500,000}{\$800,000} = 0.36 \times 0.625 = 0.225 = 22.5\%$$

2. $20,000

Profit budgeted	$180,000
Minimum required return ($800,000 × 20%)	160,000
Residual income budgeted	$ 20,000

3. RI would increase by $5,000. This can be determined either by considering the changes in the variables or by preparing new data for total operations. Considering only the changes:

Increase in sales (10,000 × $4.50)	$45,000
Increase in variable costs (10,000 × $2)	20,000
Increase in contribution margin	25,000
Increase in fixed costs	10,000
Increase in profit	15,000
Increase in minimum desired return ($50,000 × 20%)	10,000
Increase in RI	$ 5,000

A new income statement and calculation of new total RI would show the following.

Sales ($500,000 + $45,000)	$545,000
Variable costs (110,000 × $2)	220,000
Contribution margin	325,000
Fixed costs ($120,000 + $10,000)	130,000
Divisional profit	195,000
Minimum desired return ($850,000 × 20%)	170,000
Residual income	$ 25,000

The new $25,000 RI is $5,000 more than the original figure based on budgeted operations without the special order.

4. (a) $164,000. If Bartram accepts the lower price, revenue (and hence contribution margin) will be reduced by $0.80 per unit for 20,000 units. With no change in fixed costs, the drop in contribution margin, $16,000, means a similar drop in profit. An income statement under the new assumptions would show the following.

Sales [($5 × 80,000) + ($4.20 × 20,000)]	$484,000
Variable costs ($2 × 100,000)	200,000
Contribution margin	284,000
Fixed costs	120,000
Divisional profit	$164,000

(b) $145,000. If Bartram does not accept the lower price, the *full* contribution margin from sales to Jeffers will be lost. The avoidable fixed costs will be saved. The contribution margin lost would be $60,000 (20,000 units at $3) and the fixed costs saved would be $25,000. Hence, divisional profit would drop $35,000 ($60,000 − $25,000) to $145,000 ($180,000 budgeted profit − $35,000).

The answer could also be arrived at by reference to the income statement prepared in part (a). The contribution margin lost would be $44,000 (20,000 × the lower contribution margin of $2.20), with fixed costs savings of $25,000. The net decline in profits would be $19,000 ($44,000 − $25,000), which, when subtracted from the total profit shown in the income statement in part (a), $164,000, equals $145,000.

A third, somewhat longer, approach to the problem would be to prepare an income statement assuming the sales to Jeffers are not made. This approach, too, shows a new divisional profit of $145,000.

Sales ($5 × 80,000)	$400,000
Variable costs ($2 × 80,000)	160,000
Contribution margin	240,000
Fixed costs ($120,000 − $25,000)	95,000
Divisional profit	$145,000

(c) If you concluded that there would be any change in the total profit of the firm as a result of the change in the transfer price, you have forgotten a very important point made in Chapter 10. Changes in transfer prices do not, in themselves, change total profits. Only if changes in transfer prices cause managers to change their operations and actions can a change in total profits occur. In this situation, the manager of Bartram Division had planned to sell to Jeffers Division and his income statement was budgeted accordingly. If he accepts the lower price, he will still be selling to Jeffers. Similarly, the manager of Jeffers Division had planned to buy from Bartram Division. He will still buy from Bartram Division, but at a lower price. The only thing that has changed is the transfer price. Hence, the firm's total profit will not change. The reduction in the profit of the Bartram Division (because of the lower contribution margin) will be exactly offset by the increase in the profits of the Jeffers Division (because of that division's lower costs).

(d) The firm would lose $19,000 if Jeffers bought its units from an outside supplier. You should see that from the point of view of the firm as a whole, the decision is basically a make-or-buy decision such as was discussed in Chapter 5. Consider, therefore, the two possible decisions, from the total firm's point of view.

	Decision	
	Buy from Outside Supplier	Make Product Inside (Bartram)
Purchase price (20,000 × $4.20)	$84,000	
Variable cost to produce (20,000 × $2)		$40,000
Avoidable fixed costs		25,000
Costs of each decision	$84,000	$65,000

As the above analysis indicates, the decision to produce internally carries a $19,000 advantage.

Another approach to this problem is to consider the profits of the individual divisions and how those profits would differ from originally budgeted profits if a purchase were made from an outside supplier. Consider that if Jeffers is able to purchase from either Bartram or an outside supplier at a price of $4.20, *its* profits will increase $16,000 (20,000 units × $0.80 saved) over what has been budgeted with an original transfer price of $5.00. For this reason, the manager of Jeffers would be eager to obtain the lower price, however this can be accomplished. Consider, now, the position of the manager of Bartram Division, who has budgeted profits of $180,000. The profit of *his* division will decline $35,000 (budgeted profits of $180,000 − $145,000 profits, computed in part (b), if he does not get the order from Jeffers). For this reason, the manager of Bartram should not want to lose the order from Jeffers. Putting these two changes in divisional profits together, we see that there will be a $19,000 loss (a gain of $16,000 by Jeffers and a loss of $35,000 by Bartram).

The important factor in this second approach is that if each division's manager evaluates his own situation properly, each will make a decision consistent with the good of the firm as a whole. The manager of Jeffers Division will wisely seek the lower price because it will increase his profits. The manager of Bartram Division will wisely consider the lower price because failing to do so will decrease his profits.

ASSIGNMENT MATERIAL

Questions for Discussion

11-1 Alternative accounting methods   Explain how various inventory cost flow assumptions (last-in-first-out, first-in-first-out, weighted average) could affect the measurement of return on investment for a division.

11-2 Variance in performance   What implications do you see in the following two contrasting questions?
(a) What is our deviation from plan?
(b) How well are we doing compared with what we could do?

11-3 Product-line reporting   Financial analysts often express the desire that companies publish annual reports broken down by division or principal lines of activity. They have said they would like to see financial statements broken down by products, or perhaps separated into wholesale and retail business, or maybe separated into government and commercial business. What problems might arise from attempting to fulfill this desire for additional information? What recommendations might you make?

11-4 Types of responsibility centers   Assume that the following multiple-choice question appeared on an examination covering this chapter and that the instructions were to select the single best answer.
Which of the following is true?
(a) All investment centers qualify as profit centers, but not all profit centers qualify as investment centers.
(b) All profit centers qualify as investment centers, but not all investment centers qualify as profit centers.
(c) All cost centers qualify as profit centers, but not all profit centers qualify as cost centers.
(d) All cost centers qualify as investment centers, but not all investment centers qualify as cost centers.

Forced to make a choice, most students would correctly select answer (a). If, however, only the first alternative were presented and the instructions were to indicate whether the statement was true or false, some of those same students might decide that the statement was false. What line of reasoning would those students present to justify their answer and how would you respond to their position?

Exercises

11-5 RI, ROI, and volume-cost-profit analysis   The following data refer to the DCB division of Octopus Corporation. DCB sells one product.

Selling price	$ 10
Variable cost	$ 6
Total fixed costs	$100,000
Investment	$400,000

Required: Answer the following questions, considering each independently.
1. If the manager of DCB desires a 25% ROI, how many units must be sold?
2. If the division sells 60,000 units, what will ROI be?
3. The minimum desired ROI is 15%. If the division sells 60,000 units, what will RI be?
4. The manager desires a 25% ROI and wishes to sell 40,000 units. What price must be charged?
5. The minimum desired ROI is 20% and RI is $30,000. What are sales, in units?

11-6 Comparison of ROI and RI, investment decisions   The manager of a large division of a firm has developed the following schedule of investment opportunities. The schedule shows, for each possibility, the amount to be invested and the annual profit to be earned. Currently, investment in the division is $5,000,000 and profits are $1,250,000.

Investment Opportunity	Amount of Investment	Annual Profit
A	$ 500,000	$ 90,000
B	700,000	200,000
C	1,000,000	230,000
D	1,100,000	300,000
E	1,200,000	280,000

Required
1. The division manager wishes to maximize his ROI. (a) Which projects will he select? (b) What ROI will he earn?
2. The manager wishes to maximize RI. Determine which projects he will select and the RI he will earn if the minimum desired ROI is (a) 15%, and (b) 20%.
3. Assuming that the ROI on each project approximates the internal rate of return discussed in this chapter and in Chapter 8, which policy (maximizing ROI or maximizing RI) is better for the firm? Assume that the minimum desired ROI equals cost of capital.

11-7   Product line evaluation   "My division as a whole is evaluated on ROI and RI, so why shouldn't I use those measures to evaluate my product lines?" The speaker was Lynn Cathcart, manager of the Household Products Division of General Enterprises, Inc. Cathcart provided you with the following data regarding the three major lines that the division handles.

	Cleaners	Disinfectants	Insect Sprays
Margin	20%	30%	25%
Turnover	2 times	2.5 times	2 times
Annual revenues, millions	$30	$10	$20

Required
1. For each product line, determine the ROI, total investment, and annual profit.
2. Assuming that the minimum required ROI is 30%, determine the RI for each product line.

11-8   Components of ROI   The following data refer to the three divisions of International Enterprises, Inc.

	Huge Division	Giant Division	Colossal Division
Sales	$2,000	$3,000	$5,000
Profit	500	300	300
Investment	2,500	2,000	1,500

Required
1. Compute ROI for each division, using the ratios of return on sales and investment turnover.
2. Assume that each division could increase its return on sales by one percentage point

with the same sales as are currently shown. Recompute ROI for each division and comment on the differences between the results here and those in item 1.

11-9 **ROI and VCP analysis**   The following data refer to the operations of Martin Division of LND Enterprises.

Selling price per unit	$ 30
Variable cost per unit	18
Fixed costs per year	300,000
Investment	900,000

Required
1. Determine the number of units that must be sold to achieve a 25% ROI.
2. The manager has been approached by a firm that wishes to buy 10,000 units per year at a reduced price. Current volume is 43,000 units. Accepting the special order will increase fixed costs by $30,000 and investment by $80,000.
    (a) Determine ROI without the special order.
    (b) Determine the lowest price at which the manager can sell the additional 10,000 units without reducing ROI.

11-10 **Performance evaluation criteria**   Foster Company has four divisions, A, B, C, and D. Operating data for 19X7 are, in thousands, as follows.

	A	B	C	D
Divisional profit	$ 3,000	$ 2,500	$ 6,000	$1,700
Assets employed	$18,000	$14,000	$42,000	$8,000

Required
1. Rank the divisions according to (a) return on investment, (b) residual income if the minimum desired ROI is 10%, and (c) residual income if the minimum desired ROI is 15%.
2. What other information would be helpful in your evaluation of the various divisions?

11-11 **Transfer prices for service work**   The service department of an automobile dealership does two general kinds of work: (1) work on cars brought in by customers; and (2) work on used cars purchased by the dealership for resale. The service manager is often evaluated on the basis of gross profit or some other dollar measure. Because of the evaluation measure, the prices to be charged to the used-car manager for reconditioning and repair work on cars he has bought for resale are particularly important. The used-car manager is also likely to be evaluated by his profits. Thus, he would like the service work done as cheaply as possible. The service manager would naturally like the prices to be the same as those he would charge to an outside customer.

Required
1. What possible transfer prices could be used, and what are their advantages and disadvantages?
2. How might work priorities be incorporated into the pricing policy?
3. What do you recommend?

11-12 Basic RI relationships   Grendel Division had RI of $4 million, investment of $20 million, and asset turnover of two times. The minimum required ROI was 15%.

Required
1. Determine Grendel's sales, profit, and return on sales.
2. To raise its RI by $1 million, holding sales and investment constant, Grendel would need to have what return on sales?

11-13 Transfer prices and decisions   The Armonk Division of Green Industries sells its one product, a chemical compound, to outside firms and to the Braser Division. Braser pays Armonk $3 per gallon for the compound, processes it into an industrial cleaner at a variable cost of $2 per gallon, and sells it for $7 per gallon. Budgeted income statements for the two divisions appear below. Green has no other divisions.

	Armonk	Braser	Total
Sales:			
To outsiders, 200,000 gallons	$800,000		$ 800,000
60,000 gallons		$420,000	420,000
To Braser 60,000 gallons	180,000		180,000
Total sales	980,000	420,000	1,400,000
Variable costs:			
$1.50 per gallon	390,000		390,000
$3 transfer price plus $2		300,000	300,000
Total variable costs	390,000	300,000	690,000
Contribution margin	590,000	120,000	710,000
Fixed costs	475,000	80,000	555,000
Profit	$115,000	$ 40,000	$ 155,000

Required
1. Braser Division has found an outside supplier who will sell the compound at $2.10 per gallon. The supplier insists on providing all 60,000 gallons that Braser needs. If Armonk reduces the transfer price to $2.10 and keeps Braser's business, what will the income for the firm as a whole be? What will each division's income be?
2. If Armonk refuses to meet the price and Braser buys outside, what will the income for the firm and for each division be? Armonk cannot increase its outside sales.
3. Suppose that if Braser buys outside, Armonk could increase its outside sales by 45,000 gallons. Armonk's capacity is 260,000 gallons so that it cannot meet Braser's needs and also increase its outside sales. If Braser buys outside and Armonk increases its outside sales, what incomes will the firm and each of the divisions earn?

11-14 Range of transfer price   The Schonka Division of CR Industries makes a microchip that it now sells only to outside companies. The Consumer Products Division of CR is bringing out a new oven that requires a sophisticated chip and has approached the Schonka Division for a quotation. Schonka sells the chip for $32 and incurs variable costs of $9. It has excess capacity. The Consumer Products Division can acquire a suitable chip from outside the company for $25.

Required
1. Determine the advantage to CR Industries as a whole for the Consumer Products Division to buy the chip from Schonka, as opposed to buying it outside.

2. Determine the minimum price per unit that Schonka Division would accept for the chip.
3. Determine the maximum price per unit that Consumer Products would pay to Schonka for the chip.
4. How would your answers to each of the above parts change if Schonka were working at capacity?

11-15 Basic ROI relationships Gandolf Division of Nationwide Motors had sales of $28 million, ROI of 20%, and asset turnover of four times.

Required
1. Determine Gandolf's: (a) investment, (b) profit, (c) return on sales.
2. Suppose that by reducing its asset investment Gandolf could increase its asset turnover to five without affecting either sales or income. What would its ROI be?

11-16 Effects of different depreciation methods Block Company has four operating divisions; one of these, the Lastec Division, makes plastics. Ralph Remon, the manager of the Lastec Division, is in his first year with the firm and is eager to make a good showing. He has budgeted capital expenditures of $2,000,000 for the coming year and is trying to decide on a method of depreciation, straight-line or sum-of-the-years'-digits. The assets being purchased have useful lives of four years. Total assets currently employed in the division are $4,000,000, of which $2,000,000 is plant and equipment that is being depreciated at $400,000 per year; the other $2,000,000 consists of current assets.

Ralph expects to show profits, before any depreciation, of $1,600,000 in each of the next four years.

Required
1. Prepare budgeted income statements for the next four years, assuming: (a) the use of straight-line depreciation on the new assets; and (b) the use of sum-of-the-years'-digits depreciation on the new assets.
2. Determine the total assets employed in the division at the ends of each of the next four years under both depreciation methods. Plant and equipment is shown at net book value. Current assets will remain at $2,000,000 over the four years.
3. Compute return on assets for each year.
4. Compute residual income for each year, assuming a 15% minimum desired return.
5. Which depreciation method should Ralph use and why?

11-17 Relationships For each of the following independent situations, fill in the blanks. In all cases the minimum desired ROI is 20%.

	(a) Income	(b) Investment	(c) ROI	(d) RI
1.	$2,000	$10,000	——	——
2.	$3,000	——	30%	——
3.	——	$20,000	30%	——
4.	——	$30,000	——	$1,000
5.	$4,000	——	——	$ 500
6.	——	——	30%	$3,000

Problems

11-18 Performance evaluation criteria Hawthorne Company has two divisions, Hi and Lo. The firm evaluates divisional managers based on return on investment. Budgeted data for the coming year are as follows.

	Hi	Lo	Total
Sales	$ 600,000	$ 300,000	$ 900,000
Expenses	$ 300,000	$ 200,000	$ 500,000
Divisional profit	$ 300,000	$ 100,000	$ 400,000
Investment	$1,200,000	$1,000,000	$2,200,000

An investment opportunity is available to both divisions. It is expected to return $40,000 annually and requires an investment of $200,000.

Required
1. Given that the divisional managers are evaluated based on ROI, which, if either, of the managers would accept the project? Explain.
2. Assume that the managers are evaluated on residual income. If the minimum desired ROI were 18%, which, if either, of the managers would accept the project? Explain.
3. If the minimum desired ROI were 18%, should the project be accepted from the standpoint of the firm? Explain.

11-19 Components of ROI The managers of two divisions of Diversified Company were recently discussing their operations. Some of the conversation was as follows: Frank Margin, "I get a good return on sales, about 15%, but my investment is a drag. Turnover last year was only 0.75 times." Flo Turns, "My problem is margins; turnover is about six times, but return on sales is only 2%."

Required
1. Compute ROI for each division.
2. (a) Assume that Frank Margin's division will maintain the same return on sales. Determine the investment turnover he must achieve to obtain ROI of 18%.
   (b) Assume that Flo Turns' division will maintain its existing investment turnover. Determine the return on sales she must achieve to obtain an ROI of 18%.

11-20 Transfer prices and required profit margins John Roberts, the used-car manager of the Snappy Wheels automobile dealership, is distressed by the firm's transfer pricing policy. Roberts is expected to earn a gross profit of 25% of sales in the used-car operation. He is charged with the trade-in price he sets for a used car plus any reconditioning work that is performed. The charge for reconditioning is based on actual costs by the service department plus a one-third markup over cost (25% on sales). Roberts feels that he is being unduly penalized by the one-third markup. Alan Black, the service manager, is held responsible for earning a 25% gross profit on sales and he argues that it would not be fair to force him to do reconditioning work any cheaper than the work he does on customers' cars.

Roberts has recently been approached by Joe Sharp, the owner of Sharp's Garage, an independent repair shop. Sharp offers to do reconditioning work for Roberts at

20% over cost. The work would be done during Sharp's slack periods and it would generally take about four days longer than work done by the service department, which has no excess capacity.

Required: Should Roberts take his reconditioning business to Sharp?

11-21 Appropriate transfer prices   The BIG Division of HUGE Industries expects the following results in 19X6, selling its product only to outside customers.

Sales 100,000 units at $5	$500,000
Variable costs at $2	200,000
Contribution margin	300,000
Fixed costs	200,000
Profit	$100,000

Early in 19X6, the manager of LITTLE Division of HUGE asked the manager of BIG to supply 30,000 units to LITTLE. LITTLE would modify the units at a variable cost of $4 and sell the resulting product for $8. BIG Division has capacity of 120,000 units and would therefore lose 10,000 units in outside sales if it supplied the 30,000 to LITTLE. BIG's fixed costs will remain constant up to capacity.

Required
1. If BIG does transfer 30,000 units to LITTLE, which modifies and sells them as described, what will happen to the profit of HUGE Industries as a whole? That is, how much would it go up or down?
2. What is the minimum transfer price that BIG would accept from LITTLE for the 30,000 units, the price that would keep its profit at $100,000? It might be most convenient to express the price as a total for the 30,000 units instead of per-unit.
3. Suppose that BIG's capacity is 150,000 units. Its outside sales cannot increase over 100,000 units. Redo part 1 using the new information.

11-22 Service centers   The president of Algon Company has just attended a seminar on the use of profit centers, and he is very enthusiatic about their potential for his company. He is especially interested in making some of the service centers within the company into profit centers. He decides that the maintenance department will be the first to be made into a profit center and hopes that the experience gained will be helpful if other service centers are to be converted to profit centers.

The president has called a meeting to discuss the setting of prices to be charged by the maintenance department to the units that it serves. The manager of the maintenance department suggests a cost-plus basis for pricing, with labor and materials used plus a 10% markup being charged to the unit asking for maintenance services, arguing that there must be a markup over cost in order to render the department a profit center; otherwise there is no point in changing from the current status—that of a cost center. The managers of operating departments argue that a fee schedule for each kind of maintenance job should be established. They do not like the cost-plus basis, believing that inefficiencies in the maintenance department will be passed along to them.

Required
1. Evaluate each argument.
2. Are there other choices? If so, what?
3. What recommendation can you make?

11-23   Behavior of ROI and RI   The manager of the Patterson Division of MMC Industries is considering an investment of $1,000,000 in depreciable assets with a 4-year life and no salvage value. She expects annual income of the following: year 1, $160,000; year 2, $180,000; year 3, $170,000; year 4, $160,000. These incomes are after depreciation. The firm evaluates divisional managers using ROI and RI (with an 18% minimum required return). The investment base is net book value of fixed assets at the beginning of each year and the firm uses straight-line depreciation.

The investment described above has an internal rate of return, ignoring income taxes, of about 25%, which meets the firm's cut-off rate of return.

Required
1.   Calculate the ROI and RI that the division would show in each of the four years of the investment.
2.   Would the manager be likely to accept the investment? Why or why not?

11-24   Make-or-buy and transfer pricing   Lansing Enterprises, Inc. has three divisions, A, B, and C. One of the products of the firm uses components made by A and B, with the final assembly done by C. One unit from A and one from B are required.

Data for the product are as follows.

Selling price (C division)	$80
Variable costs:	
A division	$20
B division	14
C division	8
Total variable costs	$42
Volume	10,000 units

Divisions A and B charge Division C $25 and $18, respectively, for each unit. Division C has been approached by an outside supplier who will sell the component now made by Division A at $23 per unit.

Required
1.   Prepare partial income statements, down to contribution margin, for A, B, and C based on current operations.
2.   Determine whether the offer from the outside supplier should be accepted. If A meets the price offered by the outside supplier, C will continue to buy from A.
3.   Suppose that A can sell its entire output of 10,000 units per year at $30 if it performs additional work on the component. The additional work will add $5 to variable cost per unit; fixed costs will be unchanged. The capacity of Division A is 10,000 units. Should A meet the outside supplier's price or allow C to buy from the outside supplier? Support with calculations.

11-25   Goal congruence and motivation   Rex Company manufactures furniture and related products. The manager of the Redfern Division has been seeking bids on a particular type of chair to be used in a new living room suite she wants to market. No division within the firm can supply the chair because of the unique production process required to make it.

The lowest outside bid is $120 from Dorfman Chair Company. Wisner Chair Company has bid $130 and would purchase some of the materials from the Ronson

Upholstery Division of Rex Company. The Ronson Division, which has excess capacity, would incur variable costs of $25 for the amount of material needed for one chair and would be paid $46 by Wisner. The manager of the Redfern Division knows that Wisner would buy the materials from Ronson, and that Dorfman would not. Each division manager is evaluated on the basis of return on investment.

Required
1. As manager of the Redfern Division, which bid would you accept, Dorfman's or Wisner's? Explain.
2. As president of the firm, which bid would you like to see accepted? Explain.
3. What recommendation would you make?

11-26   Divisional performance—interactions   Acme Camera Company has two divisions, film and cameras. The manager of the Film Division, John Kretzmar, has just received a report from his laboratory indicating a breakthrough in a new type of film that produces much clearer pictures. The film can only be used in the X-40, a low-priced camera made by the Camera Division. The film currently sold for the X-40 has a variable cost per roll of $0.22 and sells for $0.80 per roll. The firm currently sells 2 million rolls per year.

Kretzmar is confident that if he devoted his efforts and facilities to the production and sale of the new film he could sell 2.5 million rolls of the new film at $0.70 each. Additionally, he believes, on the basis of several market research studies, that if the Camera Division produced and sold 200,000 more X-40s per year, sales of the new film could reach 4.8 million rolls. The variable cost of the new film is $0.10 per roll, additional fixed costs to produce it would be $60,000 per year, and additional investment would be required totaling $300,000.

Sam Brewer, manager of the Camera Division, is not enthralled with the proposal that he increase production of X-40s. He argues that the camera has a contribution margin of only $4 and that he would have to increase his investment by $3,000,000 and his fixed costs by $300,000 in order to increase production by 200,000 units. He is virtually certain, as is Kretzmar, that the extra units could be sold, but he is well aware also that the firm's minimum desired ROI is 20%.

Required
1. Compute the change in RI for the Camera Division if production and sales of X-40s are increased by 200,000 units to show why Brewer is not anxious to expand his production.
2. If the manager of the Camera Division will not increase production, what is the best action for the Film Division?
3. What is the best action for the firm as a whole?

11-27   RI, ROI, VCP analysis, and effects of decisions   The following data refer to the Pratt Division of Standard National Company. Pratt Division sells only one product.

Selling price	$ 40
Variable costs	$ 24
Total fixed costs	$200,000
Investment	$800,000
Planned sales in 19X9	30,000 units

Required: Answer the following questions, considering each one independently.

1. What is planned ROI for 19X9?
2. The minimum desired ROI is 20% and the division manager wishes to maximize RI. A new customer can be obtained who will buy 10,000 units at $32 each. If the order is accepted, the division will incur additional fixed costs of $40,000 and will have to invest an additional $160,000 in various assets. Should the order be accepted?
3. The minimum desired ROI is 20% and the manager wishes to maximize RI. The division makes components for its product at a variable cost of $4. An outside supplier has offered to supply the 30,000 units needed at a cost of $5 per unit. The units that the supplier would provide are equivalent to the ones now being made and the supplier is reliable. If the component is purchased, fixed costs will decline by $20,000 and investment will drop by $40,000. Should the component be bought or made?
4. Again, minimum desired ROI is 20% and the goal is maximization of RI. The manager is considering the introduction of a new product. It will sell for $20, variable costs are $12, fixed costs will increase by $80,000, and sales are expected to be 15,000 units. What is the most additional investment in assets that can be made without reducing RI?
5. Assume the same facts as in part 4 above except that investment in the new product is to be $400,000, and that the introduction of the new product will stimulate sales of the existing product. The increase in sales of the existing product is expected to be 2,000 units.
   (a) Should the new product be introduced?
   (b) By how many units must sales of the existing product increase to justify introducing the new product?

11-28 Corporate charges and behavior   MST Company charges each of its operating divisions a percentage of sales to cover corporate expenses, which are virtually all fixed. The percentage is based on budgeted sales and budgeted corporate expenses and is predetermined for each year. In 19X6 the charge is 3%. The charge is included in calculating the profit of each division and its ROI, which is the basis for evaluating the performance of divisional managers.

The Calco Division makes electronic equipment and has some excess capacity. Its manager has found a customer who would pay $10.0 million for a batch of product that would have variable costs of $8.8 million. There would be no incremental fixed costs associated with the order. The 3% charge is not included in the $8.8 million.

The divisional manager expects to earn $15.5 million with investment of $70.5 million without the order. Accepting the order would require increased investment in receivables and inventories of about $5.1 million.

Required

1. Should the divisional manager accept the order, acting in his own best interests?
2. Assuming that the minimum required ROI is 20%, is it to the firm's advantage to accept the order?

11-29 Performance measurement—athletic programs   Haltom University is a medium-sized private university with a religious affiliation. Perhaps prompted by the prospect of declining college enrollment, a number of faculty members at Haltom have become increasingly concerned about the costs of the school's athletic program. The football program has been subjected to particular scrutiny. One professor has assembled the following data and argues, based on these data, that football is clearly a drain on funds needed elsewhere in the university.

19X4 Football Program

Revenue from ticket sales		$300,000
Revenue from concessions		25,000
Total revenue		325,000
Associated costs:		
Tuition for players on scholarship	$120,000	
Room rent in dormitories for players	22,000	
Board and incidentals for players	110,000	
Coaches' salaries	90,000	
Portion of salaries of athletic director, ticket office		
personnel, attendants, etc.	17,000	
Uniforms, equipment, etc.	10,000	
Total costs		369,000
Net loss on football program		($ 44,000)

Required
1. Comment on each item. Should it be included? If you are uncertain, state the conditions under which it would be included or excluded.
2. What other information would you want before reaching a decision on the desirability of the football program?

11-30 **Transfer prices**   The following is a budgeted income statement for a division of Weaver, Inc. The division sells both to outsiders and to another division within the firm.

Income of Superdivision

	Intercompany Sales to Subdivision	Sales to Outsiders
Sales:		
100,000 units @ $10		$1,000,000
50,000 units @ $8	$400,000	
Variable costs ($4 per unit)	200,000	400,000
Contribution margin	200,000	600,000
Fixed costs		
($300,000, allocated at $2 per unit)	100,000	200,000
Profit	$100,000	$ 400,000

Required
1. Subdivision has an opportunity to buy all of its requirements from an outside supplier at $7 per unit and will do so unless Superdivision meets the $7 price. The manager of Superdivison knows that if he loses the business of Subdivision, he will not be able to increase his sales to outsiders and his fixed costs will not change. Should Superdivision meet the $7 price from the standpoint of (a) the firm, and (b) Superdivision?
2. Superdivision meets the $7 price. It then is offered the opportunity to sell 60,000 units to a chain store at $7 each. The price of the 100,000 units now being sold to outsiders would not be affected. However, Superdivision has capacity of 190,000

units and if it could not fill all of the requirements of Subdivision then Subdivision would have to buy all the units outside at $7. Should Superdivision accept the order, considering (a) the firm, and (b) Superdivision?

3. Suppose now that Subdivision has received the offer from the outside supplier, who will provide as many units as Subdivision wants to buy at $7. Superdivision no longer has the opportunity to sell the 90,000 units to the chain store. The manager of Superdivision believes that if he reduces his prices to outsiders he can increase those sales greatly. His best estimates are that if he reduces the price to $9.20 he can sell 120,000 units, to $8.40, 150,000 units, and to $7.80, 170,000 units. His capacity is 190,000 units. Superdivision can sell any amount up to 50,000 units to Subdivision. Subdivision will buy units from the outside supplier as necessary. What should be done? How many units should Superdivision sell to outsiders and how many units should it sell to Subdivision at $7?

11-31 ROI, RI, and investment decisions   The manager of the Brandon Division of Greene Industries has been analyzing her investment opportunities. The division currently has profits of $1,250,000 and investment of $5,000,000. The schedule of opportunities is given below.

Investment Opportunity	Annual Profit	Amount of Investment
A	$300,000	$ 900,000
B	300,000	1,600,000
C	240,000	1,200,000
D	280,000	800,000
E	260,000	1,000,000

Required

1. Assume that the manager wishes to earn the highest ROI possible. Determine which projects will be selected and the ROI that will be earned.
2. Assume that the division manager wishes to maximize RI. Determine which projects will be selected and the total RI that will be earned if the minimum desired return is (a) 20%, and (b) 28%.
3. Assuming that the ROI on each project approximates the internal rate of return discussed in Chapter 8, determine which policy is better from the standpoint of the firm: maximizing ROI or maximizing RI. Assume that the minimum desired ROI approximates cost of capital.

11-32 Transfer pricing   The Macron Division of 2M Company expects the following results in 19X6.

Sales 100,000 at $3		$300,000
Variable costs	$120,000	
Fixed costs	150,000	270,000
Profit		$ 30,000

The Sparkman Division of 2M Company would like to buy 30,000 units of Macron's product. Sparkman would incur an additional $0.80 per unit and would sell the resultant new product for $4.50. Macron has capacity for 120,000 units.

Required

1. What would happen to the profit of the firm as a whole if the transaction took place at a transfer price of $1.50?
2. What would happen to the profits of each division if the transaction took place at the $1.50 transfer price?
3. What is the minimum transfer price that Macron would accept for the entire 30,000 units?

11-33   ROI and RI—capitalizing human resources   The Business Products Division of Data Systems Company develops software for business applications for main-frame computers and microcomputers. The division employs 350 people, of whom 320 are accounting and data-processing professionals, the remainder being clerks, secretaries, and editors. Because the division does no manufacturing, it has a very low asset base—about $500,000, consisting of microcomputers, office equipment, and an extensive library. The division earned $1,500,000 in the latest year. The controller of the company believes that the 300% ROI ($1,500,000/$500,000) misstates the division's results because the asset base omits the costs of training the professional employees. The division spent some $750,000 this year (19X5) on such training, including sending employees to seminars and the start-up time for new employees.

The controller realizes that generally accepted accounting principles do not condone capitalizing the costs of human assets, but she nonetheless thinks it would be interesting to see how the division would look were it to capitalize these costs and amortize them over five years. She develops the following data for the past four years (the division's entire life) in thousands of dollars.

Year	Book Profit	Training Cost	Book Assets
19X2	$ 110	$400	$220
19X3	520	500	270
19X4	960	600	420
19X5	1,500	750	500

Training costs are included as expenses in the book profit figures.

Required

1. Determine ROI for each year using the data as given above and applying generally accepted accounting principles.
2. Determine the profit, investment, and ROI for each year using the controller's method. That is, capitalize training costs and amortize them over five years, beginning with the year of the expenditure.
3. Compare the results in parts 1 and 2. Comment, including statements about the advantages and disadvantages of the controller's approach.

11-34   Transfer prices and goal congruence (CMA adapted)   A. R. Oma Company manufactures a line of men's perfumes and aftershave lotions. The manufacturing process is a series of mixing operations with the adding of aromatic and coloring ingredients. The finished product is bottled and packed in cases of six bottles each.

The bottles are made by one division, which was bought several years ago. The management believed that the appeal of the product was partly due to the attractiveness of the bottles and so has spent a great deal of time and effort developing new types of bottles and new processes for making them.

The bottle division has been selling all of its output to the manufacturing division at market-based transfer prices. The price has been determined by asking other bottle manufacturers for bids on the bottles of the appropriate size and in the required quantities. At present, the firm has received the following bids from outsiders, for a year's supply.

Quantity, Cases of 6 Bottles	Price per Case	Total Price
2,000,000	$2.00	$ 4,000,000
4,000,000	1.75	7,000,000
6,000,000	1.6666	10,000,000

The bottle division has fixed costs of $1,200,000 per year and variable costs of $1 per case. Both divisions are treated as investment centers and their managers receive significant bonuses based on profitability, so the transfer price to be used is of great interest to both of them.

The perfume manufacturing division has variable costs, excluding the cost of bottles, of $8 per case and fixed costs of $4,000,000 annually. The market research group has determined that the following price-volume relationships are likely to prevail during the coming year.

Sales Volume in Cases	Selling Price per Case	Total Revenue
2,000,000	$12.50	$25,000,000
4,000,000	11.40	45,600,000
6,000,000	10.65	63,900,000

The president of the firm believes that the market-based transfer price should be used in pricing transfers. The bottle division has no outside sales potential because the firm does not wish to supply competitors with its own highly appealing bottles.

Required

1. Of the three levels of volume given, determine the one that will provide the highest profit to the (a) bottle division, (b) perfume division, (c) firm as a whole.
2. Do the results in part 1 contradict your understanding of the effectiveness of market-based transfer prices? Explain why or why not.
3. Make a recommendation to the president of the firm.

11-35 Transfer pricing (CMA adapted) The manager of the Arjay Division of National Industries, Inc. has been given the opportunity to supply a brake assembly to an aircraft manufacturer who is willing to pay $50. The manager of Arjay is willing to accept the order if he can break even on it because he has excess capacity and would be able to keep skilled workers busy who would otherwise have to be laid off. Additionally, he believes that there is a good chance of getting more business from the same firm at better prices.

The Bradley Division of National Industries makes a part that would be used in the brake assembly. Bradley is operating at full capacity and producing the part at a variable cost of $4.25. Its selling price is $7.50 to outsiders. None of the division's output is currently being sold internally.

The manager of Arjay decides to offer Bradley a price that would result in breaking even on the order. He determines that the other costs involved in filling the order are as follows, per unit:

Parts purchased outside	$23
Other variable costs	14
Fixed overhead and administration	8
Total, before fitting	$45

He decides to offer the manager of Bradley $5 per fitting, which would bring the total cost per unit to $50, the selling price of the assembly. The firm is decentralized and the managers are evaluated based on ROI.

Required
1. Determine whether the manager of Bradley would be likely to accept the $5 offer from Arjay.
2. Determine whether it would be to the firm's advantage for Bradley to supply the part at $5.
3. As the controller of National Industries, what would you advise be done?

11-36 Budgeted and actual results Managers of divisions of Wycliff Company receive bonuses based on ROI. The bonuses constitute about 30% of the total compensation of the average divisional manager. Part of the bonus depends on whether or not the manager meets the budgeted ROI.

F. C. Smith took over as general manager of the Poursh Division in late 19X1. Budgeted and actual results for 19X6 appear below, in thousands of dollars.

	Budget	Actual
Sales	$2,500	$2,480
Cost of sales	(1,250)	(1,310)
Operating expenses	(750)	(610)
Profit	$ 500	$ 560
Investment		
Current assets (50% of sales)	$1,250	$1,280
Current liabilities		
(40% of current assets)	(500)	(580)
Plant and equipment, net	1,800	1,770
Total investment	$2,550	$2,470
ROI	19.6%	22.6%

Smith received a sizable bonus. Commenting on the results, Smith said that once he saw that sales would not meet budget, he began to cut costs, especially in discretionary areas like maintenance, employee training, and engineering (engineers were responsible for improving the quality of products and methods of manufacturing). He also held off payments to suppliers, letting them finance more of the division's asset requirements.

Required: Comment on Smith's performance. Refer to specific items shown above.

11-37 Divisional performance, cost allocations, and dropping a product line Randy Rathman is the manager in charge of two product lines for Kingston Company. He has just received the following income statement for the three months ended March 31,

19X7. The statement shows Randy's two product lines and the total results for the firm. There are 10 product lines in the firm.

| | Product Lines | | Total |
	A	B	Firm
Sales	$100,000	$200,000	$2,000,000
Separable expenses:			
Cost of sales	60,000	100,000	1,050,000
Selling and general	29,000	50,000	450,000
Total separable expenses	89,000	150,000	1,500,000
Joint costs			
(allocated on basis of sales dollars)	15,000	30,000	300,000
Total expenses	104,000	180,000	1,800,000
Income (loss)	($ 4,000)	$ 20,000	$ 200,000

Randy is disturbed by the showing of product line A. He believes that the line is contributing to the joint costs of the firm and should be kept, but is worried about the effect on his performance.

Required
1. Prepare an income statement, assuming that product line A is dropped. Show the effects on both Randy's and the firm's performance. All separable costs are avoidable. Be sure to reallocate the joint costs to product line B based on its relative percentage of the new sales for the firm. Round to the nearest $500.
2. Comment on the results. Does Randy's performance look better if product line A is dropped? Is it better? Is the decision good for the firm?

11-38 Developing divisional performance data   Dixon Company has three divisions, X, Y, and Z. The following data regarding operations and selected balance sheet elements have been prepared by the firm's accountant (in thousands).

	X	Y	Z
Sales	$2,000	$3,000	$5,000
Cost of goods sold	1,000	1,400	3,300
Gross profit	1,000	1,600	1,700
Selling and administrative expense	400	900	800
Income	$ 600	$ 700	$ 900
Current assets	$ 400	$ 700	$ 600
Current liabilities	$ 300	$ 200	$ 100
Fixed assets (net)	$2,250	$3,000	$3,750

After determining the costs and assets directly traceable to the divisions, the accountant allocated the remainder in the following way:
(a) Joint cost of goods sold of $1,800 was allocated based on sales dollars.
(b) Joint selling and administrative costs of $1,000 were allocated on the basis of relative sales dollars.
(c) Joint fixed assets of $3,000 were allocated on the basis of relative shares of directly

assignable fixed assets of $1,500, $2,000, and $2,500, for X, Y, and Z, respectively.

(d) All current assets except cash (which is held and managed by corporate headquarters) are directly assignable. Cash of $200 is allocated based on sales.

Required

1. On the basis of the data developed by the firm, rank the divisions according to return on investment in net assets, and residual income. (Assume that the minimum required ROI is 15%).

2. Recast the statements, computing divisional profit and assets employed without allocations. Rank the divisions on the same bases as in part 1 above. Comment on the differences between your rankings.

11-39 Performance evaluation and behavior   The manager of the Croydan Division of General Goods, Inc. has been evaluating a proposed investment. His analysis indicates that the project will show an internal rate of return of 23% before taxes, well above the 16% required by the firm. He is, however, concerned with the effect that the investment will have on the book rate of return for his division based on beginning-of-year book value—the basis on which his annual bonus is computed. The following are budgeted for his division for the next three years without considering the effects of the proposed investment (in thousands).

	19X1	19X2	19X3
Sales	$2,600	$2,900	$3,500
Costs	1,600	1,650	2,000
Divisional profit	$1,000	$1,250	$1,500
Invested capital (beginning of year)	$4,000	$4,400	$5,000
ROI	25%	28.4%	30%

Data on the proposed project are as follows:

Cost	$600
Revenues (annually for three years)	500
Costs before depreciation (annually for three years)	200

Straight-line depreciation will be used, and a staff member has prepared the following analysis.

	Pro Forma Data		
	19X1	19X2	19X3
Revenues (prior + $500)	$3,100	$3,400	$4,000
Costs (prior + $400)	2,000	2,050	2,400
Divisional profit	$1,100	$1,350	$1,600
Invested capital	$4,600	$4,800	$5,200
ROI	23.9%	28.1%	30.7%

Required

1. Is the investment desirable if the pretax rate of return required is 16%?
2. Is it desirable from the standpoint of the manager of the Croydan Division?
3. If your answers to questions 1 and 2 conflict, can you suggest a reconciliation?

11-40 Transfer pricing   The Westfall Division of Bailey Enterprises makes stereophonic speakers and sells them to other firms for use in complete systems. The division has the capacity to make 45,000 speakers per year and cannot increase its production because of shortages of specialized skilled labor. Data for the division's product are as follows.

Selling price		$80
Variable manufacturing costs	$48	
Variable selling costs	8	56
Contribution margin		$24

The division has just lost a customer and volume is projected at 40,000 speakers per year for the next several years. Another division of Bailey, the Leakes Division, is interested in buying speakers from Westfall and combining them into sets to be sold through retail outlets. Leakes currently buys speakers of somewhat higher quality than those made by Westfall at $84 each. The speakers are of better quality than the rest of the components of the set, so the manager of Leakes intends to reduce prices and predicts higher volume if she changes to the lower-quality speakers. Volume of the set in which the speakers would be used is currently 3,500 per year. If the price were reduced from $680 to $600, volume is expected to be 4,500 units per year. Variable costs are currently $460 per set, including the $168 for two speakers now purchased outside. The Leakes Division would buy 9,000 speakers per year from Westfall and the manager has offered a price of $62 per speaker. Westfall would not incur any variable selling expenses on speakers sold to Leakes.

Required

1. Determine whether it would be in the firm's best interests if Westfall sold speakers to Leakes.
2. At the suggested transfer price, would it be in the interests of each of the managers to have Westfall sell to Leakes?
3. Determine the limits on the transfer price—that is, the highest price that Leakes would be willing to pay and the lowest price that Westfall would accept, assuming that they would not take any action that reduced their division's profits.

11-41 Problems of market-based transfer prices   The Planton Division of Borgan Industries has developed a new electronic measuring system that requires a sophisticated microprocessor. The CLI Division makes such a microprocessor and currently sells it for $200 on the outside market. CLI incurs variable costs of $50 per unit. CLI has a lot of excess capacity: it now sells 30,000 units of the microprocessor per year and could make close to 40,000 units. However, if it tried to increase outside sales to 36,000 units, it would have to reduce its selling price on all units to $160. Accordingly, it has been restricting output.

The manager of Planton received a bid of $200, the current market price, from CLI for the microprocessor and then analyzed data regarding expected volume at different selling prices. He intended to set the price of the measuring system at either $600 or $550. His analysis follows:

	Selling Price	
	$600	$550
Expected variable costs, per unit:		
Materials	$ 90	$ 90
Microprocessor from CLI	200	200
Labor and variable overhead	110	110
Total variable costs	400	400
Contribution margin	$200	$150
Expected volume	5,000 units	6,000 units

Required

1. At the $200 transfer price, what price would the manager of the Planton Division set for the measuring system in order to maximize the division's profits?
2. From the standpoint of the firm, which price for the measuring system would be better, $600 or $550?
3. The manager of CLI Division knows that Planton will buy 5,000 microprocessors at the $200 price. What is the minimum price that he would accept for 6,000 units— the price that would give him the same total contribution margin that he could earn selling 5,000 at $200?
4. Would the transfer price that you calculated in part 3 induce the manager of the Planton Division to try to sell 6,000 units of the measuring system at $550? Assume that the two managers would have to agree on both the transfer price and the quantity to be taken. That is, the alternatives that the manager of Planton Division faces are: (1) buy 5,000 microprocessors at $200; and (2) buy 6,000 at $175.

Cases

11-42 Divisional performance and accounting methods   A divisional manager for McKy Company has been under some criticism for allowing his rate of return to fall in the past two years. He has explained that the division has been making some large investments on which a 30% before-tax rate of return is expected. He complains that the use of straight-line depreciation is hurting his book rate of return, on which his performance is evaluated. Following are comparative income statements and other data for the past three years.

	19X1	19X2	19X3
Sales	$2,200	$2,900	$3,800
Variable costs	1,200	1,500	1,800
Contribution margin	1,000	1,400	2,000
Discretionary costs	300	500	700
Committed costs (largely depreciation)	300	450	700
Total fixed costs	600	950	1,400
Divisional profit	$ 400	$ 450	$ 600
Invested capital			
(principally plant and equipment)	$1,000	$1,600	$2,400
ROI	40%	28%	25%
Capital expenditures	$ 200	$ 900	$1,500

Required

1. Explain how the falling ROI (in the years indicated) may not be indicative of poor performance.
2. What possible solutions are there?

11-43 Capital budgeting and performance evaluation   Arnold Donald, manager of the Western Division of Global Enterprises, Inc., is considering an investment opportunity. He can save $10,000 in cash operating costs per year by using a machine that costs $40,000 and has a 10-year life with no salvage value. Arnold calculates the book rate of return in the first year as 15% [($10,000 − $4,000 depreciation)/$40,000]. He therefore decides that the machine is not a wise investment because his current rate of return in 20% and he is evaluated based on ROI. (His current income is $40,000 and investment is $200,000.)

The seller of the machine offers Arnold the opportunity to lease it at $8,500 per year if Arnold will accept a noncancellable lease for ten years. Arnold asks your advice and specifically requests that you consider the effect of the lease on book ROI. He wonders whether there will be a significant difference between the ROIs under the lease-purchase alternatives.

Arnold further informs you that the firm's minimum desired ROI before taxes is 12%, which approximates cost of capital.

Required: Advise Arnold regarding his choices. Comment on whether the lease or purchase alternative is better from his standpoint and from the firm's.

11-44 National Automobile Company—A; introduction of a new model   National Auto Company consists of four relatively autonomous divisions. In the past each division has concentrated on a relatively limited range of models designed to appeal to a particular segment of the automobile market. The Kalicak Division has been producing midsized cars for many years. They range in price (to dealers) from $4,000 to $5,200.

One day last August, Noel Mack, general manager of the Kalicak Division, was studying some reports prepared by the firm's Market Research Department at central headquarters. Mack had been considering for some time the possibility of bringing out a "stripped-down" version of the division's most popular model, the Panther. He had been hesitant to do so because he feared that sales of the higher-priced Panthers would suffer. The market research indicated, however, that lost sales of higher-priced versions would be negligible if a new Panther were introduced and priced to sell to the customer for about $4,100. The lowest price at retail now charged for a Panther is $4,550.

Mack was pleased at the results of the study and instructed his production manager to determine the costs that would be involved in producing 80,000 units of the new model per year—the number of units that the study indicated could be sold. Mack also asked for information about additional investment in equipment, inventories, and receivables that would be necessitated by the higher volume.

A few days later Mack had the additional information. The production manager estimated the cost per unit to be $3,600, composed of the following basic categories:

Variable costs	$3,000
Fixed costs	600
Total	$3,600

The fixed cost per unit included consideration of $10,000,000 in existing fixed costs that would be reallocated to the new model under a complicated formula used by the division's cost accounting department. The additional investment in equipment would be $80,000,000 and in receivables and inventories about $30,000,000.

Mack was reasonably certain that the information he had gathered was as accurate as estimates are likely to be. He consulted with several large dealers and concluded that the model could be priced at $3,800 to dealers. Any higher price would force the dealers to charge more than $4,100, with a consequent decline in volume below the 80,000 per year target.

Like the other divisional managers, Mack is evaluated based on the residual income earned by his division. The minimum desired return is 18%. Income taxes are ignored in determining residual income for the divisions.

Required: Determine whether the new Panther should be brought out.

11-45   National Automobile Company—B; interaction effects of decisions   While mulling over his decision whether to introduce the new Panther model, Noel Mack was eating lunch with Bob Tibbit, general manager of the Hatfield Division, which specializes in compact and subcompact cars. Mack told Tibbit about the study he had ordered and gave a general picture of the results, including the projection of 80,000 units of volume of the new model.

After lunch, Tibbit called Wallace Richards, the chief of market research for the firm, and requested more information about the study. Richards said that the study indicated a potential decline in volume of 30,000 units of one of the Hatfield Division's best-selling higher-priced models if Kalicak brought out the new lower-priced model. Tibbit asked why that datum had not been included in the report given to Mack and was told that Mack had only asked for estimates in declines in volume of Kalicak Division cars. Tibbit slammed down the telephone and called his production manager and sales manager. He informed them of the situation and demanded that they quickly collect information.

Several days later, the production manager informed Tibbit that the model in question which sold to retail dealers for $3,400 had unit costs of $2,900 at the division's current volume of 160,000 units per year. There were fixed costs of $500 included in the $2,900 figure. Tibbit asked what savings in fixed costs might be expected if volume were to fall by 30,000 units and was told that the fixed cost per unit would rise to about $560, even though some fixed costs could be eliminated.

Further conversations with other managers revealed that the division's investment could be reduced by about $70,000,000 if the drop in volume were experienced.

Tibbit was visibly distressed by what he had heard. He was concerned with his division's interests, but realized that Mack had the right to operate in accordance with his best interests. He pondered the possibility of going to the firm's executive vice president for advice.

Required

1. Determine the effects on the Hatfield Division of the introduction of the new Panther.
2. Determine the effects on the firm of the introduction of the new Panther.

11-46   ROI at Burlington Industries, Inc.[5]   Burlington Industries, Inc. is a very large and widely diversified manufacturer of textiles and associated products. The organization consists of several largely autonomous divisions, the performances of which are evaluated using, among other measures, ROI and dollar profit. Profit measures are before tax

[5]This problem was adapted from material in a paper presented by Mr. Donald R. Hughes, then assistant controller of Burlington Industries, Inc., at a symposium at Ohio State University. The symposium's papers, and discussions of them, are in Thomas J. Burns, ed., *The Behavioral Aspects of Accounting Data for Performance Evaluation* (Columbus, Ohio: College of Administrative Science, Ohio State University, 1970). We acknowledge gratefully the permission of Professor Burns to adapt the material.

but after a special deduction called the Use of Capital Charge (U. O. C. C.). The minimum required ROI for a division is the weighted average of the minimum required ROIs for three different types or classes of assets. The three classes are: (1) accounts receivable less accounts payable; (2) inventories; and (3) fixed assets.

The central managers at Burlington believe that the use of different required ROIs recognizes the different risks involved in the different types of asset investment. Fixed assets, which are committed for relatively long periods of time and lack liquidity, should, in their opinion, earn a higher ROI than assets committed for a shorter time. Receivables, which are turned into cash in a shorter period of time than inventories, would require a lower ROI. The minimum required ROIs for the three classes are 7% for receivables-less-payables, 14% for inventories, and 22% for fixed assets. These minimums are based on estimates of cost of capital and of relative investment in each class of assets for the firm as a whole.

The following data relate to a hypothetical division of Burlington, stated in thousands of dollars.

Sales	$23,450
Cost of sales	16,418
Selling and administrative expense	1,678
Other expenses, not including U.O.C.C.	1,025
Accounts receivable less accounts payable	2,540
Inventories	3,136
Net fixed assets	3,560

Required

1. Prepare an income statement for the hypothetical division. Use the same basis as is used by Burlington.
2. Compute ROI for the division and the weighted-average minimum required ROI.
3. Comment on the method used by Burlington. Does it seem to encourage desirable behavior on the part of managers? Is the use of different minimum ROIs a good idea?

CHAPTER 12

CONTROL AND EVALUATION OF COST CENTERS

In this chapter we continue the discussion of responsibility accounting, with particular emphasis on its application to cost centers. We explain how managers set performance standards, how they use them for performance evaluation, and what problems they encounter in using standards. More specifically, we examine the role of standard costs for planning, with a major emphasis on developing standards for variable costs and interpreting variances from those standards.

PERFORMANCE CONCEPTS

There are two ways of identifying achievement: as effectiveness or as efficiency. *Effectiveness* relates to whether a particular job was done or an objective achieved. *Efficiency* is a more complex concept of performance because it incorporates the cost required to accomplish the task. If you wish to rid your house of mice, an effective way to do so is to burn it down. This method is quite inefficient because it costs you your house. Setting out traps may keep the mice down to a manageable number; it is not totally effective, but is relatively efficient.

It is rare that both total effectiveness and maximum efficiency (least cost) can be attained in the same situation. Most situations required trade-offs that depend on the relative importance of the two measures in the particular case. Suppose a firm receives a rush order for its product. To fill the order within the specified time may require the incurrence of more cost than would be normal for the given quantity (overtime premium, disruption of normal production schedule, etc.). The decision to accept or reject the order would depend on the results of an analysis of incremental revenues and costs such as was shown in Chapter 5. If the analysis indicates that the order should be accepted, efficiency would be to some extent forsaken to achieve effectiveness (filling the order).

In this chapter, our concern is primarily with measures of efficiency. We describe techniques for analyzing how well managers have controlled the *acquisition* and *use* of resources in producing a given quantity of output.

STANDARDS AND STANDARD COSTS

A standard is a norm, a criterion by which performance is judged. One standard for effectiveness might be the production of a specified number of units of product. Comparison of the actual production with the standard would indicate whether the manager had been effective. If efficiency is to be evaluated, the problem is more complex because efficiency is a relationship between input and output.

The *number* of labor hours expected to be used to produce a unit of product is a standard related to input. Similarly, input standards might be set for the quantities of material required (pounds, gallons, etc.) and for the variable overhead needed to produce a unit of output.[1] The *prices* to be paid for labor hours, materials, and variable overhead items are also standards related to input. They are standard *prices* or *rates,* while the quantities of inputs required are standard *quantities.*

It is possible to exercise some control and evaluate performance by examining physical measures only. For example, we could compare the number of labor hours used to produce 1,000 units of product with the number expected to be used (the standard). And we could compare the pounds of material used with the number of pounds we expected to use. However, it is more informative to express standard and actual use in cost terms. How much cost did we incur and does that amount compare favorably or unfavorably with our standards? This approach takes account of the dollar effects of using more or less of an input factor and of paying more or less for the factor than we had planned. While the switch from physical measures to dollars is useful, the distinction in the previous paragraph between quantities and prices is still relevant. That is, the dollars of cost (either actual or standard) are influenced by the two separate factors. Hence, in order to express standards in cost terms, we must have both *standard quantities* and *standard prices.*

---

[1]Note that a standard for fixed overhead per unit of output is not listed. Since total fixed costs are, by definition, unaffected by changes in volume, the fixed cost per unit will necessarily depend on the number of units produced. Hence, an expected fixed cost per unit can serve as a standard only if the volume of production on which it is based is the volume actually achieved. Standards by which to evaluate the performance of managers responsible for fixed costs are discussed later in this chapter.

STANDARD COSTS AND BUDGETS

Before going further, it may be helpful to review some of the ideas developed in preceding chapters and see how those ideas apply here.

Beginning with Chapter 1 we described budgeting as the process of relating required resources (inputs) to planned results (outputs). This relationship was further emphasized in Chapter 6 when we dealt with a manager's responsibility for planning for profit and for the resources required to achieve the firm's profit goals. Based on planned outputs (sales and related production), the firm plans its inputs (related cost levels for the various factors involved in achieving the planned output levels). Thus, selling costs are planned on the basis of expected sales levels, and production costs on the basis of expected production levels. And, because plans do not always coincide with what occurs, we introduced the concept of a **flexible budget allowance,** a budgeted cost allowance that takes into consideration some deviation from expectations (e.g., sales or production levels that do not coincide with expectations). The ability to develop flexible budgets derives from the fact that some costs are variable. Thus, if sales levels are not as expected, a flexible budget allowance can be determined for the actual level of sales achieved. If production is not as expected, an appropriate budget allowance can be determined for the achieved level of production. In either case, the budget allowance is adjusted to recognize achieved *output* (sales or production). We cannot stress too strongly the point that evaluating efficiency requires that we compare actual costs with a flexible budget allowance based on actual output, not on budgeted output. One of the commonest errors in analyzing variances from standard cost is to compare actual costs with the flexible budget allowance based on *budgeted* output.

The relationship between standard costs and budgets is a very direct and simple one. **Standard costs** are per-unit expressions of flexible budget allowances based on output. If it takes two hours of direct labor to finish one unit of product, and if direct laborers are paid $4 per hour, the standard labor cost of one unit of output is $8. Hence, if 1,000 units are actually produced, the flexible budget allowance for labor is $8,000 (1,000 units × $8 standard labor cost per unit). If the per-unit standard cost of labor is added to the per-unit standards for materials and variable overhead, the total standard variable cost for a unit of product can be found.[2] This standard cost can be used in developing the firm's budget and subsequent flexible budget allowances.

Note, however, that for any of the required input factors (for example, labor), two factors determine its total cost: the quantity of that input used (for example, the number of hours worked by laborers); and the cost of a unit of such input (for example, the hourly wage paid to the laborer). Hence, it would be possible to establish a flexible budget allowance that takes into consideration inputs rather than outputs. For example, in the situation described above, the flexible budget allowance for total labor cost if 1,000 units of product were produced would be $8,000 (1,000 units × $8 per unit) based on *output*. On the other hand, if a total of 2,100 hours of labor were used during the period, it would be possible to identify a flexible budget allowance based on *input*. This allowance would be $8,400 ($4 per hour × 2,100 hours worked).

---

[2]Again, since fixed costs do not change as production changes, the notion of a standard fixed cost per unit of product is of doubtful value. Other approaches to controlling fixed costs are discussed later in the chapter. More will be said in Chapter 14 about the treatment of fixed costs in setting standard costs.

In this chapter, we shall use the term *total standard cost* to refer to the flexible budget allowances based on output. As we shall see, however, because the use of separate standards for quantities and prices allows the computation of flexible budget amounts based on inputs, the use of such standards assists in the fixing of responsibility, evaluation of performance, and control of operations.

Illustration of Standard Variable Cost

A manufacturer of wooden packing crates has decided to use standard variable costs to aid in planning and control. After careful study he has determined that if workers are producing at normal efficiency the direct labor time per crate is one-half hour. Also given normal efficiency, 20 feet of lumber should be used per crate. Direct laborers are normally paid $6 per hour, and lumber usually costs $0.10 per foot. Additionally, variable overhead is expected to be incurred at the rate of $2 per direct labor hour. Using these data the standard variable cost of a crate is computed as shown in Exhibit 12-1.

Exhibit 12-1
Standard Variable Costs

Cost Factor	Standard Quantity ×	Standard Price =	Standard Cost
Materials	20 feet	$0.10	$2.00
Direct labor	½ hour	$6.00	3.00
Variable overhead	½ hour	$2.00	1.00
Total standard variable cost per crate			$6.00

In practice, there might be several other materials besides lumber; there also might be several kinds of direct labor at different rates. We use a single material and a single type of direct labor to focus on the general concepts. The same reason prompts our use of a variable overhead approach that is based on hours of direct labor. Measures of activity other than labor hours could be used for determining the variable overhead rate. The selection of a measure of activity to which to relate overhead requires identification, if possible, of the "causal" factor most associated with overhead incurrence (see Chapter 3, pages 62–64). In a highly automated plant, variable overhead might be related more closely to machine-hours than to labor hours. In complex situations, the rate might be based on several factors and determined by the use of multiple regression analysis, as in the appendix to Chapter 3. The important thing is to find some reasonable way to develop an overhead rate that can be translated into a variable overhead per unit of product. For simplicity we use a single figure for variable overhead. There would be a number of costs included in this category, like the variable portions of utilities, supplies, and payroll fringe benefits.

A standard variable cost per unit is a tool a manufacturer can use for planning, control, and performance evaluation. If good, the standards can be used to plan what variable production costs should be for any level of production. When actual production is known, the standard cost per unit can be multiplied by the number of units produced to give the flexible budget allowance for that production level. If the standards used are current and reasonable, actual costs can be compared with expected costs to evaluate performance. As with previous situations where a comparison was made between budgeted and actual costs, the differences are called **variances.** The next section is devoted to the problems of computing and interpreting variances when standard costs are used.

VARIANCES

We shall begin the illustration of variance analysis with direct labor costs. With a single exception, the analysis to be shown here is the same for the other cost factors.

Labor Variances

Suppose that in one month 1,000 crates are made. What *should* the direct labor cost be? The total standard direct labor cost, or flexible budget allowance, for 1,000 crates should be $3,000, computed as follows, from data in Exhibit 12-1.

actual production × (units)	standard hours per unit	=	standard hours allowed	×	standard rate per hour	=	total standard cost
1,000	× ½ hour	=	500 hours	×	$6.00	=	$3,000

The term *standard hours allowed* describes the physical quantity of direct labor that should have been used to produce 1,000 units. We could also have computed the flexible budget allowance for 1,000 crates by simply multiplying the 1,000 crates by the $3.00 standard direct labor cost per crate. The method to be used is largely a matter of convenience.

Suppose now that direct laborers actually worked 480 hours during the month and were paid at a rate of $6.10 per hour. The total actual cost is $2,928 (480 hours × $6.10). Actual costs were $72 less than expected (standard cost of $3,000 − $2,928 actual cost), producing a *total variance* of $72. But why? And who is responsible for the difference?

In some types of performance reporting (as in Chapter 10, for example), there is no distinction made between variances in prices paid and in quantities purchased. However, in a large organization there are managers who do not control both prices and quantities. A foreman is not likely to be responsible for wage rates or material prices but only for the quantities of labor and material used.

Because different managers might control different aspects of cost, we want to isolate the type of variance involved so that we can identify the manager responsible for the variance. Hence, we want to separate the $72 total variance in the example into two components: (1) the difference due to price; and (2) the difference due to quantity. There are several ways to compute the price and quantity variances and many terms are used to describe such variances. Price variances are sometimes called *rate, budget,* or *spending variances.* Quantity variances are sometimes called *use* or *efficiency variances.* The particular term you use is not significant so long as you know which kind of variance is being referred to.

There are two common approaches to separating a total variance into its components. The first to be illustrated deals with the problem from the point of view of total costs. We will hold one of the variable factors constant (either price or quantity), and see what portion of the total variance is due to the effects of the other factor. Note first that the actual total labor cost can be separated as follows:

$$
\begin{array}{ccc}
\text{Actual} & \text{actual rate} & \text{actual cost} \\
\text{input} & \times \quad \text{for input} \quad = & \text{of input} \\
\text{quantity} & \text{factor} & \text{factor} \\
\text{480 hours} & \times \quad \$6.10 \quad = & \$2{,}928
\end{array}
$$

To accomplish our objective we need a flexible budget allowance based on our *input* factor, labor. Such a budget allowance is computed below and is $2,880, which is the standard wage rate times the number of hours actually worked.

$$
\begin{array}{ccc}
\text{Actual} & \text{standard rate} & \text{budget allowance for} \\
\text{input} & \times \quad \text{for input} \quad = & \text{actual quantity} \\
\text{quantity} & \text{factor} & \text{of input factor} \\
\text{480 hours} & \times \quad \$6 \quad = & \$2{,}880
\end{array}
$$

The only difference between the two calculations is the rate being used for the input factor. The input factor, circled in the calculations, is the same for both, 480 hours. Hence, the difference between the actual cost incurred ($2,928) and the flexible budget allowance ($2,880) is due to the difference between the standard wage rate and the actual wage rate. That $48 difference ($2,928 − $2,880) is the **labor rate variance,** and the variance in this case is said to be *unfavorable* because the actual cost is greater than the flexible budget allowance for that quantity of input (480 hours).

The variance due to quantity is calculated in much the same way. To accomplish this we calculate the flexible budget allowance based on the actual *output* (1,000 units) as opposed to the actual input (480 hours). Our objective is to determine what the total costs would be, based on output. Such a budget allowance is computed below to be $3,000.

$$
\begin{array}{ccc}
\text{Standard} & \text{standard rate} & \text{budget allowance} \\
\text{input} & \times \quad \text{for input} \quad = & \text{for actual} \\
\text{quantity} & \text{factor} & \text{quantity of output} \\
\text{1,000 units} & & \\
\times \ \tfrac{1}{2} \text{ hour per} & & \\
\text{unit} = 500 \text{ hours} & \times \quad \$6 \quad = & \$3{,}000
\end{array}
$$

Compare this formulation with the one immediately preceding it, where a budget allowance was computed for the actual quantity of the input factor, labor hours. Note that both calculations utilize the standard rate for the input factor, boxed in the calculations. The only difference between the two calculations is related to the quantity of input, labor hours. Hence, the $120 difference between the two calculated total costs ($3,000 − $2,880) is due to the difference in the quantity of labor used. This difference is called the **labor efficiency variance** and in this situation is *favorable* because workers worked fewer than the 500 standard hours allowed for 1,000 units of output. The rela-

Exhibit 12-2

Labor Variances

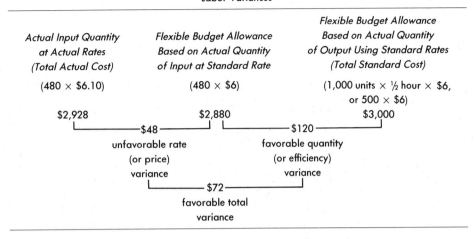

Actual Input Quantity at Actual Rates (Total Actual Cost)	Flexible Budget Allowance Based on Actual Quantity of Input at Standard Rate	Flexible Budget Allowance Based on Actual Quantity of Output Using Standard Rates (Total Standard Cost)
(480 × $6.10)	(480 × $6)	(1,000 units × ½ hour × $6, or 500 × $6)
$2,928	$2,880	$3,000

———$48———
unfavorable rate
(or price)
variance

———$120———
favorable quantity
(or efficiency)
variance

———$72———
favorable total
variance

tionships just described are diagramed in Exhibit 12-2. Our analysis shows that the total variance of $72 can be explained as follows:

Labor rate variance	$ 48 unfavorable
Labor efficiency variance	120 favorable
Total labor variance	$ 72 favorable

There is an important point to be observed in Exhibit 12-2. As you move from left to right, the cost figures could be said to become more "standard." The leftmost figure is actual cost, the next is actual quantity multiplied by the standard rate, and finally, the standard quantity multiplied by the standard rate. Thus, if the number to the left in any pair is larger than the one to the right, the variance is unfavorable. If the number to the right is larger than the one to the left, the variance is favorable.

Alternative Computation Methods

We can also isolate variances by dealing directly with the differences between the standard and actual figures for rate and quantity. For example, the labor rate variance could be computed as follows:

$$\frac{\text{Labor rate}}{\text{variance}} = \frac{\text{actual}}{\text{hours}} \times \left(\frac{\text{standard}}{\text{rate}} - \frac{\text{actual}}{\text{rate}} \right)$$

$$-\$48 \quad = \quad 480 \quad \times \quad (\$6 - \$6.10)$$

Direct laborers were paid $0.10 per hour more than standard (an unfavorable occurrence), and earned this amount over 480 hours.

The same approach could be used to calculate the labor efficiency variance.

$$\begin{array}{c}\text{Labor} \\ \text{efficiency} \\ \text{variance}\end{array} = \begin{array}{c}\text{standard} \\ \text{rate}\end{array} \times \left(\begin{array}{c}\text{standard} \\ \text{hours}\end{array} - \begin{array}{c}\text{actual} \\ \text{hours}\end{array}\right)$$

$$\$120 \quad = \quad \$6 \quad \times (500 \text{ hours} - 480 \text{ hours})$$

The firm worked 20 hours fewer than the standard hours required to produce 1,000 units (a favorable occurrence).

When the number inside the parentheses (using these alternative formulations) is negative, as in the rate variance, the variance is unfavorable. When the number inside the parentheses is positive, as in the efficiency variance, the variance is favorable.

You may use either or both methods. The difficulty with the alternative method is that sometimes the actual rate may be a number with several digits after a decimal point. Suppose that workers were paid $2,920 for 480 hours of work. The actual average rate would be $6.083333. . . . You would then have a slight difference between the rate variance computed this way and that computed under the method described earlier. Taking the standard rate multiplied by actual quantity and subtracting this from actual total cost (or vice versa, depending on which is larger) will always yield a precise answer.

In some cases one method might be simpler than the other; fewer computations might be required. If you were told that 6,000 hours were worked by direct laborers at a wage rate $0.20 less than the standard rate, you could determine that the labor rate variance was $1,200 favorable ($0.20 × 6,000), even though you knew neither the total actual cost nor the budgeted amount based on 6,000 hours.

Variable Overhead Variances

We have used labor variances to illustrate the computational procedures. We could as easily have used variable overhead. The computations are the same, extending to the use of direct labor hours if variable overhead is budgeted according to labor hours (as they are in our example).

Assume that variable overhead costs incurred during the month are $980. What are the variable overhead variances? Total standard variable overhead cost for 1,000 units of output is $1,000 ($1 standard cost per crate × 1,000 crates, or 500 standard direct labor hours at $2 standard rate per hour; refer to Exhibit 12-1). Hence, we know that the total variance is $20 favorable (actual cost of $980 compared with a standard of $1,000).

Exhibit 12-3 shows that actual direct labor hours are used to determine the middle term (the flexible budget based on actual quantity of input), and that standard labor hours are used to determine the right-hand term. (The right-hand term is also given by $1 standard variable overhead per unit × 1,000 units.) The rate variance, which is usually called the **overhead spending variance,** is calculated in the same way as the labor rate variance. The quantity variance is usually called the **overhead efficiency variance.** It is calculated using the standard variable overhead rate and the actual and standard direct labor hours.

It is possible to compute the spending variance using the alternative calculation

Exhibit 12-3
Variable Overhead Variance

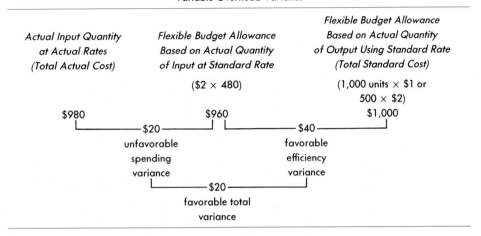

method described earlier. However, because we were given only total overhead incurred, we must divide the total cost of $980 by the actual hours of 480 to determine the actual rate at which the variable overhead was incurred. That rate is about $2.0416 ($980/480). The format of the calculation would be the same as for the computation of the direct labor variance.

$$\frac{\text{Spending}}{\text{variance}} = 480 \times (\$2.00 - \$2.0416) = -\$19.97$$

The variance, $19.97, would be rounded up to $20, the spending variance computed in Exhibit 12-3.

The variable overhead efficiency variance can also be calculated using the standard rate per direct labor hour of $2 and the difference between the actual and standard hours.

$$\frac{\text{Efficiency}}{\text{variance}} = \$2 \times (500 - 480) = \$40$$

The efficiency variance computed in this manner is the same as that shown in Exhibit 12-3.

As long as variable overhead standards are based on direct labor hours, the only difference in calculating labor and overhead variances is in the rates (prices); that is, actual and standard direct labor hours are used both for labor and overhead. Hence, the variable overhead efficiency variance will always go in the same direction as the labor quantity variance.[3]

This relationship is not surprising. In fact, the variable overhead efficiency variance is probably the result of using more or less labor than standard. Consider some of the costs that might be included in variable overhead. There might be payroll taxes, pensions and other fringe benefits, and many other costs that will be incurred whenever

[3]In addition, the two variances will bear the same ratio as the ratios of their respective standard rates; if the variable overhead rate is one-half of the direct labor rate, the variable overhead efficiency variance will be one-half of the labor quantity variance.

employees work and regardless of whether the employees work efficiently or ineffi-
ciently. If the employee puts in an hour, the other costs will follow. Hence, if there are
inefficient labor hours (an unfavorable labor efficiency variance), there will be an
unfavorable variable overhead variance, and vice versa. As long as variable overhead is,
in fact, related to labor hours, as so many overhead elements certainly are, overhead
efficiency variances do not indicate efficient (or inefficient) "use" of variable overhead
so much as efficient (or inefficient) use of direct labor.

Of course, some elements of variable overhead may be related directly to the
number of units produced, rather than to the number of labor hours worked. For example, costs like packaging materials (boxes, padding, lining) are likely to be related to
units produced. The workers who pack the products should use standard quantities of
these materials for each packaged product even if they work more or less efficiently
than standard (take more or less time to package the product). If variable overhead
contains significant amounts of cost elements of this type, the conventional calculations
of variable overhead efficiency *and* budget variances may not be appropriate for analysis and may give rise to interpretation problems.

Let us look at an example. The machining department of a large firm requires
two direct labor hours per unit of product. The department uses cutting tools with a
standard cost of $1.50 each and that must generally be replaced after (have a standard
life of) 20 hours of use. If the standard for cutting tools is based on labor hours, the
standard would be $0.15 per unit of product, computed as follows:

$$\frac{\text{Life of tool (in hours)}}{\text{Labor hours per unit}} = \frac{20}{2} = 10 \text{ units per tool}$$

$$\frac{\text{Cost per tool}}{\text{Units per tool}} = \frac{\$1.50}{10} = \$0.15 \text{ per unit}$$

Suppose now that the department showed the following results for a recent
month when cutting tools were purchased at the standard price.

Units produced	10,000
Direct labor hours worked	20,000
Cutting tools used	1,200

The calculation of overhead variances in the conventional fashion is given below.

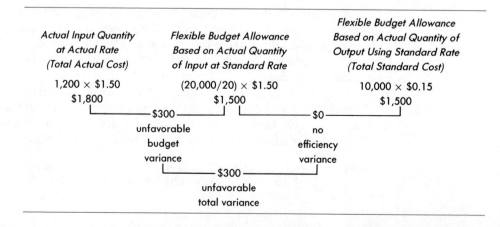

Actual Input Quantity at Actual Rate (Total Actual Cost)	Flexible Budget Allowance Based on Actual Quantity of Input at Standard Rate	Flexible Budget Allowance Based on Actual Quantity of Output Using Standard Rate (Total Standard Cost)
1,200 × $1.50 $1,800	(20,000/20) × $1.50 $1,500	10,000 × $0.15 $1,500

$300 unfavorable budget variance

$0 no efficiency variance

$300 unfavorable total variance

Does the analysis reflect the facts as we know them? No. The budget variance is not caused by paying a price different from the $1.50 standard. It arises because workers used 200 more tools than the standard quantity for the number of hours worked and the quantity of output. The budget variance for this overhead item is actually an efficiency variance, because it results from the inefficient use of the input factor (the cutting tools) by the laborers.

In a practical situation, the analyses of variable overhead variances would include the computation of variances for each cost element classified as variable overhead. And, when there are significant costs of the type just described—ones related to units of output rather than strictly to direct labor hours, it would be wise to analyze these costs separately, in a fashion similar to the analysis of materials variances, which we cover in the next section.

Materials Variances

The material price variance is slightly different from its counterparts in labor and variable overhead. Material, unlike labor, can be stored. What is purchased in one period is not necessarily used in that period. Consequently, the **material price variance** is calculated based on the quantity of material *purchased,* not the quantity *used.* The **material use variance** is calculated the same way as the labor and overhead efficiency variances.

Suppose that the firm bought 23,000 feet of lumber and paid $2,390 for it. The average price paid was about $0.1039. The standard price per foot of lumber is $0.10, as in Exhibit 12-1. In calculating the material price variance, the flexible budget allowance must be based on what you would expect to pay for the quantity *purchased.* This would be $2,300 (23,000 feet × $0.10 per foot). The material price variance is diagramed in Exhibit 12-4.

Exhibit 12-4
Material Price Variance

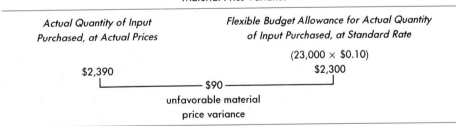

Actual Quantity of Input Purchased, at Actual Prices	Flexible Budget Allowance for Actual Quantity of Input Purchased, at Standard Rate
	(23,000 × $0.10)
$2,390	$2,300

└─────────── $90 ───────────┘
unfavorable material
price variance

Because the purchasing manager's function relates to purchasing, not using materials, the material price variance should be based on the amounts purchased during a period and not on the amounts used. If we use the alternative formula, we must remember to use the actual quantity purchased, as follows:

$$\begin{matrix} \text{Material} \\ \text{price} \\ \text{variance} \end{matrix} = \begin{matrix} \text{actual} \\ \text{quantity} \\ \text{purchased} \end{matrix} \times \left(\begin{matrix} \text{standard} \\ \text{price} \end{matrix} - \begin{matrix} \text{actual} \\ \text{price} \end{matrix} \right)$$

$$-\$89.70 = 23,000 \times (\$0.10 - \$0.1039)$$

The calculated amount, $89.70, is different from the $90 shown in Exhibit 12-4 because of rounding the calculation of the actual price paid per foot.

The material use variance is calculated in the same way as the direct labor and variable overhead efficiency variances. Assume that the firm used 19,500 feet of lumber to make the 1,000 crates. The standard quantity of lumber per crate is 20 feet (Exhibit 12-1), so the total standard quantity for 1,000 crates is 20,000 feet. The standard cost of lumber for 1,000 crates would be $2,000 (which is 20,000 feet at $0.10 per foot, or 1,000 crates multiplied by the standard material cost per crate of $2, as shown in Exhibit 12-1). The material use variance is diagrammed in Exhibit 12-5.

Exhibit 12-5
Material Use Variance

Flexible Budget Allowance for Actual Quantity of Input Used, at Standard Rate	Flexible Budget Allowance Based on Actual Quantity of Output, Using Standard Rates
19,500 × $0.10	(20,000 × $0.10 or 1,000 × $2)
$1,950	$2,000

$50
favorable
material use
variance

Alternatively, we could calculate the material use variance by using the following formula:

$$\begin{array}{ccc} \text{Material} \\ \text{use} \\ \text{variance} \end{array} = \begin{array}{c} \text{standard} \\ \text{price} \end{array} \times \left(\begin{array}{c} \text{standard} \\ \text{quantity} \\ \text{for output} \\ \text{achieved} \end{array} - \begin{array}{c} \text{} \\ \text{actual} \\ \text{quantity} \end{array} \right)$$

$$\$50 \quad = \quad \$0.10 \quad \times \quad (20,000 \quad - \quad 19,500)$$

Interaction Effects

Strictly speaking, the methods illustrated do not correctly show the effects on performance due to price differences alone. The price variances are computed using actual quantities. Hence, the managers responsible for the acquisition of resources (materials, labor, overhead) are being assigned responsibility for some of the efficiency or inefficiency of the managers who control the use of resources.

In the example on page 457 standard direct labor hours for 1,000 crates are 500, actual hours 480, and there is a $0.10 per hour unfavorable wage rate variance. The rate variance is $48 ($0.10 × 480). It can be argued that the manager responsible for wage rates should be charged with a $50 variance ($0.10 × 500 standard hours). A person in that position cannot control hours worked and it is unfair to give him or her credit for the efficient use of workers' time. The manager is responsible for the $0.10 per hour excessive cost incurred for labor.

The $2 difference between $48 and $50 is due to interaction of rate and efficiency and is not properly chargeable to either manager. It is a joint variance. The variance due to use of labor is assigned correctly to the manager of resource use; the efficiency variance is calculated based on the standard wage rate. In the earlier computations with this example on page 458, the effects of interaction were assigned to the manager responsible for acquiring labor even though some of the variance was caused by variances from standard hours. In practice, the interaction effect is not likely to be large; it is often ignored and is included in the rate variance.

VARIANCES AND PERFORMANCE EVALUATION

Isolating a variance is but the first step toward providing information that might be useful for performance evaluation. As pointed out in Chapter 10, the factors relevant to evaluating the performance of an individual manager are those that the manager is responsible for and that the manager can control. Quantifying the effects of price and quantity differences is not the same thing as identifying the *causes* of, and the responsibility for, the differences. Knowing that workers were paid more or less than the standard rate, or worked more or less than the standard hours, does not explain *why* these variances from standard occurred.

Two issues complicate the interpretation of variances for the purpose of performance measurement. First, nonstandard performance is of concern only if the standards are appropriate. That is, the standards must be up to date, reflecting current work methods and current wage rates. Consider, for example, an unfavorable labor rate variance. If a modification in the production process, with the full approval of top-level management, necessitated the use of more highly paid laborers for a particular task, the variance is the result of a failure to change the standard, not the work-assignment decisions of the manager who supervises the task. Similarly, if the standard does not include a wage increase negotiated in the most recent union contract, the standard, not the managers that control work assignments, is responsible.

The second issue that clouds the interpretation of variances is that variances are not independent of one another. That is, a variance of one type may be directly related to a variance of another type, either in the same or a different department. (We confronted a somewhat similar situation in Chapter 10, where the use of a particular transfer-pricing scheme could result in the actions of one manager affecting the reported performance of another.) For example, suppose that the purchasing manager buys lower-quality materials that cause increases in labor time. Unfavorable labor and variable overhead efficiency variances in processing departments are traceable to, and should be considered with, any favorable materials price variance from the purchase of the materials. (Note that an unfavorable material use variance might also occur in such a situation.)

Thus, knowing that there was a variance with respect to some element of cost (material, labor or overhead) is not the same as knowing why the variance occurred or which manager is responsible for it. For an identified variance to be of maximum usefulness for performance evaluation, there must be an investigation to determine the cause of the variance.

INVESTIGATION OF VARIANCES

When standards are used and there are variances, managers must decide whether: (1) the amount of the variance is sufficient to warrant investigation; (2) there is a reasonable probability that finding the cause of the variance will lead to corrective action (some variances might not be correctable); and (3) the cost of investigating the cause of the variance and correcting the problem will be less than the cost of a recurrence of the variance. As a general rule, a variance should be investigated if the inquiry is expected to lead to corrective action that will reduce costs by an amount greater than the cost of the inquiry.

Managers will usually want to investigate only significant variances. Two criteria are generally used to evaluate significance: absolute size and percentage of standard cost. A variance of $5 is almost certainly not worth investigating, whereas a variance of $100 may or may not be. If the total cost incurred is $500 and standard cost is $400, the $100 variance is 25% of standard. This large a percentage variance may well be worth investigating, whereas a $100 variance with standard cost of $85,000 may not. Thus, absolute size of a variance is probably less important than its percentage of standard cost.

The cost of investigating variances is difficult to determine. If there are personnel whose job it is to make these investigations, there is not likely to be additional cost because their salaries must be paid in any event. However, with a fixed amount of time to spend on various tasks, it is wise to concentrate on variances that are likely to be correctable and the correction of which may be expected to yield large savings.

Companies sometimes use **control charts** to decide when a particular variance should be investigated. These charts usually show the cost behavior patterns in the past so that efforts will not be wasted investigating costs that normally show wide fluctuations. A control chart is shown in Figure 12-1.

The dots, representing actual costs incurred, are scattered widely. The dotted lines represent the limits within which costs are not investigated. The lines could be set closer to or further away from the flexible budget allowance. The closer the limits, the more variances would be investigated, and vice versa. The wide scattering of costs suggests frequent variances. If the manager believes that the production process is under adequate control and that the variances are unavoidable, wide limits would be set. If the manager thought that the variances were caused by factors that could be corrected, the process would be investigated and perhaps narrow limits would be set. There are

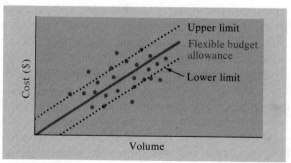

FIGURE 12-1   *Sample Control Chart*

many sophisticated ways of developing control charts; you are likely to study some of these in statistics courses.

One fact that should *not* be important in a decision about whether or not to investigate a variance is whether that variance is favorable or unfavorable. That is, a manager should avoid a tendency to believe that favorable variances can be left uninvestigated because they indicate that things are going better than expected and should not be tampered with. As we pointed out in the previous section, variances are not independent, so that a favorable variance in one responsibility area might have unfavorable effects on another segment of the firm. Moreover, favorable variances can be caused by actions that could harm the firm in the long run. For example, favorable variances in material prices or labor efficiency could indicate a lessened concern for the quality of the finished product. Sooner or later customers will see the reduced quality, and the reputation and subsequent sales of the firm will be hurt. In the short run, profits might increase because of lower costs (favorable variances); but long-run profits may suffer.

Because, as we suggested early in the chapter, standards can be useful for planning purposes, one of the most important reasons for investigating variances is simply to detect bad standards. We gave examples in the previous section of variances that could occur because of out-of-date standards. Variances could also result if standards are set at levels that are either too tight or too loose to begin with. If standards are to be used for planning and decision making, they must reflect current information about attainable performance.

Consider, for example, a company that makes several products, has limited productive capacity, and wishes to choose the most profitable mix of those products. As we saw in Chapter 4, a decision about product mix requires knowledge of the contribution margins of each product, and this knowledge depends upon knowing the variable costs of producing each product. If the standard variable cost does not approximate the actual variable cost, decisions could be made that would lead to less than optimum profits because of inaccurate information about the contribution margins from particular products.

SETTING OF STANDARDS—
A BEHAVIORAL PROBLEM

There are several ways to estimate standards for prices and quantities needed to produce a product. The most common are engineering methods and managerial estimates based on experience and knowledge of the production process. These methods are most relevant to determining quantity standards.

Engineering Methods

Some companies develop standard quantities for materials and labor by carefully examining production methods and determining how much of an input factor is necessary to obtain a finished unit. In time-and-motion studies, which are often used to set labor quantity standards, an industrial engineer breaks down the movements necessary to perform each task into smaller units. For example, a worker may have to reach into a bin, pick up a part, place it on his or her bench, drill two holes in specified places, then place the part into another bin. Each individual movement is timed. The total time required to perform the entire task becomes the standard time allowed. Similarly with materials, industrial engineers study the form and shape of raw materials and the cutting and trimming required, and determine how much material will be required per unit. (Such determinations consider the material wasted through cutting, trimming, and perhaps spoilage of partly finished units.)

Engineering methods may also be used to set standards for some overhead items, such as maintenance. The industrial engineer will try to identify the necessary components of a desirable maintenance program (much the same as automobile owners do when they set up a schedule for changing oil, tuning the engine, and replacing parts) and estimate the costs of each component. A standard is then established that allows for specified maintenance expense per machine-hour used, with an allowance for other maintenance that occurs because parts break or wear out before they are replaced.

Although some overhead items can be analyzed using engineering methods, it is usually difficult to analyze overhead by starting with a unit of product. Unlike materials and labor, most of overhead is not directly related to single units of product. It is more likely that large amounts of overhead are related to large quantities of product or labor hours. (Consider the difficulty of trying to determine the cost per labor hour of the wages of materials handlers—men who take partly finished units of product from one work station to another. Only some broad average based on sizable quantities of production can be used to estimate variable cost of materials handling per direct labor hour.) For this reason, standards for variable overhead are more often developed using methods that are illustrated in Chapter 3: high-low, scatter diagram, and regression analysis.

Managerial Estimates

Some firms rely on the judgment of managers to determine quantities of input needed to produce a unit of product. This method has several advantages: (1) line managers who are setting the standards are the ones responsible for achieving the standards, and should participate in their setting; (2) line managers may bring the workers into the process of setting standards, thereby extending participation down to still another level; (3) line managers may resent staff persons (industrial engineers) intruding into their areas of responsibility.

What Standard—Ideal, Attainable, or Historical?

What level of performance ought to be considered in developing a standard? Should the standard be based on what can be done under the best possible conditions? Should it include allowances for waste, fatigue, recurring breakdowns, and bottlenecks, that is, currently attainable performance? Should it be based on past performance, an historical measure?

An **ideal standard** is one that could be attained only under *perfect* conditions. It assumes that laborers continuously work at the peak of their abilities; that materials always arrive at work stations on time; that tools never break; that maintenance on machines never stops production; that no one makes mistakes. In short, an ideal standard is one that is not likely to be achieved under anything like normal working conditions.

Currently attainable performance as a standard is based on expectations about efficiency under *normal* working conditions. Such a standard makes allowances for unavoidable losses of efficiency due to recurring problems that can never be eliminated. But currently attainable standards are not lax. Performance requirements may be high, but are attainable if everything goes reasonably well.

Historical standards must obviously be based on experience. The use of historical performance as a standard has serious drawbacks. Past inefficiencies will be perpetuated as they become built into the standard. Changes in product design and work methods that drastically affect labor and material requirements may be ignored. Historical achievements have no particular significance *except as they may aid in predicting the future.* (Compare this reservation with those expressed earlier—particularly in Chapters 6, 7, and 11—about the usefulness of historical information for predicting the future.)

Ideal standards are sometimes argued to be the best because the resulting variances alert managers to deviations from the ideal and motivate workers to the best possible job. It is questionable whether ideal standards really do assist managers in these ways. There is some evidence from the behavioral sciences that motivation is not increased but actually reduced by the use of ideal standards. Being unattainable goals, ideal standards may foster discouragement, lack of commitment to the goal, and distrust of higher levels of management. Frustrated managers and workers may choose to ignore a standard they know to be unattainable. Variances using an ideal standard will always be unfavorable, so the managers have no idea whether their (and the workers') performances are satisfactory based on some reasonable goals.

Research in the behavioral sciences indicates that managers and workers respond well to standards as goals when there has been participation in setting the standards and when the standards are attainable. Such standards may also be used for planning, whereas ideal standards may not. A management that uses ideal standards must still make adjustments in order to *plan* accurately for expenses, pro forma financial statements, and cash flows.

Additionally, currently attainable standard costs are of more value than ideal standard costs for decision-making purposes. Acceptance of special orders, price reductions or increases, promotional campaigns, and other special decisions must be based on *expected* variable costs, not those that could be obtained only under ideal conditions, nor on historical costs that may be outmoded.

Revising Standards

We have already noted that faulty standards create problems as a manager attempts to understand variances. When should standards be revised? How often should standards be reviewed? Should we incorporate variances into the planning process or assume that standards will be met? Some accountants favor revising standards at frequent intervals because the standards will then more closely reflect currently attainable performance and will therefore be better for planning. Others advocate less frequent revision because, they say, standards lose their meaning if continually revised; standards will come to represent expected actual results with inefficiencies built in.

The middle position is the most popular. Standards should be revised when the conditions that prevailed when they were set are no longer present *and* are not expected to return in the foreseeable future. Wage increases negotiated in connection with a new union contract, price increases agreed upon with regular suppliers, and changes in work methods would justify changing standards. Several periods of above- or below-standard performance would justify changing standards only if such performance reflected changed conditions. Thus, managers would not have their standard performance levels reduced simply because they could not meet the higher levels established earlier.

STANDARD COSTS AND PERFORMANCE REPORTS

Just as with flexible budgets, standard costs can serve as bases for performance reporting. A flexible budget prepared on the basis of units produced, rather than hours worked, is the standard cost allowance for performance reporting. The basic concept underlying performance reporting is to report by responsibility. A manager should have the information needed to exercise control over operations and should be held responsible only for those costs that he or she can control.

VARIANCES AND COST CENTERS

Lower-level managers usually manage cost centers and so receive reports that show only costs. Exhibit 12-6 illustrates a performance report for a cost center. In the illustration, the number of units produced is less than the number budgeted, which difference could indicate that the manager was ineffective because he or she failed to meet the production goal. But failure to meet the production goal could have been caused by a problem in a department that had previously worked on the product, in which case *this* manager cannot be held responsible for the shortfall in production. If the production shortfall is the fault of this manager, shortfalls will appear in those departments, if any, that work on the product after this manager's department. In any case, the cause of the production shortfall must be determined before the performance of this manager can be evaluated.

Note that the actual costs reported to the manager on the sample report have already been adjusted to eliminate price variances. That is, the amounts in the *Actual* column for controllable costs are actual quantities of material, labor, and supplies multiplied by standard prices. This approach would be taken when the manager has no control over the prices paid for the factors used, only over the quantities used of each factor. If the department's manager could select personnel to assign to specific tasks, the labor rate variance might also appear on the performance report.

Exhibit 12-6
Departmental Performance Report

Month of May 19X7

Department ___Machining___   Manager ___R. Jones___
Date Delivered ___6/4___   Date Returned ___6/6___

	Budgeted	Actual	Variance
Production, in units (original budget 11,000 units)		9,000	2,000
Controllable costs, for actual production of 9,000 units:			
Materials, standard of $2	$18,000	$18,800	$800U ∗
Labor, standard of $3	27,000	28,800	1,800U ∗
Supplies, standard of $0.10	900	880	20F
Repairs	$1,100	$1,200	$100U
Power	900	900	0
Total controllable	$47,900	$50,580	$2,680U
Noncontrollable costs:			
Depreciation Machinery used in department	$1,500	$1,500	0
Heat and light (allocated)	200	220	20U
Other allocated costs	800	860	60U
Total noncontrollable	$2,500	$2,580	$80U

Comments and Explanations ∗ *Faulty materials required more time and created more waste.*

Because, as we noted earlier, the performance in one department could affect that in another, performance reports usually contain "Comment" sections that can be used to provide explanations of variances. The department manager can then concentrate on those variances that need explanation and, if the cause of the variance is in that department, comment on the prospects for improvement.

The sample performance report shows some noncontrollable costs clearly labeled as such and shown separately. Although sample reports in Chapter 10 did not include such costs, it is common for noncontrollable costs to be included in performance reports so that, as we noted in Chapter 11, the manager is kept aware that such costs exist.

In general, variable costs are controllable whereas many fixed costs are not, at least over short periods of time. Allocated costs are rarely controllable by the department to which they are allocated. Thus, the depreciation on machinery used in the machining department is separable with respect to the department, but not controllable in the short run. The allocated costs are neither controllable nor separable with respect to this department.

VARIANCES AND INCOME STATEMENTS

Higher-level managers, typically managers of profit or investment centers, receive performance reports that show both revenues and expenses—that is, they receive some type of income statement. A manager responsible for both revenues and costs is concerned with variances related to both aspects of profit. The sample income statement in Exhibit 12-7 is one of the possible formats that such a statement might use for reporting variances.

Exhibit 12-7
Sample Income Statement (Thousands of Dollars)

Sales		$14,345
Standard variable cost of sales		11,112
Standard variable manufacturing margin		3,233
Variances:		
Materials	$ 89U	
Direct labor	109U	
Variable overhead	6F	
Total		192U
Actual variable manufacturing margin		3,041
Variable selling and administrative expenses		871
Contribution margin		2,170
Fixed costs:		
Budgeted fixed manufacturing costs	1,045	
Budget variance—fixed manufacturing costs	15U	
Selling and administrative expenses	554	
Total fixed costs		1,614
Income		$ 556

Note that the sample report does not show price and use (efficiency) variances separately. This particular income statement is a summary report and would be supported by one or more schedules showing the details of the variances. The number of supporting schedules, and the details on them, would depend on the level of the manager receiving the report. The higher the level, the less supporting detail. The general manager of a large division of a large company does not need to know about labor variances by cost center, only by plant.

Unlike the typical income statement that would be presented to a manager who is responsible for both costs and revenues, the statement in the exhibit does not show, except with respect to fixed manufacturing costs, budgeted costs, and variances as well as actual amounts. We omitted these items in order to draw your attention to the basic format for reporting variances. We did, however, include a budget variance relating to the fixed costs, since such variances can occur and are, as shown in the next section, identified for reporting purposes and analyzed for possible managerial action.

One point that may not be obvious from the sample income statement is the difference in the quantity measure used for cost of sales and for the calculation of variances. Obviously, the standard variable cost of sales is based on the number of units sold. On the other hand, variances are computed, as you know, on the basis of the number of units produced. We shall see more income statements of this type in Chapter 14.

CONTROL OF FIXED COSTS

We know from earlier discussions that total cost per unit of product will change with a change in production because there is a fixed component in the total cost. For product costing purposes, discussed in Chapter 14, a standard fixed cost per unit is sometimes computed. But for *control* purposes, the notion of a standard total fixed cost per unit has little meaning. It is the total cost incurred for each element of fixed overhead that is relevant.

Fixed overhead is made up of several components, such as depreciation, property taxes, supervisory and managerial salaries, and the computed fixed component of mixed costs, such as maintenance and power. Each item is budgeted separately for the departments in which they are controllable. The budgeted amount for each element of cost is the standard.

There are, in practice, two variances computed for fixed costs, one of which is described in Chapters 13 and 14. For the current purpose, the question of cost control, only the budget variance requires comment.

Budget Variances

The **fixed overhead budget variance** is the difference between the fixed cost budgeted and incurred for a particular element of cost for a particular department. Budget variances may occur for many reasons. There may have been changes in the prices for resources (a raise in salaries, an increase in property taxes as a result of a change in rates); some discretionary costs, such as employee training or travel, might have been increased or decreased by managerial action; and quantities of resources used might have been greater or less than budgeted, as when more or fewer janitors were hired than were budgeted.

The major considerations in analyzing budget variances related to fixed costs are behavioral. A manager who is worried about exceeding his or her budget may have a tendency to postpone incurring discretionary costs (such as employee training). On the other hand, when a manager fears that being below budget will lead to a budget cut for the next period, unnecessary costs may be incurred.

A manager can manipulate some discretionary costs to achieve a low total budget variance (total fixed costs incurred less total fixed costs budgeted). If attention is focused only on the totals, critical problems can be obscured. The manager who scrimps on employee training or maintenance is improving short-run performance to the detriment of the long run. This type of undesirable action might escape notice if only the totals were considered.

There are different philosophies about the budgeting of fixed costs. There are advocates of tight budgets, loose budgets, and budgets based on currently attainable performance levels. Our preference is for the use of currently attainable budgets, with the persons whose budgets are being set participating in the determination of what is currently attainable. Likewise, the methods used in setting standard variable costs—historical analysis, engineering methods, and managerial judgment—can also be applied to the budgeting of fixed costs.

Fixed Costs on Performance Reports

The performance report shown in Exhibit 12-6 does not distinguish between controllable variable costs and controllable fixed costs. Whereas materials and direct labor can be expected to be variable, the other controllable items could be variable, fixed, or mixed. It is simple to revise such a report to show the fixed and variable components of controllable costs. A revised form of the report appears in Exhibit 12-8.

This report differs from Exhibit 12-6 in only one respect: it shows separately the fixed and variable components of controllable costs. For planning, the manager would want to know whether a variance already experienced is likely to recur. It may be easier to plan for future variances if the fixed and variable controllable costs are separated. If a fixed cost appears to be running $1,000 per month more or less than budgeted, and this variance is expected to continue, the manager can count on the variance being $1,000 per month. A direct labor efficiency variance that appears to be 10% of standard cost will be a different dollar amount in each month depending on production. Thus, planning for future operations requires different analyses for the two kinds of costs—fixed and variable.

A PROBLEM AREA: SEPARATING FIXED AND VARIABLE COSTS

In some situations the firm may not be able to isolate the variable overhead variances and the fixed overhead budget variances. This will occur when, as is often the case, it is impossible to determine how much of the *actual* overhead costs incurred is fixed and

Exhibit 12-8

Departmental Performance Report

Month of May 19X7

Department ___Machining___   Manager ___R. Jones___

Date Delivered ___6/4___   ˙Date Returned ___6/6___

	Budgeted	Actual	Variance
Production, in units (original budget 11,000 units)		9,000	2,000
Controllable costs, for actual production of 9,000 units:			
Variable:			
Materials, standard of ___$2___	$18,000	$18,800	$800U *
Labor, standard of ___$3___	27,000	28,800	1,800U *
Supplies, standard of ___$0.10___	900	880	20F
Total variable	$45,900	$48,480	$2,580U
Fixed: Repairs	$1,100	$1,200	$100U
Power	900	900	0
Total fixed	$2,000	$2,100	$100U
Total controllable	$47,900	$50,580	$2,680U
Noncontrollable costs:			
Depreciation Machinery used in department	$1,500	$1,500	0
Heat and light (allocated)	200	220	20U
Other allocated costs	800	860	60U
Total noncontrollable	$2,500	$2,580	$80U

Comments and Explanations *Faulty materials required more time and created more waste.

how much is variable. Some overhead costs will be mixed, having both a fixed component and a variable component. For example, a cost like electricity might have both fixed and variable components. For budgeting and planning, the fixed and variable components might be easy to identify by using the scatter-diagram or high-low method. And the calculated values might be quite accurate in predicting the total cost that will be incurred at a specified level of activity.

Suppose that electricity is budgeted per month using the following formula: total cost = $2,450 + ($0.80 × direct labor hours). The fixed portion is related to lighting that is not turned off when the product is not being produced. The variable portion relates to machinery that is operated only when products are being produced. Let us assume that the standard and actual cost per kilowatt hour is $0.03. Any difference between actual electricity cost and the flexible budget amount must then be caused by the quantity of electricity used. At the end of the month, the firm's managers cannot tell how much electricity was used for machinery (the variable portion) and for other purposes (the fixed portion) unless there are separate meters for the machinery.

For a particular month, suppose that the standard direct labor hours per unit are two, that production was 4,000 units, that a total of 8,100 direct labor hours were used (100 hours over standard), and that actual electricity cost was $9,210. The total standard hours allowed for production of 4,000 units would be 8,000 (4,000 × 2). The total budgeted cost for electricity would be $8,850 ($2,450 + [$0.80 × 8,000 standard labor hours]). Because we cannot, in the absence of separate meters, analyze the actual cost according to what should be its fixed and variable components, we cannot calculate separately the variances for the fixed and variable elements. In such cases, most firms calculate a single variance for the mixed cost as a whole. Using the data in our example, the variance would be calculated as follows:

$$
\begin{aligned}
\text{Budget variance} &= \text{actual cost} - \text{flexible budget based on output} \\
&= \$9,210 - \$8,850 \\
&= \$360 \text{ unfavorable variance}
\end{aligned}
$$

The variance is unfavorable simply because actual cost exceeds the budget allowance. We know that actual labor hours were 100 over standard, so we might surmise that about $80 of the total budget variance (100 hours × $0.80 per hour) was attributable to labor inefficiency, but we have no way of being sure of this.

Of course, if the firm is paying more than the budgeted price of $0.03 per kilowatt hour, it could determine how much of a variance was attributable to the price difference, and that information might be helpful in making decisions about possible alternative ways to operate. For example, the firm could consider installing machinery that would use less electricity. Reference to the total cost of electricity is not sufficient for making such decisions.

Why might a firm not work toward isolating the fixed and variable components of the actual cost? Why, for example, wouldn't the firm in the example above install meters on its machines in order to determine how much electricity related to machines and how much to lighting the factory? The answer is usually that the cost to obtain the additional information would be greater than the benefits to be achieved. True, the firm would have a better idea of why it was experiencing variances. But the cost to install and maintain the meters might be more than the savings that could be achieved through better control. A fundamental principle of managerial accounting is that obtaining additional information is desirable only if the benefits will exceed the costs.

STANDARDS AND MULTI-PRODUCT COMPANIES

So far we have, for the most part, implicitly assumed that a company that used standard costs made a single product. Standard costs are also used by many companies that produce several different products. No conceptual problems are introduced simply because a company makes more than one product; but a practical question arises about the extent to which detailed information should be produced and the cost of obtaining the additional information. This same question was addressed, in another context, in the previous section.

Though it is seldom a problem to develop standards, and hence, standard costs, for a multi-product company, it may be difficult, and in many cases, impossible, to isolate variances by product. This is true if the several products are manufactured using the same facilities and the same workers, and the company cannot determine the actual use of materials and labor for each product. That is, the costs of materials and labor may be identifiable with production as a whole, but it may be very costly, or impossible, to keep track of material use and direct labor time on the production of each individual product.

If more than one product is involved, and if actual production costs are not identified with a particular product, the variances relate to all products as a group. Whether or not it would be desirable to keep track of materials and direct labor by product depends on the relationship between the cost of obtaining the information and the potential benefits of having that information.

Managers are concerned with individual products because they are interested in whether the products are being made at or near the standard cost that they are using for planning and making decisions. Their concern, then, is with whether standards, in general, are based on current information; and they may not need detailed information on variances by type of cost and product. As a practical matter, a firm might occasionally keep track of materials and labor, by product, as a check on the standards, or might investigate efficiency variances to see if they are influenced by the product mix (a sign that the standard for one or another product may be inappropriate). As a general rule, however, isolating specific variances by product is not a common practice.

STANDARD COSTS FOR NONMANUFACTURING ACTIVITIES

Standard costs were developed for nonmanufacturing activities long after they were used for manufacturing. Nonmanufacturing activities have certain traits that render the development of standard costs difficult. Measuring output in nonmanufacturing activities is difficult. It is rare that homogeneous physical units flow out of the work done by the product design, legal, accounting, marketing, and general administration departments. There is seldom a definable measure of output because there is no standard product.

Costs associated with administrative and general work also tend to be fixed more than are those of manufacturing. Consequently, it might be impossible to develop standard variable costs per unit of output even if the appropriate unit of output could be determined. Therefore, general and administrative activities are usually controlled by static budgets, rather than by standard variable costs. Thus the earlier material on control of fixed costs is applicable to nonmanufacturing activities, but, in general, the material on standard variable costs is not.

Despite the difficulties, there have been and will continue to be numerous attempts to develop standards for nonmanufacturing activities. For example, the number of typing strokes per page has been standardized by some organizations as has the number of files processed and the number of books shelved. This is a challenging and important area of managerial accounting.

SUMMARY

Standard costs provide a tool for planning, control, and evaluation of the activities of cost centers. The manager of a cost center, and his superiors, receive information showing the efficiency of his operation. Comparisons of planned production with actual production indicate whether the manager was effective in performing assigned tasks.

The standard for each major element of product cost (material, labor, and overhead) is a combination of two separate standards: one for the quantity of the element used in the product, the other for the price of a unit of that element. The total variance between budgeted and actual cost can be analyzed into the variance related to a difference in price and the variance related to a difference in the quantity of the factor used. Since a single manager is not always responsible for both prices of resources and the quantity of resources used, the separation of total variances into price and use components assists in assigning responsibility. The separation is also helpful in planning future operations if it can be determined that a particular variance is likely to recur.

Loose standards do not encourage managers to work efficiently. Tight standards may discourage a manager. Participation by managers in standard setting can help to overcome some of these problems.

Seldom is a manager's performance, as shown in reports, a result of only his or her own actions; there are interdependencies among managerial functions. Hence, variances cannot automatically be said to be due to good or bad performance by a single manager. The causes of variances are not always easy to determine and could include not only poor management in the department showing the variance but also, though certainly not limited to, poor management in an entirely different department, or use of a bad standard.

KEY TERMS

control chart
currently attainable standards
engineered standards

fixed overhead budget variance
flexible budget allowance
historical standards

ideal standards
labor efficiency variance
labor rate variance
material price variance
material use variance

overhead efficiency variance
overhead spending variance
standard costs
variances

KEY FORMULAS

$$\begin{array}{c}\text{Total standard}\\\text{cost for}\\\text{input factor}\end{array} = \text{production} \times \begin{array}{c}\text{standard quantity}\\\text{of input factor}\\\text{per unit of}\\\text{production}\end{array} \times \begin{array}{c}\text{standard rate for}\\\text{input factor per}\\\text{unit of input}\end{array}$$

$$\begin{array}{c}\text{Total actual}\\\text{cost}\\\text{for input}\\\text{factor}\end{array} = \begin{array}{c}\text{actual}\\\text{input}\\\text{quantity}\end{array} \times \begin{array}{c}\text{actual price}\\\text{for input}\\\text{factor}\end{array}$$

$$\begin{array}{c}\text{Price}\\\text{variance}\end{array} = \begin{array}{c}\text{actual quantity}\\\text{of input acquired}\end{array} \times \left(\begin{array}{c}\text{standard price}\\\text{per unit of input}\end{array} - \begin{array}{c}\text{actual price}\\\text{per unit of input}\end{array}\right)$$

$$\begin{array}{c}\text{Quantity}\\\text{variance}\end{array} = \begin{array}{c}\text{standard price}\\\text{per unit of input}\end{array} \times \left(\begin{array}{c}\text{standard quantity}\\\text{of input required}\end{array} - \begin{array}{c}\text{actual quantity}\\\text{of input used}\end{array}\right)$$

REVIEW PROBLEM

Baldwin Company makes cabinets. One model, the Deluxe, has the following requirements.

Materials (44 feet of wood at $0.20 per foot)
Direct labor (4 hours at $7 per hour)
Variable overhead ($5 per direct labor hour)

During June 19X4 the firm made 1,200 Deluxe cabinets. Operating results were:

Material purchases	58,000 feet at $0.19	$11,020
Material used	53,200 feet	
Direct labor	4,750 hours at $7.10	$33,725
Variable overhead		$23,900

Required: Compute the standard variable cost per Deluxe cabinet and the variances for June 19X4.

Answer to Review Problem

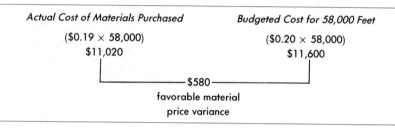

Standard Variable Cost

Material (44 feet of wood at $0.20)	$ 8.80
Direct labor (4 hours at $7 per hour)	28.00
Variable overhead at $5 per direct labor hour	20.00
Total standard variable cost	$56.80

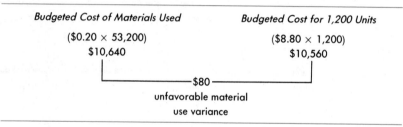

Materials Variances for June 19X4

Actual Cost of Materials Purchased
($0.19 × 58,000)
$11,020

Budgeted Cost for 58,000 Feet
($0.20 × 58,000)
$11,600

$580
favorable material
price variance

Alternatively, ($0.20 − $0.19) × 58,000 = $0.01 × 58,000 = $580 favorable

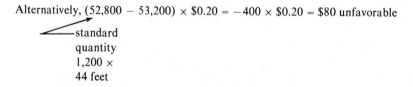

Budgeted Cost of Materials Used
($0.20 × 53,200)
$10,640

Budgeted Cost for 1,200 Units
($8.80 × 1,200)
$10,560

$80
unfavorable material
use variance

Alternatively, (52,800 − 53,200) × $0.20 = −400 × $0.20 = $80 unfavorable

standard
quantity
1,200 ×
44 feet

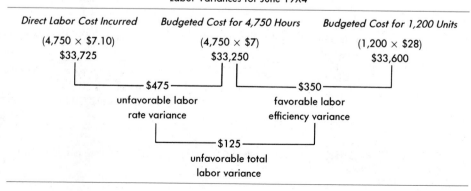

Labor Variances for June 19X4

Direct Labor Cost Incurred
(4,750 × $7.10)
$33,725

Budgeted Cost for 4,750 Hours
(4,750 × $7)
$33,250

Budgeted Cost for 1,200 Units
(1,200 × $28)
$33,600

$475
unfavorable labor
rate variance

$350
favorable labor
efficiency variance

$125
unfavorable total
labor variance

Alternatively, the labor rate variance is

$$4,750 \times (\$7 - \$7.10) = -\$475 \text{ unfavorable}$$

The labor efficiency variance is

$$\$7 \times (4,800 - 4,750) = \$350 \text{ favorable}$$

standard
hours
$1,200 \times 4$

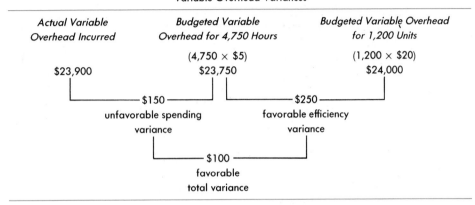

Variable Overhead Variances

Actual Variable Overhead Incurred	Budgeted Variable Overhead for 4,750 Hours	Budgeted Variable Overhead for 1,200 Units
	$(4,750 \times \$5)$	$(1,200 \times \$20)$
$23,900	$23,750	$24,000

$150
unfavorable spending
variance

$250
favorable efficiency
variance

$100
favorable
total variance

Alternatively, the spending variance could be computed by calculating the actual rate of about $5.032, and subtracting it from the standard rate of $5, then multiplying by 4,750 hours.

$$(\$5 - \$5.032) \times 4,750 = -\$152 \text{ unfavorable}$$

The efficiency variance is also given by

$$\$5 \times (4,800 - 4,750) = \$250 \text{ favorable}$$

Note that because the variable overhead standard is based on direct labor hours, the only difference between the computation of the labor efficiency variance and the variable overhead efficiency variance is the rate used.

ASSIGNMENT MATERIAL

Questions for Discussion

12-1 Budgeting and standards Budgeting aids managers in planning and control. Standard costs are useful for assisting in budgeting and for planning and control in general. What is accomplished by the use of standard costs that is not accomplished by budgeting?

12-2 Interpretation of variances For each of the following situations (a) indicate whether a variance would be expected to occur; (b) state which variance(s) would be affected and in what direction; and (c) state whether an investigation should be undertaken and whether you think corrective action could be taken.
1. Wage rates have risen because a new union contract has been signed.

2. To increase safety, the plant manager has reduced the speeds at which fork-lift trucks carrying materials and semifinished products among work stations can be driven.

3. The firm sells its wasted raw materials, chiefly metals, to a scrap dealer. Lately, revenue from sales of waste has been increasing although production has been steady.

4. Exceptionally heavy rainfall necessitates the drying out of certain materials that are stored outside.

5. The electric utility that supplies the firm with power has been having difficulty with its generators. There are frequent blackouts and brownouts.

6. Many part-time workers must be hired because of a rapid increase in production.

12-3   Revising standards   Indicate whether each of the events listed below calls for revision in standards and, if so, which standard(s). If possible, indicate the direction of the revision. Assume that currently attainable performance is the basis for all standards.

1. Complaints from customers about dullness of a metallic finish on the product have induced the production manager to assign a worker to buff the surface.

2. The labor efficiency variance has consistently been unfavorable by anywhere from 2% to 4%.

3. A new material is being used that is more expensive than the old. However, there is less waste and it is easier to handle.

4. The product is a wooden cabinet. Previously, a number of parts of the cabinet had been nailed together. Now those parts are being screwed together.

5. A strike at the plant of a supplier has forced the purchase of some raw materials at higher prices from other sources.

6. Rates for electricity have increased. The plant uses a great deal of electricity for machinery.

7. An overhead crane has been installed to speed the movement of semifinished product from one work station to another.

12-4   Effects of changed conditions   Each of the following describes a change that occurred after standards had been set for the period and then lists three of the variances that were discussed in the chapter. For each item, select the variance most likely to be affected by the described change in conditions, and explain your choice.

1. To meet a shortage of workers in the face of a steady demand for the product, the firm decided to hire workers with less experience than those hired in the past.
   Variances of concern: Material price variance, labor rate variance, labor efficiency variance.

2. Faced with the prospect of a shortage of the firm's normal raw materials, the firm decides to use a new, more expensive material that produces less waste and is easier to handle.
   Variances of concern: Labor rate variance, variable overhead spending variance, variable overhead efficiency variance.

3. Based on a suggestion from a direct laborer, the process for assembling certain parts of the final product has been changed so that a single employee assembles six components. Before the change, two employees of the same department worked independently to assemble three components each, and a third employee in that department put together the subassemblies produced by those two employees.
   Variances of concern: Material use variance, labor efficiency variance, variable overhead spending variance.

12-5   Setting standards   The controller of a large manufacturing company said: "In our company the standard cost is the true cost; actual cost is simply an aberration from true cost." Speculate on how the standards might have been set.

12-6 Responsibility for variances (CMA adapted) Phillips Company uses a standard cost system. Variances for each department are calculated and reported to the department manager. The reporting has two major purposes: for use by superiors in evaluating performance, and for use by managers in improving their own operations.

Jack Smith was recently appointed manager of the Assembly Department. He has complained that the system does not work properly and discriminates against his department because of the current practice of calculating a variance for rejected units. The procedures for making this calculation are as follows: (1) all units are inspected at the end of the assembly operation; (2) rejected units are examined to see if the cause of rejection can be assigned to a particular department; (3) units that are rejected but cannot be identified with a particular department are totaled; (4) the unidentifiable rejects are apportioned to each department on the basis of the identifiable rejects. Thus, if a department had 20% of the identified rejects, it would also be charged with 20% of the unidentified rejects. The variance, then, is the sum of the identifiable rejects and the apportioned share of unidentified rejects. Evaluate the validity of Smith's claim, and make a recommendation for resolving the problem.

Exercises

12-7 Standard cost computations Blivet Company makes a single product and has established the standard prices and quantities for a finished unit as follows.

Material	4 pounds @ $1 per pound
Direct labor	3 hours @ $8 per hour
Variable overhead	$6 per direct labor hour (DLH)

The company also has fixed overhead of $100,000 per year.

Required: Fill in the blanks in the following items.
1. The standard cost per unit of finished product is
   (a) _____ for material,
   (b) _____ for direct labor, and
   (c) _____ for variable overhead.
2. At 70,000 hours of direct labor, the total variable overhead cost should be _____.
3. At 90,000 hours of direct labor, production should be _____ units.
4. If 100,000 pounds of material are used, production should be _____ units.
5. At 60,000 hours of direct labor, the total material used should be _____ pounds.
6. If 66,000 pounds of material are used, the total variable overhead cost should be _____, and the total labor cost should be _____.

12-8 Basic material and labor variances Fergon Company makes a lamp shade and had the following budgeted and actual results in December.

	Budget	Actual
Unit production	10,000	11,000
Direct labor hours	20,000	21,700
Materials used, yards	40,000	43,200

The standard labor rate is $10 per hour and the standard material price is $2 per yard.

Required: Calculate the direct labor efficiency variance and the material use variance.

12-9   Basic variance relationships, materials   Fill in the blanks below. You can work them in order, but you do not have to.

Standard material cost per unit of product	$ 20
Material use variance	$ 2,000F
Standard material use for quantity produced, in pounds	23,600
Number of pounds of material purchased	30,000
Material price variance	$ 3,000U
Standard price per pound of materials	$ 5
Standard pounds of materials per unit of product	_____
Units produced	_____
Number of pounds of materials used	_____
Amount paid for materials purchased	_____

12-10   Basic variance relationships, direct labor   Fill in the blanks below. You can work them in order, but you do not have to.

Direct labor rate variance	$ 5,200F
Amount paid to direct laborers	$306,800
Excess of actual labor hours over standard labor hours for quantity produced	1,000
Direct labor efficiency variance	$ 6,000U
Standard direct labor hours per unit	3
Standard direct labor rate per hour	_____
Flexible budget allowance for actual hours worked	_____
Actual direct labor hours worked	_____
Total standard cost of direct labor for quantity produced	_____
Total standard direct labor hours for quantity produced	_____
Units produced	_____

12-11   Variance computations   Below are the standard variable costs for a glotto.

Material	3 pounds of lotto @ $1 per pound	$ 3.00
Labor	2 hours of gluing labor @ $6 per hour	12.00
Variable overhead	$3 per labor hour	6.00
		$21.00

Actual results in March were as follows:

Production	1,000 glottos
Materials purchased and used	3,200 pounds for $3,220
Hours of gluing labor worked	2,100 hours
Cost of labor	$12,100
Variable overhead incurred	$ 6,500

Required: Compute all variable cost variances.

12-12 Comprehensive variance analysis The 4N Company makes a number of products. Standard costs for an industrial chemical appear below, along with actual results for March.

Materials, 3 pounds at $4 per pound	$12
Direct labor @ $10 per hour	30
Variable overhead @ $6 per DLH	18
Total standard variable cost	$60

Actual results for March:
1. Production was 1,200 units.
2. Material purchases were 3,200 pounds at $3.90 per pound.
3. The firm used 3,620 pounds of material in production.
4. Direct laborers worked 3,800 hours at $10.10 earning $38,380.
5. Variable overhead was $22,000.

Required: Compute all variable cost variances.

12-13 Significance of variances Ann Jackson, the controller of Stone Company, was recently told by several production managers that "as long as total costs do not exceed budgeted costs, based on standard prices and quantities, there is no reason to do any investigating or analysis."

Required: Comment critically on the statement. Cite at least two reasons for not accepting it.

12-14 Variance computations Trivet Company makes a single product and has developed the following standard cost per unit of finished product.

Material	4 pounds @ $1	$ 4
Direct labor	2 hours @ $7	14
Variable overhead	$4 per DLH	8
Total standard variable cost per unit		$26

In 19X5, the actual results were as follows.

Direct labor hours worked	21,500
Number of units produced	11,000
Rate paid to direct laborers	$7.20 per hour
Materials purchased	50,000 pounds
Price paid for materials	$0.96 per pound
Materials used in production	45,000 pounds
Variable overhead incurred	$85,800

Required: Compute all variable cost variances.

12-15 Revision of standard costs Clarkson Company manufactures toys. One group of toys consists of small cars, each of which requires the same quantities of materials and direct labor. The cars are packaged and sold in batches of 50. The standard variable cost of a batch is given below.

Materials	$10.00
Direct labor (4 hours)	16.00
Variable overhead	12.00
Total standard variable cost	$38.00

The supervisor of the department in which the cars are made is uncertain how to prepare the budget for the coming year. He tells you the following:
(a) Material costs will be higher by an average of 20% because of price increases.
(b) Laborers will get a 5% pay raise at the beginning of the year.
(c) Increased efficiency will result in a 10% reduction in direct labor hours.
(d) The variable overhead rate will increase to $3.40 per direct labor hour.

Required: Prepare revised standard variable costs.

12-16   Relationships—labor variances   Each of the situations given below is independent. The only element of cost being considered is direct labor. Fill in the blanks.

	a	b	c	d
Units produced	2,000	————	3,000	————
Actual hours worked	4,800	4,200	————	————
Standard hours for production achieved	5,000	————	————	6,000
Standard hours per unit	————	0.5	2	3
Standard rate per hour	$ 6	$ 10	$ 4	————
Actual labor cost	————	$41,800	————	$24,500
Rate variance	$ 310U	————	$ 300U	$ 300F
Efficiency variance	————	$ 1,000U	$ 600F	$ 800U

12-17   Variances   Given the following data, compute all variable cost variances.

Standards for a Unit of Product

Material	2 pounds @ $4 per pound
Direct labor	4 hours @ $7 per hour
Variable overhead	$4 per DLH

June Activity

Production	2,000 units
Material purchases (all used)	4,400 pounds for $16,950
Laborers' earnings	8,300 hours for $58,400
Variable overhead incurred	$33,000

12-18   Variance analysis   Kuhn Company makes automobile antifreeze. The firm has developed the following formula for budgeting monthly factory overhead costs. Total overhead cost = $122,000 + ($12 × direct labor hours). Other data relating to the cost of a case of the product are given below.

Materials	4 gallons at $0.80 per gallon
Direct labor	20 minutes at $6 per hour

During a recent month Kuhn produced 15,000 cases of product and incurred the following costs.

Materials (purchased and used)	59,500 gallons	$ 48,200
Direct labor	5,100 hours	$ 30,600
Overhead		$183,500

Required: Compute the price and quantity variances for materials and direct labor and the total variance for overhead.

12-19 Performance reporting   The president of your firm has asked you to investigate some unfavorable variances that arose in one of the departments last month. The following summary of the department's performance report was given to you.

	Budget	Actual	Variance
Production (in units)	2,000	2,500	500F
Costs (based on budgeted production):			
Direct labor	$6,000	$7,000	$1,000U
Supplies	400	650	250U
Repairs	1,000	1,200	200U
Power	800	1,100	300U
Total costs (all variable)	$8,200	$9,950	$1,750U

Required
1. Was performance poor?
2. What suggestions do you have?

12-20 Variances—relationships among costs   Read the following in its entirety and then fill in the blanks.

1. Standard variable costs per unit:		
(a) Materials	4 pounds @ $____	$ ____
(b) Direct labor	____ hours @ $6.00	$12.00
(c) Variable overhead	$3 per DLH	$ ____
2. Production		8,000 units
3. Material purchases	33,000 pounds	$62,000
4. Material used, at standard prices	31,200 pounds	$ ____
5. Direct labor, actual	____ hours	$80,800
6. Material price variance		$ 4,000F
7. Material use variance		$ ____
8. Direct labor rate variance		$ 3,200F
9. Direct labor efficiency variance		$ ____
10. Variable overhead spending variance		$ 1,200U
11. Variable overhead efficiency variance		$ ____
12. Variable overhead, actual		$ ____

12-21   Standards—machine-hour basis   Wilkens Company is highly automated and uses machine-hours as the basis for setting standard variable costs per unit of product. A unit requires two pounds of material costing $3 per pound and 20 minutes of machine time to make. The standard variable overhead rate is $12 per machine-hour. There is no direct labor; all workers are classified as indirect labor and their wages are considered part of variable overhead.

During June, 15,000 units were produced using 4,800 machine-hours. Variable overhead costs incurred were $58,400. Purchases of materials were 34,000 pounds for $105,000 and 31,000 pounds were used.

Required
1. Compute the standard variable cost of a unit of product.
2. Compute the variances for June.

Problems

12-22   Investigation of variances   The production manager of Knowles Company tells you that he exercises management by exception in controlling operations. He examines a performance report and calls for further analysis and investigation if a variance is greater than 10% of total standard cost or is more than $1,000. He is not responsible for any rate or price variances, and is therefore concerned only with efficiency variances. During April, the following occurred:
1. Materials used: 4,200 gallons
2. Direct labor hours: 6,100
3. Production: 1,500 units
The standard cost of a unit is as follows:

Materials (3 gallons @ $4)	$12
Direct labor (4 hours @ $6)	24
Variable overhead ($8 per DLH)	32
Total standard variable cost	$68

Required
1. Compute the variances for which the production manager is held responsible.
2. Determine which variances should be investigated according to his criteria.

12-23   Determining a base for cost standards   The production manager of Wingate Company recently performed a study to see how many units of product could be made by a worker who had no interruptions, always had materials available as needed, made no errors, and worked at peak speed for an entire hour. It was found that a worker could make 20 units in an hour under these ideal conditions. In the past, about 15 units per hour was the average. However, some new materials handling equipment had recently been purchased and the manager is confident that an average of 17 units per hour could be achieved by nearly all of the workers.

All workers are paid $5.10 per hour. During the month after the study had been performed, workers were paid $510,000 for 100,000 hours. Production was 1,650,000 units.

Required
1. Compute the standard labor cost per unit to the nearest tenth of a cent based on the following:

   (a)   historical performance
   (b)   ideal performance
   (c)   currently attainable performance

2.   Compute the labor efficiency variance under each of the standards in part 1 above and comment on the results. Which method of setting the standard would you choose for planning purposes? For control purposes? Explain.

12-24 **Investigation of variances**   The supervisor of the stamping department is pleased with her performance this past month. Her operation showed a favorable material use variance of $1,000. The following data relate to the stamping operation:

Units produced	2,000
Standard costs for materials:	
Libidinum, 3 pounds @ $3	$ 9
Larezium, 2 pounds @ $4	8
Total standard material cost	$ 17

During the month, 5,000 pounds of libidinum and 4,500 pounds of larezium were used.

Required

1.   Verify the amount of the material use variance.
2.   Did the supervisor do a good job this month? What questions must be answered before coming to a conclusion about the manager's performance?

12-25 **Determination of standard costs**   Vernon Company makes its single product, Shine, in the following way:

      Materials Dull and Buff are mixed in batches of 500 pounds. Material is used in a ratio of three pounds of Dull for each two pounds of Buff. The mixing is done by two laborers and each batch takes three hours to mix. The resulting mixture is boiled for four hours, which process requires the services of four workers. The mixture that comes out of the boiler yields four pounds of finished product for each five pounds of raw material put in so that the 500 pounds of material mixed become 400 pounds of final product. (Evaporation during the boiling process reduces the volume of the output.)

      All laborers earn $6 per hour. Variable overhead is $3 per direct labor hour. Dull costs $2.80 per pound; Buff costs $2 per pound.

Required: Determine the standard variable cost per pound of finished product.

12-26 **Standards and variances, two products**   Bascomb Company makes two products. Both go through essentially the same process and the company does not keep records regarding the amounts of material and labor used in making each product, only for the two products as a whole. Standard cost data are:

	Product A	Product B
Materials:		
2 pounds at $4/pound	$ 8	
3 pounds at $4/pound		$12
Direct labor	16	24
Variable overhead	12	18
Total standard costs	$36	$54

All direct laborers earn $8 per hour and the variable overhead rate is $6 per direct labor hour. The same material is used in both products.

During March, the company had the following results:

Production	2,000 product A, 1,500 product B
Material purchases	9,000 pounds at $4.15 per pound
Material used	8,900 pounds
Direct labor	8,750 hours at $7.95 per hour
Variable overhead	$55,500

Required

1. Compute all variable cost variances for production as a whole.
2. Can you compute variances for each product? If not, why not? For what reasons might you want to isolate variances to the individual products?

12-27 Input standards versus output standards Cassidy Company manufactures an industrial solvent. The firm budgets its manufacturing costs based on direct labor hours. The production manager is unable to interpret the report that he has just received and asks for your assistance. The report contains the following data:

	Actual Cost at 10,000 Direct Labor Hours	Budgeted Cost for 10,000 Hours
Materials used at standard prices	$ 26,000	$ 24,000
Direct labor	67,500	68,000
Indirect labor	27,450	26,500
Other variable overhead	27,400	27,300
Total variable costs	$148,350	$145,800

Production during the period was 48,000 gallons, which would require 9,600 direct labor hours at standard performance.

Required: For each component of cost determine the variance due to efficiency (or inefficiency), and that due to spending or price.

12-28 Bases for standard costs and decisions Sewell Company uses very tight standards for determining standard costs for its products. The production manager believes that the use of standards that could be achieved only under ideal conditions helps to motivate foremen and workers by showing them how much improvement is possible and therefore giving them goals to achieve.

The sales manager has criticized the use of such high standards for performance and correspondingly low standard costs because it makes it difficult for him to determine whether business at lower than normal prices should be accepted. In one specific instance, the sales manager was offered the opportunity to sell 4,000 units at $8.50, which is $4 below the normal selling price. The standard variable cost per unit of product is as follows.

Materials (3 pounds at $0.50)	$1.50
Direct labor (½ hour at $6 per hour)	3.00
Variable overhead ($4 per direct labor hour)	2.00
Total standard variable cost	$6.50

The sales manager was uncertain whether the order should have been accepted. He knew that the standards were never met. What bothered him was the extent to which they were not met. He asked his assistant to try to determine whether the order would have been profitable. The assistant developed the following information:

Material price and labor rate variances were negligible. However, during a normal month, when 10,000 units were produced, the material use variance, direct labor efficiency variance, and total variable overhead variance were $2,000, $6,000, and $5,200, respectively, all unfavorable.

Required

1. Assuming that the experience of the month presented would have applied when the special order was being made up, should the order have been accepted?
2. Develop new standard variable costs based on currently attainable performance, assuming that the month presented reflected currently attainable performance. Be sure to include both prices and quantities for each input factor.

12-29   Analyzing results—sales and cost variances   The managers of Reed Company, which manufactures blankets, were disappointed at the shortfall in profit for 19X7, as shown below:

Reed Company
Income Statements for 19X7 (in millions)

	Budgeted	Actual
Unit sales	10.0	10.8
Sales	$120.0	$122.1
Variable manufacturing costs:		
Materials	20.0	21.8
Direct labor	15.0	17.0
Variable overhead	5.0	5.2
Total variable costs	40.0	44.0
Contribution margin	80.0	78.1
Fixed costs:		
Manufacturing	50.0	50.8
Selling and administrative	20.0	19.9
Total fixed costs	70.0	70.7
Profit before taxes	$ 10.0	$ 7.4

Required: The president of the firm would like an analysis showing why it fell short of budgeted profit. He wants you to determine the effects of the difference between budgeted and actual unit volume, budgeted and actual selling prices, and budgeted and actual costs for the volume achieved. Production equaled sales. Prepare such an analysis and be sure that it accounts for the difference between budgeted and actual profit.

12-30   Flexible and static budgets   Marvel Manufacturing Company is managed by a family; none of its members understand accounting. Ralph Marvel, one of the managers, was elated at the following performance report.

	Budget	Actual	Variance
Production	30,000	26,000	
Direct materials	$ 75,000	$ 72,000	$ 3,000F
Direct labor	45,000	40,000	5,000F
Variable overhead	90,000	86,000	4,000F
Fixed overhead	60,000	60,000	—
Totals	$270,000	$258,000	$12,000F

Ralph showed the report to Susan Roberts, the newly hired assistant controller, saying that one did not need to understand accounting to see that coming in under budget was a good thing.

Required: As Ms. Roberts, what would you say to Mr. Marvel?

12-31   Variance analysis—changed conditions   Your firm makes a product with the following standard costs:

Materials (4 pounds @ $2)	$ 8
Direct labor (2 hours @ $5)	10
Variable overhead ($4 per DLH)	8
Total standard variable cost	$26

The standards have proved to be currently attainable and are generally met within small variances each month. In August the manufacturing vice president brings in a glowing report from the purchasing department. The firm bought materials for $1.50 per pound. The new materials were different from the old, but were of equal quality for the finished product. In September the materials bought during August were used with the following results.

Production scheduled	4,000 units
Actual production	3,600 units
Direct labor (8,100 hours)	$40,000
Variable overhead	$33,000
Material used	15,840 pounds

Required
1. Compute all variances that you can.
2. Why may the variances have occurred?
3. Assuming that the experience of September will continue, should the firm continue buying the new material?

12-32   Economic cost of labor inefficiency   The Columbia Window Company makes high-quality bay windows for residences. Sales are to wholesalers who in turn sell to building contractors or to homeowners. During some months of the year the company has trouble keeping up with demand and loses sales because its customers are generally unwilling to wait and will buy from a competitor. Direct labor time available is constrained by the production process, so that the company can obtain a maximum of 280,000 direct labor hours per month. The typical product mix results in an average standard labor time of 14 hours per unit. The standard labor rate is $10 per hour and the standard variable overhead rate is $8 per direct labor hour. Average material cost is $82 per unit, average selling price $620 per unit. Results for two recent months appear below. January is typically a slow month, June a busy one, with orders for over 22,000 units.

	January	June
Units produced	12,500	19,200
Actual labor hours	179,400	280,000

Material costs were at standard. The actual labor rate equaled the standard rate, and variable overhead equaled $8 times actual direct labor hours in both months.

Required
1. Compute the labor efficiency variance and variable overhead efficiency variance for each month.
2. Do the variances for both months reflect the true cost to the firm of labor inefficiency? Why or why not?

12-33 **Standard costs, variances, and evaluation (CMA adapted)**   Bergen Company manufactures and sells a single product. The standard variable cost of a unit is given below.

Material, 1 pound plastic @ $2	$ 2.00
Direct labor, 1.6 hours @ $4	6.40
Variable overhead	3.00
Total standard variable cost	$11.40

The variable overhead cost is not related to direct labor hours, but rather to units of product because it is felt that production is the causal factor in the incurrence of the variable overhead elements. The elements of variable overhead, based on a yearly volume of 60,000 units of production, are as follows.

Indirect labor, 30,000 hours @ $4	$120,000
Supplies, oil, 60,000 gallons @ $0.50	30,000
Maintenance costs, variable portion, 6,000 hours @ $5 per hour	30,000
Total budgeted variable overhead	$180,000

Fixed overhead costs are budgeted as follows, based on 60,000 units of production.

Supervision	$ 27,000
Depreciation	45,000
Other fixed overhead (includes fixed maintenance costs of $12,000)	45,000
Total budgeted fixed overhead	$117,000

During November, 5,000 units were produced and actual costs were as follows:

Material, 5,300 pounds used @ $2	$10,600
Direct labor, 8,200 hours @ $4.10	33,620
Indirect labor, 2,400 hours @ $4.10	9,840
Supplies, 6,000 gallons of oil @ $0.55	3,300
Variable maintenance costs, 490 hours @ $5.30	2,597
Supervision	2,475
Depreciation	3,750
Other fixed overhead (includes maintenance of $1,100)	3,600
Total	$69,782

Purchases of materials were 5,200 pounds at $2.10 per pound. The firm has divided responsibilities so that the purchasing manager is responsible for price variances for material and oil, and the production manager is responsible for all quantities of materials, labor (direct and indirect), supplies, and maintenance. The personnel manager is responsible for wage rate variances and the manager of the maintenance department is responsible for spending variances.

Required

1. Calculate the following variances:
   (a) material price
   (b) material use
   (c) direct labor rate
   (d) direct labor efficiency
   (e) total variable overhead
   (f) total fixed overhead
2. Prepare a report that details the overhead variances of each element by responsibility. (A convenient method would be to list the managers across the top, and under each show the variances for which they should be charged.) You should account for the totals of the variable and fixed overhead variances. That is, the total of your answers to requirement 1 should be distributed to individual managers.

12-34 **Use of unit costs**   The foreman of the machining department of Glenmills Company has just received the following performance report, which was prepared by the new cost accountant:

	Costs per Unit		
	Budget	Actual	Variance
Materials	$ 3.00	$ 2.96	($0.04)
Direct labor (1.5 hours per unit at standard)	6.00	6.084	0.084
Variable overhead			
Indirect labor	2.40	2.48	0.08
Power	0.90	0.93	0.03
Fixed overhead	4.00	4.95[a]	0.95
Totals	$16.30	$17.404	$1.104

[a]Actual cost incurred divided by actual production in units.

Budgeted production was 12,000 units, actual production was 10,000 units. Budgeted fixed overhead per unit is based on budgeted production. You learn that actual material cost in the report is based on standard prices and that all other actual cost figures are based on actual prices and quantities.

The foreman is not responsible for direct labor rates, which were $3.90 at actual cost. He is also not responsible for variable overhead spending variances, but he is responsible for fixed overhead budget variances.

Required: Prepare a new report including only those items for which the foreman is responsible. (You may wish to use a different type of presentation from that shown above.)

12-35 **Analysis of income statement**   The controller of Taylors Company has given you the following income statement.

Sales 20,000 × $20		$400,000
Standard variable cost of sales		240,000
Standard variable manufacturing margin		160,000
Variances:		
Materials	$ 6,000F	
Direct labor	4,000U	
Variable overhead	3,000U	1,000U
Actual variable manufacturing margin		159,000
Fixed costs:		
Budgeted manufacturing costs	75,000	
Fixed cost budget variance	2,000U	
Selling and administrative costs	40,000	117,000
Income before taxes		$ 42,000

The controller gives you the following additional data. Production was 22,000 units. Material purchases were all made at standard price. Direct laborers averaged 0.85 hours per unit, which was 0.05 hours above the standard time. Actual total direct labor cost was $144,800. The standard variable overhead rate is $2 per direct labor hour.

Required: Answer the following questions.
1. What was the direct labor efficiency variance?
2. What was the direct labor rate variance?
3. What was the standard material cost per unit?
4. What was actual total variable overhead?
5. What was the variable overhead efficiency variance?
6. What was the variable overhead budget variance?
7. What was actual total fixed manufacturing cost?
8. If the standard material price is $2 per pound, how many pounds are needed at standard to make a unit of product?
9. How many pounds of material did the firm use?

12-36 Forecasting income   Robyn Company had the following income statement in 19X7.

Sales 110,000 × $20		$2,200,000
Standard variable cost of sales		880,000
Standard variable manufacturing margin		1,320,000
Variances:		
Materials	$ 2,400U	
Direct labor	1,800F	
Variable overhead	1,600F	1,000F
Actual variable manufacturing margin		1,321,000
Fixed costs:		
Manufacturing	560,000	
Selling and administrative	470,000	1,030,000
Income		$ 291,000

The details of standard cost were:

Materials 0.50 pounds at $4 per pound	$2.00
Direct labor 0.40 hours at $10 per hour	4.00
Variable overhead at $5 per direct labor hour	2.00
Total standard variable cost	$8.00

The company's industrial engineers have redesigned the product so that (1) material requirements should be 0.45 pounds; (2) direct labor hours should be 0.35. The company expects to produce 120,000 units in 19X8 and to sell 115,000. Material costs will increase to $4.20 per pound. Each element of fixed cost should increase by 5%.

The managers and engineers expect to see material use about 2% over the 0.45 pounds standard because it will take some time for the workers to learn the new production methods. They also expect direct labor for the year to be 6% or so above standard for the same reason. They do want to use the 0.45 pounds and 0.35 hours as the standards, however, because they expect workers to operate at standard by the middle of the year. The standard variable overhead rate will increase by $0.20 per hour because of rising prices for input factors like supplies and power. All elements not mentioned should remain about the same as they were in 19X7.

Required
1. Determine the standard cost for the product for 19X8.
2. Prepare an income statement for 19X8 reflecting the manager's expectations, using the same format as the one for 19X7.

12-37 Relationships among data   Dempsey Company uses standard variable costs. Variable overhead rate is based on direct labor hours. The following data are available for operations during April 19X4.

Total production	_____
Actual labor cost	$61,600
Actual materials used	5,900 pounds
Actual variable overhead	$37,150
Standard labor cost per unit	_____
Standard material cost per unit	$ 4.50
Standard variable overhead cost per unit	_____
Materials purchased	$ 2,800 (8,200 pounds)
Material price variance	$ 500U
Labor rate variance	$ 2,500U
Variable overhead spending variance	$_____ F or U
Material use variance	_____
Labor efficiency variance	$ 900F
Variable overhead efficiency variance	$_____ F or U
Direct labor hours worked	9,850
Standard labor rate	_____
Standard direct labor hours per unit	5
Variable overhead rate per DLH	$ 4

Required: Fill in the blanks. (*Hint:* You cannot do the parts of the problem in the order indicated.)

12-38 Standard costs—alternative raw materials   Visodane Company manufactures a household cleaner called Kleenall that is sold in 32-ounce (1/4-gallon) plastic bottles. The cleaner can be made using either of two basic raw materials—anaxohyde or ferodoxin. Their respective costs are $10 and $8 per pound. Whichever material is used is mixed with water and other chemical agents and is then cooked. The product is then bottled and the bottles are packed into cartons of 20 bottles each.

The basic batch size is made with 1,200 gallons of water, costing $0.30 per hundred gallons. The chemical agents other than the raw materials mentioned above cost $120 per batch. If anaxohyde is used, 100 pounds of it are mixed with the water and chemical agents. If ferodoxin is used, 110 pounds are needed. The mixing process takes three hours, requiring the services of three laborers.

The mixture is then cooked, for 80 minutes if anaxohyde is used, 90 minutes if ferodoxin is used. One worker is needed for the cooking process. Using either raw material, the output of the cooking process is 1,000 gallons because of evaporation. Bottling and packing requires one laborer working two hours.

All laborers are paid $6 per hour. Variable overhead is based on the time required in each process because the high degree of mechanization makes direct labor a poor measure of volume for variable overhead. The overhead per hour for the mixing process is $30, $120 for the cooking process, and $60 for the bottling and packing process. Bottles cost $0.04 each and the cartons cost $0.20 each.

Required
1. Compute the standard cost of a carton of 20 bottles of Kleenall, assuming (a) anaxohyde is used; and (b) ferodoxin is used.
2. Suppose that each carton sells for $20 and that cooking time available each month is 1,000 hours. Which material should be used?

12-39   Developing standard costs (CMA adapted)   The controller of Berman Detergent Company has asked for your help in preparing standard variable costs for the firm's major product, Sudsaway. The firm has never used standard costs and the controller believes that better control would be achieved if standards were used. He wants the standards to be based on currently attainable performance.

The following data are available for operations in 19X6.

Materials used 1,350,000 gallons @ $0.80 per gallon		$1,080,000
Direct labor 160,000 hours @ $5.50 per hour		880,000
Variable overhead:		
Indirect labor	$240,000	
Maintenance and repairs	80,000	
Packaging materials	370,000	
Other variable overhead	480,000	1,170,000
Total variable production costs		$3,130,000

During 19X6, 740,000 cases of Sudsaway were produced. Each case contains 12 bottles of 16 ounces each, a total of 1.5 gallons per case. During 19X6 the firm was using an inferior raw material. During 19X7 the firm expects to pay $0.90 per gallon for a better material. Even with the better material, there will still be some shrinkage during production. The controller expects that output of Sudsaway in gallons will be 90% of the raw material put into process.

The firm employed a number of inexperienced workers in 19X6. They worked about 48,000 of the total direct labor hours, which is about 12,000 more than standard hours. During 19X7 the controller expects all workers to be normally productive and to be earning an average wage rate of $5.80.

According to the controller, variable overhead costs were under control during 19X6, given the excessive labor hours worked. Packaging materials were not affected by the excessive labor hours, being related to cases actually produced. Indirect laborers will receive a 10% wage increase early in 19X7.

Required: Prepare standard variable costs, by category of cost, for a case of Sudsaway.

Cases

12-40   Standard costs—joint products   Sigmund Company buys a single raw material and processes it into two intermediate products, guild and stern. Both guild and stern are further processed into final products; neither can be sold at split-off.

The joint process is supervised by one manager; the additional processing of each product is supervised by separate managers. Based on currently attainable performance, it takes six workers three hours to process a 1-ton batch of raw material into 800 pounds of guild and 1,000 pounds of stern. The remainder is worthless waste. The raw material costs $360 per ton. All laborers are paid $6 per hour and variable overhead is $4 per direct labor hour.

Still based on currently attainable performance, it takes three workers five hours to complete the processing of an 800-pound batch of guild, and four workers three hours to complete a 1,000-pound batch of stern. When completed, guild sells for $0.75 per pound, stern for $0.90.

Required: Compute whatever standard costs you think would be helpful to the firm. Explain why you computed the ones you did.

12-41 Incurred costs and performance Weldon Oil Company operates a refinery in the northeastern United States. During the winter about 200 workers are employed as drivers of fuel-oil trucks to deliver oil for heating purposes. Drivers are paid $10 per hour. During the summer there is no need for their services as fuel-oil truck drivers and they are given low-grade jobs in the refinery. Although these low-grade jobs usually pay only $7 per hour, the drivers are given their usual $10 rate as a matter of company policy.

The manager of the refinery is charged with the $10 wage paid to the drivers while they work in the refinery. The manager of the fuel-oil distribution department bears no charge except when the workers are delivering fuel oil.

The refinery manager does not object to employing the drivers during the summer. Even with this addition to his regular work force he must hire students and other temporary employees in the summer. He does, however, object to the $10 charge in the summer, because he can obtain equally qualified (for those jobs) workers at $7 per hour and he must use the drivers as a matter of firm policy.

Required: Discuss the issues involved and make a recommendation about the charges for the drivers' wages during the summer.

12-42 Determining a standard cost Renata Tomato Company processes and cans tomato paste. The company has the capability to can whole tomatoes as well, but has not done so for about a year because of lack of profitability. The production manager and controller were recently discussing the production plan for the next several months. They agreed, on the basis of the information in the schedule below, that the firm should continue to process only tomato paste. The firm has the capacity to process 5,000,000 pounds of tomatoes per month, whether for canning whole or making into paste.

	Whole Tomatoes	Tomato Paste
Selling price per case	$6.00	$5.80
Variable costs:		
Tomatoes[a]	3.10	2.00
Direct labor	0.90	1.00
Variable overhead	1.80	2.00
Packaging	0.52	0.60
Total variable costs	6.32	5.60
Contribution margin	($0.32)	$0.20

[a]Whole tomatoes must be grade A tomatoes, which cost 15.5¢ per pound.

Paste is made from grade B tomatoes, which cost $0.08 per pound. There are 20 pounds of tomatoes in a case of whole tomatoes, 25 pounds in a case of paste.

A few days after the decision had been made to process only paste, the president of the firm received a call from a large tomato grower who offered to sell Renata as many pounds of tomatoes as it could use for the next six months. The price was to be $0.095 per pound, and the batches would be mixed A and B grades. The grower would guarantee that at least 40% of the tomatoes would be grade A.

The president told the production manager about the offer. The latter replied that it could cost $0.005 per pound to sort the tomatoes into the two grades, but that there would be no other additional costs if the offer were accepted. The firm's capacity to process 5,000,000 pounds per month would not be affected. The firm can sell all it can produce.

The production and sales managers decided to investigate the probable effects of taking the offer. They agreed that it would be profitable to can whole tomatoes if the price were much less than the current $0.155 per pound, but they were uncertain of the effects on the contribution margin of paste. They agreed to ask the controller to prepare a new analysis of relative profitability of the two products.

The controller's analysis showed that paste was now a losing proposition, while whole tomatoes were extremely profitable. The controller's analysis showed the cost of tomatoes for both products at $0.10 per pound, the purchase price and additional sorting costs.

	Whole Tomatoes	Tomato Paste
Price per case	$6.00	$5.80
Variable costs:		
Tomatoes	2.00	2.50
Other variable costs	3.22	3.60
Total variable costs	5.22	6.10
Contribution margin	$0.78	($0.30)

The production manager and sales manager wondered about the wisdom of using the $0.10 per pound cost of tomatoes for both products. "After all," said the sales manager, "aren't we paying more for the grade A tomatoes and less for the grade B? It seems unreasonable to say that they have the same cost." The controller said that other methods were possible, suggesting that the costs could also be assigned based on the ratios of costs of buying the tomatoes already sorted. "If we did it that way," he said, "we would find that if we bought 2,000,000 pounds of grade A tomatoes at $0.155 it would cost $310,000. The 3,000,000 grade B tomatoes would cost $240,000 at $0.08. The total cost would be $550,000. The cost of grade B would thus be about 43.6% of the total. So we could assign $218,000 ($500,000 × 43.6%) to the grade B tomatoes in the package deal. That would give a cost per pound of $0.07267. Doing the same with the grade A produce would give $0.141 per pound."

At this point the president entered the room and commented that it seemed to him that the firm was buying $240,000 worth of grade B tomatoes at $0.08 per pound and the rest of the purchase and sorting costs should be assigned to the grade A tomatoes. "That would give $260,000 to the grade A ($500,000 − $240,000), which is $0.13 per pound. Wouldn't that be best?"

Required
1. Determine whether the firm should buy the unsorted tomatoes.
2. Discuss the appropriateness of the methods of determining the standard cost of tomatoes suggested by each of the managers and make a recommendation.

PRODUCT COSTING

Part Four deals with product costing—determining unit costs of manufactured products. The study of product costing is important to managers who are not accountants because many reports that managers use incorporate one or another of the methods considered in the following three chapters.

An understanding of cost behavior and of the significance of unit costs is particularly important in interpreting reports of manufacturing firms. Cost allocation is further considered together with its effects—how it can obscure information necessary for planning and decision making. The discussion of product costing methods also considers the potential behavioral problems associated with such methods. Thus, product costing also has implications for control and performance evaluation.

CHAPTER 13

INTRODUCTION TO PRODUCT COSTING: JOB-ORDER COSTING

This chapter begins a sequence of three chapters devoted to **product costing**—the determination of costs of inventory and of cost of goods sold—for manufacturing firms. In this and the next two chapters we shall deal only with certain highlights of the subject, providing an introduction to the basic approaches to product costing and cost accumulation methods.

GENERAL APPROACHES

The most common approach to product costing is **absorption costing** or **full costing.** The distinctive feature of this approach to determining the cost of a product is that it includes the calculation and use of a fixed cost per unit. Such a practice, as indicated in earlier chapters, is unwise for planning, control, and decision making. An alternative approach, **direct costing** or **variable costing,** follows the principle advocated throughout this book—that managers should consider fixed costs only in total, not per unit. That approach is illustrated in Chapter 14.

Given the emphasis in managerial accounting on *not* using per-unit fixed costs, why should a manager understand absorption costing? To answer this we have to understand that an accounting system serves several purposes. From it comes information for managers. But the system must also produce information for financial reporting and taxation purposes.

As pointed out in Chapter 1, users of financial accounting reports are different from those of managerial accounting reports. External users are interested in, among other things, making comparisons among firms. For that reason, financial accounting reports are subject to certain ground rules (called generally accepted accounting principles). These ground rules provide that financial accounting and tax reports of income utilize some measure of the *total* per-unit cost of a product. That is, in such reports, a total cost is associated with each unit of product, whether the unit is sold (cost of goods sold) or is still on hand (inventory). Hence, the accounting system must produce such cost data.

Since it is not unusual for companies to use, for internal purposes, data required for external purposes, a manager is likely to encounter reports that reflect per-unit fixed costs. Managers in a nonmanufacturing firm should not be affected by the carry-over of financial accounting rules to managerial reports. This is because in such firms the only cost normally associated with a unit of product sold or in inventory is a variable cost—the purchase cost of the unit. But managers in a manufacturing firm who receive reports based on the rules of external reporting must take into consideration that the information in the reports associates both variable and fixed manufacturing costs with a unit of product. As we know from earlier chapters, per-unit total costs can be misleading. Accordingly, it is particularly important that managers in manufacturing firms understand how the information they receive was developed and, more importantly, how to interpret that information in performing their functions of planning and control.

This chapter will help you understand and use absorption-costing information. But first, you will need to acquire an understanding of the flows of major costs in a manufacturing firm.

COST FLOWS

Every firm that makes a product or renders a service incurs a variety of costs. A merchandising concern incurs the cost of purchasing a ready-for-sale product, plus the costs of selling the product and administering the firm. A manufacturing concern incurs costs for the purchase of basic materials, the labor performed to turn these materials into a finished product, the facilities needed for the manufacturing process, and, of course, its selling and administrative efforts.

The selling and administrative costs of either type of firm are normally identified with the period in which the costs are incurred, and are called expenses in that period (**period costs**). Costs more obviously (at least intuitively) related to the product are not called expenses until the product leaves the firm and are identified as **product costs.** The accounting path followed by a product-associated cost, from the time it is incurred to the time it leaves the firm, is called the **flow of costs.**

From your study of financial accounting you are familiar with the flow of product costs for a merchandising company. The cost of purchased products flows into inventory and then into cost of goods sold. For a manufacturing firm, the basic situation is the same—costs flow into inventory and then to cost of goods sold. But the situation is complicated by two facts already noted in Chapters 3 and 6: (1) manufacturers typically have not one but three types of inventory, and (2) the cost associated with manufacturers' inventories includes more than the purchase price of materials needed in the manufacturing process.

At any given time, the products of a manufacturing firm may be in any of three different forms:

1. **Finished goods inventory,** consisting of units of product that are ready for sale. This inventory is equivalent to what is called *inventory* by a merchandising concern.
2. **Work in process inventory,** consisting of units of product that are semifinished (such as automobiles without windshields, doors, or engines). Reaching this semifinished state requires not only materials but also the services of laborers and the availability of manufacturing facilities. There is no equivalent of this inventory in a merchandising concern.
3. **Raw materials inventory,** consisting of the various materials and components that go into a finished product but on which no work has yet been done. Here, again, there is no equivalent in a merchandising concern, for such a concern handles only ready-to-sell products.

Thus, although the costs of a manufacturing concern flow, as with a merchandising concern, into inventory and eventually to cost of goods sold, the process is more complicated because the flow involves more than one type of inventory and involves costs other than direct purchasing costs.

The flow of costs in a manufacturing firm is shown in Figure 13-1 (page 506). The costs of materials are first collected in the Raw Materials Inventory account.[1] As materials are requisitioned for use in production, their costs flow to the Work in Process Inventory.[2] The cost of labor is first collected in Direct Labor, and then flows to Work in Process Inventory to show that work was done to help transform basic materials to a semifinished state. Costs incurred to provide manufacturing facilities (usually called *overhead costs*) are collected in Manufacturing Overhead and then flow to Work in Process Inventory, to show that the facilities are required to accommodate the transformation of raw materials to salable product. Thus, Work in Process Inventory collects the costs of materials, labor, and manufacturing overhead.

The costs accumulated in Work in Process are transferred to Finished Goods, to reflect the cost of units ready for sale. Finally, the costs of units sold are transferred from Finished Goods to Cost of Goods Sold. Generally speaking, then, *all* manufacturing costs flow through Work in Process, to Finished Goods, and, finally, to Cost of Goods Sold.

In many companies, products are finished very soon after they are begun, making work in process a negligible quantity. In other companies, the production process is

---

[1]There are many titles used in practice to designate the same basic things. For instance, some firms use the title ' Stores" to refer to the account that contains the cost of materials and purchased components.

[2]To make it easier to follow the discussion, we shall capitalize the names of accounts, while using lowercase to denote the items themselves. Thus, "Work in Process Inventory" refers to the account, while "work in process" refers to the physical, semifinished product.

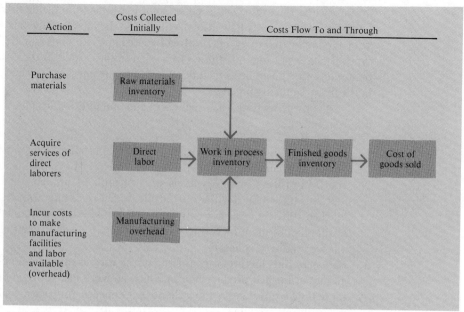

FIGURE 13-1   Flow of Costs in a Manufacturing Firm

long, perhaps a month or even more than a year, making work in process a significant amount.

Although the length of the manufacturing process can influence the accounting process, a much more influential factor is the nature of the product and of the manufacturing process. That is, the approach to collecting information about the production process can differ depending on whether the manufacturing process involves production of a variety of products quite different from one another or of what amounts to a series of production runs of identical (or very similar) products. The next section explains the significance of this distinction.

THE MANUFACTURING PROCESS

The nature of the manufacturing process that a company uses to make its products influences the way in which the firm accounts for its product costs. Consider a company that makes only one product over and over again, in a more or less continuous process. Every pound of sugar or flour or coffee, every gallon of orange or tomato juice, every individual brick, is virtually the same as any other. The nature of the manufacturing process makes it impossible to distinguish the cost of any *particular* pound of sugar or flour or coffee, or any particular gallon of orange or tomato juice, from the cost of any other, because all of the units move through the manufacturing process together. In such cases, it is quite appropriate to calculate a unit cost by dividing total production costs by the number of units (pounds, gallons, etc.) produced, and managers can be satisfied with knowing the cost of an "average" unit. Such companies would use what is called *process costing,* which is discussed in more detail in Chapter 15.

At the other end of the spectrum of manufacturing processes are situations in which the same product is rarely, if ever, produced twice. A construction company seldom builds exactly the same bridge, office building, or house twice. Each output is unique. A printer might work on 50 different books in a month, each with a different number of pages, type of ink, and quality of paper. Such companies typically produce several individual units, or several "batches" of product, with each unit or "batch" being different from the others. In such companies, a calculation of an average cost for the period (obtained by dividing total production costs for the period by the total number of units produced) is meaningless, because the units of product are so different as to make pointless a single measure of units of output. Yet the managers of such companies are keenly interested in the cost of each different unit or batch. For, while they might not make the same product again, they will make similar ones—requiring similar amounts of material and labor—in the future and therefore will want the ability to use the costs on current jobs to estimate costs of future jobs. Such companies use what is called **job-order costing,** the type of situation on which we concentrate in this chapter.

A job-order system requires keeping track of the materials and labor actually used on a particular job, and then *assigning* some amount of manufacturing overhead to each job. Tracing materials and labor to specific jobs is not a big problem; workers simply keep track of their time and of the materials they use on each job that they do. But it is impossible to trace all manufacturing overhead costs to jobs; many manufacturing overhead costs—such as heat, light, power, and machinery depreciation—do not obviously "attach" themselves to specific jobs. Hence, the costs of overhead are applied (assigned) to specific jobs indirectly, by determining an *overhead rate per unit of some input factor* (such as labor hours, machine hours, or whatever), with which total overhead costs seem to vary most closely.

Assigning overhead costs to one activity based on the level of some other activity (like labor hours) is not a new concept. We did this in Chapter 12, where we considered variable overhead as related to labor. In that chapter we used direct labor hours to determine the standard variable overhead cost per unit. In this chapter we relate all overhead costs to some input factor such as labor. Roughly speaking, when we assign overhead based on some input factor, we are saying that if a particular job requires, for example, 10% of total direct labor time, that job should also bear 10% of total overhead cost.

JOB-ORDER COSTING

Exhibit 13-1 contains some of the basic information we shall use to illustrate job-order costing, which requires that the costs of material, labor, and overhead be accumulated for specific customer orders. (For now, ignore the lower part of the exhibit which deals with budgeting information.) The Farr Company manufactures electronic sensing devices to customer order. It has two production departments through which each manufactured product must pass. Though materials and labor are added in each department, the two departments have different operating characteristics. The Machining Department is capital intensive; hence, overhead in that department is primarily related to machinery use and is assigned to products on the basis of machine hours used on a given product. On the other hand, the Assembly Department is labor intensive, so that labor hours are considered the most appropriate basis for assigning to products the overhead costs of that department. Exhibit 13-1 shows that three jobs (J-1, J-2, and J-3) were worked on in July.

As we saw earlier in the chapter, the distinctive feature of absorption costing is that it assign all costs, variable and fixed, to units of production. Thus, in determining the costs of the jobs worked on by Farr Company, it is necessary to adopt some method for making such an assignment. There are two commonly used methods for doing so: actual costing and normal costing. We shall use the data for Farr Company to illustrate the cost assignment procedures for both methods, and then we shall discuss the impact of those procedures on the financial statements, particularly on the income statement.

Actual Costing

We begin with a system called **actual job-order costing,** where all of the actual overhead incurred during the period is applied to the jobs worked on that period. The material and direct labor costs in Exhibit 13-1 were accumulated through records prepared

Exhibit 13-1
Farr Company Data for July

	Machining Department	Assembly Department
Total overhead costs	$140,000	$48,000
Total machine hours	7,000	—
Total direct labor hours	—	6,000
Overhead rates for July:		
Per machine hour	$ 20	
Per direct labor hour		$ 8

	Job Number			
Job Data:	J-1	J-2	J-3	Totals
Machine hours	2,000	1,000	4,000	7,000
Direct labor hours	1,000	3,000	2,000	6,000
Materials used	$22,000	$18,000	$34,000	$74,000
Direct labor				
at $10 per hour	$10,000	$30,000	$20,000	$60,000

Budgeted data for year

	Machining Department	Assembly Department
Machine hours	100,000	—
Direct labor hours	—	60,000
Overhead costs:		
$1,200,000 + ($5 per MH)	$1,700,000	
$300,000 + ($4 per DLH)		$540,000

by workers showing how much material and how much labor time and cost were used. All that remains is to apply overhead to the jobs. To assign all the overhead costs to the jobs, we calculate the overhead rates by dividing total actual overhead by the total amount of the relevant input factor—machine hours in the Machining Department, direct labor hours in the Assembly Department. In general form we have:

$$\frac{\text{Overhead rate}}{\text{for department}} = \frac{\text{total departmental overhead}}{\text{total departmental activity}}$$

In the specific situation here we have:

$$\frac{\text{Machining department}}{\text{overhead rate}} = \frac{\$140,000}{7,000}$$

$$= \$20 \text{ per machine hour}$$

$$\frac{\text{Assembly department}}{\text{overhead rate}} = \frac{\$48,000}{6,000}$$

$$= \$8 \text{ per direct labor hour}$$

The total costs on the three jobs can now be summarized as follows:

	Job Number		
	J-1	J-2	J-3
Machining overhead ($140,000):			
2,000 hrs. at $20	$40,000		
1,000 hrs. at $20		$20,000	
4,000 hrs. at $20			$ 80,000
Assembly overhead ($48,000):			
1,000 hrs. at $8	8,000		
3,000 hrs. at $8		24,000	
2,000 hrs. at $8			16,000
Total overhead	48,000	44,000	96,000
Materials	22,000	18,000	34,000
Direct labor	10,000	30,000	20,000
Total cost per job	$80,000	$92,000	$150,000

Notice that all $140,000 of Machining overhead cost is assigned to the three jobs ($40,000 + $20,000 + $80,000 = $140,000). All $48,000 in Assembly overhead is also assigned to the three jobs. Under actual costing, the total overhead incurred is assigned to individual jobs.

Suppose that job J-1 was the only one sold in July. Its cost would appear in the July income statement as cost of goods sold. If job J-2 was finished but not sold, then its cost would appear in the July 31 balance sheet as Finished Goods Inventory. And if job J-3 was still incomplete at the end of July, its cost would appear on the balance sheet as Work in Process Inventory.

Actual job-order costing is simple, but is not commonly used because it can produce misleading results. The cause of this problem is that overhead rates can fluctuate significantly from month to month, so that similar jobs done in different months might have quite different amounts of overhead and, hence, total cost. Perceiving the jobs as similar, managers may sell the products at about the same price, and the different gross profits (because of the differing total costs) could lead to unwarranted conclusions about profitability.

You may have already guessed, after having seen how the rates were computed, that there are two reasons for the fluctuations in overhead rates. First, activity (labor or machine hours) can differ from month to month. Such differences occur because of seasonality in the business or simply because of changes in the general economic situation. Second, the actual costs could fluctuate from period to period—heating is an obvious example. Though managers might expect higher heating costs in the winter, it is of doubtful value to say that products made in the winter "cost more." Consider the following example.

North Company normally incurs variable overhead at $2 per labor hour. In May its fixed overhead is $90,000; but in December, because of seasonal cost factors, it is $100,000. Labor hours are 10,000 in May, but 20,000 in December, again because of seasonal factors; however, in this case the seasonality relates to demand for the product. Under actual job-order costing, the overhead rates for the two months would be computed as follows:

	May	December
Total overhead costs:		
$ 90,000 + (10,000 × $2)	$110,000	
$100,000 + (20,000 × $2)		$140,000
Direct labor hours	10,000	20,000
Overhead rate per labor hour	$ 11	$ 7

Suppose, now, that North makes two similar jobs in May and December, each requiring 100 direct labor hours at $5 per hour and $800 in materials. The total costs of the jobs would be:

	Job Done in	
	May	December
Materials	$ 800	$ 800
Labor (100 × $5)	500	500
Overhead, at $11 and $7	1,100	700
Total	$2,400	$2,000

Does the job done in December really cost $400 less than the one done in May? Is it likely that a customer would be willing to pay more for a job just because it was done in one of the company's slow months? In fact, we showed in Chapter 3 that customers can usually get lower, not higher, prices in slow months, because companies need the business to keep their workers busy. Yet the profitability of the two products will *appear* different if they were sold at the same price, and this appearance could mislead a manager who is trying to develop a price quote on a similar job. To avoid encountering this problem, most companies use a technique called normal costing.

Normal Costing

The essence of **normal costing** is a smoothing of overhead rates over the year. The vehicle used to accomplish this smoothing is a **predetermined overhead rate.** That is, the firm uses a single overhead rate throughout the year, rather than an actual overhead rate computed each month. A predetermined overhead rate is just what the term suggests: an overhead rate calculated in advance. Obviously, then, it cannot be based on actual costs and activity. Rather, budgeted results are used, and the rate is calculated from the following formula.

$$\frac{\text{Predetermined}}{\text{overhead rate}} = \frac{\text{budgeted overhead for year}}{\text{budgeted production activity for year}}$$

Budgeted production activity can be expressed as direct labor hours, machine hours, or some other measure that managers think appropriate. Thus, the activity measures used in normal costing are the same as those used in actual costing; the difference is in the use of budgeted rather than actual figures.

Let us illustrate normal job-order costing with the Farr Company, using the budgeted data at the bottom of Exhibit 13-1 (page 508). Note that the budget formulas for overhead costs have the form we saw in several earlier chapters:

$$\frac{\text{Budget}}{\text{allowance}} = \frac{\text{fixed}}{\text{costs}} + \left(\frac{\text{variable cost per}}{\text{unit of activity}} \times \frac{\text{volume of}}{\text{activity}}\right)$$

Thus, total budgeted overhead in Machining is $1,700,000, which includes budgeted fixed costs of $1,200,000 per year, plus $5 of variable cost per machine hour (MH) times budgeted machine hours of 100,000. In the same fashion but using direct labor hours (DLH), total budgeted overhead for Assembly is $540,000. The *predetermined* overhead rates are $17 per machine hour ($1,700,000/100,000) for Machining and $9 per direct labor hour ($540,000/60,000) for Assembly. These rates, multiplied by the number of hours worked on each job, give the overhead costs of the jobs.

	Job Number		
	J-1	J-2	J-3
Machining overhead: 2,000 hrs. at $17	$34,000		
1,000 hrs. at $17		$17,000	
4,000 hrs. at $17			$ 68,000
Assembly overhead: 1,000 hrs. at $9	9,000		
3,000 hrs. at $9		27,000	
2,000 hrs. at $9			18,000
Total overhead	43,000	44,000	86,000
Materials, as before	22,000	18,000	34,000
Direct labor, as before	10,000	30,000	20,000
Total cost per job	$75,000	$92,000	$140,000

There are several important points in this schedule. First, notice that material cost and direct labor cost are the same for each job as they were under actual costing (schedule on page 509). But the overhead cost assignments are *not* all the same as they were under actual costing. This difference marks the distinction between the two costing methods. We shall expand on this point shortly.

The cost of job J-2 is the same as it was under actual costing because the changes in the rates canceled out. Jobs J-1 and J-3, however, show lower total costs under normal costing. Which set of costs for these specific jobs is "correct"? There is no answer to this question, much as there is no answer to the question whether first-in-first-out or last-in-first-out is the "correct" inventory cost flow assumption. A difference in results for specific jobs in specific months will appear under normal and actual costing, if for no other reason than that normal costing smooths fixed overhead over the activity for the entire year. This difference, between actual and normal overhead in a given period, is further discussed in the next section.

The following analysis should help you understand the different treatments of overhead under actual costing and normal costing. Under actual costing, the overhead cost assigned to a particular job is calculated as follows:

$$\text{Overhead assigned to job} = \frac{\text{actual hours worked on job}}{} \times \frac{\text{total actual overhead}}{\text{total actual hours}}$$

Under normal costing, the overhead assigned to a job is:

$$\text{Overhead assigned to job} = \frac{\text{actual hours worked on job}}{} \times \frac{\text{total budgeted overhead}}{\text{total budgeted hours}}$$

Thus, under actual costing, the sum of overhead assigned to jobs equals total actual overhead because the total actual hours worked on jobs equals the total actual hours. But under normal costing, in order to have total overhead assigned to jobs equal to total actual overhead, total budgeted overhead must equal total actual overhead *and* total actual hours must equal total budgeted hours. (Offsetting differences could make the assignment come out even, but that is unlikely.) The difference between actual overhead and applied overhead under normal costing is called *misapplied overhead*.

Misapplied Overhead

To explore the implications of using normal versus actual costing, let us look at the total overhead costs assigned under the two methods to jobs worked on in July:

	Overhead Applied to Jobs Using	
	Actual Costing	Normal Costing
Machining overhead (actual cost of $140,000):		
Job 1 Job 2 Job 3		
$40,000 + $20,000 + $80,000	$140,000	
$34,000 + $17,000 + $68,000		$119,000*
Assembly overhead (actual cost of $48,000):		
Job 1 Job 2 Job 3		
$ 8,000 + $24,000 + $16,000	48,000	
$ 9,000 + $27,000 + $18,000		54,000*
Total	$188,000	$173,000

*Note that total overhead assigned to jobs under normal costing could also be computed directly simply by multiplying the predetermined department overhead rate by the number of hours worked (by machines or workers) in the department. For example, total overhead assigned in Machining is 7,000 machine hours times the $17 predetermined rate.

Under actual costing, overhead assigned to jobs equals total actual overhead of $188,000. Such is not the case under normal costing, however. Machining overhead shows a $21,000 difference ($140,000 − $119,000), actual being greater than applied; Assembly overhead shows a $6,000 difference ($54,000 − $48,000), applied being greater than actual. These differences are called, respectively, **underapplied overhead** and **overapplied overhead.** (The terms **underabsorbed** and **overabsorbed overhead** are also used.) The difference in total is $15,000 of underapplied overhead (actual overhead exceeding applied overhead).

Some difference between actual and applied overhead is almost inevitable simply because overhead is applied by using a rate that is based on budgeted data. What is the significance of overapplied or underapplied overhead?

At first glance, misapplied overhead might look like the variances studied in Chapter 12. That is, if one views applied overhead as the "standard," any over- or underapplication might seem analogous to favorable and unfavorable variable cost variances. (After all, assigning to products more, or less, cost than is actually incurred does not change the total actual cost.) But it would be inappropriate to carry the analogy too far. Remember that the calculation of the predetermined overhead rate involves both budgeted costs and budgeted production activity. Part of the over- or underapplied overhead could result because actual costs are lower (a favorable variance) or higher (an unfavorable variance) than budgeted. Typically, however, some over- or underapplied overhead results from a difference between the actual level of production activity and the activity level used in the calculation of the predetermined overhead rate.

To illustrate these two points, let us look more closely at the results in the Assembly Department, which showed $6,000 overapplied overhead.

Laborers in Assembly worked 6,000 hours. The budget formula for the annual overhead cost for the department (Exhibit 13-1) is $300,000 of fixed costs plus $4 per labor hour for variable cost. Assume that monthly budgeted fixed overhead is $25,000 (one twelfth of the annual amount). We can compare July's budgeted and actual costs as follows:

Actual costs, fixed and variable	$48,000
Budgeted costs, $25,000 + ($4 × 6,000 hrs.)	49,000
Budget variance, favorable	$ 1,000

The department incurred $1,000 less total cost than was budgeted, a favorable occurrence. The calculation of a **budget variance** is not new with this chapter. In this case, we cannot determine how much of the variance relates to fixed cost and how much to variable cost, because we do not know the actual amounts of fixed and variable costs. But we do know now that part of the $6,000 of overapplied overhead in Assembly represents a favorable budget variance because actual costs were lower than budgeted costs.

Let us look at the other factor affecting the predetermined rate and, therefore, the amount of overhead applied. We know (again from Exhibit 13-1) that the department budgeted 60,000 direct labor hours for the year, for a monthly average of 5,000 hours. But in July the department worked 6,000 hours. The variance caused by a difference between actual hours worked and the budgeted hours used in the calculation of the rate that is used to apply overhead is called the **volume variance** or the **idle capacity variance.** It is computed as follows.

Budgeted cost, as computed above	$49,000
Applied cost ($9 × 6,000 actual hours)	54,000
Volume variance, favorable	$ 5,000

Note that using the budgeted cost in the calculation eliminates the effect of any budget variance. When applied overhead exceeds budgeted overhead, the volume variance is said to be favorable; when the opposite is true, the variance is said to be unfavorable. Hence, we have identified two favorable variances that add up to the $6,000 difference between actual and applied overhead in the Assembly Department for the month.

We understand the meaning of a budget variance, but does the volume variance have any economic significance? Very little, if any. Whether it is favorable or unfavorable is not, per se, good or bad, because it relates solely to the smoothing of fixed overhead, and arises only because actual hours do not equal the monthly share of budgeted hours. In order to see this, let us look still further at the $9 predetermined overhead rate.

The budgeted overhead cost used in the calculation of the $9 predetermined overhead rate has both a fixed and a variable component. The variable portion of the rate is $4 per hour, so the fixed portion is $5. (Alternatively, budgeted fixed overhead is $300,000 and budgeted hours are 60,000, also giving a $5 fixed portion.) Now, look at the difference between actual hours (6,000) and the 5,000 monthly share of the hours budgeted for the year. The volume variance is exactly that 1,000-hour difference multiplied by the $5 rate for fixed overhead. That this should be true is not surprising if you recast the calculation of the volume variance and separate budgeted and applied costs into their variable and fixed components, as below.

	Variable Portion		Fixed Portion	
Budgeted cost	(6,000 hrs. × $4)	$24,000	(5,000 hrs. × $5)	$25,000
Applied cost	(6,000 hrs. × $4)	24,000	(6,000 hrs. × $5)	30,000
Volume variance	—	—	(1,000 hrs. × $5)	$ 5,000

The total amount budgeted for variable costs depends on the actual level of activity (the flexible budget). But fixed costs are not expected to change with the level of activity, so the budgeted amount is not affected when more (or fewer) hours are worked than were budgeted. Thus, what produces the volume variance is the difference between budgeted and actual production activity, the 1,000 hours.

We now have three different, but equivalent, formulas for calculating volume variance.

$$\frac{\text{Volume}}{\text{variance}} = \frac{\text{total budgeted}}{\text{manufacturing overhead}} - \frac{\text{total applied}}{\text{manufacturing overhead}}$$

$$= \frac{\text{total budgeted fixed}}{\text{manufacturing overhead}} - \frac{\text{total applied fixed}}{\text{manufacturing overhead}}$$

$$= \frac{\text{predetermined overhead}}{\text{rate for fixed costs}} \times \left(\begin{array}{ccc}\text{budgeted} & & \text{actual} \\ \text{production} & - & \text{production} \\ \text{volume} & & \text{volume}\end{array}\right)$$

You should use the formula that is most convenient in a given situation, for they all give the same answer. The first would be used when, as was the case with the example, total budgeted and applied overhead are not separated into fixed and variable components. The next section addresses more directly the question of separate or combined rates as well as that of using rates covering more than one department.

Combining Overhead Rates

The single advantage of separating the predetermined overhead rate into fixed and variable components is that variances can then be determined for each component. Specifically, the budget variance, computed as a single amount in the example, could be further analyzed into a variance related to fixed overhead and one related to variable overhead. If, for example, we knew that the $48,000 of actual costs in the Assembly Department consisted of fixed costs of $21,000 and variable costs of $27,000, the separate budget variances could be computed as follows.

	Actual	Budget	Variance (favorable)
Fixed costs	$21,000	$25,000	($4,000)
Variable costs	27,000	24,000*	3,000
Total	$48,000	$49,000	($1,000)

*The flexible budget allowance of 6,000 hrs. at $4 per hr.

The $5,000 volume variance would not be changed by the use of separate predetermined overhead rates for fixed and variable overhead costs, since that variance is related only to fixed overhead.

In order to determine these variances, it is not sufficient to budget (and apply) the fixed and variable components separately. It must also be possible to separate the costs *incurred* (actual costs) into fixed and variable costs. Most companies use a single overhead rate encompassing both variable and fixed overhead costs. The principal reason for this is that a great many companies simply cannot make that separation when dealing with actual costs incurred. To see why this is so, recall what you learned in Chapter 3 about a mixed cost.

The variable and fixed components of a mixed cost may be identified by using various mathematical techniques (high-low, regression analysis, etc.). The ability to develop a formula that will be helpful in predicting the *total* amount of some cost (for planning purposes) does not imply the ability to recognize the variable and fixed portions of that cost *as it is incurred throughout the period.* (We saw this point in Chapter 12, pages 474–477, in connection with budget variances.) In a typical manufacturing situation, a large number of the individual overhead costs are mixed; consequently, there will be little likelihood that the firm will be able to classify *actual costs* as either variable or fixed. In the absence of such information about actual costs, the need for separate predetermined overhead rates disappears and a single rate, such as we used in the example, is the most practical.

While a firm may not be able to separate actual fixed and variable costs, it is important in many firms that there be a separation of total costs by department. Our illustration used different overhead rates for the two departments, and used different input factors as the basis for applying overhead in the departments. To use different input factors, the company must keep track of the input factors in each department by job. (That is, it must have records showing the machine hours by job and the direct labor hours by job.) The record keeping is costlier than it would be if the company used a single overhead rate for the entire factory and a single input factor as a base for applying overhead. Why, then, bother with departmental rates? The answer is that departments can differ greatly in their operating characteristics, and the job-by-job information produced using a single rate can mislead managers. As a matter of fact, a single rate can be misleading even if *all* departments use the same input factor as a base for applying overhead. An example should make the point clear.

The data given below relate to Reinhart Company, which makes electrical equipment.

	Departments		
	Fabrication	Assembly	Totals
Variable overhead rate per DLH	$8	$2	
Budgeted direct labor hours	25,000	25,000	50,000
Total budgeted variable overhead	$200,000	$ 50,000	$250,000
Budgeted departmental fixed overhead	200,000	100,000	300,000
Total budgeted overhead	$400,000	$150,000	$550,000
Direct labor hours, budgeted	25,000	25,000	50,000
Predetermined overhead rates	$16	$6	$11

The $11 plant-wide rate does not capture the differences between the two departments, and using it could lead to poor decisions. Notice that the $11 rate is only $3 higher than the *variable overhead rate* in the Fabrication Department. The $11 rate would not give a very high margin over the variable overhead in that department if the firm used the $11 rate in pricing and for other decisions.

Suppose the firm sets its prices at 120% of manufacturing costs, including overhead applied at the $11 rate. If the firm does get 25,000 direct labor hours in the Fabrication Department, the firm will charge its customers $330,000 for overhead in that department, calculated as follows:

Plant-wide rate	$11.00
Multiplied by 120% = charge to customers	$13.20
Multiplied by direct labor hours	25,000
Charges to customers for overhead	$330,000

Of course, Reinhart would also charge for materials and labor. We are concentrating on the price that it would charge related to overhead costs to illustrate the potential problem.

The charges to customers are less than the overhead for the department ($400,000), although they are greater than the variable overhead. In the long run, the firm must be able to cover all costs to earn profits, and charging $13.20 per hour for work done in fabrication will not cover that department's overhead. Of course, a charge at $13.20 per hour for overhead in the *Assembly Department* would provide a good profit, but the firm might lose customers whose jobs require a great deal of assembly time because the prices would seem high to the customers. If Reinhart had a competitor with a similar cost structure that used departmental rates, the competitor would charge only $7.20 ($6 × 120%) for work done in the Assembly Department, so that the competitor would probably get most of the business that required a high proportion of assembly time, while Reinhart would get most of the business that required a high proportion of fabrication time. The competitor would charge $19.20 ($16 × 120%) for work it did in fabrication, much more than the $13.20 that Reinhart would charge.

Finally, unless Reinhart uses departmental rates, it cannot determine contribution margins on products, nor can it make any of the volume-cost-profit analyses that would help it to make better decisions.

INCOME STATEMENTS, ACTUAL AND NORMAL COSTING

We began this chapter by pointing out that absorption costing, which involves some calculation of a *total* cost for a product, is the most commonly followed approach to product costing and is required in reports distributed outside the firm. We have also shown, using a job-order type of manufacturing process, two different methods for assigning overhead costs to product. Our illustration of the methods would not be complete without looking at how the manufacturing activity would appear in the company's income statement for July.

Exhibit 13-2 (page 518) shows the July income statement for Farr Company under the two methods. We have assumed that the firm had $40,000 of selling and administrative expenses in July and that, as suggested earlier, job J-1 was completed and was sold for $150,000. Costs accumulated on jobs J-2 and J-3 become inventory at the end of the month. In their internal reports, many companies would give further detail about the underapplied overhead, showing separately the budget and volume variances computed earlier.

Exhibit 13-2

Farr Company

Income Statement for July

	Actual Costing		Normal Costing	
Sales		$150,000		$150,000
Cost of sales:				
Beginning inventories	$ 0		$ 0	
Manufacturing costs:				
Materials	74,000		74,000	
Labor	60,000		60,000	
Overhead–actual	188,000			
–applied			173,000	
Total current costs	322,000		307,000	
Total costs	322,000		307,000	
Less, ending inventory	242,000*		232,000†	
Cost of sales		80,000		75,000
Normal gross margin				75,000
Underapplied overhead				15,000§
Actual gross margin		70,000		60,000
Selling and administrative expenses		40,000		40,000
Income		$ 30,000		$ 20,000

*Job J-2 ($92,000) + Job J-3 ($150,000) = $242,000
†Job J-2 ($92,000) + Job J-3 ($140,000) = $232,000
§Actual overhead of $188,000, less applied overhead of $173,000, as shown on page 512.

Although there is some difference in the number of entries in the statements, the most obvious, and critical difference is in the amount of income ($30,000 under actual costing and $20,000 under normal costing). What caused the $10,000 difference?

The difference between actual absorption costing and normal absorption costing lies in the treatment given to overhead. So, you were quite right if you identified the income difference as related to a difference in overhead treatment. You were wrong, however, if you thought the income difference was because normal costing ignored some of the overhead actually incurred. The total manufacturing overhead under both methods is the actual amount of $188,000. The actual-costing income statement shows the actual overhead in a single amount; the normal-costing income statement shows the actual overhead in two amounts, $173,000 assigned to production, and $15,000 as a separate deduction.

If you look closely at the statements you will see that the source of the $10,000 difference in income is a $10,000 difference in the ending inventories. Specifically, the cost of job J-3 is $10,000 greater under actual costing than under normal costing, and that difference occurs because more overhead is assigned to that job under actual costing. Remember that overhead was assigned at the actual rate under actual costing, but at a predetermined rate for normal costing, so that for a single period within the year such differences are not uncommon. However, at year end, most companies using normal costing would convert to actual costing if they have significant amounts of overapplied or underapplied overhead. In so doing, the overhead assigned to unfinished jobs would be adjusted to the actual rate, and the difference in inventory would virtually disappear.

Although we have chosen to show an amount called *normal gross margin,* and have deducted the underapplied overhead from that amount, there is another possibility. The underapplied overhead could simply be added to normal cost of sales, and the profit figure would not change. Either approach can be used in a normal-costing statement. We chose the former approach to take advantage of your familiarity with the calculation of cost of goods sold as the addition of beginning inventory and current costs, followed by the subtraction of the ending inventory. Still another possibility would be to omit the calculation of cost of goods sold, and show only the final result. The income statements in Exhibit 13-3 show the condensed format and are equivalent to those in Exhibit 13-2.

Exhibit 13-3
Farr Company
Income Statement for July

	Actual Costing	Normal Costing
Sales	$150,000	$150,000
Cost of sales (Job J-1)	80,000	75,000
Normal gross margin		75,000
Underapplied overhead		15,000
Actual gross margin	70,000	60,000
Selling and administrative expenses	40,000	40,000
Income	$ 30,000	$ 20,000

One final observation on how operating results for an interim (part-of-a-year) period can differ under actual and normal costing. In the illustration there were no unfinished jobs at the beginning of July, so the entire difference in incomes between the two methods could be identified with the different assignments of overhead to jobs in inventory at the end of the month. Had there been a beginning inventory, a difference in incomes for July would also have been affected by different assignments of overhead to jobs in that inventory. Again, year-end conversion to actual costing, prompted largely by financial accounting requirements, will make the differences disappear.

ABSORPTION COSTING IN OTHER SETTINGS

Though we illustrated absorption costing in a job-order situation, the concepts are applicable in other situations. Consider, for example, a company that manufactures a single product. Actual fixed overhead for each period could be allocated equally among all units produced during that period (actual costing). Or, for essentially the same reasons as suggested earlier, such a firm might choose to develop an overhead application rate based on expected fixed overhead and production for the year, and apply that rate to units produced in periods within that year (normal costing). (Note that, in this case, the application rate would be based on output—units produced—rather than on some input factor such as labor or machine hours or materials cost.) The calculation of unit costs in such a firm is straightforward unless there are inventories of unfinished units at the beginning or end of a period (work in process inventories). Chapter 15 discusses the computational complications of dealing with in-process units in such a firm.

Whether one, or more than one, product is manufactured, companies that establish standard costs (such as those presented in Chapter 12) can also use absorption costing. Chapter 14 discusses the calculation and usefulness of a standard fixed cost per unit.

SUMMARY

Product costing is the determination of costs of inventory and of cost of goods sold for manufacturing firms. The approach to product costing followed by virtually all such firms is absorption costing, which requires that all manufacturing costs, variable and fixed, be included in the calculation of unit cost. The approach is required for financial reporting and income tax purposes.

In a manufacturing firm, costs flow through inventory accounts to cost of goods sold. Data regarding cost flows are accumulated in various ways, depending in many cases on the nature of the manufacturing process. Companies that produce essentially identical products accumulate and evaluate costs using process costing; companies that seldom produce the same product accumulate and evaluate costs using job-order costing.

Some firms compute job costs based on the actual costs incurred. Others use a normal costing system, under which the firm applies overhead to products using a predetermined overhead rate based on budgeted manufacturing overhead and budgeted production activity. The rate is usually stated as a cost per unit of some input measure such as direct labor hours. Predetermined overhead rates can be calculated for each department or for a factory as a whole, and, on occasion, separate rates are computed for fixed and variable overhead.

KEY TERMS

absorption (or full) costing
actual absorption costing
applied (absorbed) overhead
budget variance
finished goods inventory
flow of manufacturing costs
idle capacity variance
job-order costing
normal costing

overapplied (overabsorbed) overhead
period cost
predetermined overhead rate
product cost
raw materials inventory
underapplied (underabsorbed) overhead
volume variance
work in process inventory

KEY FORMULAS

$$\text{Unit cost} = \frac{\text{total manufacturing cost}}{\text{total number of units produced}}$$

$$\text{Predetermined overhead rate} = \frac{\text{budgeted manufacturing overhead for year}}{\text{budgeted production activity for year}}$$

$$\begin{matrix} \text{Variable overhead} \\ \text{budget variance} \end{matrix} = \begin{matrix} \text{actual} \\ \text{variable} \\ \text{overhead} \end{matrix} - \begin{matrix} \text{(flexible) budget} \\ \text{allowance for actual} \\ \text{hours worked} \end{matrix}$$

$$\begin{matrix} \text{Underabsorbed} \\ \text{(overabsorbed)} \\ \text{overhead} \end{matrix} = \begin{matrix} \text{actual} \\ \text{manufacturing} \\ \text{overhead} \end{matrix} - \begin{matrix} \text{applied} \\ \text{manufacturing} \\ \text{overhead} \end{matrix}$$

$$\begin{matrix} \text{Fixed overhead} \\ \text{budget} \\ \text{variance} \end{matrix} = \begin{matrix} \text{actual} \\ \text{fixed} \\ \text{overhead} \end{matrix} - \begin{matrix} \text{budgeted} \\ \text{fixed} \\ \text{overhead} \end{matrix}$$

$$\text{Volume variance} = \begin{matrix} \text{budgeted (fixed)} \\ \text{manufacturing} \\ \text{overhead} \end{matrix} - \begin{matrix} \text{applied (fixed)} \\ \text{manufacturing} \\ \text{overhead} \end{matrix}$$

$$\text{Volume variance} = \left(\begin{matrix} \text{budgeted} \\ \text{hours} \end{matrix} - \begin{matrix} \text{actual} \\ \text{hours} \end{matrix} \right) \times \begin{matrix} \text{predetermined} \\ \text{fixed overhead} \\ \text{rate} \end{matrix}$$

$$\begin{matrix} \text{Total overhead} \\ \text{budget} \\ \text{variance} \end{matrix} = \begin{matrix} \text{actual} \\ \text{total} \\ \text{overhead} \end{matrix} - \begin{matrix} \text{budgeted} \\ \text{total} \\ \text{overhead} \end{matrix}$$

REVIEW PROBLEM—ACTUAL AND NORMAL COSTING

Boulder Machinery Company makes drill presses to customer order and uses job-order costing. The firm began the month of March with no inventories. During March, it worked on two jobs, for which data appear below.

	Job #15	Job #16
Materials used	$69,000	$45,000
Direct labor at $10 per hour	$35,000	$60,000

Boulder incurred factory overhead costs of $209,000. Budgeted monthly factory overhead is $150,000 + ($5 × direct labor hours). The firm uses a predetermined overhead rate based on 10,000 direct labor hours per month. Activity does not usually fluctuate much from one month to another.

Required
1. Calculate the predetermined overhead rate per direct labor hour.
2. Determine the amounts of overhead to apply to each job.
3. Determine the overhead budget variance and volume variance.
4. Suppose that job #15 was sold for $240,000 and job #16 remained in inventory. Selling and administrative expenses for March were $24,000. Prepare an income statement for March. Treat variances as adjustments to gross margin.
5. Suppose now that the firm used actual costing, allocating overhead to jobs based on the actual overhead rate per direct labor hour. Determine the amounts of overhead applied to each job and prepare an income statement assuming the relevant data from part 4.

Answer to Review Problem

1. $20.00 per direct labor hour, calculated as follows:

$$\text{Predetermined rate} = \frac{\text{total budgeted overhead}}{\text{total budgeted activity}}$$

$$= \frac{\$150,000 + (\$5 \times 10,000)}{10,000}$$

$$= \$20$$

The rate consists of $15 fixed and $5 variable. Because there is no significant fluctuation in activity it is perfectly reasonable to use the monthly rather than the annual figures to calculate the rate. In fact, with annual fixed overhead of $1,800,000 ($150,000 × 12) and 120,000 direct labor hours (10,000 × 12), we would have exactly the same result.

2.

	Job #15	Job #16	Totals
Direct labor hours:			
$35,000/$10	3,500		
$60,000/$10		6,000	9,500
Overhead at $20 per hour	$70,000	$120,000	$190,000

3.

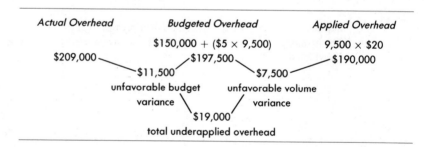

Actual Overhead	Budgeted Overhead	Applied Overhead
	$150,000 + ($5 × 9,500)	9,500 × $20
$209,000	$197,500	$190,000
$11,500		$7,500
unfavorable budget variance		unfavorable volume variance
	$19,000	
	total underapplied overhead	

4.

Sales		$240,000
Cost of sales, normal cost[a]		174,000
Gross margin on normal cost		66,000
Variances:		
Budget variance	$11,500U	
Volume variance	7,500U	19,000
Actual gross margin		47,000
Selling and administrative expenses		24,000
Income		$ 23,000

[a]Job #15, materials + direct labor + applied overhead =
$69,000 + $35,000 + $70,000 = $174,000

5. The problem here is simply to determine the actual overhead rate.

$$\text{Actual rate} = \frac{\text{actual overhead}}{\text{actual activity}}$$

$$= \frac{\$209,000}{9,500 \text{ hours}}$$

$$= \$22.00 \text{ per hour}$$

The applied amounts are:

	Job #15	Job #16	Total
Direct labor hours	3,500	6,000	9,500
Overhead applied at $22 per hour	$77,000	$132,000	$209,000

Thus, all overhead goes to individual jobs so that there are no variances. The income statement would show the following, with Job #15 costing $181,000 ($69,000 + $35,000 + $77,000).

Sales	$240,000
Cost of sales	181,000
Gross margin	59,000
Selling and administrative expense	24,000
Income	$ 35,000

The difference in incomes arises from the differences in inventory. Under actual costing the $19,000 underapplied overhead from normal costing is spread to the individual units, giving them higher costs.

REVIEW PROBLEM—OVERHEAD VARIANCES

Using the data from Exhibit 13-1 (page 508), compute the budget and volume variances for the Machining Department of Farr Company. Monthly budgeted fixed overhead is one twelfth of annual budgeted fixed overhead.

Answer to Review Problem

We already know that the overhead in the Machining Department was $21,000 underapplied in July, since actual costs were $140,000 and only $119,000 of overhead was applied (page 512). What we need to know are the budgeted costs for the same period. The annual cost formula is $1,200,000 + $5 per machine hour, with total budgeted hours of 100,000. The budgeted fixed cost for a month would be $100,000 (one twelfth of the year), and budgeted monthly production activity would be 8,333⅓ machine hours. We can now compute the budget variance.

Actual costs	$140,000
Budgeted costs, $100,000 + ($5 × 7,000 actual hours)	135,000
Budget variance, unfavorable	$ 5,000

Knowing the $5,000 unfavorable budget variance and the fact that overhead was under-applied by $21,000 for the month, we also know that the volume variance must be $16,000 ($21,000–$5,000), and that the variance must be unfavorable. But let us compute the variance separately.

Budgeted costs, as above	$135,000
Applied cost, $17 × 7,000 machine hours	119,000
Volume variance, unfavorable	$ 16,000

If we choose to separate the components of the $17 predetermined overhead rate, we could say that the fixed component is the $1,200,000 budgeted annual fixed cost divided by the 100,000 budgeted annual machine hours, or $12 per machine hour. (The variable component would be the $5 in the budget formula.) The volume variance could now be computed as follows.

Budgeted fixed costs for the month	$100,000
Fixed overhead applied, $12 × 7,000 hrs.	84,000
Volume variance, unfavorable	$ 16,000

Finally, the volume variance could be determined by looking only at the difference between actual and budgeted production.

Predetermined overhead rate for fixed costs, as above	$12 per hr.
Difference between budgeted and actual	
production activity (8,333⅓ − 7,000 hrs.)	1,333⅓ hrs.
Volume variance ($12 × 1,333⅓ hrs.)	$16,000

ASSIGNMENT MATERIAL

Questions for Discussion

13-1   Interrelationships with earlier chapters   What similarities and differences do you see between predetermined overhead rates and flexible expense budgets?

13-2   Absorbing overhead   Businesspeople sometimes make statements like the following: "Our overhead rates allow us to absorb our overhead costs at 80% of capacity."

Required: Comment on this statement. What does it mean?

13-3   Overhead application   "Underapplied overhead is a bad sign. This is because the more overhead you apply, the lower your fixed cost per unit." Discuss these statements critically.

13-4   Actual and normal costing   Suppose that a firm begins and ends the year with no inventories. Would there be any difference between its income computed using actual costing and using normal costing? Why or why not?

13-5 **"What's normal about it?"**   A student sitting near you in class just uttered the words that form the title of this question. The student does not see how you can apply overhead to work done each month, and went on to say: "If it costs you $15 in one month and $12 the next, that's the way it goes. All this 'applying' business is a bookkeeping trick, but it doesn't make any sense in the real world."

Required: Comment on the statements.

Exercises

13-6 **Job-order costing—income statement**   SBO Company uses normal job-order costing. Its predetermined overhead rate is based on the following data.

Variable overhead per direct labor hour	$4
Total budgeted fixed overhead	$800,000
Total budgeted direct labor hours	200,000

The company began 19X5 with no inventories. A summary of material and direct labor cost for 19X5 appears below. All direct laborers earn $10 per hour.

	Total	Jobs Sold	Jobs in Ending Inventories
Material costs	$ 900,000	$ 800,000	$100,000
Direct labor cost	$1,800,000	$1,600,000	$200,000

Total sales were $6,000,000; selling and administrative expenses were $400,000. Total actual manufacturing overhead was $1,540,000.

Required
1. Compute the predetermined overhead rate for 19X5.
2. Prepare an income statement for 19X5 with overapplied or underapplied overhead shown as an adjustment to cost of sales.

13-7 **Predetermined overhead rates**   For each of the following situations, fill in the missing data. The predetermined overhead rates are based on budgeted fixed costs and budgeted labor hours for the year.

	(a) Fixed Overhead Rate	(b) Budgeted Fixed Overhead	(c) Budgeted Hours	(d) Actual Hours	(e) Overhead Applied
1.	_____	$180,000	30,000	32,000	_____
2.	$5	_____	20,000	22,000	_____
3.	_____	$ 72,000	_____	11,000	$ 66,000
4.	$6	$120,000	_____	_____	$108,000
5.	$3	_____	18,000	_____	$ 45,000

13-8   Selecting an overhead base   Pruess Company does not now use predetermined overhead rates for applying fixed overhead to jobs. The controller wishes to begin doing so and has developed the following information for one department: budgeted fixed manufacturing overhead for the coming year is $450,000; budgeted direct labor hours are 60,000; budgeted machine hours are 75,000.

Required
1.   Compute two predetermined rates that could be used in this department.
2.   The results during the year were as follows: fixed manufacturing overhead, $440,000; direct labor hours 68,000; machine hours, 77,000. For each of the rates determined in part 1 above, determine (a) the amount of overhead that would be applied to jobs; and (b) the amount of overapplied or underapplied overhead.

13-9   Overhead relationships—variances   Each of the following cases is independent. Fill in the blanks, being sure to indicate whether a variance is favorable or unfavorable. The figures for "total budgeted overhead" are the flexible budget allowances based on the actual level of activity for the period. In each case, the firm uses a single rate to apply both fixed and variable overhead.

Case	(a) Total Budgeted Overhead	(b) Total Actual Overhead	(c) Total Applied Overhead	(d) Total Budget Variance	(e) Volume Variance
1	$400,000	$405,000	$390,000	_____	_____
2	$600,000	_____	$585,000	$10,000U	_____
3	$300,000	$310,000	_____	_____	$20,000F
4	$300,000	_____	_____	$ 6,000F	$10,000U

13-10   Job-order costing—assigning overhead   Marquette Machinery is a job-order company. It uses normal costing with its predetermined overhead rate based on the following information. Monthly budgeted overhead = $800,000 + ($2 × direct labor cost). Monthly budgeted direct labor cost is $1,000,000. At the end of March, the following information was available.

	Total	Jobs Sold	Jobs in Ending Inventory of Work in Process	Finished Goods
Material cost	$610,000	$500,000	$ 50,000	$60,000
Direct labor cost	$990,000	$800,000	$100,000	$90,000

Actual overhead for the month was $2,520,000.

Required
1.   Determine cost of goods sold for the month.
2.   Determine the ending inventory of work in process.
3.   Determine the ending inventory of finished goods.
4.   Determine overapplied or underapplied overhead.

13-11   Predetermined overhead rates—job-order costing   Walton Company uses predetermined rates for fixed overhead, based on machine hours. The following data are available relating to 19X5.

Budgeted fixed factory overhead cost	$160,000
Budgeted machine hours	40,000
Actual fixed factory overhead cost incurred	$158,000
Actual machine hours used	38,000

Jobs worked on:

Job No.	Machine hours used on job
12	12,000
13	16,000
14	7,000
15	3,000

Required
1. Compute the predetermined overhead rate to be used for the year.
2. Determine the overhead to be applied to each job worked on during the year.
3. Determine the budget variance.
4. Determine total over- or underapplied overhead at the end of the year.

13-12 Job-order costing Wisconsin Machinery Company makes large industrial machines. The firm uses a job-order cost system with overhead applied to jobs at $15 per direct labor hour. Direct laborers are paid $8 per hour. The following data apply to jobs worked on in March 19X4.

	4-22	4-23	4-24	4-25
Costs in beginning inventory:				
Materials	$ 34,000	$10,000	0	0
Direct labor	48,000	8,000	0	0
Overhead	90,000	15,000	0	0
Total	$172,000	$33,000	0	0
Costs incurred in March:				
Materials	$11,000	$46,000	$60,000	$ 9,000
Direct labor	$16,000	$32,000	$52,000	$12,000

Job 4-22 was completed and sold in March. Jobs 4-23 and 4-24 were also completed and sold. Job 4-25 was not finished at the end of March. Total overhead incurred during March was $212,000.

Required
1. Compute the amounts of overhead to be applied to each job.
2. Compute the amount of over- or underapplied overhead for March.
3. Compute cost of goods sold for March and the inventory at March 31.
4. Sales revenue from the three jobs sold was $860,000 and selling and administrative expenses for March were $180,000. Prepare an income statement for March.

13-13 Comparison of actual and normal costing The Riopelle Company uses actual job-order costing, assigning overhead to jobs based on direct labor cost. During March, the company had the following activity:

	Jobs Worked on in March		
	M-1	M-2	M-3
Material costs	$30,000	$41,000	$35,000
Direct labor cost	$20,000	$15,000	$25,000

Total actual overhead was $168,000, selling and administrative expenses were $24,000. Job M-1 was sold for $160,000. Jobs M-2 and M-3 were incomplete at the end of March.

Required

1. Determine the actual overhead rate per direct labor dollar.
2. Determine the overhead assigned to each job and the total cost of each job.
3. Prepare an income statement for March.
4. Suppose now that the company uses normal costing, with its predetermined overhead rate based on $2,100,000 budgeted overhead and $700,000 budgeted direct labor cost for the year. Calculate the predetermined overhead rate and redo parts 2 and 3 using normal costing. Show any misapplied overhead as an adjustment to gross margin.

13-14 Graphical analysis of overhead   The graph below shows the budgeted manufacturing overhead for Minich Company.

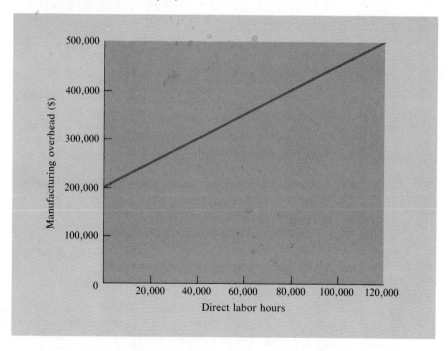

Required

1. Draw in the line that represents applied overhead for each of the following cases.
   (a) The predetermined overhead rate is $5 per direct labor hour.
   (b) The predetermined overhead rate is based on 100,000 direct labor hours.
2. Suppose that actual overhead equals budgeted overhead and that volume is 90,000

direct labor hours. What are the volume variances under each of the two cases from part 1?

13-15 Job-order costing The data below pertain to the March operations of Covera Machine Tool Company. The company ships jobs as it completes them, keeping no inventory of finished goods.

Jobs in beginning work in process:	
Materials	$243,080
Direct labor	$322,200
Factory overhead	$467,190
Materials put into process in March:	
To jobs in ending inventory	$233,430
To jobs finished and sold in March	$856,340
Direct labor:	
To jobs in ending work in process	$452,400
To jobs finished and sold in March	$892,880

The company uses normal costing and applies overhead at $1.45 per direct labor dollar. The material and labor costs for jobs finished and sold include the cost to finish the beginning inventory of work in process.

The company had sales of $4,680,000 in March, and had selling and administrative expenses of $453,650.

Required
1. Determine the overhead cost in ending inventory of work in process and in cost of goods sold.
2. If overhead was underapplied by $34,540 in March, what was actual overhead incurred?
3. Prepare an income statement for March, treating underapplied overhead as an expense.

13-16 Basic job-order costing Kelton Company makes a wide variety of gear assemblies for industrial applications. The firm uses normal costing, with a predetermined overhead rate of $4.50 per direct labor hour. During March, 19X6 Kelton worked on the jobs listed below:

	Job Number		
	311	312	313
Materials used on job	$14,510	$23,760	$ 9,540
Direct labor cost	$17,250	$12,420	$11,300
Direct labor hours	1,500	1,100	940

Required
1. Compute the amounts of overhead that would be applied to each job and the total cost of each job.
2. Actual overhead for March was $16,300. How much was overapplied or underapplied overhead?

13-17   Overhead application   The controller of Williams Company has received the following budgeted amounts for manufacturing overhead costs of 19X7.

	Fixed Amount	Variable Cost per Direct Labor Hour
Indirect labor	$ 58,000	$0.90
Supplies	19,000	0.15
Lubricants	12,000	0.08
Utilities	47,000	0.50
Repairs	18,000	0.17
Property taxes	8,000	0
Depreciation	18,000	0
Total	$180,000	$1.80

It is estimated that 60,000 direct labor hours will be worked in 19X7.

Required
1.   Compute the predetermined fixed overhead rate per direct labor hour.
2.   Assume that 62,000 direct labor hours are worked on jobs in 19X7.
    (a)   How much fixed overhead will be applied?
    (b)   How much variable overhead should be incurred? How much applied?
    (c)   If actual overhead costs are $304,000, how much overapplied or underapplied overhead results from controllable causes (budget variances)?

13-18   Overhead application   Vavasour Company is a highly automated operation that measures its activity by machine hours. Its managers have budgeted machine hours for jobs in the coming year, 19X2, at 400,000. They budget annual manufacturing overhead using the formula:

$$\text{Total budgeted overhead} = \$2,400,000 + (\$0.80 \times \text{machine hours})$$

Required
1.   Compute the predetermined overhead rate for 19X2.
2.   At the end of 19X2, the controller has collected the following information. There were no beginning inventories.

Total manufacturing overhead incurred		$2,730,000
Total machine hours		385,000
Machine hours on jobs sold	310,000	
Machine hours on jobs in ending inventories	75,000	

Determine the amounts of applied overhead in costs of goods sold and in ending inventories. Determine the amount of overapplied or underapplied overhead and break it down into the budget variance and volume variance.

13-19   Job-order costing—two departments   Barton Machinery Company makes bottle-capping equipment. Each order is somewhat different from all others, so that the firm uses job-order costing. There are two departments, Machining and Assembly. The Machining Department is highly mechanized and the Assembly Department is labor intensive. Accordingly, the firm applies overhead using machine hours in the Machining

Department, direct labor hours in the Assembly Department. Budgeted data for the two departments for 19X6 appear below.

	Machining Department	Assembly Department
Total budgeted overhead	$360,000	$144,000
Machine hours	120,000	
Direct labor hours		72,000

During March of 19X6 the firm worked on two jobs. Data on these jobs appear below.

	Job #1029	Job #1030
Materials used	$21,000	$32,000
Direct labor, Assembly Department		
at $6 per hour	$18,000	$19,200
Machine hours in Machining Department	4,000	5,000

Required
1. Calculate the predetermined overhead rate for each department using the budgeted results.
2. Calculate the amounts of overhead applied to each job and the total cost of each job.
3. Actual overhead in the Machining Department was $28,000 and in the Assembly Department was $12,100. Calculate the amounts of overapplied or underapplied overhead for each department.

Problems

13-20 **Basic job-order costing** Walker Company manufactures precision optical instruments that its customers need made to order. The firm uses normal costing, setting its predetermined overhead rate based on direct labor hours. For 19X4, the rate is $6.30 per hour, which is based on $1,890,000 budgeted overhead and 300,000 budgeted hours.

During January, the firm worked on three jobs, which we summarize below:

	Job Number		
	M-101	R-12	Z-610
Materials used	$ 47,800	$63,200	$41,600
Direct labor cost	$112,200	$96,400	$87,300
Direct labor hours	11,600	8,950	7,780

Job M-101 was completed and sold while the other two remained in inventory at the end of January. Actual overhead incurred in January was $166,400.

Required
1. Determine the amount of overhead that should be applied to each job.
2. Determine cost of goods sold for January and the ending inventory.
3. Determine the amount of overapplied or underapplied overhead for January.

13-21   Job costing in a service firm   Russell and Morrison is a firm of architectural engineers operating in a single office in a medium-sized city. The firm charges clients for the time that each person on the staff spends on the client's business, using a rate of 2½ times the person's salary, based on an 1,800-hour working year. Thus, an architectural draftsman earning a salary of $15,000 would be charged out to clients at $21 per hour [($15,000/1,800) × 2.5 = $20.83, rounded to $21]. The rate is intended to cover all costs as well as yield a profit to the firm.

Budgeted results for 19X9 are as follows:

Salaries of professional staff	$ 700,000
Salaries of support personnel (clerks, typists, etc.)	78,000
Other costs	680,000
Total expected costs	$1,458,000

The listed costs do not include any salaries for Russell and Morrison. Each partner expects to work about 1,200 chargeable hours and to bill those hours at a rate of $60 per hour. About 80% of the time of professional staff is chargeable to clients, about 40% of the time of support personnel. The nonchargeable time is for general firm business, professional activities (attending seminars and continuing-education programs), and the like.

Required
1. What income should the partners earn, in total, if their estimates of costs and performed services prove correct?
2. Suppose that two specific professional employees work on the architectural design for a particular client. One earns $18,000 per year, the other $21,000, and each works 12 hours on this particular project. How much will the firm charge the client for the project assuming that neither the partners nor the support staff is involved in this project? (Round hourly rates to the nearest dollar.)

13-22   Allocation and behavior   Brenner Company allocates joint production costs such as depreciation, property taxes, payroll office, and factory accounting on the basis of cost of materials used on jobs in each production department. Material costs for the coming year are expected to be $300,000, joint production costs $750,000.

The manager of the fabricating department has developed a new process that requires 10% more materials than the old, but 20% less labor time. Without the new process, she expects to incur materials costs of $60,000 and labor of $50,000 during the coming year.

Required: Would it be desirable to introduce the new process? Consider the viewpoints of both the firm and the manager of the fabricating department. If your answers conflict, suggest a solution.

13-23   Overhead application and pricing decisions   Grendel Company makes high-quality furniture. The company has just received an offer from a large furniture wholesaler for a single batch of goods. The sale price is $25,000, which is about $10,000 less than would ordinarily be obtained from such a batch. The sales manager is sure that existing sales would be unaffected by the special order and he would like to accept the order if any profit can be made. The production manager provides the following estimates of cost for the order.

Materials	$ 6,000
Direct labor (3,000 hours)	9,000
Overhead	15,000
Total	$30,000

The production manager informs you that the overhead cost is based on the firm's overhead application rate of $5 per direct labor hour. The rate includes both fixed and variable overhead and was determined based on 60,000 expected direct labor hours and $300,000 budgeted total overhead costs. The rate last year was $5.50, based on 50,000 direct labor hours and $275,000 total overhead costs. The production manager tells you that the difference in rates is due to the difference in direct labor hours—the cost structure is the same this year as last year.

Required
1. Determine the incremental cost of producing the order. Should the order be accepted?
2. What other factors should be considered in deciding whether to accept this special order?

13-24 **Overhead rates and cost analysis**   Walton Machinery Company makes a variety of industrial machines and uses a job-order costing system. The firm has recently been operating at well below capacity and the sales manager has been trying to increase orders. She recently received an offer to bid on a large press and submitted the specifications to Walton's cost estimators. Their estimate appears below:

Materials	$29,600
Direct labor at $9 per hour	19,800
Overhead at $12 per direct labor hour	26,400
Total manufacturing cost	75,800
Standard allowance for selling and	
administrative expenses, 10% of manufacturing cost	7,580
Total cost	83,380
Standard allowance for profit at 15% of total cost	12,507
Suggested price	$95,887

The sales manager told the executive vice president that the price above would not be low enough to get the job. She said that the customer expected a price in the neighborhood of $75,000, which another company had already bid. The vice president called in the controller, who said that the overhead rate was about 60% variable, 40% fixed, and that variable selling and administrative expenses were negligible. The vice president was reluctant to meet the $75,000 price, but agreed to think it over and get back to the sales manager.

Required: Advise the managers. Should the firm meet the $75,000 price?

13-25 **Pricing policy and profits**   Sumter Company is a job-order firm. It uses material supplied by its customers, so that virtually all of its manufacturing costs are direct labor and overhead. Jackie Wiggins, the controller, had prepared the following data for use in establishing the company's pricing policy for the coming year.

Total budgeted direct labor hours	240,000
Total budgeted manufacturing costs	$4,800,000

Total budgeted manufacturing costs were developed using the formula:

Total manufacturing costs = $1,200,000 + $15 × direct labor hours

Total selling and administrative expenses are budgeted as: $800,000 + $0.10 × revenue. The management of the company seeks an $880,000 profit.

Required
1. Determine the total revenue that Sumter must earn to achieve its profit objective.
2. Determine the price per direct labor hour that Sumter must charge to achieve the objective.
3. Suppose that the company uses the pricing policy you developed and actually works 230,000 direct labor hours. What will its profit be?
4. Suppose that the company uses your pricing policy and works 250,000 hours. What will its profit be?

13-26   Normal costing   Boardman Company is a job-order firm that manufactures equipment used to cap bottles. The following data summarize 19X3 activities.

Beginning inventories of work in process and finished goods	$ 360,000
Materials put into process	2,240,000
Direct labor	1,780,000
Manufacturing overhead incurred	2,520,000
Selling and administrative expenses	880,000
Sales	7,960,000

The firm uses an overhead application rate of $1.40 per direct labor dollar, based on budgeted direct labor cost of $1,800,000 and the following formula for budgeting manufacturing overhead:

Manufacturing overhead = $1,440,000 + ($0.60 × direct labor cost)

At the end of the year, the controller determined that the following costs were in the indicated places.

	Totals	Jobs Sold	Ending Inventory of Incomplete Jobs	Ending Inventory of Finished Jobs
Materials	$2,240,000	$1,890,000	$120,000	$230,000
Direct labor	$1,780,000	$1,480,000	$100,000	$200,000

Required: Prepare an income statement for the year, using normal costing and showing the budget variance and volume variance as separate adjustments to gross margin.

13-27   Comparison of actual and normal costing   Wharton Company began 19X5 with no inventories. It experienced the following results in that year.

	Totals	Amounts Included in Goods Sold	Amounts Included in Inventories
Materials used	$ 500,000	$450,000	$ 50,000
Direct labor	$1,000,000	$900,000	$100,000

The company had actual overhead costs of $2,200,000 and selling and administrative expenses of $700,000. Revenue was $4,500,000.

Required

1. Assume that the firm allocates overhead to jobs on an actual basis, using direct labor cost. (a) Determine the amount of overhead that would appear in cost of goods sold and in the ending inventories. (b) Prepare an income statement for the year.
2. Assume that Wharton uses a predetermined overhead rate of $2 per direct labor dollar during the year and treats any underapplied or overapplied overhead as a separate item on the income statement. (a) Determine the amounts of applied overhead that would appear in cost of sales and in ending inventories. (b) Prepare an income statement for the year.

13-28 Overhead application and levels of activity The managers of LeVine Window Company have been discussing the overhead application rate that they should use in the coming year. They agree that total manufacturing overhead should be budgeted at $1,200,000 plus $1.50 times direct labor hours, but are not sure what they should budget for direct labor hours. One manager has argued that 300,000 hours is as good an estimate as any, another that 360,000 hours would be better.

Required

1. Compute the predetermined overhead rate using (a) 300,000 hours, and (b) 360,000 hours.
2. Suppose that the firm actually works 320,000 direct labor hours and incurs total manufacturing overhead costs of $1,710,000. (a) What would the budget variance and volume variance be if the firm had selected 300,000 hours to set the predetermined rate? (b) What would the same two variances be if the firm had used 360,000 hours to set the rate?

13-29 Job-order costing and decisions Last month, Marchmont Furniture Company began work on a large number of custom-made chairs ordered by a retail store in New Jersey. When the work was nearly complete the retailer went bankrupt and was not able to pay for the chairs. The sales manager of Marchmont immediately began to call other stores in an effort to sell the chairs. The price originally agreed on was $210,000, but the best price that the sales manager could get if the chairs were finished according to the original specifications was $140,000. This offer was obtained from the Z-Store chain. Randle Company, which also operates a chain of stores, offered $158,000 for the chairs provided that some different upholstery and trim were used. The sales manager talked to the production manager about the order and got the following information.

	Costs Accumulated to Date
Materials	$ 31,500
Direct labor (7,000 hours at $5)	35,000
Factory overhead at $10 per hour	70,000
Total accumulated costs	$136,500

The factory overhead rate includes $4 variable overhead and $6 fixed overhead. The additional work required to complete the chairs was estimated as follows by the production manager.

	Original Specifications	Randle's Specifications
Materials	$4,100	$9,000
Direct labor hours	800 hours	1,800 hours

Required

1. Using the firm's costing method, determine the total costs that would be charged to the job assuming (a) the work is completed based on the original specifications, and (b) the chairs are modified as required by Randle Company.
2. Determine which offer Marchmont should accept.

13-30 Job-order costing—service business Sofdat Inc. develops computer programs for businesses, hospitals, local governments, and other organizations. Some of the work is done cost-plus, some is fixed-fee. The company has been having some difficulty in analyzing the profitability of various jobs and in estimating costs for use in bidding for fixed-fee business.

The company has hired you to develop a job-order costing system. So far, you have decided that, for this company, production costs should include the costs listed below, along with their estimated amounts for the coming year.

Programmers' salaries	$480,000
Supervisors' salaries	120,000
Other costs of programming	240,000

You decide that the company should use normal costing, treating programmers' salaries as "direct labor" with each programmer having an hourly rate equaling his or her salary divided by the normal 2,000-hour working year. You also decide to treat the other two elements of cost as "manufacturing overhead." You intend to use programming hours to set the predetermined overhead rate because programmers earn different salaries. Finally, you intend to treat the cost of idle programming time (actual salaries paid less salaries charged to jobs) and "excess cost" (amounts charged to jobs in excess of actual salaries paid) as part of overhead.

The president expects selling and administrative expenses to be $180,000. She also expects programmers to work about 24,000 hours and you decide to use this figure to compute the predetermined overhead rate.

The president is interested in seeing how the system will operate and gives you the following information for a hypothetical month.

There was no beginning inventory of jobs. Sales were $170,000. All costs incurred were one twelfth of the estimated annual amounts given above. Jobs sold had a total of 1,350 programming hours and jobs in process at the end of the month had 450 programming hours, so that actual hours for the month were 1,800 (1,350 + 450). Information on programmers' salaries is as follows:

Salaries on jobs sold	$27,000
Salaries in ending inventory	$ 9,200

Idle time was $3,800 ($40,000 incurred − $27,000 − $9,200).

Required
1. Calculate the predetermined overhead rate per hour of programmers' time.
2. Determine the cost of the ending inventory of jobs in process.
3. Determine the overapplied or underapplied overhead cost for the month, including the idle time.
4. Prepare an income statement for the month showing overapplied or underapplied overhead as a separate expense or negative expense.

13-31 Comparing actual and normal costing—seasonal business   Barnett Company has used actual job-order costing for several years. At the end of each month, a clerk divides total manufacturing overhead cost incurred during the month by total direct labor cost for the month to get an overhead rate per labor dollar. He then applies overhead at this rate to each job worked on during the month. Because the firm uses actual overhead, there is no underapplied or overapplied overhead.

The president of the firm has been unhappy with this method because it results in widely differing overhead costs in different months. The firm's work is highly seasonal, with the summer months very heavy and the winter months light. The president has asked you to show how the use of normal costing would differ from the actual costing system now in effect and has given you the following data regarding two jobs done in the past year. The jobs were quite similar.

	Job J-12	Job A-16
Material cost	$10,410	$10,310
Direct labor	16,900	16,400
Overhead	40,560	29,520
Totals	$67,870	$56,230

Job J-12 was done in January, when total overhead was $528,000 and total labor cost was $220,000. Job A-16 was done in August, when total overhead was $1,179,000 and total labor cost was $655,000. The firm budgets annual overhead using the formula

$$\text{Total annual overhead} = \$3,200,000 + (\$1.20 \times \text{direct labor cost})$$

Total budgeted labor cost for the current year is $4,000,000.

Required
1. Develop the predetermined overhead rate based on total budgeted overhead and labor cost.
2. Determine the costs of the two jobs using the rate that you calculated above.
3. Comment on the advantages of using predetermined overhead rates.

13-32 Analyzing overhead   The president of your company has come to you with some questions about overhead. You recently changed the company's accounting system from actual costing to normal costing, not without some opposition from other managers who could not see the advantages. Although the president was not happy with the actual costing system, he is not convinced that normal costing is a significant improvement.

The specific questions that he wants you to answer relate to determining whether or not costs are under control and what information he can get from the figures for underapplied and overapplied overhead. He gives you the results from the most recent three months:

	March	April	May
Direct labor hours worked on jobs	14,000	8,000	5,000
Total overhead incurred	$71,000	$52,000	$51,000
Total overhead applied at			
$6 per direct labor hour	84,000	48,000	30,000
Underapplied (overapplied) overhead	($13,000)	$ 4,000	$21,000

The predetermined rate of $6 per hour was calculated using budgeted direct labor hours for the year of 120,000 and budgeted overhead of $480,000 fixed and $2.00 variable per direct labor hour. Budgeted fixed overhead is $40,000 for each of the three months shown above.

Required: Making any calculations you consider relevant, tell the president what he can learn using the above data.

13-33   **Departmental versus plant-wide overhead rates**   Caldwell Company operates two departments, Grinding and Assembly, in its plant that makes optical devices including binoculars and telescopes. Because nearly all of its products are made to customer order, the firm uses job-order costing. In the past, the firm has used a single overhead application rate based on total budgeted direct labor hours and total budgeted overhead. The rate for 19X8 was computed using the data below.

	Grinding Department	Assembly Department	Total
Total budgeted overhead	$1,200,000	$800,000	$2,000,000
Budgeted direct labor hours	200,000	50,000	250,000
Rate $2,000,000/250,000			$8

Total budgeted overhead for each department was based on the following formulas:

Grinding Department	$800,000 + ($2 × direct labor hours)
Assembly Department	$500,000 + ($6 × direct labor hours)

The firm bases its bid prices on total estimated cost including direct labor, materials, and overhead applied at $8 per direct labor hour. The controller has been thinking about changing the system to departmental rates and has collected the following data regarding two jobs recently completed. All direct laborers in the plant earn $10 per hour.

	Job 391	Job 547
Direct labor hours—Grinding	330	80
—Assembly	30	180
Material cost	$3,000	$2,500
Direct labor cost	3,600	2,600

The firm's policy is to bid a price that is 150% of the total estimated manufacturing cost including applied overhead.

Required

1. Determine the amounts of overhead that the firm would apply to each job using the $8 plant-wide rate. Determine the total cost of each job. Assuming that the actual results for each job were also the estimated results that the firm used to set the bid prices, determine the price that the firm would have bid for each job.
2. Compute the predetermined overhead rates for the two departments separately.
3. Determine the amounts of overhead applied to each job, the total cost of each job, and the bid price for each job using the predetermined departmental overhead rates that you computed in part 2.
4. Comment on the differences in your results for the two jobs using the plant-wide rate and departmental rates. Would you recommend that the firm switch to departmental rates?

13-34 Departmental overhead rates The Jurgenson Company makes a number of different types of electric motors. The motors go through three departments: fabrication, machining, and assembly. The firm has been using a predetermined rate for variable overhead, but the results have not been satisfactory. The firm prices its motors at 250% of variable cost and has been finding that some models sell poorly, some well.

The variable overhead rate was calculated in the following way: The chief cost accountant determined the amounts of total variable overhead and direct labor hours in the three departments and based the rate on the weighted average. The schedule below shows the derivation of the rate, based on an average month's operations.

Department	Direct Labor Hours Worked	Total Variable Overhead
Fabrication	6,000	$ 48,000
Machining	10,000	60,000
Assembly	14,000	42,000
Totals	30,000	$150,000

Weighted average variable overhead rate = $5 per direct labor hour ($150,000/30,000).

The following schedule shows the determination of prices for two models, the 136 and the 260, for lots of 100 motors.

	Model 136	Model 260
Materials	$ 350	$ 410
Direct labor ($4 per hour)	320	260
Variable overhead ($5 per hour)	400	325
Total variable cost	$1,070	$ 995
Multiplied by 2.5 (250%) equals price per 100	$2,675	$2,487.50

The direct labor requirements in hours for each model, by department, are given below:

	Model 136	Model 260
Fabrication	40	5
Machining	25	10
Assembly	15	50
Total direct labor hours	80	65

The chief cost accountant realizes that the variable rates per direct labor hour are different among the departments. But he believes that it is simpler to use the weighted-average rate. He also believes that it would make little difference to use individual departmental rates.

Required
1. Compute the variable costs of each model using variable overhead rates based on the individual departmental rates.
2. Compute the selling prices that the firm would charge if it used the data given in part 1.
3. Do you think that the firm is wise to use the weighted-average variable overhead rate? Why or why not?

13-35 **VCP analysis in a job-order firm**   Carthage Machine Works manufactures industrial machinery, principally small cutting equipment. Virtually all of the machines are custom made and the firm uses job-order costing. The president of the firm has developed the following estimates for the coming year, 19X8:

Material cost	$280,000
Direct labor hours	20,000
Direct labor wage rate	$9 per hour
Variable manufacturing overhead	80% of direct labor cost
Fixed manufacturing overhead	$200,000
Selling and administrative expenses	$ 70,000

The president tells you that his pricing policy is to charge the customer 125% of material cost plus a per-hour amount for direct labor. He would like to earn a profit of $60,000 before taxes in 19X8.

Required
1. Determine the price per direct labor hour that the firm must charge to meet the target profit.
2. Suppose that the company adopts the per-hour charge that you computed above and has the following results: material costs, $300,000; direct labor hours, 18,000. All overhead costs are incurred as expected (variable per unit of activity and fixed in total). Determine the profit that the company will earn.

13-36 **Actual and normal costing—large inventory changes**   OH Company manufactures a product out of air. The plant is completely automated so that there is no direct labor. In fact, the only manufacturing cost is $300,000 annual depreciation. Selling and administrative expenses are all fixed at $100,000 per year.
    The firm began 19X6 with no inventories. During the first six months it made

150,000 units, sold 100,000. During the last six months it made 50,000 units, sold 100,000. The selling price is $3 per unit.

Required

1. Prepare income statements for each 6-month period assuming that the firm uses actual costing and incurs all costs evenly over the year.
2. Prepare income statements for each 6-month period assuming that the firm uses normal costing with the predetermined overhead rate per unit of product being $1.50, based on budgeted annual production of 200,000 units. The volume variances should appear as adjustments to gross margin.

Cases

13-37 Cost justification   The following material is taken from a column by Rowland Evans and Robert Novak that appeared in the July 8, 1976 *Knickerbocker News* (Albany, New York). At that time, the federal election laws required that candidates for the presidency limit spending before their parties' conventions to $13 million.

> When Treasury Secretary William Simon traveled to Raleigh, N.C., last Jan. 20 to address the state Chamber of Commerce and then a President Ford Committee (PFC) reception, the taxpayers' bill was $2,310. The reimbursement to Uncle Sam for the PFC for political expenses: $17.44. . . .
>
> The method used for Simon's Jan. 20 journey to North Carolina, an important primary state, is the model. The Air Force charged $2,310 for a Jetstar carrying Simon and seven others (including aides and Secret Service agents) to North Carolina. Since Simon occupied only one of eight seats, his share of the cost is $288.75. The 30 minutes spent at the PFC reception amounted to only 5 per cent of the portal-to-portal time from Washington. So, 5 percent of $288.75 is $14.44. Add $3 for the share of meals, and the cost to the PFC is $17.44.

Required

1. Suppose that you had been engaged as a consultant to President Ronald Reagan, who was President Ford's opponent in that campaign for the Republican nomination. What would you say about the method used to determine the cost billed to the PFC? What other information would you seek?
2. Suppose that you were engaged as a consultant to the PFC. How would you defend the $17.44 charge?

13-38 What is cost?—consumer action   Easy Ed Johnson's Belchfire Auto Agency has been advertising that it will sell cars at $50 over cost and that anyone who can prove that Ed is making more than $50 on a sale will get a $5,000 prize. Phyllis Henley decides to disprove Ed's claim. She obtains the following information from a consumer magazine:

Cost Data from *Consumer Scoop—*
Belchfire 8 with Standard Equipment

Invoice cost to dealer	$3,400
Commission to salesman, basic rate per car	100
Variable cost of make-ready services (lubrication, washing, etc.)	40
Total cost to dealer	$3,540

Since Phyllis knows that Ed has been selling this particular model for $3,900, she marches into the showroom and demands a $5,000 prize because she can "prove" that Ed is selling this model at $360 over his cost. Ed, with considerable aplomb, summons his accountant, who presents the following information to Phyllis.

Invoice cost to dealer	$3,400
Commission to salesman, basic rate per car	100
Cost of make-ready services	120
General overhead	230
Total cost	$3,850

The accountant points out that Phyllis has failed to consider the "real" costs that are incurred in running a large automobile dealership. He states that the make-ready and general overhead costs are based on the total service department cost and total overhead costs divided by the number of cars sold last year (500). General overhead costs are virtually all fixed. Ed pleasantly and politely offers his condolences to Phyllis for having failed to win the $5,000 and invites her back any time she wants to buy a car at $50 over cost.

Phyllis is not at all happy with her reception at Ed's or the data provided by his accountant, and she decides to sue for the $5,000 in the local court.

Required: Assume that Phyllis loses the case at the local level and appeals the decision to a higher court. The trial judge (original decision) has agreed with the explanation of Easy Ed's accountant. Nevertheless, Phyllis argues that Easy Ed is defrauding the populace and owes her $5,000. Her lawyer has asked you to serve as an expert witness. What would your testimony be?

13-39 Budgeting, cash flow, product costing, motivation   After almost two decades of profitable operations, Pennywise Company experienced its first loss in 19X6, and all the internal reports during the first 11 months of 19X7 indicated that the company would have a second loss year. At the meeting of the board of directors at the end of December 19X7, the members were given the first draft of the basic operating data for 19X7 which showed a loss. Public announcement of the data would be made shortly after the directors' meeting.

The directors had maintained the dividend record of the company so as not to antagonize the stockholders or give the impression that the recent losses were any more than a temporary setback. Most of the directors had come to realize, by the end of 19X7, that future dividends would be advisable only if the company returned to profitable operations. Consequently, the board members were willing to consider any plans which might help minimize inefficiencies, reduce costs, and build a profitable operation once again.

The chairman of the board (and principal stockholder), Mr. Ira Hayes, had recently attended a conference sponsored by the National Association of Manufacturers on motivating personnel to better performance. Mr. Hayes was not particularly impressed with most of the discussions. He told the personnel manager, Mr. Gray: "Those speakers all seemed to concentrate on qualitative and nonquantifiable issues like working conditions and improving the general atmosphere to promote creativity and individuality. There was the usual lot of noise about implementing methods of 'participatory management,' and the like, and coordinating the efforts of the management team. But really, there wasn't much in the way of concrete suggestions."

Having been closely associated with the company since its founding by Mr. Hayes 16 years before, Mr. Gray was well acquainted with Mr. Hayes' feelings on the matter of motivation. As Mr. Hayes had said on many occasions, he was convinced that the surest (and easiest) way to really motivate people was to provide monetary incentives of some kind and then let people know exactly what measures would be used to assess their performance. In keeping with this philosophy, Mr. Hayes proposed, at the first board meeting in 19X8, that the company adopt a profit-sharing plan in which all employees could participate. The other members of the board were receptive to the idea and a committee was appointed to draw up a plan.

According to the plan devised by the committee, the company would set aside cash equal to a certain percentage of before-tax profits. The cash would be distributed to all employees on the basis of a preestablished formula. Or, more correctly, a set of such formulas was needed because the performances of employees in different areas of the company had to be measured in different ways. Mr. Ira Hayes, Jr.,the president, wanted to provide his own incentives to encourage better performance by sales and production personnel. He gave the sales and production manager, individually, several long and enthusiastic pep talks on expanding their respective areas to higher levels. He further authorized an expenditure for $450,000 on a nationwide advertising program.

Production in the plant reached the normal capacity of 1,875,000 units for the year 19X8. At the board meeting in early 19X9, the president remarked: "Back in the black again. The field people did a great job pushing sales up by almost 17%." (Exhibit 2 shows the data presented to the board at that meeting. Exhibit 1 shows the basic data available to the directors at the meeting discussed in the first paragraph of the case.)

Exhibit 1
Pennywise Company
Operating Data for 19X7

Part A: Condensed Statement of Income

Sales (1,200,000 units at $12 per unit)	$14,400,000
Cost of goods sold	11,760,000
Gross margin on sales	2,640,000
Selling and administrative expenses	3,630,000
Net operating loss for the year 19X7	($ 990,000)

Part B: Miscellaneous Operating Data

Normal operating capacity, in units		1,875,000
Fixed costs:		
Manufacturing		$ 6,000,000
Selling and administrative		750,000
Variable costs, per unit:		
Manufacturing	$4.80	
Selling and administrative	$2.40	

The board was pleased with the results of their new plan and with its apparent immediate effectiveness. There was, in fact, much optimistic talk at the meeting about the effect that the new plan would have on 19X9 operations, especially because the special sales campaign would probably not be repeated regularly. The board voted to continue the plan for at least one more year. After the vote, Mr. Hayes Jr. suggested that it would probably be good for employee relations if the board would announce soon when the pool for profit sharing would be distributed in cash to the employees because the dividend announcement had already been widely publicized. In an outer room, the sales manager, the production manager, and the controller were discussing the advantages and disadvantages of nepotism and of nonoperating management on the board of directors.

Exhibit 2
Pennywise Company
Operating Data for 19X8

Sales (1,406,250 units at $12)		$16,875,000
Cost of goods sold:		
Fixed costs	$ 6,000,000	
Variable costs (1,875,000 @ $4.80)	9,000,000	
	15,000,000	
Less: Ending inventory (468,750 units @ $8.00)	3,750,000	
		11,250,000
Gross margin on sales		5,625,000
Selling and administrative expenses:		
Fixed costs	1,200,000	
Variable costs (1,406,250 @ $2.40)	3,375,000	
		4,575,000
Operating profit before taxes and allowance for profit-sharing pool		1,050,000
Provision for profit-sharing pool		210,000
Operating profit before taxes		840,000
Provision for federal income taxes		420,000
Net income for the year 19X8		$ 420,000
Dividends to common stockholders (@ $0.20)		$ 200,000

The questions following this paragraph are not designed to limit your discussion or specifically direct your analysis. Nor is there any particular significance to the order in which they are listed. You will find it worthwhile to answer the first one first because it may provide some clue as to how you might proceed. It would probably be inefficient to answer each of the questions directly and in order because some are interrelated, but you may want to incorporate some comments about each of them in your answer.
1. What is the company's break-even point?
2. What is the company's system for implementing the management functions of planning and control?
3. Are profits likely to continue?
4. Has the profit-sharing plan contributed to efficiency? to cost reduction? to a return to profitable operations?
5. Should the board announce a cash distribution to employees relatively soon?

CHAPTER 14

STANDARD COSTING: ABSORPTION AND VARIABLE

In the previous chapter we saw that the requirements of external reporting force firms to develop per-unit total costs for their products. Systems to produce such costs are called product-costing systems and involve the absorption (application) of fixed overhead into product cost. Two such systems—actual costing and normal costing—were introduced. A weakness common to both of these absorption-costing systems is that they do not offer the opportunity to analyze efficiency, an important factor if managers are to exercise control. In Chapter 12 we introduced the idea that the establishment of standards could help the manager exercise responsibility for controlling operations. This chapter describes how standard costs can be used in a product-costing system.

Under standard costing, the firm shows its inventories at standard cost. Variances appear on the income statement as expenses, or negative expenses. Standard costing is the predominant method of product costing in large firms and is a sensible alternative to actual costing or normal costing. Because most large and medium-sized firms, as well as some small ones, use standard costs for control purposes, integrating standard costs into the product-costing system is desirable. Since the accounts of the firm must provide information for product-costing purposes anyway, it is helpful to incorporate directly into the accounts the information about standards so that variance calculations need not be made outside of or apart from the records. (It is generally wise to have as much information as possible captured directly by the accounts, because the information is then easier to retrieve and more likely to be accurate.)

This chapter concentrates first on the basics of standard costs for product-costing purposes. That is, we will still be dealing with absorption costing, which requires a unit cost that includes fixed overhead. (The cost accumulation procedures for standard costing are shown in Chapter 15.) Because throughout this book we have emphasized the importance and value of using variable costs for internal purposes, this chapter also devotes some attention to a comparison of absorption costing (using standards) with the recommended approach (emphasizing variable costs). The recommended approach is called **variable costing** (or **direct costing**), which means only that fixed production costs are not considered to be part of the cost of the product but rather are expensed in the period in which they are incurred.

STANDARD ABSORPTION COSTING

As described in Chapter 12, a firm may establish standard costs for materials, direct labor, and variable overhead. Under standard absorption costing, the firm also determines a **standard fixed overhead cost** per unit of product. The resulting *total* standard cost per unit is the amount used to determine the cost of inventory on hand and the cost of goods sold. Variances of actual costs from standard, including the volume variance, are treated as expenses (or negative expenses if the variances are favorable) and reported separately in the income statement.

Chapter 12 covered the determination of standards for the variable costs of producing the product, so the only new problem to be considered here is the development of a standard for fixed overhead. The concept of the predetermined overhead rate will be useful in attacking the problem of developing a standard fixed cost.

Let us begin with a simple situation in which a firm makes only one product. (The procedures for a multiple-product firm will be illustrated in a later section.) In such a case, the firm can determine a standard fixed cost per unit simply by dividing total budgeted fixed manufacturing overhead by some number of units of product. There is no need to use direct labor hours or machine hours because, even though each unit of product will already have assigned to it a standard number of hours, *all* hours will be worked on the same kind of product. Thus, if the firm's managers expect fixed overhead to be $3,000,000 for the year and unit production to be 100,000 units, the standard fixed cost per unit can be calculated as:

$$\text{Standard fixed cost per unit} = \frac{\text{budgeted fixed overhead}}{\text{budgeted units of production}}$$

$$= \$3,000,000/100,000 = \$30$$

Exhibit 14-1 presents data for the SMP Company, which produces an automobile part. The company has standards for labor, material, and variable overhead. To simplify the situation, we will group all the standard variable costs into a single per-unit variable cost. And, because you have already learned to analyze variances in variable costs, we will further assume that variable costs were incurred as budgeted (that is, that there were no variances).

Exhibit 14-1
SMP Company
Operating Data for 19X5

Production in units	110,000
Sales in units, at $80 each	90,000
Ending inventory in units	20,000
Actual production costs:	
Variable at $20 per unit	$2,200,000
Fixed	3,200,000
Selling and administrative expenses	1,900,000
Standards and budgets:	
Budgeted fixed production costs	$3,000,000
Standard variable production costs	$20 per unit

In analyzing the year's activity we will be interested in budget variances as well as a volume variance. But in order to determine the variances, we must first decide upon a standard cost to which actual costs can be compared.

Calculating a Standard Fixed Cost

The standard fixed cost per unit depends, as it did in the development of a predetermined overhead rate, on two things: (1) the choice of a *measure* of activity (number of units, direct labor hours, or machine hours, for example); and (2) a *level* of activity (actual or budgeted units or hours, for example). Since we are dealing with a single-product firm, the most obvious measure of activity is units of product, but the level of activity to be used in the calculation of a standard cost must also be chosen.

Under normal costing, the predetermined overhead rate was established using budgeted activity for the coming year. That same level of activity could be used to establish the standard cost per unit, but there are two other commonly used levels: normal activity (or normal capacity) and practical capacity.

Normal activity (normal capacity) is the average expected or budgeted activity over the coming two or more years. Two years would be the minimum, with four or five years being the maximum. The objective in using this activity level is to develop a standard fixed cost that reflects the firm's expected long-term costs. If the firm expects to grow, it would probably want to set a selling price that reflects its average costs over the next few years rather than those over only the current year when a lower volume is anticipated.

Practical capacity is the maximum level of activity the company can achieve given the usual kinds of interruptions that managers expect but excluding strikes or severe shortages of materials. As with budgeted and normal activity, the measure of volume may be units of product, direct labor hours, or some other measure. Standard costs based on practical capacity reflect the lowest reasonable long-term average fixed cost.

Let us assume that late in 19X4 the managers of SMP decided that they would set the standard per-unit fixed cost on the basis of normal capacity of 100,000 units.

The standard would then be $30 per unit, computed as follows:

$$\frac{\text{Standard fixed}}{\text{cost per unit}} = \frac{\text{budgeted fixed overhead}}{\text{normal capacity}}$$

$$= \$3,000,000/100,000 = \$30 \text{ per unit}$$

The total standard cost per unit would be $50, consisting of the $20 standard variable cost per unit and the $30 standard fixed cost per unit. We shall use this standard fixed cost per unit to determine variances during the period. And, if variances are not significant, the standard will also be used in external financial statements for the period.

Income Statements

Using the standard cost per unit and the operating data from Exhibit 14-1, we can prepare an income statement for SMP Company for 19X5. Exhibit 14-2 contains such a statement. As you can see, the format is much the same as those used for actual and normal absorption costing in Chapter 13, which formats in turn were based on the typical income statement presentation used in financial accounting. That is, cost of sales is computed by adding the beginning inventory and the additional costs for the year, and then subtracting the ending inventory. The real difference between standard costing and either actual or normal costing is that the inventories are stated at standard rather than actual or normal cost. The amounts shown for variable production costs and applied fixed production costs are the per-unit standard costs multiplied by the number of units produced. Thus, *the standard cost of sales is simply the per-unit standard cost multiplied by the number of units sold.*

Exhibit 14-2
SMP Company
Income Statement for 19X5

Sales (90,000 × $80)		$7,200,000
Standard cost of sales:		
Beginning inventory	$ 0	
Variable production costs (110,000 × $20)	2,200,000	
Applied fixed production costs (110,000 × $30)	3,300,000	
Cost of goods available (110,000 × $50)	5,500,000	
Ending inventory (20,000 × $50)	1,000,000	
Standard cost of goods sold (90,000 × $50)		4,500,000
Standard gross margin		2,700,000
Variances:		
Fixed cost budget variance	200,000U	
Volume variance	300,000F	100,000F
Actual gross margin		2,800,000
Selling and administrative expenses		1,900,000
Income		$ 900,000

As with normal costing, the volume variance under standard costing is budgeted fixed overhead minus the amount of fixed overhead applied, the only difference being that units of product, rather than labor hours, are used in the calculation. For the

SMP Company in 19X5, the volume variance is calculated as follows:

$$\text{Volume variance} = \begin{pmatrix} \text{actual} & & \text{units at} \\ \text{units} & - & \text{normal} \\ \text{produced} & & \text{capacity} \end{pmatrix} \times \begin{array}{c} \text{standard} \\ \text{fixed cost} \\ \text{per unit} \end{array}$$

$$= (110{,}000 - 100{,}000) \times \$30$$

$$= \$300{,}000 \text{ favorable}$$

A complete analysis of fixed overhead variances is similar to that used in Chapter 13 and is also graphed in Figure 14-1.

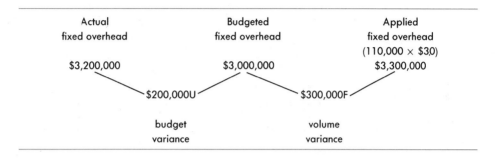

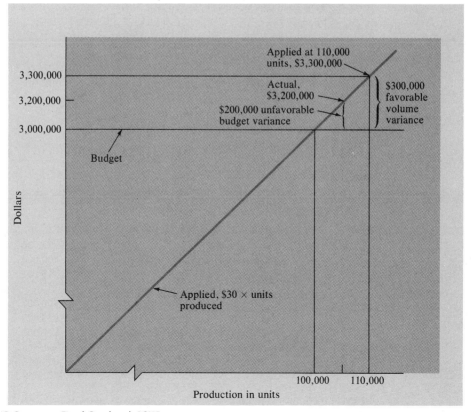

FIGURE 14-1   SMP Company, Fixed Overhead, 19X5

Since SMP Company incurred variable production costs equal to standard costs for 19X5 there are no other variances.

There is no need to show the details of the section for the standard cost of sales, since that amount is equal to the number of units sold times the standard cost per unit. Thus, an income statement such as the one in Exhibit 14-3 could also be used. The placement of variances is a matter of personal choice. Some prefer to show them as adjustments to standard cost of goods sold, others as adjustments to standard gross margin. There is no "correct" way. You should see that the final results for actual gross margin and income will be the same regardless of where the variances appear in the statement.

Exhibit 14-3
SMP Company
Income Statement for 19X5
(Alternative)

Sales		$7,200,000
Cost of sales:		
Standard cost of sales (90,000 × $50)	$4,500,000	
Variances—fixed cost budget variance	200,000U	
—volume variance	300,000F	
Cost of sales		4,400,000
Actual gross margin		2,800,000
Selling and administrative expenses		1,900,000
Income		$ 900,000

Before we see how a standard fixed cost per unit can be used in a firm that makes more than one product, make sure you understand the basics of standard absorption costing in a single-product firm by completing the following review problem.

Review Problem

The SMP Company, whose activity was the basis for the description of standard absorption costing, had the following operating data for 19X6:

Production, in units	95,000
Sales, in units, at $80 each	100,000
Ending inventory, in units	15,000
Actual production costs:	
Variable at $20 per unit	$1,900,000
Fixed	$2,950,000
Selling and administrative expenses	$1,900,000
Standard variable production cost	$20 per unit
Budgeted fixed production costs	$3,000,000

Prepare income statements for 19X6, using the formats of Exhibits 14-2 and 14-3. The solution appears in Exhibit 14-4.

Exhibit 14-4
SMP Company
Income Statement for 19X6

Sales (100,000 × $80)		$8,000,000
Standard cost of sales:		
Beginning inventory (from Exhibit 14-2)	$1,000,000	
Variable production costs (95,000 × $20)	1,900,000	
Applied fixed production costs (95,000 × $30)	2,850,000	
Cost of goods available (115,000 × $50)	5,750,000	
Ending inventory (15,000 × $50)	750,000	
Standard cost of goods sold (100,000 × $50)		5,000,000
Standard gross margin		3,000,000
Variances:		
Fixed cost budget variance	50,000F	
Volume variance	150,000U	100,000U
Actual gross margin		2,900,000
Selling and administrative expenses		1,900,000
Income		$1,000,000

Income Statement for 19X6, Alternative Format

Sales (100,000 × $80)		$8,000,000
Cost of sales:		
Standard cost of sales (100,000 × $50)	$5,000,000	
Variances—fixed cost budget variance	50,000F	
—volume variance	150,000U	
Cost of sales		5,100,000
Actual gross margin		2,900,000
Selling and administrative expenses		1,900,000
Income		$1,000,000

Calculation of Variances

Actual fixed overhead	Budgeted fixed overhead	Applied fixed overhead
		(95,000 × $30)
$2,950,000	$3,000,000	$2,850,000
$50,000F	$150,000U	
budget	volume	
variance	variance	

Multiple Products

Standard costing is especially common among firms that make several products of essentially the same design. Yet even a firm that makes each product in batches—like the job-order firms discussed in Chapter 13—can use standard costs. The necessary condition for using a standard costing system is the ability to develop reasonable standards for each input factor. Consider, for example, the Richards Company, which makes two models of tables, Model 345 and Model 788. Through engineering studies the company has determined that the standard material and labor costs for making each model are as follows.

	Model 345	Model 788
Standard material cost	$20	$60
Standard labor cost, at a standard rate of $10 per hour:		
3 hours × $10	$30	
5 hours × $10		$50

Richards Company budgets its factory overhead using a budget equation that was developed using regression analysis (see Chapter 3) and incorporates both variable and fixed factory overhead. The equation for the company is:

$$\text{Annual factory overhead} = \$2,000,000 + (\$8 \times \text{direct labor hours})$$

The budget equation reflects the company's overhead structure as consisting of $2,000,000 in fixed overhead and variable overhead that changes by $8 for each direct labor hour worked. Thus, the company can establish the standard variable overhead cost per unit *of each model* simply by multiplying the $8 rate by the number of labor hours per unit of each model—a standard of $24 ($8 × 3 hours) for Model 345, and a standard of $40 ($8 × 5 hours) for Model 788. Of course, establishing a standard fixed overhead cost for each *model* of table requires not only a knowledge of the number of labor hours worked on each table but also a predetermined overhead rate per labor hour.

Suppose that Richards uses its normal capacity of 500,000 labor hours to set the predetermined overhead rate. Knowing now that the budgeted fixed overhead of $2,000,000 is to be absorbed over 500,000 labor hours, the predetermined overhead rate for fixed overhead would be $4 ($2,000,000/500,000), and the total standard cost for each model can be determined. Using the $4 rate per direct labor hour, the total standard cost for each model would be as follows.

	Model 345	Model 788
Standard material cost	$20	$ 60
Standard labor cost, at the standard labor rate of $10 per hour		
3 hours × $10	30	
5 hours × $10		50
Standard variable overhead, at the standard rate of $8 per hour		
3 hours × $8	24	
5 hours × $8		40
Standard fixed overhead, at the standard rate of $4 per hour		
3 hours × $4	12	
5 hours × $4		20
Total standard cost per unit	$86	$170

The standard costs, as shown above, will now be used by Richards Company both for reporting inventory and cost of goods sold and for analyzing variances. For example, suppose that the firm makes 90,000 units of Model 345 and 42,000 units of Model 788. Total fixed overhead applied and the volume variance could be calculated as follows.

Total fixed overhead applied:	
Model 345 90,000 units × $12 standard	
fixed cost per unit	$1,080,000
Model 788 42,000 units × $20 standard	
fixed cost per unit	840,000
Total applied fixed overhead	1,920,000
Budgeted fixed overhead	2,000,000
Volume variance, unfavorable	$ 80,000

Comparison of Standard and Normal Costing

Although the normal-costing concept of a predetermined overhead rate is related to the development of a standard fixed cost per unit, the results reported under the two types of costing systems are not the same. Remember that, under normal costing, overhead is applied on the basis of the number of hours actually worked. In a standard costing system, overhead is applied on the basis of the number of units actually produced. Let us see how the results would differ in the case of Richards Company, using as an example the production activity given in the preceding section.

In the prior analysis, the volume variance was calculated by applying the standard fixed overhead cost per unit, which cost was based on the standard number of labor hours per unit. The actual number of hours worked on each type of product was not needed. But assume that to achieve the production levels given above the firm had to work 280,000 hours making Model 345 tables and 205,000 hours making Model 788 tables, for a total of 485,000 hours. If the firm had been using normal costing with a predetermined fixed overhead rate of $4 per hour (the same as the rate used to determine the standard cost per unit), the total fixed overhead applied for the year would have been $1,940,000 (485,000 actual hours × $4 per hour), or $20,000 more than the overhead applied under standard costing ($1,920,000).

Exhibit 14-5 shows these differences in overhead application and how the differences affect the reported volume variance. Unless standard hours are equal to actual hours, normal costing and standard costing will give different volume variances. The two systems will always give the same *budget* variance, however, because the budget variance is simply actual cost minus budgeted cost. The different volume variances arise because different amounts of fixed overhead are *applied* under the two methods. The difference in volume variances serves to remind you of what we said when the concept of a volume variance was first introduced in Chapter 13: the variance has little or no economic significance and reflects only the effect of using some activity measure or other in determining the overhead application rate.

Exhibit 14-5

Comparison of Normal and Standard Costing

Normal Costing	
Total *actual* hours worked:	
Model 345	280,000
Model 788	205,000
Total actual hours	485,000
Predetermined overhead rate	$4
Total fixed overhead applied	$1,940,000
Budgeted fixed overhead	2,000,000
Volume variance—unfavorable	$ 60,000
Standard Costing	
Total *standard* hours for output level achieved:	
Model 345 90,000 units × 3 hours per unit	270,000
Model 788 42,000 units × 5 hours per unit	210,000
Total standard hours	480,000
Predetermined overhead rate	$4
Total fixed overhead applied, equals the amount	
determined using units of product (see page 553)	$1,920,000
Budgeted fixed overhead	2,000,000
Volume variance—unfavorable	$ 80,000

We have presented several costing methods in this and the previous chapters. The table below summarizes the similarities and differences among the three methods, actual costing, normal costing, and standard costing, showing the basis for determining the inventoriable cost of a unit of product.

Element of Cost	Actual Costing	Normal Costing	Standard Costing
Materials	actual cost	actual cost	standard cost
Direct labor	actual cost	actual cost	standard cost
Overhead	actual cost	applied cost	standard cost
	(actual input × actual rate)	(actual input × predetermined rate)	(standard input × predetermined rate)

We see here that actual costing and normal costing differ only in the treatment of overhead, as explained in Chapter 13. Standard costing differs from both of the other methods in using standard costs rather than actual costs. The only difference between standard costing and normal costing with respect to overhead is, as shown earlier, that applied overhead under standard costing is based on standard quantities of the input factor (or, what amounts to the same thing, on actual unit production), while overhead applied under normal costing is based on the actual quantities of input factors.

VARIABLE COSTING

The product-costing systems discussed thus far have all been absorption costing systems, wherein some portion of a firm's fixed costs is included in inventory and thus carried over to some future year. Such systems are required for financial reporting and for income tax purposes, and are often used, as we mentioned earlier, for internal purposes also. However, throughout this book we have recommended internal reports using the contribution margin format, which treats all fixed costs of the current period as period costs. When the recommended approach is applied to product costing, the result is called variable costing.

Variable costing does not include fixed production costs in the determination of unit costs of inventories, but rather it shows all fixed costs as expenses in the period incurred. The flow of costs using variable costing can easily be shown by a slight variation of the cost-flow figure that was presented in Chapter 13. Figure 14-2 below depicts the difference in cost flows under variable and absorption costing systems. It is possible—and we think it is preferable—to use variable costing for internal reports.

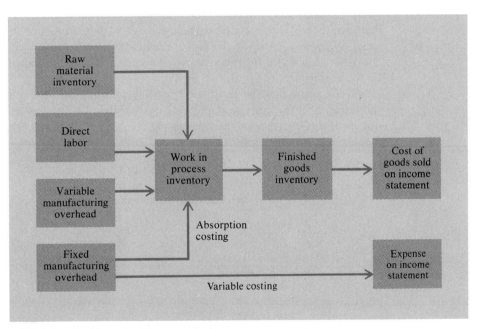

FIGURE 14-2   Flow of Costs in a Manufacturing Firm

Exhibit 14-6 (page 556) shows income statements for the SMP Company for 19X5 and 19X6 using standard variable costing and the same operating data that were presented earlier in the chapter for that company.

Because there are no variable cost variances in our example, the results using standard variable costing are the same as they would be if the firm used actual variable costing. That is, the actual variable production costs are the same as the standards for such costs, hence, the calculated per-unit cost of inventory is the total actual variable cost divided by the total number of units produced.

If you had been given exactly the same information about SMP Company in an earlier chapter, you would probably have prepared income statements like these:

SMP Company
Income Statements—Variable Costing

	19X5	19X6
Sales at $80 per unit	$7,200,000	$8,000,000
Variable costs at $20 per unit	1,800,000	2,000,000
Contribution margin	5,400,000	6,000,000
Fixed costs:		
Production	3,200,000	2,950,000
Selling and administrative	1,900,000	1,900,000
Total fixed costs	5,100,000	4,850,000
Income	$ 300,000	$1,150,000

The income statements in Exhibit 14-6 only *appear* to be different from and more complex than statements you have seen in earlier chapters. The only difference between these statements and those in Exhibit 14-6 is the amount of detail on cost of sales. Whether you use the shortened format above, or the expanded format of Exhibit 14-6, the incomes for the two years are the same and reflect an expensing of fixed costs in the year incurred.

    .   Compare now the results under variable costing with the results under absorption costing for the same economic activity (Exhibits 14-2 and 14-4). Absorption costing income is higher than variable costing income for 19X5 and lower for 19X6. Can you explain why this is so? Of course you can! Absorption costing income in 19X5 is

Exhibit 14-6
SMP Company
Standard Variable Costing Income Statements

	19X5	19X6
Sales	$7,200,000	$8,000,000
Standard variable cost of sales:		
Beginning inventory	0	400,000
Variable production costs:		
110,000 × $20	2,200,000	
95,000 × $20		1,900,000
Goods available for sale	2,200,000	2,300,000
Ending inventory:		
20,000 × $20	400,000	
15,000 × $20		300,000
Standard variable cost of sales	1,800,000	2,000,000
Contribution margin	5,400,000	6,000,000
Fixed costs:		
Budgeted fixed production costs	3,000,000	3,000,000
Fixed cost budget variance	200,000U	50,000F
Selling and administrative expenses	1,900,000	1,900,000
Total fixed costs	5,100,000	4,850,000
Income	$ 300,000	$1,150,000

higher because absorption costing transfers some of the fixed costs of 19X5 into 19X6 as part of the cost of the ending inventory of 20,000 units. Absorption costing income in 19X6 is lower because a similar shift of 19X6 costs (to 19X7) was smaller (fixed costs on an ending inventory of only 15,000 units) than the amount of fixed costs transferred in from 19X5.

In more general terms, the differences are traceable to the relationship between production and sales. *When production exceeds sales, so that ending inventory is greater than beginning inventory, absorption costing will report a higher income than variable costing. When sales exceed production, absorption costing will report a lower income than variable costing.* The difference in incomes is due entirely to the fixed costs that are carried forward in inventory under absorption costing. Such costs are shown on the balance sheet as inventory and are not considered to be expense until the goods are sold. If the amount of Year 1 fixed cost transferred in inventory to Year 2 is greater than the amount of Year 2 fixed cost transferred in inventory to Year 3, the total fixed cost expensed in Year 2 under absorption costing will be more than the fixed costs incurred in Year 2, and income will be lower than under variable costing. By the same token, if the amount of Year 1 fixed cost transferred to Year 2 is less than the amount of Year 2 fixed cost transferred to Year 3, the total fixed cost expensed in Year 2 under absorption costing will be less than the Year 2 fixed costs, and absorption costing income will be higher than variable costing. Exhibit 14-7 shows the amounts of fixed production costs expensed in each year under the two approaches, along with a reconciliation of the incomes that are produced under these approaches.

Exhibit 14-7
Reconciliation of Incomes—Variable and Absorption Costing

	19X5	19X6
Comparison of reported income:		
Variable costing (Exhibit 14-6)	$ 300,000	$1,150,000
Absorption costing (Exhibits 14-2 and 14-4)	900,000	1,000,000
Difference to be explained	($ 600,000)	$ 150,000
Explanation of income difference:		
Fixed production costs in beginning inventory		
(transferred from prior year):		
0 units × $30	$ 0	
20,000 units × $30		$ 600,000
Fixed production costs incurred during the year	3,200,000	2,950,000
	3,200,000	3,550,000
Less, fixed production costs in ending inventory		
(being transferred to a future year):		
20,000 units × $30	600,000	
15,000 units × $30		450,000
Total fixed costs expensed under absorption costing for		
the year	2,600,000	3,100,000
Total fixed costs expensed under variable costing—		
equal to total fixed costs incurred	3,200,000	2,950,000
Difference between fixed costs incurred and		
expensed for the year	($ 600,000)	$ 150,000

If, in fact, the standard fixed cost *per unit* does not change from year to year, the difference between absorption costing income and income under variable costing can be directly computed by multiplying the standard fixed cost per unit by the change in inventory from one year to the next. Thus, we could have made the reconciliation shown in Exhibit 14-7 simply by using the formula:

$$
\begin{matrix}
\text{Difference} \\
\text{in} \\
\text{incomes}
\end{matrix}
=
\left(
\begin{matrix}
\text{units in} \\
\text{beginning} \\
\text{inventory}
\end{matrix}
-
\begin{matrix}
\text{units in} \\
\text{ending} \\
\text{inventory}
\end{matrix}
\right)
\times
\begin{matrix}
\text{standard} \\
\text{fixed cost} \\
\text{per unit}
\end{matrix}
$$

$$
\begin{matrix}
\text{19X5} \\
\text{Difference}
\end{matrix}
= \quad (0 - 20{,}000) \quad \times \$30 = (\$600{,}000)
$$

$$
\begin{matrix}
\text{19X6} \\
\text{Difference}
\end{matrix}
= \quad (20{,}000 - 15{,}000) \quad \times \$30 = \$150{,}000
$$

EVALUATION OF METHODS

We have already stated that we believe variable costing to be superior to absorption costing for internal reporting purposes. Not all managers, whether in accounting or elsewhere, would agree with our position. What does seem evident is that absorption costing is used for internal reporting primarily because it is required for external reporting, so that preparing reports by any other approach must involve some incremental cost.

External Reporting

Although the arguments about the suitability of either method for external reporting are not germane to internal considerations, some are mentioned here to alert you to the principal justifications offered for absorption costing.[1]

The *matching concept,* to which you were introduced in financial accounting, holds that costs must be matched against related revenues or against the revenues of the periods that have benefitted from the costs. Under this concept, the cost of fixed assets is assigned, through depreciation, to the various periods that constitute the life of the fixed asset.

It is obvious that fixed production costs "benefit" the firm in the sense that, without them, few modern firms could produce anything at all. Having a factory building and equipment entails depreciation, property taxes, some level of maintenance, and other fixed costs. Moreover, many factory personnel, such as managers and supervisors, are compensated on a salary rather than an hourly basis. Because these fixed costs are essential to the production of goods, one could argue that they should be expensed when and only when the goods are sold and not when the goods are produced but still remain in inventory. Such an argument is made by those favoring absorption costing.

[1]For income tax reporting, the tax law, which can be extraordinarily complex, governs the determination of inventory and related costs of sales. We might point out that in a growing economy, inventories will rise. Additionally, costs rise as well. Firms probably pay more taxes under absorption costing than they would under variable costing, which could be one reason why the government requires absorption costing.

Advocates of variable costing for financial reporting purposes would offer a counterargument. They would say that fixed production costs do benefit production, but that it is production as a whole that is benefitted rather than the production of any single unit of product. In other words, fixed costs should be considered as providing the *capacity* to produce, regardless of whether the capacity is used. Thus, once the firm is in business and producing goods, fixed production costs have done their job; they are not needed for *this* or *that* unit, only for production as a whole. Accordingly, advocates of variable costing for financial reporting purposes argue that considering fixed costs on a per-unit basis is inappropriate because fixed costs cannot be identified with individual units; that is, such costs are *joint* to all the units produced. Controversy about the most appropriate method for external reporting purposes has raged for many years, and we do not expect it to stop in the foreseeable future.

Internal Reporting

The basic advantage of variable costing for internal reporting is that it presents information in a form that is most practical for managers—in the form needed for volume-cost-profit analysis.

The separation of fixed and variable costs, and the specific reporting of contribution margin enable managers to perform the volume-cost-profit analysis that cannot be done by working directly with absorption costing statements. Managers attempting to predict income for a future period would encounter difficulties using an absorption costing income statement for two reasons: (1) they must not only predict sales for that future period, but must also predict production; and (2) they must break down the cost figures into their fixed and variable components (i.e., managers must *develop* the information that is automatically *provided* when variable costing is used).

With variable costing, production has no influence on income. Managers can concentrate on the effects of changes in sales without having to allow for production. If sales fall from one period to another, variable costing income will also fall. If absorption costing is used, it is possible for income to rise in a period of falling sales if production is a good deal higher than sales. Most managers are accustomed to thinking of sales, not production, as the income-generating activity of the firm. Variable costing is therefore more in tune with the basic understanding of income than is absorption costing.

Of course, absorption costing requires making allocations of fixed costs to units of product. We have consistently argued that allocations are unwise for managerial purposes because they obscure volume-cost-profit relationships, can lead to poor decisions, and are not helpful in control and performance evaluation. Absorption costing can therefore be criticized because it requires allocations.

In a multiple-product firm using absorption costing, fixed costs of production will be allocated to the several products, and to the individual units of each product. Many costs that are joint with respect to several products (depreciation on factory building, salary of plant manager, etc.) will be allocated first to products, and then to units of each product. Thus, statements prepared by product or by product line will contain two sets of allocations, making it extremely difficult to analyze the relative profitability of a product or a product line.

In summary, the information that managers need is provided much more directly by statements prepared under variable costing than under absorption costing. Where absorption costing is used, a manager must often recast statements in order to perform many of the kinds of analyses needed to carry out functions of planning, decision making, control, and performance evaluation.

Advocates of absorption costing argue that variable costing may prompt managers to take a short-run approach to problems when a long-run approach would be more desirable. Although they acknowledge the usefulness of variable costing information for specific short-run decisions (like the acceptance of special orders), they argue that, in the long run, concentration on such information can be harmful. The major objection they have is that if fixed costs are not considered to be costs of product, the firm may tend to set prices too low to cover its fixed costs and earn profits. If managers become accustomed to reports prepared using variable costing they could come to ignore the fixed costs that might be the great bulk of production costs for some firms. In short, advocates of absorption costing argue that it is useful because it alerts a manager to the need to cover both fixed and variable costs.

There are two counterarguments to the advocates of absorption costing. One is that even absorption costing does not include *all* costs, fixed or variable, as product costs. Selling and administrative costs are excluded from inventory under both costing methods. These costs may be extremely significant for many firms. In the same vein, when a standard fixed cost per unit is used, the amount of fixed cost included in product cost (and therefore in inventory) is decided in advance. Some fixed costs will probably be overapplied or underapplied and will not enter into the determination of inventory.

The other counterargument is that it is unnecessary to allocate fixed costs to units in setting prices when the firm faces competition and cannot charge any price it chooses. A firm could analyze the expected volume-price relationships along the lines suggested in Chapter 4 (page 109) and select the best combination of price and expected volume. If a firm does have discretion over prices and can expect to sell about the same volume no matter what price is charged, there would be no harm in using a total cost per unit to set prices. However, firms in these circumstances are much less common than firms that face competition and therefore cannot charge any price they wish.

If absorption costing is to be used, it seems better to use a standard fixed cost per unit than an actual fixed cost per unit. When a standard fixed cost is used, the income effects of production's being different from sales are isolated in the volume variance. The volume variance tells us what these effects are, but is not helpful for control purposes. The use of standard fixed costs per unit would probably help to alleviate the problem of a manager's changing prices at frequent intervals just because total cost per unit is changing as production changes.

SUMMARY

Standard costing is a method of product costing that uses standard costs instead of actual costs. One major benefit of standard costing is that it ties the accounting records to the calculations of the variances that can be used for control purposes. Another benefit is that it simplifies the recordkeeping for a firm that makes several products.

The use of standard absorption costing requires the calculation of a standard fixed cost per unit. Like normal costing, standard absorption costing yields a volume variance as well as a fixed overhead budget variance; but the volume variance, under either approach, is of little, if any, economic significance. Setting a standard fixed cost per unit requires selecting a level of activity, the most common of which are normal activity and practical capacity. The magnitude, and perhaps even the direction, of the volume variance will depend on the activity level chosen for setting the standard.

The required use of some type of absorption costing for external reporting has contributed to the internal distribution of, and the need for managers to understand, reports reflecting this approach to product costing. For internal, managerial purposes, some firms use standard variable costing, or even actual variable costing, which consider only variable production costs as product costs, and treat fixed manufacturing costs as expenses in the period in which they are incurred. Variable costing is compatible with both VCP analysis and the contribution margin format of the income statement.

KEY TERMS

direct costing
normal activity (capacity)
practical capacity

standard costing (absorption or variable)
standard fixed overhead cost per unit
variable costing

KEY FORMULAS

$$\text{Standard fixed cost per unit} = \frac{\text{budgeted fixed overhead}}{\text{units of production (or other measure of activity)}}$$

$$\begin{array}{c}\text{Volume variance—}\\ \text{standard costing}\end{array} = \left(\begin{array}{c}\text{actual}\\ \text{units}\\ \text{produced}\end{array} - \begin{array}{c}\text{units at}\\ \text{selected}\\ \text{capacity}\end{array}\right) \times \begin{array}{c}\text{standard}\\ \text{fixed cost}\\ \text{per unit}\end{array}$$

$$\begin{array}{c}\text{Difference in}\\ \text{income between}\\ \text{absorption and}\\ \text{variable costing}\end{array} = \begin{array}{c}\text{fixed costs in}\\ \text{beginning}\\ \text{inventory}\end{array} - \begin{array}{c}\text{fixed costs in}\\ \text{ending}\\ \text{inventory}\end{array}$$

REVIEW PROBLEM

King Chair Company produces two types of chairs—the Junior Executive model and the Senior Executive model. Data for 19X4 are given below. There were no beginning inventories.

	Junior Executive		Senior Executive	
Selling price		$100		$250
Variable costs:				
Manufacturing	$30		$80	
Selling	4	34	8	88
Contribution margin		$ 66		$ 162
Units produced		8,000		3,000
Units sold		7,600		2,500
Direct labor hours required per unit		2		4

Budgeted fixed production costs are $600,000, selling and administrative expenses $280,000. Actual fixed production costs were $620,000, and fixed selling and administrative expenses were as budgeted. The variable costs for production given on page 561 are standard costs. All variable costs were incurred as expected. The firm uses its normal capacity of 30,000 direct labor hours per year to set standard fixed costs for its products.

Required

1. Determine the predetermined overhead rate for fixed production costs per direct labor hour.
2. Calculate standard fixed costs for each model.
3. Prepare a standard absorption costing income statement for 19X4. Show the two fixed cost variances as adjustments to obtain actual gross profit from standard gross profit.
4. Prepare a standard variable costing income statement for 19X4.

Answer to Review Problem

1. $20 per hour. $600,000 budgeted fixed production costs divided by 30,000 direct labor hours.
2. $40 for the Junior Executive, $80 for the Senior Executive.

	Junior Executive	Senior Executive
Direct labor hours required per unit	2	4
Fixed overhead rate per direct labor hour	$20	$20
Standard fixed cost per unit	$40	$80

3.

King Chair Company Income Statement for 19X4—Standard Absorption Costing

Sales [(7,600 × $100) + (2,500 × $250)]		$1,385,000
Cost of goods sold:		
Variable production costs [(8,000 × $30) + (3,000 × $80)]		480,000
Fixed production costs [(8,000 × $40) + (3,000 × $80)]		560,000
Total		1,040,000
Ending inventory [400($30 + $40) + 500($80 + $80)]		108,000
Cost of goods sold (7,600 × $70) + (2,500 × $160)		932,000
Gross profit at standard		453,000
Variances:		
Fixed cost budget variance	$ 20,000U	
Volume variance[a]	40,000U	60,000
Actual gross profit		393,000
Selling and administrative expenses:		
Variable [(7,600 × $4) + (2,500 × $8)]	$ 50,400	
Fixed	280,000	330,400
Income		$ 62,600

[a]The volume variance can be calculated in two ways:

(a) It is the difference between budgeted fixed production costs of $600,000 and fixed production costs applied of $560,000. Because application was less than budgeted, the $40,000 difference is unfavorable.

(b) It can be calculated by finding total standard direct labor hours for the output achieved and subtracting that figure from the 30,000 hours used to set the rate of $20 per hour. The difference multiplied by $20 per hour gives the variance:

Model	Units Produced × Hours per Unit = Total Hours		
Junior Executive	8,000	2	16,000
Senior Executive	3,000	4	12,000
Total hours			28,000
Hours used to set standards			30,000
Variance in hours			2,000
Multiplied by rate per hour			$ 20
Volume variance			$40,000

4.

King Chair Company
Income Statement
for 19X4—Standard Variable Costing

Sales		$1,385,000
Standard cost of goods sold		
(7,600 × $30) + (2,500 × $80)		428,000
Standard gross profit		957,000
Variable selling costs		50,400
Contribution margin		906,600
Fixed costs:		
Manufacturing	$620,000	
Selling and administrative	280,000	900,000
Income		$ 6,600
The detail of standard cost of goods sold follows:		
Variable production costs [(8,000 × $30) + (3,000 × $80)]		$ 480,000
Ending inventory [(400 × $30) + (500 × $80)]		52,000
Standard cost of goods sold		$ 428,000

ASSIGNMENT MATERIAL

Questions for Discussion

14-1 Variable and absorption costing   "The trouble with variable costing is that I have to put all of the fixed costs on the income statement right away. With absorption costing I can put some of them into inventory where they belong and take care of them later when the products are sold." Discuss these statements critically.

14-2 Period costs—product costs   The distinction between product costs and period costs is a major point of contention between the advocates of variable costing and those of absorption costing. Is the distinction important for decision making?

14-3 Variable costing   One argument for variable costing is that fixed manufacturing costs will be incurred regardless of the level of production. Does this argument consider all types of fixed costs?

Exercises

14-4 Basic standard costing—absorption and variable   Wilkinson Company makes Zuds, a cleaning product for household use. The product has a standard variable manufacturing cost of $4 per case. Fixed production costs are $500,000 per month; fixed selling and administrative expenses are $350,000 per month. The firm began March, 19X1 with no inventories and had the following activity in March, April, and May.

	March	April	May
Production in cases	120,000	100,000	110,000
Sales in cases	100,000	110,000	110,000

Zuds sells for $15 per case. The president of the company would like you to prepare two sets of monthly income statements: one showing monthly income using variable costing, the other showing monthly income using absorption costing with normal activity of 100,000 cases per month used to set the standard fixed cost.

Required: Prepare income statements by month as the president requested. Use a format that shows the details of beginning and ending inventories and of production costs in the cost of goods sold section.

14-5   Standard costing income statements   The following data pertain to the operations of the Lindsey Corporation for 19X8:

Normal capacity	200 units
Practical capacity	300 units
Budgeted production	240 units
Actual production	250 units
Actual sales ($25 per unit)	240 units
Standard variable production cost per unit	$10
Fixed production costs—budgeted	$2,400

During 19X8 there were no variable cost variances; fixed costs incurred were equal to the budgeted amount. There were no beginning inventories and no selling, general, or administrative expenses.

Required

1. Determine the standard total cost per unit assuming that standard fixed cost is based on (a) normal capacity, (b) practical capacity, and (c) budgeted production.
2. Prepare income statements for each of the three bases computed in part 1.

14-6   Standard variable costing   Arbo Company uses standard variable costing. Its product sells for $20, has standard variable manufacturing costs of $4, and budgeted total fixed manufacturing costs of $500,000. The company had no beginning inventories. It produced 110,000 units and sold 95,000. Actual variable manufacturing costs were $440,000, actual fixed manufacturing costs were $500,000. Variable selling expenses were a five percent commission on sales. Fixed selling expenses were $300,000.

Required: Prepare a standard variable costing income statement.

14-7   Standard absorption costing   XYZ Company produces a single product that sells for $15. Standard variable manufacturing cost is $3, standard fixed manufacturing cost is $4, based on normal capacity of 100,000 units. The firm began the year with no inventories, produced 110,000 units and sold 95,000. Actual total variable manufacturing costs were $330,000, actual fixed manufacturing costs $380,000. Selling and administrative expenses were $300,000.

Required: Prepare a standard absorption costing income statement showing *each* identifiable variance separately.

14-8   Absorption costing   TRS Company makes a single product that sells for $50. The standard variable manufacturing cost is $10, the standard fixed manufacturing cost is $8, based on budgeted fixed costs of $800,000 and budgeted production of 100,000 units. During 19X6, the company produced 96,000 units and sold 90,000. All manufacturing costs were incurred as budgeted, variable per unit and fixed in total. Selling and administrative expenses were $300,000. There were no beginning inventories.

Required
1.   Prepare a standard absorption costing income statement.
2.   If there had been a beginning inventory, would your income figure have been different from what you determined in part 1? Explain.

14-9   Variable costing (extension of 14–8)   Refer to the data in the previous exercise. Assume that TRS Company uses variable costing. Prepare an income statement.

14-10   Standard fixed cost and volume variance   The data below refer to the operations of Hiball Company for 19X8.

Normal capacity	100,000 units
Practical capacity	150,000 units
Budgeted production	120,000 units
Actual production	110,000 units
Fixed costs—budgeted and actual	$600,000

Required
1.   Compute the standard fixed cost per unit based on (a) normal capacity, (b) practical capacity, and (c) budgeted production.
2.   Compute the volume variances for each of the methods given in item 1.

14-11   Relationships   For each of the following situations, fill in the missing data. In all cases, the standard fixed cost per unit is based on normal capacity of 10,000 units.

	(a) Standard Fixed Cost per Unit	(b) Total Budgeted Fixed Costs	(c) Actual Production	(d) Volume Variance (Favorable)
1.	$__	$_____	8,000	$8,000
2.	$3	$_____		$6,000
3.	$__	$40,000	8,000	$_____
4.	$6	$_____	11,000	$_____
5.	$__	$30,000	_____	($7,500)

14-12 Effects of changes in production—standard variable costing The following data relate to Elliot Company's one product.

Sales (20,000 units at $10)	$200,000
Production costs:	
Variable costs, standard and actual	$4 per unit
Fixed, budgeted and actual	$ 60,000

The company has no beginning inventories and no selling and administrative expenses.

Required: Prepare income statements using standard variable costing assuming the firm produced (a) 25,000 units, and (b) 26,000 units.

14-13 Effects of change in production—standard absorption costing (extension of 14-12) Assume that Elliot Company uses standard absorption costing.

Required
1. Assume that Elliot uses a standard fixed cost per unit of $3 based on its normal activity of 20,000 units. Prepare income statements assuming that production is (a) 25,000 units, and (b) 26,000 units.
2. Assume that the firm uses a standard fixed cost per unit of $2 based on its practical capacity of 30,000 units. Prepare income statements assuming that production is (a) 25,000 units, and (b) 26,000 units.

14-14 Interpreting results The president of Stockley Company has been reviewing the income statements of the two most recent months. She is puzzled because sales rose and profits fell in March, and asks you, the controller, to explain.

	February	March
Sales ($30 per unit)	$540,000	$660,000
Standard cost of sales	270,000	330,000
Standard gross profit	270,000	330,000
Volume variance	40,000	(50,000)
Selling and administrative expenses	(150,000)	(150,000)
Income	$160,000	$130,000

The standard fixed cost per unit is $10, based on normal capacity of 20,000 units of production per month.

Required
1. Determine production in each month.
2. Explain the results to the president.
3. Prepare income statements using variable costing.

14-15 Income determination—variable and absorption costing The following data have been collected for Ronsen Company, based on activity for the year 19X4.

Sales (110,000 units)	$2,200,000
Production	80,000 units
Variable costs of production, budgeted and actual	$ 800,000
Fixed production costs, budgeted and actual	$ 360,000
Beginning inventory	50,000 units
Selling, general, and administrative costs	$ 250,000

Standard production costs for the prior year were the same as for the current year.

Required: Prepare income statements for the year 19X4, assuming (1) standard variable costing, and (2) standard absorption costing with 100,000 units being used as the basis to set the standard for fixed production costs. (*Hint:* Remember that beginning inventory in dollars will be different for each costing method.)

14-16 Income determination—standard absorption costing, practical capacity (extension of 14-15)   Assume that Ronsen Company uses standard absorption costing and has been using a standard fixed cost per unit based on practical capacity of 120,000 units.

Required: Prepare an income statement for the year 19X4. (Remember that beginning inventory in dollars will be different from those determined in 14-15.)

14-17 Relationships   Fill in the blanks for each of the following independent situations. *In all situations,* selling price is $10, standard and actual variable manufacturing cost is $6, fixed production costs, budgeted and actual, are $100,000, and the level of volume used to set the standard fixed cost per unit is 50,000 units. There are no selling and administrative expenses.

Case	(a) Unit Sales	(b) Unit Production	(c) Income— Variable Costing	(d) Income— Absorption Costing
1	70,000	————	————	$170,000
2	————	————	$ 90,000	$110,000
3	50,000	55,000	————	————
4	————	65,000	$180,000	————

14-18 Standard costing—absorption and variable   Corson Company makes a single product and uses standard absorption costing. Standard labor and materials are:

Materials, 3 gallons at $4 per gallon	$12
Direct labor, 0.50 hour at $10 per hour	5

Manufacturing overhead is budgeted according to the formula:

$$\text{Total annual manufacturing overhead} = \$500,000 + \$2 \times \text{direct labor hours}$$

The company uses its normal capacity of 25,000 direct labor hours (50,000 units) to set the standard fixed cost.

The company began 19X7 with no inventories. It produced 45,000 units and sold 40,000 at $40 each. Selling and administrative expenses were $200,000. There were no variable cost variances, and fixed production costs were incurred as budgeted ($500,000).

Required

1. Determine the total standard cost per unit.
2. Prepare an income statement for 19X7.
3. Prepare an income statement for 19X7 assuming that the company uses variable costing.

14-19 Analysis of income statement—standard costs The income statement for Bourque Manufacturing Company for 19X6 appears below. The company uses standard costs and has established the following standards for a unit of finished product.

Materials (10 pounds @ $1)	$10
Direct labor (2 hours @ $4)	8
Variable overhead ($1 per direct labor hour)	2
Fixed overhead	2
Total	$22

The standard for fixed overhead is based on a normal capacity of 20,000 units. During the year 19X6, 51,000 direct labor hours were worked and 248,000 pounds of material were used.

Bourque Manufacturing Company
Income Statement for 19X6

Sales (20,000 units @ $40)		$800,000
Cost of goods sold—at standard		440,000
Standard gross profit		360,000
Variances:		
Materials	$ 3,000U	
Labor	3,000U	
Variable overhead	3,000U	
Fixed overhead:		
Spending variance	5,000F	
Volume variance	10,000F	6,000F
Gross profit		366,000
Selling, general, and administrative expenses		220,000
Income		$146,000

Required

1. Based on the information provided, determine the following:
   (a) Number of units produced
   (b) Material use variance

(c) Material price variance
(d) Direct labor efficiency variance
(e) Direct labor rate variance
(f) Variable overhead efficiency variance
(g) Variable overhead spending variance
(h) Fixed overhead incurred

2. Prepare an income statement based on variable costing.

14-20 Conversion of absorption-costing income statement from normal to practical capacity (extension of 14-19) The standard costs and the income statement for Bourque Manufacturing Company in 14-19 assume that the standard fixed cost per unit is based on a normal capacity of 20,000 units. Assume, instead, that Bourque wants to base its standard fixed cost per unit on its practical capacity of 40,000 units.

Required
1. Determine the standard fixed cost per unit.
2. Prepare an income statement for 19X6.

14-21 Costing methods and product profitability Forman Company makes three products in the same plant. Fixed costs are applied to products based on the number of direct labor hours required to make the product. The rate of application is based on budgeted fixed costs of $900,000 and budgeted direct labor hours of 150,000. Per-unit data for the three products are as follows.

	A	B	C
Selling price	$160	$64	$90
Production costs, including applied fixed cost based			
on predetermined rate	$150	$56	$81
Direct labor hours required for one unit of product	9	4	3

Required
1. Determine variable production costs per unit for each product.
2. Assuming that variable costs of production are the only variable costs, determine which product yields: (a) the highest contribution margin per unit; (b) the highest contribution margin percentage; and (c) the highest contribution margin per direct labor hour.
3. If a manager asked you which product is the most profitable, what would you answer?

Problems

14-22 Analysis of income statements As the chief financial analyst of Markem Enterprises, Inc., you have been asked by the president to explain the difference between the two income statements prepared for his consideration. One was prepared by the controller, the other by the sales manager. Both used the same data from last year's operations.

	Statement A	Statement B
Sales (10,000 units)	$1,000,000	$1,000,000
Cost of goods sold:		
Beginning inventory	0	0
Production costs	600,000	900,000
Ending inventory	(200,000)	(300,000)
Cost of goods sold	400,000	600,000
Gross profit	600,000	400,000
Other costs	500,000	200,000
Income	$ 100,000	$ 200,000

Variable costs of production, the only variable costs, are $40 per unit.

Required

1. Determine which statement was prepared using variable costing, which using absorption costing.
2. Determine (a) fixed production costs; (b) selling and administrative costs; (c) production in units; and (d) cost per unit of inventory for both statements.
3. Which statement do you think was prepared by which manager and why do you think so?

14-23 Conversion of income statement   The manager of the Morgan Division of Rorshoot Industries has been on the job only a short time. The income statement below, for the third quarter of 19X7, is the first report he has received. He is having some difficulty in understanding it because he is familiar only with variable costing, and he has asked you to convert the statement to a variable costing basis.

Sales		$1,324,000
Cost of sales		893,700
Gross profit		430,300
Operating expenses:		
Selling and administrative	$276,300	
Unabsorbed fixed overhead	21,600	297,900
Income		$ 132,400

From reviewing internal records you have determined the following additional information:

1. Selling and administrative costs are all fixed.
2. The division sells its one product at $40 per unit.
3. Fixed manufacturing overhead is applied at $12 per unit.
4. There was no fixed overhead budget variance.
5. Production during the quarter was 38,200 units.

Required: Prepare an income statement using standard variable costing.

14-24 Effects of costing methods on balance sheet   McPherson Company has a loan with a large bank. Among the provisions of the loan agreement are (a) the current ratio must be at least 3 to 1, and (b) the ratio of debt to stockholders' equity must be no higher than 75%. The balance sheet at December 31, 19X4 is as follows.

Assets		Equities	
Cash and receivables	$ 460,000	Current liabilities	$ 200,000
Inventory (40,000 units		Long-term bank loan	300,000
at variable cost)	200,000	Stockholders' equity	760,000
Total current assets	660,000		
Fixed assets (net)	600,000		
Total assets	$1,260,000	Total equities	$1,260,000

Current ratio $660,000/$200,000 = 3.3/1
Debt/stockholders' equity $500,000/$760,000 = 65%

The budgeted income statement for 19X5 is as follows:

Sales (100,000 units)		$1,000,000
Variable cost of sales		500,000
Variable manufacturing margin		500,000
Other variable costs (variable with sales)		50,000
Contribution margin		450,000
Fixed costs:		
Manufacturing	$300,000	
Other	50,000	350,000
Income		$ 100,000

Budgeted production is 100,000 units. The president of the company anticipates substantial expenditures for fixed assets and intends to obtain a new loan to help finance these expenditures. He projects the following pro forma balance sheet for December 31, 19X5.

Assets		Equities	
Cash and receivables	$ 400,000	Current liabilities	$ 240,000
Inventory (40,000 units		Long-term bank loans	460,000
at variable cost)	200,000	Stockholders' equity	860,000
Total current assets	600,000		
Fixed assets (net)	960,000		
Total assets	$1,560,000	Total equities	$1,560,000

He sees that the firm will be in default on both provisions of the loan agreement. (Compute the current ratio and debt/stockholders' equity ratio to verify his finding.) Trying to resolve the problem, he lists the following points:
(a) Practical capacity is 150,000 units.
(b) The company could perhaps benefit if absorption costing were used.

Required
1. Recast the income statement and balance sheet using standard absorption costing with production of 150,000 units and the standard for fixed costs based on practical capacity. Assume that all increased production costs are paid in cash.
2. Is the company safely within the limits of the loan agreement?
3. Is the company better off using absorption costing?

14-25 **"Now wait a minute here."**   The title of this problem is the statement your boss made when you showed him the results of completing part 1 of this assignment.

Hownet makes panes for greenhouse windows, selling them for $10 each. Standard variable manufacturing cost is $2 and total fixed manufacturing costs are $60,000. Normal volume is 10,000 units, so that the standard fixed cost per unit is $6. Your boss had asked you to determine the firm's gross profit (after any production variances) from selling 10,000 units. The company treats all variances as adjustments to standard gross margin. Being conscientious, you decided to check your results by preparing income statements down to actual gross margin under each of the following cases. There are no beginning inventories.

1. Sales are 10,000 units, production is 10,000 units.
2. Sales are 10,000 units, production is 10,001 units.
3. Sales are 10,001 units, production is 10,001 units.
4. Sales are 9,999 units, production is 10,001 units.

Required
1. Prepare the income statements.
2. Explain why your boss gave the response he did.
3. Tell your boss why the results came out as they did.

14-26 **Incorporating variances into budgets**   Viner Company is developing its budgets for the coming year. The firm uses the standard costs shown below for its final product.

Materials	3 gallons @ $3	$ 9
Labor	4 hours @ $5	20
Variable overhead	$6 per DLH	24
Total standard variable cost		$53

Budgeted fixed manufacturing costs are $300,000. Selling, general, and administrative expenses, all fixed, are budgeted at $400,000. Generally, there is about a 10% variance over standard quantity for materials, which usually cost 5% less than the standard price. Direct laborers will receive a 6% wage increase at the beginning of the year, and labor efficiency is expected to be 4% better than standard. An unfavorable variable overhead spending variance of 5% is expected. Sales for the year are budgeted at 20,000 units at $100; production schedules indicate planned production of 24,000 units. There are no beginning inventories. The purchases of raw material are budgeted to be equal to expected material use.

Required
1. Determine the expected variable cost variances for the year.
2. Prepare a budgeted income statement for the coming year using standard variable costing.

14-27 **Costs and decisions**   "You're fired!!" was the way your boss, the controller of Saran Bathing Suit Company, greeted you this morning. His ire was based on the two income statements shown below. A few months ago you recommended accepting an offer from a national chain for 10,000 suits at $12 each. At that time, inventories were getting too high because of slow sales. Things have not improved noticeably since then. Your recommendation was based on the variable production costs of $10 per unit, which are the only variable costs. The total standard cost of $16 per suit includes $6 in fixed costs, based on normal production of 130,000 units.

Income Statements for 19X4

	If Special Order Had Not Been Accepted	Actual, with Special Order
Sales: 100,000 × $25	$2,500,000	$2,500,000
10,000 × $12		120,000
Total sales	2,500,000	2,620,000
Cost of sales at standard cost of $16	1,600,000	1,760,000
Standard gross profit	900,000	860,000
Volume variance (20,000 @ $6)	120,000U	120,000U
Actual gross profit	780,000	740,000
Selling and administrative expenses	710,000	710,000
Income	$ 70,000	$ 30,000

"Your stupidity cost us $40,000, you jerk!! Now clean out your desk and scram."

Required: Prepare an argument that will get your job back.

14-28 Basics of absorption and variable costing   Fixed Company was organized on January 1, 19X5 and began operations immediately. The balance sheet immediately after organization showed plant and equipment of $2,400,000 and common stock of $2,400,000. The plant is completely automated and makes its one product out of air. Its only cost is $240,000 depreciation, based on a 10-year life and the straight-line method. During the first two years of operation the company had the following results.

	19X5	19X6
Units produced	140,000	100,000
Units sold	120,000	120,000

All sales were at $5 per unit and were for cash. The company uses a standard fixed cost of $2 per unit based on normal volume of 120,000 units. There were no cash disbursements in either year so that cash at the end of each year was $5 multiplied by cumulative sales.

Required
1. Prepare income statements for each year.
2. Prepare a balance sheet as of the end of each year.
3. Repeat parts 1 and 2 using variable costing.

14-29 Actual versus standard costs—multiple products   Brennan Company makes luggage. For some time, there has been dissatisfaction with the firm's cost information. Unit costs have fluctuated greatly and they have not been useful for planning and control purposes.

Under the present system, unit costs are computed at the end of each month. The costs are determined by allocating all actual production costs for the month to the various models produced, with the allocation based on the relative material costs of the various models.

The controller has decided to develop standard costs for product costing purposes. He has analyzed the material and labor requirements for each model, based on what he believes to be currently attainable performance. The results of his analysis are as follows. (For simplicity, the problem is limited to only three models.)

	Briefcase #108	Cosmetic Case #380	Two-Suiter #460
Material costs	$12.00	$14.00	$18.00
Labor hours required	0.5	0.8	1.5

Workers are all paid $8 per hour, and the firm usually works about 6,000 labor hours per month. The controller intends to use the 6,000 hours to set his standard fixed cost per unit. His analysis of monthly manufacturing overhead indicates that it behaves according to the formula $90,000 + ($7 × direct labor hours).

During April the firm had the following results. There were no inventories at April 1.

	#108	#380	#460
Production in units	3,000	2,500	1,200
Sales in units	2,400	1,800	1,000
Sales in dollars	$84,000	$90,000	$85,000

There were no variable cost variances and fixed production costs were $92,000.

Required
1. Compute the standard cost for each model.
2. Compute the ending inventory of finished goods.
3. Prepare an income statement for April. Selling and administrative expenses were $28,000.

14-30 Interim results, costing methods, and evaluation of performance Kleffman Company sells a product with a highly seasonal demand. The budgeted income statement for 19X7 is given below.

Budgeted Income Statement for 19X7

Sales (240,000 units)		$2,400,000
Cost of goods sold—at standard:		
Materials	$420,000	
Direct labor	540,000	
Manufacturing overhead	600,000	1,560,000
Gross profit—at standard		840,000
Selling, general, and administrative expenses		420,000
Income before taxes		$ 420,000

Budgeted production is 240,000 units, the number used to set the standard fixed cost per unit. The controller has determined that materials, labor, 40% of manufacturing overhead ($240,000), and $120,000 of the selling, general, and administrative expenses are variable. All fixed costs are incurred evenly throughout the year.

January and February are relatively slow months, each with only about 5% of annual sales. March is the first month of a fairly busy period and production in February is generally high in order to stock up for the anticipated increase in demand. The actual income statements for January and February 19X7 are shown below.

	January	February
Sales (12,000 units)	$120,000	$120,000
Cost of goods sold—at standard	78,000	78,000
Gross profit—at standard	42,000	42,000
Manufacturing variances:		
Variable costs	3,000F	4,000U
Fixed cost—budget	2,000F	3,000U
Fixed cost—volume	9,000U	7,500F
Gross profit—actual	$ 38,000	$ 42,500
Selling, general, and administrative expenses	31,000	31,000
Income	$ 7,000	$ 11,500

Although the president is pleased that performance improved in February, he has asked the controller why there is a difference in profits in the two months, since sales were the same. He also wonders why profits were not about 5% of the amount budgeted for the year, since each month's sales were 5% of the annual budget.

Required
1. Explain to the president why profits in January and February would be expected to be less than 5% of the budgeted annual profit, even though each month's sales were 5% of the budgeted annual amount.
2. Explain to the president why profits differed in the two months. Comment on the president's being pleased that "performance improved in February." Support your answers with calculations.

14-31 Income statements and balance sheets Arens Company makes a single product, a microwave oven that sells for $300. The standard variable cost of production is $180 per unit and the only other variable cost is a 10% sales commission. Fixed production costs are $3,600,000 per year, incurred evenly throughout the year. Of that amount, $800,000 is depreciation and the remainder all require cash disbursements. Fixed selling and administrative expenses of $200,000 per month all require cash disbursements.

For inventory costing Arens uses a standard fixed cost of $45 per unit, based on expected annual production of 80,000 units. However, during 19X6 the firm experienced the following results, by 6-month periods.

	January–June	July–December
Sales in units	30,000	40,000
Production in units	32,000	42,000

The firm sells for cash only and pays all of its obligations as they are incurred.

Its balance sheet at December 31, 19X5 was as follows:

Arens Company Balance Sheet as of
December 31, 19X5 (In Thousands of Dollars)

Assets		Equities	
Cash	$ 400		
Inventory (1,000 units)	225	Common stock	$3,000
Plant and equipment (net)	3,000	Retained earnings	625
Total assets	$3,625	Total equities	$3,625

During 19X6, all costs were incurred as expected, variable costs per unit and fixed costs in total.

Required
1. Prepare income statements (in thousands of dollars) for each of the two 6-month periods and the year as a whole.
2. Prepare balance sheets as of June 30 and December 31, 19X6, in thousands of dollars.

14-32 **Pricing dispute**   Calligeris Company manufactures brake linings for automobiles. Late in 19X2 the firm received an offer for 10,000 linings from Phelan Company. Phelan was unwilling to pay the usual price of $5 per lining, but offered to buy at a price that would give Calligeris a $0.50 gross profit per lining.
        Without consideration of the order, Calligeris expected the following income statement for the year.

Sales (100,000 linings at $5)		$500,000
Cost of goods sold at standard:		
Beginning inventory (20,000 × $4)	$ 80,000	
Variable production costs (100,000 units at $2.50)	250,000	
Fixed production costs at $1.50 per unit	150,000	
Cost of goods available for sale	480,000	
Ending inventory (20,000 × $4)	80,000	
Cost of goods sold at standard		400,000
Standard gross profit		100,000
Volume variance (20,000 × $1.50)	30,000F	
Selling and administrative expenses	50,000	20,000
Income		$ 80,000

The production manager decided that the order could be readily filled from units in the firm's inventory, so no additional production was planned. The firm shipped 10,000 linings to Phelan Company, billing that firm for 10,000 units at $4.50 per lining. No additional costs were incurred in connection with this order.

Required
1. Prepare an income statement for 19X2 assuming that the actual results for the year were as planned except that the additional sale was made to Phelan Company. Do the results show that the firm earned the agreed gross profit?

2. Suppose that you were the controller of Phelan Company. Would you dispute the $4.50 price? If so, why? What price would you propose and why?

14-33 Predetermined overhead rates—multiple products The controller of Salmon Company has been working on the development of a new costing system. He believes that the use of standard costs would reduce the cost of recordkeeping and simplify the firm's internal reporting to managers. He has asked your assistance and you have collected the following information relating to the firm's three products.

		Product	
	Model 84	Model 204	Model 340
Variable production costs	$4	$7	$11
Direct labor hours required	0.50	0.80	1.50

The firm works 50,000 direct labor hours per year at normal operating level and the controller wishes to use that figure to set the predetermined overhead rate for the budgeted fixed production costs of $300,000

Operating results for 19X4 are given in the table below. There were no beginning inventories.

	Production in Units	Sales in Units	Sales in Dollars
Model 84	30,000	25,000	$250,000
Model 204	24,000	20,000	$280,000
Model 340	20,000	18,000	$450,000

All production costs were incurred as expected, variable costs per unit and total fixed costs. Selling and administrative expenses were $140,000.

Required
1. Compute standard fixed costs per unit for each model.
2. Compute the ending inventory in dollars for each model.
3. Prepare an income statement for 19X4.

14-34 Standard costs and pricing The controller of Carolina Mills has been discussing costs and prices with the treasurer. The controller wants to use 2,400,000 machine hours to set standard fixed costs while the treasurer would prefer to use 3,000,000 hours. The controller feels that the lower base would make it easier for the company to absorb its fixed overhead, but the treasurer is concerned that the company might set its prices too high to be competitive with other companies.

"Look," the treasurer said, "suppose we use our formula for budgeting total manufacturing costs, materials, labor, and overhead."

Total manufacturing cost = $7,680,000 + $4.25 per machine hour

"Now," he went on, "if we use your basis of 2,400,000 hours and our usual pricing formula, setting prices at 150% of total manufacturing cost, we will have higher prices than competition will permit, with consequent loss of volume."

The controller replied, "I can't agree with you. Your basis of 3,000,000 hours is very close to practical capacity and we'd be taking the risk of having a significant amount of underabsorbed overhead that would really hurt our profits."

Required
1. Suppose that selling and administrative expenses are $6,200,000, all fixed. What profit will the company earn if it uses 2,400,000 hours to set standard fixed costs, sets prices using the formula given above, and sells output requiring 2,400,000 machine hours? (Assume no inventories.)
2. Repeat part 1 substituting 3,000,000 machine hours for 2,400,000 hours.
3. Is the real issue here the selection of the base for applying fixed overhead? Why or why not? What is the real concern?

14-35 **Product costing methods and VCP analysis**   Tollgate Company expects to produce 190,000 units of product in 19X6. The firm uses a predetermined overhead rate for fixed overhead based on 210,000 units, which is its normal capacity. Over- or underabsorbed overhead is shown separately in the income statement. The firm's selling price is $16 per unit. At the expected level of production Tollgate expects the following costs:

Variable production costs	$1,330,000
Fixed production costs	630,000
Fixed selling and administrative costs	434,000

In addition, there are variable selling costs of $2 per unit. The firm has no inventory at the end of 19X5.

Required
1. Determine the break-even point assuming that variable costing is used.
2. Determine the number of units that must be sold to break even given that production will be 190,000 units. Assume absorption costing.
3. If your answers to the first two parts are different, explain the difference, showing calculations.
4. Would your answer to part 2 be different if the firm had had a beginning inventory of 10,000 units costed at the same per-unit amount that the firm will use in 19X6? Explain why or why not, with calculations.

14-36 **Comprehensive review, budgeting, overhead application**   Ruland Company makes and sells a single product. The product sells for $20 and Ruland expects sales of 880,000 units in 19X5. The distribution of sales by quarters is expected to be 20%, 25%, 25%, and 30%. The firm expects the following costs in 19X6.

Manufacturing Costs

	Fixed	Variable per Unit
Materials (4 pounds at $0.80)	—	$3.20
Direct labor (0.5 hour at $5)	—	2.50
Maintenance	$ 46,000	0.20
Indirect labor	422,000	0.40
Supplies	316,000	0.05
Power	186,000	0.10
Depreciation	1,900,000	—
Supervision	310,000	—
Miscellaneous	320,000	0.05
Totals	$3,500,000	$6.50

Selling, General, and Administrative Expenses

	Fixed	Variable per Unit
Salesperson compensation		$2.00
Other salaries and wages	$1,200,000	—
Other expenses, including interest on debt	4,350,000	
Totals	$5,550,000	$2.00

Budgeted production and purchases are:

Quarter	Production (Units)	Raw Material Purchases (Pounds)
1	210,000	733,000
2	220,000	950,000
3	260,000	904,000
4	210,000	795,000
Totals	900,000	3,382,000

Other information relating to Ruland's operation is given below:

1. The firm uses a standard fixed cost of $3.50 per unit for product costing purposes.
2. Sales are collected 60 days after sale.
3. Purchases of raw materials are paid for in the month after purchase.
4. Direct labor costs unpaid at the end of a quarter are about 10% of the cost incurred that quarter. All other manufacturing costs requiring cash disbursements (all but depreciation) are paid as incurred, except for raw material purchases.
5. All selling, general, and administrative expenses require cash disbursements and are paid as incurred except for salesperson's commissions. These are paid in the month after incurrence.
6. The firm has a 40% income tax rate. At the end of any year, the amount of unpaid taxes is about 25% of the total expense for the year.
7. A dividend of $300,000 will be paid to shareholders in 19X5.
8. Purchases of plant assets will total $2,100,000 in 19X5 and will be paid for in cash.
9. You may assume that sales, production, and purchases of raw materials are spread evenly over the months of each quarter (one-third of quarter in each month of the quarter).

The balance sheet at the end of 19X4 follows, in thousands of dollars.

Assets		Equities	
Cash	$ 840	Accounts payable (materials)	$ 240
Accounts receivable	2,800	Accrued commissions	120
Inventory—finished goods		Accrued payroll (direct labor)	64
(146,000 units)	1,460	Income taxes payable	80
Inventory—materials		Long-term debt	4,000
(530,000 pounds)	424	Common stock	7,000
Plant and equipment	16,200	Retained earnings	1,820
Accumulated depreciation	(8,400)		
Total	$13,324	Total	$13,324

Required

1. Prepare a budgeted income statement for 19X5.
2. Prepare a cash budget for 19X5 for the year as a whole, not by quarter.
3. Prepare a pro forma balance sheet for the end of 19X5.
4. Without preparing new statements, describe the differences there would be in those you have prepared if the firm were using variable costing.

Cases

14-37 Costing methods and evaluation of performance   Ralph Sampson is the manager of the Wallace Division of Fizer Industries, Inc. He is one of several managers being considered for the presidency of the firm, as the current president is retiring in a year.

All divisions use standard absorption costing for inventories; normal capacity is the basis for application of fixed overhead. Normal capacity in the Wallace Division is 40,000 units per quarter, and quarterly fixed overhead is $500,000. Variable production cost is $50 per unit. Ralph has been looking at the report for the first three months of the year and is not happy with the results.

Wallace Division Income Statement for First Quarter

Sales (25,000 units)		$2,500,000
Cost of goods sold:		
Beginning inventory (10,000 units)	$ 625,000	
Production costs applied	1,562,500	
Total	$2,187,500	
Less: Ending inventory	625,000	1,562,500
Gross profit		937,500
Volume variance		(187,500)
Selling and general expenses		(500,000)
Income		$ 250,000

The sales forecast for the second quarter is 25,000 units. Ralph had budgeted second-quarter production at 25,000 units, but changes it to 50,000 units which is practical capacity for a quarter. The sales forecasts for each of the last two quarters of the year are also 25,000 units. Costs incurred in the second quarter are the same as budgeted, based on 50,000 units of production.

Required

1. Prepare an income statement for the second quarter.
2. Does the statement for the second quarter reflect Ralph's performance better than that for the first quarter? Can you make any suggestions for reporting in the future? Do you think Ralph should be seriously considered for the presidency of the firm? Why or why not?

14-38 Cost justification   Many states operate Medicaid and other programs designed to provide health services for their citizens. Sometimes these services are reimbursed by the state on a cost-plus basis. The following testimony took place at a hearing of the State Senate committee on nursing home costs. Nursing home care is one of the many types of health services covered by Medicaid programs. In most cases, the nursing homes are privately owned and operated.

Senator: Now, as I understand it, the state pays you for the costs to run the home plus 10% of cost, but you are allowed a maximum profit of 15% return on investment. Is that correct?

Nursing Home Manager: That's right. And we have a very big investment in the home. About $70,000 per bed in building and equipment alone, which does not count our major asset, those dedicated employees. Now, a lot of hospitals and nursing homes try to get away with less, but we want our guests to have the finest possible accommodations.

Senator: I see by the drawings of the building that about 60% of the space is devoted to offices. Your own office is 40 by 35 feet and has a fireplace, two couches, 12 chairs, and a Louis XIV desk. Is that, too, correct?

Nursing Home Manager: Well, Senator, I do need a lot of space for conferences and other activities. For example, I often hold small social functions in my office for staff personnel. It helps to keep up morale, which is very important.

Senator: Commendable. Now about these charges for laundry.

Nursing Home Manager: We are very proud of our cost-cutting efforts there, Senator. We used to do the laundry ourselves, but it was costing too much. My brother-in-law's firm does it for only $0.60 per pound. Why, in 19X7 it cost us $117,000 to process 100,000 pounds of laundry. Soap and detergents were $12,000, power and water amounted to $8,000, salaries were $35,000, depreciation on our equipment was $7,000, and depreciation on the building was $55,000. Of course, the building depreciation is only for the basement, where the laundry was located. We don't use that space now that we have the laundry done outside. Now in 19X8 it cost us $121,000 to process 120,000 pounds of laundry, which is $1.01 per pound. We could have processed about 340,000 pounds with the equipment and personnel we had, but we knew we would never get that high, so we sold the equipment to the laundry service that we use now. We took a pretty big loss on that sale, as a matter of fact. Now we are sending out about 200,000 pounds of laundry per year.

Senator: I see. I wonder if you could explain to us the $350,000 management fee that was charged to the home for 19X8.

Nursing Home Manager: I'm glad you asked about that, Senator. Did you notice that it has gone down since the prior year? You see, our home is owned by a large corporation and it has opened several new homes, so naturally that cuts down on our share of the fee. The fee is based on the number of guests served.

The home office of the corporation incurs a lot of costs on behalf of all of the homes. You remember, for example, Senator, the large press party given to announce the opening of several new homes and the overall plans for growth and improved services to guests. I believe you were quite impressed at the time with the corporation's plans.

Senator: Well, yes, that's true. I do think it is wise to get to know more about the people you deal with; it gives you an idea of what type of people they are. But I have one last thing I'd like to cover here, the fees for laboratory tests. They seem to be awfully high for an operation the size of yours.

Nursing Home Manager: I suppose they could appear so. But we are concerned about the health of our guests and so we test their blood every day. You can't be too careful, you know. I know that a lot of the homes wouldn't do that $5 test for bubonic plague, but you never can tell when an outbreak might occur.

Senator: Frightful thing, the plague. Well, I think that about covers everything I wanted to get to. And I must say that you were very well prepared for your testimony here.

Nursing Home Manager: Thank you, Senator. It has been a pleasure to clear up these little points for your committee.

Required: Comment on the practices described.

14-39   **Costing methods and performance evaluation**   Warren Progman, the new manager of the Oliver Division of General Products Company, was greatly displeased at the income statements that his controller, Hal Gannon, had been giving him. Progman had recently been placed in charge of the division because it had not been showing satisfactory results. Progman was upset because, although sales had risen in each of the last two months, profits had not kept pace. Income statements for the last three months are given below:

	March	April	May
Sales	$360,000	$440,000	$560,000
Cost of sales	198,000	264,000	381,000
Gross profit	162,000	176,000	179,000
Other expenses	142,000	150,000	162,000
Profit before taxes	$ 20,000	$ 26,000	$ 17,000

Progman asked Gannon why profits had declined when sales had increased, and why a substantial increase in sales from March to April had produced only a small increase in profits. Gannon's reply was simply that operations had gone according to plans that Progman had set, and that the problems that Progman wanted to know about were due to the method of accounting for product costs and the relationships of sales to production.

Progman was unimpressed with this explanation, and rather testily pointed out that he had been put in charge of the division to "turn it around," and he was not about to let accounting conventions give the corporate management second thoughts about placing him in charge. Gannon, who was fully aware of the claims Progman had made when being considered for the manager's job, had not liked Progman from the start. To the suggestion that accounting conventions were standing in the way of Progman's performance, Gannon replied only that the reports for all divisions were prepared from the same uniform accounting system and in the form required for corporate reporting. He told Progman that the reports were prepared using generally accepted accounting principles, which was necessary because the corporation was publicly held and had to issue reports to shareholders. He did not tell Progman that he believed the methods used by the firm for external reporting were inappropriate for internal purposes.

Later, at lunch with Frank Holloway, the division's sales manager, Gannon related the conversation that he had with Progman. Holloway, who had also wondered about the firm's accounting methods, asked Gannon why he didn't just explain the statements to Progman. "Not on your life," said Gannon. "I see no reason to help that braggart. Let *him* explain to the top brass why things aren't going the way he said they would if he were put in charge instead of me."

"Actually," Gannon continued, "what he's worried about just isn't a difficult problem. Cost of sales included both standard cost and the adjustment needed when production for the month did not equal the 25,000-unit volume that was used to set the standard fixed cost of $9 per unit. In fact, things have gone very well. We have had no variances at all except for volume. Selling prices have held very well at $20 per unit, and the division is doing much better now. But would I like to be there when the brass asks Progman why things are not going so well! Why, even production in April was right on target at 25,000 units budgeted."

Required
1. Explain the results in the three-month period. You may wish to compute standard fixed costs per unit and production in each month.
2. Prepare income statements for the three months using variable costing.

14-40 Costing methods and product profitability   At a recent meeting, several of the managers of Cornwall Valve Company were discussing the firm's costing and pricing methods. Although there was general agreement that the methods to be used should be helpful to managers in determining which products to emphasize, there was considerably less agreement on which methods would accomplish this.

The sales manager, Ralph Stokes, expressed his preference for product costs based on variable costs only. "I see no reason to charge a product with fixed costs. Contribution margin is, after all, the critical question in selecting the products to push."

"I just can't agree with you," said Bill Rollo, the production manager. "If you'd just take a walk through the plant you'd be reminded that men and materials aren't the only things thay you need to produce one of our valves. There are tons of machinery that cost money too. Ignoring those costs can only get you into trouble and it sure isn't very realistic anyway. You've *got* to consider the machine time required for each product, and that can only be accomplished by allocating the fixed production costs to products. Machining time is critical, and production costs should be allocated on a machine-hour basis."

To make this point, Bill put an example on the conference room blackboard. "Look, let me show you. Let's take just three of our basic products that all require time in the grinding department. That department has a capacity of 1,000 machine hours a month, and the monthly fixed costs of the department are $10,000." Below is the schedule Bill put on the board.

	101-27	*101-34*	*101-56*
Selling price	$9.00	$12.00	$17.40
Variable costs	5.00	6.00	8.40
Contribution margin	4.00	6.00	9.00
Fixed costs (see below)	1.00	1.25	2.50
Profit per unit	$3.00	$ 4.75	$ 6.50
Number of valves processed per hour	10	8	4

Bill continued, "Now what I've done is compute a fixed cost per unit by dividing the $10 per hour fixed cost by the number of valves of each type that we can process in one hour. You can see that what I use the grinding machinery for *does* make a difference. It seems to me that an approach like this is much better for showing what products to emphasize. This shows that the 56 is the best bet and the 27 is the worst."

"But Bill," said Ralph, "we don't disagree. The 56 is a winner because it has the highest contribution margin, and the 27 we wouldn't push because it contributes the least. What are we arguing about?"

Bill was not too happy about having his own example used to counter his argument. He admitted that, in the case he used, the relative rankings of the products were the same as they would be using the contribution margin approach. But he still felt that his method would be more valuable to the sales manager than a simple contribution margin approach, and he looked around the room for support.

"Well, now, it's nice to hear that you two are so interested in the information my staff has to offer," commented Joe Anderson, the controller. "But if you want to be realistic, let's consider something else. We're committed to making some of each of these valves, though not nearly enough to keep the grinding department operating at capacity. So the big decision isn't really which valve to produce and sell. What we really need to know is which one to produce after we've met the commitments we made. And the kicker is that we could probably sell all of whatever we produce. The way I see it, we have about 600 hours of grinding time available for discretionary production. So what do we do?"

Bill continued to argue for his approach, and he specifically attacked the question of pricing. "The way we price our products just isn't rational; I know we could do better if we considered the fixed costs the way I said. We should be selling the 27s for $12.50 if we want to make them as profitable as the 56s, and we'd have to jack the price of 34s by $1.75 to equal the profit on the 56s. Okay, okay, I can see you're getting upset about the idea of such increases, Ralph. I know the customers would be unhappy. But if we cater to their needs by producing these models, we ought to get a fair return for doing it."

Required: Determine which valve should be produced once the committed demand is satisfied. Criticize the analyses of the sales manager and the production manager, including their comments about pricing.

CHAPTER 15

PROCESS COSTING AND THE COST ACCOUNTING CYCLE

In Chapter 13 you were introduced to product costing—the determination of a cost for a unit of manufactured product. Most of the concepts introduced (such as cost flows, application of overhead) apply to all types of manufacturing situations, but the emphasis was on job-order costing, the cost accumulation method most relevant to a company producing several different and nonstandard products. For companies that manufacture a single, homogeneous product, or a group of such products, another cost accumulation method is used—process costing. The first part of this chapter discusses the concepts peculiar to product costing for such firms.

Finally, to complete our study of product costing and place the flow of manufacturing costs in an *accounting* framework, we illustrate the cost accounting cycle. The illustrations cover the journal entries and accounts employed in the two types of cost accumulation systems, job-order costing and process costing. In addition, we illustrate the accounting cycle for a costing system that incorporates standard costs. The cost control benefits of using standard costs are significant, and standard costs can be used by either job-order or process-costing firms.

PROCESS COSTING

As we stated in Chapter 13, many companies make a single, homogeneous product in more or less continuous processes. Some examples are producers of sugar, bricks, cement, various chemicals, instant coffee, etc. While the production of such a product may include several phases, each unit of product must proceed through each phase at the same time as many other units. All the units in a group receive the same treatment. (If more than a single product is involved, a particular product must still go through one, two, or more separate processes.) Companies operating in this fashion use what is called **process costing**.

The essence of process costing is the accumulation of costs by process, by each phase in the production operation. The firm obtains per-unit costs for goods passing through a process by dividing costs for the process by the number of units produced. Hence, the result is an average cost per unit. Such an averaging is necessary because all units are worked on together, and it is impossible to identify the costs of a process with anything other than the entire batch.

A process costing firm, like a job-order firm, could, for internal reporting, determine inventoriable unit costs using either variable or absorption costing, as described in Chapter 14. We know, however, that for financial reporting and tax purposes, all firms must use absorption costing, so we shall concentrate on that approach for process costing. As we also showed in Chapter 13, the assignment of overhead to production in a job-order type of manufacturing situation can be accomplished using either actual or normal costing. These options are also available to a firm using process costing.

The only new problems introduced by the process-nature of a manufacturing operation arise because, at any given time and in any given phase of production, there is often a batch of product that is not completely through that phase. (That is, the entire batch is "in process" and thus is complete only to a certain extent.) Specifically, this fact creates a problem: (1) in determining the number of units to use in computing the per-unit cost, and (2) in raising the need for some type of cost-flow assumption (first-in-first-out or weighted-average) in order to follow the product through the individual processes. Thus, while the calculation of per-unit costs takes the general form:

$$\text{Unit cost} = \frac{\text{total production cost}}{\text{units produced}},$$

the process-nature of the production operation makes this calculation more complicated than it first appears.

To illustrate the special problems arising in a process-costing situation, consider the Ronn Company, which produces a single product in a single manufacturing process. Exhibit 15-1 shows the relevant data for the company's operations in the months of August and September. The goal is to compute the cost of a unit produced in each of those months and, of course, the cost of any ending inventory.

The data include for each month the total production costs, the number of units completed, and some information about how much work has been done on those units that were still in process at the beginning and the end of each month (work-in-process inventories). Thus, while 100,000 units were completed in August, another 5,000 units were still in process and only 60% complete at the end of that month. Similarly, the

Exhibit 15-1

Data for Ronn Company

	August	September
Production costs	$206,000	$191,400
Unit data:		
In process at beginning of month	0	5,000
Completed during month	100,000	90,000
In process at end of month	5,000	10,000
Percentage of completion for end-of-period work	60%	40%

work done in September to incur the indicated production costs involved not only work on new units but also the completion of some units started in August and the starting of work on some units still incomplete at the end of September. To compute the cost of a unit in a given month, the first problem is to determine an appropriate denominator for the general formula given above. That determination requires an understanding of the concept of equivalent production.

Equivalent Production

Total production costs for a given month relate to the work done on units both finished and in process at month end. It would not, therefore, be appropriate to calculate a cost of finished units simply by dividing total costs incurred by the number of units *finished*. For example, while Ronn Company incurred some of its August production costs to start and finish some units in that month, there is no doubt that some of those costs were also incurred in starting the work on units that were still in process at the end of the month. Thus, some of the $206,000 in production costs in August involved doing 60% of the work on the 5,000 units still in process at the end of that month. Hence, you could not compute a per-unit cost for the 100,000 units completed simply by dividing the total costs of $206,000 by those 100,000 units. Some consideration must be given to the work done on units still in inventory.

The situation in September has still another dimension, for that month's production costs were incurred for three types of work: (1) work to finish those units in process at the beginning of the month; (2) work to start and finish some units within the month; and (3) work to finish partly those units still in process at the end of the month. Here, again, the calculation of a per-unit cost for the 90,000 finished units cannot involve just the total production costs of $191,400 and the 90,000 units completed. We must consider not only the work on the ending inventory, but also the work done to finish the units started in August (the beginning inventory).

To see how ending and beginning in-process inventories are handled in computating per-unit costs, let us take each in its turn, beginning with August, when the only complication is in-process units at the end of the period.

Ending Inventory   To determine the cost of work on a unit of product when there is an inventory of partially completed units on hand at the end of the period, we must include the amount of work done during that period on those partially finished units. Thus, for

Ronn Company, work was completed on 100,000 units plus 60% of the work done on another 5,000 units. To calculate a unit cost, we must calculate an **equivalent production** of complete units in the following way.

Units completed this period	100,000
Completed units *equivalent* to the work done on partially completed units:	
5,000 units × 60% complete	3,000
Total equivalent production	103,000

In general terms, the formula for equivalent production is this:

$$\frac{\text{Equivalent}}{\text{production}} = \frac{\text{units}}{\text{completed}} + \left(\frac{\text{units in}}{\text{ending inventory}} \times \frac{\text{percentage}}{\text{complete}}\right)$$

With this equivalent production, we can compute the unit cost of a completed unit in August as follows:

$$\frac{\text{production costs}}{\text{equivalent production}} = \frac{\$206,000}{103,000 \text{ units}} = \$2.00 \text{ per unit}$$

Thus, we can account for the total production costs of $206,000 as follows:

Cost of finished units transferred to finished goods (100,000 × $2 per unit)	$200,000
Cost of ending inventory (5,000 units × $2 to complete a unit × 60%)	6,000
Total production costs accounted for	$206,000

What this calculation says, in effect, is that 5,000 units that are 60% complete are the equivalent of 3,000 units that are 100% complete, and the cost of a single complete unit is $2. When there are no beginning inventories, the unit cost of production is computed by dividing the total production costs for the period by the number of units completed *plus* the equivalent completed units in the ending inventory.

Beginning Inventory   The second problem that arises in computing unit costs in a process-costing setting appears when there are units in process at the beginning of the period. These units will be completed during the current period, but costs will have been incurred on them in both the prior and the current periods. To compute a unit cost for the current period we must decide whether to combine the costs carried over in the beginning inventory (an averaging approach), or to restrict the unit-cost calculation to costs only for work done in the current period. The decision is essentially a choice of a cost-flow assumption, such as you learned about in financial accounting. Combining the costs is a weighted-average approach; maintaining a separate identity for the costs in the beginning inventory is a *first-in-first-out (FIFO)* approach. In this chapter we shall use the weighted-average cost-flow. The appendix to this chapter describes the calculations of equivalent production and unit costs using the FIFO method.

The per-unit cost for a given period still involves dividing total production costs by equivalent units, as noted in an earlier section. But if there are units in process at the beginning of the period and we adopt the weighted-average approach to the flow of costs, what we have is a *merging* of the current production costs with those costs incurred to start work on the beginning inventory. We can see how this merging occurs by considering the Ronn Company activity in September.

The total production cost to be considered is the combination of the costs incurred in August on the September beginning inventory, and the costs incurred to work on units started in September. Thus, the total cost to be considered is $6,000 (the costs determined above as related to the units 60% finished at the end of August), plus $191,400 of costs incurred in September—or $197,400. Since the weighted-average approach merges costs for doing basically the same thing, we need not consider the beginning inventory *units* in the calculation of equivalent production. That is, we can merge those beginning units with all those units started and finished this period, so that the calculation of equivalent production is the same as it was when there was no beginning inventory:

Units completed during September	90,000
Completed units *equivalent* to the work done	
in September on partially completed units:	
10,000 × 40%	4,000
Equivalent production	94,000

Using the weighted-average assumption, equivalent production is calculated as before:

$$\begin{matrix} \text{Equivalent} \\ \text{production---} \\ \text{weighted} \\ \text{average} \end{matrix} = \begin{matrix} \text{units} \\ \text{completed} \end{matrix} + \left(\begin{matrix} \text{units in} \\ \text{ending} \\ \text{inventory} \end{matrix} \times \begin{matrix} \text{percentage} \\ \text{complete} \end{matrix} \right)$$

Although it is not necessary to do so, we could give separate recognition to the completed units that were started in the prior period. This could be done as follows:

Units started in August and completed	
in September (beginning inventory)	5,000
Units started and completed in September	
(90,000 − 5,000)	85,000
Completed units *equivalent* to the work done	
in September on partially completed units	
(ending inventory):	
10,000 × 40%	4,000
Equivalent production	94,000

There is no need to consider the percentage of the work that was done each month on the items in process at the beginning of the period, because we are combining the costs of the incomplete work from August with the costs of completing the work in September. Thus, the cost of completing a unit in September can be computed as follows:

$$\text{Cost per unit—weighted average} = \frac{\text{cost of beginning inventory} + \text{costs incurred during the period}}{\text{equivalent production—weighted average}}$$

For Ronn Company, the unit cost for September would be:

$$\text{Unit cost (weighted average)} = \frac{(\$6,000 + \$191,400) = \$197,400}{94,000} = \$2.10$$

All this means is that, on average, it took $2.10 to make a unit of product in September. The total costs (remember we are merging the costs from the beginning inventory with the production costs in September) of $197,400 are accounted for as follows:

Costs of finished units transferred to finished goods (90,000 × $2.10)	$189,000
Cost of ending inventory (10,000 units at $2.10 to complete a unit × 40%)	8,400
Total cost accounted for	$197,400

Notice that, in both August and September, we showed that the total costs incurred were "accounted for" by the costs transferred out of the process plus the costs remaining "in process." This calculation, because it uses the computed unit cost, offers a check on your work. If the total costs accounted for as either transferred out or still in process do not agree with the total costs incurred, you have made an error.

Although no other conceptual problems arise with the use of process costing, there is one very common, practical situation that can complicate the calculation of equivalent production, and still another common, very practical situation that requires special care in computing the cost of ending inventory. The first complication arises simply because it is unusual for all three of the basic components of manufacturing cost (material, labor, and overhead) to be equally complete (or incomplete) at a given time. The second complication arises in situations—which, unfortunately, constitute the majority of manufacturing situations—in which the production of a product involves more than one department, phase, or process. The next two sections discuss how these common situations can be dealt with, using the basic idea of equivalent production and work in process.

Materials and Conversion Costs

Our example with the Ronn Company assumed that the percentage-of-completion figure applied to all productive factors alike—material, labor, and overhead. However, such a situation is quite unlikely. Materials are usually put into a process at an early stage, so that work-in-process inventories often include all, or nearly all, the materials but significantly less than the total expected labor and overhead. Consider, for example, the production process of a company that manufactures sugar from sugar beets.

While the process of grinding beets into sugar takes a certain amount of time and certain types of facilities, all the sugar beets are added at the start of production. It would be unreasonable to suggest that the production process was equally complete with respect to materials, labor, and overhead.

It generally takes some labor to convert raw materials into a product, and manufacturing overhead is usually incurred throughout a process. Hence, labor and overhead are called **conversion costs**. It is generally assumed that when a specific portion of the labor involved in a manufacturing process has been completed, the same completion percentage is applicable to overhead.

Though differing degrees of completion for materials and conversion costs do not change the general formula for computing unit costs, they do necessitate separating the total costs and determining a separate equivalent production for materials and conversion costs. We shall illustrate this computational difference using the data from Exhibit 15-2.

Exhibit 15-2
Production Data for Borne Company for May

		Materials	Conversion Costs
Costs for beginning inventory		$ 4,000	$ 5,600
Production costs incurred in May		$36,000	$52,000
Unit data:			
Units completed	45,000		
Units in process	5,000		
Percentage of work complete		100%	60%

First, an equivalent production must be computed for the two types of costs.

	Materials	Conversion Costs
Units completed during the period	45,000	45,000
Completed units *equivalent* to the work done on partially completed units:		
5,000 units × 100%	5,000	
5,000 units × 60%		3,000
Equivalent production	50,000	48,000

The production cost to be used in the calculation of unit cost is, based on a weighted-average cost-flow assumption, the combination of the costs in the beginning inventories and the costs of the current period. The unit cost calculation would, therefore, be as follows:

$$\frac{\text{Unit cost}}{\text{for materials}} = \frac{\$4,000 + \$36,000}{50,000} = \$0.80 \text{ per unit}$$

$$\frac{\text{Unit cost for}}{\text{conversion costs}} = \frac{\$5,600 + \$52,000}{48,000} = \$1.20 \text{ per unit}$$

Using these unit costs, we can compute the cost of a unit transferred to finished goods as $2.00 (the $0.80 cost of materials, plus the $1.20 labor and overhead cost to complete each unit). The cost of the ending inventory of work in process would be computed as follows:

Material cost: 5,000 units × 100% × $0.80	$4,000
Conversion cost: 5,000 units × 60% × $1.20	3,600
Total cost of ending work in process inventory	$7,600

Taking advantage of the check-point presented in earlier sections, we can see that the total costs incurred are fully accounted for through the transfer of completed units and the costs assigned to the ending inventory.

Total costs to be accounted for:	
Costs in beginning inventory ($4,000 + $5,600)	$ 9,600
Costs for current month ($36,000 + $52,000)	88,000
Total	$97,600
Total costs accounted for as:	
Cost of finished units transferred	
to finished goods (45,000 × $2.00)	$90,000
Cost of ending inventory, computed above	7,600
Total	$97,600

Thus, the only complications that occur because of different percentages of completion for materials and conversion costs are the needs to compute different amounts of equivalent production and to separate total costs by type. Since the normal accounting process would separate the costs of each of the three cost elements, and since the people in charge of a particular process are well aware of the potential for differing degrees of completion for some cost elements, the complications posed by the different completion percentages are usually easy to deal with.

The only other computational complication that warrants mention in this introduction to process costing is the problem created when there is more than one process in the manufacturing operation, so that products move from one process to another. That complication is really a special case of the situation just discussed, a situation in which units are complete to differing degrees for some types of costs.

Multiple Processes

If a product moves from one process to another, it is obvious that the *total* cost of the product includes the costs of all the processes. Suppose, for example, that the manufacture of a particular product includes both a forming phase (which involves cutting large blocks of some raw material into smaller blocks of roughly equal size) and a sanding phase (which involves refining the shapes to common specifications). The cost of a unit transferred from sanding to finished goods would include the cost of both the forming and the sanding processes. The cost of a unit in process in the sanding phase would include not only the cost of that phase but also the cost of the forming phase.

To illustrate the implications of multiple processes for the computation of unit costs and the costs of ending work in process inventory, let us extend the example of Borne Company, for whom the basic production data for May are provided in Exhibit 15-2. Let us assume that the 45,000 units that were completed in May, at a unit cost determined earlier to be $2, are transferred to a finishing department. No materials are added during the finishing process, and overhead in that department is closely associated with labor hours worked. Operating data for June for the finishing process are as follows:

Unit data:	
On hand at beginning of June	0
Transferred in from prior department	45,000
Transferred to finished goods	40,000
On hand at end of period (70% complete)	5,000
Cost data:	
Beginning inventory	0
Transferred in from prior department	
(45,000 × $2 per unit)	$ 90,000
Department's conversion costs for June	$156,600

What is the cost of a single unit transferred in June from the finishing process?

The first step, of course, is to calculate the equivalent production for the finishing process.

Units completed during the period	40,000
Completed units equivalent to the work	
done on partially completed units	
5,000 × 70%	3,500
Equivalent production	43,500

Dividing equivalent production into the conversion costs for the month ($156,600) yields a unit cost for the finishing process of $3.60. The cost of a unit transferred to finished goods would be the $2.00 from the prior department plus the $3.60 cost from the finishing department, or $5.60. The cost of the ending in-process inventory would be as follows:

Prior department costs, 5,000 × 100% × $2.00	$10,000
Conversion cost for finishing	
5,000 × 70% × $3.60	12,600
Total cost of ending inventory	$22,600

The total cost to be accounted for by the finishing department consists of the costs transferred in ($90,000), the costs in the beginning inventory (none), and the month's production costs ($156,600), or $246,600. That total is accounted for as follows.

Cost of units transferred to finished goods (40,000 × $5.60)	$224,000
Cost of ending in-process inventory, computed above	22,600
Total cost accounted for	$246,600

Thus, the transferring in of units from an earlier manufacturing process does *not* affect the calculation of equivalent production, or of the unit cost for the department.

Summary of Process Costing

Process costing, which is used by companies whose product does not change significantly from one period to the next or does not differ much from unit to unit, requires use of the new concept called equivalent production. A unit cost is computed for each phase of the production process, and the computation may require separating the costs of materials from the costs of converting those materials into the final product. Overhead costs for a given process may be collected using either actual or normal costing, but the manner of collection does not change the calculations of either equivalent production or per-unit costs.

The rest of this chapter is devoted to illustrating the *accounting framework* not only for process costing but also for the other product-costing options.

THE COST ACCOUNTING CYCLE

In Chapter 13 we presented an overview of the flow of costs in a manufacturing firm (Figure 13-1, page 506), noting that costs are first accumulated by their basic nature (materials, labor, and overhead) and are then passed on, through work in process, to finished goods, and, ultimately, to cost of goods sold. In Chapter 14 we noted that the choice between absorption and variable costing determines whether some of the costs (fixed manufacturing costs, in particular) would pass through work in process or be assigned directly to expense for the period. At no time, however, have we described these cost flows in terms of accounts and journal entries. The major purpose of the final section of this chapter is to place previously described cost flows into an accounting framework.

The transition from a set of ideas to an accounting flow is not difficult. Figure 15-1, which is but a minor variation of similar figures in Chapters 13 and 14, translates cost flows to changes in specific accounts. Figure 15-1 points out the critical difference between absorption and variable costing, the latter of which assigns fixed manufacturing overhead to expense in the period in which those costs are recognized. Absorption costing assigns such costs to Work in Process, hence they are allowed to flow through

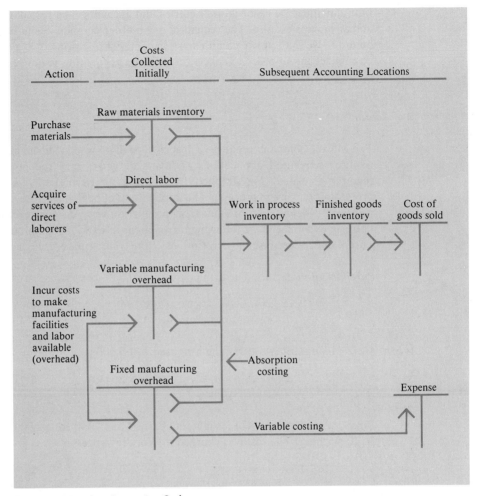

FIGURE 15-1   Cost Accounting Cycle

Finished Goods and, ultimately, to Cost of Goods Sold.[1] We shall concentrate our discussion of accounting entries on those relevant to absorption costing.

The two major cost accumulation systems, based on the nature of the manufacturing operation, are *process* and *job-order costing*. Either actual or normal costing can be used under either system, and standard costs can often be incorporated under either system. Despite the differences between the various combinations available, the general form of the journal entries to formalize the flow of costs does not differ much from one system to another. This situation is true because, as Figure 15-1 shows, there is a limited number of places for costs to be collected or transferred. Thus, we shall

[1]Following the pattern introduced in Chapter 13, we have chosen to indicate the names of accounts by using captial letters, while using lowercase letters to denote the objects themselves. Thus, "Work in Process" refers to an account, while "work in process" refers to the physical, semifinished product.

limit our illustrations of journal entries and accounts. The first illustration will be of actual process costing. The second of a job-order company using normal costing. In addition, we shall provide an illustration of standard costing in a very simple, process-costing setting in order to concentrate on the accounting issues peculiar to standard costing.

Illustration of Actual Process Costing

The Mason Company produces a special type of plywood. The manufacturing process requires sequential applications of layers of wood until the plywood reaches the required thickness. For simplicity, we have assumed that there were no beginning inventories of work in process. (The implications of beginning work-in-process inventories for the calculation of equivalent production were discussed on pages 588–590.) The firm experienced the following transactions in 19X5. (We omit explanations of the journal entries because the descriptions of the transactions serve the same purpose.)

Purchase of materials: The firm bought 1,400,000 feet of wood at $0.095 per foot.

1.	Materials Inventory (1,400,000 × $0.095)	$133,000	
	Cash or Accounts Payable		$133,000

Materials put into process: The firm used 1,300,000 feet of wood.

2.	Work in Process Inventory (1,300,000 × $0.095)	$123,500	
	Materials Inventory		$123,500

Direct labor incurred: Direct laborers earned $344,400 for 82,000 hours of work at $4.20 per hour. The cost was charged to Work in Process.

3a.	Direct Labor	$344,400	
	Cash or Accrued Payroll		$344,400
3b.	Work in Process Inventory	$344,400	
	Direct Labor		$344,400

Overhead costs incurred: The firm incurred the following overhead costs. For brevity we list only a few individual items, lumping the bulk of overhead costs into the "Other" category.

Variable overhead:	
Indirect labor	$ 84,000
Supplies	12,000
Other	155,300
Total variable overhead	$251,300
Fixed overhead:	
Supervision	$ 74,000
Depreciation	96,000
Other	291,000
Total fixed overhead	$461,000

Overhead costs are first recorded by type of cost.

4.	Indirect Labor	$ 84,000	
	Supplies	12,000	
	Other Variable Overhead	155,300	
	Supervision	74,000	
	Depreciation	96,000	
	Other Fixed Overhead	291,000	
	Accumulated Depreciation		$ 96,000
	Cash, Accrued Payables		616,300

Overhead costs are not usually put directly into Work in Process Inventory. Instead, they are gathered together into an account called Manufacturing Overhead, or into two such accounts: one for variable overhead and one for fixed overhead.

5a.	Variable Manufacturing Overhead	$251,300	
	Indirect Labor		$ 84,000
	Supplies		12,000
	Other Variable Overhead		155,300
5b.	Fixed Manufacturing Overhead	$461,000	
	Supervision		$ 74,000
	Depreciation		96,000
	Other Fixed Overhead		291,000

The manufacturing overhead accounts are for convenience and are especially helpful when standard costing is used, as we shall show shortly. The amounts put into the manufacturing overhead accounts are now transferred to Work in Process Inventory.

6.	Work in Process Inventory	$712,300	
	Variable Manufacturing Overhead		$251,300
	Fixed Manufacturing Overhead		461,000

Production: During the year the firm finished 40,000 square yards of plywood and transferred them to the storage area for finished goods. Another 3,000 square yards were still in process at the end of 19X5. These 3,000 square yards were two-thirds finished. That is, on the average, the plywood remaining in process had two thirds of the materials and two thirds of the labor required to make a finished square yard.

To transfer the cost of finished units to Finished Goods Inventory, we need to know the per-unit cost of those units finished. But, as pointed out in the discussion of process costing, it is not appropriate to compute the unit cost simply by dividing the total cost by the 40,000 square yards of product finished. (The reason is that some of the work that relates to that total cost was performed on the 3,000 square yards of material still in process at the end of the period.) Therefore, what is needed is the equivalent production. Because there are no beginning inventories of work in process, the calculation of equivalent production requires no cost flow assumption and can proceed as follows.

$$\text{Equivalent production} = 40,000 + (3,000 \times 2/3) = 42,000 \text{ sq. yds.}$$

The 42,000 equivalent production figure is used to determine the cost per unit. At this point we have $1,180,200 in the Work in Process Inventory account, composed of the following costs. The numbers in parentheses refer to journal entries.

Materials (2)	$ 123,500
Direct labor (3b)	344,400
Variable overhead (6)	251,300
Fixed overhead (6)	461,000
Total	$1,180,200
Divided by equivalent production	42,000
Equals cost per unit	$28.10

The $28.10 cost per unit is used for the transfer to Finished Goods Inventory.

7.	Finished Goods Inventory (40,000 × $28.10)	$1,124,000	
	Work in Process Inventory		$1,124,000

Sales: The firm sold 35,000 square yards at $40 each.

8a.	Cash or Accounts Receivable (35,000 × $40)	$1,400,000	
	Sales		$1,400,000
8b.	Cost of Goods Sold (35,000 × $28.10)	$ 983,500	
	Finished Goods Inventory		$ 983,500

Selling and administrative expenses: The firm incurred $340,000 in selling and administrative expenses.

9.	Selling and Administrative Expenses	$ 340,000	
	Cash, Accrued Payables		$ 340,000

At this point the accounts for direct labor, variable overhead, and fixed overhead would all have zero balances. The other key accounts would show the following:

Work in Process Inventory					Finished Goods Inventory			
(2)	$ 123,500				(7)	$1,124,000	$983,500	(8b)
(3b)	344,400				Bal.	$ 140,500		
(6)	712,300	$1,124,000	(7)					
	1,180,200	1,124,000						
Bal.	$ 56,200							

Cost of Goods Sold		
(8b)	$ 983,500	

Materials Inventory			
(1)	$ 133,000	$123,500	(2)
Bal.	$ 9,500		

An income statement for the Mason Company is given in Exhibit 15-3.

Exhibit 15-3
Income Statement for Mason Company—
Actual Process Costing

Sales (8a)[a]	$1,400,000
Cost of goods sold (8b)	983,500
Gross profit	416,500
Less: Selling and administrative	
expenses (9)	340,000
Income	$ 76,500

[a]Figures in parentheses indicate journal entry numbers from the
earlier illustrations.

Our illustration of actual process costing incorporates three simplifying assumptions. First, there is no beginning inventory of plywood in process. This assumption simplifies the calculation of equivalent production and eliminates the need for a cost-flow assumption (weighted average or FIFO). We have already shown how the calculations change when there is a beginning inventory and the weighted-average method is adopted; an appendix (page 612) covers the situation where the FIFO approach is adopted.

Second, the illustration covers only one manufacturing process, though, as already indicated, processing a given product may require that the product undergo more than one process. The *accounting* in a multiple-process system is not significantly different from that in a single-process system. The only difference might be that a firm could maintain separate work-in-process accounts for the different processes. Should that be the case, the cost of goods finished in one process would be transferred to a separate work-in-process account for a subsequent process. However, the cost of goods finished in the final process would, as shown in Figure 15-1, be transferred to Finished Goods.

The third simplifying assumption is that the completion percentage at the end of a given period is the same for all three components of manufacturing cost (materials, labor, and overhead). As shown earlier, completion percentages differing in respect to materials and conversion costs require the calculation of different amounts of equivalent production for the various cost components, thus affecting the calculations of unit costs for those components. But differences in unit costs do not change the basic journal entries to record the flow of costs. The only effect of such unit-cost differences is to change the dollar amounts of such entries. Thus, none of the simplifying assumptions affects the journal entries that record the basic flow of costs.

Illustration of Job-Order Costing

Portland Mill Works makes various industrial products that require work in two departments, stamping and assembly. The Stamping Department uses large pieces of costly machinery and relatively little direct labor. Accordingly, the managers of the firm believe that machine hours is the appropriate measure of activity in that department. The Assembly Department is relatively labor intensive, with machinery limited to small devices. The managers use direct labor hours as the measure of activity in the Assembly Department.

Analysis of the company's operations has produced the following equations to describe total budgeted overhead for each of the firm's departments.

Budgeted overhead—Stamping = $400,000 + ($1 × machine hours)
Budgeted overhead—Assembly = $100,000 + ($1.50 × direct labor hours)

Based on forecasts of activity for 19X6 the company has established predetermined overhead rates as follows.

	Stamping Department	Assembly Department
Budgeted machine hours	200,000	
Budgeted direct labor hours		100,000
Total budgeted overhead:		
$400,000 + ($1 × 200,000)	$600,000	
$100,000 + ($1.50 × 100,000)		$250,000
Divided by budgeted levels of activity	200,000	100,000
Equals predetermined overhead rates	$3.00	$2.50
	per machine hour	per direct labor hour

During the year, the company keeps track of the machine hours spent on each job in the Stamping Department and the direct labor hours in the Assembly Department. Exhibit 15-4 presents the actual results for the year, including the overhead applied for each department.

Exhibit 15-4
Portland Mill Works
Results for 19X6

Activity Data	Totals	Jobs Sold	Jobs in Ending Work in Process Inventory	Jobs in Ending Finished Goods Inventory
Direct labor hours in Assembly Department	95,000	80,000	5,000	10,000
Machine hours in Stamping Department	210,000	190,000	7,000	13,000
Cost Data				
Materials used	$ 650,000	$ 580,000	$30,000	$ 40,000
Direct labor	800,000	720,000	20,000	60,000
Applied overhead:				
Assembly Department at $2.50[a]	237,500	200,000	12,500	25,000
Stamping Department at $3.00[b]	630,000	570,000	21,000	39,000
Total costs	$2,317,500	$2,070,000	$83,500	$164,000
Actual Overhead				
Assembly	$ 244,000			
Stamping	$ 608,000			
Total	$ 852,000			

[a]Total, 95,000 × $2.50 = $237,500; jobs sold, 80,000 × $2.50 = $200,000, etc.
[b]Total, 210,000 × $3.00 = $630,000; jobs sold, 190,000 × $3.00 = $570,000, etc.

The information in Exhibit 15-4 enables us to determine the budget and volume variances for each department, as well as the totals.

Stamping Department

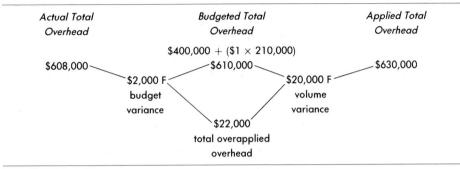

| Actual Total Overhead | | Budgeted Total Overhead | | Applied Total Overhead |

$400,000 + ($1 × 210,000)

$608,000 — $610,000 — $630,000

$2,000 F budget variance

$20,000 F volume variance

$22,000 total overapplied overhead

Assembly Department

$100,000 + ($1.50 × 95,000)

$244,000 — $242,500 — $237,500

$1,500 U budget variance

$5,000 U volume variance

$6,500 total underapplied overhead

The totals are:

Budget variance,	$2,000 F − $1,500 U	$ 500 F
Volume variance,	$20,000 F − $5,000 U	15,000 F
Total overapplied overhead		$15,500

We can easily verify this total by comparing the totals of actual and applied overhead from Exhibit 15-4.

Total actual overhead, $244,000 + $608,000	$852,000
Total applied overhead, $237,500 + $630,000	867,500
Total overapplied overhead	$ 15,500

The journal entries and accounts of a job order firm are not different in kind from those of a process costing firm (or a firm that uses standard costs). Essentially, job-order costing is a specific identification method, so that transfers from Work in Process Inventory to Finished Goods Inventory and to Cost of Goods Sold are based on the particular jobs finished and sold. For Portland Mill Works, the following entries summarize the flows that we know about. All of the information comes from Exhibit 15-4.

Materials used

1.	Work in Process Inventory	$ 650,000	
	Materials Inventory		$ 650,000

Direct labor

2a.	Direct Labor	$ 800,000	
	Cash or Accrued Payroll		$ 800,000
2b.	Work in Process Inventory	$ 800,000	
	Direct Labor		$ 800,000

Overhead incurrence and application

3a.	Factory Overhead—Stamping Department	$ 608,000	
	Factory Overhead—Assembly Department	244,000	
	Various Credits, Cash, Accrued Expenses,		
	Accumulated Depreciation		$ 852,000
3b.	Work in Process Inventory	$ 867,500	
	Factory Overhead—Stamping Department		$ 630,000
	Factory Overhead—Assembly Department		237,500

Completion of jobs

4.	Finished Goods Inventory	$2,234,000	
	Work in Process Inventory		$2,234,000

This entry is the total cost of all jobs completed during the year, which consists of the $2,070,000 cost of goods sold plus the $164,000 cost of jobs still in Finished Goods Inventory at year end.

Cost of sales

5.	Cost of Goods Sold	$2,070,000	
	Finished Goods Inventory		$2,070,000

At this point, the various manufacturing overhead and inventory accounts would appear as follows:

Factory Overhead—Stamping					Factory Overhead—Assembly			
(3a)	$ 608,000	$ 630,000	(3b)		(3a)	$ 244,000	$ 237,500	(3b)
		22,000	Bal.		Bal.	6,500		

Work in Process Inventory					Finished Goods Inventory			
(1)	$ 650,000				(4)	$2,234,000	$2,070,000	(5)
(2)	800,000				Bal.	$ 164,000		
(3)	867,500	$2,234,000	(4)					
	2,317,500	2,234,000						
Bal.	$ 83,500							

Cost of Goods Sold		
(5)	$2,070,000	

The amounts shown as ending balances in Cost of Goods Sold and the two inventory accounts agree with the amounts shown in Exhibit 15-4. The balances of the factory overhead accounts represent the overapplied or underapplied overhead for the departments. The net overapplied overhead is $15,500 ($22,000 overapplied in stamping minus $6,500 underapplied in assembly).

What happens to the balances representing misapplication (actual different from applied) of overhead? As stated in Chapter 13, there are two possibilities. The $15,500 can be shown in the income statement, either as an adjustment to cost of goods sold or to gross margin. Or, the company could convert to an actual costing basis by assigning the misapplied overhead to all the work done in the departments during the year.

Illustration of Standard Costing

The final illustration of the cost accounting cycle deals with standard costing systems. Virtually all such systems require that transfers of costs *from* Work in Process Inventory to Finished Goods Inventory be made at the total standard cost of units completed and transferred. But the mechanics of such systems differ in ways to put costs *into* Work in Process Inventory. Specifically, there are two alternatives: (1) put in actual quantities of inputs at standard prices, or (2) put in standard quantities of inputs at standard prices. We shall illustrate the latter technique.

Data for DMV Company appear in Exhibit 15-5. For simplicity, we shall assume that the firm has no inventories of work in process—that it finishes the units it starts each day.

Exhibit 15-5
DMV Company
Data for Illustration

Standard Costs	Model A	Model C
Materials at $3 per pound	$ 9 (3 pounds)	$ 12 (4 pounds)
Direct labor at $8 per hour	16 (2 hours)	32 (4 hours)
Variable overhead at $6 per DLH	12	24
Fixed overhead at $10 per DLH[a]	20	40
Total standard cost	$57	$108

Results for March, 19X6	Model A	Model C
Beginning inventories at standard cost:		
500 units of model A, 200 of model C	$28,500	$21,600
Units produced in March	5,000	2,000
Units sold in March	5,200	1,700
Ending inventories in units	300	500

Costs in March		
Materials purchased		
(no beginning inventory)	30,000 pounds	$ 92,000
Materials used	24,000 pounds	
Direct labor	19,000 hours at $8.20	$155,800
Variable overhead		$112,000
Fixed overhead		$198,000

[a]Budgeted fixed overhead $200,000 per month/normal capacity of 20,000 direct labor hours

To avoid interrupting the discussion of the journal entries for standard costing, we shall calculate the variances before beginning. First, the following schedule shows the standard quantities of materials and labor hours for the level of output that the firm achieved in March.

	Model A	Model C	Total
Standard quantity of material needed for achieved output:			
3 pounds × 5,000 units	15,000		15,000
4 pounds × 2,000 units		8,000	8,000
Total standard pounds			23,000
Standard quantity of labor hours allowed for achieved output:			
2 hours × 5,000 units	10,000		10,000
4 hours × 2,000 units		8,000	8,000
Total standard hours			18,000

With the information regarding the standard quantities of input factors we can now calculate the several variances as follows:

Materials Variances	
Price variance ($3 × 30,000 pounds) − $92,000	$ 2,000 unfavorable
Use variance (23,000 − 24,000) × $3	3,000 unfavorable
Labor Variances	
Rate variance ($8.00 − $8.20) × 19,000 hours	3,800 unfavorable
Efficiency variance (18,000 − 19,000) × $8	8,000 unfavorable
Variable Overhead Variances	
Budget variance ($6 × 19,000) − $112,000	2,000 favorable
Efficiency variance (18,000 − 19,000) × $6	6,000 unfavorable
Fixed Overhead Variances	
Budget variance, $200,000 − $198,000	2,000 favorable
Volume variance (20,000 − 18,000) × $10	20,000 unfavorable

One objective of a standard costing system is to isolate variances in the accounts as quickly as possible, instead of just making separate calculations outside of the accounting system. Timely determination of variances helps in control because the sooner the managers know about variances, the sooner they can decide whether or not to investigate and possibly act.

The journal entries describing the events of March appear below. The basic pattern of the entries is that *price* variances are isolated when the cost is incurred, which is when the variance first becomes known, and *quantity* variances are isolated when costs are put into process. Thus, the entries putting costs into process are made at the end of the period, when production is known, because you must know production to be able to determine the efficiency variances and fixed overhead volume variance. As we have said, there are other possible patterns, but they all share the essential characteristic of standard costing: all inventories appear at standard cost at the ends of periods.

Material purchases

1.	Materials Inventory (30,000 pounds × $3)	$ 90,000	
	Material Price Variance	2,000	
	Cash or Accounts Payable		$ 92,000

Material use

2.	Work in Process Inventory (23,000 pounds × $3)	$ 69,000	
	Material Use Variance	3,000	
	Materials Inventory (24,000 pounds × $3)		$ 72,000

Direct labor

3a.	Direct Labor (19,000 × $8)	$152,000	
	Direct Labor Rate Variance	3,800	
	Cash or Accrued Payroll		$155,800
3b.	Work in Process Inventory (18,000 × $8)	$144,000	
	Direct Labor Efficiency Variance	8,000	
	Direct Labor		$152,000

Variable overhead

4a.	Variable Manufacturing Overhead (19,000 × $6)	$114,000	
	Variable Overhead Spending Variance		$ 2,000
	Various Credits, Cash, Accrued Expenses		112,000
4b.	Work in Process Inventory (18,000 × $6)	$108,000	
	Variable Overhead Efficiency Variance	6,000	
	Variable Manufacturing Overhead		$114,000

Fixed overhead

5a.	Fixed Manufacturing Overhead	$200,000	
	Fixed Overhead Budget Variance		$ 2,000
	Various Credits, Cash, Accumulated Deprecia-tion		198,000
5b.	Work in Process Inventory (18,000 × $10)	$180,000	
	Fixed Overhead Volume Variance	20,000	
	Fixed Manufacturing Overhead		$200,000

Completion of goods

6.	Finished Goods Inventory [(5,000 × $57) + (2,000 × $108)]	$501,000	
	Work in Process Inventory		$501,000

Cost of sales

7.	Cost of Goods Sold [(5,200 × $57) + (1,700 × $108)]	$480,000	
	Finished Goods Inventory		$480,000

The T-accounts for each type of inventory and for Cost of Goods Sold appear below. The beginning balance in Finished Goods Inventory is the standard cost of the 500 units of model A and 200 units of model C on hand at the beginning of March (from Exhibit 15-5). The ending balance reflects the standard cost of the 300 units of Model A and 500 units of Model C [($57 × 300) + ($108 × 500) = $71,100]. Materials Inventory shows the standard price of the 6,000 pounds in the ending inventory, which is the 30,000 pounds bought less the 24,000 used.

Work in Process Inventory				Finished Goods Inventory			
(2)	$ 69,000			3-1 Bal.	$ 50,100		
(3b)	144,000			(6)	501,000	$480,000	(7)
(4b)	108,000				551,100	480,000	
(5b)	180,000	$501,000	(6)	3-31 Bal.	$ 71,100		
	501,000	501,000					

Materials Inventory				Cost of Goods Sold		
(1)	$ 90,000	$ 72,000	(2)	(7)	$480,000	
3-31 Bal.	$ 18,000					

At this point, all of the variances have been isolated in separate accounts the balances of which are as follows.

	Dr. (Cr.)
Material price variance	$ 2,000
Material use variance	3,000
Direct labor rate variance	3,800
Direct labor efficiency variance	8,000
Variable overhead spending variance	(2,000)
Variable overhead efficiency variance	6,000
Fixed overhead budget variance	(2,000)
Fixed overhead volume variance	20,000
Net variance, unfavorable	$38,800

What is the disposition of these account balances? There are usually two alternatives. The variances can be carried to the period's income statement as adjustments to either cost of goods sold or gross margin. Or, they can be prorated among Cost of Goods Sold, Finished Goods Inventory, and Work in Process Inventory. Since in the present example, for DMV Company, there is no in-process inventory at the end of the period, a proration would involve only Finished Goods Inventory and Cost of Goods Sold. As stated earlier, the need for a proration depends on the magnitude of the variances and the ending inventories, since generally accepted accounting principles would accept standard costs for financial reporting purposes as long as the income-statement results of using such costs did not differ materially from the results under actual costing. Unfortunately, what constitutes a "material" difference has never been defined.

Final Comparative Comments

We have illustrated the cost accounting cycle in three situations. First, we showed a company that used actual process costing; next, a job order firm that used normal costing; and finally, a process costing operation that used standard costs. At this point it is desirable to review briefly not only the illustrations but also the many topics covered as part of our three-chapter discussion of product costing.

Any cost accounting system can be classified as either variable costing or absorption costing, the difference being that only the latter assigns fixed manufacturing overhead to specific units of product. Any system will use actual, normal, or standard costs. The nature of the manufacturing operation tends to separate cost accumulation systems into job order and process. Both types of firms could use either absorption or variable costing, and actual, normal, or standard costs. (It is unlikely, however, that many job order systems would use standard costs because of the major differences among the products produced on the various jobs.)

Yet, with all these possibilities, the only real differences among the various methods, systems, and techniques relate to the valuation of the inventories. That is, since the costs incurred by a firm in a given period are whatever they are, the different techniques that have been discussed are simply different ways of assigning those costs to two different sets of units: those sold and those still on hand. If a company has no inventories, all of the various approaches and combinations thereof will produce the same amount of income on the income statement.

Thus, managers, who must use accounting reports to help them in decision making, must also know on what basis those reports were prepared and must comprehend the effects that any given approach or technique will have on those reports. Since any of the approaches and techniques will have an effect on the valuation of inventories, a manager's first concern should be about what constitutes *inventoriable cost*.

SUMMARY

The nature of a manufacturing operation determines whether a company will use job-order or process costing. The calculation of unit costs under process costing is complicated by the existence of incomplete units of inventory at the beginning and/or end of a period. The concept of equivalent production was developed to overcome this complication, but the existence of beginning inventories requires further refinement of the concept to take into account some type of cost-flow assumption (weighted average or first-in-first-out).

The flow of costs through a manufacturing firm can be accounted for by using several methods or systems regardless of whether a company uses job-order or process costing. Specifically, a firm can use either actual or normal costing in the assignment of manufacturing overhead, or use standard costs for some or all components of manufacturing cost. (In addition, of course, a firm could use either variable or absorption costing, but the latter is required for external reporting and therefore is likely to be used for internal reports.)

The journal entries to reflect cost flows are, in general form, quite similar for job-order and process costing, They are, however, somewhat more complex when standard costs are used, because entries in that situation must isolate variances into separate accounts.

KEY TERMS

conversion costs	job-order costing
cost accounting cycle	process costing
equivalent production	standard costing
inventoriable cost	

KEY FORMULAS

$$\text{Equivalent production—weighted average} = \text{units completed} + \left(\text{units in ending inventory} \times \text{percentage complete} \right)$$

$$\text{Equivalent production—first-in-first-out} = \text{units completed} + \left(\text{units in ending inventory} \times \text{percentage complete} \right) - \left(\text{units in beginning inventory} \times \text{percentage complete in prior period} \right)$$

$$\text{Cost per unit—weighted average} = \frac{\text{cost of beginning inventory} + \text{costs incurred during the period}}{\text{equivalent production—weighted average}}$$

REVIEW PROBLEM—PROCESS COSTING

Stambol Manufacturing Company makes a single type of chemical solvent. Data for April 19X8 are as follows.

Beginning inventory of work in process	$ 6,000
Materials used	$485,000
Direct labor incurred	$648,000
Overhead incurred	$604,000
Gallons completed and sent to finished goods	800,000
Gallons in ending inventory (75% complete)	40,000

Required
1. Determine equivalent production and cost per unit. Use the weighted-average method.
2. Determine the cost of the ending inventory of work in process.
3. Prepare a T-account for Work in Process Inventory. Check the ending balance with your answer to part 2.
4. Assume that there was no inventory of finished product at the beginning of April. During April, 730,000 gallons were sold, and 70,000 gallons remained in ending finished goods inventory. Determine the cost of goods sold and the cost of the ending inventory of finished product.

Answer to Review Problem

1. Equivalent production and cost per unit:

Equivalent Production

Gallons completed	800,000
Equivalent production in ending inventory (40,000 × 75%)	30,000
Equivalent production for April	830,000

Cost per Unit—Weighted Average

Beginning inventory of work in progress	$ 6,000
Costs incurred:	
Materials	485,000
Direct labor	648,000
Overhead	604,000
Totals	$1,743,000
Divided by equivalent production	830,000
Equals cost per unit	$2.10

2. Ending inventory of work in process, $63,000 (30,000 equivalent units × $2.10)

3.   Work in Process Inventory

Beginning balance	$ 6,000		
Materials	485,000		
Direct labor	648,000		
Overhead	604,000	$1,680,000 transferred out (800,000 × $2.10)
	1,743,000	1,680,000	
Ending balance	$ 63,000		

The $63,000 balance equals the answer to part 2.

4. Cost of goods sold is $1,533,000, which is 730,000 gallons multiplied by $2.10. Ending inventory of finished goods is $147,000, which is 70,000 gallons (800,000 − 730,000) multiplied by $2.10.

REVIEW PROBLEM—STANDARD COSTING

Assume that Mason Company, whose actual operations we accounted for in the chapter (pages 596–599), decided to change to standard costing. It developed the following standards per square yard of plywood.

Materials (30 feet of wood at $0.10 per foot)	$ 3
Direct labor (2 hours at $4 per hour)	8
Variable overhead ($3 per direct labor hour)	6
Fixed overhead[a]	9
Total standard cost	$26

[a]Based on budgeted fixed overhead of $450,000 and normal capacity of 50,000 square yards ($450,000/50,000 = $9 per square yard).

Required

1. Using the actual results detailed in the chapter, calculate the variances from standard cost.
2. Prepare journal entries to record the events.
3. Prepare T-accounts for Work in Process Inventory, Finished Goods Inventory, Materials Inventory, and Cost of Goods Sold at standard.
4. Prepare an income statement for the year and contrast it with the one shown in Exhibit 15-3 that uses actual costing.

Answer to Review Problem

1.

Materials Variances

Price variance [1,400,000 feet at $0.005 ($0.10 − $0.095)]	$ 7,000	favorable
Use variance [1,300,000 − (42,000 × 30 feet)] × $0.10	4,000	unfavorable

Direct Labor Variances

Rate variance [82,000 hours × ($4.20 − $4)]	$16,400	unfavorable
Efficiency variance [82,000 hours − (42,000 × 2)] × $4	8,000	favorable

Variable Overhead Variances

Spending variance [$251,300 − (82,000 × $3)]	$ 5,300	unfavorable
Efficiency variance [82,000 hours − (42,000 × 2)] × $3	6,000	favorable

Fixed Overhead Variances

Budget variance ($461,000 − $450,000)	$11,000	unfavorable
Volume variance [(50,000 − 42,000) × $9]	72,000	unfavorable

2.

1.	Materials Inventory (1,400,000 × $0.10)	$ 140,000	
	Material Price Variance		$ 7,000
	Cash or Accounts Payable		133,000
2.	Work in Process (1,260,000 × $0.10)	$ 126,000	
	Material Use Variance	4,000	
	Materials Inventory		$ 130,000
3(a).	Direct Labor (82,000 × $4)	$ 328,000	
	Direct Labor Rate Variance	16,400	
	Cash		$ 344,400
3(b).	Work in Process Inventory (42,000 × 2 × $4)	$ 336,000	
	Direct Labor Efficiency Variance		$ 8,000
	Direct Labor		328,000

4.	Indirect Labor	$ 84,000	
	Supplies	12,000	
	Other Variable Overhead	155,300	
	Supervision	74,000	
	Depreciation	96,000	
	Other Fixed Overhead	291,000	
	Accumulated Depreciation		$ 96,000
	Cash, Accrued Payables		616,300
5(a).	Variable Manufacturing Overhead		
	(82,000 hours × $3)	$ 246,000	
	Variable Overhead Spending Variance	5,300	
	Indirect Labor		$ 84,000
	Supplies		12,000
	Other Variable Overhead		155,300
5(b).	Fixed Manufacturing Overhead		
	(budget of $450,000)	$ 450,000	
	Fixed Overhead Budget Variance	11,000	
	Supervision		$ 74,000
	Depreciation		96,000
	Other Fixed Overhead		291,000
6(a).	Work in Process Inventory (42,000 × $6)	$ 252,000	
	Variable Overhead Efficiency Variance		$ 6,000
	Variable Manufacturing Overhead		246,000
6(b).	Work in Process Inventory (42,000 × $9)	$ 378,000	
	Fixed Overhead Volume Variance		
	(8,000 × $9)	72,000	
	Fixed Manufacturing Overhead		$ 450,000
7.	Finished Goods Inventory (40,000 × $26)	$1,400,000	
	Work in Process Inventory		$1,040,000
8(a).	Cash or Accounts Receivable		
	(35,000 × $40 selling price)	$1,400,000	
	Sales		$1,400,000
8(b).	Cost of Goods Sold (35,000 × $26)	$ 910,000	
	Finished Goods Inventory		$ 910,000
9.	Selling and Administrative Expenses	$ 340,000	
	Cash, Accrued Payables		$ 340,000

3.

Work in Process Inventory

(2)	$ 126,000		
(3b)	336,000		
(6a)	252,000		
(6b)	378,000	$1,040,000	(7)
	1,092,000	1,040,000	
Bal.	$ 52,000		

Finished Goods Inventory

(7)	$1,040,000	$910,000	(8b)
Bal.	$ 130,000		

Materials Inventory

(1)	$ 140,000	$ 130,000	(2)
Bal.	$ 10,000		

Cost of Goods Sold

(8b)	$ 910,000	

Income Statements for Mason Company—Absorption Costing

	Actual Process Costing		Standard Process Costing
Sales (8a)[a]	$1,400,000		$1,400,000
Cost of goods sold (8b)	983,500		910,000
Gross profit	416,500		490,000
Manufacturing variances:			
Material price (1)		$ 7,000F	
Material use (2)		4,000U	
Direct labor rate (3)		16,400U	
Direct labor efficiency (3)		8,000F	
Variable overhead spending (5)		5,300U	
Variable overhead efficiency (6)		6,000F	
Fixed overhead budget (5)		11,000U	
Fixed overhead volume (6)		72,000U	87,700U
Actual gross profit			402,300
Less: Selling and administrative			
expenses (9)	340,000		340,000
Income	$ 76,500		$ 62,300

[a]Figures in parentheses indicate journal entry numbers.

APPENDIX: PROCESS COSTING—THE FIFO ASSUMPTION

We stated in this chapter that so long as there is no beginning inventory of work in process, there is no need for a choice of a cost-flow assumption (between weighted average and first-in-first-out). The need for a cost-flow assumption arises because, for various reasons, the cost to work on a unit of product in one period may not be the same as the cost to work on a unit in the next period.

If we merge the costs of the prior period and the current period to compute the cost of a finished unit, we adopt, as we did in the chapter, the weighted-average assumption. But it is just as reasonable—and intuitively more appealing—to suggest that the costs incurred in the current period apply only to that portion of the work done in the current period on the beginning inventory. This alternative assumption is the **first-in-first-out (FIFO)** assumption. Adopting this assumption changes the calculation of the unit cost for the current period, because it changes both components of the calculation of current-period unit cost: (1) the total costs that are to be considered, and (2) the equivalent production.

Illustration of FIFO

To illustrate FIFO, let us return to the data used in this chapter to illustrate the weighted-average assumption. For your convenience, the data in Exhibit 15-1 are reproduced in Exhibit 15-6. The company starts the month of August with no beginning

Exhibit 15-6

Data for Ronn Company

	August	September
Production costs	$206,000	$191,400
Unit data:		
In process at beginning of month	0	5,000
Completed during month	100,000	90,000
In process at end of month	5,000	10,000
Percentage of completion for		
end-of-period work in process	60%	40%

inventory of in-process units. Hence, there is no need to know the company's cost flow assumption. The unit cost of completing a unit in August would be computed, as we showed in the chapter, by dividing the total manufacturing costs in August ($206,000) by the equivalent production in that month (103,000), for a unit cost of $2.00. That is, whatever work was done on whatever units were processed in August (started and finished during the month, or still unfinished at the end of the month), the total costs were $206,000. The cost of processing a full unit was $2.00 ($206,000/103,000). The situation in September is different.

In September, 90,000 units were completed and 10,000 were on hand, 40% complete. But of the 90,000 units completed, we know that 5,000 units were partially complete at the beginning of the period, so that the production costs for September could be considered as applying to those beginning-inventory units *only* to the extent that work was done in September. Therefore, we calculate the cost of processing a unit of product in September by using only September's costs and an equivalent production that reflects only September's work. We already know that the production costs in September were $191,400, so the only issue is calculating an equivalent production related only to the September costs. What we need is a production number that relates only to the work done in September.

Three types of work were done in September: (1) work to finish the units that were partially finished in August (beginning in-process inventory); (2) work to complete units that were started *and* finished in September; and (3) work to partially complete units that were started in September but not finished. Thus, equivalent production could be computed as follows:

Work done on September's beginning inventory:	
5,000 units × 40% completed in Sept.	2,000
Work done on units started and completed in Sept.	
(90,000 − 5,000) × 100% completed in Sept.	85,000
Work done on units partially complete at the end of Sept.	
10,000 × 40%	4,000
Equivalent production, FIFO	91,000

Although this three-step approach defines the types of work done in September, a more straightforward approach would involve making a simple adjustment to the weighted-average calculation of equivalent production. Remember that equivalent production using the weighted-average approach adds the finished units to the equivalent units in ending inventory (see page 589). If we started with the number of finished units (90,000 in September, in the present example), we need only subtract the amount of work done on some of those units *prior* to September. Thus, the calculation of equivalent production for September using the FIFO assumption would be:

Units completed in September (90,000 × 100%)	90,000
Work done on units partially complete at the end of Sept.	
10,000 × 40%	4,000
	94,000
Less, work done in August on units completed in Sept.	
5,000 units × 60%	3,000
Equivalent production, FIFO	91,000

We could generalize this calculation in this way:

$$\begin{array}{l}\text{Equivalent}\\\text{production}\\\text{—first-in-}\\\text{first-out}\end{array} = \begin{array}{l}\text{units}\\\text{com-}\\\text{pleted}\end{array} + \left(\begin{array}{l}\text{units in}\\\text{ending}\\\text{inven-}\\\text{tory}\end{array} \times \begin{array}{l}\text{percent-}\\\text{age}\\\text{complete}\end{array}\right) - \left(\begin{array}{l}\text{units in}\\\text{beginning}\\\text{inventory}\end{array} \times \begin{array}{l}\text{percentage}\\\text{complete}\\\text{in prior}\\\text{period}\end{array}\right)$$

The unit cost calculation under FIFO differs from that under weighted-average in that the former does not merge the costs from one period to the next and uses a different equivalent production calculation. The general formula for calculating unit cost under FIFO is simply:

$$\text{unit cost—FIFO} = \frac{\text{production costs for the period}}{\text{equivalent production—FIFO}}$$

In the example, the unit cost would be $2.1033 (September production costs of $191,400 divided by equivalent production of 91,000 units).

Regardless of the cost-flow assumption, the total costs that must be accounted for are the costs in the beginning inventory plus the production costs for the period.

Costs of beginning inventory	
5,000 units × 60% × $2	$ 6,000
Production costs for September	191,400
Total cost to be accounted for	$197,400

These costs either have been transferred to finished goods (for the completed units) or are associated with the units still in process. With the FIFO assumption, the cost relevant to the units in process at the end of the period is the unit cost for work done this period, or $2.1033. The cost assigned to the ending inventory of 10,000 units that are 40% complete would be $8,413 (10,000 × 40% × $2.1033).

The costs transferred to finished goods can be determined by analyzing the units transferred.

Transfer of units that were in process at the beginning of the month:

Cost from prior period (beginning inventory) (5,000 × 60% × $2)		$ 6,000
Completion costs	(5,000 × 40% × $2.1033)	4,207
Total		10,207
Transfer of units started and completed in September		
(90,000 − 5,000) × $2.1033		178,780
Total		$188,987

Thus, the total cost of $197,400 can be accounted for as:

Costs transferred to finished goods	$188,987
Costs in ending inventory	8,413
Total cost accounted for	$197,400

If you compare the FIFO results with those for the weighted-average assumption, you will see that the unit cost for September under FIFO ($2.1033) is slightly higher than that under weighted-average ($2.10, page 590). As a result, the total cost assigned to the ending work in process under FIFO ($8,413) is slightly higher than under weighted-average ($8,400, page 590). The magnitude of the difference is a function of the illustrative data; you should not assume that the difference will always be so small that the extra calculations (for FIFO) are not warranted.

The next section discusses one major reason for adopting the FIFO assumption.

Why Choose FIFO?

As we suggested at the start of this appendix, the FIFO method is intuitively appealing, for it suggests that the costs incurred in a given period are applicable only to whatever work is actually done during that period. This intuitive appeal is supported by a manager's normal (and required) interest in controlling costs. The per-unit cost given by the weighted-average method is not particularly suitable for control purposes because it mixes performance (cost) in the current period with performance in prior periods.

The FIFO assumption, with its calculation of an equivalent production that includes only current work, and its calculation of current unit costs using only the production costs incurred in the current period, separates performance data for different periods. From Chapter 12 we know that some companies establish *standard* costs for certain aspects of the manufacturing process, and that comparisons of actual costs with preestablished standards give managers useful information for control and performance evaluation. For a company that uses standard costs and process costing, the FIFO assumption is particularly useful simply because it does not intermingle actual costs from two periods.

ASSIGNMENT MATERIAL

Questions for discussion

15-1 "True" fixed cost Is there any meaning to the statement that there is a "true" fixed cost per unit of product? Discuss.

15-2 Kinds of standards If you were president of a manufacturing firm, which of the following kinds of income statement would you prefer to receive and why?
(a) One showing actual costs only.
(b) One showing standard costs and variances, with standard costs based on ideal standards.
(c) One showing standard costs and variances, with standard costs based on currently attainable standards.

Exercises

15-3 Overhead rates, standard cost income statement The following data pertain to the operations of Dickson Company for 19X5.

Budgeted production	100,000 units
Actual production	90,000 units
Budgeted costs—manufacturing:	
Materials	$ 400,000
Direct labor	300,000
Variable overhead	200,000
Fixed overhead	300,000
Actual costs:	
Materials	$ 350,000
Direct labor	280,000
Variable overhead	190,000
Fixed overhead	320,000
Administrative	400,000
Actual sales (80,000 units)	$1,600,000

There were no beginning inventories. Dickson uses a standard fixed cost based on budgeted production.

Required: Prepare a standard cost income statement. Show variances separately for each category of manufacturing cost.

15-4 Straightforward process costing TUV Company uses weighted-average process costing. It has no material costs. The data below relate to July.

Beginning inventory, 2,000 units 60% complete	$1,210
Units completed in July	20,000 units
Units in ending work in process, 30% complete	4,000 units

Conversion costs incurred in July were $22,110.

Required
1. Determine equivalent production for July.
2. Determine the cost of the ending inventory of work in process.
3. Determine the cost of goods transferred to finished goods.

15-5 Basic process costing—weighted average   The data below relate to the operations of Houston Milling Company for March. The company puts materials, labor, and overhead into process evenly throughout.

Beginning inventory, 10,000 units 70% complete	$19,100
Units completed in March	100,000 units
Ending inventory, 40% complete	5,000 units

Production costs incurred in March were $190,000. The company uses the weighted-average method.

Required
1. Compute equivalent production.
2. Compute unit cost.
3. Compute the cost of the ending inventory.
4. Compute the cost of units finished and transferred to finished goods inventory.

15-6 Basic process costing—FIFO (extension of 15-5, related to Appendix)   Refer to the data in the previous assignment. Redo it using the first-in-first-out method.

15-7 Standard cost system—journal entries   Watson Company makes a single product. Its standard cost is given below.

Materials (2 pounds @ $4)	$ 8
Direct labor (3 hours @ $5)	15
Variable overhead ($6 per direct labor hour)	18
Fixed overhead (based on normal	
capacity of 50,000 units)	10
Total standard cost	$51

At the beginning of 19X9 there were no inventories. During 19X9 the following events occurred.
(a) Material purchases were 120,000 pounds for $455,000.
(b) Direct laborers were paid $790,000 for 151,000 hours of work.
(c) Variable overhead of $895,000 was incurred.
(d) Fixed overhead incurred was $490,000.
(e) Materials used were 95,000 pounds.
(f) Production was 48,000 units. All units started were finished.
(g) Sales were 45,000 units at $100 each.

Required
1. Prepare journal entries to record the above events. Isolate variances as early as possible. Assume that the department managers are responsible for all variances except material price and direct labor rate.

2. Calculate ending inventory and cost of goods sold assuming (a) standard process costing, and (b) actual process costing.

15-8 Relationships, volume variances, and production Ayres Inc. began 19X8 with 20,000 units of product on hand. During the year, 90,000 units were sold, and there were 15,000 units in inventory at the end of the year. Standard fixed cost per unit is $5 based on budgeted fixed overhead of $400,000 for the year.

Required
1. Compute the volume variance for 19X8.
2. Determine what would have happened to Ayres's total income if production had increased by 1,000 units but sales had remained the same.

15-9 Relationships—income, production, and volume variance Fosheim Company sells a single product at $10 per unit. There are no variable manufacturing costs, and fixed manufacturing costs are budgeted at $300,000. In 19X5 the company showed a standard gross profit of $160,000 and an income of $58,000; sales that year were 40,000 units. Selling and administrative expenses in 19X5 were $90,000, and fixed manufacturing costs were incurred as budgeted.

Required
1. Compute the standard fixed cost per unit.
2. Compute the volume variance for 19X5.
3. Determine how many units were produced in 19X5.
4. Determine what Fosheim would have shown as income in 19X5 if the company had used variable costing.

15-10 Relationships—income, sales, and volume variance In 19X3 Bishop Company sold 101,000 units of product. Variable cost per unit was $12, both budgeted and actual. The standard fixed manufacturing cost per unit is $8 and there are no selling or administrative expenses. Fixed manufacturing costs were incurred as budgeted. Income for 19X3 was $332,000 after considering an unfavorable volume variance of $72,000. There was no change in inventories over the year 19X3.

Required
1. Determine the selling price of a unit of product.
2. Determine what level of volume was used to set the standard fixed cost per unit.
3. Determine the budgeted amount of fixed manufacturing costs.

15-11 Process costing—unit costs Valley Manufacturing Company uses a process costing system. The following data apply to July 19X9. Percentages of completion are the same for materials and for conversion costs.

	Units
Beginning inventory, 20% complete	4,000
Finished during July	60,000
Ending inventory, 60% complete	8,000
Production costs:	
Cost in beginning inventory	$ 5,840
Incurred during July	$208,000

Required

1. Compute the cost per unit of the units finished during the period, using the weighted-average costing method.
2. Compute the amount of ending work in process inventory in dollars.
3. Prepare a T-account for Work in Process Inventory.

15-12 **Process costing (extension of 15-11, related to Appendix)**   Redo 15-11, using first-in-first-out.

15-13 **Process costing—two departments**   Berke Manufacturing Company makes a single product, a chemical called Argot. The product is made in two processes, mixing and boiling. The following data apply to May 19X7. There were no beginning inventories. Percentages of completion are the same for materials and for conversion costs.

	Mixing	Boiling
Barrels completed during May	80,000	80,000
Barrels on hand at May 31	6,000	
Percentage complete	70%	
Production costs incurred	$42,100	$64,000

Required

1. Compute the cost per barrel for each process.
2. Compute the amount of ending work in process inventory in the Mixing Department.
3. The firm had no finished product on hand at the beginning of May. Of the 80,000 gallons finished during May, 70,000 were sold. Compute cost of goods sold and ending inventory of finished goods.

15-14 **Process costing**   Hittite Company makes a water-soluble paint. All materials are put into process and are then mixed for several hours. Data for July are given below:

Unit Data

Gallons completed in July	130,000
Gallons in ending inventory	24,000
Percentages complete:	
Materials	100%
Labor and overhead	75%

Cost Data

	Materials	Labor and Overhead
Beginning inventory	$ 3,200	$ 9,600
Incurred during July	$29,140	$82,160

Required

1. Using the weighted-average method, compute equivalent production for (a) materials, and (b) labor and overhead for the month of July.

2. Compute unit costs for each cost factor using the weighted-average method.
3. Prepare the journal entry to transfer the cost of finished gallons to Finished Goods Inventory.
4. Prepare a T-account for Work in Process Inventory.
5. Prove that your ending balance in Work in Process, from part 4, is correct.

Problems

15-15 Equivalent production and unit costs   Borr Company manufactures a single type of fertilizer in a single process. Data for April are as follows:

Beginning inventory of work in process	20,000 pounds
Completed in April	200,000 pounds
Ending inventory of work in process	30,000 pounds
Cost of materials used in production	$322,000
Conversion costs incurred	$651,100
Costs in beginning inventory:	
Materials	$ 34,500
Conversion costs	$ 46,500

The inventories were 100% complete for materials. The beginning inventory was 75% complete for conversion costs, the ending inventory 60% complete. The company uses the weighted-average method.

Required
1. Determine equivalent production for materials and for conversion costs.
2. Determine unit costs for materials and for conversion costs.
3. Determine the cost of the ending inventory of work in process and the cost transferred to finished goods inventory.

15-16 Equivalent units and standard costs (related to Appendix)   The production manager of Kneehi Company has just received his performance report for June 19X9. Among the data included are the following:

	Costs		
	Budgeted	Actual	Variance
Material	$10,000	$11,500	$1,500U
Direct labor	20,000	21,300	1,300U
Variable overhead	15,000	15,400	400U
Fixed overhead	18,000	18,800	800U
Totals	$63,000	$67,000	$4,000U

The budgeted amounts are based on 2,000 units, the number actually completed during June. The production manager is upset because 800 half-finished units are still in process at the end of June and are not counted as part of production for the month. However, at the beginning of June, there were 300 units one-third completed.

Required
1. Compute production in equivalent units on a first-in-first-out basis.
2. Prepare a new performance report.

15-17 Costing methods and pricing The sales manager and the controller of Emerson Company were discussing the price to be set for a new product being brought out by the firm. They had accumulated the following data:

Variable costs	$8 per unit
Fixed costs	$80,000 per year

The sales manager had set a target volume of 10,000 units per year. He determined that average fixed cost would be $8 per unit, bringing average total cost per unit to $16. The firm follows a policy of setting prices at 200% of cost, so the sales manager stated that the price would be $32 per unit.

The controller said that $32 seemed high, especially as competitors were charging only $30 for essentially the same product. The sales manager agreed, stating perhaps only 8,000 units per year could be sold at $32. However, he was convinced that the price should be set at 200% of cost. He added that it was unfortunate that fixed costs were so high, because he felt that 10,000 units could definitely be sold if the price were $30, and probably 12,000 at $28. However, it would not be possible to achieve the desired markup at those prices.

Required
1. Point out the fallacies in the reasoning of the sales manager. (You might wish to show what would happen at the $32 price. Would the firm achieve the desired markup?)
2. Determine which of the three prices ($32, $30, $28) will give the highest annual profit.

15-18 Process costing—journal entries Swanson Company makes a single type of pump on an assembly line. The firm uses process costing and applies manufacturing overhead at the rate of $12 per direct labor hour. Inventories at the beginning of 19X6 were as follows.

Raw material	$ 34,000
Work in process	67,000
Finished goods	125,000

During 19X6 the following transactions took place:
1. Material purchases were $286,000.
2. Wages earned by direct laborers for 35,000 hours were $289,000.
3. Raw materials costing $271,000 were put into process.
4. Other manufacturing costs incurred were
   (a) Indirect labor $ 46,000
   (b) Supervision and other salaries   182,000
   (c) Utilities and insurance   23,500
   (d) Depreciation   72,000
   (e) Other miscellaneous costs   112,000

5. Transfers from Work in Process to Finished Goods were $863,000.
6. Sales were $1,314,000.
7. Cost of goods sold was $818,000.
8. Selling and administrative expenses were $387,000.

Required
1. Prepare journal entries to record the above events.
2. Determine the ending balance in each inventory account.
3. Prepare an income statement for 19X6.

15-19   Product costing and volume-cost-profit analysis   The president of Landry Company asked you for assistance in analyzing the firm's revenue and cost behavior. You gathered the following data relating to the firm's only product.

Selling price		$10
Variable costs:		
Production	$4	
Selling	2	6
Contribution margin		$ 4
Fixed production costs	$120,000 per month	
Fixed selling and administrative		
expenses	$ 30,000 per month	

You calculated the firm's break-even point as 37,500 units per month and the volume required to earn the president's target profit of $8,000 per month as 39,500 units.

Three months after you provided the analysis, the president called you. On your arrival at his office he gave you the following income statements.

	April	May	June
Sales	$380,000	$395,000	$420,000
Cost of goods sold	243,200	269,300	316,125
Gross profit	136,800	125,700	103,875
Selling and administrative costs	106,000	109,000	114,000
Profit (loss) before taxes	$ 30,800	$ 16,700	($ 10,125)

The president is extremely upset at the results. He asks why your analysis does not hold, particularly because he has been assured by the production manager that variable costs per unit and fixed costs in total were incurred as budgeted during the three months. The sales manager has also assured the president that selling prices and variable costs per unit, as well as fixed costs in total, were as expected.

After a few minutes you talk to the controller, who tells you the firm uses actual absorption costing and produced the following quantities of product during the three months: April, 50,000 units; May, 40,000 units; June, 32,000 units. There were no inventories on hand at the beginning of April.

Required: Explain the results to the president. Show calculations of the determination of cost of goods sold for each month.

15-20   Process costing   Stockton Company makes a chemical spray that goes through two processes. Data for February are as follows:

	Mixing Department	Boiling Department
Gallons transferred to Boiling Department	75,000	
Gallons transferred to finished goods		68,000
Gallons on hand at end of month	9,000	15,000
Percent complete:		
Prior department costs	—	100%
Materials	100%	—^{a}
Labor and overhead	60%	40%
Costs incurred during February:		
Materials	$18,480	—
Labor and overhead	$32,160	$25,900
Beginning inventories:		
Gallons	8,000	8,000
Costs:		
Materials	$ 1,680	—
Prior department costs	—	$ 6,350
Labor and overhead	$ 4,020	$ 2,220

^{a}No material is added in this department.

Required

1. Determine the weighted-average equivalent production by cost category for each department.
2. Determine the per-unit cost by category for the Mixing Department.
3. Prepare the journal entry to record the transfer from the Mixing Department to the Boiling Department.
4. Determine the cost per unit by cost category for the Boiling Department.
5. Prepare the journal entry to record the transfer of product from the Boiling Department to Finished Goods.
6. Prepare the T-accounts for Work in Process for each department. Verify the ending inventory balances.

15-21 Process costing (related to Appendix, extension of 15-20)   Assume that Stockton Company uses the FIFO assumption for costing purposes, and that the beginning inventory in the Mixing Department was 60% complete as to materials and 70% complete as to conversion costs.

Required

1. Determine the FIFO equivalent production by cost category for the Mixing Department, and the unit cost for each category.
2. Determine the total cost to be transferred to the Boiling Department.
3. Prepare a T-account for Work in Process in the Mixing Department and verify the ending inventory balance.

15-22 Standard costs—performance evaluation   Topham Company is opening a new division to make and sell a single product, the Wally. The product is to be made in a factory that has a practical capacity of 150,000 units per year. Production is expected to average 120,000 units after the first two years of operation. During the first two years, sales are expected to be 80,000 and 100,000 respectively, with production being 100,000 and 110,000 in those years.

The Wally is to sell for $20, with variable manufacturing costs of $8. Fixed production costs are expected to be $360,000 annually for the first several years. Selling and administrative costs, all fixed, are budgeted at $300,000 annually.

Ronald Yost, controller of the firm, has suggested that the normal capacity of 120,000 units be used to set the standard fixed cost per unit. The other managers agree that Ron's idea is sound and Bill Roberts, the controller of the new division, is given the task of developing budgeted income statements based on the data given.

The operations of the first year are summarized as follows:

Sales (78,000 units)	$1,560,000
Production	115,000 units
Costs incurred:	
Variable production costs	$ 930,000
Fixed production costs	370,000
Selling and administrative costs	300,000

Required

1. Prepare a budgeted income statement based on the expected results in the first year of operations.
2. Prepare an income statement based on actual results.
3. Comment on the results. Was performance better than expected or worse? Explain.

15-23 Standard cost income statement—relationships and variances The income statement for Rider Company for 19X6 appears below. Other data are as follows:

(a) There were no beginning inventories.
(b) Fixed overhead absorbed per unit is $2, based on budgeted production of 250,000 units, and budgeted fixed costs of $500,000.
(c) The standard direct labor rate is $4 per hour.
(d) Variable overhead standard cost is based on a rate of $2 per direct labor hour.
(e) Direct laborers worked 116,000 hours.
(f) The standard price for materials is $0.50 per pound.
(g) Material purchases were 800,000 pounds at $3,000 over standard price.

Sales (200,000 units)		$2,000,000
Cost of sales:		
Materials	$300,000	
Direct labor	400,000	
Overhead	600,000	1,300,000
Standard gross profit		700,000
Manufacturing variances:		
Materials	$ 12,000U	
Direct labor	18,000F	
Variable overhead spending	4,000U	
Variable overhead efficiency	8,000F	
Fixed overhead budget	7,000F	
Other underabsorbed overhead	20,000U	3,000U
Actual gross profit		697,000
Selling and administrative expenses		600,000
Income		$ 97,000

Required: Determine the following:
1. Standard cost per unit, including standard prices and quantities for each element of cost.
2. Standard variable cost per unit.
3. Production for the year.
4. Ending inventory at standard cost.
5. Fixed overhead costs incurred.
6. Cost of materials purchased.
7. Material use variance.
8. Pounds of material used in production.
9. Direct labor efficiency variance.
10. Direct labor rate variance.
11. Direct labor costs incurred.
12. Variable overhead costs incurred.
13. Amount by which income would have increased if one more unit had been sold, no more produced.
14. Amount by which income would have increased had one more unit been produced and sold.

15-24 Interpretation of standard cost statement   The income statement presented below represents the operations of Thomas Company for June. Variable manufacturing costs at standard are 50% of total standard manufacturing cost. Standard fixed costs per unit are based on normal activity of 30,000 units per month.

Thomas Company
Income Statement for June, 19X4

Sales (20,000 units)		$200,000
Standard cost of sales		120,000
Standard gross profit		80,000
Manufacturing variances:		
Materials	$2,000U	
Direct labor	1,000F	
Overhead budget	1,000U	
		2,000U
		78,000
Volume variance		24,000U
Gross profit, actual		54,000
Selling, general, and administrative costs		48,000
Income		$ 6,000

Required: Answer each of the following questions.
1. What are fixed and variable standard costs per unit?
2. What are monthly fixed manufacturing costs?
3. How many units were produced in June?
4. If beginning inventory of finished goods was $60,000 at standard cost, how much is ending inventory at standard cost? (*Hint:* Prepare an expanded cost-of-goods-sold section.)

15-25 Income statement for standard costing, practical capacity (extension of 15-24)   Assume the same facts as in 15-24, except for the following:
(a) Production is 22,000 units.
(b) Total fixed production costs are $90,000.

(c)   Thomas bases its standard fixed cost per unit on its practical capacity of 40,000 units per month.

(d)   There were no beginning inventories.

Required: Prepare a new income statement. (*Hint:* The standard fixed cost per unit will not be the same as that determined in 15-24.)

15-26   Standard costs, budgets, variances, journal entries   The following data relate to the operations of Warner Company for 19X2.

Budgeted sales (100,000 units)	$1,000,000
Budgeted production	140,000 units
Budgeted costs:	
Materials (2 pounds per unit)	$ 210,000
Direct labor (1 hour per unit)	420,000
Variable overhead ($1 per direct labor hour)	140,000
Fixed overhead—manufacturing	300,000
Selling and administrative (all fixed)	180,000

The firm uses a standard cost system; the production costs above are based on standard cost per unit. Standard fixed cost per unit is based on 150,000 units of production at practical capacity. The inventory of finished goods at December 31, 19X1 is 13,000 units at standard cost. There were no inventories of work in process or materials at December 31, 19X1.

Actual results for 19X2 are as follows:

Sales (95,000 units)	$950,000
Production	130,000 units
Materials purchased (250,000 pounds)	$192,500
Materials used	236,000 pounds
Direct labor (133,000 hours)	$402,000
Variable overhead	128,000
Fixed overhead	285,000
Selling and administrative expenses	175,000

Required

1.   Prepare a budgeted income statement for 19X2.
2.   Prepare all necessary journal entries to record events in 19X2. The production manager is responsible for all variances except material price and labor rate.
3.   Prepare an income statement for 19X2.

15-27   Actual process costing, journal entries, and income statement   Wilberforce Company now uses actual process costing. The following data relate to its operations in July 19X7. There were no beginning inventories.

1.   Material purchases were $39,600 for 12,000 pounds ($3.30 per pound).
2.   Payments to direct laborers were $28,850 for 7,300 hours of work.
3.   Variable overhead costs incurred were $58,510.
4.   Fixed overhead costs incurred were $86,500.
5.   Material use was 11,000 pounds.
6.   Units completed totaled 7,200. Units in process at the end of July 19X7 were 500, 40% complete.

7. Sales were 6,500 units at $50 per unit.
8. Selling and administrative expenses were $106,000.

Required
1. Prepare journal entries for July.
2. Prepare an income statement for July.

15-28 **Standard process costing, journal entries, and income statement (extension of 15-27)** The president of Wilberforce Company has asked for your assistance. He would like to know whether standard costing could be used by his firm and how it would work. He makes available to you all the information from 15-27. He believes that if Wilberforce were to use standard costing the following standards would be appropriate.

Materials (1.5 pounds at $3.20)	$ 4.80
Direct labor (1 hour at $4)	4.00
Variable overhead (at $8 per direct labor hour)	8.00
Fixed overhead (at $12 per direct labor hour)	12.00
	$28.80

The president tells you that the per-unit fixed overhead figure of $12 is based on normal capacity of 7,000 direct labor hours per month.

Required:
1. Prepare journal entries for July using standard process costing.
2. Prepare an income statement for July using standard process costing.

15-29 **Special order** Western Corn Oil Company has found that its sales forecast for 19X6 was too high by about 40,000 cases of oil. Because the production budget was not revised, inventory is expected to be about 40,000 cases above normal at year end. In early December the sales manager was offered the opportunity to sell 25,000 cases at $4.80, well below the normal price of $8. Regular sales would not be affected if the order were accepted. He asked the controller for an analysis indicating whether the order should be accepted and was given the partial income statement shown below. The controller said that because there would be no effect on general and administrative expenses, it was only necessary to determine the unfavorable effect on gross profit.

Expected Income Statements

	Without Order	With Order
Sales	$2,400,000	$2,520,000
Standard costs of sales, $6 per case	1,800,000	1,950,000
Standard gross profit	$ 600,000	$ 570,000
Volume variance	(120,000)	(120,000)
Actual gross profit	$ 480,000	$ 450,000

The sales manager was puzzled and asked the controller about the volume variance. The controller replied that the volume variance related to production, not sales, and that production would not be increased because inventory was already too high. She said that the volume variance resulted because the firm used 400,000 cases on which to base the standard fixed cost, and actual production was expected to be only 340,000 cases.

Required
1. Determine whether the order should be accepted.
2. Prepare new income statements, down to actual gross profit, using variable costing.
3. Prepare a new partial income statement assuming that production would be increased by 25,000 cases if the order were accepted.

15-30 Job-order costing—standards and variances   Carlson Company makes a variety of types of furniture. The company has established standard variable costs for some of its high-volume models like the ones described below.

	Chair Model 803	Sofa Model 407
Materials:		
Wood	$ 24	$ 58
Fabric	46	92
Other	13	21
Total materials	83	171
Direct labor at $5 standard rate per hour	65	90
Variable overhead at $8 per direct labor hour	104	144
Total standard variable cost	$252	$405

During June the firm worked on two job orders. Order 82 was for 80 units of Model 803, order 83 was for 50 units of Model 407. Both jobs were finished and sold for $97,000.
Cost data are as follows:

Materials used, at standard prices:	
Wood	$ 4,855
Fabric	8,360
Other	2,090
Direct labor, 2,050 hours at $5 per hour	10,250
Variable overhead incurred	16,850

Fixed production costs were incurred as budgeted, $24,600. Selling and administrative expenses were $18,700. There were no material price variances.

Required
1. Determine the standard cost of each job order, by individual cost category.
2. Determine the following variances: material use, by type of material; direct labor efficiency; variable overhead spending; variable overhead efficiency.
3. Prepare an income statement for June using standard variable costing. Show the variances calculated in part 2 as a single lump sum.

15-31 **Comprehensive problem in costing methods** The following data relate to Gagner Company operations for 19X5.

	Budgeted	Actual
Production (units)	200,000	180,000
Sales (units)	190,000	160,000
Direct materials	$400,000	$375,000
Direct labor	$600,000	$580,000
Variable overhead	$400,000	$395,000
Fixed overhead	$200,000	$208,000
Selling, general, and administrative expenses	$700,000	$700,000

There were no beginning inventories; sales prices averaged $15 per unit; practical capacity is 250,000 units.

Required
1. Prepare income statements based on the following costing methods:
   (a) actual absorption costing
   (b) standard absorption costing—fixed overhead based on budgeted production (show the total variance for each element of cost)
   (c) standard absorption costing using practical capacity as the fixed overhead allocation base
   (d) standard variable costing
   (e) actual variable costing
2. Compare and contrast the results obtained in part 1.

15-32 **Comprehensive problem in costing methods (extension of 15-31)** The Gagner Company now has data regarding operations for 19X6, during which selling prices again averaged $15 per unit. The following data relate to 19X6 activity:

	Budgeted	Actual
Production (units)	150,000	190,000
Sales (units)	140,000	200,000
Direct materials	$300,000	$400,000
Direct labor	$450,000	$590,000
Variable manufacturing overhead	$300,000	$410,000
Fixed manufacturing overhead	$200,000	$215,000
Selling, general, and administrative expenses	$700,000	$720,000

Required: Prepare income statements for 19X6, using each of the methods listed in 15-31.

15-33 **Standard costs and product profitability** Tucumcary Office Products Company makes three sizes of file folders. The company has practical capacity of 50,000 machine hours per year and uses that figure to set standard fixed costs for each size of folder. At the beginning of 19X6 the controller had prepared the following data regarding the three sizes of folders (all data per carton of 50 folders):

	Two-inch	Three-inch	Four-inch
Selling price	$17.00	$24.00	$31.00
Standard variable costs	8.00	11.00	16.00
Standard fixed costs	4.80	6.40	9.80
Total standard costs	12.80	17.40	25.60
Standard gross profit	$ 4.20	$ 6.60	$ 5.40
Expected sales in cartons	44,000	25,000	30,000
Machine hours required per carton	0.3	0.4	0.6

The sales manager has informed the controller that he has been approached by a large office supplies chain. The chain wants to buy 24,000 cartons of a six-inch folder and is willing to pay $40 per carton. The sales manager had discussed the offer with the production manager who stated that the folders could be made using the existing equipment. Variable costs per carton would be $19, and 0.8 machine hours would be required per carton.

Because the chain would take not fewer than 24,000 cartons, the sales manager was fairly sure that the firm would not have the capacity to fill the special order and still manufacture its other products in the volumes required by the expected sales. He therefore asked the controller to develop data on the proposed order and to decide which of the existing products should be partially curtailed. The controller then prepared the following analysis, which is incomplete because he was called away before finishing it. The sales manager was not sure how to proceed from this point and asked you to help him make the decision.

	Six-inch Folder
Selling price	$40.00
Standard variable cost	19.00
Standard fixed cost	12.80
Total standard cost	$31.80
Standard gross profit	$ 8.20

The controller has also prepared the following analysis of budgeted profit for the year:

	Two-inch	Three-inch	Four-inch	Total
Standard gross profit per carton	$4.20	$6.60	$5.40	
Expected volume	44,000	25,000	30,000	
Total expected gross profit—standard	$184,800	$165,000	$162,000	$511,800
Expected volume variance				140,800
Expected actual gross profit				371,000
Budgeted selling and administrative expenses, all fixed				327,000
Budgeted profit before taxes				$ 44,000

The firm generally manufactures about as many cartons of each size of folder as it sells. Because it rarely experiences differences between standard and actual machine hours for given levels of production, it computes its volume variance based on the difference between 50,000 hours and actual hours worked.

Required: Prepare an analysis for the sales manager showing him whether the special order should be accepted and for which products, if any, production and sales should be reduced.

15-34 Review problem   Sally Ann Frocks is a manufacturer of dresses. Its relevant range is 1,500 to 5,000 dresses per month. For the month of May 19X5, it has prepared the following forecast:

Sales (2,500 dresses @ $30 each)
Variable manufacturing costs per dress:
   Materials (3 yards @ $2 per yard)
   Direct labor (2 hours @ $0.50 per hour)
   Variable overhead ($1 per DLH)
Fixed manufacturing overhead ($3,000)
Variable selling costs (commissions at 10% of sales)
Fixed selling and administrative costs ($6,000)
Inventories:
   May 1, 19X5   none
   May 31, 19X5   materials 500 yards, finished dresses 500

Normal capacity is 3,000 dresses per month, which is the basis for overhead application.

Required: Answer the following questions.
1. What is practical capacity?
2. What is budgeted production for May?
3. How many yards of materials should be purchased during May?
4. How many hours does it take to produce a dress?
5. What are total variable manufacturing costs per dress?
6. What are total manufacturing costs per dress?
7. What is contribution margin per dress?
8. What is the cost per dress of the ending inventory if variable costing is used?
9. What is the cost per dress of the ending inventory if absorption costing is used without a predetermined fixed overhead rate?
10. What is the cost to produce one additional dress?
11. What is the cost to produce and sell an additional dress?
12. What is the predetermined fixed overhead rate per direct labor hour?
13. What are total budgeted manufacturing costs for May?
14. Give a formula for total manufacturing costs in the range of 1,500 to 5,000 dresses per month.
15. What would the predetermined fixed overhead rate be per direct labor hour if practical capacity were used as the base?
16. What is budgeted income for May?
17. What is the break-even point, in dresses?
18. By how much could budgeted sales fall before a loss was incurred?
19. By how much would income increase for each unit sold above budgeted volume?

15-35 Comprehensive review   McLeod Company produces and sells a single product, the Winser. Standard manufacturing costs for a unit of Winser, which sells for $20, are as follows:

Materials:	
Wyn (2 pounds @ $1 per pound)	$2.00
Luz (1 yard @ $0.50 per yard)	0.50
Forming labor (½ hour @ $6 per hour)	3.00
Variable overhead ($4 per hour of forming labor)	2.00
Fixed overhead ($7 per hour of forming labor)	3.50

The standard for fixed overhead is based on normal productive capacity of 10,000 units. The company has also established standards for marketing and administrative costs as follows, based on a normal sales volume of 10,000 units.

Marketing costs:	
Variable	$2.50 per unit sold
Fixed	$2.50 per unit sold
Administrative costs:	
Fixed	$1.50 per unit sold

A budgeted statement of cash flows for 19X1 appears below.

McLeod Company Budgeted Cash Flows for 19X1

Sources of cash:		
Operations		$25,000
Uses of cash:		
Dividends	$10,000	
Purchases of equipment	4,000	
Retirement of bonds	10,000	
Purchase of marketable securities	8,000	
		32,000
Decrease in cash balance		$ 7,000

The balance sheet of McLeod Company at December 31, 19X0 is shown below. The last column in the balance sheet indicates the budgeted change in each balance sheet item for 19X1.

McLeod Company Balance Sheet

	December 31, 19X0	19X1 Budgeted Change
Assets		
Current assets:		
Cash	$ 31,000	$− 7,000
Marketable securities	—	+ 8,000
Accounts receivable, net of allowance for doubtful accounts	40,000	+15,000

Inventories:			
Finished product	$ 55,000		0
Raw materials	20,000		+ 5,000
		75,000	
Prepaid expenses		4,000	− 1,000
Total current assets		150,000	
Property, plant, and equipment:			
Land	50,000		0
Building, net of accumulated depreciation	100,000		− 8,000
Equipment, net of accumulated depreciation	100,000		−18,000
		250,000	
Total assets		$400,000	

Equities

Current liabilities:			
Accounts payable		$ 45,000	+ 5,000
Notes payable		30,000	0
Total current liabilities		75,000	
Bonds payable		150,000	− 10,000
Total liabilities		225,000	
Stockholders' equity:			
Common stock	$100,000		0
Retailed earnings	75,000		− 1,000
Total stockholders' equity		175,000	
Total equities		$400,000	

For the year 19X1, McLeod planned to produce and sell 8,400 units of Winser, and succeeded in achieving the production and sales goals. A total of 17,000 pounds of Wyn and 8,000 yards of Luz were used and 4,400 hours were worked by forming laborers. At the end of 19X1, the following income statement was prepared:

McLeod Company Income Statement for 19X1

	Budget	Actual	Difference
Sales	$168,000	$172,200	$4,200F
Variable costs:			
Wyn	16,800	18,500	1,700U
Luz	4,200	4,000	200F
Forming labor	25,200	24,500	700F
Manufacturing overhead	16,800	18,000	1,200U
Marketing overhead	21,000	21,000	—
Fixed costs:			
Manufacturing	35,000	34,000	1,000F
Marketing	25,000	23,000	2,000F
Administrative	15,000	15,000	0
Total costs	159,000	158,000	1,000F
Income	$ 9,000	$ 14,200	$5,200F

Required: On the basis of the information provided, complete the following sentences.

1. The budgeted return on average owners' equity is $_____ divided by $_____.
2. The budgeted cash to be received from customers (ignoring bad debts) is $_____.
3. The budgeted raw material purchases are $_____.
4. Budgeted expiration of prepaid expenses exceeds new prepayments by $_____.
5. The budgeted change in equipment can be explained by a purchase of equipment of (a) $_____ and depreciation charges of (b) $_____.
6. The budgeted increase in working capital is $_____.
7. The budgeted working capital from operations is $_____.
8. The budgeted pounds of Wyn used for production are _____.
9. The total budgeted standard costs of Wyn are $_____.
10. The material use variance for Wyn for 19X1 is $_____.
11. The material price variance for Wyn for 19X1 is $_____.
12. The budgeted yards of Luz to be used for production are _____.
13. The total budgeted standard cost of Luz is $_____.
14. The material use variance for Luz is $_____.
15. The material price variance for Luz is $_____.
16. The total budgeted standard cost of forming labor is $_____.
17. The labor rate variance is $_____.
18. The labor efficiency variance is $_____.
19. The number of labor hours reported as inefficient is _____.
20. The total budgeted manufacturing cost for 19X1 is $_____.
21. The efficiency variance for variable manufacturing overhead is $_____.
22. The spending variance for variable manufacturing overhead is $_____.
23. The budget variance for fixed manufacturing overhead is $_____.
24. The predetermined rate for fixed manufacturing overhead was calculated by dividing $_____ by _____ units.
25. The volume variance for fixed manufacturing overhead is $_____.
26. If the predetermined overhead rate for fixed manufacturing overhead had been set at 8,800 units rather than at the normal capacity of 10,000, the volume variance would have been $_____.
27. If the predetermined overhead rate for fixed manufacturing overhead had been calculated by using 7,000 units of Winser, the rate would have been $_____ per hour of labor.
28. The amount of total manufacturing overhead in the 8,400 units of product transferred to finished goods is $_____.
29. The reported variance most likely attributable to the Purchasing Department is the _____ variance.
30. From the budgeted cash flows, it _____ (is, is not) possible to determine that for any time period during the year, cash inflows from normal operations are greater than cash outflows from such normal operations.
31. An unfavorable labor efficiency variance _____.
    (a) is always attributable to poor supervision or inept laborers.
    (b) could result from excess time spent in processing substandard materials.
    (c) must be investigated, regardless of the cost of the investigation.
    (d) could not be self-correcting.
    (e) could not be attributable to action by the Purchasing Department.
32. The predetermined total manufacturing overhead absorption rate is $_____ per hour of forming labor.
33. Of the sales, cash, direct labor, direct materials, and manufacturing overhead budgets, the one most likely to be prepared first would be the _____ budget.

34. The total cost of producing one more unit of Winser than budgeted would be $_____.

35. The cost of producing and selling one more unit of Winser than budgeted would be $_____.

15-36 Process costing, second department (related to Appendix, extension of 15-21) The beginning inventory in the Boiling Department of Stockton Company was 50% complete as to conversion costs.

Required: Using the data from 15-20 and 15-21 and the above information, do the following:

1. Determine the FIFO equivalent production for conversion costs in the Boiling Department, and the per-unit conversion cost.
2. Determine the total cost to be transferred from the Boiling Department to Finished Goods.
3. Prepare a T-account for Work in Process in the Boiling Department and verify the ending inventory balance.

15-37 Review of Chapters 12, 13, 14, and 15 ARC Industries makes fiberglass insulation, selling it for $20 per roll. The standard variable cost per roll is as follows:

Material (25 pounds at $0.20 per pound)	$5
Direct labor (0.20 hour at $10 per hour)	2
Variable overhead at $5 per direct labor hour	1
Total standard variable cost per roll	$8

Budgeted fixed production costs are $1,500,000 per year.

ARC began 19X3 with no inventories. Actual results for 19X3 were as follows:

Sales (230,000 rolls)	$4,600,000
Production	260,000 rolls
Production costs:	
Materials purchased (7,000,000 pounds)	$1,425,000
Materials used	6,450,000 pounds
Direct labor (53,000 hours)	$ 520,000
Variable manufacturing overhead	$ 270,000
Fixed production overhead	$1,480,000
Selling and administrative costs, all fixed	$ 800,000

The firm uses actual absorption costing for most purposes, though it has established standard variable production costs. The treasurer of the firm would like to see how standard costing would work for income determination and wants you to prepare income statements using the two approaches. One statement would be a standard variable costing statement, the other a standard absorption costing statement with 250,000 rolls used to set the standard fixed cost.

Required

1. Determine all variances from standard costs, including the fixed overhead budget and volume variances.
2. Prepare the income statements that the treasurer requested. On each, show the variances as a lump sum subtracted from the standard gross margin or contribution margin.

15-38 Review of Chapters 12, 13, 14, and 15 (extension of 15-37)   During 19X4 ARC
Industries produced 240,000 rolls and sold 250,000. The same standards and budgets in
effect in 19X3 applied to 19X4, and the selling price remained at $20 per roll. Actual
costs were as follows:

Materials purchased (6,200,000 pounds)	$1,210,000
Materials used	5,900,000 pounds
Direct labor (47,000 hours)	$ 475,000
Variable overhead	$ 240,000
Fixed production overhead	$1,510,000
Selling and administrative costs	$ 810,000

Required: Prepare income statements using the same bases as for 15-37. Again, calculate all variances and show the appropriate total as a lump sum on each statement.

PART FIVE

SPECIAL TOPICS

The last part of this book covers three special topics that are often treated in managerial accounting courses, but which are also frequently included as parts of other courses.

Chapter 16 introduces several quantitative decision-making techniques that are increasingly being employed in approaching real-world problems. Chapter 17 covers the statement of changes in financial position, including both cash flow and working capital flow. Chapter 18 introduces financial statement analysis. The chapter is geared primarily to the uses of financial statements by managers, creditors, and stockholders.

CHAPTER 16

QUANTITATIVE METHODS AND MANAGERIAL ACCOUNTING

We have stated throughout this book that making decisions requires considering both quantitative and qualitative factors. Because of the increasing mathematical sophistication of managers and the availability of computers, much attention has been given in recent years to refining the uses of quantifiable data in the decision-making process. These refinements have been applied, for the most part, to determine the best course of action in very complex situations. But the principles on which the techniques are based are equally applicable in less complex cases.

A sizable number of managers may not fully understand all of the mathematics that underlie some of the quantitative techniques that have come into use. Nevertheless, there are compelling reasons why any manager, and most certainly a managerial accountant, should be aware of these techniques, their uses, and their limitations. First, the manager must be able to describe the problems to the specialist who sets up and solves them and identify the information relevant to the problems. Second, the manager must be able to communicate effectively with the specialist; he or she must comprehend what the specialist is saying, and grasp the basics of the solution being offered. Third, the manager must know and understand the limitations of a given technique, so that he or she is able to evaluate the applicability of a proposed technique to the problem at hand and to suggest possible changes if the solution appears to be ineffective.

QUANTITATIVE METHODS— AN OVERVIEW

The term *quantitative methods* describes sophisticated mathematical techniques for solving managerial problems. Other terms are operations research, model building, and quantitative analysis. You have used quantitative methods throughout this book. VCP analysis uses simple algebra; budgeting uses mathematically stated relationships among variables (collections on receivables are 40% of the current month's sales, 60% of the preceding month's sales); and capital budgeting utilizes present values.

Almost all of the quantitative techniques in this book require that managers state their expectations about the future. They predict prices, costs, demand, and so on. Often, the quantifiable factors are stated in equations [income = (sales price × units sold) − (variable costs × units sold) − fixed costs]. Operations research techniques and models work the same way. We determine which quantifiable factors are relevant to a decision, express relationships among those factors in equations, and solve the equations to obtain the answers. The major difference between operations research models and the techniques you have been using is the level of complexity.

In one respect all the quantitative methods are the same: a solution will be only as good as the predictions about future conditions. If these predictions do not turn out to be true, the best result might not be realized. Hence, when developing predictions about future conditions, there must be close cooperation and communication between manager and specialist.

STATISTICAL DECISION THEORY

We introduced the concept of **expected value** in Chapter 6. We applied the concept to sales forecasting under conditions in which managers believed that several possible outcomes were possible and assigned probabilities to each of these outcomes. The concept is applicable to many other situations, some of which we illustrate here. Following these illustrations we discuss some questions involving the ways probabilities are developed.

Suppose your company is considering alternative methods of acquiring computer time. You have identified three feasible choices:

(a)   You can rent one make of computer for a flat rate of $6,000 per month, using as much computer time as you need.

(b)   You can rent another make of computer for $2,000 per month plus $40 per hour of use.

(c)   You can use the computer at a service bureau (a firm that rents computer time to others) for $80 per hour.

Study of the three computers indicates that all will meet your computing needs, and you have assessed the likelihood of your needs as follows:

(1) Event (Estimated Hours of Computer Time Needed per Month)	×	(2) Estimated Probability of Occurrence	=	(1) × (2) Expected Value
30		.10		3
60		.15		9
100		.25		25
150		.30		45
200		.20		40
		1.00		122

The expected value of required time is 122 hours. You can now compare the costs related to the three choices at 122 hours as follows:

Alternative	Cost
(a) Rent for $6,000 per month	$6,000
(b) Rent for $2,000 plus $40 per hour	
122 hours at $40 per hour = $4,880 + $2,000	$6,880
(c) Buy time from the service bureau at $80 per hour	
122 hours × $80 per hour	$9,760

Renting the computer for $6,000 per month is the least-cost choice.

Sometimes the costs of choices can be directly associated with the probabilities of occurrence. You could have computed the expected values of the costs of each outcome in the problem above. The situation for choice (b) could have been analyzed as follows:

(1) Hours Required	(2) Probability	×	(3) Conditional Value[a]	=	(2) × (3) Expected Value
30	.10		$ 3,200		$ 320
60	.15		4,400		660
100	.25		6,000		1,500
150	.30		8,000		2,400
200	.20		10,000		2,000
	1.00				$6,880

[a]Cost incurred if the event in column 1 occurs. For example, $3,200 = $2,000 + ($40 × 30 hours).

The cost for choice (c) would have been computed as follows:

Hours Required	Probability	×	Conditional Value	=	Expected Value
30	.10		$ 2,400		$ 240
60	.15		4,800		720
100	.25		8,000		2,000
150	.30		12,000		3,600
200	.20		16,000		3,200
	1.00				$9,760

Choice (a) has the same cost no matter what the hourly rate. Therefore, the expected value is 100% certain to be $6,000.

Variance Investigation

As stated in Chapter 12, a variance should be investigated when the expected savings from investigation exceed the cost of the investigation. The expected value framework is helpful in deciding whether or not to investigate.

Assume that a $300 variance has occurred and is expected to continue for six months if not corrected. An investigation to find the exact cause of the variance will cost nothing. The chances are about 80% that even after identifying the cause, the variance cannot be corrected. The expected values of the costs of investigating and not investigating are summarized below.

Choice 1—Do Not Investigate

An expected cost of $300 for six months	$1,800

Choice 2—Conduct an Investigation

Possible Outcome	Probability of Outcome	×	Conditional Value	=	Expected Value
Cause is correctable	.20		0		0
Cause is not correctable	.80		$1,800		$1,440
Total	1.00				$1,440

It is worthwhile to investigate the variance; it costs nothing to investigate and there are potential savings of $360 ($1,800 − $1,440).

The $360 difference has special significance; it is the maximum amount you would be willing to *spend* to investigate whether the variance can be corrected. The amount is called the **value of perfect information,** which is defined as the difference between: (1) the expected value of the best alternative, given the existing information; and (2) the expected value of alternatives when you know in advance what event will occur.

To confirm that the computed difference is the maximum you would pay to investigate the variance, suppose that it will cost $360 to investigate. What would be the expected values (costs) of the two choices?

Choice 1—Do Not Investigate

A cost of $300 for six months	$1,800

Choice 2—Conduct an Investigation

Possible Outcome	Probability of Outcome ×	Conditional Value =	Expected Value	
Cause is correctable	.20	$ 360[a]	$ 72	
Cause is not correctable	.80	2,160[b]	1,728	
Total	1.00			$1,800

[a] The cost to investigate will be incurred.
[b] The cost to investigate plus the cost of the continued variance will be incurred.

Thus, the expected cost of both choices is the same.

Let us introduce two modifications of the variance investigation circumstances: (1) the cost to investigate a variance is $200; and (2) there is a 30% probability that the variance was caused by a random disturbance and will not continue beyond the first period in which it occurs. The usual expected value approach can be used under these circumstances also. The analysis would be as follows:

Choice 1—Do Not Investigate

Possible Outcome	Probability of Outcome ×	Conditional Value =	Expected Value	
Variance is random, will stop without action	.30	0	$ 0	
Variance will continue	.70	$1,800	1,260	
Total	1.00			$1,260

Choice 2—Conduct an Investigation

Possible Outcome	Probability of Outcome ×	Conditional Value =	Expected Value	
Variance is random, will stop without action	.30	$ 200	$ 60	
A problem exists that can be corrected	.14[a]	200	28	
A problem exists that cannot be corrected	.56[b]	2,000	1,120	
Total	1.00			$1,208

[a] The 20% chance of being able to take corrective action now applies to only 70% of the cases. The probability thus becomes 70% × 20%, or 14%. (Remember the total probabilities must be 1.0.)
[b] Same reasoning as in above note except that the probability of there being an uncorrectable problem is 70% × 80%, or 56%.

Under the new conditions, an investigation should be undertaken because the expected value (expected cost) of investigating is smaller than that of not investigating.

Another approach available to solve the problem is the **decision tree,** a commonly used device that offers a graphical representation of the problem. The decision tree for this decision, shown in Figure 16-1, works in essentially the same way as the tabular format, but has the advantage of allowing a step-by-step determination of probabilities when there are several possible events within other events (the 80%–20% probabilities within the 70% probability).

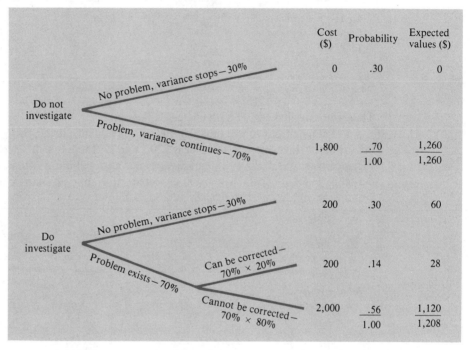

FIGURE 16-1   Decision Tree

Using either format, the expected cost of investigating is less than the expected cost of *not* investigating. The difference between the expected costs of the two choices ($1,260 − $1,208 = $52) is smaller now than it was before ($52 as opposed to $360). This makes sense because now there is a 30% chance that you do not have to do anything and the variance will stop anyway. This condition should make the investigation less attractive, as does the new cost to investigate.

Capital Budgeting Application

Firms frequently have investment opportunities that promise either high rewards (high net present values) or large losses (high negative net present values). Such opportunities are called risky because they involve potential loss, but they can also be rewarding. (Chapter 3 discusses cost structure and risk; the substitution of fixed costs for variable costs could be either beneficial or disastrous, depending on the future levels of sales.) Consider a manufacturer of toys who is trying to decide whether to market a new toy.

The manufacturer believes that the toy has a chance to be a big seller, but could also be a flop.

Assume the following possibilities for net cash flows after taxes in the two circumstances described: the toy sells well; the top is a flop.

	Sells Well	Flops
Years 1–5	$15,000	$1,000

What should the manufacturer do? A common approach is to find the expected value of the future cash flows based on the probabilities of their occurrences. The expected value is the sum of the individual flows under the possibilities stated, multiplied by the probability of occurrence. Assume that the marketing group believes there is a 60% chance of the toy's being a big seller and a 40% chance of its being a flop.

	Cash Flow	×	Probability of Occurrence	=	Expected Value
Sells well	$15,000		.60		$9,000
Flops	1,000		.40		400
Totals			1.00		$9,400

The cash flows are now expressed as an expected value of $9,400 based on the probabilities of occurrence of each situation. The $9,400 can then be discounted at cost of capital to determine whether the present value is greater than or less than the investment required.

There are times when it may be unwise to rely solely on expected values. Suppose you were given the following choices: (1) take $10,000 now; or (2) flip a coin, heads you get $40,000, tails you lose $20,000. Compute the expected values (assuming an honest coin, of course).

Choice 1—A certain gain of $10,000.
Choice 2—An expected value of $10,000, as indicated below.

Event	Probability	×	Conditional Value	=	Expected Value
Heads	.5		$40,000		$20,000
Tails	.5		−20,000		−10,000
	1.00				$10,000

At first glance, the two choices are equally valuable, since both provide an expected value of $10,000. But as with most decisions, nonquantifiable factors would influence your decision. In this case, unless you have a great deal of money, you would probably not select choice 2. The difficulty with relying solely on the expected value may be described, though in an oversimplified fashion, like this: the expected value concept is based on probabilities, and probability theory is based on mathematical laws that assume large numbers of occurrences. If you had 1,000 chances to play the coin flip game just described, it would not matter much whether you took the $10,000 or tossed the coin. You could expect to win about 500 times, lose about 500 times. But with only one try, you are staking a great deal on only one coin toss.

Operations researchers have tried to incorporate such considerations into the simple expected value model by attaching "utilities" to the various outcomes. (Utility represents the degree of "better-offness" or "worse-offness" associated with the events.) Using utilities, operations researchers have tried to recognize that generally it detracts more from your well-offness to lose $20,000 than is added by winning $40,000. But assigning values to the utilities remains a matter of judgment, and assigned values may differ markedly depending on who is doing the choosing. Different managers will make different decisions, even if they all use the same data. Some are more willing to take risks in the hope of earning higher profits. We consider this point in more detail in the following section.

The use of probabilities can provide more rational evaluations of the consequences of decisions than can guesswork. Provided that they understand the limitations of the analysis, managers can make better decisions.

Payoff Tables

Managers use the expected value concept most often when they have several available strategies with probabilities attached to the outcomes of each and when they must make the same decision several times. A typical application would be a firm's decision on how many units of a product to buy (or make) when there are given probabilities for sales and the unsold units are discarded or sold at substantial losses.

For example, suppose that a florist must decide how many units of a particular corsage to buy each week. All units must be bought in advance and no additional purchases are possible. Unsold corsages will have to be discarded. The florist has estimated the demand for the corsage as given below. (For computational simplicity we shall assume that no other outcomes are possible. Computers make it possible to analyze more realistic situations quickly.)

Demand in Units	Probability of Demand
4,000	20%
8,000	50%
12,000	30%

The variable cost per corsage is $6 and the selling price is $10. Please notice the difference between this situation and the toy situation described on page 645. Here, the firm must buy a specific number of corsages, and so if the demand does not at least equal the number purchased, the firm has a loss of $6 per unit in discarding the corsages. The approach to this kind of problem is to prepare a **payoff table** which shows the outcome of each possible strategy. We assume that the florist will buy either 4,000, 8,000, or 12,000 units. The conditional payoff of each of those strategies is computed in Exhibit 16-1.

Exhibit 16-1

Payoffs of Various Strategies—Conditional Values

Event:	Action: Purchases of		
Demand	4,000	8,000	12,000
4,000	$16,000	($ 8,000)	($32,000)
8,000	16,000	32,000	8,000
12,000	16,000	32,000	48,000

The values are computed as follows. Each individual entry in the table is the contribution margin that would be gained, or lost, given the combination of sales and purchases. Thus, if the firm *bought* 4,000 units, it would sell 4,000 units no matter what the demand because it could not buy any more even if it learned that 8,000 or 12,000 units would be demanded by buyers. Hence, if purchases are 4,000 units, the firm will earn a $16,000 contribution margin by selling 4,000 units ($4 per unit × 4,000 units) and will lose nothing by having to discard units bought but not sold.

If the firm buys 8,000 units and can only sell 4,000, costs will be $48,000 (8,000 × $6) and revenues only $40,000 (4,000 × $10), for a loss of $8,000. Or, put another way, the firm would earn $16,000 contribution margin on the 4,000 units sold, but would lose $6 per unit for the 4,000 units not sold and discarded. If the firm did sell 8,000 units, it would earn revenues of $80,000, have costs of $48,000, and a contribution margin of $32,000 ($4 × 8,000). The same contribution margin would be earned if the firm could have sold 12,000 units, but only sold 8,000 because only 8,000 were purchased.

The next step is to compute the expected value of each possible outcome, using the probabilities of demand. A summary of the expected values is shown in Exhibit 16-2.

Exhibit 16-2

Expected Values of Strategies

		Action: Purchases of					
		4,000		8,000		12,000	
Demand	Probability	CV^a	EV^b	CV^a	EV^b	CV^a	EV^b
4,000	.20	$16,000	$ 3,200	($ 8,000)	($ 1,600)	($32,000)	($ 6,400)
8,000	.50	16,000	8,000	32,000	16,000	8,000	4,000
12,000	.30	16,000	4,800	32,000	9,600	48,000	14,400
Expected values			$16,000		$24,000		$12,000

^{a}Conditional values from Exhibit 16-1.
^{b}Conditional value multiplied by probability.

Notice that the expected value of the strategy of purchasing 4,000 units is equal to the conditional value of each outcome: demands of 4,000, 8,000, and 12,000. This should not be surprising, because the firm can sell only 4,000 units if it buys only that many. The problem with that strategy is that the firm loses contribution margin if it could have sold more than 4,000 units.

Notice also that the outcomes of buying 12,000 units are much more widely dispersed than the others, which is also to be expected. The more you buy *and* sell, the higher the profit; the more you buy and do *not* sell, the lower the profit or higher the loss.

Using the expected value criterion, a manager would select the strategy of buying 8,000 units. But remember that we are dealing with expectations: the actual values might be different from the ones expected. At this point, most managers would recognize how important to the results the estimated probabilities are and would attempt some type of "what if" analysis (the sensitivity analysis discussed in earlier chapters). For example, the manager might compute what happens if the probability of selling 12,000 units increases to 40%, with an offsetting decrease in the probability of selling 8,000 units, or try several combinations of probabilities that he considers plausible. Using a microcomputer (or a desk-top terminal connected with a company's main computer) and one of the many available software packages, a manager could obtain information about more than a dozen such combinations in just a few minutes.

Again, we stress the point that no quantitative method, from VCP analysis through expected value calculations, *tells* you what to do. It tells you only what will happen *if*—and "if" is a big word—all of your predictions are correct. Accordingly, this type of analysis is usually applied in firms that continually have to make decisions about production or purchasing. Examples are firms that sell perishable goods. (A vendor of fresh fruits and vegetables must buy them in advance and cannot keep unsold quantities in stock.)

The value of perfect information can also be computed from payoff tables. It is, in this application, the difference between the contribution margin that would be earned if the firm knew how many units would be demanded and therefore purchased exactly that many, and the expected value of the strategy it would follow using only probabilities.

If the firm knew in advance how many corsages would be demanded, it would buy exactly that many and would have the following expected value of contribution margin, selling 4,000 units in 20% of the weeks, 8,000 units in 50% of the weeks, and 12,000 units in 30% of the weeks.

Sales	Contribution Margin, Conditional Value (Exhibit 16-1)	Probability	Expected Value
4,000	$16,000	.20	$ 3,200
8,000	32,000	.50	16,000
12,000	48,000	.30	14,400
Expected value			$33,600

Notice that the expected values correspond to those in Exhibit 16-2 for the entries in the same row and same column. That is, the entry in the row for 4,000 here is $3,200 as in the 4,000 row and column in Exhibit 16-2. In the 8,000 row, 8,000 column is $16,000; and in the 12,000 row 12,000 column is $14,400. The same is true of the conditional values.

In this case, then, the value of perfect information is $9,600 ($33,600 − $24,000). We can make this clear by showing the expected sales for a 10-week period, following the strategy of buying 8,000 units each week and following the optimal strategy when we know in advance what the week's demand will be.

During the 10-week period we would expect to sell 4,000 corsages twice (20% × 10 weeks); 8,000 corsages five times; and 12,000 corsages three times. If we follow the strategy of buying 8,000 each week we would have losses of $8,000 twice and gains of $32,000 eight times. (When we sell only 4,000 corsages we lose $8,000, and when we sell 8,000 we gain $32,000, from Exhibit 16-1.) Total contribution margin for the 10-week period would then be $240,000, which is ($32,000 × 8) − ($8,000 × 2). With perfect information, we would buy and sell 4,000 corsages twice, buy and sell 8,000 corsages five times, and buy and sell 12,000 corsages three times. The contribution margin for the period would be as follows:

Sales	Number of Weeks	×	Contribution Margin per Week	=	Total
4,000	2		$16,000		$ 32,000
8,000	5		32,000		160,000
12,000	3		48,000		144,000
Total					$336,000

The difference between the expected contribution margin with perfect information ($336,000) and using the optimal strategy without having perfect information ($240,000) is $96,000, which is ten times (for ten weeks) the value of $9,600 that we calculated before.

In the real world it is impossible to obtain *perfect* information, but the concept is still valuable. *Some* additional information can almost always be obtained at a price—test-marketing of new products is an example of an effort to obtain more information. The questions are whether the information gained would result in a change in your strategy, whether your decisions would be better if you did obtain the information, and whether the cost is less than the added benefits.

Developing Probabilities

The probabilities to be used in computing expected values can be intuitive and judgmental, or they can be developed by using more objective, sophisticated statistical techniques.

At one extreme, probabilities might be "best estimates" of experienced managers. There might be some historical basis for the estimates, as when managers have developed rules of thumb through past experience and believe that the current situation is similar to previous situations. For example, if a machine is not operating at peak efficiency the manager might believe that the probability is about 60% that an internal part is wearing out, 40% that some random factor is at work that will not continue. Tearing down the machine to examine and perhaps replace the part could be very costly both in labor and in lost production while the machine is idle. The manager might decide to wait for another week or so to get a better idea.

At times the manager may have fairly objective probabilities based on the presence or absence of external factors. A good example is provided by a firm whose business depends greatly on the weather. A firm that sells hot dogs and soft drinks at baseball parks might be able to develop probabilities of sales based on weather forecasts. The hotter the day is expected to be, the more soft drinks the firm can expect to sell. Of course, the validity of the manager's estimates depends on the validity of the weather forecasts.

Often, firms will try to narrow down the range of estimates by getting additional information and using statistical techniques to evaluate the information. One common example is in the area of market research. A firm might be considering the introduction of a new product that would require a nationwide advertising and promotional campaign. Because such campaigns can be very costly, the company might test-market the product using a regional promotional campaign. The area or areas selected should be fairly representative of the entire country for the results to be useful. After the small-scale campaigns are underway the managers can analyze the information and gain a better perspective on probable nationwide sales. You may study some of these techniques in later courses in marketing and statistics.

Citing the fact that probabilities are only estimates, some managers react negatively to the use of quantitative techniques requiring their use. Such managers argue that "sound business judgment" is better than quantitative analysis because the former does not require a lot of assumptions. It is true, of course, that quantitative techniques require the use of estimates, and that quantitative analyses do not tell managers what to do. Managers must make the decisions. But it is also true that when a manager makes a decision, with or without the help of quantitative analysis, the decision *implies* the existence of some beliefs about the future. Consider a decision to set a production level without first examining the probable demand for the product. Such a decision implies *some* expectation about demand. Any manager who selects a particular course of action—say, ordering 4,000 corsages—is making assumptions about the future, whether or not those assumptions (expectations) are specifically stated. All that the payoff table shows is that there is a higher profit potential in a decision to order 8,000. One of the major benefits of quantitative analysis is that it shows what must happen for the manager's decision to be correct.

INVENTORY CONTROL MODELS

Inventory is one of the most important assets a company owns. It usually makes up a large proportion of the current assets, and its level will have a significant effect on the rate of return earned by the firm.

The ideal situation is to immediately sell the merchandise that has just been bought or made. In the ideal case, the investment in inventory awaiting sale is minimized—at zero. Unfortunately, the ideal situation is seldom found, because of the leads and lags between purchases or production and sales. That is, most firms must stock inventory well in advance of selling it. Moreover, in most retail businesses there must be a supply sufficient to attract customers. Yet, if a firm carries too large an inventory, it will incur excessive **inventory carrying costs.** There are costs related to carrying inventory in a manufacturing firm also, but, in addition, failure to have sufficient inventory of raw materials can result in production delays, idle workers, and dissatisfied customers. Thus, there has been considerable research in the area of inventory control.

The Problem

There are three basic kinds of costs associated with inventory: the costs of ordering and receiving inventory items; the costs of having inventory on hand; and the costs of *not having enough* inventory. Examples of specific costs in each of these categories appear in Exhibit 16-3.

Exhibit 16-3

Costs of Ordering (including Receiving)

1. Processing the order
2. Forms used
3. Time spent (opportunity cost)
4. Order follow-up time
5. Unloading and inspection

Costs of Carrying Inventory

1. Cost of capital on investment
2. Space used
3. Wages of personnel in storage section
4. Personal property taxes
5. Fire and theft insurance
6. Clerical costs
7. Risks of obsolescence and deterioration

Costs of Not Having Enough Inventory

1. Lost contribution margin from sales
   (a) Particular sales are lost because customers could not get what they wanted.
   (b) Later sales may be lost because the dissatisfied customers do not return and other customers may not come because of word-of-mouth notification that your selection is inadequate.
2. Bottlenecks in production because of the lack of one material.

We are seeking an inventory policy that will minimize total costs. A major difficulty is that the three types of costs are not independent. The more you order at one time, the lower the ordering costs. But the more you order, the higher is your average inventory, thus increasing the carrying costs. On the other hand, the higher your average inventory, the less likely you are to lose sales (incur opportunity costs).

Only incremental costs are relevant in determining the desired level of inventory. Hence, in any particular situation one or more of the costs listed in Exhibit 16-3 may not be relevant to the solution of the cost minimization problem. For example, if a firm has large amounts of space for which there are no alternative uses, there is no incremental storage cost. If insurance premiums are based on the quantity of goods carried, they are relevant; if the premium is a flat amount no matter how much inventory is carried (unlikely, but possible), it is irrelevant. The only costs to be considered are those that will change with the level of inventory.

Determining the costs of carrying too little inventory, called **stockout costs,** can be very difficult. These costs are opportunity costs and do not normally appear in accounting records. For this reason, such costs may be inadvertently ignored, or their significance downplayed, even though such costs are as real as those that are recorded and can, in a given situation, be far greater than recorded costs. When goods have a relatively high contribution margin, the cost of stockouts could well exceed, by several times, the total costs associated with carrying inventory sufficient to ensure against stockouts.

We shall deal with the problem of minimizing costs in two stages: (1) the manager must determine *when* to order, that is, how low to allow inventory to fall before ordering a new supply; and (2) the manager must determine *how much* to order at a time. Ordering only as much as you need and at exactly the right time will minimize costs.

When to Order—The Reorder Point

How low should we allow inventory to fall before ordering more? The answer to this question is called the **reorder point** and can be expressed either in units or dollars. In determining the reorder point, we are trying to minimize the total costs of being out of stock when the item is needed for production or sale, and the cost of carrying the inventory.

The reorder point depends on two things: the amount of inventory that can be expected to be used or sold between the times of placing the order and receiving the new stock; and **safety stock.** Safety stock is the quantity of inventory that serves as a cushion in case the order comes in late or use is greater than normal from the time the order is placed to the time it is received.

The period of time between placing an order and its receipt is called **lead time.** The lead time in days multiplied by the expected daily use of inventory is one component of the reorder point; the other is the safety stock. Suppose it takes ten days to receive an order, daily use of the part is 20 units, and no safety stock is provided. The reorder point is 200 units (20 units × 10 days). *If* your predictions are accurate, you will not run out of inventory. As you use the last unit, the new units will have just come in. If the manager believes that a safety stock of 100 units is desirable, the reorder point will be set at 300 units (200 + 100). Then, if the order arrives late, or there is an unexpected need for more than 20 units on one or more days, there will be enough stock to last until the order is received. The behavior of inventory for this situation is depicted in Figure 16-2. It is assumed in that graph that 800 units are ordered at a time.

In some cases, expected daily use will be computed by reference to annual use and the number of working days during a year. Suppose that records reveal the annual use to be $60,000 (at cost), that there are 200 working days in the year, that lead time is 15 working days, and a safety stock of $5,000 is desired. The reorder point in dollars would be $9,500, computed in the following manner:

$$\begin{array}{c} \text{Inventory} \\ \text{reorder} \\ \text{point} \end{array} = \begin{array}{c} \text{safety} \\ \text{stock} \end{array} + \left(\begin{array}{c} \text{daily} \\ \text{use} \end{array} \times \begin{array}{c} \text{lead} \\ \text{time} \end{array} \right)$$

Estimating average daily use as $300 ($60,000 annual use divided by 200 working days), and considering the 15-day lead time and the safety stock, the reorder point is $9,500:

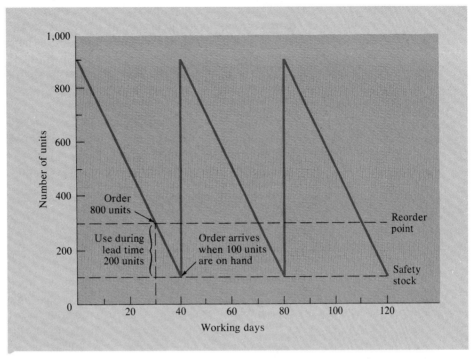

FIGURE 16-2   Behavior of Inventory Level

$$\begin{array}{l} \text{Inventory} \\ \text{reorder} \\ \text{point} \end{array} = \$5,000 + (\$300 \times 15)$$

$$= \$9,500$$

Determining Safety Stock

One of the most critical aspects of inventory management is deciding on the safety-stock level. The costs of not having enough inventory are most closely related to the amount of safety stock carried.

Safety stock is required because two factors are uncertain: lead time and use during the lead time. If both factors were known, there would be no reason to carry safety stock. Suppose that normal lead time is 10 days but can be as long as 15 days. Suppose that average daily use is $300 but can be as high as $420. Based only on the averages, the reorder point before consideration of safety stock is $3,000 (10 days × $300). But using the extreme possibilities for lead time and daily use, the computed reorder point is $6,300 (15 days × $420). If we reorder when inventory is $6,300, we are virtually certain to never run out. But the cost of carrying so much inventory might be prohibitive. Moreover, while we might expect occasionally to experience 15-day lead time or daily use of $420, it is unlikely that both would be encountered at the same time. Hence, a compromise is in order. We would select a reorder point between $3,000 (no safety stock) and $6,300 ($3,300 safety stock). To arrive at a compromise, a manager might investigate not only how *often* the lead time exceeds ten days and daily use exceeds $3,000, but also the importance of the item in the sales or production picture. For example, a higher safety stock is warranted for a high-volume, high-contribution-margin item. Similarly, a higher safety-stock level would be set for a part used in several of the firm's major products than for one used in only a few, slow-moving products.

In practice, detailed analyses might be made for only a few items of especial importance. Low-cost, nonessential items might be given reorder points based solely on the intuition of an experienced manager. It can be very expensive to make extended studies of the flows of inventory items. Extensive analysis should not be undertaken unless the potential benefits exceed the investigative costs.

How Much to Order—
The Economic Order Quantity

The answer to the question "how much to order at a time?" is called the **economic order quantity (EOQ)**. (The question is often stated in terms of how often an order should be placed.) Our examples use firms that do not manufacture the item but order it from a supplier. The analysis would be the same if the item were produced internally, but the term *economic lot size* would be used.

In determining how much to order at a time, the goal is to minimize the sum of the costs of ordering and the costs of carrying inventory. Suppose that a firm uses 12,000 units of product during a year. ("Uses" can mean either sells or uses in some other way. Supplies and raw materials are used, but not "sold" in the usual sense.) The firm has estimated incremental costs of carrying inventory to be $0.60 per unit per year. The incremental cost of placing an order has been determined to be $250 (including incremental clerical costs, forms, data processing, delivery, etc.).[1] If use is even throughout the year, we can prepare a schedule showing how ordering costs and carrying costs would behave as the number of orders changes. The assumption that use is even throughout the year is critical to the EOQ model. If use varies from month to month or week to week, the model will not give the correct solution.

The cost of carrying inventory is based on the average number of units held *over and above safety stock*. (The cost of carrying safety stock should be excluded because it is the same under all alternative ordering schemes.) Since we have relatively even use throughout the year, the average inventory over the safety stock will be one half of the order size, as can be seen by considering the possible inventory levels. The highest level occurs when an order has just been received; inventory equals safety stock plus the order size. The lowest point occurs just prior to the receipt of the order, when inventory equals safety stock.

Carrying costs are variable with the level of inventory, so the incremental carrying costs are the cost per unit per year multiplied by the average number of units in inventory above the safety-stock level. The costs for our example are shown in Exhibit

---

[1] If we were dealing with a manufactured item, the costs to be considered would be those of setting up to make a batch of the product (for example, changing dies, and idle time during the changeover).

16-4. The EOQ is 3,000 units ordered four times a year. When solving for EOQ in this way, you know you have reached the answer when the total cost begins to rise after having fallen.

Exhibit 16-4
Determination of EOQ

(a)	(b)	(c)	(d)	(e)	(f)
			Annual	Annual	Total
Number of	Number of	Average	Ordering	Carrying	Annual
Orders	Units Ordered	Inventory	Costs	Costs	Costs
per Year	12,000/(a)	(b)/2	$250 × (a)	$0.60 × (c)	(d) + (e)
1	12,000	6,000	$ 250	$3,600	$3,850
2	6,000	3,000	500	1,800	2,300
3	4,000	2,000	750	1,200	1,950
4	3,000	1,500	1,000	900	1,900
5	2,400	1,200	1,250	720	1,970

Figure 16-3 shows the behavior of each element of cost and total cost as the number of orders increases. The total cost does not change very much over a fairly wide range. In the example, the costs of ordering three, four, and five times per year are fairly close together. This phenomenon occurs because one component of cost is rising while the other is falling.

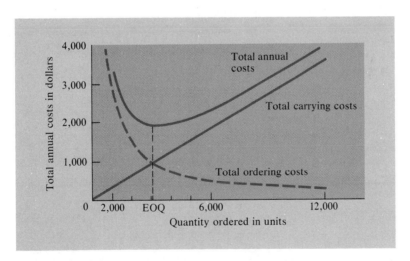

FIGURE 16-3   Behavior of Inventory Costs

We can also approach the problem by examining the costs based on the number of units ordered at a time. Exhibit 16-4 shows the costs of ordering 12,000, 6,000, 4,000, 3,000, and 2,400 units at a time. We add 3,500 units and 2,800 units and determine the results, which are shown in Exhibit 16-5. The number of orders per year is not even for either alternative; this means that you might order three times in one year, four times the next year. The ordering cost computed based on fractional orders is an average annual ordering cost, not the cost to order in any one particular year. Neither of the order sizes in Exhibit 16-5 produces a more economical result than the one produced with an order size of 3,000 units as shown in Exhibit 16-4.

Exhibit 16-5
Annual Costs of Ordering and Carrying
for Order Sizes of 3,500 and 2,800 Units

(a)	(b)	(c)	(d)	(e)	(f)
			Average		Average
	Number of		Annual	Annual	Annual
Number of	Orders	Average	Ordering	Carrying	Total
Units	per Year	Inventory	Costs	Costs	Costs
Ordered	12,000/(a)	(a)/2	$250 × (b)	$0.60 × (c)	(d) + (e)
3,500	3.43	1,750	$ 857.50	$1,050	$1,907.50
2,800	4.29	1,400	1,072.50	840	1,912.50

There is a formula which is used to determine the lowest possible cost. The exact EOQ is given by:

$$EOQ = \sqrt{\frac{2CD}{k}}$$

where

C = the incremental order cost;
D = the number of units used in a year;
k = the annual carrying cost per unit.

Applying the formula to the example gives:

$$EOQ = \sqrt{\frac{2 \times \$250 \times 12,000}{\$0.60}}$$

= 3,162 units (rounded)
or 3.8 orders per year (12,000/3,162)

Total costs at this order quantity would be:

Order costs (3.8 × $250)	$ 950.00
Carrying costs [$0.60 × (3,162/2)]	948.60
Total cost	$1,898.60

Note that the difference in cost between the exact EOQ and the cost based on ordering 3,000 units at a time is only $1.40 per year.

The formula can be used to find the exact EOQ when data about the use of the product are given in units. In some situations, however, use of the product is more easily determined in dollars and carrying costs more easily stated as a percentage of dollar costs. In such cases, another technique is available for determining EOQ stated in dollars of inventory rather than in units. The method is no different from the one illustrated earlier, but it applies in situations in which it may not be feasible to compute the necessary data per unit.

Consider the task of a manager in a hardware store, who wants to determine an economic order quantity but does not wish to keep track of individual items such as screws and nails of various sizes. Instead, he may wish to order a batch of various sizes when the dollar amount of his inventory reaches a reorder point. We shall use the data from the earlier example, but express the annual use of the item in dollars, assuming an average unit cost of $4. Thus, the annual use becomes $48,000 (12,000 × $4). Carrying costs are now 15% of cost ($0.60/$4). In Exhibit 16-6 only dollar amounts are used, but the ordering and carrying costs are exactly the same as those computed in Exhibit 16-4.

Exhibit 16-6
Determination of EOQ
(In Dollars)

(a)	(b)	(c)	(d)	(e)	(f)
	Dollar Amount		Annual	Annual	Annual
Number of	Ordered	Average	Ordering	Carrying	Total
Orders	at Cost	Inventory	Costs	Costs	Costs
per Year	$48,000/(a)	(b)/2	$250 × (a)	15% × (c)	(d) + (e)
1	$48,000	$24,000	$ 250	$3,600	$3,850
2	24,000	12,000	500	1,800	2,300
3	16,000	8,000	750	1,200	1,950
4	12,000	6,000	1,000	900	1,900
5	9,600	4,800	1,250	720	1,970

LINEAR PROGRAMMING

In Chapter 5 we noted that profits are maximized when the firm makes the combination of products that maximizes the contribution margin per unit of the fixed resource. In the example given on page 159, only one resource was fixed, machine-hours available. It is more likely that several resources will be fixed and that there will be many products from among which to choose. Often there is also a constraint on the production of alternative products because it is unlikely that very large quantities of any single product can be sold at the same prices as smaller quantities.

When several constraints are present and several products can be manufactured, **linear programming** can be used to determine the combination of products that will maximize profits. Linear programming can also be used to find the combination of input factors that minimizes the cost of performing a certain activity. A cattle feeder can determine the least-cost method of mixing various feeds to provide a specific level of nourishment for the cattle. Or, a firm with several factories and warehouses can determine the least-cost method of moving the required quantities of finished product from the factories to the warehouses.

The mathematics involved in linear programming is complex and will not be dealt with in this book. You should be able to recognize the kinds of problems that can be solved with linear programming, understand the formulation of the problem, and see what is being done when the problem is solved.

Essentially, linear programming is the solving of a system of simultaneous linear equations that include an **objective function** specifying what is to be maximized (usually contribution margin) or minimized (usually cost). The rest of the equations state the **constraints.**

A firm makes two products, X and Y. Both products require time in two production departments, the Assembly Department and the Finishing Department. Data on the two products are as follows:

	X	Y
Hours required in Assembly Department	2	4
Hours required in Finishing Department	3	2
Total hours required	5	6
Variable cost per hour, both departments, labor and overhead	$ 5	$ 5
Total variable labor and overhead	$25	$ 30
Materials	15	30
Total variable cost	$40	$ 60
Selling price	$65	$100
Contribution margin	$25	$ 40

Each week, 100 hours are available in the Assembly Department, and 90 hours in the Finishing Department. Using these data we can formulate the linear program in the following steps.

Step 1.   Formulate the objective function, which in this case is to maximize total contribution margin per week.

$$\text{Maximize: contribution margin} = \$25X + \$40Y$$

where X and Y stand for the numbers of units of each product that will be produced.

Step 2.   Formulate the constraints as inequalities.

$$2X + 4Y \leq 100$$

$$3X + 2Y \leq 90$$

Each inequality describes the constraint of available time in a department. The first one states that the number of units of X multiplied by 2 (hours per unit of X assembled), plus the number of units of Y multiplied by 4 (hours per unit of Y assembled), cannot exceed (must be equal to or less than) 100, which is the available capacity of the Assembly Department. The second inequality states that the number of units of X multiplied by 3, plus the number of units of Y multiplied by 2 cannot exceed 90, the number of hours available in the Finishing Department.

Two other constraints are required but may not seem obvious at first glance. They are "nonnegativity" constraints.

$$X \geq 0$$

$$Y \geq 0$$

The reason for these constraints is that if they were not introduced it would be possible, mathematically, to arrive at a solution that represented, in effect, negative production.

We can now show the entire set of equations and inequalities that would be used if we were going to solve the problem using mathematical techniques.

$$\text{Maximize: contribution margin} = \$25X + \$40Y$$

Subject to the constraints:

$$2X + 4Y \leq 100$$

$$3X + 2Y \leq \ 90$$

$$X \qquad\ \geq\ \ 0$$

$$Y \geq\ \ 0$$

Step 3. Draw the lines representing constraints on a graph. The constraints on the capacities of the two departments are shown in Figure 16-4. The nonnegativity constraints are implicit because we show only the upper right-hand side of the graph, where production of both products is zero or positive.

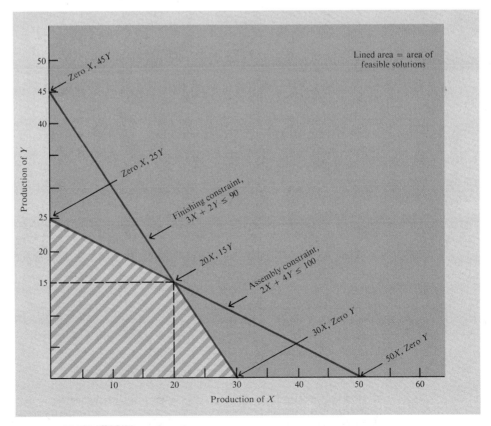

FIGURE 16-4 Graphic Solution of Constraints on Capacity

Drawing the lines representing the capacity constraints can be done intuitively. For example, the assembly constraint is $2X + 4Y \leq 100$. Thus, if only product X is made, maximum production is 50 units, which is $100/2$. If only Y is made, maximum production is 25 units, which is $100/4$. Hence, the points on the axes are determined and the line is drawn to connect them. Each point on the line represents a possible combination of production.

For example, assembling 30 units of X would require 60 hours of assembly time. There would be 40 hours left $(100 - 60)$ to assemble units of Y. In that time, 10 units of Y could be assembled. Notice on the graph that the point $30X$, $10Y$ is not inside the shaded area, the area of feasible, possible solutions. Though the firm can *assemble* that combination of units, it cannot *finish* that combination because the point $30X$, $10Y$ lies above the line representing the Finishing Department constraint. All points within the area of feasible solutions are achievable combinations of production, all points outside the area are unachievable.

Step 4.   Determine the contribution margin at all of the corners in the area of feasible solutions. In linear programming an optimal solution always occurs at a corner, an intersection of two lines. The axes are considered to be lines.[2]

Corner		Production		Contribution Margin		Total Contribution Margin
X	Y	X	Y	X	Y	
0	0	0	0	0	0	0
30	0	30	0	$750	0	$750
20	15	20	15	$500	$600	$1,100
0	25	0	25	0	$1,000	$1,000

The corner $20X$, $15Y$ produces the best solution.

In certain cases it is possible to solve for the intersections of constraints using simultaneous equations.[3] This enables you to find the intersection of two constraints without having to draw an accurate graph. Using the illustration in the text, we turn the inequalities into equations:

$$(1) \ 2X + 4Y = 100$$

$$(2) \ 3X + 2Y = \ \ 90$$

Multiplying equation (2) by 2 and subtracting equation (1) we obtain:

$$4X = 80$$

$$X = 20$$

Substituting 20 for X in equation (1) gives:

$$40 + 4Y = 100$$

$$4Y = \ \ 60$$

$$Y = \ \ 15$$

[2]There may be other solutions that also yield the best possible result, but none yields a better result than is achieved at an intersection.

[3]The most widely used technique for solving large linear programming problems is called the *simplex method*. It requires finding solutions to a set of simultaneous equations until the optimal solution is found.

This approach is helpful in some cases, but the introduction of additional constraints warrants the use of the more complex approach.

Many other types of constraints are possible. Figure 16-5 shows the graph when the sales of product X are assumed to be limited to 16 units per week because of market conditions. The formerly optimal solution of $20X$, $15Y$ is no longer feasible. Two new corners have been created, $16X$, zero Y; and $16X$, $17Y$. Clearly, $16X$ and zero Y is less desirable than $16X$ and $17Y$. The question is now whether $16X$, $17Y$ is better than zero X, $25Y$, which was the second best solution in the original problem. At $16X$, $17Y$, total contribution margin per week is $1,080 [($25 \times 16) + ($40 \times 17)]$. This is better than the $1,000 that would be earned producing only 25 units of Y.

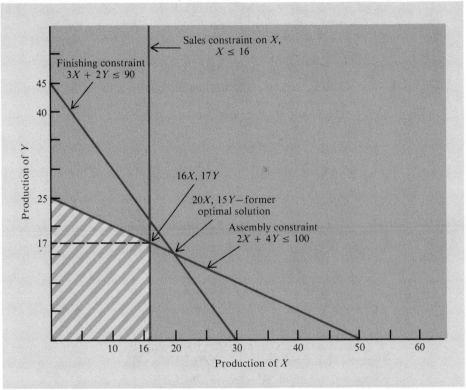

FIGURE 16-5 Linear Programming: Graphic Solution of Constraints on Capacity and on Sales of X

The constraint of the Finishing Department is no longer critical. It now lies completely outside the area of feasible solutions and therefore the time in the Finishing Department will not be fully utilized. The Finishing Department will have eight hours of unused capacity because 16 units of X and 17 of Y can be finished in 82 hours.

$$3X + 2Y \leqq 90$$
$$3 \times 16 = 48$$
$$2 \times 17 = \underline{34}$$
$$\text{Total} \qquad 82$$

Management would consider reducing the available capacity of the finishing department if it expected the constraint on sales of X to continue and if there would be savings in cost accompanying a reduction in capacity. Linear programming does not consider fixed costs, but in a situation like the one described, management should consider the possibility of reducing capacity.

Sensitivity Analysis

Sensitivity analysis, the testing of a solution to see how much it would change if one or more of the variables were to change, is an important part of decision making. Let us consider the original situation in which there was no constraint on the sales of product X. The manager of the firm might expect the price of product X to fall, which would lower its contribution margin. Total contribution margin would also fall so long as the firm stayed with its original plan to produce 20 units of X and 15 of Y. At some point the drop in contribution margin would make it more profitable for the firm to produce 25 units of Y, none of X, than to continue with the original plan.

The manager is interested in knowing how far the contribution margin of product X would have to fall before he should stop producing it. He can make that determination in the following way. If he produces 25 units of Y, none of X, the firm will earn $1,000 contribution margin per week. Therefore, when the total contribution margin from producing 20 units of X and 15 of Y drops to $1,000 he would be indifferent between the two mixes.[4] Total contribution margin at the optimal solution is now $1,000, which is $100 more than that earned if 25 units of Y are produced. Therefore, if the contribution margin from X drops by more than $100, when 20 units of X are made, it would pay the firm to stop producing X. Because 20 units are being produced, a drop of more than $5 per unit ($100/20) would make it more profitable to produce only 25 units of Y. A $5 drop would put contribution margin for a unit of X at $20.

We can also solve this problem using the following equation, where C equals the contribution margin of X per unit that would make the firm indifferent between producing $20X$, $15Y$ and zero X, $25Y$.

$$\$40 \times 25 = (\$40 \times 15) + (C \times 20)$$

This equation says simply that when contribution margin per week from producing 25 units of Y, none of X, equals that earned from producing 15 units of Y, 20 of X, the manager is indifferent. Solving for C,

$$\$1,000 = \$600 + (C \times 20)$$
$$\$400 = C \times 20$$
$$C = \$20$$

Consequently, if the contribution margin per unit of product X went below $20, the firm would stop producing X and devote its facilities solely to making Y.

Similarly, a rise in the price and contribution margin per unit of Y would tend to make the firm more likely to stop producing X and produce more of Y. The equation below states that when the contribution margin of 25 units of Y equals that of 15 units of Y plus 20 units of X, the firm would earn the same with either production mix. C represents contribution margin per unit of Y.

---

[4] In fact, any combination of production along the line representing assembly capacity, from 20 X, 15 Y down to zero X, 25 Y would give the same total contribution margin per week.

$$C \times 25 = (C \times 15) + (\$25 \times 20)$$
$$C \times 25 = (C \times 15) + \$500$$
$$C \times 10 = \$500$$
$$C = \$50$$

If contribution margin of product Y goes above \$50 per unit, the firm will earn more total contribution margin producing $25Y$, zero X, than $15Y$, $20X$.

Sensitivity analysis is essentially the repetitive performance of calculations that differ only in the values used for some of the variables. The increased availability of computers to individual managers has significantly reduced the time required for such analysis.

Shadow Prices

A manager who has solved a linear programming problem might wish to know whether it would be beneficial to add capacity in a particular department. He or she would be interested in the value of adding, say, an hour per week of assembly time. The value of adding an additional hour of capacity is the additional contribution margin that could be earned. This amount is called the **shadow price** of the resource.[5]

A shadow price is an opportunity cost—the cost of not having an additional unit of capacity. It can also be interpreted as the value of the last hour, the amount of contribution margin that would be *lost* if the firm had one hour fewer than it actually does have.

We shall calculate the shadow price of the assembly constraint using our original illustration in which there was no constraint on the sales of product X. To make it easier to show graphically, we shall add 8 hours of capacity to the Assembly Department, rather than 1 hour. Figure 16-6 (page 664) shows the new assembly constraint. It also shows the former optimal solution, where the assembly constraint and finishing constraint lines intersected when capacity in the Assembly Department was 100 hours per week. Notice that the new corner, $18X$, $18Y$ shows the firm making fewer units of X than before, but more units of Y. Because the contribution margin of Y is higher than that of X the company would be willing to give up two units of X $(20-18)$ to add three units of Y $(18-15)$.

Checking the new corners for the optimal solution, we have

Corner		Contribution Margin		Total Contribution
X	Y	X	Y	Margin
18	18	$450	$ 720	$1,170
0	27	0	$1,080	1,080

The new optimal solution of $18X$, $18Y$ has total contribution margin of \$1,170 per week. That is \$70 higher than the \$1,100 earned under the optimal solution of $20X$,

---

[5]Stated generally, a shadow price is the value of being able to relax any constraint by one unit. A unit could be an hour, or it could be a unit of product. For example, in the illustration in which sales of X were limited to 16 units per week, a shadow price could be computed for that constraint. It would be the difference between contribution margin at $16X$, $17Y$ and at the optimal solution if 17 units of X could be sold.

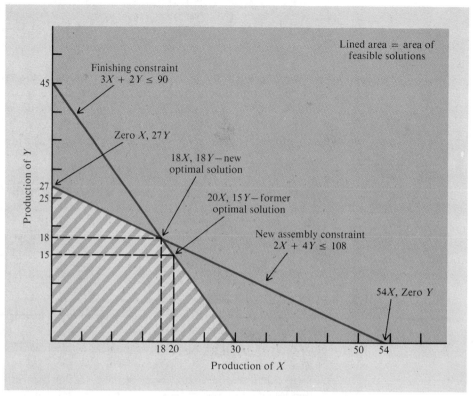

FIGURE 16-6 Linear Programming: Graphic Solution of Increased Assembly Capacity

15Y when the Assembly Department had 100 available hours. Therefore the firm would be willing to pay up to $70 per week to get an additional 8 hours of assembly capacity.

The shadow price is $8.75, which is $70/8 hours. If we had used 101 hours, we would have had contribution margin of $1,108.75. We would also have had a noninteger solution, with fractional units of both products being made. In linear programming, capacity is fixed for the planning period (a week, day, month, or year). In the long run the firm can add to capacity or reduce it. Shadow prices give an idea of the value of adding capacity and are important information for long-run planning.

SUMMARY

The use of statistical decision theory enables a manager to incorporate the effects of uncertainty about future results into his or her analysis. Inventory control models provide more rational ways of evaluating inventory policy than do guesses and intuitive methods. Linear programming is a useful tool when a manager must decide how best to use existing resources.

Much of the information needed for using these techniques is supplied by the managerial accountant. Therefore, he or she must be aware of the objectives and information requirements of such techniques. The managerial accountant will sometimes have to assist in formulating the problem and must therefore be aware of the capabilities and limitations of the techniques available.

KEY TERMS

decision tree
economic order quantity
expected value
inventory carrying costs
lead time
linear programming

payoff table
reorder point
safety stock
shadow price
stockout costs
value of perfect information

KEY FORMULAS

$$\text{Economic order quantity} = \sqrt{\frac{2(\text{incremental order cost})(\text{no. of units used in a year})}{\text{annual carrying cost per unit}}}$$

Inventory reorder point = safety stock + (daily use × lead time)

REVIEW PROBLEM—EXPECTED VALUES

In March, Grauger Company experienced an unfavorable cost variance of $2,000. Based on experience and judgment, the production manager believes that there is a 40% probability of the variance being due to random causes and therefore not continuing. There is a 60% probability that there is some difficulty in the production process and that the variance will continue at $2,000 per month for the next two months. Investigating the variance would cost $800. If the variance is investigated and something is wrong with the process, there is a 70% probability that corrective action could be taken, a 30% probability that nothing can be done.

Required: Determine the expected costs of investigating and of not investigating the variance.

Answer to Review Problem

1.

Event	Cost	Probability	Expected Value
	Expected Cost of Investigating		
Variance is random and will not continue	$ 800	.40	$ 320
Variance is caused by problem in process that can be corrected	$ 800	.42[a]	336
Variance is caused by problem that cannot be corrected	$4800	.18[b]	864
Expected cost of investigating		1.00	$1,520

[a] 60% × 70%
[b] 60% × 30%

2.

Expected Cost of Not Investigating

Event	Cost	Probability	Expected Value
Variance is random	0	.40	0
Variance is caused by problem in process and will continue	$4000	.60	$2,400
Expected cost of not investigating		1.00	$2,400

The variance should be investigated because the expected cost to investigate is less than that of not investigating.

REVIEW PROBLEM—INVENTORY CONTROL

The following data apply to one of the products of Tebbetts Company.

Annual use	12,000 units
Annual carrying cost	$0.80 per unit
Order cost	$300 per order
Safety stock	500 units

There are 200 working days per year and the lead time is 12 days.

Required
1. Determine the reorder point.
2. Determine the total annual cost of ordering (a) twice a year, (b) three times a year, (c) four times a year, and (d) five times a year.

Answer to Review Problem

Safety stock	500			
Use during lead time	720 12 × (12,000/200)			
Reorder point	1,220			

	(a)	(b)	(c)	(d)
1. Orders per year	2	3	4	5
2. Order cost at $300 each	$ 600	$ 900	$1,200	$1,500
3. Quantity ordered 12,000/orders per year	6,000	4,000	3,000	2,400
4. Average inventory (quantity ordered/2)	3,000	2,000	1,500	1,200
5. Carrying cost (average inventory × $0.80)	$2,400	$1,600	$1,200	$ 960
6. Total cost (order cost + carrying cost)	$3,000	$2,500	$2,400	$2,460

The lowest cost is achieved by ordering 3,000 units four times per year. In fact, in this case the exact EOQ is 3,000 units. We can tell this because the carrying costs and order costs are exactly the same, $1,200. The lowest total cost is achieved when carrying costs and order costs are both the same. We can verify this fact by using the EOQ formula.

$$\text{EOQ} = \sqrt{\frac{2 \times \$300 \times 12,000}{\$0.80}} = \sqrt{\frac{\$7,200,000}{\$0.80}} = \sqrt{9,000,000} = 3,000 \text{ units}$$

ASSIGNMENT MATERIAL

Questions for discussion

16-1 Optimum order size—changing conditions   Explain the effect that each of the following would tend to have on the optimum order size for product X at Company A.
  (a)   Leading banks have announced a reduction in the prime interest rate.
  (b)   The selling price of product X declines with no change in its purchase cost.
  (c)   The company moves to a high-crime, inner-city area.
  (d)   The city in which Company A is located increases the personal property tax rate.
  (e)   There is a substantial increase in the demand for product X.
  (f)   The company decides to change from the straight-line method of depreciating its warehouse to the sum-of-the-years'-digits method.

16-2 Reorder point   Indicate how each of the following factors, considered independently, would influence your establishing the reorder point for inventory (relatively high, relatively low, or no effect). Explain.
  1.   Your company has very low fixed costs, very high variable costs (about 85% of sales).
  2.   Your product is stored in specially designed and built freezers that cost a great deal of money.
  3.   Your product is ice cream, sold from a store located in a large shopping center.
  4.   Your suppliers have seen falling profits because of intensive competition.
  5.   Your major supplier is having difficulties because two factions of its stockholders have been fighting for control.

Exercises

16-3 Inventory control   Ridley Company uses $60,000 (at cost) of a particular raw material during the year. The material is used evenly throughout the year. Order costs are $400 per order, and carrying costs for inventory are 18% of carrying value. The firm carries a safety stock of $2,000 (at cost), has a lead time of 12 days, and works 300 days per year.

Required
  1.   Determine the reorder point.
  2.   Prepare a table to determine the economic order quantity.

16-4 Variance investigation   Cole Company's controller has determined that it costs $400 to investigate a variance and that in one out of four cases investigated corrective action is possible. An unfavorable variance of $1,000 has been experienced. The production process will be changed after next month, so any savings would be only for one month if corrective action can be taken. Should the variance be investigated?

16-5 Inventory control   Using the following data, determine the economic order quantity and the reorder point for Part No. 368. Round your computations to even units and dollars.

Cost per unit	$20
Use per year	12,000 units
Carrying costs	15% of cost
Order costs	$1,000 per order
Lead time	8 days
Safety stock	800 units
Working days in a year	200

16-6 Linear programming, formulation of problem   XY Company makes two products, X and Y. Data are:

	X	Y
Selling price	$80	$100
Material requirements, pounds	2	1
Labor time, hours	2	3

Materials cost $8 per pound and the combined labor and variable overhead rate is $12 per labor hour. The company has 400 pounds of material and 500 hours of labor available. It can sell all of either product that it can make. Fixed costs are $2,000, of which $700 is depreciation. All fixed costs are unavoidable.

Required: Formulate the objective function and constraints.

16-7 Linear programming (extension of 16-6)   Refer to the previous exercise. Determine the optimal product mix.

16-8 New products—expected values and risk   The sales manager of Happy Toy Company is considering two new toys. One is a doll, the other a game. She has, on the basis of market research and experience, formulated the following table of cash flows and probabilities.

	Doll		Game	
Event	Cash Flow	Probability	Cash Flow	Probability
Big success	$40,000	.1	$76,000	.3
Fair success	32,000	.7	38,000	.4
Flop	16,000	.2	(20,000)	.3

Required
1. Determine the expected value of cash flows associated with each new toy.
2. Which one would you select, and why?

16-9 Linear programming—formulation of problem   Garson Company makes three products, A, B, and C. Their respective contribution margins are $60, $70, and $80. Each product goes through three processes: cutting, shaping, and painting. The numbers of hours required by each process for each product are as follows.

Hours Required in Each Process

Product	Cutting	Shaping	Painting
A	4	2	4
B	3	5	3
C	5	2	2

The following numbers of hours are available per month in each process: cutting, 8,000; shaping, 6,000; and painting, 4,000.

Required: Formulate the objective function and constraints to determine the optimal production policy.

16-10 Linear programming   The PQ Company makes two products. Data are:

	P	Q
Selling price	$50	$30
Variable costs	$20	$15
Labor hours required per unit:		
Grinding department	3	1
Assembly department	2	2

The firm has 900 hours of labor time available in the grinding department, 800 in the assembly department.

Required: Determine the optimal product mix.

16-11 Sensitivity analysis   The florist for whom you prepared the payoff table on page 647 is not impressed. He has decided to order 4,000 corsages per week because he does not want to be stuck with unsold goods. Because you own a share of the business, you would like him to order 8,000 per week. In an effort to show him that he is being unduly conservative, you decide to show him how low the risk is by using more pessimistic probabilities. Because you would not order 12,000 corsages, you can lump together the probabilities of selling 8,000 and 12,000. (The contribution margin from ordering 8,000 corsages is the same whether demand is 8,000 or 12,000.)

Required: Determine the expected values of ordering 8,000 corsages with the following probabilities:

Case	Demand in Units	Probability of Demand
1	4,000	.30
	8,000	.70
2	4,000	.40
	8,000	.60
3	4,000	.50
	8,000	.50

16-12 Cost structure and probabilities   The production manager of Omega Company is considering modifying one of his machines. The modification will add $10,000 per month to the cost of running the machine, but will reduce variable operating costs by $0.20 per unit produced. The modification itself costs nothing and the machine can be returned to its regular operating method at any time.

The product made on the machine has an uncertain demand; the best estimates available are as follows:

Monthly Demand	Probability
25,000	.30
40,000	.30
60,000	.30
70,000	.10

Required
1. Determine the number of units that must be produced to justify the modification.
2. Determine the expected value of making the modification. Should it be made?

16-13 Payoff table   Campus Program Company sells programs for football games. The owner of the company believes that the following data reflect the pattern of sales.

Quantity Sold (Cases)	Probability
100	.30
150	.50
200	.20

The owner is uncertain of the number of cases of programs to order. He must order one of the quantities given above. A case of programs sells for $200 and the purchase price is $100. Unsold programs are thrown away.

Required: Construct a payoff table to determine the number of cases of programs the firm should order.

16-14 Cost of investigating variances   Farnham Company's production manager has determined that it costs about $500 (incremental cost) to investigate a variance. About one in four investigations results in corrective action.

Required: Determine how high the potential savings from corrective action should be to make it worthwhile to investigate a variance.

16-15 Inventory control—sensitivity   Morton Company sells a product that has the following attributes:

Annual demand	12,000 units
Annual carrying cost per unit	$3
Order cost	$125

Required

1. Determine the EOQ using the formula. Determine the annual cost associated with this policy.
2. Suppose that the firm doubles the order quantity, halving the number of orders from the one you calculated in part 1. What is the cost of following the nonoptimal policy?

Problems

16-16 Expected values—a law firm The firm of Smith, Jones, and Jankowski has been approached by Hirt, a victim of a whiplash injury suffered in an automobile accident. He wants the firm to represent him in a court suit, with the firm's fee being one third of the total judgment given by the court.

Jankowski states that 2,000 hours would be needed to prepare and try the case, with the opportunity cost being $80 per hour. Based on experience with similar cases, he believes that the following judgments and associated probabilities are reasonable estimates on which to decide whether to accept the case.

Judgment for Hirt	Probability of Judgment
0	.40
$180,000	.20
$300,000	.30
$420,000	.10

Required: Determine whether the firm should accept the case.

16-17 Inventory control Blitzen Industries makes products in individual production runs, because all its products must go through one particular machine. Each time a new production run is set up, the firm incurs incremental costs of $800.

The cost to carry a unit of product A is $2 per year, including taxes, insurance, spoilage, and the required return on investment. Sales of product A are 12,000 units per year.

Required

1. Determine the number of times that A should be made in a year.
2. The company carries a safety stock of 300 units of A, the working year is 200 days, and production of a batch requires eight days. At what inventory level will a production run be made?

16-18 Variance investigation Edwards Company has just experienced a $3,000 unfavorable variance. The production supervisor believes that there is a 30% chance that the variance was a one-time thing and will not continue. He believes that if an investigation is made, the chance of correcting the variance is 40% and of not correcting it is 60%. It costs $800 to investigate a variance. The most that will be lost if the variance continues is $3,200.

Required: Compute the expected costs of investigating and not investigating the variance. Determine whether an investigation should be made.

16-19 Linear programming Fast Class Company makes two products, the Fast and the Class. Fasts sell for $12 and have variable costs of $5. Classes sell for $14 and have variable costs of $6. Both products are put through two processes—cutting and forming. Each unit of Fast requires two hours of cutting and four hours of forming. Each unit of Class requires three hours of cutting and two of forming. The company has available 300 hours of cutting time and 240 hours of forming time per month.

Required
1. Determine the number of Fasts and Classes that should be produced each month.
2. Determine the total contribution margin that will be earned per month.

16-20 Product selection Henson Electronics Company is trying to decide which of three products to introduce for the coming season. It is felt that only one should be brought out because the company is relatively small and needs to concentrate its promotional effort. Information about the products being considered is as follows.

	Radio	Toaster	Coffee Maker
Selling price	$22	$37	$45
Variable cost	13	20	25
Contribution margin	$ 9	$17	$20
Sales forecasts, in units, with prob-	25,000 (20%)	12,000 (10%)	15,000 (60%)
abilities in parentheses	40,000 (40%)	19,000 (25%)	20,000 (20%)
	50,000 (30%)	25,000 (50%)	20,000 (20%)
	75,000 (10%)	38,000 (15%)	

Required
1. Compute the expected values of contribution margins for the three products.
2. Which product would you select, and why?

16-21 Make or buy Walters Company manufactures ceramic figurines. Sometimes the company subcontracts production of its designs to other companies, paying a set amount per piece. The chief designer for the company has come up with a new item that most of the managers expect will be a best seller. Some of the managers are less sure, and want to be as cautious as possible.

   If Walters is to manufacture the item, it must lease some additional space and machinery at a cost of $80,000 for the coming year. The lease could not be canceled for one year. Unit variable cost would be $14 and the selling price $36. Alternatively, the company could subcontract production. A local outlet has agreed to produce the item and sell it to Walters Company at $23.

   The company's sales manager has developed the following estimates of demand and probabilities for the new figurine, using her experience with other, similar items.

Demand	Probability
7,000	.20
9,000	.30
12,000	.30
14,000	.20

Required: Determine the expected value of the profit on the figurine if Walters (a) makes it internally, and (b) subcontracts it.

16-22 **Inventory control—effects of errors in policy**   The purchasing manager of Kensington Company buys one of its principal products in batches of 2,000, basing the amount of the purchase on his personal judgment. Data for the product are:

Order cost	$800
Carrying cost, annual per unit	$2
Annual demand	20,000

Required
1. Determine the EOQ using the formula.
2. Determine the cost to the firm of not following the optimal purchasing policy. That is, determine the difference between total costs under the existing policy and under the optimal policy.
3. Determine how high the carrying costs would have to go to make the EOQ 2,000 units.
4. Determine how low order costs would have to go to support an EOQ of 2,000 units, assuming that the carrying costs are $2.

16-23 **Inventory control—determination of incremental costs**   Rankin Company currently has no stated inventory policy. The sales manager and controller have asked you to assist in preparing a policy. Two of the factors to be determined are the cost of carrying inventory and the cost of ordering. The following information pertains to the company's only product.

Cost per unit	$90
Sales per year	15,000 units
Required return on investment	15%
Insurance	$500 per year plus $1.70 per unit of average inventory
Taxes	$2 per unit of average inventory
Storage	The firm leases a warehouse that can hold 20,000 units. Rent is $1,000 per year
Costs of purchasing department:	
Salaries	$12,000 per year fixed, plus $50 per order
Forms, postage	$10 per order

In addition, each time an order is received, the company hires men from a local employment service to unload the order. On any size order, three men are hired at $30 each per day.

Required: Determine the EOQ, using the formula. Be sure to determine which costs shown above are relevant to the analysis, which are not.

16-24 **Special order decision—probabilities**   The sales manager of Schieren Company has been approached by a chain store that would like to buy 10,000 units of the firm's product. The sales manager believes that the order should be accepted because the price offered is $6 and variable costs of production are $5.

In a conversation with the production manager, the following information was developed by the sales manager: (1) Sufficient capacity exists to meet the special order. (2) Prices for materials and wage rates are expected to increase by the time the order would be manufactured, but the amounts of the increases are not certain. The best estimates of the probabilities are as follows:

New Variable Cost	Probability
$5.20	.30
5.70	.40
6.60	.30

Required
1. Determine whether the special order should be accepted based on the data given.
2. What other factors might be taken into consideration in reaching a decision?

16-25 Standard costs with fluctuations   Corman Company produces its major product under uncertain conditions. Due to differences in the quality of raw materials received from suppliers, it may take anywhere from eight to ten pounds of material to make a unit of product. The production manager believes that it is foolish to try to set standard costs for materials under present circumstances. As the controller, you are reluctant to forgo completely the opportunity to collect information that could aid in the control process; so you decide to make further investigation.

   You find that the production manager is essentially correct about the fluctuations in the amount of raw materials required. However, the quantity of materials required is eight pounds about 20% of the time, nine pounds about 70% of the time, and ten pounds only 10% of the time.

Required
1. Can standard costs for materials be developed that will aid in both control and planning?
2. What would you suggest as a standard quantity for materials?

16-26 Cost of investigating a variance   Chapman Company's production manager has been trying to decide whether a particular variable overhead variance should be investigated. The variance was $300 unfavorable this past month, and it is expected that the variance will continue at the rate of $300 for five more months if nothing is done. The estimated cost to investigate the variance is $600 and the chances are four out of five that nothing can be done to correct the variance even if its cause could be isolated. If the variance is investigated and found to be correctable, the total savings, not considering the cost of the investigation, will be $1,500 (the total cost of the variance over the next five months).

Required: Determine whether the variance should be investigated.

16-27 Expected values and utilities   The sales manager of Winston Toy Company has been studying a report prepared by an outside consultant. The company has asked the consultant to study the advisability of bringing out a new doll that would be quite different from anything else on the market. The report indicated that there was considerable variation in expectations of sales of the new doll. The consultant concluded that there was about a 60% chance of selling 50,000 dolls and a 40% chance of selling only 10,000 dolls.

   The doll would be priced at $24, with variable costs of $20. Incremental fixed costs, primarily for advertising, would be $120,000.

   The sales manager decided, on the basis of the expected value of profit, that the doll should be introduced, but the president of the firm was leery. The president said there was a good chance the doll would lose money, and the company has had too many duds in recent years. After some discussion, the president decided that losing a dollar was twice as bad as earning a dollar was good. He instructed the sales manager to prepare a new analysis incorporating his utility, although he did not call it that.

Required
1. Prepare a schedule showing the expected value of profit without consideration of the president's views.
2. Prepare a new schedule in which the president's views are incorporated. Determine whether the doll should be brought out.

16-28 Variance investigation   Richter Company has experienced an unfavorable variance of $2,000 in May. The production manager found, from past data, that 30% of the time a variance of this size is experienced there is nothing wrong with the process and the variance stops. When there is a problem with the process, 60% of the time the variance continues for two additional months, at $2,000 per month, and 40% of the time it continues for three additional months, also at $2,000 per month.

Investigating the variance would cost $800. If there is a problem with the production process, it can be corrected 40% of the time. The other 60% of the time nothing can be done. The 40% and 60% probabilities apply both to variances that would continue for two additional months and to those that would continue for three additional months. Once the investigation has been carried out, if it has been determined that the cause of the variance can be corrected, correcting it costs an additional $600.

Required
1. Determine the expected cost of not investigating the variance.
2. Determine the expected cost of investigating the variance.

16-29 Capital budgeting probabilities   The following estimates and probabilities have been prepared by the production manager of Hector Company. They relate to a proposed $60,000 investment in a machine that will reduce the cost of materials being processed by the firm. The cost of capital is 16%. Ignore taxes.

Annual Cash Savings		Useful Life	
Event	Probability	Event	Probability
$20,000	.30	9 years	.40
14,000	.30	8 years	.40
12,000	.40	6 years	.20

Required
1. Compute the expected values of annual cash savings and useful life. Determine whether the machine should be purchased.
2. The production manager wishes to see whether the machine would be a good investment if each of his most pessimistic estimates, but not both at the same time, came true. Determine whether the investment would be desirable if (a) the useful life is the expected value computed in part 1, and annual cash flows are only $12,000; (b) the annual cash flows are equal to the expected value computed in part 1, and the useful life is only six years.

16-30 Expected values   The managers of Hawkins Company are trying to decide how to operate in the coming year. The company rents a machine that performs essential operations on the product; the rental period is one year. The product sells for $10 per unit and has variable costs of $1.

There are three machines available; operating and other data are summarized below.

Machine	Productive Capacity	Annual Rental
Standard	11,000 units	$50,000
DeLuxe	12,000	54,000
Super	13,000	55,500

The sales forecast for the coming year has been based on the 10,000 units sold the prior year; it is expected that demand for the product will increase, but the size of the increase is uncertain. The best estimates are as follows:

Sales in Units	Probability
11,000	.30
12,000	.50
13,000	.20

Required: Determine the best course of action for the company to take and defend your answer.

16-31 Inventory control—quantity discounts   Alexander Company buys one of its principal products from Zephyr Company in batches of 2,000. The product costs Alexander $10 and annual demand is 20,000 units. Annual carrying costs are $1.60 per unit, which includes a required rate of return of 10% (all other carrying costs are related to units, not cost), and incremental ordering costs are $160 per order. The current batch size is the EOQ for this product.

Zephyr sells this product only to Alexander and has to set up a production run every time an order is received. There are no carrying costs because Zephyr maintains no inventory, and setup costs are $1,000 per production run. The production manager of Zephyr asked the sales manager whether it might not be a good idea to offer Alexander a price reduction if Alexander would agree to buy half as often, and double the usual quantity each time. After some discussion, it was agreed that Alexander would be offered a $0.20 price reduction for buying in batches of 4,000 units or more.

Required
1. Compute the annual gain or loss to both Alexander and Zephyr if the price reduction is granted.
2. Suppose that Zephyr offers to supply all 20,000 units at a single time. Determine the lowest price per unit that Zephyr could charge and not reduce its income below the level it would earn supplying the product in batches of 4,000.
3. Determine whether Alexander should buy all of its annual requirements at once, at the price you computed in part 2. (Assume that Alexander would still get the $0.20 reduction if it decided to buy 4,000 units at a time.)

16-32 Payoff table   *The Evening News* is a large metropolitan newspaper. The paper is sold through dealers who are charged $0.20 per copy that they sell. Unsold copies are returned to *The News* and full credit is given. The unsold copies are sold as waste paper for $0.02 each.

The News is currently printed in daily batches of 500,000. Management is considering a change in this policy and has asked for your help. A recent study showed the following results.

Papers Returned	Percentage of Time
100,000	20%
50,000	20%
-0-	60%

The study also indicated that when 500,000 copies were all sold, there were often more papers demanded. The demand could not be met because of the limit of 500,000 copies available. The best estimates are that 25% of the time 500,000 copies are demanded, 25% of the time 550,000 are demanded, and 10% of the time 600,000 papers could be sold if they were available.

The variable cost of producing a paper is $0.10.

Required
1. Determine the best strategy for *The Evening News.*
2. Determine the value of perfect information.

16-33 Linear programming, graphical solution Salinas Furniture Company makes two types of sofas, traditional and modern. Because of their different types of construction they require different amounts of machine time and skilled labor time. The company has available, per week, 1,000 hours of skilled labor and 1,200 hours of machine time. The variable costs associated with skilled labor, including both wages and variable overhead, are $7 per hour; for machine time, the variable costs are $6 per hour. The firm can sell all of the modern sofas it can make, but only 200 traditional sofas per week.

Additional data on the two sofas are as follows:

	Traditional	Modern
Selling price	$240	$180
Material costs (the only other variable cost)	$ 80	$ 60
Labor hours required, per unit	4	2
Machine hours required, per unit	3	4

The following figure plots the above constraints:

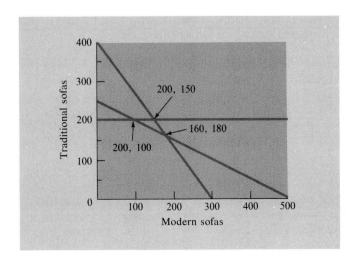

Required

1. Determine the number of each sofa that should be produced each week.
2. Assuming that the price of modern sofas remains constant, at what price for traditional sofas would the firm increase its production of traditional sofas and reduce that of modern sofas?

16-34 **Expected values—capital budgeting**   Fleming Company plans to build a factory to manufacture a new product. The product and the factory are expected to have useful lives of ten years. No salvage value is expected for any of the components of the factory. The firm's marketing research staff has studied the potential demand for the product and has provided the following information.

Expected Annual Demand	Probability of Demand
200,000 units	60%
250,000 units	40%

The firm can build a factory with capacity of either 200,000 or 250,000 units. Data on the two possible factories are given below:

Capacity	Total Cost, All Depreciable Assets	Annual Fixed Costs Requiring Cash
200,000	$1,500,000	$300,000
250,000	1,800,000	380,000

The product will sell for $5 and have variable costs of $1. The tax rate is 40% and cost of capital is 16%. Straight-line depreciation would be used for tax purposes.

Management has decided to base its decision on net present value. Whichever factory shows the greater favorable difference between the present value of the expected value of future cash flows and the investment required will be built.

Required: Prepare analyses of the expected values of future cash flows under the two investment possibilities. Determine which factory should be built.

16-35 **Expected values (AICPA adapted)**   Wing Manufacturing Company makes a chemical compound, product X, that deteriorates rapidly. Any compound left unsold at the end of the month in which the firm makes it becomes worthless. The total variable cost of manufacturing the product is $50 per pound and the selling price is $80 per pound. The demand for the product, with associated probabilities, appears below.

Monthly Demand	Probability
8,000	.25
9,000	.60
10,000	.15

The management of Wing believes that it is necessary to supply all customers who order product X. Failing to do so would result, in the managers' judgment, in losing not only sales of product X, but also sales of other products. Wing has found a company that will sell product X to it at $80 per pound, plus $10 freight per pound. The managers would like to develop a policy regarding production. Some have argued that the high cost of obtaining additional amounts of product X from the outside supplier makes it desirable to produce 10,000 pounds per month. Others have argued that it is safer to produce fewer pounds and to buy from the supplier as needed.

Required: Determine what production strategy maximizes the expected value of profit.

CHAPTER 17

STATEMENT OF CHANGES IN FINANCIAL POSITION

We have seen throughout this book that the accounting information system must serve the needs of both financial and managerial accounting. Much of the information prepared for distribution outside the firm is used, in the same or somewhat different form, by the firm's managers. For example, data from income statements and balance sheets will be used for such purposes as performance measurement and budgeting.

A third formal statement commonly used in financial accounting is the statement of changes in financial position.[1] This chapter discusses the use and development of the statement of changes in financial position in its two most common forms.

THE INTEREST IN RESOURCE FLOWS

Managers of the firm, as well as its creditors, suppliers, and stockholders, know that the profitability of current operations is but one of the factors important to survival and

---

[1]Since the publication of *Accounting Principles Board Opinion No. 19* (New York: American Institute of Certified Public Accountants, 1971), the statement of changes in financial position has been a required part of any set of financial statements purporting to show financial position and results of operations in accordance with generally accepted accounting principles.

growth. Also important are the current inflows of resources (for the moment, think of resources as cash), and the uses to which these resources are put. Managers develop cash budgets to anticipate potential deficiencies of resources for carrying out the firm's plans.

Upper-level managers in large, divisionalized firms are always concerned with whether particular divisions are generating resources for use by the firm, or are consuming them. A division that is consuming more resources than it generates could become a serious problem, and the firm's managers would want to spot such a tendency as early as possible. At times, managers will decide to seek additional resources in the form of debt or common stock; at other times, they will decide to curtail budgeted activities. In either case, the goal is to balance resources available and resources needed. *How* the managers accomplish this balancing is of interest to both creditors and investors.

Inflows of resources provide the means for repaying debts, bringing out new products, replacing worn-out equipment, etc. These inflows constitute the firm's **financing activities.** The uses of available resources, called the firm's **investing activities,** affect its future. Decisions to invest in new or replacement equipment affect the future profitability of the firm. By the same token, timely repayments of debt help to preserve the firm's credit standing and its access to additional resources. Hence the creditor's and investor's interest in the firm's resource flows: Where did the firm obtain the resources to support its current operations and its outlays for long-term investments? Is the firm making significant investments for the future?

The current year's income statement shows the current effects of *past* financing and investing activities. It shows the current revenues and expenses from past investment, the current interest on all borrowing, and the current return to stockholders. The current year-end balance sheet shows the *cumulative* financing and investing activities of the firm—assets the firm still has, the total remaining unpaid on borrowings, the accumulated stockholders' investment. A statement of changes in financial position is needed because neither of the other statements provides enough data on the firm's *current* investing and financing activities—important activities that will affect the firm's future. Though the statement is, like the others, after-the-fact or historical in nature, it provides the interested reader with further information with which to assess the decisions and performance of the firm's managers and to gain some insight into the firm's prospects.

THE FORMAL RESOURCE STATEMENT

We have already noted that both the managers of a firm and external parties are interested in the flows of resources into and out of the firm. Statements of resource flows may differ slightly depending upon how the preparers of the statements define *resources,* but the major parts and format of the statements are very similar.

Concepts of Resources

Cash is an extremely important asset and the firm cannot get along without it. But both managers and external parties recognize that cash flows alone seldom reflect all of the firm's investing and financing activities. Hence, the statement of changes in financial position often uses a concept of resources other than cash, so as to describe more fully those activities. For example, a financial manager would be concerned that temporarily available cash in excess of immediate needs be invested for short periods in highly liquid, income-producing securities such as government notes. In the view of that manager, the firm's immediately usable resources would include not only cash but also those highly liquid securities. A statement of resource flows sometimes reflects this point of view.

An even broader concept of resources is commonly found in formal statements of resource flows. Under this concept, resources are defined as **working capital** (current assets − current liabilities). Reported resource inflows (or outflows) are those transactions or events that give rise to increases (decreases) in working capital rather than cash or the combination of cash and short-term investments. There are at least two reasons to extend the concept of resources beyond cash or near-cash items.

First, because cash is of critical importance, it is not only wise to know something about what is happening to cash, but also to know about the prospects for cash flows over the near future. For the most part, current assets and liabilities are known items that will be turned into cash or require the use of cash within a year. Managers, accountants, and external users of financial statements believe that looking at flows of working capital, which encompass cash-to-be-received and cash-to-be-paid, affords a broader view of the firm's liquidity than an examination of cash alone.

A second reason for the use of the working capital concept in a statement of resource flows is that such statements usually cover relatively long time periods, such as a quarter or a year. Very short-term timing differences between making a sale and collecting cash, or purchasing inventory and paying cash, can be removed from the resource-flow picture over a longer period by using the working capital concept. (Working capital includes short-term receivables, payables, and inventory.) With longer periods of time, the importance of the timing of the actual flows of cash declines relative to the total flows of cash.

Thus, a statement of resource flows can be based on flows of cash, cash and short-term investments, working capital, or even some other concept of resources. Regardless of the concept used, items included in the definition of resources are often referred to as *funds*. For some years the statement now called the statement of changes in financial position was called the *funds flow statement* or simply the **funds statement.** You will still see the term *funds* used in many published financial statements and we use it interchangeably with *resources.*

One way in which a formal statement of resource flows may differ from a resource statement based solely on cash flows involves the reporting of transactions and events that, no matter what the concept of resources used, do not technically change resources. For example, suppose that a firm issued a 10-year note payable in a transaction to acquire machinery. Since no cash was involved, a report of the firm's cash flows would not include this transaction. And, since neither the machinery nor the 10-year note payable would affect working capital, a report of the firm's resource flows using the working capital concept would also omit this transaction. Yet acquiring machinery is obviously an investment; and issuing the note is a financing activity of the firm. So that *all* important investing and financing activities of the firm will be reported, a formal statement of resource flows will include information about significant transactions that did not technically affect resources as defined for that statement.

Categories of Resource Flows

Because the statement of changes in financial position is distributed and used outside the firm, its format and content are governed by official pronouncements on generally accepted accounting principles, the ground rules of financial accounting. Official and firm rules regarding the funds statement are few and relatively simple, and apply regardless of the concept of resources used. The statement should:

1. Have two basic parts: *resource inflows,* often called *funds provided,* and *resource outflows,* often called *funds used* or *funds applied;*
2. Identify a net flow relating to the firm's basic operating activities, such flow being called **funds** (or resources) **provided by operations,** if resources increased as a result of such activities, or *funds used for operations,* if such activities resulted in a decrease in resources;
3. Report those financing and investing activities that did not affect resources (under whatever definition is being used).

An example of the type of activity that would require reporting under the last rule is acquiring assets by issuing stock.

To meet the information needs of external parties, it is perhaps universal practice to show the relationship between the funds statement and the firm's income statement by specifically showing the net income on the funds statement. Net income is, of course, related to the flow of funds from the firm's basic operating activities. Hence, the amount of net income is, when specifically reported, included in the section of the funds statement that identifies the net operating flow as required by the second rule. Because net income is not likely to equal the operating resource flows of the firm under any of the common definitions of resources, the statement invariably includes an explanation of the differences between net income and the net resource flow from operations.

Format of the Statement

Exhibit 17-1 shows a skeleton outline of a formal statement of changes in financial position. Since a firm's normal operations are expected to produce a net inflow of resources, rather than a net outflow, the outline shows that funds were *provided by* operations (that is, that resources increased as a result of basic operating activities). Practice varies considerably when operations result in a net *outflow* of resources. Some firms will report net operating flows in the resources-provided section of the statement regardless of whether the operating flow that year is positive (an inflow) or negative (an outflow). Still others would include a net operating outflow under the resources-used section of the statement. All of these approaches are acceptable at the present time.

Exhibit 17-1
Example Company
Statement of Changes in Financial Position
for the Year 19X7

Resources provided by:		
Operations:		
Net income		XXX
Adjustments for items that affected net income but did not affect resources in the same way:		
	XXX	
	XXX	XXX
Funds provided by operations		XXX
Other sources:		
	XXX	
	XXX	XXX
Total resources provided during the year		XXX
Resources used for:		
	XXX	
	XXX	
Total resources used during the year		XXX
Net increase in resources		XXX
Other financing and investing activities:		
	XXX	
	XXX	
	XXX	

The section of the statement entitled "Adjustments for items that affected net income but did not affect resources in the same way" contains the explanation of the difference between net income and the resources flowing from operations. The content of this section depends on the concept of resources used to develop the statement. The concept of resources also determines what items will be shown as resources provided by other sources, as resources used, and as other financing and investing activities. But in most cases, it makes little difference in the nonoperating sections whether the cash or the working-capital concept of resources is used.

With this outline in mind, we shall show the development of a statement of changes in financial position under the cash concept and the working-capital concept of resources, using the same basic data in both cases.

Data for Illustration

We shall illustrate the preparation of a statement of changes in financial position with the USL Corporation, a retailing firm. Because the statement describes changes in the balance-sheet items during the period and relates directly to the income statement for the period, we have provided these financial statements for the company in Exhibits 17-2 and 17-3.

Exhibit 17-2

USL Corporation

Combined Statement of Income and Retained

Earnings for the Year 19X5

Sales		$1,000,000
Cost of goods sold:		
Beginning inventory	$100,000	
Purchases	540,000	
Cost of goods available for sale	640,000	
Less: Ending inventory	190,000	
Cost of goods sold		450,000
Gross profit		550,000
Operating expenses:		
Depreciation	56,000	
Other operating expenses	264,500	
Total operating expenses		320,500
Net income		229,500
Retained earnings at the beginning of the year		190,000
		419,500
Dividends declared and paid during the year		30,000
Retained earnings at the end of the year		$ 389,500

Exhibit 17-3

USL Corporation

Balance Sheets as of December 31

Assets	19X5	19X4	Increase (Decrease)
Current assets:			
Cash	$ 239,500	$ 360,000	($120,500)
Accounts receivable	280,000	150,000	130,000
Inventory	190,000	100,000	90,000
Total current assets	709,500	610,000	
Noncurrent assets:			
Plant and equipment, at cost	890,000	600,000	290,000
Less: Accumulated depreciation	115,000	60,000	55,000
Total noncurrent assets	775,000	540,000	
Total assets	$1,484,500	$1,150,000	
Equities			
Current liabilities:			
Accounts payable	$ 85,000	$ 55,000	30,000
Accrued expenses	50,000	5,000	45,000
Total current liabilities	135,000	60,000	
Bonds payable, due 19X9	100,000	100,000	—
Total liabilities	235,000	160,000	
Owners' equity:			
Common stock	860,000	800,000	60,000
Retained earnings	389,500	190,000	199,500
Total owners' equity	1,249,500	990,000	
Total equities	$1,484,500	$1,150,000	

RESOURCES AS CASH

From the comparative balance sheets we can see that USL's cash decreased by $120,500 during the year. Our objective is to develop a statement showing the basic sources of cash inflows and the basic purposes of cash outflows that produced this decrease.

The typical statement of changes in financial position not only identifies the major components of resource flows, but also offers a direct link to the income statement. That is, the net flow from operations begins with net income, and shows how the net flow from operations is derived from the reported amount of net income. This derivation is sometimes called a **reconciliation of net income and cash provided by operations,** and gives the content of that section of the statement entitled "adjustments."

Reconciliation of Net Income and Cash from Operations

Deriving net operating cash flow from net income is not difficult if you keep in mind the makeup of the income statement and the balance sheet. *Why* would the revenues on the income statement differ from the cash collections from customers? *Why* would the cost of goods sold and operating expenses not be the same as the cash disbursed for purchases and expenses?

Revenues Versus Cash Inflows.   The difference between sales and cash receipts has two causes. First, early in the year cash was received from customers for sales made in the prior year and included in the sales for that year's income statement. (This amount was the beginning balance in accounts receivable.) Second, late in the year, sales were made but cash will not be collected until next year. (Amounts still due at year's end from such sales constitute the accounts receivable at the end of the year.) Thus, net income reflects sales made this year regardless of the period in which cash was collected, while cash receipts would reflect cash collected this year regardless of the period in which the sales were made. *Hence, to move from the amount of net income to the cash flow for the year, we must: (1) add the accounts receivable at the beginning of the year, and (2) subtract the accounts receivable at the end of the year.* In the case of USL Corporation, we would add $150,000 and subtract $280,000, or we can simply subtract the increase of $130,000. This is the first "adjustment" on the formal statement. (You may want to look briefly now at the completed statement shown in Exhibit 17-4 on page 690.)

Cost of Sales Versus Cash Outflows.   Consider next why there would be a difference between cost of goods sold ($450,000) on the income statement and the amount of cash actually disbursed for merchandise. Two major factors create a difference.

First, the beginning and ending inventories affect cost of goods sold for the year regardless of the period in which payments for those inventory items occurred. In USL's case, the beginning inventory increased cost of goods sold by $100,000, and the ending inventory decreased cost of goods sold by $190,000. Because of these inventories, cost of goods sold this year was lower, and net income higher, by $90,000 ($190,000 − $100,000), and that amount completely disregards the timing of the cash payments for those inventories. Thus, net income reflects the effects of inventories, while cash payments for merchandise are not tied to whether the items were or are on hand. *Hence, to remove from net income the effect of inventories which have no direct relationship to cash flows, we must (1) add the beginning inventory, and (2) subtract the ending inventory.* In USL's case, we would add $100,000 and subtract $190,000, or we can simply subtract the $90,000 increase in inventory. This is the second "adjustment" in the final statement.

The second reason for a difference between the cost of goods sold and the cash outflows for merchandise is that cost of goods sold shows the purchases made this year regardless of when the purchased merchandise was paid for. From your knowledge of financial accounting you know two things: (1) Early in the year, cash was paid for purchases made in the prior year (the unpaid amounts at the end of the last year being shown as the beginning balance in accounts payable); and (2) purchases made late in the year will not be paid for until the next period (the unpaid amounts at the end of the current year being shown as the ending balance in accounts payable). Thus, cost of goods sold, as shown in this year's income statement, may be higher or lower than cash payments for merchandise, depending on the relationship between the beginning and ending balances in accounts payable. *Hence, to move from net income to the cash flow for the year, we must (1) subtract the accounts payable at the beginning of the year, and (2) add the accounts payable at the end of the year.* In the case of USL, we would subtract $55,000 and add $85,000, or we can simply add the $30,000 increase in accounts payable. This is the third "adjustment" in the completed statement.

Operating Expenses and Cash Outflows.   Finally, let us consider why the operating expenses shown on the income statement would not equal the actual cash disbursements for such expenses. One reason for a difference is well known to you. Operating expenses include depreciation, which, as you know, requires no current disbursement of cash. Depreciation expense reduced net income without having any effect on cash flows this period. *Hence, to remove from net income the effect of depreciation expense, we must add the amount of depreciation* (in USL's case, $56,000) *to reported net income.* This is the fourth "adjustment" on the formal statement.

There is a second set of reasons for the difference between operating expenses and the cash disbursements for such expenses. In the early part of the year cash will be paid to liquidate liabilities for expenses of the prior year (called accrued expenses), while in the latter part of the year expenses will be incurred for which cash will not be disbursed until next year. Thus, net income for the current period has been reduced by this year's expenses regardless of the year in which the expenses were paid for, while disbursements for the year cover cash payments for expense items regardless of the year in which the expense is incurred. *Hence, to move from net income to the cash flow for the year, we must (1) subtract the accrued expenses at the beginning of the year, and (2) add the expenses accrued but unpaid at the end of the year.* In the case of USL, we would subtract $5,000 and add $50,000, or we could simply add $45,000. This final "adjustment" completes the explanation of the difference between USL's net income and its cash flow from operations, and the remainder of the funds statement can be prepared.[2]

---

[2]Though a given practical situation may involve many adjustments other than those explained in detail in this chapter, the additional adjustments can be determined by following the same reasoning processes as

Nonoperating Flows

Look again at the comparative balance sheets in Exhibit 17-3. Almost every item on the balance sheet showed a change between the two years. We know that the changes in accounts payable, accounts receivable, inventory, accrued expenses, and part of the change in accumulated depreciation relate to operations. What brought about the other changes? They must be related to other financing and investing activities of the firm. By applying a little common sense, we can reach tentative conclusions about the nature of those other activities, and then, with a few inquiries, we can complete the funds statement.

Below is a summary of the changes in balance-sheet items other than those related to normal operations:

Item	Change Increase (Decrease)
Retained earnings	$199,500
Common stock	60,000
Accumulated depreciation	55,000
Plant and equipment	290,000

The combined statement of income and retained earnings (Exhibit 17-2) tells us that the change in retained earnings is due to the net income and the payment of dividends. So we know that there was a nonoperating outflow of cash for dividends. The increase in common stock must have been brought about by the issuance of additional stock; whether or not the stock was issued for cash can be determined by inquiry. If for cash, we can include the issuance among the nonoperating sources of cash in our statement. If the stock was issued in return for plant and equipment, we have a financing and investing activity that did not affect cash and should be reported separately in the final section of the funds statement.

The increase in accumulated depreciation requires a little more analysis. From the income statement we know that the depreciation for the year was $56,000, which *should* have increased accumulated depreciation by the same amount. Since the actual increase is only $55,000, something must have happened during the year to decrease accumulated depreciation by $1,000. From your knowledge of financial accounting you know that accumulated depreciation decreases when a depreciable asset is sold.[3]

---

those offered for the explained adjustments. For example, consider what adjustment might be necessary if a firm has Prepaid Expenses at the beginning and end of the year under consideration. Income will have been reduced by the amount of the operating expenses paid for last year but not used until the current year (beginning balance in Prepaid Expenses); cash disbursements for operating expenses will include payments for items that will not show as expenses in this year's income statement (ending balance in Prepaid Expenses). The appropriate "adjustment" would be to add the beginning balance in Prepaid Expenses and subtract the ending balance in that account. Similarly, since depletion of natural resources and amortization of intangible assets are like depreciation (allocations of previously incurred costs, with no requirements for current cash outlays), these expenses would require "adjustments" like the one for depreciation.

[3]The cost of the asset is removed from the asset account, and the accumulated depreciation on that asset is removed from the Accumulated Depreciation account.

You could then conclude that some asset was sold and inquire further as to its cost and selling price. Let us assume we learn that some equipment that had cost $10,000 and had accumulated depreciation of $1,000 was sold for $9,000. The $9,000 would be reported as cash provided by other sources.

Plant and equipment decreased by $10,000 when equipment was sold, as we determined above. Yet over the year plant and equipment increased by $290,000; therefore, there must have been additions to plant and equipment of $300,000. Here again, inquiry would determine whether or not the acquisition involved only cash. If only cash was involved (as in USL's case), this outflow would show as a use of resources. If the acquisition involved both cash and, say, common stock issued during the year, the resource statement would show both.

To summarize briefly, we started with comparative balance sheets for USL and noted that cash had decreased by $120,500. To explain that change, we analyzed the changes in all other balance sheet accounts. The results of that analysis are presented in a formal statement of changes in financial position, as discussed in the next section.

The Formal Statement

The funds statement for USL, using the cash concept of resources, is shown in Exhibit 17-4. Because such statements can utilize different definitions of resources, the title of the statement specifically refers to the resource definition used. The five adjustments appearing in the reconciliation of net income and funds provided by operations are listed in the order in which they were discussed in the preceding section. It is, however, almost universal practice for the depreciation adjustment to be shown first.

If you reflect for a moment about all of the adjustments, you will see that the first three and the fifth are quite different from the fourth. The depreciation adjustment, required because depreciation expense appears on the income statement, has no relation at all to the operating inflows or outflows of funds for the current period. The other four adjustments directly relate to specific operating flows of funds. These four adjustments are needed because of the relatively short-term timing differences between cash flows and appearance on the income statement. Once you understand the reasoning for the treatment of these items in the reconciliation, you may find the following general rules helpful:

1. Add to net income a decrease in a current asset item or an increase in a current liability item; and,
2. Subtract from net income an increase in a current asset item or a decrease in a current liability item.

Note that the net change in cash, as shown on the statement (a decrease of $120,500) agrees with the decrease in cash as shown in the comparative balance sheets (Exhibit 17-3). The two statements are thus linked together, with the funds statement describing the cash inflows and outflows that contributed to the decline in the resource, cash, as shown on the balance sheet. The name, "changes in financial position," is derived from this link with the balance sheet, which is called, on occasion, a statement of financial position.

Exhibit 17-4

USL Corporation

Statement of Changes in Financial Position—Cash Basis

for the Year 19X5

Resources provided by:		
Operations:		
Net income		$229,500
Adjustments for items that affected net income but		
did not affect resources in the same way:		
Increase in accounts receivable	($130,000)	
Increase in inventory	(90,000)	
Increase in accounts payable	30,000	
Depreciation for the year	56,000	
Increase in accrued expenses	45,000	
Total adjustments		(89,000)
Funds provided by operations		140,500
Other sources:		
Issuance of common stock	60,000	
Sale of plant and equipment	9,000	
Funds provided by other sources		69,000
Total resources provided during the year		209,500
Resources used for:		
Purchase of plant and equipment	300,000	
Dividends	30,000	
Total resources used during the year		330,000
Net decrease in cash resources		$120,500

It is possible, as we have shown, to develop the information for a statement of changes in financial position by analyzing the other financial statements and asking a few questions. For the managers of the firm with access to information about actual cash flows, the task is relatively easy. Without access to information about actual flows, the task is still not impossible. And for anyone—manager, stockholder, or creditor—presented with a statement of changes in financial position, the main task is to understand its contents and implications. Before discussing the information presented in the statement we will develop another funds statement, based this time on the working capital concept of resources.

RESOURCES AS WORKING CAPITAL

The objective of a funds statement using the working capital concept of funds is to describe the inflows and outflows of working capital. Because cash is a part of working capital, changes in cash may change working capital. But many transactions that change cash do not change working capital at all. For example, neither collections of accounts receivable nor payments on accounts payable affect working capital. The former increase one current asset (cash) and decrease another (accounts receivable); the latter decrease one positive element of working capital (cash), but also decrease one negative element (accounts payable). Similarly, purchases of inventory on account do not affect total working capital (a current asset increases and a current liability increases by the same amount).

You should recognize that these examples were among the factors involved in reconciling reported net income and the cash flows from operations. When the concept of resources is broadened from cash to working capital, the funds statement is less complex, primarily because the reconciliation of net income and resources provided by operations is less complex.

Reconciliation of Net Income and Working Capital from Operations

Most of the factors that create differences between net income and cash provided by operations do not create differences between net income and working capital provided by operations.

As an example, consider the difference between reported revenues and cash receipts from customers. The difference relates solely to the accounts receivable at the beginning and the end of the year. In our reconciliation of net income and cash from operations we had to add the collections of prior years' accounts receivable because these collections increased cash this year without increasing this year's income. But both cash and accounts receivable are current assets and hence components of working capital. The collection of cash on old accounts receivable does not increase working capital this year. Cash goes up and accounts receivable go down; there is no increase (inflow) of working capital. Similarly, in our reconciliation of net income and cash from operations we had to subtract the amounts relating to sales for which no cash was collected this year; we did this because net income had been increased by such sales while cash had not. But the sale of merchandise on account this year increases both net income *and* working capital this year: sales (and net income) go up, and working capital, in the form of accounts receivable, goes up.

Look again at the reconciliation of net income and cash flow from operations (Exhibit 17-4). Almost all of the adjustments involve items that are not cash but are part of working capital. In a statement of resource flows based on the working capital concept, these adjustments are not necessary because the components of net income reflect increases or decreases consistent with the increases or decreases in working capital.

Let us illustrate by analyzing one more of the adjustments—that for the change in accrued expenses. We had to subtract from net income the accrued expenses at the beginning of the year because cash was used to pay for them even though they were not included in this year's expenses. But this payment for last year's expenses reduced neither current income nor working capital. (The payment reduced current liabilities and current assets by the same amount.) Hence, in reconciling net income and working capital from operations, the cash payment of the previous year's accrued expenses is irrelevant and no adjustment is required. Neither is there a need to adjust for the accrued expenses at the end of the year. Net income was reduced because of the recognition of these expenses, and working capital was also reduced because a current liability was increased.

Analysis would show that none of the adjustments related to components of working capital are needed to reconcile net income and working capital from operations. Are there *any* differences between net income and working capital provided by operations? Without looking at the adjustments you should be able to develop a *general* answer to the question. The only differences between net income and working capital provided by operations must result from items that affected net income but did not have a similar effect on working capital.

Very few items meet this description. The most obvious is depreciation expense, which reduces net income but does not involve any components of working capital. For USL Corporation, the only difference between net income and working capital from operations is depreciation expense. In other cases, expenses similar to depreciation (depletion of natural resources, amortization of intangible assets such as franchises or patents) would fit the description and thus qualify as adjustments.[4]

The Formal Statement

With respect to nonoperating flows of resources, all other items appearing in the statement of changes in financial position under the cash concept would also appear in the statement based on the working capital concept. In each item, cash and working capital were both affected by the same amount. A formal statement using the working capital concept appears in Exhibit 17-5.

Exhibit 17-5
USL Corporation
Statement of Changes in Financial Position—Working Capital Basis
for the Year 19X5

Resources provided by:		
Operations:		
Net income		$229,500
Adjustment for items that affected net income but did not		
affect resources in the same way:		
Depreciation for the year		56,000
Funds provided by operations		285,500
Other sources:		
Issuance of common stock	$ 60,000	
Sale of plant and equipment	9,000	
Funds provided by other sources		69,000
Total resources provided during the year		354,500
Resources used for:		
Purchase of plant and equipment	300,000	
Dividends	30,000	
Total resources used during the year		330,000
Net increase in working capital resources		$ 24,500

[4]Those familiar with the accounting for bonds payable and income taxes should recognize that bond discount or premium amortization and deferred taxes would also qualify as adjustments.

The statement shows that working capital increased during the year by $24,500, and we can prove this by referring to the comparative balance sheets and computing the change in working capital for the year. A schedule computing the change is shown in Exhibit 17-6. The schedule shows that working capital did indeed increase by $24,500, from $550,000 at December 31, 19X4, to $574,500 at December 31, 19X5.[5] Thus, this formal statement, like the one prepared using the cash concept of resources, is directly linked to the balance sheet (through the working capital change) and to the income statement (through the reference to net income).

Exhibit 17-6
USL Corporation
Schedule of Working Capital
at December 31

	19X5	19X4	Increase (Decrease) in Working Capital
Current assets:			
Cash	$239,500	$360,000	($120,500)
Accounts receivable	280,000	150,000	130,000
Inventory	190,000	100,000	90,000
Total current assets	709,500	610,000	
Current liabilities:			
Accounts payable	85,000	55,000	(30,000)
Accrued expenses	50,000	5,000	(45,000)
Total current liabilities	135,000	60,000	
Working capital	$574,500	$550,000	$ 24,500

We noted earlier that an individual trying to develop a cash-basis resource statement might not have immediate access to the details of actual cash flows for the period but could still, with careful analysis and some inquiries, accomplish the task. The same applies to a statement using the working capital concept of resources. The comparative balance sheets would be studied to identify changes, and the statement of income would be reviewed for clues to the reasons for the changes. With the answers to a few careful questions (such as those raised in the analysis of the cash basis statement), a statement not significantly different from that in Exhibit 17-5 could be developed.

OPERATING FLOWS—A SPECIAL PROBLEM

In illustrating the development of a statement of changes in financial position under either concept of resources, we have used very common transactions. For example,

---

[5]In published financial statements, which are governed by *Accounting Principles Board Opinion No. 19,* a schedule of working capital such as that shown in Exhibit 17-6 is generally required as part of the statement of changes in financial position.

depreciation was the only item affecting income and not affecting one of the current asset or liability accounts. Stock was issued for cash and equipment was acquired for cash. The sale of plant and equipment was at book value, so no gain or loss appeared in the income statement.

Of the illustrative transactions, the one least likely to occur in a more realistic situation is the sale of a plant asset at its book value. When a noncurrent asset is disposed of at any price other than its book value, a gain or loss on the sale appears in the income statement. The cash or other working capital flow associated with the sale is its selling price, while net income will be affected not by the funds received but by the gain or loss on the sale. Such a transaction produces an inflow of resources, but the inflow is not related to operations; the gain or loss produces a change in net income, but the change is not because of operations. In a reconciliation of net income with resources provided by operations, the effect of the gain or loss must be removed from net income, and whatever resources are provided by the sale should be shown under "other sources of funds."

For example, suppose a particular long-term investment that had cost $30,000 was sold during the year for $45,000. The cash (or working capital) provided by this sale was $45,000 and this amount should be reported as a nonoperating source of funds. But the $15,000 gain on the sale will have been included in the net income for the year. Hence, net income has increased by $15,000 as a result of a nonoperating inflow of resources of $45,000. In the statement of changes in financial position for this firm, the $15,000 gain should be *subtracted* from net income as one of the adjustments to arrive at funds from operations, and the total selling price, $45,000, should be shown as a nonoperating source of funds.

If the sale of a noncurrent asset results in a loss rather than a gain, the same line of reasoning would lead to an adjustment of net income that *added* the loss. For example, suppose that the long-term investment described above as costing $30,000 was sold for $20,000 during the year. Net income will have been lower because of the $10,000 loss. Yet there would have been no outflow of resources at all; rather, the sale would have produced a $20,000 inflow of resources. In the statement of changes in financial position, the $10,000 loss would be added to net income as one of the adjustments to arrive at funds from operations in order to remove the effect of this nonoperating transaction. The $20,000 inflow of resources as a result of the sale would be shown among the nonoperating sources of funds.

Exhibit 17-7 contains a statement of changes in financial position for a company that sustained both a loss and a gain as a result of sales of noncurrent assets. Note that this statement is not significantly different from previous examples except for the additional adjustments to net income.

CONCLUDING COMMENTS

The headings and descriptions used in a funds statement may vary from company to company. A company may use the words *cash, working capital, resources,* or *funds* where we have used other terms. The heading "Adjustments for items that affected net income but did not affect resources in the same way" is actually a rather uncommon description for the items used to reconcile net income and resources provided by opera-

Exhibit 17-7

Lenseth Company

Statement of Changes in Financial Position—Working Capital Basis

for the Year 19X7

Resources provided by:		
Operations:		
Net income		$203,000
Adjustments for items that affected net income but		
did not affect resources in the same way:		
Depreciation for the year	$ 25,000	
Loss on sale of equipment	12,000	
Gain on sale of investment in stock of Girard		
Company	(15,000)	
Total adjustments		22,000
Funds provided by operations		225,000
Other sources:		
Sale of equipment	13,000	
Sale of investment in the stock of Girard Company	45,000	
Funds provided by other sources		58,000
Total resources provided during the year		283,000
Resources used for:		
Dividends	143,000	
Purchases of new equipment	110,000	
Total resources used during the year		253,000
Net increase in working capital resources		$ 30,000
Other financing and investing activities:		
Issuance of long-term notes for new equipment		$180,000

tions. A more common heading would be "Adjustments for items that did not affect working capital (or cash)." In any case, the title used for the adjustments section should be descriptive of the purpose of the adjustments.

A common misconception has arisen over the years that depreciation is a source of funds. This misconception is understandable when we consider that depreciation is added to net income to arrive at funds provided by operations. The misunderstanding has not been reduced by carelessly prepared funds statements that provide no heading at all for the adjustments but simply list the individual adjustments, starting with depreciation, after the net income. As you know, depreciation is neither a use nor a source of funds. It requires no current outlay of cash or working capital; an outflow of funds occurred at the time the depreciating asset was acquired.

There is, however, one sense in which it could be said that depreciation influences current funds flows. Because depreciation is deductible for tax purposes, a firm's income tax payment (which *is* an operating use of funds) is lower than it would have been had there been no depreciation to deduct. Hence the net funds from operations are larger than would be the case had there been no depreciation. But if the firm had no revenues and still had depreciation, there would be no funds from operations. Thus, depreciation can help the firm *retain* funds, but only when there is some source producing an inflow of funds to be retained.

Because a funds statement is required for companies that distribute their financial statements publicly, it will normally be prepared by the firm's accountants (as are
the balance sheet and income statement). Nevertheless, the nonaccountant, inside or
outside the firm, must have a basic understanding of the development of the statement
and of the alternative concepts of resources on which the statement is based.

SUMMARY

Information on flows of working capital or cash is important to readers of financial statements.
The statement of changes in financial position, or funds statement, provides information on the
sources and uses of the firm's financial resources. This information can be used to determine
how the firm was financed, whether from internal generation of resources, from long-term creditors, from stockholders, or from combinations of all of these sources. The information in the
statement also enables the reader to determine how the firm used its financial resources,
whether it bought plant assets, retired long-term debt, paid dividends to its stockholders.

Two approaches to preparing the statement are commonly used, a working-capital
basis and a cash basis. The user can convert a statement from one basis to the other by using
data from comparative balance sheets.

KEY TERMS

financing activities
funds provided by operations
funds statement
investing activities

reconciliation of net income and cash
    (working capital provided by operations)
statement of changes in financial position
working capital

KEY FORMULA

$$\text{Working capital} = \text{current assets} - \text{current liabilities}$$

REVIEW PROBLEM

Comparative balance sheets and a combined statement of income and retained earnings for
Harold Company are given on page 697.

Harold Company
Balance Sheets at December 31

Assets	19X7	19X6	Change Increase (Decrease)
Current assets:			
Cash	$ 205	$ 190	$ 15
Accounts receivable	420	430	(10)
Inventory	350	310	40
Total current assets	975	930	
Investments	120	160	(40)
Plant and equipment	2,500	2,250	250
Accumulated depreciation	(800)	(720)	80
Total assets	$2,795	$2,620	
Equities			
Current liabilities:			
Accounts payable	$ 210	$ 220	(10)
Accrued expenses	65	70	(5)
Total current liabilities	275	290	
Long-term debt	100	250	(150)
Total liabilities	375	540	
Owners' equity:			
Common stock, no par value	1,800	1,600	200
Retained earnings	620	480	140
Total owners' equity	2,420	2,080	
Total equities	$2,795	$2,620	

Harold Company
Combined Statement of Income and Retained Earnings
for the Year 19X7

Sales		$1,950
Cost of goods sold:		
Beginning inventory	$ 310	
Purchases	890	
Cost of goods available for sale	1,200	
Less: Ending inventory	350	
Cost of goods sold		850
Gross profit on sales		1,100
Operating expenses:		
Depreciation	100	
Other operating expenses	300	
Total operating expenses		400
Operating income		700
Other income—gain on sale of investments		30
Net income		730
Retained earnings at December 31, 19X6		480
		1,210
Dividends declared and paid		590
Retained earnings at December 31, 19X7		$ 620

The following additional information is also available to you.
1. Common stock was issued for $200 cash this year.
2. Investments costing $40 were sold at a gain of $30.
3. Equipment costing $30 and with accumulated depreciation of $20 was sold for $10.

Required

1. Determine the cash provided by operations.
2. Prepare a statement of changes in financial position using the cash concept of resources.
3. Determine the change in working capital for the year 19X7.
4. Determine the amount of working capital provided by operations for the year 19X7.
5. Without preparing a formal statement, reconcile the change in working capital as computed in part 3, with the working capital provided by operations, as computed in part 4.

Answer to Review Problem

1. We must compute the cash flow from operations by making the adjustments to net income. Review of the company's income statement reveals the need for three adjustments: (a) depreciation, a noncash expense, has reduced income; (b) the sale of a long-term investment, a *nonoperating* transaction, has increased income to the extent of the gain on the sale; and (c) the change in inventory, which is not directly related to cash flows, has increased net income. The change in inventory (an increase) produced an increase in net income because the ending inventory (which reduced cost of goods sold and hence increased income) was greater than the beginning inventory (which increased cost of goods sold and hence decreased income).

    We can then turn to the comparative balance sheets for any other facts that might cause the reported components of net income (revenues, cost of goods sold, and operating expenses) to be different from the actual cash flows relating to operations. Review of the comparative balance sheets reveals the need for three additional adjustments: (d) the change in accounts receivable means there is a difference between the cash inflows from operations and the reported revenues; (e) the change in accounts payable means there is a difference between cash outflows for operations and the reported cost of goods sold because there is a difference between cash outflows for purchases and the reported purchases; and (f) the change in accrued expenses means that there is a difference between the operating cash outflows for expenses and the reported operating expenses.

    Changes in the other balance-sheet items, though they may have affected cash, would not have given rise to operating cash flows. If such changes affected net income, their effect should be eliminated from net income as we compute the cash flow from operating activities. Let us look at the other balance-sheet changes.

    A change in noncurrent investments would be a nonoperating change, a sale or purchase. A cash flow from such a change does not result from operations. We have already recognized that net income must be adjusted to remove the effect of the sale of investments on net income [adjustment (b) above]. A change in plant and equipment too would be a nonoperating change, a sale or purchase. The income statement shows no evidence that either type of nonoperating change affected net income. The only operations-related change in accumulated depreciation is the depreciation for the year, which has no effect on cash flow from operations. We have already identified an adjustment (a) to remove the effect of the depreciation expense from the net income.

    The changes in long-term debt and common stock, whatever their causes, would give rise to nonoperating flows. Again, there is no evidence (such as a gain from retirement of debt) in the income statement that such nonoperating changes affected net income. The change in retained earnings is explained by net income, which we have already considered, and the payment of dividends, which is a nonoperating flow that did not affect net income.

Thus, we can compute the cash provided by operations by starting with net income and making the six adjustments (a) through (f):

Reconciliation of Net Income and Cash from Operations

	Net income		$730
	Adjustments for items that affected net income but		
	did not affect cash the same way:		
(a)	Depreciation for the year	$100	
(b)	Gain on sale of long-term investment	(30)	
(c)	Increase in inventory	(40)	
(d)	Decrease in accounts receivable	10	
(e)	Decrease in accounts payable	(10)	
(f)	Decrease in accrued expenses	(5)	
	Net adjustment		25
	Cash provided by operations		$755

2. In part 1, the information needed for one section of the statement, cash provided by operations, was developed. Our objective now is to find any other inflows or outflows of cash (nonoperating flows). For this information we refer again to the balance-sheet changes that did not affect the cash flow from operations. The changes, already discussed briefly, are summarized below.

Item	Change Increase (Decrease)
Investments	($40)
Plant and equipment	250
Accumulated depreciation	80
Long-term debt	(150)
Common stock	200
Retained earnings	140

Let us examine each of these changes carefully.

The decrease in investments was the result of a sale which produced a gain of $30. Since the investments that were sold cost $40 (the amount of the balance sheet decrease in investments), the proceeds from the sale must have been $70. Hence we have a nonoperating cash inflow of $70 to be reported on the statement.

The normal reason for an increase in plant and equipment would be a purchase of new equipment. Remember, however, that each change shown in the comparative balance sheets is a *net* change which could be the result of more than one transaction. We already know that during the year the company sold equipment that originally cost $30. This transaction *reduced* plant and equipment by $30. Thus, the purchases of new plant and equipment must have been enough to offset this decrease and produce a net increase in plant and equipment of $250, or $280 ($250 + $30). We have, then, two transactions: sale of equipment and purchase of equipment, both of which involve nonoperating cash flows. The old equipment was sold for $10, which amount should be reported as a nonoperating cash flow. The new equipment must have cost $280, reported as a nonoperating use of cash.

Depreciation, as we know, neither produces nor uses cash. Hence, the change in accumulated depreciation is not a cash inflow or outflow. We can explain the change from what we already know about the firm's activities for the year. Accumulated depreciation increased by $100 because of the current year's depreciation expense as shown on the income statement. Accumulated depreciation decreased by $20 because an asset on which depreciation of $20 had accumulated was sold. The net change is an increase of $80 (an increase of $100 offset by a decrease of $20). We already determined, in our analysis of plant and equipment, that a nonoperating cash inflow of $10 should be reported in connection with the sale of equipment.

The normal reason for a decline in long-term debt is that some of the debt was repaid. Such a repayment would be a nonoperating outflow or use of cash. Since we have no evidence to indicate some other reason for the decrease, we shall report the decline as a nonoperating use of cash in the amount of $150.

Common stock increased by $200 during the year; the usual explanation for such an increase is that additional shares of stock were issued. This conclusion is confirmed by the information obtained at the beginning of the problem, and we can include among the nonoperating sources of cash the issuance of additional stock for $200.

The lower portion of the combined statement of income and retained earnings reports that the net change in retained earnings resulted from an increase because of net income and a decrease because of dividends. The net income is an operating source of cash and we have already dealt with cash from operations. The payment of dividends should be reported on our statement as a $590 nonoperating use of cash.

Having analyzed and explained all the changes in balance sheet accounts during the year, we can incorporate our conclusions into a formal statement of changes in financial position, as shown below.

Harold Company
Statement of Changes in Financial Position—Cash Basis
for the Year 19X7

Resources provided by:		
Operations:		
Net income		$ 730
Adjustments that affected net income but did not affect cash the same way:		
Depreciation for the year	$100	
Gain on sale of long-term investment	(30)	
Increase in inventory	(40)	
Decrease in accounts receivable	10	
Decrease in accounts payable	(10)	
Decrease in accrued expenses	(5)	
Net adjustment		25
Cash provided by operations		755
Other sources:		
Sale of investments	70	
Sale of equipment	10	
Issuance of common stock	200	
Cash from other sources		280
Total cash provided during the year		1,035
Resources used for:		
Acquisition of plant and equipment	280	
Retirement of long-term debt	150	
Dividends on common stock	590	
Total cash used during the year		1,020
Net increase in cash		$ 15

3. Although this requirement could be completed on a less formal basis, following is a schedule of working capital that would appear as part of a statement of changes in financial position. The amounts are taken directly from the comparative balance sheets.

Harold Company Schedule of Working Capital
at December 31

	19X7	19X6	Change in Working Capital Increase (Decrease)
Current assets:			
Cash	$205	$190	$15
Accounts receivable	420	430	(10)
Inventory	350	310	40
Total current assets	975	930	45
Current liabilities:			
Accounts payable	210	220	10
Accrued expenses	65	70	5
Total current liabilities	275	290	15
Working capital	$700	$640	$60

4. From part 1 we already know those items that caused a difference between net income and cash from operations. Cash is one component of working capital. If any of the items already identified is also a part of working capital, the difference between net income and working capital from operations would disappear. Reviewing the list of adjustments in the cash basis statement of changes in financial position, we see that the last four relate to changes in other working capital accounts. Hence, the only adjustments still needed are the first two, and we can compute working capital from operations as follows:

Net income		$730
Adjustments for items that affected net income but did not affect working capital in the same way:		
Depreciation for the year	$100	
Gain on sale of investments	(30)	
Net adjustment		70
Working capital provided by operations		$800

5. The total change in working capital was an increase of $60. Although the working capital provided by operations was $800, there were other sources of working capital during the year, and the company used working capital for various reasons. We can refer to the cash basis statement of changes in financial position which was prepared earlier. Those nonoperating transactions which provided or used cash resources during the year also provided or used working capital resources during the year. (This might not always be the case, but it is true for Harold Company this year.) Without preparing a formal statement of changes in

financial position based on the working capital concept, we can reconcile the $800 and the $60 as follows:

Funds provided by operations (from part 4)		$ 800
Funds provided by other sources:		
Sale of investments	$ 70	
Sale of equipment	10	
Issuance of common stock	200	280
		1,080
Funds used for:		
Dividends	590	
Debt retirement	150	
Acquisition of plant assets	280	1,020
Increase in working capital (from part 3)		$ 60

APPENDIX: A WORKSHEET APPROACH TO PREPARING STATEMENTS OF CHANGES IN FINANCIAL POSITION

The commonsense approach to preparing the statement of changes in financial position used in the chapter can be supplemented with a more systematic approach, the use of a worksheet. The worksheet does not replace a basic knowledge of accounting; rather it organizes the elements of the statement and serves as a means to account for all its necessary components.

The worksheet technique is especially helpful when the problem is complex and some data are missing. You know from the chapter and the review problem that you sometimes have to make judgments about the most probable cause of a change in a noncurrent account like accumulated depreciation, bonds payable, or common stock. The use of a worksheet enables you to determine more systematically whether you have considered all of the transactions that affect the statement.

The rationale of the worksheet is straightforward. It is used to *reconstruct* the transactions that affected working capital or cash during the year and to identify the effects of those transactions as sources and uses of funds. We shall use the data from the review problem on pages 696–698 to illustrate the preparation of a worksheet for a working capital basis statement of changes in financial position.

Preparing the Worksheet

The worksheet is prepared in two basic steps. First we enter the beginning and ending balances of all noncurrent accounts and of a single summary account for working capital for Harold Company, as shown in the partially completed worksheet in Exhibit 17-8. The lower part of the worksheet will then serve as the basis for preparing the formal statement after the transactions for the year have been entered in the two middle columns.

Exhibit 17-8

Harold Company Worksheet for Statement of Changes in
Financial Position for Year Ended December 31, 19X7

	Beginning Balance		Analyses of Transactions		Ending Balance	
	Dr.	Cr.	Dr.	Cr.	Dr.	Cr.
Noncurrent accounts:						
Investments	160				120	
Plant and equipment	2,250				2,500	
Accumulated depreciation		720				800
Long-term debt		250				100
Common stock		1,600				1,800
Retained earnings		480				620
Subtotal	2,410	3,050			2,620	3,320
Various working capital accounts						
(net debit balance)	640				700	
Working capital provided						
by operations:						
Net income						
Adjustments:						
Depreciation						
Other sources of working capital:						
Uses of working capital:						
Totals	3,050	3,050			3,320	3,320

Please notice three points about the worksheet. First, it is set up in debit-credit form. The total debits are equal to the total credits at both the beginning and end of the year, reflecting a basic accounting formula. Second, working capital is shown as a single figure; the individual current assets and current liabilities are not shown. The reason for using this summary account is that we do not care about *particular* current assets and current liabilities, only about the net amount of working capital. We can derive the single summary amount in the manner shown in part 3 of the review problem (page 701).

Notice also that we have filled in part of the bottom of the worksheet. We would not normally know exactly what items the statement will contain, but we can be fairly sure that there will be an operations section which includes net income and depreciation. We can also be reasonably confident that there will be some other sources and uses. As we reconstruct the year's transactions we shall fill in appropriate titles for the individual sources and uses.

The second step in preparing the worksheet is to reconstruct the transactions that affected working capital over the year. This is done by working with the information available and making the most plausible assumptions about items for which information is not available. The reconstruction is done in journal entry form.

As we make the journal entries we shall be accounting for the changes in noncurrent accounts and in working capital at the same time. Again, because we are not concerned with particular current asset and current liability accounts we shall use the account title Various Working Capital Accounts to designate sources and uses of working capital that will appear on the formal statement.

Reconstruction of Transactions

We shall begin the reconstruction of transactions by considering retained earnings. We know that net income for the year was $730 and that dividends were $590. Net income, of course, is not a single transaction, but rather the net effect of a great many transactions affecting a number of working capital and noncurrent accounts. In journal entry form we show the effect of net income on working capital:

1.	Various Working Capital Accounts	$730	
	Retained Earnings		$730
	To record net income as a source of working capital.		

Dividends are recorded in the following entry:

2.	Retained Earnings	$590	
	Various Working Capital Accounts		$590
	To record dividends as a use of working capital.		

Common stock: We know that the Harold Company issued $200 of common stock for cash. However, even if we did not know that, we would still assume the $200 increase in the Common Stock account to be the result of an issuance. Again, because we are concerned with working capital, the fact that cash was received for the stock is not important. The entry below recognizes the issuance.

3.	Various Working Capital Accounts	$200	
	Common Stock		$200
	To record issuance of common stock as a source of working capital.		

Long-term debt: The balance sheets of Harold Company and the partially filled-in worksheet tell us that long-term debt decreased by $150. The most likely explanation is that there was a retirement of long-term debt. The entry below gives effect to that transaction:

4.	Long-Term Debt	$150	
	Various Working Capital Accounts		$150
	To record retirement of long-term debt as a use of working capital.		

Accumulated depreciation and plant and equipment: These two accounts have to be considered together because the sale of equipment affected both of them. The sale of equipment with a cost of $30 and accumulated depreciation of $20 for its book value of $10 is recorded in entry 5:

5.	Various Working Capital Accounts	$10	
	Accumulated Depreciation	20	
	Plant and Equipment		$30
	To record sale of plant assets as a source of working capital.		

We must also give effect to depreciation expense, which did not use working capital, but was included in the determination of net income.

6. Adjustments $100
       Accumulated Depreciation $100
    To record depreciation as an adjustment that did not affect
    working capital the same way it affected net income.

Entries 5 and 6 fully account for the change in Accumulated Depreciation, but not for the change in Plant and Equipment. Plant and Equipment began with a balance of $2,250 and increased to $2,500, a change of $250. The $30 credit made in entry 5 tells us that the firm must have added $280 in plant assets. This inference is recorded in entry 7.

7. Plant and Equipment $280
       Various Working Capital Accounts $280
    To record purchases of plant assets as a use of working capital.

Investments: The only noncurrent account left is Investments, which decreased by $40, from $160 to $120, as the result of a sale of investments. The sale brought a price of $70, giving a $30 gain. We know that the formal statement must show the $70 price as an "other source," not as an operating source. We also know that the gain was included in the determination of net income and must therefore be subtracted in the adjustments section. In journal entry form we can take care of this transaction by showing a debit to working capital of $70 for the selling price and a credit to income adjustments of $30 for the gain. The credit will then become a deduction in the operations section of the formal statement.

8. Various Working Capital Accounts $70
       Investments $40
       Adjustments   30
    To record a $70 source of working capital from the sale of investment and a
    $30 adjustment in working capital provided by operations from the gain on
    the sale.

At this point all of the accounts are fully reconciled. The completed worksheet appears in Exhibit 17-9. The lower part of the worksheet provides all of the information needed to prepare a formal statement. The debit entries are either sources of working capital or adjustments in the operations section, the credit entries are either uses of working capital or adjustments in the operations section.

As we noted earlier, the major advantage to the worksheet approach to developing a funds statement is that it provides a systematic way of dealing with the changes in resources. Ending balances in the balance sheet accounts reflect all activity during the year. The beginning balances on the worksheet, adjusted for the entries in the "Analyses of Transactions" column, must agree with the "Ending Balances." If they do not, further analysis is necessary until all balance sheet changes have been explained.

Exhibit 17-9

Harold Company Worksheet for Statement of Changes in
Financial Position for the Year Ended December 31, 19X7

	Beginning Balance		Analyses of Transactions		Ending Balance	
	Dr.	Cr.	Dr.	Cr.	Dr.	Cr.
Noncurrent accounts:						
Investments	160			40 (8)	120	
Plant and equipment	2,250		280 (7)	30 (5)	2,500	
Accumulated depreciation		720	20 (5)	100 (6)		800
Long-term debt		250	150 (4)			100
Common stock		1,600		200 (3)		1,800
Retained earnings		480	590 (2)	730 (1)		620
Subtotal	2,410	3,050			2,620	3,320
Various working capital accounts						
(net debit balance)	640				700	
Working capital provided						
by operations:						
Net income			730 (1)			
Adjustments:						
Depreciation			100 (6)			
Gain on sale of investments				30 (8)		
Other sources of working capital:						
Issuance of common stock			200 (3)			
Sale of investments			70 (8)			
Sale of equipment			10 (5)			
Uses of working capital:						
Dividends				590 (2)		
Retirement of debt				150 (4)		
Purchases of plant assets				280 (7)		
Totals	3,050	3,050	2,150	2,150	3,320	3,320

ASSIGNMENT MATERIAL

Questions for Discussion

17-1 Depreciation and working capital   It is often said that working capital, or cash, generated by operations consists of net income and depreciation. Explain why this statement is or is not true.

17-2 Net income and cash flow   Bryant Machine Shop was started by Walter Bryant five years ago. The shop has been fairly profitable and Mr. Bryant has been withdrawing cash in an amount equal to net income for each year. He has taken out an amount equal to nearly half of his original investment of $80,000, which was used mainly to purchase machinery. Mr. Bryant's customers pay cash on completion of work. He keeps very little inventory and pays his bills promptly. He is puzzled because the cash balance continues to increase despite his withdrawals. Can you offer any explanation for the increase in cash?

17-3 Net income and working capital Suppose that a large retail chain and a railroad earned the same net income. Which firm would you expect to show the higher working capital provided by operations? Explain your answer.

17-4 Explanation of cash-based statement You have provided the president of Ralston Company with a full set of financial statements, including a statement of changes in financial position on a cash basis. He understands everything except some of the adjustments in the operations section of the funds statement. He has three specific questions:

1. "Why do you subtract the increase in accounts receivable? We don't pay out cash for our accounts receivable, we collect it."
2. "And the inventory, which you show as an addition because our inventory decreased during the year. We sure didn't get any cash because our inventory decreased. In fact, the decrease means that we have less to sell next year and will have to spend more cash to replenish our supply. So why add it back to net income?"
3. "Our accrued expenses increased and you showed this as a source of cash? Look, we had especially heavy payroll costs at the end of the year and we paid them the third day of the new year. So it seems to me that we had to use more cash because of the increase, not less."

Required: Explain each of the items to the president.

Exercises

17-5 Relationships Answer the questions for each of the following independent situations.

1. At year end ABC Company had current assets of $120,000, which were $18,000 higher than at the beginning of the year. Working capital at year end was $64,000, which was $4,000 lower than at the beginning of the year.
   (a) What were current liabilities at the end of the year?
   (b) What were current liabilities at the beginning of the year?
2. Noncurrent assets of NMO Company increased by $160,000 and noncurrent equities (equities other than current liabilities) declined by $40,000 over the past year. What was the change in working capital over the year?
3. Working capital of XYZ Company increased by $50,000 over the past year. Current assets other than cash increased by $35,000 and current liabilities decreased by $7,000 over the year. What was the change in cash over the year?
4. Working capital provided by operations was $70,000. Current assets other than cash increased by $16,000 and current liabilities increased by $12,000 over the year. What was cash provided by operations?
5. Working capital provided by operations was $90,000 and depreciation expense was $52,000. What was net income?

17-6 Working capital—operations Drew Company had net income of $28,000 in 19X6. The following were included in the determination of net income:

1. Depreciation expense of $85,000.
2. Amortization of intangible assets of $22,000.
3. Loss on sale of plant assets of $3,000.
4. On one sale for $24,000, the customer gave Drew Company a 5-year note bearing 9% interest.

Required: Compute the amount of working capital provided by operations.

17-7   **Cash from operations (continuation of 17-6)**   Drew Company experienced the following changes in its current accounts during 19X6:

Accounts receivable	+$17,000
Inventory	−$ 9,000
Accounts payable	−$14,000
Accrued expenses	+$ 2,000

All other data are given in Exercise 17-6.

Required: Determine cash provided by operations.

17-8   **Working capital from operations**   Below is an income statement for Julon Company, a sole proprietorship, for 19X9.

Julon Company—Income Statement for 19X9

Sales		$140,000
Cost of goods sold		70,000
Gross profit		70,000
Operating expenses and losses:		
Wages	$30,000	
Insurance	500	
Bad debts	1,000	
Depreciation	12,000	
Patent amortization	2,000	
Loss on sale of equipment	200	
Taxes	9,300	
		55,000
Net income		$ 15,000

Required: Compute working capital provided by operations for 19X9.

17-9   **Converting cash flow to income**   The following data were prepared by the controller of Boyd Company. They relate to 19X7.

Cash collections from customers		$910,000
Payments to suppliers of merchandise	$470,000	
Wage and salary payments	160,000	
Other-payments of operating expenses	120,000	750,000
Cash provided by operations		$160,000

Other data taken from the firm's records show the following:
1. Accounts receivable increased by $20,000.
2. Accounts payable decreased by $8,000.
3. Inventory remained constant.
4. Accrued wages and salaries increased by $3,000.
5. Depreciation expense was $45,000.

Required: Determine the net income for 19X7.

17-10 Converting cash flow to working capital flow (continuation of 17-9)   Using the information in 17-9, compute the working capital provided by operations for Boyd Company for 19X7.

17-11 Reconciliation of net income and cash from operations   Select from the list below those items that would be relevant to a reconciliation of net income and cash from operations, and prepare such a reconciliation.

Gain on sale of long-term investment	$82,000
Increase in accounts receivable	12,500
Increase in land	48,000
Increase in accrued expenses payable	6,800
Decrease in inventory	6,500
Decrease in accounts payable	12,000
Decrease in prepaid insurance	1,500
Increase in common stock	85,000
Net income	174,000
Depreciation expense	61,000
Decrease in cash	14,000
Cash received from sale of long-term investment	228,800
Cash provided by operations	143,300

17-12 Reconciliation of net income and working capital from operations (continuation of 17-11)   Using the relevant information from 17-11, prepare a reconciliation of net income and working capital from operations.

17-13 Analysis of noncurrent accounts   The following data were taken from the records of Miller Mining Company:

	End of Year	
	19X6	*19X5*
Plant and equipment	$2,240,000	$1,980,000
Accumulated depreciation	(980,000)	(740,000)
Mineral properties, net of depletion	3,750,000	2,950,000

You have also determined that plant and equipment costing $240,000 and with accumulated depreciation of $90,000 was sold for $80,000 and that depletion expense related to mineral properties was $440,000. The only other transactions affecting the accounts shown were depreciation expense, purchases of plant and equipment, and purchases of mineral properties.

Required
1. Determine the amount of working capital provided by sales of plant and equipment.
2. Determine the gain or loss to be added or subtracted in the operations section of the statement of changes in financial position.
3. Determine the amount of depreciation expense to be added to net income in the operations section of the statement.
4. Determine the amount of working capital used to buy plant and equipment.
5. Determine the amount of working capital used to buy mineral properties.

17-14 Working capital—transactions Fisher Company began 19X4 with $110,000 working capital. During 19X4 the following occurred.
1. Net income was $115,000.
2. Depreciation expense was $70,000.
3. The firm retired bonds that were due in 19X9. The amount of cash spent to retire them was equal to their book value of $60,000.
4. The firm paid $90,000 for plant and equipment.
5. The firm declared dividends of $15,000, to be paid in January 19X5.
6. The firm wrote off as expense the book value of some long-term investments in stock of companies that went bankrupt in 19X4. The expense was $30,000.

Required: Prepare a statement of changes in financial position on a working capital basis.

17-15 Effects of transactions Determine the effect, if any, of each transaction listed below on (a) net income, (b) working capital, and (c) cash. Show the amount of the change and its direction (+ or −).
1. Common stock was issued in exchange for equipment. The agreed price was $300,000.
2. A dividend payable in cash of $120,000 was declared, but not paid.
3. The dividend in item 2 was paid.
4. An account receivable of $10,000 was written off against the Allowance for Doubtful Accounts.
5. Marketable securities classified as a current asset were sold for $30,000 cash. They had been shown at their cost of $27,000.
6. A customer who owed the firm $12,000 on account receivable gave the firm equipment with a fair market value of $12,000 in settlement of the receivable.
7. Interest payable was accrued in the amount of $14,000.
8. The interest payable in item 7 was paid.
9. The firm bought 100 shares of its own stock for the treasury. The cost was $4,600, paid in cash.
10. Inventory with a cost of $18,000 was written off as obsolete.
11. Plant assets that had cost $45,000 and were one third depreciated were sold for $12,000 cash.

17-16 Working capital flow (related to Appendix) The most recent income statement and condensed comparative balance sheets for Stout Company are as follows:

Stout Company Balance Sheets as of June 30

Assets	19X6	19X5
Current assets	$ 325	$ 350
Plant and equipment	1,290	1,110
Accumulated depreciation	(640)	(590)
Totals	$ 975	$ 870
Equities		
Current liabilities	$ 210	$ 195
Long-term debt	200	150
Common stock	300	300
Retained earnings	265	225
Totals	$ 975	$ 870

Stout Company Income Statement
Year Ended June 30, 19X6

Sales		$1,240
Cost of sales		710
Gross profit		530
Operating expenses:		
Depreciation	$ 50	
Other operating expenses	240	290
Income		$ 240

Stout declared and paid dividends of $200. There were no sales or retirements of plant assets. Plant assets were bought for $180 cash and $50 in long-term debt was issued to ease a cash shortage.

Required
1. Determine the change of working capital over the year 19X6.
2. Prepare a worksheet for a statement of changes in financial position.

17-17 Statement preparation—cash basis Below is a list of items that would appear in the statement of changes in financial position for Collins Company for the year 19X8.

Net income for the year	$346,000
Dividends paid during the year	140,000
Proceeds from sale of a 10-year bond issue	300,000
Amortization of the company's patents	7,000
Depreciation expense	153,000
Cash received on sale of land	80,000
Increase in inventory	17,000
Increase in accounts receivable	74,000
Loss on the sale of land	20,000
Decrease in accrued expenses	12,000
Cash purchase of new equipment	400,000
Cash purchase of a long-term investment	265,000
Increase in income taxes payable	6,000
Increase in accounts payable	48,000
Purchase of land and buildings by giving a 20-year note	350,000

Required: Prepare a cash basis statement of changes in financial position using all the items given. (*Hint:* The change in cash was an increase of $52,000.)

17-18 Statement preparation—working capital basis (continuation of 17-17) Using the information given in 17-17, (1) prepare a statement of changes in financial position using the working capital concept, and (2) verify the change in working capital, which was an increase of $101,000.

17-19   Funds statement from comparative balance sheets   Below are the balances of certain items for Lorelei Company at December 31, 19X5 and 19X6.

	December 31	
	19X5	19X6
Cash	$ 4,000	$17,000
Accounts receivable, net of the allowance		
for doubtful accounts	5,000	9,000
Inventory	10,000	12,000
Long-term investments	2,000	—
Property, plant, and equipment	30,000	47,000
Totals	$51,000	$85,000
Accumulated depreciation on plant and		
equipment	$ 5,000	$ 7,000
Accounts payable	3,000	5,000
Notes payable, due in 1 year	4,000	3,000
Long-term notes payable	10,000	18,000
Common stock	25,000	40,000
Retained earnings	4,000	12,000
Totals	$51,000	$85,000

The following information is also available about the firm's transactions in 19X6.
1. Net income for the year was $26,000.
2. Depreciation on plant and equipment for the year was $2,000.
3. Long-term investments were sold during the year at cost.
4. Property, plant, and equipment costing $5,000 was purchased for cash.
5. Dividends of $7,000 were declared and paid.
6. Some equipment was purchased by giving a $12,000 long-term note.
7. The company liquidated a $4,000 long-term note payable by issuing capital stock to the holder of the note.
8. A stock dividend was distributed to common stockholders. Retained Earnings was charged for $11,000 for this dividend, and the full $11,000 was added to Capital Stock.

Required: Prepare a statement of changes in financial position using the working capital definition of resources.

17-20   Cash basis funds statement from comparative balance sheets (continuation of 17-19)   Using the information provided in 17-19, prepare a statement of changes in financial position using cash as the definition of resources.

Problems

17-21   Working capital flows—balance sheets   Condensed comparative balance sheets and other data pertaining to LMN Company are as follows:

LMN Company
Balance Sheets as of December 31

Assets	19X5	19X4
Current assets	$ 78,000	$ 84,000
Investments	60,000	110,000
Plant and equipment	450,000	400,000
Accumulated depreciation	(250,000)	(220,000)
Total assets	$338,000	$374,000
Equities		
Current liabilities	$ 32,000	$ 36,000
Long-term debt	30,000	100,000
Common stock, no par value	210,000	180,000
Retained earnings	66,000	58,000
Total equities	$338,000	$374,000

Other data:
1. Net income was $21,000 in 19X5. Dividends were $13,000.
2. No plant assets were sold or retired in 19X5.
3. Investments costing $50,000 were sold for $55,000.
4. Depreciation included in expenses for the year was $30,000.

Required
1. Determine the change in working capital for the year 19X5.
2. Prepare a statement of changes in financial position on a working capital basis. When information is unavailable about a change in a noncurrent account, make the most likely assumption.
3. Comment briefly on the firm's major financing and investing activities.

17-22 **Working capital and cash—transactions** The transactions of Martin Company for 19X6 and other selected data are given below:
1. Sales, all on account, were $800,000.
2. Cost of goods sold was $360,000.
3. Depreciation expense was $60,000.
4. Other operating expenses, all paid in cash, were $210,000.
5. Equipment was purchased for $220,000 cash.
6. Long-term investments were sold at an $8,000 gain. They had cost $57,000.
7. Common stock was issued for cash of $150,000.
8. A building that had cost $80,000 and had accumulated depreciation of $72,000 was destroyed by fire. There was no insurance coverage.
9. Over the year, the following changes occurred in the current accounts of the firm:

Cash	+$ 17,000
Accounts receivable	+ 140,000
Inventory	+ 82,000
Accounts payable	+ 14,000

Required

1. Determine net income for the year.
2. Prepare a statement of changes in financial position on a working capital basis. The change in working capital can be determined from the information in item 9.
3. Prepare a statement of changes in financial position on a cash basis.

17-23   Balance sheet   The following condensed balance sheet and statement of changes in financial position for Quatro Company are available. Notice that working capital is shown as a single figure.

Quatro Company Balance Sheet
as of June 30, 19X7

Working capital	$ 50,000		
Investments	80,000	Long-term debt	$ 90,000
Plant and equipment	280,000	Common stock, no par	100,000
Accumulated depreciation	(160,000)	Retained earnings	60,000
Total	$250,000	Total	$250,000

Quatro Company Statement of Changes
in Financial Position Year Ended June 30, 19X8

Resource provided by:		
Operations:		
Net income		$ 34,000
Adjustments:		
Depreciation		18,000
Working capital provided by operations		52,000
Other sources:		
Sales of investments		30,000
Sale of common stock		40,000
Total resources provided		$122,000
Resources used for:		
Dividends	$14,000	
Purchases of plant assets	80,000	
Retirement of long-term debt	20,000	114,000
Increase in working capital		$ 8,000

Investments were sold at book value. No plant assets were sold or retired.

Required: Prepare a balance sheet for Quatro Company as of June 30, 19X8. Show working capital as a single figure.

17-24   Balance sheet (extension of 17-23)   Refer to the data in 17-23. Assume that the balance sheet given is for June 30, 19X8, instead of June 30, 19X7. The statement of changes in financial position is still for the year ended June 30, 19X8. Prepare the balance sheet for June 30, 19X7. That is, instead of preparing the ending balance sheet, you are to prepare the beginning balance sheet.

17-25   Cash flow   As you were walking down the hall to your office at Complan Company, you met the president of the firm. She was disturbed at the latest financial statements and wanted your help. She explained that the firm was faced with a serious shortage of cash even though profits were high and working capital increased. She showed you the following condensed financial statements. (All data are in thousands of dollars.)

Complan Company Income Statement for 19X7

Sales	$6,720
Cost of sales	3,850
Gross profit	2,870
Operating expenses	2,140
Net income	$ 730

Complan Company Balance Sheets as of December 31

Assets	19X7	19X6	Change
Cash	$ 25	$ 380	($355)
Accounts receivable	990	860	130
Inventory	1,445	1,200	245
Plant and equipment (net)	3,850	3,370	480
Totals	$6,310	$5,810	
Equities			
Accounts payable	$ 190	$ 280	($90)
Accrued expenses	110	200	(90)
Long-term debt	2,250	2,200	50
Common stock	2,080	2,080	0
Retained earnings	1,680	1,050	630
Totals	$6,310	$5,810	

The president told you that it had been touch-and-go whether the firm would have enough cash to pay a $100,000 dividend that had been declared when the directors realized that the firm was having an excellent year. In order to pay the dividend, the firm had to increase its long-term borrowings by $50,000. "We made $730,000," she went on, "and had depreciation expense of $150,000. We did buy $630,000 worth of plant assets, but I figured that our cash would stay about the same as it was last year. Look at this stuff and tell me what happened."

Required: Explain the results to the president.

17-26 **Working capital—comprehensive problem (related to Appendix)** Condensed comparative balance sheets and other data for Rhonda Company are given below.

Rhonda Company Balance Sheets

Assets	End of Year	Beginning of Year
Current assets	$130,000	$100,000
Investments, long-term	100,000	140,000
Plant and equipment	450,000	400,000
Accumulated depreciation	(110,000)	(80,000)
Intangible assets	54,000	60,000
Total assets	$624,000	$620,000

Equities	End of Year	Beginning of Year
Current liabilities	$ 45,000	$ 90,000
Long-term debt	140,000	200,000
Common stock, $10 par value	80,000	50,000
Paid in capital	270,000	220,000
Retained earnings	89,000	60,000
Total equities	$624,000	$620,000

Other data:
1. The change in working capital was an increase of $75,000.
2. Net income was $41,000; dividends were $12,000.
3. Sales of plant assets for $12,000 resulted in a loss of $10,000. The assets had cost $40,000 and had accumulated depreciation of $18,000. Purchases of plant were $90,000. Depreciation expense for the year was $48,000.
4. Amortization of intangible assets was $6,000.
5. Investments costing $40,000 were sold for $51,000.
6. Long-term debt in the amount of $60,000 was retired.
7. Common stock was sold for a total price of $80,000 cash.

Required
1. Prepare a worksheet to reconstruct the events of the year and make the necessary entries.
2. Prepare a statement of changes in financial position on a working capital basis.

17-27 **Funds statement from comparative trial balances**   Below are the beginning and ending balances of the balance sheet accounts for Truitt Company for 19X3.

	Beginning of Year		End of Year	
	Dr.	Cr.	Dr.	Cr.
Cash	$ 22,000		$ 16,000	
Marketable securities,				
temporary investment	14,000		10,000	
Accounts receivable	50,000		60,000	
Allowance for bad debts		$ 10,000		$ 12,000
Inventory	70,000		85,000	
Buildings and equipment	190,000		240,000	
Patents	26,000		20,000	
Accounts payable		30,000		40,000
Accrued wages payable		4,000		5,000
Accumulated depreciation on				
buildings and equipment		96,000		100,000
10-year bonds payable		80,000		104,000
Premium on bonds payable		—		1,000
Treasury stock	—		4,000	
Common stock		100,000		135,000
Retained earnings		52,000		38,000
Totals	$372,000	$372,000	$435,000	$435,000

The following information is also available about the firm's activities in 19X3.
1. Net income was $14,000.
2. Dividends of $8,000 were declared and paid.

3. A stock dividend was declared and distributed, and for this reason $20,000 was charged to Retained Earnings, which amount represented the par value of the stock issued in connection with the dividend. (The market value at the date the dividend was declared was equal to the par value of the stock.)

4. Depreciation in the amount of $8,000 was recorded as expense this year.

5. Machinery costing $6,000 and having a book value of $2,000 was sold for $3,000 cash in 19X3.

Required: Prepare a statement of changes in financial position (working capital basis) for Truitt Company for 19X3. You may assume that any changes other than those described above are attributable to reasonable transactions with which you should be familiar.

17-28 **Cash basis funds statement from comparative trial balances (continuation of 17-27)**   Using the information provided in 17-27, prepare a statement of changes in financial position using cash as a definition of resources.

17-29 **Treatment of transactions**   Explain how each of the following transactions would be reflected on a statement of changes in financial position prepared on (a) the working capital basis, and (b) the cash basis. Be specific.

1. Depreciation expense was $340,000.

2. A $110,000 dividend, payable in cash, was declared late in the year and will be paid early next year.

3. Fixed assets costing $380,000 with accumulated depreciation of $170,000 were sold for $80,000 cash.

4. Long-term investments were written off because the firms issuing the securities went bankrupt. The write-off was $220,000.

5. The firm issued long-term debt in exchange for land. The value of the land was $640,000, which equaled the value of the debt.

6. Near the end of the year the firm sold a parcel of land for $300,000, which was $60,000 more than its cost. The buyer gave the firm a 5-year, 8% note for $300,000.

7. The firm was required to pay $50,000 in settlement of a dispute relating to its income tax return of three years ago. The firm debited Retained Earnings for $50,000.

17-30 **Statements from limited data**   The following *changes* in the balance sheet accounts for Rohmer Company occurred during 19X8:

	Change	
Account	Debit	Credit
Cash	$120	
Accounts receivable		$180
Inventory	120	
Plant and equipment	350	
Accumulated depreciation		90
Accounts payable	80	
Accrued expenses		30
Long-term debt	15	
Common stock		200
Retained earnings		185
Totals	$685	$685

The firm had net income of $225 and paid dividends of $40. No plant assets were sold or retired.

Required
1. Prepare a statement of changes in financial position on a working capital basis. In the absence of available information, make the most reasonable assumption about the cause of a change. Be sure to find the change in working capital first.
2. Prepare a statement of changes in financial position on a cash basis.

17-31 Working capital and net income   Walter Rimstone, president of Piedmont Enterprises, was recently talking to his banker. The banker had just received Piedmont's most recent financial statements and was disturbed by the decline in working capital, which he called "deterioration of the current position." Mr. Rimstone said that he was surprised because the year had been the best in the firm's history. Condensed financial statements are given below, in thousands of dollars.

Piedmont Enterprises Income Statement for 19X5

Sales	$860
Total expenses, including $30 depreciation	620
Net income	$240

Piedmont Enterprises Balance Sheets
as of June 30

Assets	19X5	19X4
Current assets	$180	$160
Plant and equipment	740	560
Accumulated depreciation	(140)	(110)
Total assets	$780	$610
Equities		
Current liabilities	$115	$ 48
Long-term bank loan	110	125
Common stock	200	200
Retained earnings	355	237
Total equities	$780	$610

Mr. Rimstone asks you to figure out why working capital declined in the face of record income.

Required: Prepare a statement of changes in financial position on a working capital basis. Make whatever assumptions you think are reasonable when information is lacking.

17-32 Cash flow and income   Hamer Company is currently negotiating a bank loan with Eighteenth National Bank of Mardel. The bank's officers would like a statement showing the estimated cash flow that Hamer expects in the coming year. They need this information to be able to decide on the likelihood that Hamer will be able to repay the loan of $100,000 at the end of the year. Hamer's current balance sheet is given below, along with other data.

Hamer Company Balance Sheet
as of December 31, 19X6

Assets		Equities	
Cash	$ 15,000	Accounts payable	$ 48,000
Accounts receivable	110,000	Wages and salaries payable	12,000
Inventory	130,000	Common stock	300,000
Plant and equipment	750,000	Paid in capital	250,000
Accumulated depreciation	(300,000)	Retained earnings	95,000
Total assets	$705,000	Total equities	$705,000

Other data:

1. Sales for 19X7 are expected to be $1,030,000. Accounts receivable are expected to be $140,000 at the end of 19X7.
2. Cost of goods sold is expected to be $480,000 and year-end inventory is expected to be $150,000.
3. Accounts payable are expected to be $15,000 higher at the end of 19X7.
4. Wages and salaries payable are expected to be $22,000 at the end of 19X7, with wages and salary expense expected to be $215,000 for 19X7.
5. Depreciation expense for 19X7 is expected to be $60,000.
6. Other expenses, all to be paid in cash, are expected to be $95,000, including the interest on the loan being negotiated.
7. Cash expenditures for plant and equipment are expected to be $140,000 in 19X7.
8. Hamer expects to pay a dividend of $30,000 in 19X7.

Required

1. Determine the expected net income for 19X7, including as an expense the interest on the loan.
2. Prepare a statement of changes in financial position on a cash basis for the expected transactions of 19X7. Include the bank loan as a source of cash, but not as a use. Determine whether the company will be able to repay the loan on January 1, 19X8.

17-33 Working capital and cash requirements   Pittston Valve Company is expanding its plant to meet increased demand for its products. The expansion will enable the firm to increase its annual sales by $2,000,000. Additional expenses will be $1,700,000, including $140,000 in depreciation. During the first year of operation of the expanded plant, accounts receivable are expected to rise by $600,000 and inventory by $450,000 to support the higher sales levels. Accounts payable will increase by about half of the increase in inventory. In later years these accounts will remain at their higher levels, but will not increase any further.

Required

1. Determine the amount of working capital that is expected to be provided by operations related to the expansion for the first year and the second year.
2. Determine the amount of cash expected to be provided by operations related to the expansion for the first year and the second year.
3. What do your results tell the managers?

17-34 Comprehensive problem (related to Appendix)   Comparative balance sheets and an income statement for RJM Company are given below. All data are in millions of dollars.

RJM Company Balance Sheets as of June 30

Assets	19X7	19X6
Cash	$ 9.5	$ 28.7
Accounts receivable	125.8	88.6
Inventories	311.4	307.0
Prepayments	12.6	11.4
Total current assets	459.3	435.7
Investments	68.3	71.8
Plant and equipment	1,313.9	1,240.6
Accumulated depreciation	(753.1)	(687.4)
Intangible assets	42.5	46.2
Total assets	$1,130.9	$1,106.9

Equities		
Accounts payable	$ 62.6	$ 59.8
Taxes payable	32.4	29.6
Accrued expenses	38.9	52.6
Total current liabilities	133.9	142.0
Long-term debt	505.3	496.2
Common stock, no par value	384.2	377.4
Retained earnings	107.5	91.3
Total equities	$1,130.9	$1,106.9

RJM Company Income Statement for 19X7

Sales and other revenue		$896.3
Expenses:		
Cost of goods sold	$493.2	
Depreciation	69.3	
Amortization	3.7	
Other expenses	288.5	854.7
Net income		$ 41.6

Sales and other revenue includes a gain of $0.8 million on sale of investments. Amortization expense is related to intangible assets. Other expenses include losses of $1.3 million on sales and other disposals of equipment. These assets had cost $9.6 million and had accumulated depreciation of $3.6 million. Long-term debt and common stock were issued for cash.

Required

1. Prepare a worksheet for a statement of changes in financial position on a working capital basis.
2. Prepare a section on operations only for a cash basis statement of changes in financial position.

17-35 Classification of items in funds statements—alternative bases A list of items follows, most of which would appear on a statement of changes in financial position for Brillan Company for the year 19X8 if such a statement were prepared on the cash basis or the working capital basis, or both. That is, some items might appear only on one statement, some items might appear on both, and some items might appear on neither. During the current year, cash increased by $101,000 and working capital increased by $125,000.

1. Dividends declared during the year were $125,000, but dividends actually paid in cash were $103,000.
2. An issue of 10-year bonds payable was sold for $275,000 cash.
3. Amortization of the company's franchise cost was $6,000.
4. Depreciation on the company's tangible fixed assets was $159,000.
5. Land was sold at a loss of $14,000; cash received for the sale was $74,000.
6. Decrease in inventory, $6,000.
7. Increase in accounts receivable, $81,000.
8. Increase in accrued expenses payable, $11,000.
9. Decrease in income taxes payable, $24,000.
10. Increase in accounts payable, $51,000.
11. Decrease in prepaid expenses, $1,000.
12. Increase in Allowance to Reduce Short-term Investments to Lower-of-Cost-or-Market, $3,000.
13. Decrease in short-term bank borrowings (debt), $13,000.
14. Cash paid for new equipment, $500,000.
15. Cash paid for a long-term investment, $158,000.
16. Note payable given to acquire land and building, $200,000. This is a 10-year note.
17. Amortization of discount on the 10-year bond issue mentioned in part 2, $2,000.
18. Cash received as dividend on stock held as a long-term investment and accounted for on the equity basis, $25,000.
19. Amortization of discount on a long-term investment in bonds, $3,000.
20. Cash received from sale of treasury stock, $6,000; the stock had cost the company $4,000.
21. Increase in credit balance of Deferred Taxes account, $4,000.
22. Brillan's portion of net income of company whose stock is mentioned in part 18, $56,000.
23. Net income for the year, $402,000.

Required: Prepare a statement of changes in financial position for Brillan Company for 19X8 using the (a) cash concept of funds, and the (b) working capital concept of funds.

17-36 Funds statement from comparative trial balances   Below are the trial balances for Mesmer Company at the beginning and the end of 19X5.

	Beginning of Year		End of Year	
	Dr.	Cr.	Dr.	Cr.
Cash	$ 50,000		$ 60,000	
Accounts receivable	150,000		200,000	
Inventory	250,000		270,000	
Prepaid expenses	50,000		70,000	
Land	250,000		307,000	
Buildings and equipment	700,000		838,000	
Bond discount—5% bonds	—		8,000	

| | Beginning of Year | | End of Year | |
	Dr.	Cr.	Dr.	Cr.
Allowance for bad debts		$ 25,000		$ 35,000
Accumulated depreciation		300,000		421,000
Accounts payable		170,000		220,000
Accrued expenses		105,000		115,000
Bonds payable—5% bonds		—		200,000
—6% bonds		175,000		—
Bond premium—6% bonds		4,000		—
Long-term notes payable		—		80,000
Capital stock—par value		450,000		475,000
Paid-in capital in excess of par		81,000		83,500
Retained earnings		140,000		123,500
	$1,450,000	$1,450,000	$1,753,000	$1,753,000

The following information is also available regarding Mesmer Company's activities in 19X5.

1. Net income for the year was $70,000, which amount included gains and losses on transactions relating to fixed assets and bond retirements.

2. Land costing $100,000 was purchased, paying 20% in cash and giving long-term notes payable for the remainder of the purchase price. The only other transaction related to land was a sale that produced a gain of $12,000.

3. Equipment that had originally cost $82,000 and had a book value of $23,000 was sold for $8,000 cash. Additional equipment was purchased for cash.

4. At the beginning of the year, bonds payable carrying an interest rate of 5% and a maturity value of $200,000 were sold for $190,000 cash. Very shortly thereafter, the 6% bonds which had previously been outstanding (and which had originally been issued at a premium) were purchased on the open market for $159,000 and were retired.

5. During the year, a stock dividend was declared and issued and was appropriately accounted for by a charge against Retained Earnings for $27,500, the market value of the stock distributed in connection with the dividend. The market value was 10% higher than the par value for the shares issued. Cash dividends were declared and paid as usual.

Required: Prepare a statement of changes in financial position using the working capital definition of resources.

CHAPTER 18

ANALYZING FINANCIAL STATEMENTS

For many reasons, managers are interested in relationships among selected items in the firm's financial statements. From Chapter 2 we know that managers often establish a target profit expressed as a ratio of income to sales (return on sales). We have also seen that the ratio of income to total assets (or some other measure of return on investment) is commonly used in measuring divisional performance. The chapters on comprehensive budgeting stressed the development of pro forma financial statements and the cash squeeze that can accompany buildups of inventories and receivables. This chapter addresses directly the topic of analyzing financial statements. Such analysis includes the calculation, interpretation, and evaluations of ratios of one element of the financial statements to another.

Many outsiders, like suppliers, investors in debt or equity securities, and brokerage firms that give (or sell) advice on investments, are extremely interested in the activities of a firm. Our approach to the topic of analyzing financial statements will be the viewpoint of a financial analyst, who makes recommendations to potential investors after studying financial statements and other sources of information about a business entity. The analyst's conclusions, opinions, and recommendations can affect the entity's ability to obtain credit, sell stock, and secure new contracts. Therefore, the manager must be aware of the financial analyst's viewpoint. But as we proceed, it should become obvious that managers and analysts share many of the same concerns.

THE PURPOSE AND APPROACH
OF THE ANALYST

Financial analysts use financial statement information in their analyses for decision making. Banks that provide short-term loans, insurance companies that buy long-term bonds, brokerage firms that make recommendations to their customers, mutual funds that buy stocks or bonds—all of these, and many other institutions, employ financial analysts to help them make decisions about individual firms. Individual investors also perform financial analysis in making their investment decisions.

Financial analysts, like company managers, base their decisions on expectations about the future. Thus, just as a manager's analysis focuses on forecasts of the future, that of the financial analyst must concentrate on what the future holds. Analysts want to know what to expect from a firm—whether it is likely to be able to pay its bills, repay loans with interest, pay dividends on stock, or expand into new areas. It should not be surprising, then, that the financial analyst, like the firm's managers, is concerned with what happened in the past only insofar as the past can be considered a reliable guide to the future. For example, a company might have an extremely impressive history of regular growth in net income and sales, financial stability, and capable management. But if its major product becomes illegal (e.g., the insecticide DDT), or obsolete (e.g., early types of computers and calculators), the firm's prospects would be severely impaired. Nevertheless, like managers who use information such as a cost prediction formula based on past experience, the analysts approach their task with the assumption that what has held true in the past is likely to continue *unless* they have information that indicates otherwise. Hence, an analyst, like one of the firm's managers, will be continually on the lookout for any signs that the future will be different from the past.

In addition to having in common a focus on the future, the firm's managers and the financial analyst share, for several reasons, an interest in the same analytical approaches. First, because it is important to the firm that investors continue to be willing to supply capital at reasonable rates, internal managers want to duplicate the analyses made by outsiders (viz., financial analysts) so as to look at the firm in the way it is seen by those outsiders. The managers review these analyses to see whether the firm's ratios are out of line with those of other firms in the industry, or with what the managers believe to be the expectations of outsiders.

Second, ratios offer the internal manager an opportunity to view operating results in a way that reflects relationships not readily discernible from a review of the ratio's components. For example, one might expect the levels of sales returns, bad debts, and accounts receivable to be related to sales volume. Hence, a more efficient implementation of the principle of management-by-exception could result from internal analyses that reflect the relationships of these items to sales rather than from reports that show only the individual values for these items in relation to prior periods. It is not surprising, then, that internal managers often use ratios, and trends or changes in ratios, as starting points in analyzing their firm's operations.

For obvious reasons, the internal manager has more information than the external analyst and can study ratios, and their underlying components, in more depth. For example, using a technique described later in this chapter, an outsider might calculate the *average* age of a firm's accounts receivable. The internal manager could, however, obtain a more precise picture of the age of outstanding receivables by requesting, periodically, an aging schedule of receivables, which schedule would show exactly how much of the total receivables are under 30 days old, 31 to 60 days old, and so on. In effect, the external analyst obtains a general picture of the firm's operation and financial position, while the internal analyst is interested in, and can obtain information about, the details of that picture. This difference is consistent with the interests of the two analysts. The external analyst is interested in the firm as a whole, its prospects for the future and the results of decisions by management as a team. The internal analyst, on the other hand, is interested also in what specific actions can be taken by which individual managers.

GENERAL METHODS OF ANALYSIS

Financial analysis consists of a number of interrelated activities. Among the most important of these activities are considerations of ratios and trends and the comparison of ratios and trends against some norms. (A norm is a standard for comparison, which could be an average value for a particular industry or for all firms in the economy.) Trends are of interest, of course, as clues to what the future holds.

Areas of Analysis

Different types of investors are interested in different aspects of a firm. Short-term creditors, such as suppliers and banks considering loans of relatively short duration (90 days or six months), are concerned primarily with the firm's short-term prospects. They want to know whether there is a significant danger that the firm will not be able to pay its obligations in the near future. Banks, insurance companies, pension funds, and other investors considering relatively long-term commitments (e.g. 10-year loans), are also concerned with the firm's short-term prospects, but are more concerned with its long-term outlook. If such investors are satisfied that the firm has no short-term problems, they still might not make a loan unless they are reasonably sure that the firm has good prospects for long-term financial stability and can be expected to repay the loan and interest.

Current stockholders, and potential individual or institutional stockholders, are also interested in both the short- and long-term prospects of the firm. But they are concerned with more than the ability to repay loans and make interest payments. They are interested in the firm's potential profitability—its ability to earn satisfactory profits and pay dividends; and, with profitability comes the likelihood that the market price of the stock will increase.

We have divided the discussion of these aspects of the prospects of a firm into three major areas: liquidity, solvency, and profitability. For the most part we shall be working with ratios, the results of dividing numbers by other numbers. Ratios are particularly useful because they enable analysts to compare firms of different sizes.

Sample Financial Statements

In our discussion we shall use the financial statements and some additional financial information about Graham Company (Exhibit 18-1). The analysis has actually begun in the exhibit because it shows the percentages of sales for each item on the income statement and the percentage of total assets or total equities for each balance sheet item. These percentage statements, or **common size statements,** are used to spot trends. They can sometimes help an analyst to see signs of either trouble or improvement.

Exhibit 18-1

Graham Company Balance Sheets as of December 31

	19X6 Dollars	19X6 Percent	19X5 Dollars	19X5 Percent
Current assets:				
Cash	$ 80,000	5.2%	$ 50,000	3.6%
Accounts receivable	180,000	11.6	120,000	8.7
Inventory	190,000	12.2	230,000	16.7
Total current assets	450,000	29.0	400,000	29.0
Plant and equipment—cost	1,350,000	87.1	1,150,000	83.3
Accumulated depreciation	(340,000)	(21.9)	(250,000)	(18.1)
Net plant and equipment	1,010,000	65.2	900,000	65.2
Other assets	90,000	5.8	80,000	5.8
Total assets	$1,550,000	100.0	$1,380,000	100.0
Current liabilities:				
Accounts payable	$ 110,000	7.1%	$ 105,000	7.6%
Accrued expenses	40,000	2.6	15,000	1.1
Total current liabilities	150,000	9.7	120,000	8.7
Long-term debt	600,000	38.7	490,000	35.5
Total liabilities	750,000	48.4	610,000	44.2
Common stock, 22,000 shares	220,000	14.2	220,000	15.9
Paid-in capital	350,000	22.6	350,000	25.4
Retained earnings	230,000	14.8	200,000	14.5
Total stockholders' equity	800,000	51.6	770,000	55.8
Total equities	$1,550,000	100.0	$1,380,000	100.0

Graham Company Income Statements
for the years ended December 31

	19X6 Dollars	19X6 Percent	19X5 Dollars	19X5 Percent
Sales	$1,300,000	100.0%	$1,080,000	100.0%
Cost of goods sold	800,000	61.5	670,000	62.0
Gross profit	500,000	38.5	410,000	38.0
Operating expenses	280,000	21.6	210,000	19.4
Income before interest and taxes	220,000	16.9	200,000	18.6
Interest expense	48,000	3.7	42,000	3.9
Income before taxes	172,000	13.2	158,000	14.7
Income taxes at 40% rate	68,800	5.3	63,200	5.9
Net income	$ 103,200	7.9	$ 94,800	8.8

Other information:

Dividends declared and paid were $73,200 in 19X6, $63,000 in 19X5
Operating expenses include depreciation of $90,000 in 19X6, $75,000 in 19X5.

Two of the more important percentages on the income statement are the **gross profit ratio,** which is gross profit divided by sales, and **return on sales,** which is net income divided by sales. These ratios for Graham Company in 19X6 are 38.5% and 7.9%, respectively. The gross profit ratio improved in 19X6 over 19X5, but return on sales declined.

Return on sales and the gross profit ratio are interesting to financial analysts and to internal managers because these ratios indicate, to some extent, how valuable a dollar of sales is to the firm. The ratios do not correspond to the contribution margin ratio, but they do give a rough idea of the profit/sales relationship. A relatively low return on sales, combined with a normal gross profit ratio, could indicate that the firm's operating expenses are out of line with those of other firms. As we shall mention several times in this chapter, ratios give clues or provide indicators, but do not tell you that a firm is acting wisely or unwisely.

Balance-sheet ratios are used to see whether the proportions of particular assets or liabilities are increasing or decreasing, and whether they are within reasonable bounds. We shall explore balance-sheet ratios in more detail later in the chapter.

LIQUIDITY

Liquidity is the ability of a firm to meet its short-term liabilities. The more liquid a firm, the more likely it is to be able to pay its employees, suppliers, and holders of its short-term notes payable. Analysis of liquidity is most important to short-term creditors, but is also of concern to long-term creditors and stockholders. Even if a company has excellent long-term prospects, it could fail to realize them because it was forced into bankruptcy when it could not pay its short-term liabilities. In order to get to the long term, a firm has to get through the short term.

Working Capital and the Current Ratio

Working capital, the difference between current assets and current liabilities, is a very rough measure of liquidity. The Graham Company had the following amounts of working capital at the ends of 19X5 and 19X6:

	19X6	19X5
Current assets	$450,000	$400,000
Current liabilities	150,000	120,000
Working capital	$300,000	$280,000

We see that working capital increased, but this does not necessarily mean that the firm became more liquid. For one thing, working capital is stated in absolute dollar terms and hence is greatly influenced by the size of the firm. Most analysts look at changes in working capital only as a very rough indication of changes in liquidity, and will supplement their analysis with several other calculations.

The **current ratio** is a measure of relative liquidity, which takes into account differences in absolute size. It can be used to compare firms that have different total current assets and liabilities as well as to offer a basis for comparison for the same firm in years when the components of the ratio change.

$$\text{Current ratio} = \frac{\text{current assets}}{\text{current liabilities}}$$

Graham Company has current ratios of 3.33 to 1 in 19X5 ($400,000/$120,000) and 3 to 1 in 19X6 ($450,000/$150,000). We would therefore say that, on the basis of the current ratio, the firm seemed to be less liquid at the end of 19X6. There is a very good reason for saying "seemed to be less liquid." One major problem that arises with the use of any ratio, but especially the current ratio, is that of composition. The **composition problem** concerns the use of a total, like total current assets (or current liabilities), that might mask information that would be conveyed by looking at the individual components. How soon will the current assets be converted into cash so that they can be used to pay current liabilities? How soon are the current liabilities due for payment? You already know that current assets are normally listed in the order of their liquidity, from cash, the most liquid, to prepaid expenses. (In fact, prepaid expenses will not be converted into cash at all, so technically they are not liquid at all.) The analyst can obtain a general idea of the potential magnitude of the composition problem by reviewing the common size balance sheet to see the extent to which current assets are made up of relatively liquid items. Some analysts compute the proportion of total current assets represented by each component, and compare those proportions from year to year.

Quick Ratio (Acid-Test Ratio)

The **quick ratio,** or **acid-test ratio,** is computed by dividing cash plus accounts receivable plus marketable securities by current liabilities. Thus it is similar to the current ratio but with inventories and prepayments eliminated from the numerator. Only those assets that are cash or "near cash" (called **quick assets**) are included, so that the ratio gives an indication of debt-paying ability in the very near term.

$$\text{Quick ratio} = \frac{\text{cash} + \text{marketable securities} + \text{receivables}}{\text{current liabilities}}$$

Graham Company had no marketable securities at the end of either year, hence its quick ratios are as follows:

$$19X5 \quad \frac{\$50,000 + \$120,000}{\$120,000} = 1.42$$

$$19X6 \quad \frac{\$80,000 + \$180,000}{\$150,000} = 1.73$$

Graham Company seems to have increased its liquidity because its quick ratio increased. We could say that the firm was better able to meet current liabilities at the end of 19X6 because the ratio of its most liquid assets to its current liabilities has increased. We would still like to know more. For example, we would want to know how soon its current liabilities have to be paid, and how rapidly the firm can expect to turn its receivables and inventory into cash. The payment schedules for current liabilities cannot be determined simply by examination of financial statements, but we can gain some insight into the liquidity of receivables and inventory.

Working Capital Activity Ratios

Neither the acid-test ratio nor the current ratio indicates the time within which the firm expects to realize cash from its receivables and inventories. Nor does either tell us the time within which the firm must pay its various current liabilities. Three ratios are commonly used to gain some insight into the answers to these important questions.

Accounts Receivable Turnover.   This ratio is calculated by dividing credit sales for the year by average accounts receivable:

$$\text{Accounts receivable turnover} = \frac{\text{credit sales}}{\text{average receivables}}$$

In general, average receivables are defined as the beginning balance plus the ending balance, divided by 2. This simple averaging procedure is satisfactory so long as there are no extremely high or low points during the year (including the end of the year). If a firm has widely fluctuating receivable balances, it would be better to take a monthly average instead of using only the beginning and ending balances for the year. For illustrative purposes we assume that all of Graham Company's sales are on credit. Because we do not have the beginning balance for 19X5, we can only calculate the turnover for 19X6 for Graham Company.

$$\frac{\$1,300,000}{(\$120,000 + \$180,000)/2} = \frac{\$1,300,000}{\$150,000} = 8.67 \text{ times}$$

Receivable turnover is a measure of how rapidly the firm collects its receivables. In general, the higher the turnover the better. Analysts will sometimes make a related calculation called number of **days' sales in accounts receivable.** This figure indicates the average age of ending accounts receivable and is calculated as follows:

$$\text{Days' sales in accounts receivable} = \frac{\text{ending accounts receivable}}{\text{average daily credit sales}}$$

Average daily sales is simply credit sales for the year divided by 365. For Graham Company, assuming that all sales are on credit, we have average daily credit sales of about $3,562 ($1,300,000/365).

$$\text{Days' sales in receivables} = \frac{\$180,000}{\$3,562} = 51 \text{ days}$$

Graham Company's accounts receivable are, on the average, 51 days old. The firm therefore will probably collect all of its outstanding receivables by about 51 days after the balance-sheet date.

The two receivables ratios are interrelated. If receivables at the beginning and end of the year were the same, we could calculate days' sales in receivables by dividing the number of turnovers into 365 days. [In this case we would get about 42 days (365/ 8.67 turnovers), which is somewhat less than the 51 days we calculated before. The difference arises because the beginning balance in receivables was a good deal lower than the ending balance.] Similarly, we could divide the number of days' sales in receivables into 365 days to get the turnover. (Again, the result would be different from our previous calculation of 8.67 because of the lower beginning balance.)

The faster customers pay, the better. An increase in turnover (or decrease in days' sales in receivables) indicates that the firm is becoming more efficient in collecting its accounts. But there are always trade-offs; if the firm loses sales because of tight credit policies, the advantage of faster collection might be more than offset by the loss of profits because of lower total sales. (Remember, the collection period can be reduced to zero days if the firm sells only for cash.)

Using the total sales of Graham Company in the computations of the two receivables-related ratios was justified because we knew that all sales were on credit. An analyst outside the firm would not usually be able to determine what portion of a firm's sales is on credit and would use total sales for the analysis for lack of better information. The ratios so computed would not be misleading as long as the proportions of cash and credit sales did not change significantly (another instance of "the composition problem.") An internal manager would, of course, have access to information about the composition of total sales and could make a more precise calculation of the receivables ratios. Moreover, the internal manager would be extremely interested in the precise patterns of customer payments, for cash budgeting and control purposes; hence the manager would be concerned with individual customers that are large enough to have a significant impact on the pattern of cash collections. Nevertheless, as a first step in his analysis, the internal manager is likely to use the same general ratios as the external analyst.

Inventory Turnover.   The same type of analysis applies to the firm's inventory. Inventory turnover is calculated as follows:

$$\text{Inventory turnover} = \frac{\text{cost of goods sold}}{\text{average inventory}}$$

Again, average inventory is usually considered to be the sum of the beginning and ending balances divided by 2. If the firm has higher inventories and lower inventories for significant portions of the year because of seasonal business, it would be better to use monthly figures to determine the average.

Graham Company's inventory turnover for 19X6 is about 3.8 times, calculated as follows:

$$\frac{\$800,000}{(\$230,000 + \$190,000)/2} = \frac{\$800,000}{\$210,000} = 3.8$$

We cannot compute the 19X5 turnover because we do not know the beginning balance.

This measure indicates the efficiency with which the firm uses its inventory. Turnover of inventory is critical for many businesses, especially those that sell at relatively low markup (ratio of gross profit to cost) and depend on high volumes of sales to earn satisfactory profits. Discount stores and food stores rely heavily on rapid turnover of inventory to keep up their profitability. Other firms, like jewelry stores, with very high markups do not need such rapid turnovers to be profitable.

Investment in inventory can be very expensive. Some costs—insurance, personal property taxes, interest on the funds tied up in inventory, and obsolescence—can be very high. Therefore, a firm would prefer to keep its inventory as low as possible. The problem is that if inventory is too low, particularly in firms such as retail stores, sales might be lost because customers cannot find what they want. Such firms must balance the need to maintain fairly high inventories to keep sales up with the additional costs of having high inventories.

Analysts will also sometimes calculate the number of **days' sales in inventory,** which is a measure of the supply that the firm maintains. This ratio is calculated as follows:

$$\text{Days' sales in inventory} = \frac{\text{ending inventory}}{\text{average daily cost of goods sold}}$$

Average daily cost of goods sold is simply cost of goods sold for the year divided by 365. For the Graham Company this figure is $2,192 ($800,000/365) and the number of days' sales in inventory is about 87 ($190,000/$2,192).

As you may remember from your study of financial accounting, generally accepted accounting principles allow several different formats for the income statement. In some acceptable formats, no single number is given for cost of goods sold, and the outside analyst cannot, therefore, determine inventory turnover using the approach presented above. In such cases, the analyst will use total sales as a substitute for cost of goods sold, even though sales and inventory are not measured in the same way. (Sales is measured in selling prices, while inventory is measured in cost prices.) The inventory turnover so derived is, of course, overstated—a unit costing $1 and sold for $2 will reflect two inventory turnovers when only one unit has been sold—and the analyst must recognize the automatic overstatement in the calculation. As long as analysts understand the effect of using the substitute (sales), they will not be misled by the results. But note that comparisons between firms must be made more carefully because different firms may have differing policies on markup. The internal analyst who is trying to compare his or her firm with others in the same industry will face the same problems as the external analyst, will probably use the same substitute measure, and must, therefore, be as cautious as the external analyst in interpreting the results of the computations.

One last matter warrants comment here. As you will recall from Chapter 13, a manufacturing firm has not one but three types of inventory: raw materials, work in process, and finished goods. The calculation of inventory turnover, as described above, relates to the finished goods inventory of a manufacturing firm, since only that inventory is measured on the same basis (full cost of a completed unit) as cost of goods sold. An internal analyst should be able to compute not only the turnover of finished goods inventory but also the turnover for the firm's inventory of raw materials:

$$\frac{\text{Turnover of}}{\text{inventory of}} = \frac{\text{raw materials used in production}}{\text{average raw materials inventory}}$$
$$\text{raw materials}$$

An external analyst is seldom able to compute this second inventory turnover because the financial statements available externally seldom, if ever, provide sufficient information to determine the value of the numerator of the ratio.

Days' Purchases in Accounts Payable.   This ratio, of special concern to creditors and the firm's managers, is computed as follows:

$$\frac{\text{Days' purchases in}}{\text{accounts payable}} = \frac{\text{ending accounts payable}}{\text{average daily purchases}}$$

The calculation of this ratio by an internal analyst in a merchandising firm is relatively easy because such an analyst may have direct knowledge of the firm's total purchases for the year and can readily compute average daily purchases (total purchases/365). The analyst could also compute total purchases as follows:

$$\text{Purchases} = \frac{\text{cost of}}{\text{goods sold}} + \frac{\text{ending}}{\text{inventory}} - \frac{\text{beginning}}{\text{inventory}}$$

For Graham Company, the days' purchases in accounts payable can be computed as about 53 days:

$$\frac{\text{Days' purchases}}{\text{in accounts payable}} = \frac{\$110,000}{(\$800,000 + \$190,000 - \$230,000)/365}$$

$$= \frac{\$110,000}{\$2,082} = 52.8 \text{ days}$$

We cannot compute the ratio for 19X5 because we do not know the beginning inventory for that year. The value for 19X6, about 53 days, must be interpreted in light of the normal credit terms offered by suppliers. If the normal terms for purchases require payment in 60 days, the ratio indicates no significant problem; if normal credit terms are cash in 30 days, the ratio suggests that a problem may exist. Of course, it pays a firm to take as long as possible to pay its suppliers, so long as it does not incur high interest charges or damage its credit rating. Reducing payables by paying faster may require that the firm obtain additional financing, and such financing would have some cost (interest on a short- or long-term loan, or the opportunity cost of capital).

PROFITABILITY

Profitability can be measured in absolute dollar terms, like net income, or by using ratios. The most commonly used measures of profitability fall under the general heading of return on investment. As described in Chapter 11, return on investment is actually a family of relationships having the general form

$$\frac{\text{Return on}}{\text{investment}} = \frac{\text{income}}{\text{investment}}$$

External investors, especially stockholders and potential stockholders, are interested in the return that they can expect from the investment that they make. Managers within the firm are concerned with earning satisfactory returns on the investment that they can control. As a practical matter, then, different analysts and managers will define both income and investment differently when trying to measure the same basic relationship. In this section, we present some of the most often used alternative ways of looking at this basic relationship of accomplishment (return, income) to effort (investment).

Return on Assets (ROA)

ROA is a measure of operating efficiency, of how well the firm (or, more correctly, its management team) has used the assets under its control to generate income. The ratio below is one way to make the calculation:

$$\frac{\text{Return on}}{\text{assets}} = \frac{\text{net income} + \text{interest} + \text{income taxes}}{\text{average total assets}}$$

For Graham Company, ROA was about 15% for 19X6, calculated as follows:

$$\frac{\text{Return on}}{\text{assets}} = \frac{\$103,200 + \$48,000 + \$68,800}{(\$1,380,000 + \$1,550,000)/2}$$

$$= \frac{\$220,000}{\$1,465,000} = 15.0\%$$

We add back interest expense because we are trying to determine how profitably the firm uses its assets regardless of how the acquisition of those assets was financed. We are interested here in the operating efficiency of the firm. Net income will be higher if the firm has no long-term debt and therefore no interest expense, but the interest expense (or lack thereof) does not change the firm's operating efficiency. Accordingly, we eliminate the expense that relates only to the way the firm was financed.

We add back income taxes because the amount of tax depends on whether the firm uses debt or equity capital to finance the acquisition of its assets. (As you will recall, interest expense is tax deductible, while dividends are not.) Since our concern, when looking at return on assets, is to determine how efficiently the firm uses the assets that it has acquired, we add back income taxes to eliminate the effect of having chosen a particular way to finance the asset acquisitions. (Some analysts would add back interest but not taxes; others would add to net income only the after-tax effect of interest—interest expense times one minus the tax rate. There are arguments to support almost any definition of the numerator in the return-on-investment calculation. Choosing one alternative over another is largely a matter of personal preference.)

Average total assets is normally the sum of the beginning and ending balance-sheet amounts divided by 2. Here again, there are alternatives. If there are significant fluctuations from month to month, it is probably better, as we said in earlier discussions of ratios that involved averages, to use monthly data to determine the average. Moreover, some analysts would use, in the denominator, end-of-year assets, some would use beginning-of-year amounts, and still others would use total assets minus current liabilities. (Analysts in the latter group would argue that current liabilities are "automatic" sources of financing and typically relate to operating, rather than financing, decisions.)

In this chapter, we use average total assets, with no consideration of current liabilities, but we caution you that this is a matter of choice and preference.

In a typical company, both internal and external analysts will be able to obtain the information they need directly from publicly available financial statements, and direct comparisons with firms in the same industry can be made. However, it may be extremely difficult to make interfirm comparisons when the firm under study is highly diversified.

Return on Common Equity (ROE)

Return on assets is a measure of operating efficiency. Common stockholders are also concerned with the return on *their* investment, which is affected not only by operations but also by the amount of debt and preferred stock in the firm's capital structure. Graham Company has no preferred stock but it does have debt.

ROE is computed as follows:

$$\begin{matrix} \text{Return on} \\ \text{common equity} \\ \text{(ROE)} \end{matrix} = \frac{\text{net income}}{\text{average common stockholders' equity}}$$

Average common stockholders' equity, in the absence of preferred stock, is simply the sum of the beginning and ending amounts of stockholders' equity divided by 2. If there is preferred stock, preferred dividends must be subtracted from net income in the numerator, and the amount of total stockholders' equity attributable to preferred stock is subtracted in the denominator to obtain common stockholders' equity.[1]

ROE for Graham Company in 19X6 is a bit over 13%:

$$\frac{\$103,200}{(\$770,000 + \$800,000)/2} = \frac{\$103,200}{\$785,000} = 13.1\%$$

Notice that ROE in the example is somewhat less than ROA. If a firm finances its assets solely with common stock, such a relationship will hold between ROE and ROA because ROE is computed using after-tax income. But debtholders do not participate in the earnings of the firm; they received a stipulated, constant amount of interest. Hence the firm can increase its ROE if it uses debt, provided that ROA is greater than the interest rate it must pay to debtholders. This method of using debt (or preferred stock) to increase ROE is called **leverage** or **trading on the equity.** It involves risk as well as the potential for greater return.

The Effects of Leverage

We can illustrate the effects of leverage by considering the ROE that would be achieved under different financing arrangements. Suppose that a firm requires total

[1]There are several ways of determining the amount of total stockholder equity attributable to preferred stock. The best method, where possible, is to use the call value of preferred stock. Call value is the amount that the firm would have to pay to retire the preferred stock, and it is usually more than par value. In the case of preferred stocks that have no call value, par value could be used.

assets of $1,000,000 to earn $180,000 per year before interest and income taxes, for an ROA of 18%. The tax rate is 40%. Three alternative financing plans are possible: (1) all common stock; (2) $400,000 common stock and $600,000 in 7% bonds (interest expense of $42,000); and (3) $400,000 in common stock and $600,000 in 8% preferred stock (dividends of $48,000). We can prepare condensed income statements under the three methods as follows:

	(1) All Common Stock	(2) Debt and Common Stock	(3) Preferred Stock and Common Stock
Income before interest and taxes	$ 180,000	$180,000	$180,000
Interest expense at 7%	0	42,000	0
Income before taxes	180,000	138,000	180,000
Income taxes at 40%	72,000	55,200	72,000
Net income	$ 108,000	$ 82,800	$108,000
Less: Preferred stock dividends	0	0	48,000
Earnings available for common stock	$ 108,000	$ 82,800	$ 60,000
divided by			
Common equity invested	$1,000,000	$400,000	$400,000
equals			
Return on common equity	10.8%	20.7%	15%

The plans that include debt or preferred stock both result in lower earnings available for common equity, but a higher ROE than would be achieved if all common equity were used.

Before we go on, please do not get the impression that dividends on preferred stock are an expense. They are not, but they must be subtracted from net income to reach earnings available for common stockholders because the preferred shareholders have a prior claim on the earnings of the firm. They must receive their dividends before common stockholders can receive dividends, thus reducing the amount left for possible distribution to common stockholders.

Unfortunately, leverage works both ways. It is good for the common stockholder when earnings are high, bad when they are low. Suppose that the firm earns only $60,000 before interest and taxes. We would then have the following results:

	(1) All Common	(2) $600,000 Debt	(3) $600,000 Preferred
Income before interest and taxes	$60,000	$60,000	$60,000
Interest expense	0	42,000	0
Income before taxes	60,000	18,000	60,000
Income taxes at 40% rate	24,000	7,200	24,000
Net income	36,000	10,800	36,000
Preferred stock dividends	0	0	42,000
Earnings available for common	$36,000	$10,800	($6,000)
Common equity	$1,000,000	$400,000	$400,000
ROE	3.6%	2.7%	negative

As you can see, ROE is highest if all common equity is used, but the return is very low. Firms that have relatively stable revenues and expenses, like public utilities, can use considerable leverage. It is risky for firms in cyclical businesses like automobiles, aircraft, and construction, where income fluctuates greatly from year to year. A couple of bad years in a row could bring a heavily leveraged firm into bankruptcy.

Some managers find it useful to expand the ROE calculation as follows:

$$\text{ROE} = \left(\frac{\text{net income}}{\text{sales}}\right) \times \left(\frac{\text{sales}}{\text{average total assets}}\right) \times \left(\frac{\text{average total assets}}{\text{average common stock-holders' equity}}\right)$$

The first factor is return on sales, discussed earlier. The second factor is called **asset turnover,** and is designed to show the dollars of revenue produced by the average dollar invested in assets. The third factor is a type of leverage factor, one of the several ways of reflecting the extent to which the firm has financed its operations with debt. Notice that sales cancels out in the denominator of the first factor and the numerator of the second, while total assets cancels with the denominator of the second factor and the numerator of the third. Thus, the equation reduces to net income/average common stockholders' equity, the ROE formulation we introduced originally.

Partitioning ROE into the three factors might give managers some hints for increasing ROE. Comparisons of the individual ratios with those of similar firms would not only indicate where a firm is falling behind its competitors, but also could enable managers to see more quickly how an improvement would affect ROE.

Using the results for Graham Company for 19X6 produces the following:

$$\text{ROE} = \left(\frac{\$103,200}{\$1,300,000}\right) \times \left(\frac{\$1,300,000}{(\$1,380,000 + \$1,550,000)/2}\right)$$
$$\times \left(\frac{(\$1,380,000 + \$1,550,000)/2}{(\$770,000 + \$800,000)/2}\right)$$
$$= 0.079 \times 0.887 \times 1.866 = 0.131, \text{ or } 13.1\%$$

Earnings per Share (EPS)

An investor considering the purchase of stock in a firm is not concerned as much with the total income of the firm as with his or her share of that income. That share is his or her proportional interest in the firm. Publicly owned companies present earnings per share data. Earnings per share, or EPS, is the most widely cited statistic in the financial press, business section of newspapers, and recommendations by brokerage firms and other investment advisers. In relatively simple cases, EPS is calculated as follows:

$$\frac{\text{Earnings per}}{\text{share (EPS)}} = \frac{\text{net income} - \text{dividends on preferred stock}}{\text{weighted-average common shares outstanding}}$$

The weighted average of common shares outstanding is used because it represents the best measure of the shares outstanding throughout the period, rather than just at the end of the period. If we assume that Graham Company had 22,000 shares outstanding all through 19X5 and 19X6, as well as at the ends of those years, its EPS figures would be:

$$19X5 \quad \frac{\$94,800 - 0}{22,000} = \frac{\$94,800}{22,000} = \$4.31$$

$$19X6 \quad \frac{\$103,200 - 0}{22,000} = \frac{\$103,200}{22,000} = \$4.69$$

EPS in 19X6 was $0.38 higher than in 19X5. This is an 8.8% growth rate, which can be calculated as follows:

$$\text{Growth rate of EPS} = \frac{\text{EPS current year} - \text{EPS prior year}}{\text{EPS prior year}}$$

For Graham Company:

$$\frac{\$4.69 - \$4.31}{\$4.31} = 8.8\%$$

The growth rate of EPS is an extremely useful piece of information to a financial analyst interested in the common stock of a firm. In general, the higher the growth rate the investing public as a whole expects from a firm, the more it will be willing to pay for the common stock.

Growth rates should be calculated over a number of years, rather than for a single year as we have done here. A single large increase in EPS does not mean that the firm is growing. It might simply reflect a rebound from a particularly poor year.

Dilution of EPS.   Recent years have seen the increasing use of **convertible securities,** bonds and preferred stock that can be converted into common stock at the option of the owner. The fact that these securities can be converted into common shares poses the problem of potential **dilution** (decreases) in EPS, because earnings would have to be spread over a greater number of shares. The calculation of EPS when dilution is possible can be incredibly complex.[2] We shall show you a single illustration, which is necessarily quite simple. Assume that a firm has net income of $200,000, 80,000 common shares outstanding, and an issue of convertible preferred stock. The preferred stock has dividends of $20,000 per year and is convertible into 30,000 common shares. Using the basic formula, EPS would be as follows:

$$\text{EPS} = \frac{\$200,000 - \$20,000}{80,000} = \frac{\$180,000}{80,000} = \$2.25$$

In some cases the $2.25 would be presented on the income statement and called *primary earnings per share.* Then, another EPS calculation, called *fully diluted earnings per share,* would be made. Fully diluted EPS is calculated assuming that the convertible securities had been converted into common stock at the beginning of the year. Had this occurred, there would have been no preferred dividends, but there would have

---

[2]The computation of EPS is governed by *Accounting Principles Board Opinion No. 15* (New York: American Institute of Certified Public Accountants, 1969) and *Unofficial Accounting Interpretations of APB Opinion No. 15* (New York: American Institute of Certified Public Accountants, 1970). Together, these two documents contain about 100 pages.

been an additional 30,000 common shares outstanding for the entire year. We would calculate fully diluted EPS by adding back the preferred dividends on the convertible stock to the $180,000 earnings available for common stock and adding 30,000 shares to the denominator:

$$\text{Fully diluted EPS} = \frac{\$180,000 + \$20,000}{80,000 + 30,000} = \frac{\$200,000}{110,000} = \$1.82$$

Price-Earnings Ratio (PE)

The price-earnings ratio is the ratio of the market price of a share of common stock to its earnings per share. The ratio indicates the amount an investor is paying to buy a dollar of earnings. PE ratios of high-growth companies are often very high, while those of low-growth or declining firms tend to be low. Assume that Graham Company's common stock sold at $60 per share at the end of 19X5 and $70 at the end of 19X6. The PE ratios are

$$\frac{\text{Price-}}{\text{earnings}} = \frac{\text{market price per share}}{\text{earnings per share}}$$
$$\text{ratio}$$

$$19X5 \quad \frac{\$60.00}{\$4.31} = 14$$

$$19X6 \quad \frac{\$70.00}{\$4.69} = 14.9$$

The PE ratio increased from 19X5 to 19X6. This could have happened because the firm's EPS had been growing rather slowly until 19X6 and investors believed the rate would increase in the future. Such a situation would justify a higher PE ratio. It is also possible that PE ratios as a whole increased across the market because of good economic news and expectations of good business conditions.

Dividend Yield and Payout Ratio

We have been viewing earnings available for common stockholders as the major return that accrues to owners of common stock. However, investors do not "get" EPS. They receive dividends and, they hope, increases in the market value of their shares. The **dividend yield,** calculated as the ratio of dividends per share to market price per share, is a measure of the current cash income that an investor can obtain per dollar of investment in common stock. In 19X6 the Graham Company declared and paid $73,200 in dividends, which comes to $3.33 per share on 22,000 shares. At the market price of $70, the dividend yield is about 4.76%.

$$\text{Dividend yield} = \frac{\text{dividend per share}}{\text{market value per share}}$$

$$= \frac{\$3.33}{\$70.00} = 4.76\%$$

The **payout ratio** is the ratio of dividends per share to earnings per share. For Graham Company the payout ratio in 19X6 is 71% ($3.33/$4.69). In general, companies with high growth rates show relatively low dividend yields and payout ratios. Such companies invest the cash that could be used for dividends. Investors who favor high-growth companies are not looking for dividends so much as increases in the market price of the common stock. Because such hoped-for increases may or may not come about, investing in high-growth companies is generally riskier than investing in companies that pay relatively high, stable dividends. Companies will therefore tend to attract investors who have particular philosophies about risk and return.

SOLVENCY

Solvency refers to long-term safety, to the likelihood that the firm will be able to pay its long-term liabilities. It is related to liquidity, but has a much longer time horizon. Both long-term creditors and stockholders are interested in solvency—the long-term creditor, because of a concern about receiving interest payments and a return of principal; the stockholder, because he or she cannot hope to receive dividends and increased market prices unless the firm survives.

Debt Ratio

One common measure of solvency is the debt ratio, which is calculated as follows:

$$\text{Debt ratio} = \frac{\text{total liabilities}}{\text{total assets}}$$

This ratio measures the proportion of debt in the firm's capital structure. It is also called the debt-to-assets ratio. Like some other ratios, there are variations that provide much the same information. For example, some analysts will calculate a debt-to-equity ratio as total liabilities divided by stockholders' equity. This variation gives debt as a percentage of the amount invested by stockholders. Some analysts calculate a ratio of long-term liabilities to total assets, or of long-term liabilities to fixed assets like property, plant, and equipment. The basic objective is the same with all of these ratios: to determine how debt-laden the firm is. The higher the proportion of debt in the capital structure, the riskier the firm. Firms in different industries can handle different percentages of debt. For example, public utilities typically have very high percentages of debt, manufacturing firms somewhat less.

We can calculate the debt ratio for Graham Company for both 19X5 and 19X6. The results are:

$$19X5 \quad \frac{\$610,000}{\$1,380,000} = 44.2\%$$

$$19X6 \quad \frac{\$750,000}{\$1,550,000} = 48.4\%$$

Notice that if we subtract the debt ratio from 1, we get the proportion of stockholders' equity in the capital structure. This is usually called the *equity ratio*. It is, like the debt ratio, a way of measuring solvency, but from a different standpoint.

The debt ratio increased from 19X5 to 19X6, but whether it is near a dangerous level we cannot tell without knowing a good deal more. We can obtain some additional information by calculating the burden that interest expense places on the firm.

Times Interest Earned

Times interest earned measures the extent to which operations cover interest expense. The higher the ratio, the more likely that the firm will be able to continue meeting the interest payments. It is calculated in this way:

$$\text{Times interest earned} = \frac{\text{income before interest and taxes}}{\text{interest expense}}$$

We use income before interest and taxes because interest is a tax-deductible expense. If a firm had income before interest and taxes that was exactly equal to interest expense, it would pay no taxes and show a zero net income. In this situation, times interest earned would be 1, which is extremely low.

Graham Company had interest coverage of 4.8 times in 19X5, but slipped to 4.6 times in 19X6.

$$19\text{X}5 \quad \frac{\$200,000}{\$42,000} = 4.8 \text{ times}$$

$$19\text{X}6 \quad \frac{\$220,000}{\$48,000} = 4.6 \text{ times}$$

Some analysts prefer a variation of this ratio. They add depreciation back to income before interest and taxes in the numerator. Reasoning that depreciation does not require cash payments, these analysts believe that their calculation approximates the total amount of cash available to pay interest.

Cash Flow to Total Debt

A major study involving ratios computed for actual companies showed that the single best ratio for predicting failure of a firm was the ratio of cash flow to total debt.[3] In that study, cash flow was defined as net income plus depreciation plus amortization plus depletion, and total debt as total liabilities plus preferred stock. The ratio is therefore computed as

$$\frac{\text{Cash flow to}}{\text{total debt}} = \frac{\text{net income} + \text{depreciation} + \text{amortization} + \text{depletion}}{\text{total liabilities} + \text{preferred stock}}$$

Graham Company has no amortization or depletion that we can identify, and

---

[3]See William H. Beaver, "Financial Ratios as Predictors of Failure," Empirical Research in Accounting, Selected Studies, 1966, *Journal of Accounting Research,* 1967, pp. 71–111.

no preferred stock. The values of the ratio are therefore:

$$19X5 \quad \frac{\$94,800 + \$75,000}{\$610,000} = \frac{\$169,800}{\$610,000} = 27.8\%$$

$$19X6 \quad \frac{\$103,200 + \$90,000}{\$750,000} = \frac{\$193,200}{\$750,000} = 25.8\%$$

The decline in the ratio does not seem serious, though comparison of the ratio with the industry average might indicate a potential problem.

RATIOS AND EVALUATION

Calculating ratios is but the starting point in the analysis of a firm's operations and prospects. A number of factors besides the magnitudes of the ratios must be considered, and comparisons are critical.

The ratios for the firm must be compared with ratios calculated for that firm in prior years, and trends must be evaluated. (Is the firm becoming more or less liquid? Have credit policies loosened, producing lower turnover of receivables? Have looser credit policies produced an offsetting increase in sales? Has more rapid inventory turnover resulted in greater ROA?) The ratios must also be compared, if possible, with those of similar firms, or with ratios for the industry as a whole. (Are the firm's ratios consistent with, and moving in the same direction as, those for the industry? Are out-of-line ratios explainable?)

Several factors make interfirm and industry comparisons difficult. Industry comparisons become more difficult as a firm diversifies its operations—a major trend in recent decades. Some extremely diversified companies operate in 15 or more different industries. A recent trend, welcomed by financial analysis, is increased public disclosure of detailed information about the many segments that make up diversified companies. Such additional disclosure has helped analysts make comparisons that were not possible when only overall results were available.

Even comparisons with very similar companies should be made with care. Critical to such comparisons is an understanding of the differences that can result when the companies being compared do not use the same accounting methods. The accounting method used for inventory determination, for example, may greatly influence the current ratio, inventory turnover, return on sales, and earnings per share, to name but a few of the affected ratios. Two firms identical in all respects except that one uses LIFO and the other uses FIFO can show quite different ratios. If prices have generally been rising, the LIFO firm will show a lower inventory, current ratio, return on sales, and EPS, and a higher inventory turnover. The longer the price trend has continued and the longer the firm has used LIFO, the more marked the effects of the difference in inventory method. Or, consider the effects of different depreciation methods. A firm using the sum-of-the-years'-digits method will show lower net book values for its fixed assets than one using the straight-line method; there will be corresponding differences in both total assets and net income (as well as in EPS and related ratios).

Until 1977, profitability measures could be significantly influenced by whether a firm acquired its major fixed assets through the issuance of long-term debt or stock, or through the use of long-term leasing arrangements. To a great extent, the effects of this particular difference in financing arrangements were eliminated by the issuance of *Financial Accounting Standard No. 13*,[4] but some differences may still remain.

Even comparisons among similar companies using similar accounting methods can be misleading in the sense that a firm that shows up better than another in several measures of liquidity, profitability, or solvency might not be more successful, better, or stronger than another. For example, a company might be too liquid. (Too much cash is not as bad as too little cash; but having excessive cash may also be unwise, because cash does not earn profits unless it is used for something.) Faster turnover of inventory could result from unnecessarily low selling prices. As we noted earlier, a shorter collection period on receivables could result from too restrictive credit policies. A relatively higher EPS and ROE during the upturn in the business cycle could result from over-reliance on debt financing. In short, no single ratio, or group of ratios, should be considered in a vacuum.

Another factor that should be considered in evaluating a firm by comparisons of ratios is the extent to which one or more ratios can be affected by a single transaction. For example, consider the effect of a cash payment for current liabilities. Such a payment reduces both cash and current liabilities, has no effect on total working capital, but can improve the current ratio. We can illustrate this by looking at the ratios for Graham Company at the end of 19X6 and assuming that it paid current liabilities of $30,000 just before the end of the year. Its current assets before the payment would have been $480,000 ($450,000 + $30,000), and its current liabilities $180,000 ($150,000 + $30,000), giving a current ratio of 2.67 to 1. This is lower than the 3 to 1 we calculated earlier. Before the payment the acid-test ratio would have been 1.6 to 1 [($80,000 + $180,000 + $30,000)/($150,000 + $30,000)]. This is also lower than the ratio calculated earlier (1.73 to 1). Actions taken to improve ratios in this manner are sometimes called **window dressing.** This particular type of window dressing is possible only if the current ratio and acid-test ratio are greater than 1 to 1. If they are less than 1 to 1, paying a current liability will reduce them.

Consider also the number of ratios that have net income as a component (return on sales, return on assets, return on common stockholders' equity, times interest earned, etc.). Occurrence of an *extraordinary item* (nonoperating, nonrecurring gain or loss) during the year will affect all of these ratios. Many analysts calculate ratios excluding the effect of such extraordinary items.

Finally, any evaluation based on ratios and comparisons of them, must consider the relative importance of each type of ratio to the particular industry in question. The nature of the product and of the production process, the degree of competition in the industry, and many other industry-related factors are relevant in interpreting the liquidity, profitability, and solvency ratios of a particular firm. For example, consider the utility industry. Because a utility is a monopoly, the governmental unit granting the monopoly right also regulates many of the utility's actions. In most cases, the regulating authority both ensures and limits the profitability of the utility. For a utility, liquidity problems are unlikely because their cash flows are relatively stable, they have no need to build up inventories in advance (they sell a service), and uncollectible accounts are limited by the ability to close off service. (The relatively low importance of liquidity

---

[4]Financial Accounting Standards Board, *Statement of Financial Accounting Standards No. 13, Accounting for Leases* (Stamford, Connecticut: Financial Accounting Standards Board, 1976).

concerns to public utilities is evidenced by the fact that most of these companies report current assets below plant and equipment in their balance sheets.) For the same reasons, the investing public is likely to tolerate in a utility a higher degree of leverage, a lower, if more stable, level of profitability, and a higher dividend yield and payout ratio.

All of the above considerations point out the need for understanding (1) the company being analyzed, and (2) the industry in which the company operates. That a company's ratios differ from those in the past, or are in-line or out-of-line with those of other companies in the industry, is not, *per se*, good or bad. (Knowing that, between 1980 and 1982, Chrysler Corporation improved its liquidity, profitability, and prospects for solvency, in relation to both its prior performance and to the average for the industry, does not change the fact that the entire industry performed poorly at this time.)

SUMMARY

Ratio analysis is used in making investment decisions. Analysts are concerned with trends in ratios and with whether ratios of a particular firm are in line with those of other firms in the same industry. Ratio analysis can be classified into three major types: liquidity, profitability, and solvency.

Which ratios are used and the emphasis placed on each depend on the type of decision to be made. Short-term creditors are primarily concerned with liquidity. Long-term creditors are more concerned with solvency than with liquidity and profitability, but the latter aspects are still important. Common stockholders and potential stockholders are most concerned with profitability, but liquidity and solvency are still significant.

Ratio analysis must be used with care. Ratios provide information only in the context of a comparison, and comparisons with other firms must be more than simple ratio comparisons. Different accounting methods like LIFO and FIFO, sum-of-the-years'-digits depreciation and straight-line depreciation can cause similar firms to show quite different ratios.

KEY TERMS

common size statements
composition problem
convertible securities
dilution (of earnings per
    share)
leverage

liquidity
quick assets
return on investment
solvency
window dressing
working capital

KEY FORMULAS

Liquidity Ratios

$$\text{Current ratio} = \frac{\text{current assets}}{\text{current liabilities}}$$

$$\text{Quick ratio (acid-test ratio)} = \frac{\text{cash} + \text{marketable securities} + \text{receivables}}{\text{current liabilities}}$$

$$\text{Accounts receivable turnover} = \frac{\text{credit sales}}{\text{average accounts receivable}}$$

$$\text{Days' sales in accounts receivable} = \frac{\text{ending accounts receivable}}{\text{average daily credit sales}}$$

$$\text{Inventory turnover} = \frac{\text{cost of goods sold}}{\text{average inventory}}$$

$$\text{Days' sales in inventory} = \frac{\text{ending inventory}}{\text{average daily cost of goods sold}}$$

$$\text{Inventory turnover (raw materials)} = \frac{\text{raw materials used in production}}{\text{average raw materials inventory}}$$

$$\text{Days' purchases in accounts payable} = \frac{\text{ending accounts payable}}{\text{average daily purchases}}$$

Profitability Ratios

$$\text{Asset turnover} = \frac{\text{sales}}{\text{average total assets}}$$

$$\text{Return on assets (ROA)} = \frac{\text{net income} + \text{interest} + \text{income taxes}}{\text{average total assets}}$$

$$\text{Return on common equity (ROE)} = \frac{\text{net income}}{\text{average common stockholders' equity}}$$

$$\text{Return on common equity (ROE)} = \frac{\text{net income}}{\text{sales}} \times \frac{\text{sales}}{\text{average total assets}} \times \frac{\text{average total assets}}{\text{average common stockholders' equity}}$$

$$\text{Earnings per share (EPS)} = \frac{\text{net income} - \text{preferred stock dividends}}{\text{weighted-average common shares}}$$

$$\text{Price-earnings ratio (PE)} = \frac{\text{market price per share}}{\text{earnings per share}}$$

$$\text{Dividend yield} = \frac{\text{dividend per share}}{\text{market price per share}}$$

$$\text{Gross profit ratio} = \frac{\text{gross profit}}{\text{sales}}$$

$$\text{Return on sales} = \frac{\text{net income}}{\text{sales}}$$

$$\text{Payout ratio} = \frac{\text{dividends per share}}{\text{earnings per share}}$$

Solvency Ratios

$$\text{Debt ratio} = \frac{\text{total liabilities}}{\text{total assets}}$$

$$\text{Times interest earned} = \frac{\text{income before interest and taxes}}{\text{interest expense}}$$

$$\text{Cash flow to debt} = \frac{\text{net income} + \text{depreciation} + \text{amortization} + \text{depletion}}{\text{total liabilities} + \text{preferred stock}}$$

REVIEW PROBLEM

Financial statements for Quinn Company are given below:

Quinn Company Balance Sheets as of December 31

Assets	19X7	19X6
Cash	$ 180,000	$ 200,000
Accounts receivable	850,000	830,000
Inventory	620,000	560,000
Total current assets	1,650,000	1,590,000
Plant and equipment	7,540,000	6,650,000
Accumulated depreciation	(1,920,000)	(1,500,000)
Total assets	$7,270,000	$6,740,000

Equities	19X7	19X6
Accounts payable	$ 220,000	$ 190,000
Accrued expenses	450,000	440,000
Total current liabilities	670,000	630,000
Long-term debt	1,000,000	950,000
Total liabilities	1,670,000	1,580,000
Common stock, no par value	4,000,000	4,000,000
Retained earnings	1,600,000	1,160,000
Total equities	$7,270,000	$6,740,000

Quinn Company Income Statement for 19X7

Sales		$8,650,000
Cost of goods sold		4,825,000
Gross profit		3,825,000
Depreciation	$ 420,000	
Other operating expenses	2,135,000	2,555,000
Income before interest and taxes		1,270,000
Interest expense		70,000
Income before taxes		1,200,000
Income taxes at 30% rate		360,000
Net income		$ 840,000

During 19X7 the firm declared and paid cash dividends of $400,000. There were 200,000 shares of common stock outstanding throughout the year. The market price of the stock at year end was $65. All sales are on credit.

Required: Compute the following ratios as of the end of 19X7 or for the year ended December 31, 19X7, whichever is appropriate:

1. Current ratio
2. Quick ratio
3. Accounts receivable turnover
4. Days' credit sales in accounts receivable
5. Inventory turnover
6. Days' sales in inventory
7. Days' purchases in accounts payable
8. Gross profit ratio
9. Return on sales
10. Return on assets (ROA)
11. Return on equity (ROE)
12. Asset turnover
13. Earnings per share (EPS)
14. Price-earnings ratio (PE)
15. Dividend yield
16. Payout ratio
17. Debt ratio
18. Times interest earned
19. Cash flow to debt ratio

Answers to Review Problem

1. Current ratio

$$\frac{\$1,650,000}{\$670,000} = 2.46 \text{ to } 1$$

2. Quick ratio

$$\frac{\$180,000 + \$850,000}{\$670,000} = 1.54 \text{ to } 1$$

3. Accounts receivable turnover

$$\frac{\$8,650,000}{(\$850,000 + \$830,000)/2} = 10.3 \text{ times}$$

4. Days' sales in accounts receivable

$$\frac{\$850,000}{\$8,650,000/365} = 36 \text{ days}$$

5. Inventory turnover

$$\frac{\$4,825,000}{(\$620,000 + \$560,000)/2} = 8.2 \text{ times}$$

6. Days' sales in inventory

$$\frac{\$620,000}{\$4,825,000/365} = 47 \text{ days}$$

7. Days' purchases in accounts payable

$$\frac{\$220,000}{(\$4,825,000 + \$620,000 - \$560,000)/365} = 16.4 \text{ days}$$

8. Gross profit ratio

$$\frac{\$3,825,000}{\$8,650,000} = 44.2\%$$

9. Return on sales

$$\frac{\$840,000}{\$8,650,000} = 9.7\%$$

10. Return on assets

$$\frac{\$840,000 + \$70,000 + \$360,000}{(\$7,270,000 + \$6,740,000)/2} = 18.1\%$$

11. Return on equity

$$\frac{\$840,000}{(\$5,600,000 + \$5,160,000)/2} = 15.6\%$$

12. Asset turnover

$$\frac{\$8,650,000}{(\$7,270,000 + \$6,740,000)/2} = 1.23 \text{ times}$$

13. Earnings per share

$$\frac{\$840,000}{200,000} = \$4.20$$

14. Price-earnings ratio

$$\frac{\$65}{\$4.20} = 15.5 \text{ times}$$

15. Dividend yield

$$\frac{\$2}{\$65} = 3.1\%$$

16. Payout ratio

$$\frac{\$2}{\$4.20} = 47.6\%$$

17. Debt ratio

$$\frac{\$1,670,000}{\$7,270,000} = 23.0\%$$

18. Times interest earned

$$\frac{\$1,270,000}{\$70,000} = 18 \text{ times}$$

19.   Cash flow to debt ratio

$$\frac{\$840,000 + \$420,000}{\$1,670,000} = 75.5\%$$

ASSIGNMENT MATERIAL

Questions for Discussion

18-1   **Dividend yield**   A friend of yours told you that he bought some stock in NMC Corporation five years ago for $20 per share. The firm is now paying a $5 dividend per share and the stock sells for $100. He says that the 25% dividend yield he is getting is an excellent return. How did he calculate the dividend yield? Is he correct? What would you say the dividend yield is?

18-2   **Ratios and accounting methods**   LIFO Company uses the last-in-first-out method of inventory determination. FIFO Company uses first-in-first-out. The firms have virtually the same operations, same physical quantities of inventory, same sales, same fixed assets. What differences would you expect to find in ratios of the two firms?

18-3   **Ratios and operating decisions**   Bronson Company and Corman Company are in the same industry and have virtually identical operations. The only difference between them is that Bronson rents 60% of its plant and equipment on short-term leases, while Corman owns all of its fixed assets. Corman has long-term debt of about 60% of the net book value of its fixed assets. Bronson has none. The two firms show about the same net income because Bronson's rent and depreciation are about the same as Corman's depreciation and interest. What differences would you expect to find in the ratios of the two firms?

18-4   **Ratios and accounting methods**   SYD Company uses sum-of-the-years'-digits depreciation. SL Company uses straight-line depreciation. Both firms have about the same original cost invested in fixed assets. Their operations are also about the same. They have both been growing rapidly, in sales, profits, and amounts invested in all assets. What differences would you expect to find between the two firms in their income statements, balance sheets, and ratios?

18-5   **Liquidity**   Suppose that you are the chief loan officer of a medium-sized bank. Two firms have applied for short-term loans, but you can only grant one because of limited funds available for lending. Both firms have the same working capital and the same current ratio. The firms are in the same industry and their current ratios are well above the normal industry averages. What additional information about the firms' current positions would you seek in making your decision?

18-6   **Seasonality and ratios**   The following independent questions deal with the problems of seasonality that must be confronted when performing ratio analysis.
   1.   The inventory turnover of Robertson Toy Store, which does about half of its business in November and December, was computed at 22 times. The computation was based on the average of the beginning and the ending inventories. The firm has a fiscal year end of January 31. Does the turnover figure reflect the firm's actual activity?

2. The president of Skimpy Bathing Suit Company was bragging that his current ratio was 5 to 1 and his acid-test ratio 4 to 1. The ratios were computed on October 31. Would you expect the firm to have such ratios throughout the year? Explain your answer.

3. The accounts receivable turnover for Long Golf Ball Company, which sells golf balls only in the northeastern United States, was only 2 times. The computation was based on the receivables at June 30, 19X7, and June 30, 19X8. Does the firm seem to have problems collecting its accounts?

18-7 Price-earnings ratio   A friend of yours tells you that his investment strategy is simple. He looks around for the stocks with the lowest price-earnings ratios and buys them. He reasons that he is getting the most for his money that way. Do you agree that this is a good strategy?

18-8 Relevance of ratios to industry   The annual report of the GTE (General Telephone and Electronics) Corporation for 1982 contained the normal complement of financial statements. The major sections and amounts in its balance sheet were as follows (listed in the order, and with the same major headings, as in the statement):

	December 31	
	1982	1981
Assets	*(in millions of dollars)*	
Property, plant, and equipment	$18,236	$16,927
Investments and other assets	561	506
Current assets	3,497	3,532
Totals	$22,294	$20,965
Shareholders' Equity and Liabilities		
Shareholders' equity	$ 5,816	$ 5,071
Minority interests in equity of subsidiaries	597	592
Preferred stock	744	701
Long-term debt	8,304	7,979
Reserves and deferred credits	3,251	2,912
Current liabilities	3,582	3,710
Totals	$22,294	$20,965

Required: Discuss the relevance of the three ratio groups to the analysis of a firm such as GTE.

18-9 Ratio variations   The Financial Highlights section of the 1982 annual report of Motorola Inc. includes the values of the following ratios for 1981 and 1982:
(1) Return on average invested capital (stockholders' equity) plus long- and short-term debt, net of marketable securities;
(2) Percent of total debt less marketable securities to total debt less marketable securities plus equity.
To which of the three general categories of ratios do each of the above ratios belong? How would you explain why the components of these ratios differ from those given in the chapter?

Exercises

18-10   Effects of transactions   For each of the transactions listed below, indicate its effects on the firm's (a) current ratio and (b) acid-test ratio. There are three possible answers: ($+$) increase; ($-$) decrease; and (0) would have no effect. Before each transaction takes place, both ratios are greater than 1 to 1.

Transaction	Effects on	
	(a) Current Ratio	(b) Acid-Test Ratio
Example: Purchase inventory for cash	0	—
1. Purchase inventory on account	___	___
2. Pay a current account payable	___	___
3. Borrow cash on a short-term loan	___	___
4. Sell, at a loss, marketable securities held as a temporary investment	___	___
5. Borrow cash on a long-term loan	___	___
6. Collect an account receivable	___	___
7. Record accrued expenses payable	___	___
8. Sell a plant asset for cash at a profit	___	___
9. Sell a plant asset for cash at a loss	___	___
10. Buy marketable securities, for cash, for a short-term investment	___	___
11. Purchase inventory for cash	___	___

18-11   Relationships   Answer the questions for each of the following independent situations.

1. A firm has a current ratio of 4.4 to 1. Its current liabilities are $50,000. What are its current assets?

2. A firm has return on assets of 15%, return on equity of 18%. There is no preferred stock. Net income is $900,000, and average total assets are $8,000,000.
    (a)   What is average total stockholders' equity?
    (b)   What is interest expense? (There are no income taxes.)

3. A firm has a current ratio of 3 to 1, an acid-test ratio of 1.8 to 1, and its cash and receivables are $18,000. Its only current assets are cash, receivables, and inventory.
    (a)   What are current liabilities?
    (b)   What is inventory?

4. A firm has accounts receivable turnover of five times, inventory turnover of six times. Both accounts receivable and inventory have remained constant for several years. On January 1, 19X8 the firm bought inventory. All sales are on credit.
    (a)   On the average, how long will it be before the new inventory is sold?
    (b)   On the average, how long after the inventory is sold will cash be collected?

5. A firm had current assets of $200,000. It then paid a current liability of $40,000. After the payment, the current ratio was 2 to 1. What were current liabilities before the payment was made?

6. A firm normally has accounts receivable equal to 35 days' credit sales. During the coming year it expects credit sales of $730,000 spread evenly over the year. What should its accounts receivable be at the end of the year?

18-12 Leverage Balance Company is considering the retirement of $600,000 in 10% bonds payable. These bonds are the only interest-bearing debt the company has. The retirement plan calls for the firm to issue 20,000 shares of common stock at a total price of $600,000 and use the proceeds to buy back the bonds. Stockholders' equity is now $1,000,000, with 25,000 shares of common stock outstanding (no preferred stock). The firm expects to earn $300,000 before interest and taxes in the coming year. The tax rate is 40%.

Required
1. Determine net income, EPS, and ROE for the coming year, assuming that the bonds are retired before the beginning of the coming year. Assume no change in stockholders' equity except for the new stock issue.
2. Determine net income, EPS, and ROE for the coming year assuming that the bonds are not retired. Again, assume that year-end stockholders' equity will be the same as at the beginning of the year.
3. Is the proposed retirement wise? Why or why not?

18-13 Return on assets and return on equity Travis Company has annual sales of $15,000,000 and return on sales of 8%. Interest expense is $600,000. Total assets are $12,000,000 and the debt ratio is 40%. The firm has no preferred stock. (Ignore taxes.)

Required
1. Determine income, return on assets, and return on equity.
2. Suppose that the firm could increase its return on sales to 8.5% and keep the same level of sales. What would net income, return on assets, and return on equity be?
3. Suppose that Travis reduced its debt ratio to 30% by retiring debt. New common stock was issued to finance the retirement, keeping total assets at $12,000,000. Sales are $15,000,000 and return on sales is now 9.2% because of lower interest expense that now totals $270,000. What are income, return on assets, and return on equity?

18-14 Financing alternatives Marmex Company has just been founded by three people. The founders are trying to decide how to finance the firm. There are three choices:
1. Issue $2,000,000 in common stock.
2. Issue $1,200,000 in common stock, $800,000 in 10% bonds.
3. Issue $1,200,000 in common stock, $800,000 in 12% preferred stock.

Income before interest and taxes is expected to be $500,000 per year. The tax rate is 40%.

Required
1. Compute net income, earnings available for common stock, and return on equity for each financing choice.
2. Suppose that the tax rate increases to 60%. Redo part 1. Can you draw any conclusions about the effects of tax rates on the relative desirability of the three choices?

18-15 Effects of transactions For each transaction listed below, indicate its effects on the firm's (a) receivables turnover; (b) inventory turnover; (c) gross profit ratio. The possible answers are: (+) increase; (−) decrease; and (0) would have no effect. Before each transaction takes place, the ratios are as follows: (a) receivable turnover of 8 times; (b) inventory turnover of 6 times; (c) gross profit ratio of 25 percent.

	Effects on		
	(a)	(b)	(c)
Transaction	Receivables Turnover	Inventory Turnover	Gross Profit Ratio
1. Purchase inventory on account	____	____	____
2. Sell merchandise, for cash, at the normal price	____	____	____
3. Sell a plant asset, at a profit, for some cash and a short-term note	____	____	____
4. Sell merchandise, on account, at a bargain (lower than normal) price	____	____	____
5. Receive merchandise returned by a customer for credit	____	____	____

18-16 Return on assets and equity   Randolph Company has average total assets of $4,000,000 and a debt ratio of 30%. Interest expense is $120,000 and return on average total assets is 12%. The firm has no preferred stock. (Ignore taxes.)

Required

1.   Determine income, average stockholders' equity, and return on equity.
2.   Suppose that sales have been $3,600,000 annually and are expected to continue at this level. If the firm could increase its return on sales by one percentage point, what would be its income, return on assets, and return on equity?
3.   Refer to the original data and your answers to part 1. Suppose that Randolph retires $600,000 in debt and therefore saves interest expense of $60,000 annually. The firm would issue additional common stock in the amount of $600,000 to finance the retirement. Total assets would remain at $4,000,000. What would be the income, return on assets, and return on equity?

18-17 Effects of transactions—returns ratios   For each of the transactions listed below, indicate its effects on the firm's (a) return on sales; (b) return on total assets; and (c) earnings per share. There are three possible answers: (+) increase; (−) decrease; and (0) would have no effect. Before each transaction takes place, the ratios are as follows: (a) return on sales, 10 percent; (b) return on assets, 5 percent; (c) earnings per share, $0.25.

	Effects on		
	(a)	(b)	(c)
	Return on Sales	Return on Assets	Earnings per Share
1. Sell a plant asset for cash, at twice the asset's book value	____	____	____
2. Declare and issue a stock dividend	____	____	____
3. Purchase inventory on account	____	____	____
4. Purchase treasury stock for cash	____	____	____
5. Acquire land by issuing common stock	____	____	____

18-18 Ratios   The financial statements for Massin Company, a merchandising firm, appear on the opposite page.

The company has 200,000 common shares outstanding. The price of the stock is $21. Dividends of $0.80 per share were declared. The balance sheet at the end of 19X5 showed approximately the same amounts as that at the end of 19X6.

Required: Calculate the following ratios.

1. Current ratio
2. Acid-test ratio
3. Accounts receivable turnover
4. Inventory turnover
5. Day's purchases in accounts payable
6. Gross profit ratio
7. Return on sales
8. Return on assets
9. Return on equity
10. Earnings per share
11. Price-earnings ratio
12. Dividend yield
13. Payout ratio
14. Debt ratio
15. Times interest earned
16. Cash flow to debt

Massin Company Income Statement
19X6 (In Thousands of Dollars)

Sales		$3,200
Cost of goods sold		1,400
Gross profit		1,800
Operating expenses:		
Depreciation	$ 240	
Other	1,060	1,300
Income before interest and taxes		500
Interest expense		60
Income before taxes		440
Income taxes at 40% rate		176
Net income		$ 264

Massin Company Balance Sheet as of
December 31, 19X6 (In Thousands of Dollars)

Assets			Equities	
Cash		$200	Accounts payable	$210
Accounts receivable		400	Accrued expenses	280
Inventory		350		
Total current assets		950	Total current liabilities	490
Plant and equipment	$3,200		Long-term debt	680
Accumulated			Common stock	920
depreciation	1,200	2,000	Retained earnings	860
Total assets		$2,950	Total equities	$2,950

18-19 **Analyzing ROE (adapted from a paper by Professor William E. Ferrara)**
Chapter 11 introduced the idea of separating the components of return on investment as follows:

$$ROI = \frac{\text{net income}}{\text{sales}} \times \frac{\text{sales}}{\text{investment}}$$

Applying this separation to the calculation of return on stockholders' equity we could express ROE as:

$$ROE = \frac{\text{net income}}{\text{sales}} \times \frac{\text{sales}}{\text{stockholders' equity}}$$

This separation is less enlightening than it might be, however, because net income combines the effects of financing choices (leverage) with the operating results. Letting total assets/stockholders' equity stand as a measure of financial leverage, we can express return on stockholders' equity as follows:

$$ROE = \frac{\text{net income}}{\text{sales}} \times \frac{\text{sales}}{\text{total assets}} \times \frac{\text{total assets}}{\text{stockholders' equity}}$$

Sales and total assets cancel out, leaving the ratio net income/stockholders' equity. The three-factor expression allows the analyst to look at operations (margin × turnover, the first two terms) separately from financing (the last term).

The separation is not perfect because interest (financing expense) is included in calculating net income, but the expansion is adequate for many purposes. Thus, the product of the first two terms is a measure of operating efficiency, while the third is a measure of leverage and therefore of financial risk.

The following data summarize results for three companies.

| | Company Results (dollars in thousands) | | |
	A	B	C
Sales	$4,500	$6,000	$5,000
Net income	$ 450	$ 400	$ 480
Total assets	$4,500	$4,500	$4,400
Stockholders' equity	$3,000	$2,000	$4,000
ROE	15%	20%	12%

Required: Calculate ROE for each company using the three-factor expression and comment on the results. You should be able to draw tentative conclusions about the relative operating and financing results of the companies.

18-20 **Current asset activity**   The treasurer of Billingsgate Company has asked for your assistance in analyzing the firm's current liquidity. She provides the following data:

	19X6	19X5	19X4
Total credit sales	$480,000	$440,000	$395,000
Cost of goods sold—all sales	320,000	290,000	245,000
Accounts receivable at year end	64,000	48,000	31,000
Inventory at year end	50,000	44,000	38,000
Accounts payable at year end	37,000	29,000	28,000

Required
1. Compute accounts receivable turnover for 19X5 and 19X6.
2. Compute days' credit sales in accounts receivable at the ends of 19X5 and 19X6.
3. Compute inventory turnover for 19X5 and 19X6.
4. Compute days' sales in inventory at the end of 19X5 and 19X6.
5. Compute days' purchases in accounts payable at the ends of 19X5 and 19X6.
6. Comment on the trends in the ratios. Do the trends seem to be favorable or unfavorable for each ratio?

18-21 **Constructing financial statements from ratios** The following information is available concerning the Warnock Company's expected results in 19X7 (dollars in thousands). Turnovers are based on year end values.

Return on sales	8%
Gross profit percentage	30%
Inventory turnover	4 times
Receivables turnover	5 times
Current ratio	3 to 1
Ratio of total debt to total assets	40%

Condensed Income Statement

Sales	$800
Cost of sales	——
Gross profit	——
Operating expenses	——
Net income	$——

Condensed Balance Sheet

Cash	$ 30	Current liabilities	$__
Receivables	——	Long-term debt	__
Inventory	——	Stockholders' equity	600
Plant and equipment	——		
Total	$__	Total	$__

Required: Fill in the blanks.

Problems

18-22 **Effects of transactions on ratios** For each of the following transactions, indicate its effects on the firm's current ratio, acid-test ratio, and debt ratio. There are three possible answers: (1) increase, (2) decrease, and (3) no effect. Before each transaction takes place, the current ratio is greater than 1 to 1, the acid-test ratio less than 1 to 1.

	Effects		
	Current Ratio	Acid-Test Ratio	Debt Ratio
Example: An account payable is paid.	+	—	—
1. Inventory is bought for cash.			
2. A sale is made on account, with cost of sales being less than the selling price.			
3. Long-term bonds are issued for cash.			
4. Land is sold for cash at its book value.			
5. Marketable securities being held as temporary investments are sold at a gain.			
6. Common stock is issued in exchange for plant assets.			
7. An account receivable is collected.			
8. Long-term debt is issued for plant assets.			
9. A dividend payable in cash is declared, but not paid.			
10. The dividend in item 9 is paid.			
11. A short-term bank loan is paid.			
12. Depreciation expense is recorded.			
13. Obsolete inventory is written off, with the debit to a loss account.			

18-23 **Comparison of firms** Condensed financial statements for Amex Company and Corex Company are given below. Both companies are in the same industry and use the same accounting methods. Balance-sheet data for both companies were the same at the end of 19X4 as at the end of 19X5.

Balance Sheets End of 19X5
(In Thousands of Dollars)

Assets	Amex Company	Corex Company
Cash	$ 185	$ 90
Accounts receivable	215	170
Inventory	340	220
Plant and equipment (net)	850	810
Total assets	$1,590	$1,290
Equities		
Accounts payable	$ 150	$ 140
Other current liabilities	80	90
Long-term debt	300	500
Common stock	700	300
Retained earnings	360	260
Total equities	$1,590	$1,290

Income Statements for 19X5

	Amex Company		Corex Company	
Sales		$3,050		$2,800
Cost of goods sold		1,400		1,350
Gross profit		1,650		1,450
Operating expenses:				
Depreciation	$ 280		$240	
Other	1,040	1,320	900	1,140
Income before interest and taxes		330		310
Interest expense		30		55
Income before taxes		300		255
Income taxes at 40% rate		120		102
Net income		$ 180		$ 153
Earnings per share		$ 0.90		$ 0.77
Dividends per share		$ 0.40		$ 0.20
Market price of common stock		$12.00		$11.50

Required: On the basis of the data given, determine the following:
1. Which company seems to be more liquid?
2. Which company seems to be more profitable?
3. Which company seems to be more solvent?
4. Which stock seems to be a better buy?
Support your answers with whatever calculations you believe appropriate.

18-24 Effects of transactions—selected ratios At the left, below, are several transactions or events. On the right are the names of various ratios and the value of that ratio before the associated transaction. Indicate the effect of the transaction on the specified ratio. There are three possible answers: ($+$) increase; ($-$) decrease; and (0) no effect.

Transaction	Effect on Ratio	Ratio of Concern
1. Write off an uncollectible account receivable	_____	Current ratio of 3 to 1
2. Sell merchandise, on account, at less than normal price	_____	42 days' sales in accounts receivable
3. Borrow cash on a short-term loan	_____	Acid-test ratio of 0.9 to 1
4. Write off an uncollectible account receivable	_____	Return on sales of 18%
5. Sell treasury stock at a price greater than its cost	_____	Return on equity of 20%
6. Acquire plant asset by issuance of long-term note	_____	Debt ratio of 40%
7. Record accrued salaries payable	_____	Times interest earned of 3.2
8. Record depreciation on plant assets	_____	Cash flow to debt ratio of 60%

	Transaction	Effect on Ratio	Ratio of Concern
9.	Return inventory items to supplier, for credit	____	Inventory turnover of 8 times
10.	Acquire plant asset by issuance of common stock	____	Debt ratio of 60%

18-25 Construction of financial statements using ratios   The following data are available for Wasserman Pharmaceutical Company as of December 31, 19X4 and for the year then ended:

Current ratio	3 to 1
Days' sales in accounts receivable	60 days
Inventory turnover	3 times
Debt ratio	40%
Current liabilities	$300,000
Stockholders' equity, all common stock	$1,200,000
Return on sales	8%
Return on common equity	15%
Gross profit ratio	40%

Wasserman has no preferred stock, no marketable securities, and no prepaid expenses. Assume that beginning-of-year balance-sheet figures are the same as end-of-year figures. All sales are on credit and the only noncurrent assets are plant and equipment.

Required: Prepare a balance sheet as of December 31, 19X4, and an income statement for 19X4 in as much detail as you can with the available information. Round the calculation of average daily credit sales to the nearest dollar.

18-26 Dilution of EPS   Boston Tarrier Company has been very successful in recent years, as shown by the income statement data given below. The treasurer of the firm is concerned because he expects the holders of the firm's convertible preferred stock to exchange their shares for common shares early in the coming year. All of the company's preferred stock is convertible, and the number of common shares issuable on conversion is 300,000.

Boston Tarrier Company
Selected Income Statement Data

	19X6	19X5
Net income	$3,400,000	$2,600,000
Preferred stock dividends	800,000	800,000
Earnings available for common	$2,600,000	$1,800,000

Throughout 19X6 and 19X5 the firm had 500,000 shares of common stock outstanding.

Required
1. Compute primary EPS for 19X5 and 19X6.
2. Compute fully diluted EPS for 19X5 and 19X6.

18-27 Inventory turnover and return on equity Timmons Company is presently earning net income of $300,000 per year, which gives a 10% return on equity. The president of the firm believes that inventory can be reduced through the use of tighter controls on buying. Any reduction of inventory would free cash, which would be used to pay a dividend to stockholders. Hence, stockholders' equity would be reduced by the same amount as inventory.

Inventory turnover is now three times per year. Cost of goods sold is running at $2,700,000 annually. The president hopes that the turnover can be increased to five times. He also believes that sales, cost of goods sold, and net income would remain at their current levels.

Required
1. Determine the average inventory that the firm currently holds.
2. Determine the average inventory that would be held if turnover could be increased to five times per year.
3. Determine the return on equity that would be earned if Timmons could increase turnover and reduce stockholders' equity by the amount of the reduction in investment in inventory.

18-28 Ratios—industry averages The president of Brewster Company has been concerned about the operating performance and financial strength of the firm. She has obtained data from a trade association that shows the averages of certain ratios for all firms in the industry. She gives you these ratios and the most recent financial statements of the firm. The balance-sheet amounts were all about the same at the beginning of the year as they are now.

Brewster Company Balance Sheet
as of December 31, 19X6 (In Thousands of Dollars)

Assets		Equities	
Cash	$ 860	Accounts payable	$ 975
Accounts receivable	3,210	Accrued expenses	120
Inventory	2,840	Taxes payable	468
Total current assets	$ 6,910	Total current liabilities	$ 1,563
Plant and equipment (net)	7,090	Bonds payable, due 19X9	6,300
		Common stock, no par	4,287
		Retained earnings	1,850
Total assets	$14,000	Total equities	$14,000

Brewster Company Income Statement for 19X6

Sales	$11,800
Cost of goods sold	7,350
Gross profit	4,450
Operating expenses, including $650 depreciation	2,110
Operating profit	2,340
Interest expense	485
Income before taxes	1,855
Income taxes at 40% rate	742
Net income	$ 1,113

Brewster has 95,000 shares of common stock outstanding, which gives earnings per share of $11.72 ($1,113,000/95,000). Dividends are $5 per share and the market price of the stock is $120. Average ratios for the industry are:

Current ratio	3.8 to 1	Return on equity	17.5%
Quick ratio	1.9 to 1	Price-earnings ratio	12.3
Accounts receivable turnover	4.8 times	Dividend yield	3.9%
Inventory turnover	3.6 times	Payout ratio	38.0%
Return on sales	7.6%	Debt ratio	50.0%
Return on assets	17.6%	Times interest earned	6 times
		Cash flow to debt	25.0%

Required
1. Compute the ratios shown above for Brewster Company.
2. Prepare comments to the president indicating areas of apparent strength and weakness of Brewster Company in relation to the industry.

18-29 Generation of cash flows Humbert Company must make a $600,000 payment on a bank loan at the end of March 19X9. Selected data for December 31, 19X8 are:

Cash	$95,000
Accounts receivable	355,000

Estimated cash payments required during the first three months of 19X9, exclusive of the payment to the bank, are $315,000. Humbert expects sales to be $810,000 in the three-month period, all on credit. Accounts receivable are normally equal to 40 days' credit sales.

Required
1. Determine the expected balance in accounts receivable at the end of March 19X9. Assume that the three-month period has 90 days.
2. Determine whether the firm will have enough cash to pay the bank loan on March 31, 19X9.

18-30 Evaluation of trends and comparison with industry Comparative balance sheets and income statements for Marcus Manufacturing Company appear below. Your boss, who is the chief financial analyst for Catch Hanmattan Bank, has asked you to analyze certain trends in the firm's operations and financing and to make some comparisons with the averages for firms in the same industry. The bank is considering the purchase of some shares of Marcus for one of its trust funds.

Marcus Manufacturing Company Balance Sheets
as of December 31 (In Thousands of Dollars)

Assets	19X7	19X6
Cash	$ 170	$ 180
Accounts receivable	850	580
Inventory (finished goods)	900	760
Total current assets	1,920	1,520
Plant and equipment (net)	2,050	1,800
Total assets	$3,970	$3,320

Equities	19X7	19X6
Current liabilities	$ 812	$ 620
Long-term debt	1,640	1,300
Common stock	1,000	1,000
Retained earnings	518	400
Total equities	$3,970	$3,320

Marcus Manufacturing Income Statements
(In Thousands of Dollars)

	19X7	19X6
Sales, all on credit	$4,700	$4,350
Cost of goods sold	2,670	2,460
Gross profit	2,030	1,890
Operating expenses	1,470	1,440
Income before interest and taxes	560	450
Interest expense	130	100
Income before taxes	430	350
Income taxes at 40% rate	172	140
Net income	$ 258	$ 210
Earnings per share	$2.58	$2.10
Market price of stock at year end	$32	$28
Dividends per share	$0.96	$0.80

Selected data from the 19X5 balance sheet:

Accounts receivable	$ 510
Inventory (finished goods)	620
Total assets	2,940
Stockholders' equity	1,320

The following ratios are averages for the industry in which Marcus operates.

Current ratio	2.7 to 1	Receivable turnover	8.5 times
Quick ratio	1.4 to 1	Inventory turnover	4.2 times
Debt ratio	52%	Return on assets	15%
Price-earnings ratio	11.5	Return on equity	13.5%
Dividend yield	4.5%	Return on sales	5.0%
Payout ratio	48.0%		

Required: Compute the above ratios for Marcus Company for 19X6 and 19X7 and comment on the trends in the ratios and on relationships to industry averages.

Cases

18-31   Trends in ratios   As the chief investment officer of a large pension fund, you must make many investing decisions. One of your assistants has prepared the following ratios for MBI Corporation, a large multinational manufacturer:

	Industry Average All Years	Years		
		19X7	19X6	19X5
Current ratio	2.4	2.6	2.4	2.5
Quick ratio	1.6	1.55	1.6	1.65
Receivable turnover	8.1	7.5	7.9	8.3
Inventory turnover	4.0	4.3	4.2	4.0
Debt ratio	43.0%	38.0%	41.3%	44.6%
Return on assets	17.8%	19.1%	19.4%	19.5%
Return on equity	15.3%	15.1%	15.6%	15.9%
Price-earnings ratio	14.3	13.5	13.3	13.4
Times interest earned	8.3	9.7	9.5	8.9
Earnings per share growth rate	8.4%	7.1%	6.9%	7.0%

Required: What would your decision be in the following cases? Give your reasons.
1. Granting a short-term loan to MBI.
2. Buying long-term bonds of MBI on the open market. The bonds yield 7%, which is slightly less than the average for bonds in industry.
3. Buying the common stock of MBI.

18-32 **Financial planning with ratios** The treasurer of MaxiMart, Inc., a large chain of stores, has been trying to develop a financial plan for the firm. He has, in conjunction with other managers, developed the following estimates, in millions of dollars:

	Year			
	19X3	19X4	19X5	19X6
Sales	$100	$120	$150	$210
Fixed assets, net	80	95	110	125

In addition, for planning purposes he is willing to make the following estimates and assumptions about other results:

Cost of goods sold percentage of sales	60%
Return on sales	10%
Dividend payout ratio	30%
Turnovers based on year-end values:	
Cash and accounts receivable	4 times
Inventory	3 times
Required current ratio	3 to 1
Required ratio of long-term debt to stockholders' equity	50%

At the beginning of 19X3 the treasurer expects the firm to have stockholders' equity of $60 million and long-term debt of $30 million.

Required: Prepare pro forma balance sheets and any supporting schedules you need for the end of each of the next four years. Determine how much additional common stock, if any, the firm will have to issue each year if the treasurer's estimates and assumptions are correct.

18-33 **Leverage**   Mr. Harmon, the treasurer of Stokes Company, has been considering two alternative plans for raising $2,000,000 that is needed for plant expansion and modernization. One choice is to issue long-term debt bearing 9% interest. The other is to issue 25,000 shares of common stock. The common stock is now selling at $80 per share.

The modernization and expansion can be expected to increase operating profit, before interest and taxes, by $320,000 annually. Depreciation of $200,000 annually is included in the determination of the $320,000. The firm's condensed financial statements for 19X4 are given below:

Stokes Company Balance Sheet
as of December 31, 19X4

Assets		Equities	
Current assets	$ 3,200,000	Current liabilities	$ 1,200,000
Plant and equipment (net)	7,420,000	Long-term debt, 7%	3,000,000
Other assets	870,000	Stockholders' equity	7,290,000
Total assets	$11,490,000	Total equities	$11,490,000

Stokes Company Condensed Income
Statement for 19X4

Sales		$8,310,000
Cost of sales	$5,800,000	
Operating expenses	1,200,000	7,000,000
Operating profit		1,310,000
Interest expense		210,000
Income before taxes		1,100,000
Income taxes at 40% rate		440,000
Net income		$ 660,000
Earnings per share, based on 100,000 outstanding shares		$6.60
Dividends per share		$3.30

Mr. Harmon is concerned about the effect that issuing debt might have on the firm. The average debt ratio for companies in the industry is 42%. He believes that if this ratio is exceeded, the price-earnings ratio of the stock will fall to 11 because of the potentially greater risk. If Stokes increases its common equity substantially by issuing new shares, he expects the price-earnings ratio to increase to 12.5. He also wonders what will happen to the dividend yield under each plan. The firm follows the practice of paying dividends equal to 50% of net income.

Required

1. For each financing plan, calculate the debt ratio that the company would have after the securities (bonds or stock) are issued.
2. For each financing plan, determine the expected net income in 19X5, expected earnings per share, and the expected market price of the common stock.
3. Calculate, for each financing plan, the dividend per share that Stokes would pay following its usual practice and the yield that would be obtained at the market prices from your answer to part 2.
4. Suppose that you now own 100 shares of Stokes Company. Which alternative would you prefer the firm to use? Why?

TIME VALUE OF MONEY

What would you do if you had the choice between receiving a dollar from someone now and receiving a dollar from that person at some specified time in the future? Suppose you could be absolutely sure that you would receive the dollar at the specified later time. Almost everyone would choose the first alternative as being the more desirable. We could say, generally, that a dollar now is worth more than a dollar to be received later. This statement sums up an important principle: **money has a time value.**

The truth of this principle does not assume that inflation might make the dollar received at a later time worth less in buying power. The reason that a dollar now is worth more than the certainty of a dollar to be received in the future is that you could invest the dollar now and have more than a dollar at the specified later date.

Suppose you could put the money into a savings account and earn 10% interest. If you did this with the dollar you received now, at the end of the year you would have $1.10—more than the dollar being offered to you at the later specified date. The advantage in taking the dollar now is that with this alternative you can have both the dollar and the earnings on it between now and the later date. The $0.10 is what you would lose if you chose to wait for the $1 until the end of the year. For the two alternatives to be *equivalent,* you would have to have a choice of $1 now and $1.10 a year later. The $1.10 is called the **future value** of $1 invested for one year at 10%.

The decision to take the dollar now can be viewed as the result of an analysis involving a comparison of the values of two alternatives at a specific point in time. In this case, the point in time is one year later and the comparison is between future values of $1 and $1.10. Another way to analyze the situation is to compare (1) the worth *now* of receiving a dollar now, with (2) the worth *now* of receiving a dollar later. This phrasing comes closer to describing the alternatives as they were originally presented. We could say, then, that the *present* worth (called the **present value**) of receiving a dollar now is greater than the present value of receiving a dollar later.

We could develop an analysis that focused on comparing the present values of the two alternatives: a dollar now versus a dollar a year later, given an earnings rate of 10%.[1] The present value of the dollar now is obviously $1. The present value of a dollar to be received one year later is equal to the amount of money you would have to invest now in order to have $1 at the end of the year. That amount is $0.91 [$0.91 + (10% × $0.91) = $1.00]. Later in this appendix you will see an easy way to determine the $0.91. At this point you need only be convinced that the amount *must be less than $1*. The decision facing you, then, is between an alternative with a present value of $1 and one with a present value of $0.91. The intuitive choice of the first alternative is supported now by mathematical analysis, whether the analysis concentrates on values at some common future date or on values at another common date, today.

Many economic decisions involve investing money now in the hope of receiving more money later on. Any analysis of such decisions must consider the time value of money. Suppose you have the chance to invest $10,000 today with a promise that you will receive $11,000 at the end of one year. Should you make the investment? To choose between receiving two equal sums at two different times is easy. The wiser choice is not always so obvious when, as in the present example, the alternatives are a given sum of money now and a larger sum at a specified later time. We know that if we must wait for the money, the amount to be received should be larger than the amount available to us now, but how much larger? It depends on what else you could do with the cash you have to make the investment.

Suppose you could earn a rate of 12% per year by making some other investments. If you invest $10,000 at 12% per year, you have $11,200 at the end of one year [$10,000 + ($10,000 × 12%)]. Comparing the two alternatives, you could have $11,200 at the end of the year as a result of a $10,000 investment now; or you could have $11,000 at the end of the year for a $10,000 investment now. All other things being equal, you would choose the first alternative.

What happens when the time horizon is extended beyond one period? Suppose you can invest $10,000 today and receive $12,000 at the end of two years. Should you make the investment if the prevailing, relevant interest rate is 10%? First determine how much you would have at the end of two years if you invested at a rate of 10%, as follows:

Now	You have $10,000
At the end of year 1	You have $11,000 [$10,000 + ($10,000 × 10%)]
At the end of year 2	You have $12,100 [$11,000 + ($11,000 × 10%)]

The interest earned in the second year is 10% of the total amount that you would have

---

[1]Although we are using years in the example, the more general notion used in practice is that of a *period*, which could be any length of time. At the end of the Appendix we illustrate the use of periods other than one year. For now, because it is simpler and because interest rates are usually stated as rates per year, we shall assume that a period is one year.

at the end of the first year, *not* 10% of the $10,000 you originally invested. This is the unique feature of **compound interest:** you earn the quoted interest rate both on the original amount invested and on the interest that you subsequently earn. Thus, if you put $10,000 into a bank account paying 10% interest, at the end of the first year you could withdraw $11,000 and then redeposit it to earn 10% on the entire amount for the second year.

When we compare the values of each available alternative at the end of the two years, we can see that it is not desirable to invest $10,000 now in order to receive $12,000 at the end of the two years. We could have $12,100 by investing elsewhere. In this instance, the comparison is between the two values at the *end* of the investment term. It is more common practice to compare present values.

PRESENT VALUE OF A SINGLE AMOUNT

To evaluate an opportunity to receive a single payment at some date in the future at some interest rate, we must determine the present value of that choice. Instead of determining how much we would have at some future date if we invested $1 now, we want to know how much we would have to invest now to receive $1 at some future date. In an earlier example we saw that if the interest rate is 10%, an investment of $1 will accumulate to $1.21 at the end of two years ($12,100 on a $10,000 investment). The present value of $1.21 two years from now is thus $1. The procedure to determine present values is called **discounting,** and the interest rate used is called the **discount rate.**

Formulas are available for determining the present value of a sum of money to be received in the future. However, tables have been developed that enable you to determine present values without the formulas. Suppose we wanted to find the present value of $1.21 to be received two years from now when we know that the interest rate is 10%. (We know already that the present value is $1, and this is the answer the table should give us.) Table A on page 779 shows the present value of $1 to be received at various times in the future, at various interest rates. Referring to the 10% column and the row for two periods, we find the factor .826. This means that the present value of $1 to be received two years from now is $0.826 when the interest rate is 10%. Because we expect to get $1.21, not $1, we must multiply the factor by 1.21. This multiplication produces a present value of $0.99946, which is not significantly different from $1. (The slight difference is due to rounding in preparing the table.)

A few characteristics of Table A are significant and should be understood. First, as you move down any column in Table A, the factors become smaller. You should expect this because the longer you must wait for a payment, the less it is worth now. If a dollar now is worth more than a dollar in one year, then surely a dollar one year later is worth more than a dollar two years later. Second, the factors become smaller as you move across the table in any row. As the interest rate increases, the present value of the amount to be received in the future decreases. This should also be expected. The higher interest rate you can expect to earn on the sum invested now, the less you need to invest now to accumulate a given amount at the end of some number of years.

In summary, the longer you have to wait for your money and the higher interest rate you can earn, the less it is worth to you now to receive some specified amount at a future date. The concept of present value must be understood to make decisions affecting more than a single period of time.

PRESENT VALUE OF A STREAM OF EQUAL RECEIPTS

Sometimes it is necessary to compute the present value of a *series* of equal amounts to be received at the ends of a series of years. Such a stream is called an **annuity,** and would describe bond interest received annually for a number of years. It is possible to find the present value of an annuity by finding the present values of each component of the stream and adding them. For example, what is the present value of an annuity of $1 per year for four years at 10%?

Received at End of Year	Amount to Be Received	Present Value Factor (From Table A)	Present Value of Future Receipt
1	$1	.909	$0.909
2	$1	.826	0.826
3	$1	.751	0.751
4	$1	.683	0.683
Present value of this annuity			$3.169

This procedure is cumbersome, especially if the annuity is to last for many years. You are multiplying the same number ($1) by several different numbers (the present value factors). From your study of mathematics, you know that the sum of these multiplications is equal to the product of the constant number ($1) and the sum of the different numbers. If you add up the present value factors (3.169) and multiply that sum by $1 you will get the same answer. (This can be verified at a glance because we are using an annuity of $1.)

In many practical situations you will be dealing with a series of equal receipts over several periods of time. These could be analyzed by using Table A and the lengthy procedure exemplified above. But the task is made simpler by using a table like Table B on page 779, which adds the present value factors for you. Look at Table B in the column for 10% and the row for four periods. The factor is 3.170. This is the present value of a series of four $1 receipts when the interest rate is 10%. (The factor, 3.170, is rounded up from the sum of the factors given in Table A.)

In general, the values shown in Table B are the cumulative sums of the factors from Table A. The factor for an annuity for one period in Table B is the same as the factor for a single receipt in Table A, at the same interest rate. Try adding down Table A and checking each successive sum with the factor in Table B. Any differences are due to rounding.

All the factors in both tables relate to future receipts (or payments) of $1. When dealing with amounts other than $1, the factor must be multiplied by the number of dollars involved to compute the present values. But remember that you can use Table B only when the individual payments in the stream are equal.

STREAMS OF UNEQUAL AMOUNTS

What if the payments to be received in the future are not equal in amount? The method just described to arrive at the present values of such a stream, using only Table A, is cumbersome. In some cases it can be avoided.

If most of the payments are equal, you can find the present value of the equal portions of each payment using Table B, then discount separately the remainder. We shall illustrate this method by modifying the previous example. Instead of receiving $1 per year for four years, you will receive $1 at the end of each of the first three years and $2 at the end of the fourth year.

From Table B we know that $1 per year for four years has a present value of $3.170 at 10%. We can find the present value of the stream except for the extra $1 to be received at the end of year four. Looking in Table A for the present value of $1 to be received at the end of four years, we find that the extra $1 has a present value of $0.683. Adding the $0.683 to the $3.170, we obtain $3.853. We can check this by discounting each receipt separately.

Received at End of Year	Amount to Be Received	Present Value Factor (From Table A)	Present Value of Future Receipt
1	$1	.909	$0.909
2	$1	.826	0.826
3	$1	.751	0.751
4	$2	.683	1.366
Present value of this series of payments			$3.852

The difference ($0.001) is due to rounding.

Suppose that only $0.60 is to be received at the end of the fourth year. We now have a stream of equal payments of $1 for three years, then a $0.60 payment at the end of the fourth year. Two shortcuts can be used: (1) use Table B to find the present value of a stream of $1 payments for three years, then add to it the present value of $0.60 to be received at the end of four years (from Table A); or (2) find the present value of a stream of $1 payments for four years, and subtract the present value of $0.40 at the end of four years. (The $0.40 is the difference between the $1 payment included in the annuity and the payment actually to be received.) The two solutions are as follows:

1.	Present value of $1 per year for 3 years at 10% ($1 × 2.487)	$2.4870
	Present value of $0.60 at end of year 4 at 10% ($0.60 × .683)	0.4098
	Present value of this series of payments	$2.8968
2.	Present value of $1 per year for 4 years at 10% ($1 × 3.170)	$3.1700
	Present value of $0.40 at end of year 4 at 10% ($0.40 × .683)	(0.2732)
	Present value of this series of payments	$2.8968

COMPUTATIONS FOR PERIODS OTHER THAN YEARS

In many instances where present values of future payments are to be computed, the payments may be made more frequently than once a year. A savings bank may credit interest quarterly or even daily. The interest on most bonds is paid semiannually. Nevertheless, it is common practice to quote an annual interest rate.

If interest is *compounded* more often than annually, the rate of interest actually being earned for the year is different from the quoted interest rate. Suppose a savings bank pays 6% interest compounded semiannually. How much will you have at the end of a year if you deposit $1,000 today? You will earn $30 for the first six months ($1,000 × 0.06 × ½). For the second six months, interest will be earned on the $1,030 ($1,000 + $30) and the interest earned will be $30.90 ($1,030 × 0.06 × ½). Hence, at the end of the year you will have $1,060.90. You could say that you earned at the rate of 6.09% per year, because the interest of $60.90 for one year is 6.09% of the $1,000 invested for that year. The 6.09% is called the **effective interest rate** and must be distinguished from the quoted or **nominal interest rate** of 6%. We could say that the investment is earning 3% *per period* (6% divided by the two compoundings per year). Each period you are earning 3% on whatever sum is invested during that period.

For any particular nominal interest rate, the effective interest rate will be higher the greater the number of compoundings per year. Turning the situation around, for a given nominal rate, it will take a smaller investment at the present time to obtain a fixed amount of money at a future date, the greater the number of compoundings per year. To prove this we shall return to our example of the savings bank. If you desired to receive $1,060.90 at the end of a year, you would have to put in $1,000 now if the interest rate is 6% compounded semiannually. If the interest were compounded annually, you would have to put in more than $1,000 now, because a $1,000 investment would only earn $60 in that year. The present value of $1,060.90 a year from now when the rate is 6% compounded semiannually ($1,000) is thus smaller than the present value of $1,060.90 a year from now when the rate is 6% compounded annually.

Compound interest tables are constructed on the basis of an interest rate *per period*. Therefore, you must be careful to identify what interest rate you are dealing with in any given situation. If you are interested in the present value of an amount to be received ten years from now using an effective rate of 10%, you would look in Table A in the 10% column and the row for ten periods. (Remember that an effective rate is a rate per year.) If, on the other hand, you were interested in the present value of an amount to be received ten years from now using an interest rate of 10% compounded semiannually, you would look in Table A in the *5% column* (10% divided by the number of compoundings per year) and the row for *20 periods* (10 years × the number of compoundings per year).

In most situations you will know the nominal interest rate. Therefore, to complete the desired computation you must convert the nominal rate to a rate per compounding period and revise the number of periods to take into account the compoundings.

Suppose you want to know the present value of a stream of receipts of $1,000, which will be collected every six months for the next five years. Assume that the discount rate is 10%. The annual rate is 10% and the receipts are to be collected semiannually, so we must divide the annual rate by 2 to get a rate of 5% per 6-month period. You are now using a 6-month period, so you find the factor for 5% for ten periods, the number of actual receipts in the stream. The factor from Table B is 7.722, and the present value of the stream is therefore $7,722 ($1,000 × 7.722). If the discounting had been done incorrectly using 10% for five periods (to correspond with the five years) for $2,000 (the total of the receipts in each of the five years), the present value computed from the table would have been $7,582 ($2,000 × 3.791). The present values show that it is more advantageous to receive $1,000 twice a year than $2,000 once a year. This confirms the general notion introduced at the beginning of this appendix: *the sooner cash is received, the better.*

The number of periods to be used when consulting the tables for a given situation is the number of years times the number of compoundings per year. The interest rate to be used when consulting the tables is the nominal annual rate divided by the number of compoundings per year. In this manner you are stating the interest rate per compounding period.

A practical example involves applying almost every technique in this appendix. Suppose you could buy a bond that will mature (be retired) in ten years. The bond carries a nominal interest rate of 6%, and interest is paid semiannually. On your investment you desire to earn 10% compounded semiannually. How much would you be willing to pay for a bond with a face (maturity) value of $10,000?

First you must recognize that your investment is really two investments in one. If you buy the bond you will be contracting to receive (1) $10,000 ten years from now; and (2) regular payments of $300 ($10,000 × 0.06 × ½) every six months for ten years. What is each of these investments worth to you now? The price you would be willing to pay for the bond is the sum of the present value of each of these investments.

To compute the price you would pay for the bond, you need the following:

1. The present value of $10,000 to be received ten years from now. You desire to earn 10% compounded semiannually, so you refer to Table A for the present value factor for 20 periods (10 years × 2 compoundings) at 5% (10% divided by 2 compoundings). The factor is .377, so the present value you are looking for is $3,770 ($10,000 × .377).
2. The present value of an annuity of $300 to be received each six months for ten years. You desire to earn 10% compounded semiannually, so you refer to Table B for the present value factor for 20 periods (10 years × 2 compoundings) at 5% (10% divided by 2 compoundings). The factor is 12.462, so the present value you are looking for is $3,739 ($300 × 12.462).

Thus, the price you would pay for this $10,000, 6% bond is $7,509 ($3,770 + $3,739).

USES AND SIGNIFICANCE OF PRESENT VALUES

Should you invest a sum of money now in order to receive a larger amount later (the amount could be a single payment or a stream of payments)? Your decision should be based on the amounts of the cash to be invested and received later, the length of time over which the inflows are received, and the interest rate.

Where the dollars to be received in the future are known, it is necessary only to refer to the tables for an appropriate factor, multiply by the number of dollars to be received in the future, and compare that amount with the dollars that must be invested now to receive the amount or amounts in the future. If the result of the multiplication is greater than the amount to be invested now, the present value of the future returns is greater than the investment and the investment is desirable. Such an investment is said to have a positive *net present value.* If the result of the multiplication is smaller than the required investment, the opportunity is not desirable and we say it has a negative net present value.

The use of present values is not limited to accounting. You may apply your knowledge of present values in the study of economics, finance, and statistics. Some specific applications of present values in accounting are discussed in Chapters 8, 9, and 16.

The most common use of present value tables is to find values of future payments. In some situations, however, you may wish to find the interest rate that will be earned if so many dollars are invested now and so many returned in the future. The procedures to follow when using the tables for that purpose are discussed in the next section.

DETERMINING INTEREST RATES

When you wish to know what interest rate is being earned on a given investment with known future receipts, you also use the present value tables. The interest rate so determined is called the *discount rate,* the *time-adjusted rate of return,* or the *internal rate of return.*

To find the present value of a stream of equal future receipts, you multiplied the amount of the regular receipt by a factor that incorporated both the length of the series of receipts and the interest rate being earned. This can be shown mathematically as follows:

$$\text{Present value of future receipt(s)} = \text{amount of each future receipt} \times \begin{array}{c}\text{factor for interest}\\ \text{rate and waiting period}\\ \text{(present value factor)}\end{array}$$

In prior examples, we were looking for the value to the left of the equal sign. In trying to find the interest rate you would be earning on a given investment when you know the future receipts, you are looking for the interest rate that *equates* the present values of the future receipts with the investment required to produce those receipts. Using the mathematical representation above, you are stating that the value to the left of the equal sign is the investment required now. You know the amount of the future receipts and you know one element in determining the factor required—the waiting period. We shall illustrate the method of determining the missing element in our equation—the interest rate.

Suppose you have an opportunity to invest $3,791 today and receive $1,000 per year for five years beginning one year from now, and you want to know the interest rate you would be earning. Substituting in the above formula yields:

$3,791 = $1,000 × (the factor for the interest rate for five periods)

The solution is 3.791, which is obtained by rearranging the equation to show

Present value factor for five periods = $3,791/$1,000 = 3.791

Because the $1,000 payments are an annuity, we can look in Table B for the factor in the five-period *row* that is closest to 3.791. That exact factor is found in the 10% column, so the investment yields a rate of return of 10%. We can check this by multiplying $1,000 by 3.791, giving $3,791 as the present value. In general terms, the basic equation above can also be shown as

$$\text{Present value factor} = \frac{\text{present value of receipts (required investment)}}{\text{periodic receipts}}$$

The formula can also be used in situations in which a single payment is involved. Suppose you could receive $1,450 at the end of four years if you invested $1,000 today. The factor to be found in Table A would be 0.690 (rounded), which is $1,000/$1,450. Looking across the four-period row in Table A we come to .683 in the 10% column. The rate of return is therefore a bit less than 10%.

You can also use this modification of the basic equation if you know the amount of receipts, the amount of investment (which is the present value), and the interest rate, but want to know the length of time. Suppose you could invest $1,000 now and receive $300 per year, but the number of years is uncertain. If you desire a 14% rate of return, you can compute the number of years over which you would have to receive the $300 payments:

$$\text{Present value factor} = \frac{\$1,000}{\$300} = 3.333$$

This factor is for 14% and an unknown number of years. Therefore we look down the 14% column in Table B and find that 3.433 is the factor for five years. If you received five $300 annual payments you would earn slightly more than the desired 14%.

DETERMINING REQUIRED RECEIPTS

In some decision-making situations you want to know the receipts, either single payment or annuity, that would give a particular rate of return, given the necessary investment and the life of the receipts. The basic formula can be rearranged as follows:

$$\text{Periodic receipt} = \frac{\text{present value of receipts (required investment)}}{\text{present value factor}}$$

Suppose you can invest $10,000 now and hope to receive $3,000 per year for six years. You would like to earn a 12% return. If you do receive $3,000 per year your return would be about 20% ($10,000/$3,000 = 3.33, which is close to the factor for 20% and six years). However, you are uncertain whether you will actually receive

$3,000 and want to know the minimum annual receipt for six years that will give a 12% return:

$$\text{Periodic receipt} = \frac{\$10,000}{4.111 \text{ (the factor for six years and 12\%)}} = \$2,432$$

Thus, if you receive at least $2,432 each year for the next six years you will earn at least a 12% return.

This method can also be applied to single payments, and the only difference is the table to be used. Suppose you can invest $1,000 and receive a single payment at the end of five years. If you wish to earn a 14% return, you would have to receive $1,927 (rounded), which is $1,000/.519, the factor for a single payment at 14% at the end of five periods.

SUMMARY

Many situations or decisions arise that involve cash inflows and/or outflows at different points in time. Such situations require recognition of the time value of money. To compare or evaluate a situation that involves cash flows occurring at different points in time, it is necessary to use the values of those flows at the same point in time.

Almost all managerial accounting decisions involving cash flows at different times use, as the point of analysis, the *present value* of those flows. The present value of a single cash flow at some time in the future can be computed manually or determined with the help of published tables such as Table A. When a number of future cash flows are involved, it is usually easier to compute their present value by using published tables such as Table B. Although tables such as Table B are constructed using the assumption that the individual amounts in the series of cash flows are equal, it is possible to deal with uneven cash flows by using Tables A and B.

The present value of a future cash flow (or a series of future cash flows) depends on the amount of the flow(s), the interest rate, and the length of the waiting period. In some situations, the present value is known, but one of the other elements is not known. The tables can also be used to determine the value of the unknown element.

Applications of the concept of present values include the computation of bond prices and the evaluation of other long-term investment opportunities. Chapters 8, 9, and 16 of this book all include managerial problems that must be analyzed using present values.

KEY TERMS

annuity
compound interest
discounting
effective interest rate
future value

nominal interest rate
present value
time value of money

KEY FORMULAS

$$\frac{\text{Present value of}}{\text{future receipt(s)}} = \frac{\text{amount of each}}{\text{future receipt}} \times \frac{\text{factor for interest rate}}{\text{and waiting period}}{\text{(present value factor)}}$$

$$\text{Present value factor} = \frac{\text{present value of receipts (required investment)}}{\text{periodic receipt}}$$

$$\text{Periodic receipt} = \frac{\text{present value of receipts (required investment)}}{\text{present value factor}}$$

REVIEW PROBLEMS

1. Find the present value of the following sets of payments if the discount rate is (a) 10%, (b) 16%, (c) 20%.

Received at	Amounts					
End of Year	i	ii	iii	iv	v	vi
1	$1,000	$1,000	$1,500	$2,000	$ 0	$1,000
2	1,000	1,000	2,000	2,000	3,000	3,000
3	1,000	1,000	2,000	2,000	3,000	3,000
4	1,000		2,000	2,000	3,000	0
5				5,000	4,000	5,000

2. Find the discount rates for the following situations.

Case	Investment Required Now	Periodic Receipts	Number of Years for Receipts
i	$ 3,605	$1,000	5
ii	$12,300	$2,000	10
iii	$20,860	$4,000	10
iv	$ 9,380	$3,000	5
v	$10,000	$3,050	5

3. Fill in the blanks for each of the following situations. All involve a single payment to be received at the end of the number of years given.

Case	Investment	Year in Which Payment to Be Received	Payment to Be Received	Interest Rate
i	$____	4	$4,000	14%
ii	$1,000	5	$1,464	____
iii	$3,000	____	$5,290	10%
iv	$5,000	7	____	14%

4. Fill in the blanks for each of the following situations. All involve streams of equal annual payments. Round dollar calculations to the nearest $1.

Case	Investment	Annual Cash Payments	Number of Years Payments to Be Received	Interest Rate
i	_____	$1,000	10	14%
ii	$10,000	_____	8	10%
iii	$10,000	_____	8	14%
iv	$20,000	$5,000	_____	8%
v	$10,000	$2,000	8	_____

Answers to Review Problems

1.   i. Stream of equal payments of $1,000 per year for four years.
    (a) At 10%—3.170 × $1,000 = $3,170
    (b) At 16%—2.798 × $1,000 = $2,798
    (c) At 20%—2.589 × $1,000 = $2,589

  ii. Stream of equal payments of $1,000 per year for three years.
    (a) At 10%—2.487 × $1,000 = $2,487
    (b) At 16%—2.246 × $1,000 = $2,246
    (c) At 20%—2.106 × $1,000 = $2,106

  iii. Stream of unequal payments for four years. The easiest method is to find the present value of a $2,000 stream of payments for four years and subtract the present value of $500 at the end of one year.

    (a) At 10%—3.170 × $2,000 $6,340.00
        (Table A, one year, 10%) .909 × $500   (454.50)
                                    $5,885,50

    (b) At 16%—2.798 × $2,000 $5,596.00
        (Table A, one year, 16%) .862 × $500   (431.00)
                                    $5,165.00

    (c) At 20%—2.589 × $2,000 $5,178.00
        (Table A, one year, 20%) .833 × $500   (416.50)
                                    $4,761.50

  iv. Stream of four equal payments and larger amount at end of fifth year. Either method discussed can be used. We will discount the four equal payments and add the present value of the fifth one.

    (a) 10%—3.170 × $2,000 $6,340
        (Table A, five years, 10%) .621 × $5,000   3,105
                                      $9,445

    (b) At 16%—2.798 × $2,000 $5,596
        (Table A, five years, 16%) .476 × $5,000   2,380
                                      $7,976

    (c) At 20%—2.589 × $2,000 $5,178
        (Table A, five years, 20%) .402 × $5,000   2,010
                                      $7,188

v.   Stream of unequal payments beginning at the end of year two. Although there are shortcuts, it is probably simplest to discount separately.

(a)   At 10%

Received at End of Year	Amount to Be Received	Present Value Factor (From Table A)	Present Value of Future Receipt
1	0		
2	$3,000	.826	$2,478
3	$3,000	.751	2,253
4	$3,000	.683	2,049
5	$4,000	.621	2,484
Present value of this series			$9,264

(b)   At 16% the present value is $7,712.
Computations are similar to those for (a), only using the factors for 16%.

(c)   At 20% the present value is $6,873.

2.
$$\frac{\text{Investment required}}{\text{periodic receipt}} = \text{the factor}$$

i. $\dfrac{\$3,605}{\$1,000} = 3.605$ for five years, $= 12\%$ in Table B

ii. $\dfrac{\$12,300}{\$2,000} = 6.15$ for ten years; 6.145 for 10% is the closest factor

iii. $\dfrac{\$20,860}{\$4,000} = 5.215$ for ten years; closest factor is 5.216 for 14%

iv. $\dfrac{\$9,380}{\$3,000} = 3.126$ for five years; closest factor is 3.127 for 18%

v. $\dfrac{\$10,000}{\$3,050} = 3.278$ for five years; closest factor is 3.274 for 16%

3.   All of these problems require the use of Table A.
   i. $2,368. $4,000 × .592 (the factor for 14% for four years)
   ii.   About 8%. $1,000/$1,464 = .683, which is very close to .681, the factor for a single payment in five years at 8%.
   iii.   About six years. $3,000/$5,290 = .567, which is very close to the 6-year factor at 10% (.564). In this case, you know the interest rate, so you are looking for the factor in that column which is closest to .567.
   iv. $12,500. $5,000/.400 (.400 is the factor for seven years at 14%)

4.   All of these problems can be solved by using the equation:

Present value = annual payment × present value factor

The present value, in each case, is the amount of the investment.
   i. $5,216. $1,000 × 5.216 (the factor for ten periods at 14%)
   ii. $1.874. $10,000/5.335 (the factor for eight periods at 10%)
   iii. $2,156. $10,000/4.639 (the factor for eight periods at 14%)   Notice that the cash payment is higher here than in ii because the interest rate is higher.

iv. About five years. $20,000/$5,000 = 4.0, which is the factor for 8% and an unknown number of years. Moving down the 8% column in Table B we find 3.993, which is the closest factor to 4.0 under 8%.

v. About 12%. $10,000/$2,000 = 5.0, which is the factor for eight years and an unknown interest rate. The closest factor in the 8-period row is 4.968, which is the factor for 12%. The true rate is slightly less than 12%.

ASSIGNMENT MATERIAL

1. **Computations—present values**   Find the present value of the following sets of payments if the discount rate is as noted for each set.

Received at End of Year	Set A at 8%	Set B at 10%	Set C at 12%	Set D at 14%	Set E at 20%
1		$2,000	$1,500	$3,000	($3,000)
2		2,000	1,500	3,000	$4,000
3		2,000	1,500	4,000	$4,000
4		2,000	1,500	4,000	$4,000
5		2,000	1,500		$4,000
8	$10,000		2,500		

2. **Missing factors**   Fill in the blanks for each of the following independent investment opportunities.

Case	Investment Required Now	Periodic Receipt	Number of Years of Receipt	Interest (Discount) Rate
A	$16,950	$3,000	10	_____
B	$16,775	_____	10	8%
C	$_____	$5,000	13	18%
D	$10,000	$2,500	____	24%
E	$34,340	$8,500	7	_____

3. **Computation of bond prices**   You are considering investing in some corporate bonds. Each bond is different and because the companies are different you believe you should earn a different rate of interest (effective interest rate) on each investment. The relevant data for each bond are provided below.

	Bond of Company			
	A	B	C	D
Face value	$10,000	$5,000	$20,000	$20,000
Nominal (stated) interest rate	10%	8%	6%	12%
Years to maturity	7	8	7	7
Interest paid	Annually	Annually	Semiannually	Semiannually
Desired interest rate	12%	10%	10%	10%

Required: Compute the price you would pay for each bond.

4. **Present values and rates of return**   The following information is available about two investment opportunities:

	A	B
Required investment now	$10,000	$20,000
Cash flows, annually for 7 years	$ 2,500	$ 4,700

Required
1. Compute the approximate rate of return that each investment yields.
2. Compute the present value of each investment if the desired rate of return is 10%.
3. Repeat requirement 2 assuming that the desired rate of return is 18%.
4. Determine the annual cash flows that would have to be received for each year in the 7-year period to make each investment provide a 16% return.
5. For each investment, determine the number of years that the stated annual cash flows would have to be received to make the investment provide a 20% return.

5. **Present values—unusual timing**   Although many situations involve cash flows occurring at or near the end of a period, still others involve flows at or near the beginning of a period. It is possible to use Tables A and B to deal with such situations also. For each of the situations below, compute the present value of the cash flows described.
   (a) A receipt of $5,000 exactly four years from today; the interest rate is 9%.
   (b) A receipt of $1,000 per year at the beginning of each of five years beginning today; the interest rate is 8%.
   (c) A receipt of $10,000 per year for seven years, the first receipt to arrive exactly six years from today; the interest rate is 12%.

6. **Relationships**   Fill in the blanks for each of the following independent investment opportunities.

			Case		
Item	*1*	*2*	*3*	*4*	*5*
a. Investment required now	———	$416,250	$32,280	———	$135,600
b. Present value at desired rate of return	———	———	$31,080	$358,000	$161,040
c. Annual cash receipt	$9,000	$125,000	———	$ 50,000	———
d. No. of years cash to be received	16	8	4	———	———
e. Desired rate of return	16%	14%	———	9%	8%
f. Rate of return yielded	20%	———	18%	14%	12%

Table A
Present Value of $1

Number of Periods	5%	6%	8%	9%	10%	12%	14%	16%	18%	20%	22%	24%	25%
1	.952	.943	.926	.917	.909	.893	.877	.862	.847	.833	.820	.806	.800
2	.907	.890	.857	.842	.826	.797	.769	.743	.718	.694	.672	.650	.640
3	.864	.840	.794	.772	.751	.712	.675	.641	.609	.579	.551	.524	.512
4	.823	.792	.735	.708	.683	.636	.592	.552	.516	.482	.451	.423	.410
5	.784	.747	.681	.650	.621	.567	.519	.476	.437	.402	.370	.341	.328
6	.746	.705	.630	.596	.564	.507	.456	.410	.370	.335	.303	.275	.262
7	.711	.665	.583	.547	.513	.452	.400	.354	.314	.279	.249	.222	.210
8	.677	.628	.541	.502	.467	.404	.351	.305	.266	.233	.204	.179	.168
9	.645	.592	.500	.460	.424	.361	.308	.263	.225	.194	.167	.144	.134
10	.614	.558	.463	.422	.386	.322	.270	.227	.191	.162	.137	.116	.107
11	.585	.527	.429	.387	.350	.287	.237	.195	.162	.135	.112	.094	.086
12	.557	.497	.397	.355	.319	.257	.208	.168	.137	.112	.092	.076	.069
13	.530	.469	.368	.326	.290	.229	.183	.145	.116	.093	.075	.061	.055
14	.505	.442	.340	.299	.263	.205	.160	.125	.099	.078	.062	.049	.044
15	.481	.417	.315	.274	.239	.183	.140	.108	.084	.065	.051	.040	.035
16	.458	.394	.292	.251	.218	.163	.123	.093	.071	.054	.042	.032	.028
20	.377	.312	.215	.178	.149	.104	.073	.051	.037	.026	.019	.014	.012
30	.231	.174	.099	.075	.057	.033	.020	.012	.007	.004	.003	.002	.001

Table B
Present Value of $1 Annuity

Number of Periods	5%	6%	8%	9%	10%	12%	14%	16%	18%	20%	22%	24%	25%
1	.952	.943	.926	.917	.909	.893	.877	.862	.847	.833	.820	.806	.800
2	1.859	1.833	1.783	1.759	1.736	1.690	1.647	1.605	1.566	1.528	1.492	1.457	1.440
3	2.723	2.673	2.577	2.531	2.487	2.402	2.322	2.246	2.174	2.106	2.042	1.981	1.952
4	3.546	3.465	3.312	3.240	3.170	3.037	2.914	2.798	2.690	2.589	2.494	2.404	2.362
5	4.329	4.212	3.993	3.890	3.791	3.605	3.433	3.274	3.127	2.991	2.864	2.745	2.689
6	5.076	4.917	4.623	4.486	4.355	4.111	3.889	3.685	3.498	3.326	3.167	3.020	2.951
7	5.786	5.582	5.206	5.033	4.868	4.564	4.288	4.039	3.812	3.605	3.416	3.242	3.161
8	6.463	6.210	5.747	5.535	5.335	4.968	4.639	4.344	4.077	3.837	3.619	3.421	3.329
9	7.108	6.802	6.247	5.996	5.759	5.328	4.946	4.607	4.303	4.031	3.786	3.566	3.463
10	7.722	7.360	6.710	6.418	6.145	5.650	5.216	4.833	4.494	4.192	3.923	3.682	3.571
11	8.306	7.887	7.139	6.805	6.495	5.988	5.453	5.029	4.656	4.327	4.035	3.776	3.656
12	8.863	8.384	7.536	7.160	6.814	6.194	5.660	5.197	4.793	4.439	4.127	3.851	3.725
13	9.394	8.853	7.904	7.487	7.103	6.424	5.842	5.342	4.910	4.533	4.203	3.912	3.780
14	9.899	9.295	8.244	7.786	7.367	6.628	6.002	5.468	5.008	4.611	4.265	3.962	3.824
15	10.380	9.712	8.559	8.061	7.606	6.811	6.142	5.575	5.092	4.675	4.315	4.001	3.859
16	10.838	10.106	8.851	8.313	7.824	6.974	6.265	5.669	5.162	4.730	4.357	4.033	3.887
20	12.462	11.470	9.818	9.129	8.514	7.469	6.623	5.929	5.353	4.870	4.460	4.110	3.954
30	15.372	13.765	11.258	10.274	9.427	8.055	7.003	6.177	5.517	4.979	4.534	4.160	3.995

INDEX

A

Absorption costing, 503–20, 546–54. *See also* Job order costing; Journal entries; Process costing; Product costing
  actual job order costing, 508–10
  applying overhead, 511–2, 553
  defined, 503
  and external reporting, 588–9
  and managerial information, 559–60
  misapplied overhead, 512–5
  normal costing, 511–7
  predetermined overhead rates, 511, 546, 547
  single-product situations, 519–20
  standard costing, 546–54
Accelerated Cost Recovery System, 285–7, 326, 327–30
Accounting cycle. *See* Flow of costs
Accounts payable budgeted. *See* Budgets, cash disbursements
Accounts receivable budgeted. *See* Budgets, cash receipts
Accounts receivable turnover, 729
Acid-test ratio, 728–9
ACRS depreciation. *See* Accelerated Cost Recovery System
Activity level, 547. *See also* Volume, measures of
Actual costing, 508–10, 545, 596–9. *See also* Absorption costing; Income statements; Job order costing; Process costing

Allocated costs, 145–7. *See also* Absorption costing; Joint costs; Responsibility accounting
  and joint products, 156
  in make-or-buy-decisions, 152–3
  multiple allocations, 379–82
  in performance measurement, 369–77, 420–1
  in segment analysis, 146
  step-down approach, 379–82
  transfer prices and, 370
  uses of, 375, 377
Analyzing financial statements, 723–43
  general methods, 725–7
  liquidity analysis, 727–32
  profitability analysis, 732–9
  purpose and approach of the analyst, 724–5
  ratios and evaluation, 741–3
  solvency analysis, 739–41
Annual budgets. *See* Budgeting; Budgets
Annuity, present value of, 767. *See also* Present Value
Application of overhead, 511–2, 545. *See also* Absorption costing; Normal costing; Predetermined overhead rates; Standard costing; Variances
Artificial profit center, 359, 372
Asset turnover, 736
Assets in performance measurement:
  allocations to segments, 415–7
  measurement of, 413–4, 418–9
Average total cost, 21–22, 161, 504, 547. *See also* Absorption costing; Full cost

Avoidable costs, 60, 107, 141, 144, 145. *See also* Discretionary costs; Fixed costs; Joint costs; Separable costs; Transfer prices

B

Behavior. *See* Behavioral considerations; Cost classification; Cost behavior; Qualitative factors in decision making
Behavioral considerations. *See also* Goal congruence; Motivation; Responsibility accounting; Transfer prices
  of accounting reports, 7
  in budgeting, 204–6, 249
  and decentralization, 405–7
  of divisional performance measures, 411–4, 418
  in planning step-variable costs, 59
  in setting standard costs, 465, 467–70
  in transfer pricing, 370–7
Behavior of costs. *See* Cost behavior
Benefit-cost analysis, 110–2, 250. *See also* Not-for-profit organizations
Benefit-cost ratio. *See* Profitability index
Book rate of return, 291–2, 411, 413
Book values. *See also* Analyzing financial statements
  in capital budgeting, 317
  in divisional performance measurement, 411, 413, 418–9
  in short-term decision making, 142–3
Break-even point, 24. *See also* Volume-cost-profit analysis
  formula, 25
  graph, 23–26
Budget allowance, 200, 511. *See also* Flexible budget allowance
Budgeting, 2. *See also* Budgets; Capital budgeting; Sales forecasting
  capital, 195, 276–94, 313–33
  comprehensive, 191–211, 230–9
    compared with VCP analysis, 192
  conflicts, 204
  discretionary costs, 203–4
  financial, 196, 230–9
  and human behavior, 204–6
  incremental, 249
  leads and lags, 196, 232, 233, 281
  line-by-line approval in, 248, 249

  long-term, 239–47
  in not-for-profit entities, 247–51
  operational, 191–211
  planning and, 3, 192–3
  program, 250–1
  revised financial statements, 235–7
  sales, 196–200
  for step-variable costs, 58–59
  time periods, 194, 234, 239–47
  and VCP analysis, 192
  zero-based, 249–50
Budgets. *See also* Budgeting; Capital budgeting; Comprehensive budgeting; Standard costs; Variances
  annual, 239–45
  capital, 195, 238
  cash, 195, 234–5. *See also* Cash
    disbursements, 232–4
    receipts, 231–2
  as "check-up" devices, 206
  continuous, 195
  and control, 193–4
  detail in, 192. *See also* Performance reports
  and divisional performance, 420–1
  expense, 200–4
  as feedback devices, 206
  financial, 196
  flexible, 200
  imposed, 204–5
  long-term, 239–47
  for manufacturing firms, 201–3, 209–11, 238–9
  operating, 196
  organization of, 194–5
  and planning, 192–3
  production, 209, 239
  project, 195
  purchases, 208–10
  sales, 192. *See also* Sales forecasting
  and standard costs, 455–7
  static, 200
  time periods of, 194, 195, 200
  unwise adherence to, 206, 249
Budget variances. *See* Variances

C

Capacity. *See also* Linear programming; Relevant range

(Capacity continued)
constraints
intercompany sales, 423–5
special order situations, 158
fixed costs as costs of, 59, 559
fixed facilities, use of, 159–60
normal, 547
practical, 547–8
Capital budgeting, 276–94, 313–33
application of statistical decision theory, 644–6
basic example, 380–3
cash flow and book income, 279–80
cost of capital, 277–8
decision rules, 288–9, 318, 323
decisions, 276
effects of taxes and depreciation, 283–4
income taxes in, 283–4, 326–32
investing decisions vs. financing decisions, 293–4
mutually exclusive alternatives, 319–24
ranking investment opportunities, 322–4
replacement decisions, 315–9
and resource allocation, 277–8
salvage values in, 287–8
sensitivity analysis, 324–6
techniques, 279
book rate of return, 291–2
evaluation of, 293
internal rate of return, 279, 281–2
net present value, 281
payback period, 289–91
profitability index, 322–3
types of situations, 278–280
unequal lives in, 320–2
uneven cash flows in, 284–8
utility issues in, 645–6
working capital investment, 314–5
Capital gains, 327
Carrying costs of inventory. *See* Inventory
Cash. *See also* Budgets; Budgeting; Statement of changes in financial position
budget, 195, 206, 230–9
disbursements budget, 232–4
flows, 192
and book income, 279–80, 412–4
in capital budgeting, 279
and income taxes, 279–80
uneven, 284–8, 768
idle, 238, 742
minimum balance, 235, 236–7, 240
receipts budget, 192, 231–2
resources as, 686–90
Cash-flow-to-debt ratio, 740–1
Centralization, 361. *See also* Decentralization; Responsibility accounting
Certified Management Accountant, 10
C.M.A. examination, 10
Committed costs, 60–62, 107–8, 368. *See also* Allocated costs; Fixed costs; Joint costs; Separable costs
budgeting of, 200–1
Common costs, 107. *See also* Allocated costs; Joint costs
Common-size statements, 726
Complementary effects, 150–3
Complementary products, 102
Composition problem, 728, 730. *See also* Liquidity analysis
Compound interest, nature of, 766
Comprehensive budgeting, 191, 195–6, 230–9, 276. *See also* Budgeting; Budgets
illustration, 206–9, 230–9
Conflicts in budgeting, 204
Continuous budgets, 195
Contribution margin. *See also* Variable costing
in analyzing sales variances, 99–102
defined, 19
income statement compared to financial accounting, 21, 64
negative, 151
percentage, 25, 27–28
weighted-average, 102–5
Control chart, 466
Control function, 2, 5. *See also* Budgets; Budgeting; Responsibility accounting; Standard costs; Variances
Control reports, 5
Conversion costs, 591. *See also* Manufacturing costs
Convertible securities, 737
Cost:
allocations. *See* Allocated costs
allowable, 377
analysis in not-for-profit organizations, 109–12
average total cost, 21–22
avoidable, 60. *See also* Discretionary costs; Fixed costs; Joint costs

(Cost continued)

behavior, 18–22. *See also* Volume-cost-profit analysis

analyzing, 52–69

misconceptions, 21–22, 60

mixed costs, 52–57

step-variable costs, 57–59

classification

behavior, 8, 18–22, 52–69

controllability, 8

depends on the decision, 9, 145, 156

difficulties, 53, 60, 63, 150

functional, 8, 17

object, 8, 52

by responsibility, 8. *See also* Responsibility accounting

committed, 60–62. *See also* Fixed costs

common, 107. *See also* Joint costs

controllable. *See* Responsibility accounting

conversion, 591

differential, 140–1

direct, 369

discretionary, 59–60. *See also* Avoidable costs; Fixed costs; Joint costs

distribution, 161

engineered, 59

estimation techniques

high-low method, 54–55, 57, 72, 75

regression analysis, 56, 57, 72–77

scatter-diagram method, 55–56, 57, 72, 75

fixed, 19–20

committed, 60–62

control of, 473–4

discretionary, 59–60

managerial actions and, 59–62

on performance reports, 474

standard, 455n, 547–8

flows, 504–6, 594–606. *See also* Manufacturing costs

full. *See* Absorption costing; Full cost; Pricing

incremental, 140–1. *See also* Differential costs

indirect, 369

inventoriable, 554. *See also* Absorption costing; Inventory

joint, 107

of joint process, 153–4

manufacturing, 62–64, 504

mixed, 52–57

nonvariable, 20

opportunity, 143–4

period, 504

product, 504

programmed, 59

replacement, 144, 419

semivariable, 52

separable, 107

social, 332

standard, 454

step-variable, 57–59

sunk, 142–3

total, 20

traceable, 369

unallocated, 366

unavoidable, 60

variable, 18

versus expense, 17n

Cost Accounting Standards Board, 377

Cost center, 359. *See also* Responsibility accounting; Standard costs

Cost flows in a manufacturing firm, 504–6, 555, 594–6

Cost of capital, 277–8. *See also* Capital budgeting

Cost structure, 52, 63, 67–69, 426. *See also* Transfer prices

and managerial actions, 20, 60

and managerial attitudes, 67–69

Cost systems. *See also* Absorption costing; Variable costing

job-order, 507–19, 599–603

journal entries, 594–606

process, 506, 586

standard, 545–60, 603–6

types of, 506–7, 585

Currently attainable performance, 469–474

Current ratio, 241, 727–8

Cutoff rate of return, 278. *See also* Capital budgeting; Cost of capital

D

Days' purchases in accounts payable, 732

Days' sales in accounts receivable, 729–30

Days' sales in inventory, 731

Debt ratio, 739–40

Decentralization, 361, 405–7. *See also* Organization structure; Responsibility accounting

Decision making:
 under environmental constraints, 161
 function, 2, 4–5
 long-term, 140. *See also* Capital budgeting
 qualitative factors in, 5, 61, 111–2, 140
 short-term, 139–61
 social consequences of, 332–3
Decision package, 249
Decision rules:
 in capital budgeting, 288–9, 319, 323
 dropping a segment, 149
 further processing of joint products, 155
 in short-term decisions, 140–1
 undertaking a joint process, 155
Decision tree, 644
Depreciation:
 accelerated, 284–7. *See also* Accelerated Cost Recovery System
 and cash flows, 279–80, 695
 in divisional performance measurement, 418–9
 and ratio analysis, 741
 and retention of funds, 694–5
 and taxes, 279–80, 283–4, 326–32
 tax shield of, 283, 286
Differential costs, 140–1. *See also* Incremental costs and revenues, 140
Dilution of earnings per share, 737–8
Direct cost, 369
Direct costing, 503, 546. *See also* Variable costing
Direct labor, 62. *See also* Manufacturing costs; Standard costs; Variances
Direct materials. *See* Manufacturing costs; Materials
Disbursements. *See* Cash
Discounted cash flow techniques, 293. *See also* Capital budgeting; Present value
Discounting, 766. *See also* Capital budgeting; Present value
Discount rate, 282, 766, 771
Discretionary costs, 59–60, 107–8. *See also* Fixed costs
 budgeting of, 60, 200, 203–4
 effects of reducing, 60, 205
 in responsibility accounting, 360–1
Discriminatory pricing, 161
Dividend yield, 738–9
Divisional income, 407. *See also* Divisional performance

Divisional investment, 408, 414–9. *See also* Divisional performance
Divisional performance, 405–26
 assets
  allocation of, 415–7
  measurement, 413–4, 418–9
 basis for evaluation, 419–21
 behavioral problems, 411–4
 income, 413–4
 liabilities, 417–8
 measures
  net income, 407
  residual income, 409–11
  return on investment, 407–9
 problems in measurement, 414–21
 subject of evaluation, 419–21
Divisional profit, 407
Dropping a segment, 108, 147–52

E

Earnings per share, 736–8
Economic lot size, 654
Economic order quantity, 654–7
Economic Recovery Tax Act, 328, 331
Effective interest rate, 277, 769
Effectiveness, 453
Efficiency, 408, 453, 545. *See also* Standard costs
Efficiency variances. *See also* Variances
 labor, 458–9, 460
 material use, 464
 variable overhead, 460–1
Engineered costs, 59. *See also* Discretionary costs; Fixed costs
Engineering standards, 467–8
Equity ratio, 740. *See also* Debt ratio; Leverage; Ratios, solvency
Equivalent production, 587–90, 613–4
 for different cost elements, 590–2
 first-in-first-out, 613–4
 weighted average, 587–90
Estimates. *See also* Expected value; Sales forecasting; Sensitivity analysis; Statistical decision theory
 in capital budgeting, 324–6, 380
 developing probabilities for, 649–50
 in managerial and financial accounting, 20
 in overall planning, 106

(Estimates continued)

predominance of, in managerial accounting, 20, 640

in profit planning, 29–30, 57

in setting standards, 468

in short-term decision making, 139, 140, 160

Evaluation criteria. *See* Budgets; Divisional performance measurement; Responsibility accounting

Excess present value, 279. *See also* Capital budgeting; Net present value

Expected value, 199, 640. *See also* Statistical decision theory; Sales forecasting, 199–200

Expense. *See* Cost

Expense budgets, 200–4. *See also* Budgeting; Budgets; Fixed costs

Extraordinary items, 742

F

"Fair share" of costs, 146, 369, 377

Federal Trade Commission, 161

Financial accounting. *See also* Allocated costs; Product costing

cost and expense, 17n

income statement contrasted with contribution margin approach, 21, 64

and managerial accounting, 8–9

Financial budgeting, 196, 230–47. *See also* Budgeting; Budgets

Financial statements. *See* Budgeting; Budgets, Financial accounting; Pro forma financial statements

Financing activities, 293–4. *See also* Statement of changes in financial position

Financing decisions vs. investing decisions, 293–4

"Financing gap," 245

Financing requirements, 240–1. *See also* Budgeting; Leverage; Statement of changes in financial position

Finished goods inventory, 505, 595. *See also* Cost systems; Product costing

Fixed costs, 19–20. *See also* Allocated costs; Joint costs

average, 21

avoidable, 60

budgeting for, 200–1, 203–4, 474. *See also* Budgeting; Expense budgets; Variances

changing, 29–30, 59–60

committed, 60–62, 107–8

control of, 473–4

discretionary, 59–60, 107–8

managerial actions and, 59–62

and multiple products, 107–8

on performance reports, 474

separable, 107

separating from variable costs, 474

standards for, 455n, 454–8. *See also* Standard costs

unavoidable, 60

volume variance, 514–5

Fixed facilities, use of, 159–60, 423. *See also* Linear programming

Fixed manufacturing overhead. *See* Absorption costing; Manufacturing costs; Predetermined overhead rates; Variances

Flexible budget, 200

Flexible budget allowance, 200, 201, 202, 455

Flow of costs, 504–6, 555, 594–5

Forecasting. *See* Budgeting; Estimates; Sales forecasting

Formulas:

acid-test ratio, 728

accounts receivable turnover, 729

book rate of return, 291

break-even point, 25

cash flow to total debt, 740

contribution margin, 19

as a percentage, 25

cost of goods sold, 208

current ratio, 241, 728

days' purchases in accounts payable, 732

days' sales in inventory, 731

days' sales in receivables, 729

debt ratio, 729

dividend yield, 738

earnings per share, 736

dilution of, 737

growth rate of, 737

economic order quantity, 656

equivalent production, 588

first-in-first-out, 614

weighted average, 589

fixed cost factor in mixed cost, 54

flexible budget allowance, 201

inventory reorder point, 652

inventory turnover, 730

investment turnover, 408

(Formulas continued)
labor variances, 457–60
margin of safety, 69
material variances, 463–4
multiple regression, general form, 76
normal equations of simple regression, 72
payback period, 289
payout ratio, 739
predetermined overhead rate, 511
present value of future flows, 282
price-earnings ratio, 738
profitability index, 323
purchases, 208
quick ratio, 728
residual income, 410
return on assets, 733
return on common equity, 734
return on investment, 408
return on sales, 22, 408
sales price variance, 101
sales volume variance, 101
standard fixed cost per unit, 546, 548
target profit, 26, 28, 66
total overhead budget variance, 476, 515–7
variable cost factor of mixed cost, 54
variable overhead variances, 460–3
volume variance, 515–549
working capital, 240, 727
Full cost, 146, 369, 377. *See also* Absorption costing
Full costing, 503. *See also* Absorption costing
Fully diluted earnings per share. *See* Earnings per share
Functional areas, 1, 191
Funds flows. *See* Statement of changes in financial position
Future value, 765. *See also* Present value

G

Generally accepted accounting principles, 9, 504, 606, 680n, 683. *See also* Financial accounting
Goal congruence, 357–8. *See also* Behavioral considerations; Motivation; Responsibility accounting
Gross profit ratio, 727

H

High-low method of cost estimation, 54–55, 468
compared to regression analysis, 57, 72, 75
compared to scatter-diagram method, 56, 57, 65
Historical costs. *See also* Analyzing financial statements; Book values
in divisional performance measurement, 418–9
obscure cost behavior, 60
standards based on, 469
as sunk costs, 142
House brands, 157, 158

I

Ideal capacity. *See* Practical capacity
Ideal standards, 469
Idle capacity variance, 415. *See also* Volume variance
Imposed budgets, 204–5
Income statements. *See also* Absorption costing; Budgeting; Product costing; Variable costing
actual and normal costing, 517–9
budgeted, 196, 207–8, 235–6
financial accounting and the contribution margin approach, 21, 64
standard costing, 548–50
variable costing, 555–6
and variances, 472–3
Income taxes:
Accelerated Cost Recovery System, 285–7, 326–30
in capital budgeting, 283–4, 326–32
capital gains, 327
depreciation and, 283–4, 326–32
investment tax credit, 327, 330–2
operating loss carryovers, 327
and profit planning, 66–67
progressive tax rates, 326
and target profits, 66
Incremental budgeting, 249
Incremental costs, 140–1, 146, 651. *See also* Differential costs
and discriminatory pricing, 161
and revenues, 140–2, 147, 277
Incremental profits and losses, 141, 149

Indicator methods of sales forecasting, 196–7

Indirect cost, 369

Indivisibility of resources, 57

Inflation, 20, 419

Intercompany transactions. *See* Transfer prices

Interim periods. *See also* Seasonality
and actual costing, 510
cash deficits, 234
and normal costing, 512
sales forecasting, 200

Internal rate of return, 281–2, 411, 412, 771. *See also* Capital budgeting; Divisional performance; Present value

Inventoriable cost, 554, 586, 607. *See also* Absorption costing; Product costing

Inventory:
carrying costs, 65, 204, 650–2
control models, 650–7
cost flows, 504–6, 594–5
finished goods, 505, 731
lead time, 413, 652
methods
and equivalent production, 588–9
and ratio analysis, 741
order quantity, 654–7
policy, 204, 208, 209, 210, 234
raw materials, 210, 505, 731–2
reorder point, 652
safety stock, 652–4
stages of completion. *See* Equivalent production
stockout costs, 651
turnover, 730–1
valuation. *See* Absorption costing; Inventoriable cost; Product costing
work in process, 505, 731

Investigation of cost variances, 466–7, 642–4

Investing activities, 681. *See also* Statement of changes in financial position

Investing decisions and financing decisions, 293–4

Investment center, 359, 405. *See also* Divisional performance; Responsibility accounting

Investment tax credit, 327, 330–2

Investment turnover, 408

Investment in working capital, 314–5

J

Job-order costing, 507. *See also* Absorption costing; Cost systems; Product costing
actual costing, 508–10
illustration of, 599–603

Joint assets. *See* Divisional performance

Joint costs, 107. *See also* Allocated costs; Discretionary costs; Responsibility accounting; Separable costs
in joint products, 153, 155–6

Joint process, 153

Joint products, 153, 426

Journal entries,
actual process costing, 596–9
job-order costing, 599–602
standard costing, 602–6

L

Labor. *See* Direct labor; Manufacturing costs

Labor variances, 457–60

Law of demand, 109

Leads and lags, 196, 279

Lead time, 413, 652

Leverage, 734–6, 743. *See also* Capital budgeting

Liabilities in divisional performance measurement, 417–8

Linear programming, 657–64

Line function, 3

Liquidity analysis, 727–32

Long-term budgets, 239–47, 277
asset requirements, 240
financing requirements, 240-1

Long-term decision making. *See* Capital budgeting

Losses and seasonality, 24

Loss leaders, 150

M

Make-or-buy decision, 152–3

Management:
by exception, 2, 5, 365, 406, 724
functions, 2–3
and managerial accounting, 3–8
by objectives, 2

Managerial accountants:
  activities of, 9–10
  professional examination, 10
Managerial accounting:
  and financial accounting, 8–9
    book values as sunk costs, 142, 153
    cost of goods sold differences, 63–64
    income statement differences, 21, 64
  and functions of management, 3–8
Managerial estimates for setting standards, 468
Manufacturing costs, 62–63. *See also* Absorption costing; Inventoriable cost; Product costing; Variable costing
  flows of, 505–6, 555, 594–5
  purchases budget, 208–11
  types of, 62–63, 504–5
Manufacturing overhead, 62. *See also* Absorption costing; Fixed costs; Manufacturing costs; Predetermined overhead rates; Product costing
Margin of safety, 69
Materials:
  inventory, 210, 505, 731
  variances, 463–4. *See also* Variances
Measures of volume. *See* Volume, measures of
Minimum cash balance. *See* Cash
Minimum rate of return:
  in capital budgeting. *See* Cutoff rate of return
  in divisional performance measurement, 409
Misapplied overhead, 512–5. *See also* Absorption costing; Variances
Mixed cost, 52–57, 62, 200
  estimation methods
    high-low method, 54–55
    regression analysis, 56, 72–77
    scatter-diagram method, 55–56
  manufacturing overhead as a, 62–63
  step-variable costs, 57–59
Money, time value of, 279, 764–73. *See also* Present value
Motivation, 357, 406. *See also* Behavioral considerations; Transfer prices
Multiple products. *See also* Allocated costs; Job order costing; Joint products; Measures of volume; Predetermined overhead rates
  complementary products, 102
  dropping a product, 107, 147–52

fixed costs and, 107–8
job-order costing, 507–17
joint and separable costs, 107–8, 146
sales mix, 102, 105–6
and standard costs, 477, 551–3
weighted-average contribution margin, 102–5
Mutually exclusive alternatives, 319–24. *See also* Capital budgeting

N

National Association of Accountants, 10
Natural profit center, 359
Negative contribution margin, 151
Net income as a divisional performance measure, 407
Net present value, 279, 771. *See also* Capital budgeting; Present value
Nominal interest rate, 769
Nonvariable costs, 20. *See also* Fixed costs
Normal activity, 547
Normal costing, 511–2, 545, 547. *See also* Absorption costing; Predetermined overhead rates
  compared with standard costing, 553–4
  income statement, 517–9
  interim results and, 512
  predetermined overhead rates for, 511, 547
Not-for-profit organizations, 1, 24
  benefit measurement, 110
  budgeting in, 247–51
  capital budgeting in, 283
  fixed expenditures approach, 111, 248
  service-level approach, 111
  social benefits and costs, 332–8
  volume-cost-profit analysis in, 109-12

O

Operating loss carryovers, 327
Operational budgeting, 191–211. *See also* Budgeting
Opportunity costs, 143–4, 423
  in inventory control, 651
  in make-or-buy decisions, 153
  in segment analysis, 149
  shadow prices, 663–4

Organizational structure, 361–9. *See also* Responsibility accounting
centralized, 361
choice of structure, 368–9
decentralized, 361, 405–7
line and staff, 3
Overabsorbed overhead, 513. *See also* Absorption costing; Predetermined overhead rates
Overapplied overhead, 513. *See also* Absorption costing; Predetermined overhead rates
Overhead. *See* Absorption costing; Fixed costs; Manufacturing costs; Variable costs
Overhead application. *See* Absorption costing; Predetermined overhead rates

P

Payback period, 289–91. *See also* Capital budgeting
Payoff table, 646–9
Payout ratio, 739
Perfect information, value of, 642, 648
Performance evaluation function, 2, 5–6. *See also* Behavioral considerations; Budgeting; Divisional performance; Responsibility accounting
Performance reports, 201, 202. *See also* Budgeting; Budgets; Responsibility accounting
and allocations, 369–77
and fixed costs, 474
and standard costs, 465–470
Period cost, 504
Planning. *See also* Budgeting; Decision making; Profit planning and budgeting, 3–4, 192–3
function, 2
Practical capacity, 547
Predetermined overhead rates, 511, 546, 547. *See also* Absorption costing; Standard costing; Variances
departmental and plant-wide rates, 516–7
in normal costing, 511
a single rate for fixed and variable overhead, 515–6
Present value, 765. *See also* Capital budgeting
in computing bond prices, 769–70

determining interest rates, 771–2
determining required receipts, 772–3
for periods other than years, 769–70
of a single amount, 766–7
of a stream of equal receipts, 767–8
of a stream of unequal payments, 768
tables, 779
uses and significance of, 770–1
Price determination. *See* Pricing; Target profit
Price-earnings ratio, 738
Price variances, 454. *See also* Variances
labor, 458, 459
material, 463
sales, 101
variable overhead, 460, 461
Price-volume relationships, 108–9
Pricing. *See also* Special orders; Transfer prices
discriminatory, 161
full-cost, 146
target, 28–29
variable costing and, 559–60
Primary earnings per share. *See* Earnings per share
Process costing, 506, 585, 586–94, 612–5
actual, illustration of, 596–9
equivalent production, 587–90, 613–4
multiple processes, 592–4
summary of, 594
Product cost, 504
Product costing, 503. *See also* Absorption costing; Cost systems
Production budget, 194, 209–10, 238–9
Product line, 106. *See also* Segment analysis
Product margin, 108, 147
negative, 150
Profitability index, 322–3
Profitability ratios, 732–9
Profit center, 359. *See also* Responsibility accounting
Profit planning, 17–30
and budgeting, 3–4, 192–3
income taxes and, 66–67
Pro forma financial statements, 4. *See also* Budgeting; Budgets; Financial accounting; Income statements
Program budgets, 250–1
Programmed costs, 59. *See also* Discretionary costs

Progressive tax rates, 326
Project budgets, 195
Purchases budget, 208–11, 232
    in a manufacturing firm, 209–10

Q

Qualitative factors in decision making, 5, 61,
    111–2, 140, 152
Quantity variances, 454. *See also* Variances
    labor, 458–9, 460
    materials, 464
    variable overhead, 460–2
Quick ratio, 728

R

Ranking investment opportunities, 322–4
Rate of return. *See also* Capital budgeting
    book, 291–2, 411, 412, 413
    cutoff, 278
    internal, 281–2, 771
    minimum, 278, 409
    target, 278, 409
    time-adjusted, 282
Rate variances, 454. *See also* Variances
    labor, 458, 459
    materials, 463
    variable overhead, 460, 461
Ratios. *See also* Formulas
    and evaluation, 741–2
    liquidity, 727–32
    in long-term budgeting, 241–7
    profitability, 732–9
    solvency, 739–41
Raw materials, 62. *See also* Manufacturing
    costs; Materials; Variances
Receipts. *See* Cash receipts budget
Regression analysis, 56–57, 72–77, 196, 468
    multiple regression, 66, 76–77, 456
    simple regression, 72–76
Relevant range, 22–23, 52, 54, 75
    price-volume relationships, 108–9
    and step-variable costs, 57, 58
    time periods, 22, 61
Reorder point, 652
Reorder quantity, 654–7
Replacement costs in divisional performance
    measurement, 419

Replacement decisions in capital budgeting,
    315–9
    incremental approach, 316–7
    total-project approach, 317–9
Residual income, 409–11
Resource flows. *See* Statement of changes in
    financial position
Resources, indivisibility of, 57
Responsibility accounting, 357–77. *See also*
    Divisional performance; Standard
    costs; Transfer prices
    allocations, 369–77
    controllability principle, 358, 367, 414
    cost centers, 359
    evaluation criteria, 360–1
    investment centers, 359–60. *See also* Divi-
        sional performance
    profit centers, 359
        artificial, 359
    relationship to organizational structure,
        361–9
    reporting
        for cost centers, 362–5
        for profit centers, 365–8
Responsibility centers, 358–61. *See also* Re-
    sponsibility accounting
Return. *See also* Analyzing financial state-
    ments; Divisional performance
    on assets, 408, 417
    on capital employed, 408
    on common equity, 734, 736
    on equity, 408, 417, 734
    on investment, 407–9, 732–3
    on sales, 22, 27, 408, 727, 736
Risk. *See also* Leverage
    and capital budgeting, 276–7, 290–1
    and cost structure, 67–69
Robinson-Patman Act, 161

S

Safety stock, 652–4
Sales budget, 192. *See also* Sales forecast-
    ing
Sales forecasting, 196–200, 248
    expected values and, 199–200
    historical analysis, 198
    indicator methods, 196–7
    interim periods, 200

(Sales forecasting continued)
  judgmental methods, 198
  which method to use, 198–9
Sales mix, 102, 105–6. *See also* Multiple
  products
Sales price variance, 101
Sales volume variance, 101
Salvage values in capital budgeting, 287–8
Scatter diagram, 55–56, 196, 468
  compared to high-low method, 56, 57, 65
  contrasted with regression analysis, 56,
    57, 72, 75
Seasonality, 24, 62, 195
  and budgets, 195
  losses, 24
  and ratios, 741–3
  sales forecasting, 200
Segment analysis, 107–8, 144–7, 147–52.
    See also Allocated costs; Divisional
    performance; Fixed costs; Joint costs;
    Multiple products
Semivariable costs, 52. *See also* Fixed costs;
    Step-variable costs
Sensitivity analysis:
  in capital budgeting, 324–6
  in linear programming, 662–3
Separable costs, 107, 145, 369. *See also*
    Avoidable costs; Joint costs; Multiple
    products; Segment analysis
Service departments, 369. *See also* Step-
    down allocations; Transfer prices
Shadow prices, 663–4
Short-term decision making, 139–61. *See*
    also Decision making
Simulation, 106. *See also* Sensitivity analy-
    sis
Social benefits and costs, 332
Social consequences of decision making,
  332–3
Solvency analysis, 739–41
Special orders, 157–9, 423, 560
Spending variances, 474. *See also* Vari-
    ances
Split-off point for joint products, 153, 426
Staff function, 3
Standard costing, 545. *See also* Standard
    costs
  absorption costing, 546–54
    compared with normal costing, 553–4
    fixed cost per unit, 455n, 547–8
    income statement, 548–50

  multiple products, 551–3
  evaluation of methods, 558–60
  process costing illustration, 596–60
  variable costing, 554–8
Standard costs, 455, 545. *See also* Capacity;
    Variances
  and budgets, 455–7
  currently attainable, 469
  for fixed costs, 455n, 546–8
  ideal, 469
  and multi-product companies, 477, 551–3
  for nonmanufacturing activities, 477–8
  performance level for, 469, 547–8
  and performance reports, 470
  for prices, 454
  for quantities, 454
  revising, 469–70
  setting of, 467–70
    engineering methods, 467–8
    historical, 469
    managerial estimates, 468
  and variable costing, 554–8
  variances. *See* Variances
Standard fixed cost, 455n, 546–8. *See also*
    Fixed costs
Statement of changes in financial position,
    680–96
  cash flows and the formal statement,
    686–9
  cash resources, 686–90
  categories of resource flows, 683–4
  concepts of resources, 681–3
  depreciation and funds retention, 695–6
  formal statement, 681–5, 689–90, 692–3
  the interest in resource flows, 680–1
  reconciliation of net income
    and cash from operations, 686–7
    and working capital from operations,
    691–2
  working capital resources, 690–4
  worksheet approach to developing, 702–6
Static budget, 200
Statistical decision theory, 640–50
  in capital budgeting, 644–6
  decision trees, 644
  developing probabilities, 649–50
  expected values, 199–200, 640–50
  payoff tables, 646–9
  in sales forecasting, 199–200
  "utilities" in, 645–6
  in variance investigation, 642–4

Step-down allocations, 379–82
Step-variable costs, 57–59
    defined, 57
    philosophies of planning for, 58–59
Stockout costs, 651–2
Sunk cost, 142–3, 154, *See also* Fixed costs
    book values as, 142, 153
    costs of joint process as, 154
Sunset legislation, 250

T

Target profit, 26–30
    formulas, 26, 28, 66
    and price determination, 28–29
    as return on sales, 27
    after taxes, 66
    volume, 26–27
Target rate of return, 278, 409
Tax basis for assets, 317n
Tax Equity and Fiscal Responsibility Act,
    331
Tax shield of depreciation, 283, 284, 322
Time-adjusted rate of return. *See* Capital
    budgeting; Internal rate of return;
    Present value
Times interest earned, 740
Time value of money, 279, 764–73
Traceable cost, 369. *See also* Separable
    costs
Trading on the equity, 734. *See also* Lever-
    age
Transfer prices, 359, 370, 421–6. *See also*
    Responsibility accounting
    allocations and, 371–5
    in divisional performance measurement,
        421–6
    effects of, 375–7, 421–3
    illustrations, 423–6
    methods of setting, 372, 421–3
True rate of return. *See* Capital budgeting;
    Internal rate of return
Turnover:
    asset, 736
    inventory, 730–1
    investment, 408
    receivables, 729
Two-point method of cost estimation. *See*
    High-low method of cost estimation

U

Unallocated costs. *See* Divisional perfor-
    mance
Unavoidable costs, 60, 107, 145, 146, 153,
    156. *See also* Avoidable costs; Joint
    costs; Separable costs; Transfer
    prices
Underabsorbed overhead, 513. *See also* Ab-
    sorption costing; Variances
Underapplied overhead, 513. *See also* Ab-
    sorption costing; Variances
Unequal lives in capital budgeting, 320–2
Uneven cash flows:
    accelerated depreciation, 284–7
    in capital budgeting, 284–8
    present value of, 768
    salvage values as, 298–8
    working capital investment, return of,
        314
Unit cost. *See* Absorption costing; Average
    total cost; Cost; Equivalent produc-
    tion; Inventoriable cost; Standard
    costs
Use variances. *See* Quantity variances; Vari-
    ances

V

Variable costing, 554–8
    compared to absorption costing, 558–60
    defined, 503, 546
    for external reporting, 558–9
    for internal reporting, 559–60
Variable costs, 18. *See also* Mixed cost;
    Standard costs; Step-variable costs;
    Variable costing
Variable overhead variances, 460–3
Variances. *See also* Budgets; Standard costs
    budget, 212, 547
    control charts, 466
    and cost centers, 470–2
    efficiency
        labor, 458–9, 460
        variable overhead, 460–1
    fixed overhead
        budget, 473
        volume, 515
    and income statements, 472–3, 548

(Variances continued)
   interaction effects, 464–5
   investigation of, 466–7, 642–4
   labor
      efficiency, 458–9, 460
      rate, 458, 459
   material
      price, 463
      use, 464
   and performance evaluation, 465
   problems in separating actual fixed and
      variable overhead costs, 474–7
   sales
      price, 101
      volume, 101
   variable overhead
      efficiency, 460–3
      spending, 460–3
   volume, 514–5, 549
Volume, measures of, 18, 26, 52, 55, 62–66,
   72, 75, 201–3, 547. *See also* Capacity; Predetermined overhead rates
   manufacturer, 62–64, 201–3
   normal activity, 547
   for overhead rates, 456
   practical capacity, 547
   selling and administrative costs, 64–66,
      203
Volume-cost-profit analysis, 17. *See also*
   Target profit
   and budgeting, 192
   graph, 23–26
   income taxes in, 66–69
   in multiple product firms, 102–5
   in not-for-profit organizations, 109–12

   price-volume relationships, 108–9
   relevant range, 22–23
   and variable costing, 559–60
Volume variance, 514–5, 546, 547, 549
   economic significance of, 514, 553–4
   fixed manufacturing overhead, 515
   normal costing compared with standard
      costing, 553–4
   sales, 101

W

Weighted-average contribution margin,
   102–5
Weighted-average equivalent production,
   589
Window dressing, 742
Working capital, 240. *See also* Analyzing
   financial statements; Long-term budgets; Liquidity analysis; Statement of
   changes in financial position
   and the composition problem, 728
   and the current ratio, 727–8
   defined, 240
   investment in, for capital budgeting,
      314–5
   ratio, 728
   resources as, 690–3

Z

Zero-based budgeting, 249–50